Office 365

Migrating and Managing Your
Business in the Cloud

Matthew Katzer
Don Crawford

Apress
open

Office 365: Migrating and Managing Your Business in the Cloud

Matthew Katzer and Don Crawford

ISBN 978-1-4302-6526-9

ISBN 978-1-4302-6527-6 (eBook)

President and Publisher: Paul Manning
Lead Editors: Jeffrey Pepper (Apress), Steve Weiss (Apress), Stuart Douglas (Intel)
Coordinating Editor: Christine Ricketts
Cover Designer: Anna Ishchenko

Distributed to the book trade worldwide by Springer Science+Business Media New York, 233 Spring Street, 6th Floor, New York, NY 10013. Phone 1-800-SPRINGER, fax (201) 348-4505, e-mail orders-ny@springer-sbm.com, or visit www.springeronline.com.

For information on translations, please e-mail rights@apress.com or visit www.apress.com.

About ApressOpen

What Is ApressOpen?

- ApressOpen is an open-access book program that publishes high-quality technical and business-information texts.

- ApressOpen eBooks are available for global, free, noncommercial use.

- ApressOpen eBooks are available in PDF, ePub, and Mobi formats.

- The user-friendly ApressOpen free eBook license is presented on the copyright page of this book.

We dedicate the book to our wives, who have stood by us as we learn how to be one with the cloud. Without their support, we could never achieve what we dream to accomplish.

Contents at a Glance

Contents

About the Authors

Matthew Katzer created KAMIND in 1998 to supply solutions using Microsoft and Intel Technologies for small- and medium-size businesses. Prior to creating KAMIND, he worked for Intel Corporation for 17 years, managing engineering development and IT projects. After leaving Intel, he pursued the development of technology-related inventions and holds 19 domestic and international patents in related areas. Katzer's focus with cloud solutions started in 2009, looking at ways that businesses could improve productivity and reduce operating costs. He holds a B.S.E.E. from the University of Michigan and an Executive M.B.A. from the University of Oregon.

Don Crawford brings more than 40 years of experience in database systems, online systems, networks and security, business and project management, and strategic planning. He has worked for large and small companies and organizations, including local government in Oregon, Software AG, First Interstate Bancorp (now Wells Fargo), Tektronix, CACI, Oregon Health & Science University, and LocalDial. He built a consulting business supporting industries such as hospitals and medical organizations, technology companies, service companies, startups, and nonprofits. Crawford is a partner in KAMIND.

About the Technical Reviewers

We have taken a different approach to the technical review of this book. This book is a collection of "notes from the field"—documents that we have generated to help us educate our customers as we partner with them to move to Microsoft Office 365, a cloud service that simply works. These chapters are a collection of the experiences of more than 8,200 users, as they migrated to Office 365. Their tireless feedback and the questions from our customers have helped us hone this book to be a practical reference document, not only for moving to Office 365, but also as a tool to manage businesses on Office 365.

Acknowledgments

We want to thank our Office 365 customers; Stuart Douglas and the Intel Press staff; Steve Weiss, Troy Mott, and the Apress staff; Justin Bowers, our Microsoft Business Development Manager; Neal Potter, General Manager SMB West Region, and the countless support staff at Microsoft; Jerry Fletcher of Z-axis Marketing; Dan Pearson of the WWW Group; and our wives, Barbara and Gayle, for their support. Without the assistance of all these individuals and companies, this book would never have been written.

Each of the chapters includes additional information on various blogs and Internet postings, to assist readers in searching out information on Office 365 and Microsoft's other cloud services. If we have missed a credit or an acknowledgment, please let us know.

—Matt Katzer & Don Crawford

Introduction

Why Office 365 and why this book? We are cloud solution consultants. Our mission is to make companies more successful through our knowledge of Office 365. We help companies assess, migrate, and manage cloud-based solutions.

Office 365 is a cloud-based service; it is what you know—the Microsoft Office suite. It simply works, plus you do not have to give up your intellectual property to use the service. This is important. Not all cloud solutions are this forthright. Our customers who use Office 365 have significantly reduced their IT services costs and their concerns in the areas of data security, compliance, and discovery.

This is a living book. We approached our publisher with the idea that this book should morph over time. We suggested that a living book could be created about Microsoft cloud services, based on our experience both now and in the future. It agreed.

KAMIND, a Microsoft Tier 1 Champion and a multiyear Microsoft Partner award winner, presents a unique value proposition for our Office 365 customers. Our approach has been to partner with our clients to journey to the cloud together. That experience is reflected in this book and will continue to be.

Join us in this journey to the cloud with Office 365.

Chapter 1–What Is Office 365?

This chapter is focused on why you should move your organization to Office 365. The decision to move to Office 365 is a business, rather than a technical, decision. Like any business change, the objective is to reduce your operational costs and to improve your organization's productivity, to gain a competitive advantage. The chapter ends with a hypothetical customer making the business tradeoffs toward moving to the cloud.

Chapter 2–Using Office 365 and Windows Intune

The best way to understand Office 365 is to experience it. We explore the Office 365 capabilities in a demonstration site, with a focus on how this helps your business productivity. We use a day in the life of a user to demonstrate the capabilities of Office 365. The chapter closes with a reference section on the most common end-user configurations.

Chapter 3–Office 365 Planning and Purchase

The secret to a successful migration to Office 365 is picking the correct plan that supports your business. There are three different categories of plans. The key to a successful migration to Office 365 is the planning and purchase process. Once you select a plan, your primary consideration must be to ensure that the migration process is seamless for your organization. This chapter describes the basic purchase information and details the choices. It concludes with information about pre-deployment, deployment, and post-deployment.

Chapter 4–Office 365 Setup and Migration

After you have selected your Office 365 plan and completed the planning process, the next step is the migration process. There are different ways you can migrate to Office 365 and different migration techniques. This chapter covers the most common approaches to Office 365 migration.

Chapter 5–SharePoint Administration

SharePoint administration and design can be simple or complex, depending on your business needs. This chapter provides a basic overview of the configuration necessary to be up and running using the SharePoint team site of Office 365. This chapter describes site design and construction issues and offers an overview of the SharePoint administration functions.

Chapter 6–Building Your Web Site

Office 365 includes a public-facing web site and the necessary developer's tools to build out the site. This chapter takes you from the basic Office 365 site to a fully functioning web site. The Office 365 public-facing web site fulfills the Web needs of 90% of the businesses on Office 365. This chapter describes how to configure and build the public-facing web site for your business, using the integrated Office 365 web site tools and SharePoint Designer, a design tool that is included with your Office 365 subscription.

Chapter 7–Windows Intune Administration

The secret to an optimal Office 365 site is the management of the desktop to ensure that updates are current and that the user antivirus is functioning. Windows Intune is a desktop management tool that addresses these issues, reduces the administrator's effort in desktop management, and improves the user's experience.

Chapter 8–Office 365 Administration

This chapter describes the different administration centers in Office 365 and the most common tools that you would use to administer Office 365. Depending on your Office 365 plan, there are five possible administration tools. This chapter focuses on the Office 365, Exchange, and Lync administration centers. The SharePoint and Windows Intune administration centers are described in their own chapters. The chapter closes with how to use PowerShell to manage your Office 365 environment.

Chapter 9–Compliance and Data Loss Prevention

Businesses must now adapt their e-mail document-storage systems to correctly process their electronic communication in consideration of regulatory requirements. The compliance and data loss prevention (DLP) features of Office 365 provide the capability to allow a business to manage its communications and protect against simple mistakes. Office 365 includes integrated discovery that supports legal discovery and audit requirements.

Chapter 10–Exchange Online Protection Administration

Office 365 is composed of a set of services. The Exchange Online Protection (EOP) service is the front end of Office 365 that handles all the external e-mail front-end processing and filtering. If you have smart devices that e-mail to Office 365, you will use EOP to manage the interaction.

Chapter 11–DirSync, AD FS, Single Sign-On, and Exchange Federation

Active Directory Federation Services and single sign-on is the integration of the Office 365 Active Directory with an on-premises Active Directory. This allows one sign-on (controlled by on-premises servers) to give access to both cloud and on-premises resources. Password Sync can be a simpler implementation that meets many requirements. Federation allows on-premises and cloud Exchange servers to work together.

Microsoft Office 365 releases updates every 90 days. The Authors have committed to updating this book on a similar timeline. The latest updates to this book may be found at www.getoffice365now.com.

■ ■ ■

## CHAPTER 1

Office 365: Moving to the Cloud

We plan and design for change. After it happens, we plan for the next change. What drives change? With information technology there are many factors—lower cost of equipment, better computing power, greater bandwidth, new software, and so on.

Office 365 is a cloud solution that is having a significant impact on information technology and its role in business. Office 365 represents change—change from the way we used to work to a new way of working. Its proven benefits include lowering the cost of IT services and enabling higher user productivity. Most of us would agree that Office 365 and cloud computing are helping to make our organizations more efficient and more profitable.

The profit factor is a universal driving force for business. Profit generation also drives the information technology function to become more efficient. When times are good, organizations have more resources and there is less pressure on the IT function to become more efficient. However, when a downturn in business happens, IT is frequently the first to suffer budgets cut. The only option is to become more efficient in the use of resources. IT people, whether staff or contractors, are often viewed as "the first to be cut, and the last ones around to turn off the lights."

Small businesses are particularly sensitive to change. Most do not have the capital to handle long downturns, and many look at IT as an "optional" expense. To combat this perception, many IT partner programs (like the Microsoft Partner network made up of hundreds of independent IT service providers) encourage their partners to become trusted business advisors as well as IT experts. The clear objective is to change the business owner's view of IT from an optional expenditure to an essential investment.

The challenge for IT professionals, whether they are staff or contractors, is to evaluate the business processes and technologies available and apply those that improve business efficiency. Cloud computing is one technology that can make a big difference quickly. Why Office 365? There are three reasons why Office 365 is the choice for businesses.

1. You do not assign your intellectual property rights to a third party to use their cloud service.

2. It is what you know—Microsoft Office.

3. Microsoft cloud services reduce operating costs and increase worker productivity.

This book addresses these issues. It also outlines a host of business efficiency opportunities that are to be realized with cloud computing and demonstrates how to make this happen. This book is a collection of our Best Known Methods (BKM) and processes. We want to provide you with the knowledge and tools necessary so you can move your business to the cloud using Microsoft Office 365.

Office 365: The New Cloud Challenge

When commercial cloud services were introduced more than 10 years ago, initial prices were high. Products were, admittedly, not mature and robust. This is the case with most innovations. Customer feedback was mixed and there were issues with how services were delivered and what customers really needed or wanted. In the early days of cloud services, internet connections were slow (~56Kbits to 1.2Mbits); today, internet connections are extremely fast

(100Mbits), which leads to a better user experience. Looking at today's environment, there is a lot of opportunity to fine-tune product services to meet the needs of small businesses in particular. The opportunities for small businesses include the ability to improve worker productivity and reduce (and control) IT operations costs. With this in mind, this book will use examples of integrated cloud migration solutions that we at KAMIND (IT cloud consultants and provider of services for Office 365) have engaged for this tier of user.

Like other companies, over the years Microsoft[†] has developed an increasingly more complete set of services for businesses—from small (less than 250) to large enterprises with a scalable solution offering. The current Microsoft cloud solutions have evolved from the Microsoft on-premises offerings for the 2007–2013 class of server and application products and Hotmail cloud services offering. Microsoft's first commercial service was Microsoft's Online Services (2007–2010), known as the Business Productivity Online Services (BPOS) which included Exchange[†], SharePoint[†], Office Communicator[†], and Live Meeting[†].

In February 2013, Microsoft deployed Office 365 Wave 15, the third generation of online services. This generation of Office 365 supports client desktop software for PC (Office Professional Plus) and Macs (Mac Office 2011 and later). It also allows installation of desktop software on five devices per user. This is the New Office 365[†] (see Figure 1-1).

Office 365 Feature Comparison

	Exchange Online Plans			Office 365 Plans							
				Small Businesses	Midsize Businesses	Enterprise Businesses			Kiosk	
	Kiosk	Plan 1	Plan 2	P	M1	E1	E3	E4	K1	K2
	$2 (per user/ per month)	$4 (per user/ per month)	$8 (per user/ per month)	$6 (per user/ per month)	$15 (per user/ per month)	$8 (per user/ per month)	$20 (per user/ per month)	$22 (per user/ per month)	$4 (per user/ per month)	$8 (per user/ per month)
Each user receives an email account, individual calendar, and contact list	●	●	●	●	●	●	●	●	●	●
Send and receive email from a custom domain	●	●	●	●	●	●	●	●	●	●
Web browser access to Outlook Web App for email, calendar and contacts	●	●	●	●	●	●	●	●	●	●
Access to email, calendars, and contacts from phones capable of receiving email	●	●	●	●	●	●	●	●	●	●
Connect to Microsoft Outlook 2007 and newer versions of Outlook		●	●	●	●	●	●	●		
25 MB maximum attachment size	●	●	●	●	●	●	●	●	●	●
Premium anti-spam and antivirus filtering	●	●	●	●	●	●	●	●	●	●
Configurable anti-spam filtering	●	●	●		●	●	●	●	●	●
Legal hold capabilities for deleted and edited mail			●				●	●		
Email storage per user	1 GB	25 GB	unlimited	25 GB	25 GB	25 GB	unlimited	unlimited	1 GB	1 GB
Microsoft community support (online)	●	●	●	●	●	●	●	●	●	●
Live 24 x 7 IT customer phone support	●	●	●		●	●	●	●	●	●

Figure 1-1. Office 365 feature set (courtesy of Microsoft)

Customer Segments

When KAMIND migrates customers with fewer than 250 users, our approach differs based on workforce size. We have developed distinct service packages for businesses smaller than 25 end users (be they employees, contractors, or others in the network), 26–75 end users, and 75–250 end users. This helps maintain focus on one of the main deciding factors for small business—cost. It also accommodates growth trajectory, allowing small companies to start small and invest more in cloud IT services only when the return on investment justifies it. These are considerations that KAMIND customers tell us are key to their decision making. Enterprise customers, those with more than 250 users, have different requirements then the smaller clusters, but the needs are very much the same—to reduce ongoing operation costs.

Developing affordable, flexible, powerful cloud solutions has involved a number of interim approaches. Knowing the evolution of today's IT landscape provides some insight into the current tools available from the major suppliers. For example, prior to 2013, Microsoft served the less-than-75-end-users market with Microsoft Small Business server. Enterprises with more than 75 end users tended to use Microsoft traditional server products such as Windows Server[†] 2008R2 and 2012. For a short period between 2008 and 2010 Microsoft offered the Essential Business Server[†] (EBS) product family, which was not a good fit for the 75-350 end user market. EBS was designed to provide a graceful path between Small Business Servers (SBS) and traditional Microsoft server products. An EBS Version 2 was under development until it was canceled on March 4, 2010.

The EBS server product offering was one of the first solutions that addressed both on-premises and cloud integration of cloud computing. Its cancelation was a precursor to a change that would be introduced by Office 365. The EBS solution was a three-server solution. It was designed for virtualization and integration of all SBS product features, with remote access and the management tools of System Center essentials. When EBS was aborted, Microsoft lost their leading integrated solution for the 75-plus end user market. This left the traditional Microsoft server products and the Microsoft Online Services to do the job.

The less-than-75 user market has a large set of solutions including Microsoft Home Server[†], Foundation Server[†], Windows Server and Small Business Server[†]. In July 2009, KAMIND made a comparison of SBS, EBS, and Microsoft Online Services to determine the return on investment (see Figure 1-2). The crossover point was identified at about 15 users. In other words, with fewer than 15 users, it appeared to be less expensive to deploy Microsoft Online Services than it is to use on-premises services.

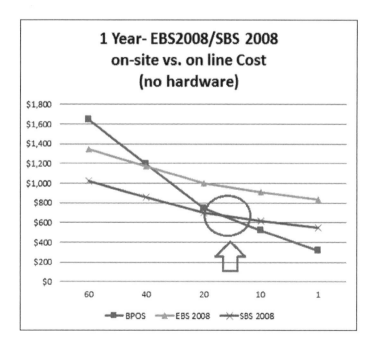

Figure 1-2. *2009/2010 on-site vs. online (cloud) comparison (Intel Case Study, Wimaxforum)*

As we moved into 2010 and incorporated March 2010 pricing of $10 per user for Microsoft Online Services, the crossover point shifted to between 100 and 150 users. Microsoft Online Services' price was at $22.50 per user at this time. The corresponding Office 365 subscription E1 is $8 per user today, demonstrating a 65 percent cost reduction.

So, in March 2010, KAMIND changed its managed services offering to address the new Microsoft Online Services pricing model. We found SBS to be our only option, and it tops out at 75 users. We found that other on-premises solutions were even more expensive.

If we look at the pricing and features of Office 365 today (Figure 1-3), there is no longer a business case to stay on-premises. The cloud-based Office 365 solution is currently the most cost-effective one for any size business. Office 365 today adapts to small one-site enterprises as well as global operations, and it has been growing in size every day. As of late 2013, a reported 69 percent of companies with 20 or fewer employees were using some type of cloud-based IT solution. At the upper end, for example, costs for an enterprise with an on-premises server supporting 1000 users are reduced by 52 percent with deployment of an Enterprise E3 license ($20 per user per month).

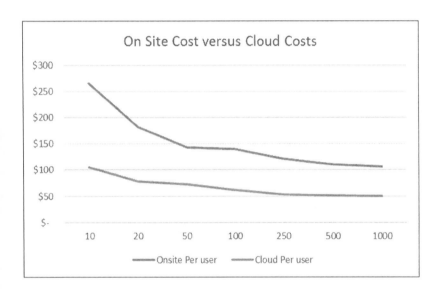

Figure 1-3. *2013 Cost comparison of on-site vs. the cloud (no cloud deployment costs included)*

Unless there is a compelling reason to use an on-premises solution, currently available IT resources make it more cost-effective to use a cloud service. There are advantages and disadvantages to whichever solution you use, and you need to understand your business requirements and how well a particular IT approach integrates with your business strategy.

Microsoft defines small business as an enterprise with fewer than 250 end users. A few other definitions will be useful at this point. The following terms will aid further understanding cloud migration and how it applies to business:

- *On-premises:* Software and hardware devices located at a user's physical location. As an example, you may have an on-premises Exchange server handling mail services.

- *Off-premises:* Often used as a synonym for the cloud, this actually denotes software and hardware devices that are located off-site for which the user of the cloud services has contracted out the physical hardware and software maintenance. As an example, with Microsoft Online Services, the user owns and is responsible for the data, but not the software or the physical server. Microsoft is responsible for backups and server maintenance.

- *Cloud:* Any cloud service that is maintained by a third party. Examples are Hotmail and Microsoft Online Services called Office 365.

- *Office 365:* The Microsoft cloud services suite solution supporting collaboration site, dynamic document synchronization, enterprise voice, compliance, Office software subscriptions (Word, Excel, PowerPoint, etc.) for PC and Mac as well as Office productivity subscriptions for Project and Visio.

- *Intel Server:* The next-generation high-density compute server that supports an integrated SAN and switch control modules. These servers handle virtualization of line of business applications. These servers may be the physical hardware on premises or off premises.

- *Hosted:* Any cloud service owned by the user but maintained by a third party. As an example, the user may host web servers on either third-party equipment or customer-owned equipment.

- *Virtualization:* A server or desktop operating system running on a virtual host. The server or desktop operating systems are run in a hardware-agnostic mode, since the hardware services are supplied by the virtual host.

- *Virtual Host:* The hosted operating environment that allow virtualization of the operating systems. Microsoft Azure services are examples of a cloud-based virtual host.

All of us who own or run a business would like to increase efficiency and reduce operational costs. It does not matter the business size. What matters is what customers want. Most customers want the businesses they use for services to be competitive in terms of services and price. In order to be competitive, owners want capability at the lowest possible price. As business owners, we make investments and want our businesses to scale, so we can grow the business and generate resources for expansion.

Table 1-1 details an example of the on-premises cost of a business that has 50–250 users. It includes a set of core functions that all businesses have: mail, document storage, web conferencing, and line of business (LOB) applications (such as a payroll application or accounting packages). In this example, the IT costs for a small business with 50 end users are about $269 per user per month. The IT cost for a business with 250 end users is about $67 per user per month. The infrastructure required to support the business is roughly the same. Cloud migration clearly enables IT infrastructure cost reduction. Table 1-2 shows the expected cost for a 50-user company with an on-premises and a cloud comparison.

Table 1-1. *On-Premises Infrastructure Costs for 50 and 250 Users (Courtesy of Microsoft)*

	50 Users Cost (USD)	250 Users Cost (USD)
Hardware and Maintenance	$70,413	73,123
Software	107,738	128,078
Operations	207,297	298,827
Deployment	98,951	101,802
	484,399	601,830
	$269	67
Cost per user		$

▓ **Note**   Core services costs are provided by Microsoft Online Services.

Table 1-2. *On-Premises vs. Cloud Comparison for a 50-User Company*

	On Premises 50 Users Cost (USD)	Cloud 50 Users Cost (USD)
Hardware and Maintenance	70,413	0
Software	107,738	36,270
Operations	207,297	100,456
Deployment	98,951	28,886
	484,399	165,612
	269	92
Cost per user		

■ **Note** The 250-user company on-premises cost is $67 per user and the cost for the cloud is $30 per user.

When a business moves to Office 365, there are three driving factors.

- The business retains ownership of its intellectual property.

- It is what they know (Microsoft Office).

- Business productivity increases, and operating costs decreases.

In Table 1-2, note that the cost for a 50-user company drops from $269 per user per month to $92 per user per month. Expand this to a 250-user company and the cost per user per month drops from $67 per user/month to $30 per user per month. This is a cost savings of more than 50 percent. The reasons for this are the following:

- Elimination of in-house maintenance and upgrades to new server software.

- Shortening the time and expense for rollouts of new features.

- Gaining the efficiency of IT services and software features that are usable anywhere.

- Reduction in IT operation costs for energy consumption and hardware updates.

Once Microsoft reduced the entry prices for online services to as low as $2 per user per month, it became more expensive to deploy on-premises equipment in virtually every enterprise. The challenge for the IT professional is how to help businesses adapt to change while balancing on-premises and cloud requirements. Our approach with all businesses is to examine the business processes of the company to understand the balance. Once the business processes are known, we examine the steps required to deploy a cloud solution to meet the business needs. This is why the approach to the cloud as a solution is so different than a traditional IT solution. The cloud solution for a business is a business process change that reduces the operating costs of the business and improves productivity.

To assist you in your understanding, we have created a small company called Ready Design Custom Cupcakes (RDCC). We will look at RDCC business requirements and how these requirements compare to on-premises and cloud needs for cloud services.

Ready Design Custom Cupcakes IT Requirements

RDCC has a unique business model as compared to other cupcake bakers. Years ago, RDCC discovered that they could simulate the cupcake design and place the simulated cupcakes of various designs into a virtual environment to gauge consumer reactions. They discovered that cupcakes that were simulated and later baked enjoyed four times the sales of "regular" cupcakes.

RDCC corporate headquarters supports 20 retail cupcake outlets. The IT organization has deployed Microsoft Exchange Server† 2007 with Live Meeting. The remote locations use Microsoft Outlook† web access, and documents are e-mailed to all franchise owners. To meet the demands of the cupcake design team, the IT organization deploys LOB applications with a clustered SQL Server 2005 to support the cupcake simulation. The RDCC IT infrastructure consists of seven servers: three support the LOB simulation application and four support core operations. The deployment is as follows:

- One server for the LOB with Access Simulation database

- One server for Microsoft Exchange Server 2007 with 18 local users and 150 remote web mail accounts

- One server for Microsoft Systems Management Server† for application deployment and management

- One Microsoft SharePoint† 2003 server

- One server running Threat Management Gateway (TMG)

- Support of 150 remote mail users with iPhone† and Phone 7

- 30 WebEx† accounts and 25 GoToMeeting† accounts

Strategic Overview

RDCC management wants an IT system focused on supporting the LOB applications rather than supporting commodity software. The IT staff at RDCC has submitted a capital expenditure (CAPEX) spending request to upgrade the aging RDCC servers. RDCC management is seeking alternatives to reduce both CAPEX and operational expenses (OPEX).

RDCC's corporate objective is to make the organization more agile and increase productivity. Management evaluated one of the online alternatives, Microsoft Office 365, to host their core software. RDCC management summarizes their priorities as follows:

- 100% ownership if the companies intellectual property (IP); no IP rights assignments to use third party services.

- Reduce capital equipment expenditures (CAPEX).

- Reduce operational expenditures with predictable IT costs.

- Work on the business with a focus on market differentiation.

- Reduce energy consumption; become more energy-efficient.

- Access latest software versions with no server upgrade.

- Achieve the ability to share cupcake recipes with the franchises from the internal document storage site.

The following is a summary of RDCC's IT management requirements with a focus on determining potential commodity products plus a comparison of them with the various business needs to design a solution addressing both on-premises and cloud needs.

On-Premises and Cloud Resource Requirements

Many different arguments are made to justify keeping servers on-premise vs. moving them into the cloud. They range from control over the data (intellectual property rights) to reducing costs. The secret is to look at the problem from a service level, to differentiate services that provide a competitive advantage from those that are a commodity. In other words, identify the business processes, and look at those processes from an IT services point of view that promotes business growth. Differentiate those capabilities from those that are core to the business, but have no strategic value. Commodity services (those that are not core to the business) move to the cloud.

If a cloud migration is approached correctly, you can achieve both objectives—promoting business and reducing cost for core commodity services. This seems like a simple problem, but it is actually very complex. To help address this, we look at the business from a capability point of view, and we will use that point of view to help us in our decision process.

The following core IT considerations are common to all businesses when viewed from the perspective of an IT solution. When looking at cloud solutions, it helps to look at each distinctive business unit and business processes before deciding what is best for the whole enterprise.

- Core business software

- LOB solutions

- Requirements for on-premises and cloud data

- E-mail utilization and retention

- Network infrastructure

- Desktop support and upgrade

- Information security

- Monitoring

- Budget: CAPEX versus Operational Expenditure (OPEX)

- Hosted web site

What IT elements will help sustain competitive advantage? That is the overriding question in each of these categories. Each business is different, depending on of its needs. An obvious example is the e-mail capabilities for business. A few years ago, a business needed to place on-site servers to have ownership and control of their e-mail (intellectual property). This need drove the Microsoft Small Business Server market. Today, e-mail is a commodity, so unless there is a different business need for an on-site mail server, it no longer makes business sense (see Figure 1-3) to manage.

In all cases, it is wise to seriously look at the cloud and the impact on the business. At KAMIND we looked at our customers, from the small five-person law firm to the larger 2,000-employee business. We looked at the impact from a commodity services perspective, and in all cases, we found that the cloud cost at least 50 percent less than on-premises equipment. The only caveat was bandwidth (the ability to transfer large amounts of data at fast speeds to cloud services). If the bandwidth was not available, then it did not make sense to migrate to the cloud.

Core Business Software

What is core software? Core software has many different meanings depending on the business. As an example, in retail businesses, the core software helps manage point of sale and inventory control. In a marketing company, it is e-mail and web conferencing software. An insurance company's core software will include e-mail and an application for managing the insurance offerings.

Core software products are usually word processing, spreadsheet, and e-mail software. If you add other application software stacks like web conferencing and presentation software, the core can expand, but this can limit an organization's ability to exchange information with other organizations.

For example, how many of us have e-mailed a Microsoft Word document or a PowerPoint presentation and just assumed that the other party could read the file? The simplest definition you can use for core software is to define it as "those software programs and services that facilitate information exchange."

Information Exchange

Information exchange refers to the action of exchanging information between multiple parties. Examples include e-mail, web conferencing, document storage/retrieval, and instant messaging. Software that assists the user in handling information exchange includes Microsoft Office, Google Apps, and OpenOffice. The specific tools engaged are a word processing application (such as Microsoft Word), presentation software (such as Microsoft PowerPoint), spreadsheet software (such as Microsoft Excel), and an instant messaging application. The business segment does not matter. The core software product is the standard tool for that segment when information is exchanged. As an example, with RDCC, the simulation tool is not applicable to the marketing segments, but web conference and e-mail are. The core products are the commodity products that are used to conduct business. Core products are drivers for efficiency and cost reduction.

More Ready Design Cup Cakes (RDCC) IT Issues

As noted earlier, RDCC was running on Exchange Server 2007 using ISA Server 2004 as a security server. They were deployed on older Dell servers. In this configuration, RDCC did not have Microsoft software assurance, so all software licenses for the upgrades would need to be purchased. Figure 1-3 shows the current service level breakdown and Table 1-3 shows the deployment cost breakdown for the on-premises and cloud options. The support costs are not shown, but the IT professionals who handled on-premises equipment support know that management of that equipment would require at least half of an IT professional's time. Both options are listed in Table 1-3.

Table 1-3. *Ready Design Cup Cakes Deployment Comparison*

Microsoft Online Services: Office 365						
Description	Users	Service	Cost per User (USD)	Deployment Costs (USD)	One Time Cost (USD)	Monthly Cost (USD)
Franchise Owner	100	E2	$16	$10 per user	$1,000	$1,600
Users	50	E3	24	100 per user	5,000	1,200
					$6,000	$2,800

Onsite Server				
Description	Users	Deployment Costs (USD)	One Time Cost (USD)	Monthly Average Cost (USD)
Users	150	200 per user	$30,000	$2,500
Server Installation			15,000	1,250
Server Hardware (Intel° Modular Server + three compute modules)			29,392	2,449
Microsoft Software (Exchange + TMG + Enterprise + CAL			49,309	4,109
			$123,701	$10,308

The RDCC IT manager reviewed the support requested and proposed a budget of $123,000, approximately $10,000 per month. The IT manager expects this will consume half of the on-staff IT professional time at a cost of about $70,000. RDCC management looked at the cost and requested the IT manager do a comparison against the monthly costs using a subscription (cloud) model.

The IT manager reviewed the information and was shocked to see that the on-premises solution costs $7,000 per month more than the Microsoft Office 365 solution. He also became aware that he could free up half of his time not having to manage an on-premises server. RDCC's management reviewed the financials and chose the Microsoft Office 365 solution, saving $150,000 in a one-year period. RDCC management also committed to having all of their franchise users use Microsoft Office applications as the office standard and decided to deploy two distinct offerings for franchises. At the franchise level, they specified the E1 service with Office Web applications. This allowed the franchise owner to use either the web applications or purchase the retail version of the Office software. At RDCC corporate offices, they can either use the Office subscription service (E3) or deploy the Office 2013 software through a volume license.

RDCC's decision to use Microsoft Online Services reduced the CAPEX and OPEX for the fiscal year. RDCC IT staff estimated that the deployment costs were between $50 and $100 per person in one-time fees, for a total of $6,000. The $6,000 migration cost for the RDCC deployment was one-fifth the estimated cost of the Exchange 2010 deployment. RDCC management realized that the selection of online services significantly reduced the cash outlay for the organization.

Line of Business Applications

LOB applications are unique to a business or a business segment. A good example of a LOB application is an insurance documentation archive system designed to handle insurance agency data. This LOB application is not relevant to, for example, a retail segment that does not handle insurance agency documents. Likewise, an LOB application of a point-of-sale (POS) system would not be a relevant application for a RDCC cupcake simulation.

RDCC's LOB application consists of the simulation application and the Microsoft Access database that is used in the simulation. The Access database is known to consume network bandwidth. However, with Office 365, the Access database can be shared from the cloud SharePoint service, so the database that is used locally is cached, and changes are replicated to the cloud. The Access database can also be linked to Windows Azure (an extension of Office 365 cloud services) and integrated with Office 365. Thus, the user accesses the database locally, and transaction change records are replicated to the cloud. This allows multiple users to have access to the information in real time without over-using available bandwidth. This is possible because updates are driven to client desktops only as they are "cached."

RDCC IT staff concluded that the LOB application no longer needed a server to support the application. The IT manager reviewed SharePoint online services and decided that this software only needed minor customization to make it useful. This decision allows the IT management to reduce the server "farm" by one more server, with a savings of about $20,000 on top of the budget savings of $90,000—all made possible by not deploying on-premises equipment.

Requirements for On-Premises and Cloud Data

The final concern for RDCC was how to address backup data issues. RDCC has a business requirement under Sarbanes-Oxley (SOX) that all financial data needs to be recoverable. RDCC has also been involved in much litigation, so they are well aware of the e-discovery impact to the business. In recent litigation RDCC was required to process all of the e-mails on their Exchange server and turn over the e-mail data as part of the litigation. Because RDCC did not have an archive retention policy, they received a federal court order that mandated a freeze in the deletion of data and placed all RDCC hardware on a legal hold. The IT staff had to recall all laptops from the field and copy the users' personal archives to the server so the data could be processed for electronic discovery. This was extremely expensive.

E-Mail Utilization and Retention

RDCC management sought to avoid this type of expense in the future and to make any discovery process more automated and less labor intensive. RDCC policy is to have a 10-year compliance archive segmented into different groups: the factory workers archive is one year, middle managers are two years, and sales and management are 10 years.

■ **Note**   Microsoft views an archive as a duplicate mailbox where data is copied from the primary mailbox. In the E1/E2 versions of Office 365, the archive is 50 GB; in versions E3/E4, it is unlimited in size.

There are three types of archives in Office 365: personal archives (local PSt and cloud), shown in Figure 1-4, and compliance archives. Personal archives (local or PST) are files in which the content is controlled by the user. A compliance archive must have data immutability; the user cannot change the data. The Office 365 (versions E1 and E2) personal archives are limited to 50GB. Office 365 archives in E3 and E4 are unlimited in size and can be made immutable (for compliance requirements). The compliance archive is controlled by business policies governed by the organization business processes and federal regulation.

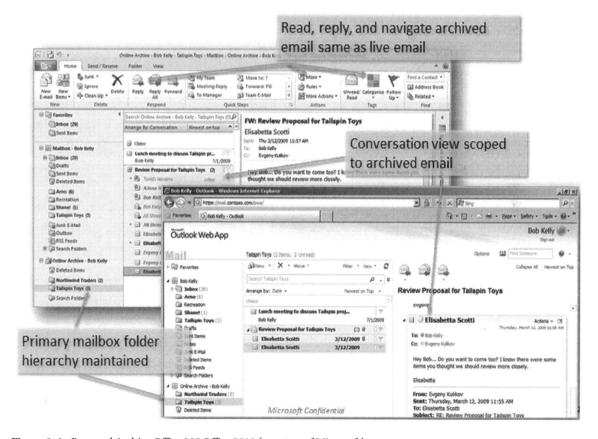

Figure 1-4. Personal Archive Office 365 Office 2010 (courtesy of Microsoft)

Network Infrastructure

RDCC has a large, robust network infrastructure to support user requirements of 200-plus employees and franchise owners. The franchise owners' businesses run seven days a week, from 5 a.m. to 10 p.m. (Pacific Standard Time).

To keep the network capability as it is, RDCC IT staff was faced with upgrading an aging on-premises data center with the latest Intel® processor-based servers from Intel, Dell, or IBM. The IT design staff proposed replacing the data center in Figure 1-5 with an Intel Server. The RDCC IT staff felt that this approach would provide the most comprehensive set of features for the cupcake virtualization and would accommodate growth. The unresolved issue was how much to deploy on the Intel Server vs. the cloud.

Figure 1-5. *RDCC private data center (courtesy of Microsoft)*

The Intel Server is 6U in size and allows up to 14 high-speed SAS drives to be arranged in a data storage pool. RDCC IT staff is planning to use the 1TB SAS drives, which allows a storage pool size of 14,366GB, with an online hot spare. As far as RDCC IT staff is concerned, this allows them to reduce the size of the data center (Figure 1-5) to a single 82-inch rack. RDCC IT staff selects the Intel Server over other vendors' products based on the following considerations:

- Lower power consumption
- More flexibility in adding computing capacity
- Intel Xeon 6-core processors will enable support up to 12-24 virtual machines with a combined memory size of over 256GB
- Fault-tolerant compute module support with auto failover
- Fault-tolerant storage module with external SAN support

To help them in their decision process RDCC IT staff modeled storage pool consumption on the Intel Server test drive site (see www.intelmodularserver.com). This site allows them to try different configurations and out-of-band management systems to develop the best solution. Figure 1-6 shows a storage pool view of the Intel Server with a modular server with a RAID 1 and a RAID 5 subsystem.

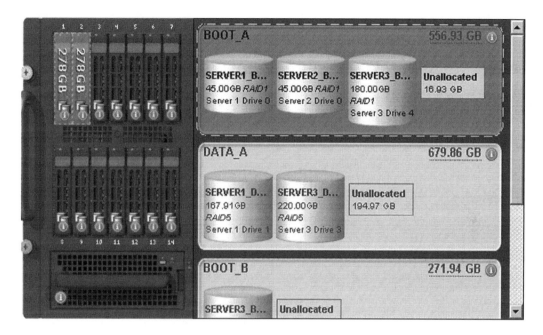

Figure 1-6. *Storage pool organization and allocation*

The Intel Server allows for organizing the Storage Access Network (SAN) or the attached SAN into a set of storage pools. The storage pools are then allocated to the individual *compute module*. In Figure 1-6, they added two SAS drives to the storage pool. However, when they built their virtual drives, they decided to organize the data in a RAID 1 configuration. KAMIND recommends that the RDCC IT staff deploys the Intel Server storage with a global hot spare.

Desktop Support and Upgrade

The RDCC IT staff needs to complete not only a data center upgrade, but also a software upgrade. In the past, they purchased a Microsoft Open License that did not include software assurance, so they had a group of deployed desktops using Office 2003 software under Windows XP. Some of the newer software uses Windows 8, so RDCC is faced with replacing all XP systems before the end of support from Microsoft, which is less than a year away.

RDCC IT examined the different pricing options for the new software. The software deployment cost is the same in all cases except for the retail product. The retail product requires that the IT staff physically enter a different serial number for each version of Office 365 software installed.

Office 2013 prices ranged from $432 to $699 (see Table 1-4) for Office 2013 software. The software that cost the most was the retail version. The cost was higher since it required an IT professional to install the software on every desktop and deploy a unique serial number key; RDCC IT staff could not do an automated "push" install for mass deployment of the software and upgrades.

Table 1-4. *Office 2013 Professional Plus License Prices (as of Publication Date, Prices Subject to Change)*

Office 2013 Professional Plus			
Option	Cost (USD)	Yearly Costs (USD)	Notes
Full Retail Product	$399	$399	No upgrade, limited installs
Volume License (L/SA)	699	233	Three-year agreement, either spread payment option
Volume License (SA)	444	148	Agreement exists for License portion
Volume License Subscription	432	144	Three-year subscription, upgrades included
Office 365 Subscription	+12 per user/month	144	Microsoft Online one-year agreement, requires Suite

Information Security

RDCC's information security requirements are similar to those of most companies. RDCC wants to make sure their data is kept private. They want to control access to their data and the computing resources. These are their business needs. RDCC doesn't want to use any cloud service that required an intellectual property transfer. Some cloud services companies use IP rights assignment as a way to sell additional product and services to the companies' employees.

All of us have heard of reports of credit card numbers being stolen from retail store point-of-sale computers. How about a government employee leaving a laptop that contains thousands of social security numbers in a car and that laptop is stolen? There are countless stories of identity theft. The stories all come down to this: How safe is your data? The safety of your data is what information security is all about, and the crux of the problem is data access and control.

Realistically, it does not matter where your data is located. It can be safe anywhere—with the right precautions. The processes and security around your data and how it is controlled is what matters. As an example, does the network administrator have access to your e-mail? What password policies are in place to ensure that your data is under control? What is the physical security like? Who picks up the trash in the evening in your data center? Who has access after-hours to the information? All that matters is how data is managed. Data loss prevention is critical for RDCC's business to ensure confidential information stays inside the company and there is no IP rights assignment to use the Office 365 cloud service.

There are many aspects of physical data security. Figure 1-7 is a picture of a Microsoft data center. All server access is controlled and limited to a few select individuals. Microsoft also has controls on who accesses the data. This is a critical aspect of data security that is often overlooked.

Figure 1-7. *Microsoft version 4 data center (courtesy of Microsoft)*

■ **Note**   Microsoft's policy is that the customer owns the data, not Microsoft.

Microsoft believes that the data is owned by the customer, and the customer has 100 percent control over the data. To put this in perspective, the customer must grant Microsoft permission to access the data. This philosophy limits data access and establishes the controls necessary for data security.

The next part of data security is built around the standards necessary for access and control of the data. The Microsoft software design philosophy is built from an idea of secure code design. Secure code design means that the software is designed using best practices from the ground up. To put this in perspective, the code in the data centers is built from a best practice software design known as *code secure*. Michael Howard and David LeBlanc wrote the Microsoft book *Writing Secure Code*. This is a must-read book if you are doing any software development.

Writing Secure Code walks a developer through the process of software development and describes the way to prevent attacks on software. This book provides examples of how software developers must padlock their code to prevent unknown attacks. The philosophy of Microsoft security begins at the core of the product design lifecycle—the developer. If you do not put the correct processes in place, then the products built on top of those products will not be secure. This philosophy of security permeates modern Microsoft products as well as the data center.

■ **Note**   Employ a risk-based, multidimensional approach to safeguarding services and data. All products must go through the secure development cycle to release code publicly. The secure development lifecycle ensures threat development management.

Microsoft supplies a multi-tenant architecture based on Active Directory and built from secure code design. Microsoft has scaled the data security problem and discovered the weaknesses of various security products. Microsoft discovered that when a deployment is scaled beyond certain practical limits, security issues that no one else has thought of emerge. Microsoft deployment of the Exchange data infrastructure goes beyond the limits of whatever has been tested before. Microsoft has greater than 40M mailboxes that use Windows Azure Active Directory security. Microsoft augments the design with data access policies that prohibit the unauthorized access of data. To ensure compliance, these policies are monitored automatically within Microsoft Office 365 software, a feature that meets RDCC design goals.

With its security requirements met, RDCC is ready to use the Windows Azure Active Directory services (see Figure 1-8) to manage the entire business and ultimately move all on-site servers to the cloud and Office 365. The following are approaches to achieving this phased "migration." RDCC's long term plan is to move the database to a hosted service in Azure and add a WordPress site that will be integrated to the Office 365 environment. RDCC felt that Azure allowed the company to expand to the cloud for all commuting services in a secured manner.

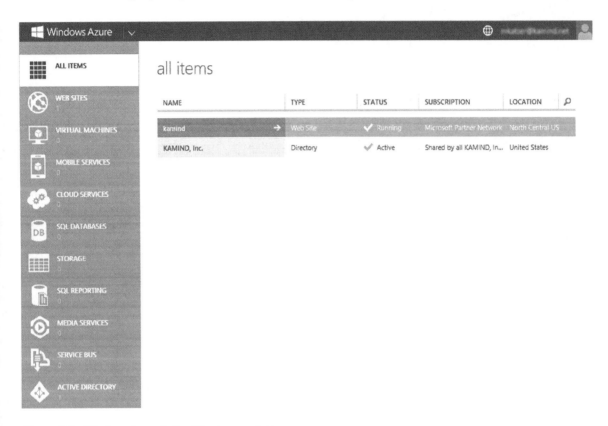

Figure 1-8. *Windows Azure Active Directory services*

Monitoring

There are two different monitoring approaches used to manage the on-site equipment and off-site equipment. These involve Microsoft Systems Center and Microsoft Windows Intune. Each has different capabilities and features depending on the needs of the client and the type of existing on-premises equipment.

Microsoft Systems Center

There are several services available for systems monitoring. There are those available from managed service providers like Level Platforms and on-premises monitoring using Microsoft Systems Center (SCC). The objective of both is the proactive monitoring of servers and clients. Why proactive monitoring? The simplest explanation is productivity. As users become more dependent on computers for daily activity, there is an expectation that it "just works."

SCC is a software management tool that runs on-premises equipment and provides complete monitoring and updates management. This software is typically used in environments with 50-500 client PCs. SCC's goal is to unify the organization under one management console with the objective of reducing IT costs. From an IT perspective,

SCC provides a proactive view of the on-premises network and has the capabilities to distribute patches (temporary fixes), install software updates, and troubleshoot network issues. SCC also has the capability to manage an unlimited number of servers, either virtual or physical. Small businesses can now manage their on-premises desktops and remaining servers at a fraction of the cost per user available to larger enterprises.

Microsoft Windows Intune—Desktop Management

The second type of monitoring product that RDCC is looking at is Microsoft Windows Intune. This is an agent (software that is installed on the device to monitor operation) product designed for small businesses. This product allows the management of updates, limited group policy control, and antivirus monitoring. The monitoring is completed at a host level. Windows Intune is integrated into Microsoft Systems Center or as a separate cloud monitoring service for small companies. Windows Intune directly controls systems updates, addresses virus issues, and manages software licenses and deployment for the business. A RDCC test confirms that all these two environments can be used simultaneously in the management of their systems.

RDCC Cloud Solution

RDCC's IT requirements are typical: improve access to technology, enhance access to data, lower operations cost, and raise product efficiency. The RDCC IT department prepared various options for deployment ranging from 100 percent on-premises to 100 percent cloud. RDCC management directed the IT organization to focus on areas that engage commodity IT services and find the best alternatives. The following was agreed upon as a balanced solution:

- Migrate all e-mail users to Microsoft Office 365 hosted Exchange Mail Services. There are 18 local users and 150 remote mail users.

- Move the SharePoint services to SharePoint in the cloud as part of the Exchange Mail migration.

- Move the 55 web conferencing accounts (Webex/GoToMeeting) to Microsoft Lync as part of the migration.

- Eliminate the need for ISA server and replace this with local firewalls (fortinet or sonicwall) since remote users will use the cloud.

Cloud Requirements

The commodity products that are readily available externally include Microsoft Exchange, SharePoint, web conferencing, virus management, and spam/virus filters. RDCC IT estimated that 35 percent of their IT resources could immediately be saved by moving to the cloud.

Office 365 Business Savings for RDCC

Principal savings came from reducing the number of servers from 12 to three. This would also eliminate the corresponding three Windows 2012 upgrades, Exchange 2013, SharePoint services, 168 Exchange CALs, and SharePoint CALs. Other "hidden" costs eliminated included the expense for backup software from the Exchange and SharePoint servers and the off-site disaster recovery backup. RDCC IT management realizes that they are allocating three-quarters of the time of a full-time IT employee to managing these environments, and skipping the expenses on server refresh.

Summary of RDCC On-Premises Requirements

Moving RDCC's core IT services to the cloud frees up budget for additional development. RDCC IT wants to migrate the cupcake simulation tool from an access database to SQL Server, and implement some other management and consolidation projects. RDCC's IT needs for on-premises services are summarized as follows:

- Use Active directory (password synchronization) for on-site security integration to Microsoft Online Services (they only have to manage 19 users; the 150 users are franchise owners).

- Use Microsoft Windows Intune for antivirus and update management.

- Deploy a blade server with two virtual machines to support the LOB application.

- Contract with a third-party managed service provider to provide a monitoring solution and hosted backup.

With the savings realized by the proposed cloud solution, RDCC is able to significantly restructure the business process and focus the organization on business productivity gains. They will be able to realize two big priorities: upgrading their servers to the new Intel Server and cleaning up their data center. RDCC will be able to dispose of two of the three computer racks and reduce all servers to one 6U unit with an integrated SAN.

RDCC IT presents the comprehensive plan. RDCC management is thrilled with the direction reallocates IT resources to improve the cupcake design simulation by moving it from an Access/SQL Server Express to SQL Azure and Windows Azure.

Migration Cost and Approaches

Granted, Table 1-4 (covered earlier in the "Desktop Support and Upgrade" section) makes many assumptions about hardware and software costs and support. However, it provides a good illustration that the total cost of ownership is quite different if the costs of server upgrades and software upgrades are considered. That is, when one compares apples with apples.

If it takes at least three years to receive a payoff from an on-premise solution, it is worthwhile to look at the cost tradeoffs and other business and technical assumptions. As an example, Table 1-2 illustrates cloud deployment costs to be less than 30 percent of the deployment costs for an equivalent on-premises solution for 50 people.

It is possible to overlook the deployment costs associated with hardware, software, infrastructure, and security required for a server-based solution. The other factor for migration to the cloud depends on employees. Small business migration can be greatly aided by IT skillsets among employees—and on whether they have accepted the migration as a positive thing. It is good practice to involve end users in the planning and transition, and to thoroughly communicate its benefits at key points in the process.

The cloud migration cost for small organizations will vary depending upon the organization skills. Office 365 migrations are about business process changes. In organizations that tend to have well-known business process, migration is quick. Organizations that change the business process experience longer cloud migration.

The business process change for a 20-user business may involve creating a program to train administrative assistants in handling the day-to-day issues like password changes, spam issues, and Outlook configurations. In this specific case, there was an initial cost in setting up the training, but rapidly dropped as soon as trained administrators took over.

Contrast this 20-user migration with an international organization that was more end-user literate with computers and technology. This was a 35-person company that was migrated to online services in three days across four different countries. The users were migrated from an on-premises solution to Microsoft Online Services.

Larger companies are business process driven. As an example, the migration of a 400-person public library in Denver Colorado had two business goals: to reduce operation costs and to retrain IT staff on new technologies. The technical migration was simple; move mail from server x to the cloud. However, the business process change was complex. In this case, a program was designed to grow grass roots support in the company and build a peer user support network. The migration, which was originally forecasted for four months, reduced the schedule by one month. Office 365 is about business process changes and how to empower and organization to embrace the change.

These are just some examples. There are different costs associated with all migration. You need to look at the business processes of the organization. This book is designed to address components in each of these costs areas. Looking at migrations, they fall into three categories: low, medium, and high. The migration costs are directly related to the organization's skills.

- *Low.* This is a do-it-yourself (DYI) migration. The IT professional (or business owner) provides the basic configuration and setup, and acts as backup support if needed. Usually the mail is uploaded using PST (since the source environment is usually POP mail).

- *Medium.* The IT professional partners with the customer for the migration. The IT professional directs customer resources remotely to complete the migration. The IT professional trains the local IT staff. The organization may need password synchronization and has a local LOB server resource.

- *High.* The IT professional handles the migration from start to finish. The cost depends on the configuration of the on-site mail server and SharePoint usage as well as the security requirements. As an example (discussed later), there may be a need for tightly integrated security; in this case a federation security server is installed.

The migration environment differs depending on the business. Some businesses are running under the Microsoft Active Domain architecture, such as SBS or equivalent. In some cases where there is a non-Microsoft OS, the mail migration cost depends on the OS where the mail and documents reside. There are other factors in the migration costs, and the solution comes down to the business processes.

Remote Monitoring with Windows Intune and Systems Center

Remote monitoring and management allows a group of computers to be managed and controlled from a central location. The rationale for remote management and monitoring is to contain operations costs. As organizations' computing infrastructure becomes more complex, we are always looking for ways to reduce the complexity of the environment. There are many different sets of remote management and monitoring tools. Typically, remote monitoring is looking for a way to aggregate data to allow a proactive analysis of the work environment. Figure 1-9 replicates the Windows Intune Monitoring dashboard for a typical small business.

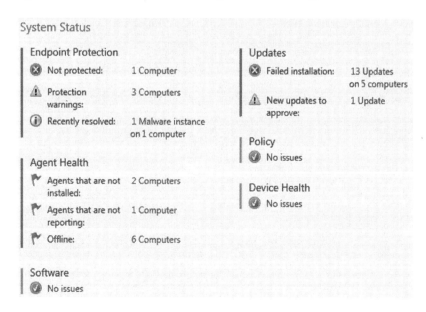

Figure 1-9. *Windows Intune Monitoring dashboard*

Microsoft recently introduced Windows Intune†, a desktop management tool for inventory, updates, and security policies, which can be purchased by end users through Microsoft Online Services. The Office 365 user accounts are linked into Windows Intune, providing better desktop management. It is highly recommended to deploy some type of tool to determine systems health. Office 365 requires that the desktop user systems be up to date and patched with the latest security patches. These desktop management tools are used to identify problems so proactive action may be taken to resolve issues before they become serious problems and affect business continuity.

The Big Decision: On-Premises or Cloud Solutions?

The line in the sand for IT change is whether to keep data on-site or off-site. The most frequent motivator for data migration to the cloud is cost. Whether it is savings realized through reduced labor, more efficient equipment, or general "operations" expenses, cost is king. Still, the best solution sometimes straddles the line, because there can be a case for equipment and services that are both on-premises and hosted by the cloud. The decision process is known as resource optimization. Resource optimization consists of the following:

- *Server Consolidation:* Reducing the number of servers to improve overall operations costs (see Figure 1-10).

Before:

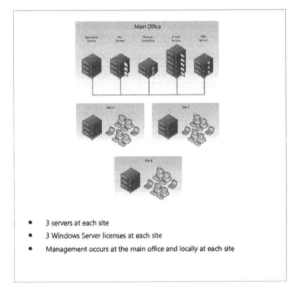

After:

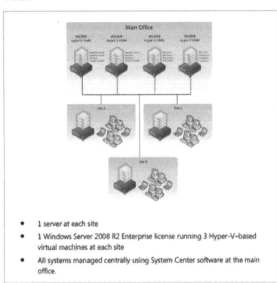

Figure 1-10. Virtualization and branch office design (courtesy of Microsoft)

- *Hardware Consolidation:* Optimizing the server hardware to reduce overall systems cost.

- *Core Services Consolidation:* Removing core services that can be purchased in the cloud at a lower rate than keeping those services on-premises.

As part of this process, illustrated in Figure 1-10, the server was optimized, enabling it to handle a more integrated workload. In this case, the server is a high density blade server such as the Intel Server platform. Many different types of servers can be used for hardware consolidation. Dell, HP, and Lenovo offer other choices. The driving factor in the optimization decision should be the integration cost.

The branch office design (Figure 1-10) demonstrates a reduction of the on-premise servers from three to one Intel Server, with six compute modules hosting the virtual machines. The Intel Server (see Figure 1-11) allows the addition of an integrated SAN with 14 SAS (1TB) drives in a RAID 10 configuration (providing a raw space of 14TB). A second integrated networked switch is also added.

Figure 1-11. *High Density Modular Server (courtesy of Intel)*

The server also supports six compute modules with 32GB to 256GB memory and dual Intel® Xeon® processors. Each compute module host OS is Windows 2008R2 Enterprise or Microsoft Windows Server 2012. The Microsoft Hyper-V software can support up to 15 additional virtual machines, with the appropriate licenses, or three additional licensed Windows Enterprise VMs. The redesign reduces the number of servers to one device and adds capabilities to support disaster recovery and business continuity.

Optimizing Core Services with the Cloud

Core services are those basic services that all businesses require including e-mail, file and print services, and document storage/management. Internal web sites, web/video conferencing, and instant messages are core cloud services that are also used in day-to-day business. All other services used to conduct business can be best described as LOB applications or services on-premises. When we look at the core services, we are looking for ways to optimize the business for productivity and operating efficiency.

Business Efficiency

Optimizing business efficiency involves looking at the core services that make businesses work and making them work as well as possible (see Figure 1-12). Supporting core IT services on-premises involves hiring information technology workers, ordering new server software, and planning migration of users on workstation software to support the new software releases. This is an ongoing struggle in all businesses, and it costs resources to perform it adequately.

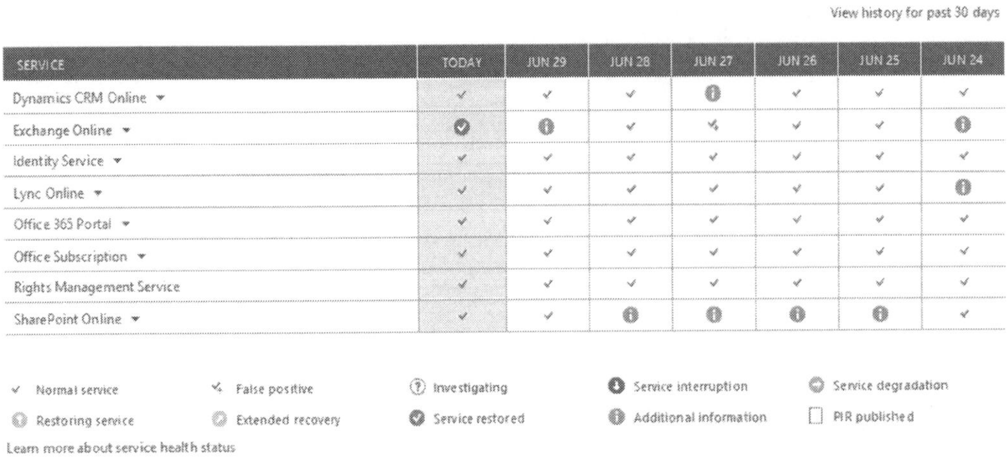

View history for past 30 days

SERVICE	TODAY	JUN 29	JUN 28	JUN 27	JUN 26	JUN 25	JUN 24
Dynamics CRM Online ▾	✓	✓	✓	ⓘ	✓	✓	✓
Exchange Online ▾	⊘	ⓘ	✓	✓	✓	✓	ⓘ
Identity Service ▾	✓	✓	✓	✓	✓	✓	✓
Lync Online ▾	✓	✓	✓	✓	✓	✓	ⓘ
Office 365 Portal ▾	✓	✓	✓	✓	✓	✓	✓
Office Subscription ▾	✓	✓	✓	✓	✓	✓	✓
Rights Management Service	✓	✓	✓	✓	✓	✓	✓
SharePoint Online ▾	✓	✓	ⓘ	ⓘ	ⓘ	ⓘ	✓

✓ Normal service	⚲ False positive	ⓘ Investigating
⟳ Restoring service	⚲ Extended recovery	⊘ Service restored

⊙ Service interruption	⊙ Service degradation
ⓘ Additional information	☐ PIR published

Learn more about service health status

Figure 1-12. *Service Health, Office 365 services*

A complete cloud services migration involves moving the on-premises infrastructure to the cloud. As noted earlier, moving to the cloud can allow businesses to either reduce the IT support staff necessary to maintain the on-premises solution or reallocate the resources for different IT projects. Operational costs can be reduced for additional services such as business continuity and disaster recovery. These services are standard with all cloud services partners. Microsoft Online Services offers 30-day mailbox content and SharePoint recoverability and 14-day recoverability on a mailbox deletion. Additional Microsoft Online Services include e-mail point-to-point encryption and immutable compliance archive (such as legal hold and the Finra – Financial Industry Regulatory Authority (www.finra.org).

Typical migrations involve removing on-premises e-mail (the internal SharePoint web site) to Microsoft Online Services and centralizing conferencing from a third-party supplier to Microsoft Live Meeting. There are sometimes differences in the user interface, but the Microsoft Online Services Business Productivity Online Suite helps resolve them. Services that are left on-site are designed around existing LOB applications using CRM systems and SQL LOB applications, as well as the traditional file/print services.

Next Steps for RDCC

Before RDCC migrates their business to the cloud and Office 365, there is planning to be done. To help plan for the migration, the management team attended a demonstration event as participants in the Microsoft Experience Center (MEC). The MEC demo walks the user through the experience using different persona to fully understand the capabilities of Office 365. This is a key step in the planning cycle for Office 365 migration. As RDCC looks at their business in detail, they will go through a typical planning and evaluation process. Office 365 migration is smooth, but it is essential to plan and test. The next few chapters will detail RDCC's experience.

Summary

This chapter focused on why businesses move to Office 365. It included a review of the business reasons and provided a cost comparison of different approaches. Like any business change, the objective is to reduce operating costs and improve productivity to build a competitive advantage. The conclusion is that Office 365 solutions can provide that competitive advantage.

Next Steps

The next chapter will cover using Office 365 and Windows Intune, starting with a day in the life of an Office 365 user and a follow-on section that helps you set up your computer to use Office 365.

Here is a list of chapters you may want to read next:

- *Chapter 2*: Using Office 365 and Windows Intune

  We explore the Office 365 capabilities in the demonstration site with a focus on how this helps your business productivity. The best way to understand is to experience Office 365. We use a day in the life of a user to demonstrate the capabilities that you have with Office 365. We close the chapter with a reference section on the most common end user configurations when you use Office 365.

- *Chapter 3:* Office 365 Planning and Purchase

  The key to a successful migration is the planning and purchase process of Office 365. There are three different categories of plans you may purchase from, but the secret to a successful migration to Office 365 is picking the correct plan that supports your business. Once you pick the plan, it is about planning the migration to Office 365 to ensure the process is seamless for your organization. This chapter describes the basic purchase information and offers more details about the choices. We close this chapter with information about pilots and e-mail migration.

- *Chapter 4*: Office 365 Setup and Migration

  Once you have selected your Office 365 plan and completed the planning process, the next step is the migration process. There are different ways you can migrate to Office 365 and different migration techniques, such as using cut over migration or federation. This chapter covers the most common approach to Office 365 migration in a non-federated environment.

- *Chapter 8*: Office 365 Administration

  This chapter describes the different administration centers in Office 365 and the most common tools that you will use to administrate your Office 365 company. Depending on your Office 365 services, there are five possible administration tools. This chapter focuses on the Office 365, Exchange, and Lync administration centers. The SharePoint and Windows Intune administration centers are described in their own chapters. We close the chapter with using PowerShell to manage your Office 365 environment.

CHAPTER 2

■ ■ ■

Using Office 365 and Windows Intune

Office 365 is a family of products organized in three product plans. Each plan is designed with features to best meet the needs of businesses based upon their size or other factors. The plans are referred to as small business, midsize business, and enterprise business. Office 365 Small Business and Midsize Business are fixed in size and configuration. Users of these plans must purchase all of the same subscription. The Enterprise plan has all of the different Office 365 options. The Office 365 Enterprise configuration allows mixing and matching features to create a customized subscription within the enterprise plan. The midsize and small business suites are restricted only to those products in those specific Office 365 plans.

Office 365 is scalable for all business. An enterprise Office 365 subscription can be created for one user or 100,000 users. The scalability is achieved with service reliability, ease of use of the administration center, and flexible mixing of the different Office 365 plans. Our approach to an Office 365 configuration is to select the suite of products that best matches the roles of the employees and needs of the organization. The Office 365 Enterprise Suite allows the most flexibility in choosing product features.

This chapter details a day in the life of an Office 365 user and material for setting up one computer to use Office 365. This approach enables most end users to start an Office 365 trial subscription and successfully configure the service.

"A Day in the Life of an Office 365 User" explores the Office 365 capabilities in the Microsoft demonstration site and details the features of Office 365. Taking the time to test the service offering in this way tends to result in the most successful migrations. With a basic understanding of the service offerings, identifying the ones that match your business needs becomes simple.

A Day in the Life of an Office 365 User

In the previous chapter, the Ready Design Cupcake Company (RDCC) completed a business analysis of the Office 365 cloud services and was ready to move to Office 365. The IT manager, Tom, looked at his total company spending, and with the help of his Microsoft Partner, determined that his on-site cost was about $115 per user per month; and the Office 365 cost would be approximately $53 per user per month (see Figure 2-1). These costs included ongoing support.

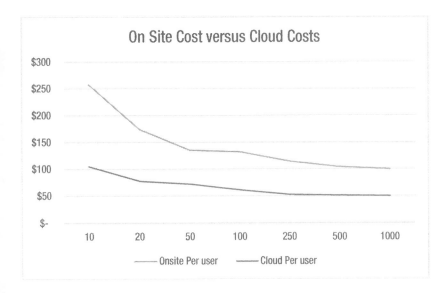

Figure 2-1. *On-site costs versus cloud costs*

However, Tom had questions about how Office 365 services would benefit his users at RDCC. He and his Microsoft Partner set up a demonstration. Most Microsoft Partners can set up different types of test environments, but in the RDCC case, the Microsoft Partner, KAMIND, choose to use an interactive training session using the Microsoft Customer Immersion Experience center (CIE), which provides a fully configured Office 365 experience. This exercise exposes Tom to the full range of Office 365 capabilities and features in such a way that he is able to relate his new knowledge to the Office 365 migration project for RDCC.

The Microsoft CIE is a preconfigured Office 365 organization that supports all of the Office 365 services, including Yammer, Project, Exchange, Lync, SharePoint, and CRM. RDCC is not interested in the CRM option at this time, but they are interested in using Windows Intune. Tom was looking for a way to reduce the costs of managing the Office 365 user's devices with a cloud solution so RDCC would not need to manage an On Premises solution using Microsoft System Center. Kamind1 suggested that Tom play the role of an end user in the Microsoft demonstration company, Contoso, Inc. Tom was assigned an Office 365 user account, and he assumed the hypothetical identity of a Contoso sales associate, Karen.

■ **Note**   "Where to start with Office 365" is a *hands-on tutorial*, not a *configuration guide*. In the second part of this chapter, we have all of the necessary configuration information to set up your desktop. The tutorial serves only to show the features of Office 365, so the ones you really need can be selected and applied to your specific work environment.

Where to Start with Office365? A Hands-On Tutorial

Start by opening up a web browser and logging in into the Office 365 site at `http://office.microsoft.com` (see Figure 2-2).

Figure 2-2. *Log in to Office 365: login screen*

Once you have entered your email address, Microsoft online services will determine if there are multiple accounts for different Microsoft services under your email address. Microsoft offers two different services for users: consumer services and business services. These services are represented as a Microsoft account and an Organization account. The Microsoft account is for Microsoft services that require a unique ID, such as your email address. Examples of these accounts are Hotmail, Microsoft Passport, Xbox Live, and volume license services (to name a few; there are other consumer services).

The Organization account is your Office 365 company business service account. The services of these two accounts are different and isolated from each other on different servers in one or more Microsoft Data Centers. It is very common that a user will have both an Organization account and a Microsoft account. When you access Office 365 services, you always use the Organization account.

▩ **Note**   You do not need to have a Microsoft account to use Office 365, only an Organizational account.

Logging into Office 365

After you have opened a browser to Office.microsoft.com, select the sign-in (Figure 2-2, upper right-hand corner) and enter your Office 365 company email address. If you have added consumer capabilities to your email address (found at account.live.com), then you will be presented with two choices (Figure 2-3). If you are going to access the Office 365, then select the Organizational account.

Figure 2-3. *Access Office 365 using the Organization account*

Once you have entered your password you will log in to Office 365 services. The next step is to explore the interface of Office 365. RDCC's IT manger chose to use the hypothetical persona of Karen Berg, a Sales Associate in the Contoso Company. He wanted to experience the operation of Office 365 from a productivity point of view as a user. When you log into Office 365 for the first time, a normal Office 365 user (like Karen Berg) sees an initial configuration screen that introduces Office 365 services to the user in the self-service portal (see Figure 2-4). Tom liked this approach because the self-service portal reduces the calls to his help desk and improves his users' satisfaction.

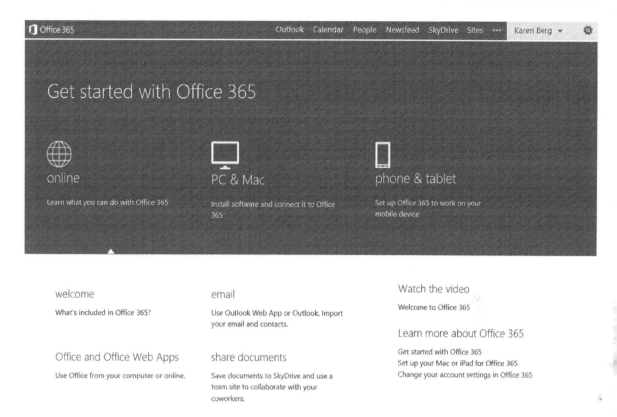

Figure 2-4. Office 365 first-time login

Tom, acting as Karen Berg, sees that he can continue to install the Office 365 software for his PC/Mac, phone, and tablet without any help desk support. He watches the "getting started" video to get a feel for the organization of Office 365. Tom explores the different services, such as Web Outlook and his personal cloud document storage, SkyDrive Pro. The self-service welcome portal (Figure 2-4) will stay visible until the Outlook services are accessed. Tom selects the Outlook tab (Figure 2-5) to see Karen's email.

Figure 2-5. Accessing Outlook: Office 365

Office 365 Outlook mail services are designed to provide data synchronization between all devices that are are using Office 365. The simplest way to look at this is that all information is synchronized, so in using email on his smartphone, Web browser, or local Outlook, Tom only needs to "read once" and/or "delete once" and all devices connected to Office 365 email services will sync his actions.

Accessing Outlook–WebApp

Tom begins to explore the Office 365 web site. The Microsoft Partner informs him that after the initial login, all future logins to Office 365 will replace the user start page to either use Outlook or the Team site, depending on the license that is assigned to the user. As an example, if the user only has a SharePoint license the user will land on the "sites" page. If the user has an email license, then the user will land on the Outlook page (Figure 2-6). Karen's license is a full Office 365 that includes access to SharePoint and Office 2013, so her default page is Outlook WebApp.

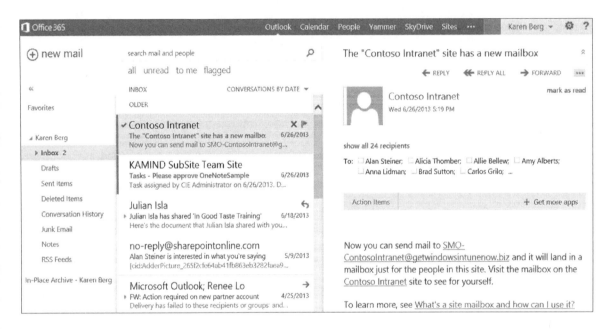

Figure 2-6. *Office 365 landing page for user with an email account*

Tom notices that the Office 365 web Outlook (Outlook WebApp) looks very similar to the Outlook client. The interface is crisp and simple to understand. The Outlook email, calendar, and People (contacts) are easily navigated. Tom notices that the Outlook WebApp supports right-click actions on the interface (Figure 2-7). This is important to Tom so that the sales staff may color code their email into different categories.

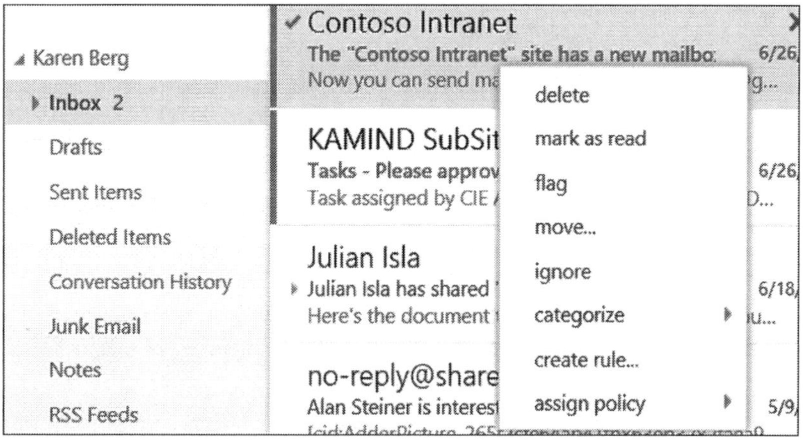

Figure 2-7. *Outlook WebApp with right-click support*

Tom also notices that he can assign an individual retention policy on his email. He right-clicks the message and selects "Assign Policy" (Figure 2-8) for email retention. In this case, he selects "never delete." The Microsoft Partner informs Tom the email size is 50GB per user, and the per-user archive is unlimited. Tom quickly realizes that this is a big benefit to his users. They are constantly getting midnight calls from the president of the company, complaining about the limited size of user's mailboxes. Most of us have, at some point, suffered the frustration of an over-full mailbox either as a sender or as a receiver.

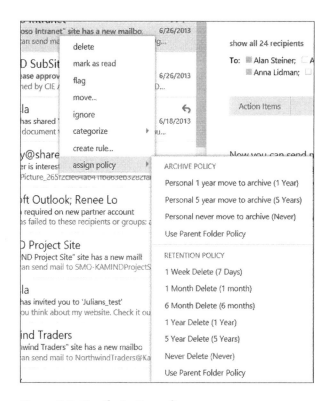

Figure 2-8. *Email retention policy*

■ **Note**   IT polices can override individual polices on email retention. The default is to allow the user to determine the best way to save email. We have seen corporate email retention polices provide as little as 90 days history. Many of us expect to retain years of old emails.

SkyDrive Pro–Overview

Tom reviews the Office 365 features and notices that there is support for SkyDrive, Sites, and Yammer. The Microsoft Partner explains that Office 365 document synchronization is part of SkyDrive. SkyDrive is Microsoft's document synchronization tool that synchronizes documents with Office 365 and all of the user's desktop or mobile devices. This allows the user Karen to access work documents on her phone, laptop, or desktop computer. The Microsoft Partner instructs Tom to access SkyDrive and select the SkyDrive menu item (Figure 2-9) to edit documents in the Office 365 cloud.

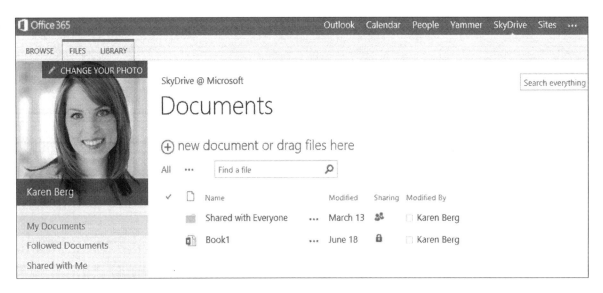

Figure 2-9. *Karen's personal document storage in SkyDrive*

■ **Note**   if this is the first time you are accessing the SkyDrive, setup can take a few minutes.

Once the setup is completed, Karen's private SkyDrive Pro cloud storage is built. Karen's initial SkyDrive Pro storage capacity can be set at levels between 25GB and 100GB. Tom thinks of RDCC sales associates who have a mobile laptop, iPad, and smartphone and considers that they are located in several different parts of the world. He realizes that SkyDrive Pro storage solves a problem for RDCC by easily maintaining control of company documents in a centralized team storage, without the associated overhead costs. His Microsoft Partner informs him that the SkyDrive is included in the subscription he plans to use for RDCC at no additional cost. The initial SkyDrive Pro size is set at 25GB.

Tom explores other aspects of using documents in the cloud and discovers that any document that is uploaded to the cloud can be used in any collaboration. Office 365 has two document storage areas. One is the personal SkyDrive site and the other is the company's "Team Site". The difference is that the personal SkyDrive site is managed by the user (Karen), and the Team Site is managed by the IT department.

Document Collaboration

The Office 365 SkyDrive and Team Site allow you to create documents specifically for collaboration. Just select the "new document" option in the "Create Document" box (see Figure 2-10) and proceed.

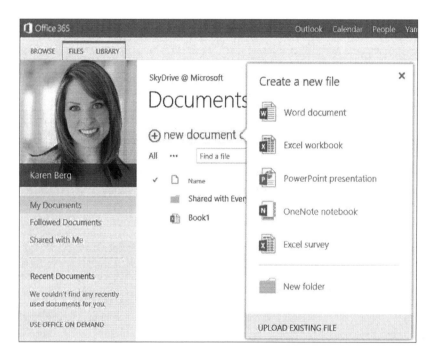

Figure 2-10. *Office 365 document creation*

You can also upload documents from other systems to Office 365 using a drag-and-drop interface. Tom discovered that when he used Windows 8.1, he could easily drag documents (Figure 2-11) to the SkyDrive Pro site in the web browser and place those documents in his personal area on Office 365. He also experimented with the Team Site and discovered that he had the same capability there.

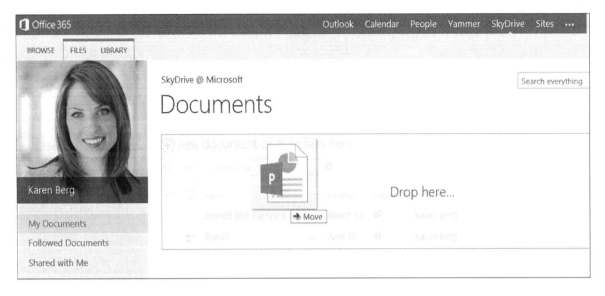

Figure 2-11. *Uploading documents to Office 365*

Once saved in Tom's personal area of Office 365, documents could be shared with other members of the team as needed. Once the documents are uploaded, they also can be edited with Office 365 web applications (Word, Excel, OneNote, PowerPoint) or with the desktop (or mobile) Office Professional Plus software, which supports PC, Mac and Android devices.

Tom discovered that Office 365 documents can be shared between designated team members using the personal "share everyone" folder, or externally to users outside the company. Tom experimented with sharing documents by selecting the ellipses (…) and later the "Share" option in the pop menu. Tom was surprised to see a preview of the file with an option to allow you to explicitly share the document (Figure 2-12).

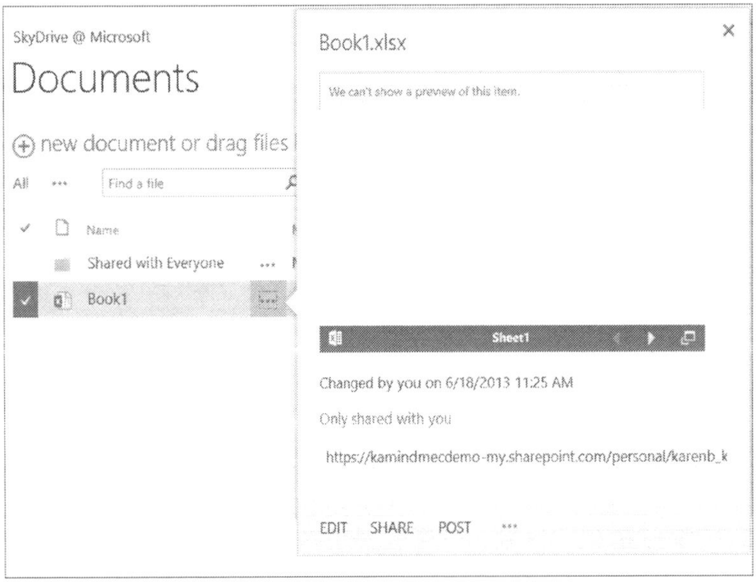

Figure 2-12. *Sharing documents in Office 365*

Once the sharing options are visible, just select "Share" and enter the necessary information (such as the user's email address) to share the directory or the file for collaboration. The files/folders that are shared show the people icon (Figure 2-13). The files/folders that are not shared show the lock icon.

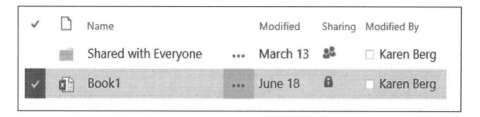

Figure 2-13. *Office 365 sharing icons*

Office 365 Yammer Configuration

Tom has been impressed with the capabilities that he has encountered so far. He sees that Office 365 offers the opportunity to reduce both operational costs and license costs while rolling out new capabilities to his users. However, he still has questions. One of his unresolved concerns is compliance issues. As an example, his legal department has asked him to restrict social media access for users in the company. The legal department feels that too much proprietary information (company confidential information) is being discussed on external social media sites such as Facebook and Google Plus.

The legal department advises that loss of company information could hurt business growth and give RDCC competitors advance information on the direction of RDCC products. The Microsoft Partner suggested that Tom consider the Yammer social media service that is part of Office 365 as a solution. Yammer is a service, similar to Facebook, used to handle group interactions in a free-form manner. It is explained that with Yammer, the company information exchanged on this channel is owned by the company and not licensed to a third party. Usually, a free service has an intellectual property rights assignment that overrides the confidentiality of the company information.

Tom selected the Yammer login from Office 365 page (Figure 2-14) and logs into Yammer using Karen Berg's Office 365 account. The first thing that Tom noticed (Figure 2-15) was the interaction of the different teams and the discussion groups. There were discussion groups for events, HR, and using Yammer itself. Tom could see that Yammer addressed one of RDCC business objectives: to make the company more integrated in their internal communications to improve productivity. The productivity gain addressed this directive and Yammer received full endorsement by the legal department.

Figure 2-14. *Yammer access: Office 365 menu option*

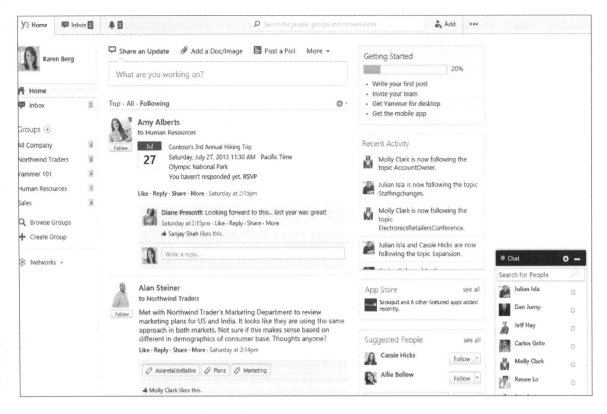

Figure 2-15. *Yammer integration for Office 365*

Tom quickly realized that one of the benefits of Yammer is that the service provides a tool for the group's communications that can be kept internal to the company. The problem with the traditional social media solutions is that RDCC proprietary information can be accidentally leaked to the public. Legal informed Tom that last year, some employees were using some free social media site to share information about a project. The legal department discovered the project discussed in the trade press. Tom was told about the data leak of company information at a company senior management meeting. Tom feels that Yammer will allow RDCC to control potential data leaks.

Public Web Site

The final service that Tom reviews is the Team Site and the public web site. Tom has a business requirement to create a new company intranet and to help the company reduce the carbon footprint. He has a secondary objective to reduce the use of other file sharing services enabling the exchange of information with external parties. To access the Team Site, Tom returns to the main Office 365 page and selects "Sites" (Figure 2-16).

Figure 2-16. *Selecting the Team Site from "Sites" menu*

After selecting the sites, Tom is presented with two choices: accessing the "Team Site" (intranet) or the public web site. Office 365 supports multiple sites depending on the configuration of Office 365 services. All Office 365 configurations include a public web site. Tom selects the public web site icon (Figure 2-17) to see the public web site. Tom accessed Karen's site, to discover that the user has the ability to follow changes made by others in the Team Site and to personalize their experience in using Office 365. Personalization allows you to follow changes in a team site, so if there are changes in the content, you are notified of the change.

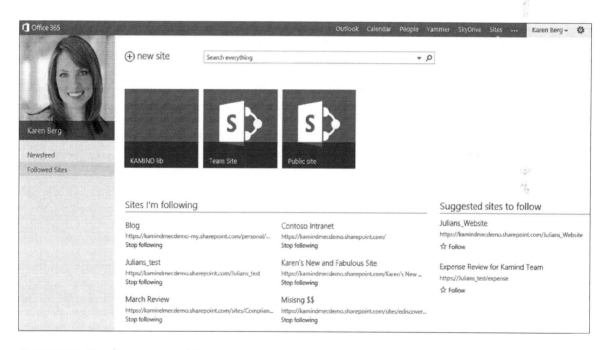

Figure 2-17. *Sites that are accessed by users*

Tom selected the "public site" icon to see the capabilities of the public site. The Office 365 public web site can be changed by the users using the web site integrated editor, using SharePoint designer (supplied as an optional tool download in Office 365).

Tom discovered that his access to the public web site configuration tools is based on permissions. If he changes from the user "Karen Berg" to a user that has permission to edit the web site, he can log into the web site (Figure 2-18, upper right-hand corner, sign in) and enter his administrator credentials. Once Tom logs into the administration panel of the public web site (Figure 2-19), he can use the Microsoft integrated tools to build the web site (see chapter 6 for more information). The "public web site" is a SharePoint site.

Figure 2-18. Office 365 public web site

Figure 2-19. Accessing the administration tools on the public web site

Tom discovered that the "public web site" in Office 365 is a private web site. The initial state of the public web site is offline. To convert the public web site to a visible web site, he simply assigned a domain to Office 365 and placed the web site online. Tom finishes exploring the public web site, returns back to the "Sites" menu, and then selects the "Team Site". The Team Site is the company's Intranet site (Figure 2-20).

Figure 2-20. *Office 365 Team Site*

Office 365 Team Site

The Microsoft Partner explains to Tom that the MEC demo Contoso site is a fully functional SharePoint site complete with document retention polices, work flows, and other productivity features. The Partner also explains that these capabilities can be used to improve the operation of RDCC business. Tom selects the "Team Site" icon and launches the Intranet site (Figure 2-20).

Tom looks at the team site and the servers they use in RDCC and realizes that he can add the functionality needed for each of the various teams to function. Tom realizes that he can assign user permissions, so individuals can have access to the different business areas. As an example, Karen can access the sales resources but have access to HR, IT, Operations, and account team only as it relates to her business role.

Office 365 and Windows Azure Active Directory Security

Tom realizes that he can use either his on-premises servers' Active Directory, to manage security, or the Office 365 security groups, to grant permissions. As an IT manager, Tom must have the maximum flexibility to restrict information as appropriate for individuals' roles. The Microsoft Partner suggested that Tom review Microsoft's Windows Azure Active Directory integration (Figure 2-21).

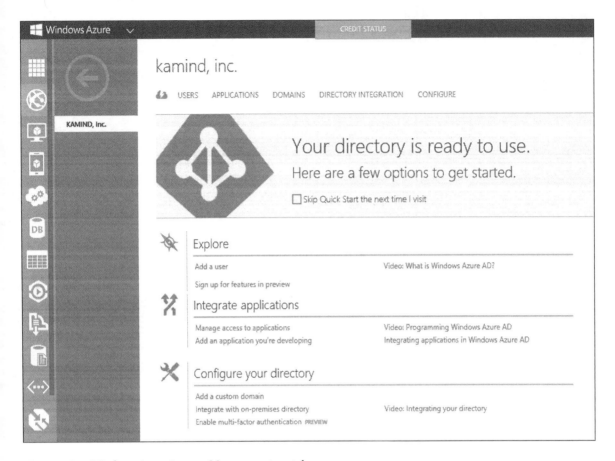

Figure 2-21. *Windows Azure Account Management portal*

Windows Azure is integrated into Office 365 Active Directory. This makes it simpler to have a single sign-on for RDCC users. If an on-premise server is integrated into Office 365 (using any Active Directory integration tools), those on-premise security objects are also copied into Windows Azure. Tom feels that with this integration approach, he can manage the user security access using either on-premise services or Office 365. As an example, Tom was thinking of placing the accounting line of the business in a Virtual Windows Azure Server and integrating that sever into Office 365 Active Directory.

RDCC's long-term strategy is to remove all on-premise servers and move them to the cloud. Tom feels there is no longer a business need for an on-premise Active Directory server. After looking at Windows Azure Active Directory integration and virtual server management, Tom recognizes that he may accomplish the server migration to the cloud as part of the move of RDCC to Office 365. This would significantly reduce RDCC's operation costs. Tom makes a note of this to discuss with the Microsoft Partner after the migration to Office 365 is completed.

Office 365 Desktop Tools

The only issue Tom has not reviewed is desktop tools for Office 365. Tom returned to the Office 365 portal and installed the Client software. Tom has a misconception that Office 365 office tools only run in the cloud and that there is no desktop software. Tom learned that Office 365 is a suite of products, namely, desktop and cloud services, and that these products work together. While using the "Karen Berg" login address, Tom was able to use the cloud tools on Office 365 and use the desktop tool without being hooked to the internet, to do work offline on his PC or his home Mac (Figure 2-22). The Microsoft Partner explains that Office 365 allows each user to have up to five copies of Office desktop software installed under the subscription. Tom thought about the cost savings from using subscription services to manage his software assets. Tom realized that he would no longer need to manage serial numbers or manage employees installing software on their own computers. Office 365 allowed Tom to remove the user software subscription when an employee leaves the company and no longer have any responsibility to remove the software. This is a business liability and huge labor effort that Tom realized he no longer needs to manage. Office 365 will significantly reduce his operations costs.

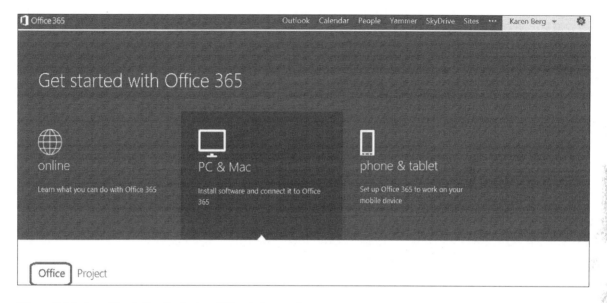

Figure 2-22. *Installing Office Professional Plus desktop software*

Tom remembers a discussion with one of his users on the differences between Office 2007 and 2010. His comment was that Office is Office; only the menus are different. The 2013 Office 365 is very similar to Office 2010. The major change is that Office 2013 is "aware" of the cloud so documents can be saved on the desktop and synced to Office 365 (using the SkyDrive Pro background synchronization tool), directly to the cloud or in the user's local documents directory.

Tom begins the installation process of the Office Professional Plus software (Figure 2-23). He returns to the Office 365 portal, selects PC/Mac, and then selects Office software to begin the installation process. He notices that he can also add Microsoft Project to his plan by purchasing a license. Microsoft Project is an optional software package that Tom has licensed in Office 365. Tom clicks the install button to install the Office Professional Plus software on his desktop.

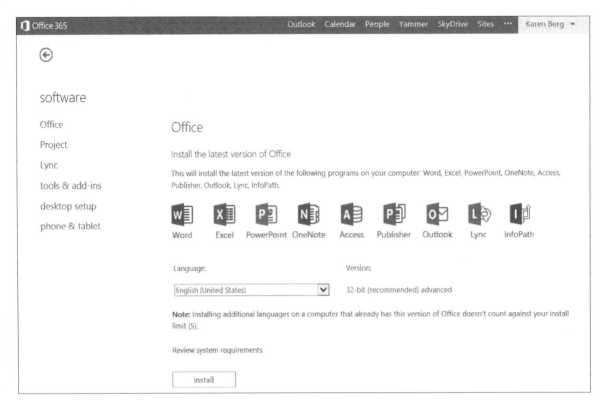

Figure 2-23. *Office desktop software installation*

The Office installation software is streamed (Figure 2-24 and Figure 2-25). Streaming means that the user can continue to work while the new software is being delivered from the Microsoft Office servers.

Figure 2-24. *Streaming Office 365*

Figure 2-25. *Streaming Office 365*

Tom started the Office Professional Plus installation (Figure 2-24 and Figure 2-25). Once this was completed, he started up Outlook using Karen Berg's email address for the demonstration account. Tom started Outlook and selected a "New Profile." The installation process required Tom to enter Karen's email address, name, and password (see Figure 2-26). Outlook discovered the cloud service and downloaded Karen's email.

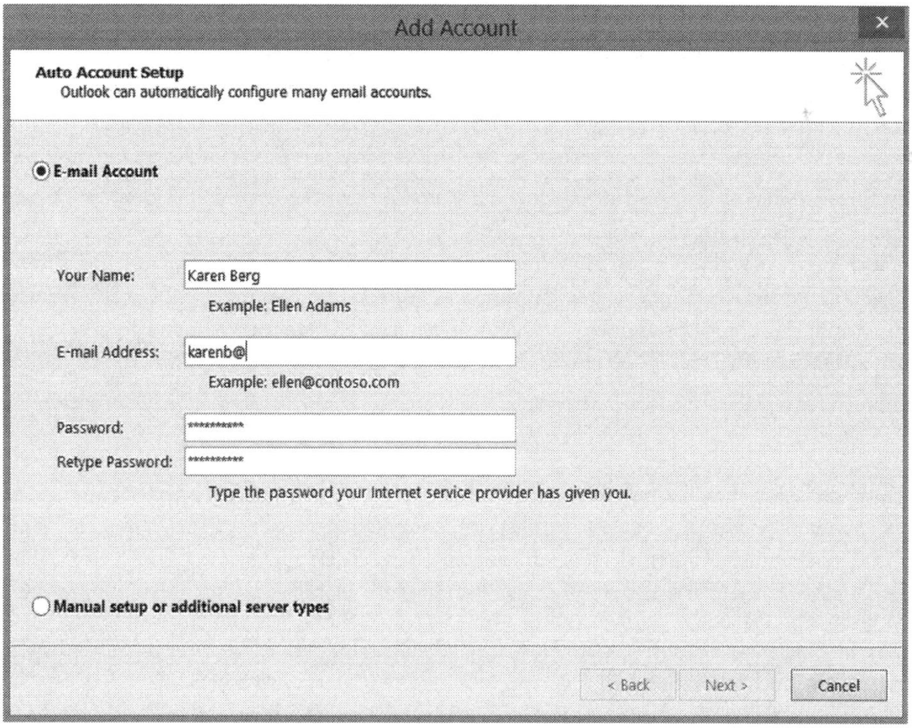

Figure 2-26. *Outlook startup screen: creating new profile*

Tom was off and running with Outlook. He selected finished (when prompted) and started Outlook. Karen's email is downloaded to Tom's client. Tom started the desktop Outlook (Figure 2-27), and he noticed that when he read an email in the desktop Outlook, the Office 365 Outlook WebApp had the same changes. Then, Tom noticed that his actions to email (reads deleted moves) were synced to the cloud. His users have always complained that the smartphones did not update the email status after a message was read or deleted. Tom no longer has to worry about this issue; all email is synced to the latest activity. Tom wanted to try one other test, so he disconnected his network connection, created a new email in Outlook, and sent it. Tom then connected his laptop back into the network and discovered that the offline email that was sent when Outlook was updated in the cloud.

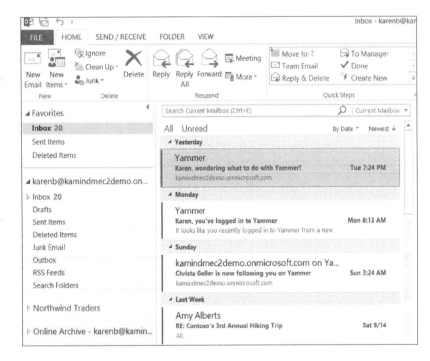

Figure 2-27. *Karen's desktop Outlook*

This solved a big problem for his users. Tom now had full business email, calendar, and contacts synchronization not only to his desktop Outlook, but also to his smartphone and iPad. He realized that the variety of third-party programs that his users were using to synchronize their contacts and calendars were no longer needed.

Using Lync

One of the problems that Tom has is web conferencing. When he installed Office on the desktop, the web video conferencing tool Lync was also installed. His users currently use Skype over the public network to talk about business needs and issues. As Tom explored Lync (the Office 365 collaborative and video conferencing tool), he realized that he can now use Lync to talk to external Lync and Skype users outside of the company as well as internal RDCC employees. Using Lync, conversations (and text in Instant Messaging Windows) can be recorded (Figure 2-28). Lync is also an Enterprise voice solution, where both users can speak at the same time (Skype does not support this feature), and Lync can also replace his desktop phone and be placed on user's mobile devices (laptop, iPad, and smartphone). Tom was pleased to see this, since many new federal regulations require conversation recording to meet compliance rules.

Figure 2-28. *Lync video conferencing and IM tool*

Tom discovered that Lync is integrated into Outlook and he can send a meeting invite out to all employees from Outlook. Tom also discovered that Lync can support external voice conferencing such as intercall conferencing. This way Tom can send out meeting requests and have the meeting either as a web conference or as a video conference (Figure 2-29). Lync allows both sides to talk at the same time, compared to other services where only one person can talk. The ability for multiple people to talk simultaneously is important for enterprise business voice.

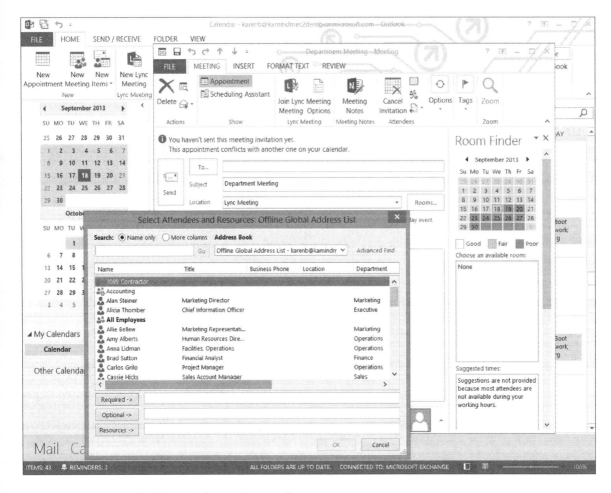

Figure 2-29. *Outlook scheduling a video conference call using Lync*

Data Loss Prevention

Tom explored some of the additional features in Office 365. One item he wanted to verify was what happens if credit card information (embedded in emails or documents) is emailed externally from RDCC. So he emailed a test message to an external user, and the email was rejected (not delivered to the external user) with the following rejection message:

```
TRANSPORT.RULES. Reject Message; the message was rejected by organization
```

The Microsoft Partner explains that Data Loss Prevention (DLP) is a configured service that is part of Office 365. This service processes the email message content against various rules. One of the rules that emails can be processed against is a Personal Information Identification rule that detects credit card numbers in email and documents. Microsoft supplies a standard set of DLP template rules, but you can also have custom DLP templates built. As an example, if RDCC has internal proprietary information, you can construct a word template for those documents and an appropriate DLP rule that manages the information so it is not emailed externally. This way, RDCC will have maximum control (as much as possible) over the external communications to ensure that only appropriate information is delivered externally. The Partner showed Tom the available DLP rules (Figure 2-30) that can be easily added to Office 365.

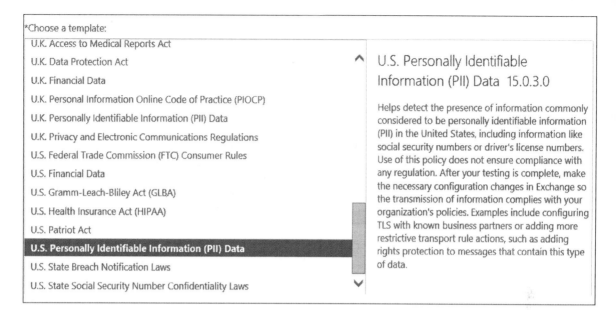

Figure 2-30. *Office 365 data loss standard rules*

Tom thought about his business requirements and the services that are part of Office 365. When he looked at the overall costs, Office 365 made business sense, and it reduces his overall expenses. With the different licensing models, Tom has the flexibility to purchase the services on a monthly invoice, or on a yearly invoice through a traditional reseller.

Device Configuration

One of the last things that Tom looked at was the smart device support. With everything else that he has experienced, he was not surprised to see that his iPhone was fully supported with Office 365 as well as the Android devices and iPads (Figure 2-31).

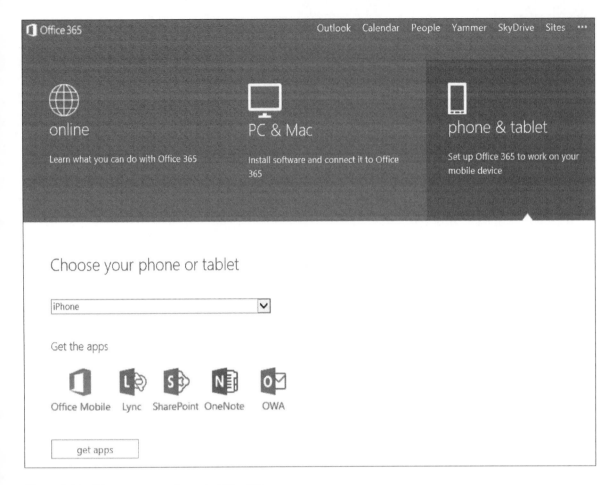

Figure 2-31. *iPhone-supported apps in Office 365*

As Tom looked over Office 365, he became aware of its different configurations. Office 365 is a cloud-based service that does not care who is the manufacturer of the user's device. Tom's users have iPhone, Macs, PCs, laptops, and the new Chrome notebooks. Tom realizes that Office 365 supports all of these devices.

Windows Intune

The Microsoft Partner suggested that Tom look at Windows Intune, so Tom enters the URL for Windows Intune (https://account.manage.microsoft.com) and starts to access the service (Figure 2-32). The Microsoft Partner remarked that Windows Intune is an integrated service that uses Office 365 Active Directory to manage desktop and mobile devices.

Figure 2-32. *Windows Intune user page:* `account.manage.microsoft.com`

Windows Intune (see Chapter 7) allows the IT organization to fully manage the user mobile devices and desktop devices with antivirus, policy management, updated management, and hardware and software inventory management. Windows Intune monitors the end user devices and sends notification to the administrator when there are issues associated with the user's system. Tom logged into Windows Intune (`https://account.manage.microsoft.com`), looked at the start screen (Figure 2-32), and proceeded to log in to the company portal (Figure 2-33).

Figure 2-33. *Windows Intune company portal*

The Microsoft Partner explained that Windows Intune is designed for the IT staff to reduce the cost of desktop management deployment. Windows Intune has a self-service portal that allows users to register their devices (mobile, laptops, desktop) into the Windows Intune deployment center. This allows the IT staff to manage those systems. Windows Intune also supports custom application deployment for mobile devices. Controlling the deployment of custom applications is a key benefit for RDCC because they no longer need to publish the mobile application to the Public cloud.

MEC Summary

Using a "walk-through" approach has exposed you to the different capabilities of Office 365 from a very practical point of view: how you use the features. There is much more to Office 365 than we discussed, and we will cover that information in subsequent chapters. At this point, if you have a trial subscription, you are ready to try Office 365. The next section contains helpful hints on Office 365 configuration of your mobile devices and workstation.

User Setup and Configuration

In our walk-through example, we wanted to give you a feeling of the capabilities of Office 365 and how to use those capabilities. We purposely skipped over the configuration: how to set up Office 365 and how to configure SkyDrive Pro and Lync. As you saw earlier, configuration is not difficult. The key to stressless configuration is noting where information is located. We have included additional workstation setup information on the following topics:

- Workstation Guides
  - Setup
  - Creating New Outlook Profile
  - Desktop Setup (office 2007/2010)
- SkyDrive Pro
  - Configuration
  - Planning
  - Team Site Caution
  - Changing Configuration
  - Office 2010 Support
  - Checking Storage Allocation
- Smartphone
  - Android (Motorola V2.2) and Other Devices
  - Windows Phone Office 365
  - Windows Phone Adding Multiple Exchange Accounts
- Lync
  - Skype Configuration
  - Creating a Microsoft Account for Skype
  - Using Skype to Call Lync
  - Troubleshooting
  - Firewall Ports

Please check `www.getoffice365now.com` for the latest information on Office 365 configurations.

Workstation: Setup Guide

The following steps are used by an individual who has Office Professional Plus licenses assigned to the users.

1. Start a web browser and sign in to Office 365 at portal.microsoftonline.com

2. On the right-hand side, select the Gear, then "Office 365 settings" (Figure 2-34)

3. Follow these steps

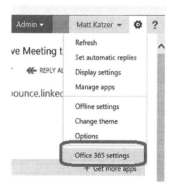

Figure 2-34. *Office 365 software download*

Step 1: Install Office 2013 or Desktop Configuration

Select the gear, then "Office 365 settings" or, as an administrator, select software download (Figure 2-34).

1. You have two options to download software in Office 365. You can download the complete Office 2013 suite, or you can download the desktop setup (for older systems using Office 2007 or Office 2010). Select one of the options shown in Figure 2-35.

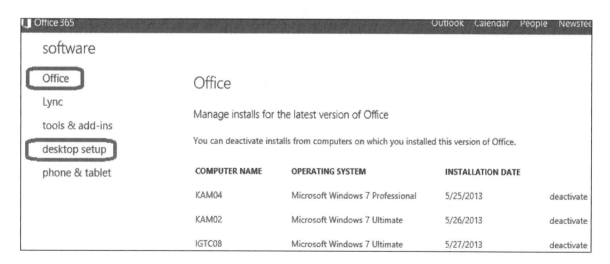

Figure 2-35. *Software selection download showing three additional systems already running Office 2013*

2.   If you choose to install the full Office 2013, select "Office" to install the software (Figure 2-36). This option is available only if the Office Professional Plus software is part of your subscription.

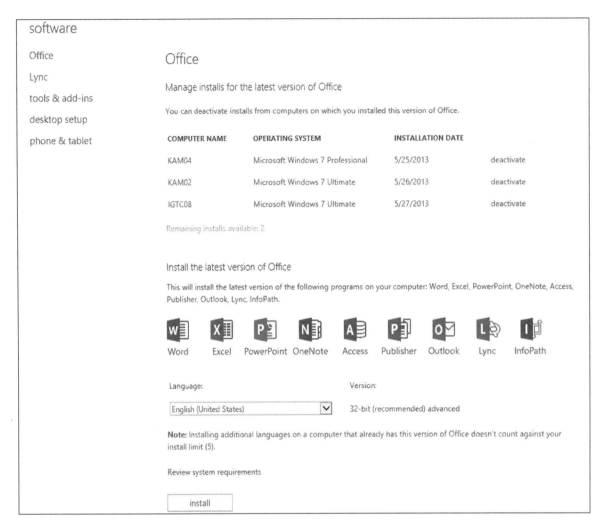

Figure 2-36.   *Installing full Office 2013*

3.   If you choose not to install Office 2013 or if you do not have the Office Professional Plus as part of your subscription, then you must install the desktop setup (Figure 2-37).

Figure 2-37. *Installing desktop setup*

4. After you have installed the desktop setup, you can install software for your phone and tablet. Please see our phone tablet setup document for installation and configuration of these features.

Step 2: Configuration of Lync

1. After you have installed Office 2013 or Lync, you need to configure Lync for your use. To use Lync, just log in using your Office 365 account.

2. Start Lync 2013 from your device and sign in (Figure 2-38 and Figure 2-39).

Figure 2-38. *Starting up Lync*

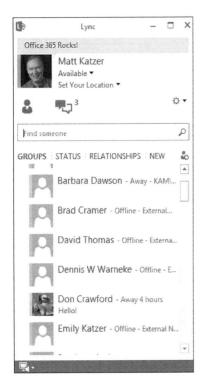

Figure 2-39. *Starting up Lync*

3. Skype Integration: If KAMIND has configured your site, it is enabled for Skype access. To send an Instant Message (IM) to a Skype user, use the formatted email address similar to "mjones(company.com)@msn.com" (example: mjones@kamind.net@msn.com), where the Microsoft Account for the Skype user to log in is mjones@company.com.

4. If your Lync client does not start up with a screen similar to the one in Figure 2-39, refer to the Lync troubleshooting notes for additional information.

Step 3: Configuration of Outlook

Your network has been set up to support automatic Outlook configuration. (Your System Administrator has done this for you already when Office 365 was set up.) If this is a new installation for Office, to configure Outlook, select "New Profile" when prompted, enter the username and password, and then select "Next" (see Figure 2-40). If there is an existing Outlook profile, you need to enable a new profile option so you can create a new Outlook profile.

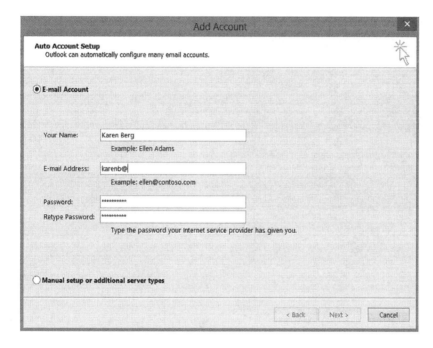

Figure 2-40. *Outlook setup*

If you wish to speed up the configuration of Outlook to Office 365, log in to the Office 365 web site www.Office365.com as the user you entered in the Outlook startup screen (Figure 2-40). Outlook uses a secured https connection and will use the same connection details that you enter for your browser. The Outlook screen will complete, and you are ready to use Office 365. Close and restart Outlook. At this point you are finished with the installation! Enjoy using Office 365.

Workstation: Creating a New Outlook Profile

Outlook operates on user profiles. You can have multiple profiles in Outlook; you just need to select which profile to use. This is useful if you need to have different email accounts running in separate Outlook profiles and isolated from each other's mail service. The normal operation for Outlook is to autoload a profile.

During Office 365 testing, it works best if you use multiple profiles and configure Office 365 in the second profile. To create a new profile, enable the "Prompt for Profile" option in the control panel. Follow the next steps:

1. Open up the control panel on your Windows 7 or Windows 8

2. In the upper right-hand corner, select "Display All Icons"

3. Select the "Mail" icon (see Figure 2-41)

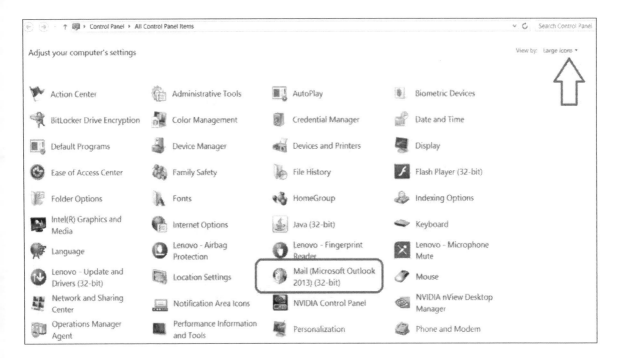

Figure 2-41. *Control panel: changing mail profile*

4. Select "Profiles" (see Figure 2-42)

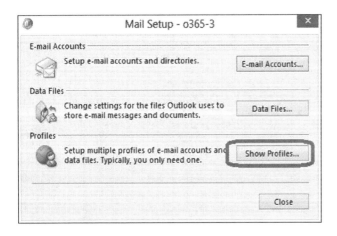

Figure 2-42. *Configuring for multiple profiles*

5. Select "Show Profiles"

6. Change to "Prompt for a profile to be used" (Figure 2-43), then exit

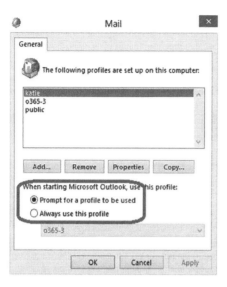

Figure 2-43. *Set to "Prompt for a profile to be used"*

7. Select OK; then close. Now start up Outlook and the dialog box will prompt you for a new profile. Select "new," repeat step 3, and enter the new email account information.

Workstation: Desktop Setup Configuration

Office 2007 and Office 2010 require additional software to be installed on your desktop. When you run the desktop setup (Figure 2-44), Office 365 will download a setup configuration tool that will update your desktop and Office software with the latest patches and security information. Office 2013 was designed for the cloud and does not require any additional desktop configuration.

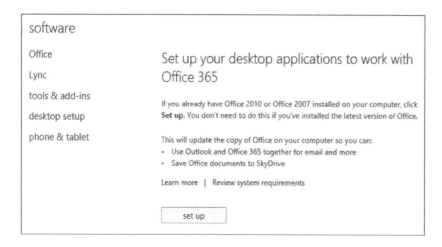

Figure 2-44. *Installing desktop setup*

To install the desktop configuration tool, select "Setup." This action will download the desktop configuration tool that will be streamed from the Office 365 servers. Once the desktop configuration tool is installed, click Setup in "Set up and configure your Office desktop apps" and follow the next steps:

1. Click the check box beside applications that need to be configured (Figure 2-45). Normally, the startup process will check the correct items. Click Continue. Close any applications that you need to.

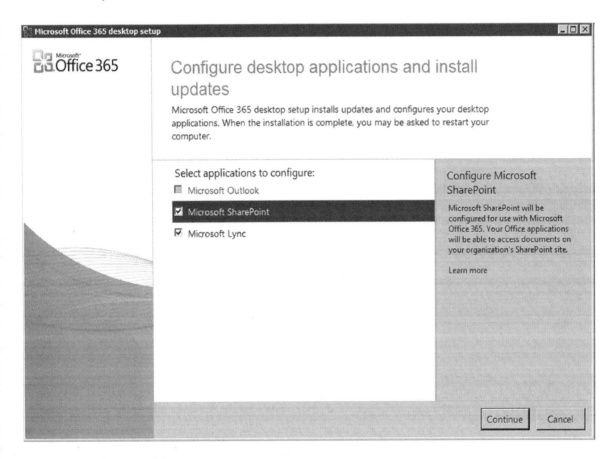

Figure 2-45. *Office 365 validation options*

2. Click Finish (Figure 2-46). You might need to restart your computer.

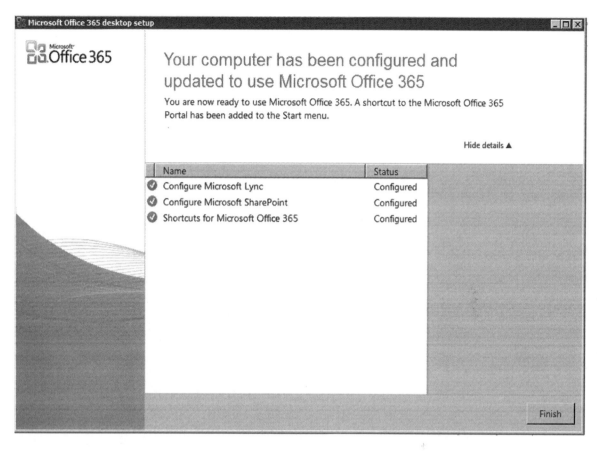

Figure 2-46. *Office 365 successful configuration update*

SkyDrive Pro: Configuration

Office 365 SkyDrive Pro is a configuration tool that is designed to sync documents from your computer to Office 365. SkyDrive Pro automatically copies your documents to the cloud. This cloud synchronization tool can sync your desktop files (up to 100GB) to Office 365. You can synchronize one directory or multiple directories on your desktop, laptop, or smartphone. The maximum file size that can be synced is 2GB.

There are two versions of SkyDrive: SkyDrive Pro (for businesses) and SkyDrive (for consumers). You select the SkyDrive based on the login ID (Figure 2-47), in this case your Office 365 Organization Account.

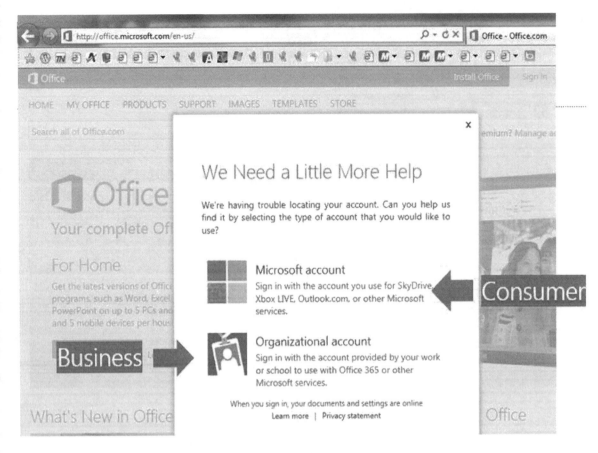

Figure 2-47. SkyDrive Pro (business) or SkyDrive (consumer)

Any data you changed in the cloud is synchronized to your desktop. Files and directories that are synchronized with the cloud (SkyDrive Pro) are shown with green check marks (see Figure 2-48). You also can share the data with external users or members of your company from SkyDrive Pro (Figure 2-49) in Office 365.

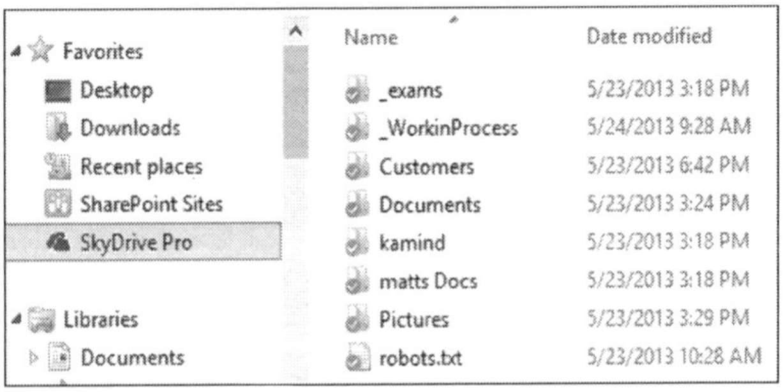

Figure 2-48. Desktop SkyDrive Pro

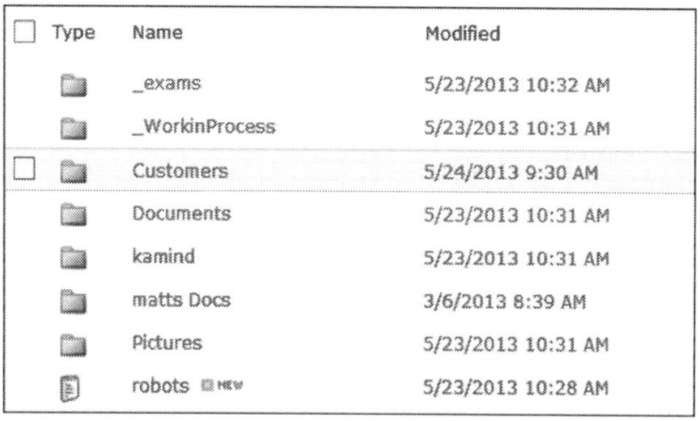

Figure 2-49. Office 365: SkyDrive Pro: cloud directory

SkyDrive Pro is automatically installed when you install Office Professional Plus. You can edit files, copy new files, or delete files from SkyDrive Pro directory with any Microsoft Office application. All changes are copied to Office 365 without any actions on your part. If you edit documents offline and then connect to the Internet, the changes are uploaded to Office 365 automatically when you connect.

You can use SkyDrive Pro with your own personal site or with the Team Site. However, it is recommended that you use your personal document site (called "SkyDrive"). SkyDrive Pro is limited to 20,000 files and up to 100GB of data on your personal site. If you use SkyDrive Pro with the Team Site, you are limited to 7GB and 5,000 files.

SkyDrive Pro: Planning for Personal and Team Site Document Storage

The following are common questions: What information do you place in SkyDrive Pro and what information do you place in your Office 365 team site? Typically, your work product can be classified in one of two categories: current or reference/archive. Current information is what you are currently using as a work in process. Reference/archive is information that is part of an older project which you may need to access every now and then.

If you look at the way you work, current information is what you want to replicate to your workstation, laptop, or tablet. It is information that you need to have access at any moment to complete a task. That is the information that you place in SkyDrive Pro and replicate to your device.

When you complete a project, you typically archive the project because the access is not needed on a daily basis. You are accessing the old project as needed. Completed projects should be placed in your Team Site, and not replicated to the desktop. If you are not going to access the information, why replicate the data? Documents in the Team Site still can be searched and downloaded when you need them.

As you start to use SkyDrive Pro, remember these rules:

— If you exceed the limits or have a replication error, SkyDrive Pro stops working.

— SkyDrive Pro is limited to 100GB.

— SkyDrive Pro can replicate multiple libraries.

— SkyDrive Pro is limited to 20,000 files and the maximum file size cannot be over 2GB.

— Team Site replication is limited to 7GB and 5,000 files per Team Site library.

Follow the next steps to set up SkyDrive Pro.

Step 1: Add SkyDrive Pro to Your Desktop

There are two ways to add SkyDrive Pro: as part of the Office 2013 download (Figure 2-50 and Figure 2-51) or as a separate download from www.microsoft.com for Office 2007 or Office 2010. The simplest way to use SkyDrive Pro is to install Office 2013. To download Office 2013, log in to Office 365 (at http://office.microsoft.com) and download the Office 365 2013 software.

Figure 2-50. *Selecting Office 365 software*

Figure 2-51. *Selecting software download*

1.   Go to http://office.microsoft.com

2.   Sign in (upper right-hand corner)

3.   Select Organization Account

4.   Click "gear" in upper right corner

5.   Select Office 365 Settings

6.   Select Software, and install

Step 2: Office 365 SkyDrive Pro Configuration

The Office 365 SkyDrive Pro configuration is simple. You need to log in to Office 365 and select SkyDrive (see red arrow in Figure 2-52). If you have not accessed this site before, there is a 5–10 minute configuration (first time). This action will build your SkyDrive site. After you have built the SkyDrive Pro site, you are ready for step 3: adding libraries to sync to your device.

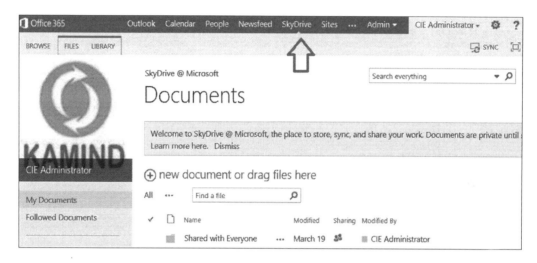

Figure 2-52. *Accessing SkyDrive Pro*

Once you have accessed SkyDrive Pro, you are ready to sync your data to the cloud.

Step 3: Launch SkyDrive Pro on Your Local System

Depending on your system, the SkyDrive Pro software may not be installed. Check to see if the software is installed on your system (see Figure 2-53). If SkyDrive Pro is installed, then skip to step 4.

Figure 2-53. *SkyDrive Pro icon*

If you do not see the cloud icon, then you need to install the SkyDrive Pro desktop software. On Windows 8, click the SkyDrive Pro icon (Figure 2-54). If you are running **Windows 7**, select the SkyDrive Pro software from the *Program files - Office 2013* menu. You need to perform this action only once to install the SkyDrive Pro software.

Figure 2-54. *SkyDrive Pro icon*

Step 4: Office 365 SkyDrive Pro Configuration

If you have not installed Office 2013 or desktop tools, return to step 1 and install the software. Once you have installed the software all that is left is to start the SkyDrive Pro and sync the cloud to your desktop. Return to the Office 365 site, select "SkyDrive" (Figure 2-55), and then select the "sync icon" and identify the local system directory for synchronization (see Figure 2-56).

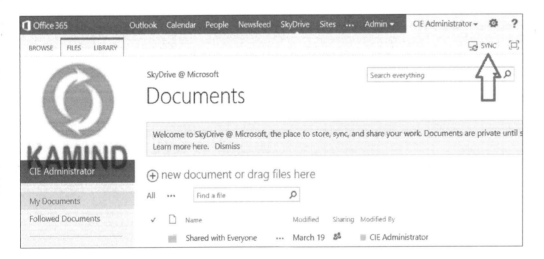

Figure 2-55. *Setting up SkyDrive Pro Sync*

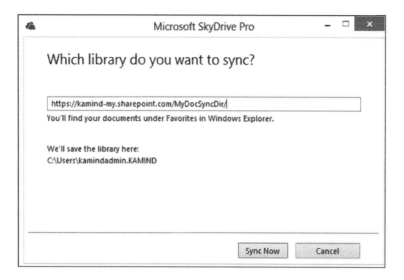

Figure 2-56. *Linking SkyDrive Pro to a local desktop location*

Office 365 will begin the process to sync the cloud with your desktop. You will be prompted to identify an area where the synchronization folder should be added to your local system. Just click OK after you verify the location.

You do not need to configure anything else. The files and documents you place in the local SkyDrive Pro folder will be copied to Office 365. If you copy files to the SkyDrive Pro folder while you are not connected to the Internet, those files will be copied when you are back online.

■ **Note**   If the URL does not appear in the SkyDrive Pro library, you can manually insert the URL from your SkyDrive site or the Team Site. In Figure 2-56, the URL is truncated at the directory to sync.

SkyDrive Pro: Team Site Caution

SkyDrive Pro is limited to 100GB of storage. Your Office 365 Team Site can be expanded to 2TB of storage. Typically, users have two types of data: personal files and team files. SkyDrive is designed for personal files. If you have a large number of pictures and you want to store them in the cloud, it is better to store them in the Office 365 Team Site than in your personal SkyDrive. Do not sync them to your desktop.

Many Office 365 users ask how they can bulk-add documents to the cloud. This is a very simple process. Just drag and drop the documents using Windows Explorer and your HTML5-compatible browser (Figure 2-57).

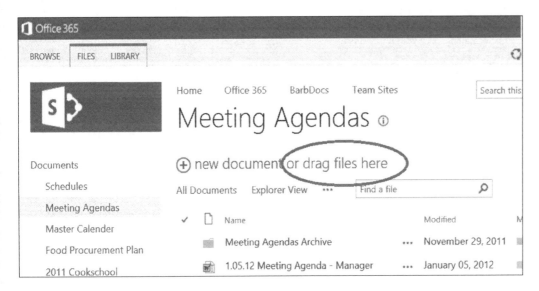

Figure 2-57. *Drag-and-drop window*

Figure 2-57 is the Team Site document window. The area in the circle is the destination for files or folders copied to Office 365. Just select a file from your desktop and drag it over to the "drop here" location (Figure 2-58). This will upload the files to the Team Site or your personal SkyDrive Pro site.

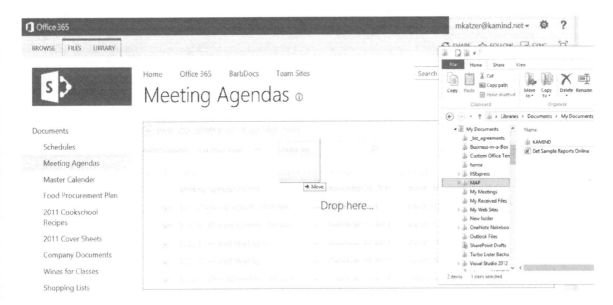

Figure 2-58. *Drag-and-drop example in the Team Site*

SkyDrive: Configuration Changes

You can add multiple libraries to synchronize with Office 365. However, when adding files from the "Team Site," there are limits to the number of files and the size of files you can sync. A different Team Site location can be added from the hidden icons by right-clicking the SkyDrive Pro icon as seen in Figure 2-59. To add a different library to sync to your desktop, select "Sync a new library." If you wish to stop the Office 365 sync or to add a different location to sync content, right-click the SkyDrive icon and make the necessary changes.

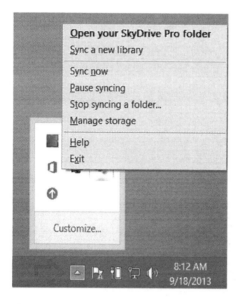

Figure 2-59. SkyDrive Pro configuration changes

___

■ **Note**   If you stop syncing a folder, the desktop folder will be converted to a non-synced folder. You will not lose any data in this process.

___

SkyDrive Pro: Support for Office 2010 Users

You may download the standalone SkyDrive Pro sync client, which allows users of SharePoint 2013 and SharePoint Online in Office 365 to sync their personal SkyDrive Pro. SkyDrive Pro client can be installed side-by-side with previous versions of Office (Office 2010, Office 2007); see Figure 2-60. To download SkyDrive Pro, go to the Microsoft download site at www.microsoft.com/en-US/download/details.aspx?id=39050

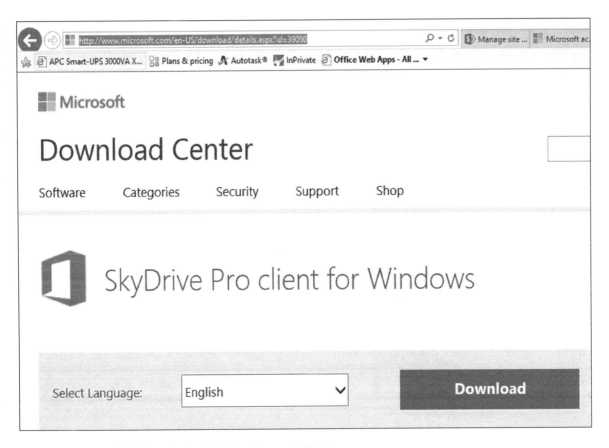

Figure 2-60. *Download SkyDrive Pro: MS doc reference: 390050*

SkyDrive: Checking Storage Allocation

Office 365 SkyDrive Pro supports up to 100GB of personal SkyDrive storage. To determine the storage you are using, access the SkyDrive status folder.

Once you have found the SkyDrive Pro icon from the hidden icons (Figure 2-61), right-click the SkyDrive Pro icon (blue cloud) and select "Manage storage" (Figure 2-62). This will launch the status of the SkyDrive Pro storage site. You have two options: view SkyDrive Pro Storage or open the SkyDrive Pro recycle bin. Select view "SkyDrive Storage" site. The personal SkyDrive storage (Figure 2-63) shows the storage allocation free in MB.

Figure 2-61. *Finding SkyDrive Pro icon from the hidden icons*

Figure 2-62. *Selecting managed storage option*

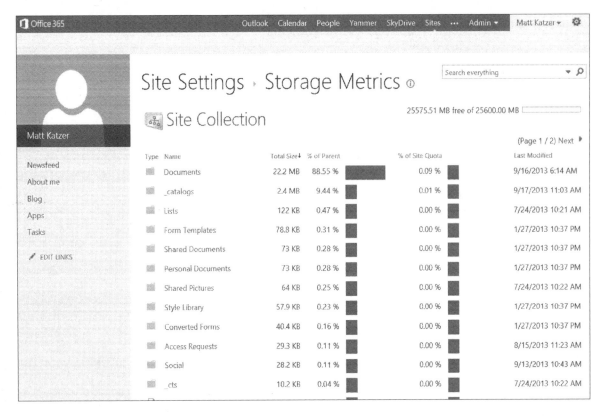

Figure 2-63. Displaying the SkyDrive storage allocation

Figure 2-63 shows that 25.6G were allocated and that 25GB are free for personal use. Your Office 365 administrator can increase your personal storage allocation to a maximum of 100GB.

Smartphone: Configuration

Configuring your smartphone for Office 365 is simple. All you need is the same information that you used to configure Outlook: your email address and password (and sometimes the Exchange Server name: m.outlook.com). Depending upon your organization's password change policy, you may need to change your smartphone's password every 90 days. In the same screens that you use to initially set up email there should be a Password Change option.

Key Configuration Items

1. The User ID is your email address

2. Always leave the Domain Name blank

3. Generic Hosted Exchange server name: m.outlook.com

iPhone

Apple products have a very controlled environment. The current versions support the ability to have multiple exchange email accounts. Here is the process:

1. Delete any previous account(s).

2. On your iPhone or iPad, under Settings, select "Mail, Contacts, and Calendars."

3. Press "Microsoft Exchange" to add your new account.

4. Enter your fully qualified email name (e.g., info@kamind.net) in both the email and username fields and your email password. Click "Next."

5. The iPhone or iPad will use Office365's autodiscover feature to fill in the server box. Click "Next."

6. Synchronize contacts and email.

At this point, you have completed the necessary steps and your device will synchronize.

Android Devices: Motorola Droid v2.2 (and Above)

The Droid environment is much less regulated (compared to iPhone or Windows Phone). These instructions may be slightly different depending upon your phone's vendor (and carrier). Android uses the term "Corporate Email" for integration into Microsoft exchange server (Office 365 service). If you do not see "Corporate Email," check with your phone supplier to verify that you have the latest version of the Android operating system on your phone.

1. Start by selecting: Home/"Settings" button (2nd from left)/Settings/Accounts & sync/ "Add account"

2. Select "Corporate"

3. Enter your fully qualified email name (e.g. info@kamind.net) and password. Click "Next."

4. This may fail. You will see a screen to allow you to re-enter your information. Re-enter your email at Domain\Username (the backslash is OK). (Your password has been kept from the previous entry.)

5. For Office 365, enter "m.outlook.com" in "Server." (This should be automatic, but may not be.)

6. Keep "Use secure connection (SSL)" checked.

7. Press "Next."

8. As part of the original setup, or later by selecting Home/"Settings" button (2nd from left)/ Settings/Accounts & sync/your account ("under Manage accounts"), you can set the check boxes for "Sync Contacts" and "Sync Calendar". Just above these Sync buttons is "Incoming settings." Change your password here.

9. Under "Account settings" you can set:

   a. "Account name" to a recognizable name (like 'your org name here')

   b. "Your name"

   c. "Signature"

   d. "Amount to synchronize" (pick two weeks)

   e. "Email check frequency" (choose Automatic (Push))

    f.   "Default account" (check box for Yes: this is the one that email will be sent from)

    g.   "Email notifications" (check box for Yes: show email available in status bar)

    h.   "Select Ringtone"

    i.   "Vibrate" options

    j.   Incoming settings: This is also where you change your password (if it changes for your Office 365 account).

    k.   Click "Sync Contacts" and "Sync Calendar"

At this point, you have completed the necessary steps and your device will synchronize.

Windows Phone: Office 365

The Windows 7 Phone environment is very controlled, and also from the same vendor that makes the Exchange Server. You may have multiple email accounts.

This procedure connects your Windows Phone 7 (version 7.5 or later) to both your Hosted Exchange and SharePoint accounts.

1. Select Settings

2. Select Office Hub

3. Select Office 365 and Setup

4. Select Add an Account – Outlook

5. You will receive a message that allows you access to the Team Site (Office 365 SharePoint)

6. Select Finish

■ **Note**   When you access the Office 365 team site, you will be prompted for username and password. Select "Always connected" to not be prompted for password.

At this point, you have completed the necessary steps and your device will synchronize.

Windows Phone: Adding Another Exchange Account

Windows Phone allows connections to multiple Exchange Servers. This procedure connects your Windows Phone to another Exchange Server.

1. Select Settings

2. Select Email+ accounts

3. Select Add an Account

4. Select Outlook

5. Enter the email address and password

6. Select "sign in"

7. If prompted that credentials are bad, check your password with "show password"

8. Change username to email address

9. Select "sign in"

10. If promoted, select "advance"

11. Enter the server name: `m.outlook.com` or the physical exchange server (see Outlook Web Access)

12. Select "sign in"

At this point, you have completed the necessary steps and your device will synchronize.

Lync: Skype Configuration

Lync is the business communications software that is included in Office 365. Lync supports enterprise voice (both users can speak at the same time) and has all of the features that Skype does, and many more. KAMIND configures Lync in Office 365 to allow Lync to be used to with Skype. Adding Skype users to Lync is simple; the same as adding contacts. Once you have added the Skype users to your Lync contacts, you can call those users using Lync. Likewise, a Skype user can contact you via your email address. This allows you to invite Skype users in Lync meetings and use Lync for web conferencing and other meetings. To add a Skype user, just select the contacts (see Figure 2-64) and add the Skype user using the option "Add a contact not in my Organization" with Skype icon.

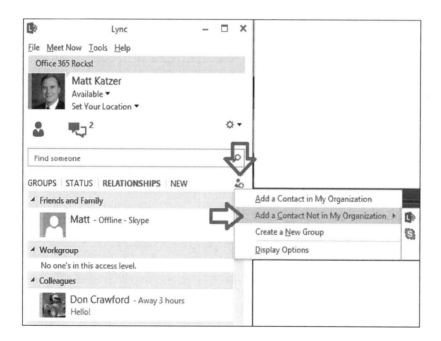

Figure 2-64. *Adding Skype via contacts*

Once you select "Add the contact," select the Skype user and fill out the additional information. In Figure 2-65, we have added the Skype user to the "Other Contacts" and set the privacy to the same as "friends and family." With external contacts you set the relationship as needed. When you enter a Skype user, the green check is displayed.

Add Skype contact

Enter Skype contact information or send invitation

IM Address:

mkatzer(kamind.com)@msn.com

Example: someone@domain.com

Add to contact group:

Customers

Set privacy relationship:

Friends and Family

Share my note, location, and all my contact information
except meeting details

OK   Cancel

Figure 2-65. *Adding the Skype contact*

When you add a Skype user, the format must be in the form similar to "mjones(company.com)@msn.com." This is the same format that you would use for other IM providers. To ensure that you can add the Skype user, make sure your client is set up to allow external contacts and that Lync is set up to communicate with Skype (steps follow).

Step 1: Enable Lync Client to Accept Skype User Calls

Enable the Lync client to accept calls from external users. Select the Lync options, then set to allow anyone to contact me (Figure 2-66). If you cannot connect to Skype users, verify the Service settings (step shown in Figure 2-67).

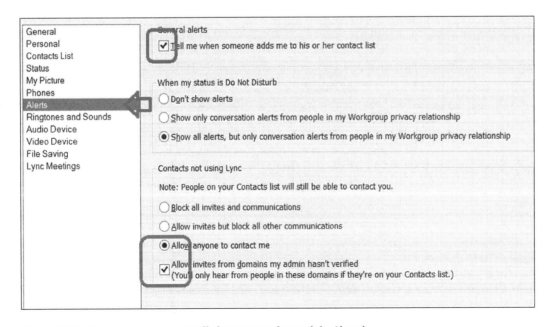

General
Personal
Contacts List
Status
My Picture
Phones
Alerts
Ringtones and Sounds
Audio Device
Video Device
File Saving
Lync Meetings

General alerts

☑ Tell me when someone adds me to his or her contact list

When my status is Do Not Disturb

○ Don't show alerts

○ Show only conversation alerts from people in my Workgroup privacy relationship

◉ Show all alerts, but only conversation alerts from people in my Workgroup privacy relationship

Contacts not using Lync

Note: People on your Contacts list will still be able to contact you.

○ Block all invites and communications

○ Allow invites but block all other communications

◉ Allow anyone to contact me

☑ Allow invites from domains my admin hasn't verified
(You'll only hear from people in these domains if they're on your Contacts list.)

Figure 2-66. *Setting Lync to accept calls form external users (aka Skype)*

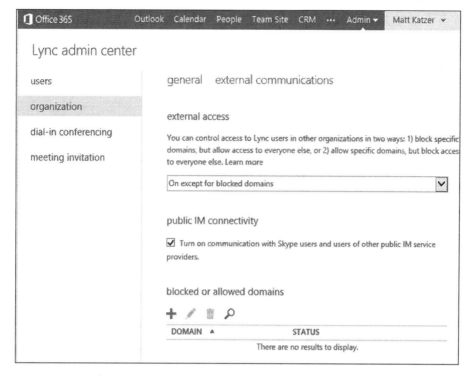

***Figure 2-67.** Enabling external communications*

Step 2: Verify Configuration of Office 365 with External Users

In the Office 365 admin center, select the Office 365 admin dashboard, service settings, and Lync. Enable the public IM connectivity (Figure 2-67) to allow Lync users to speak to Office 365 and Skype user external to your company.

Lync: Linking Microsoft Account to Skype

Office 365 is integrated with Skype, and we covered how Lync talks to Skype users. But how do Skype uses talk to Lync? When Skype was created the account names were random. Skype has changed its model to require an email address to log in rather than using the Skype "handle." The email address in Skype is already linked to the Skype account; you just need to let Microsoft know that you want to link the email address to a Microsoft account (used for password security management). Most users by now will have a Microsoft account that is linked to Skype, so you may have done this already and are using the free SkyDrive. If you do not have an account that is linked, you will need to create one. Just follow the next steps to accomplish this. Log in to Skype with a Microsoft account (Figure 2-68).

Figure 2-68. *Log in to Skype using a Microsoft account*

■ **Note**   Lync users can call any Skype users, but Skype users need to ask permission (send a contact) before they can speak to Lync users.

Then link your Microsoft account to your Skype account (Figure 2-69). If you do not have a Microsoft account, you need to create one. A Microsoft account is nothing more than your email address with security extensions. Skype and other Microsoft services use these security extensions to grant access to different services. To add Microsoft security to your email address, go to `http://accuount.microsoft.com` and select "new." Fill in your email address for the account ID. You added consumer security to your email address. Remember that the Microsoft account is the consumer account and not your organization ID, unless you have previously linked them together (Figure 2-70).

Figure 2-69. Selecting Skype account to link to Microsoft account

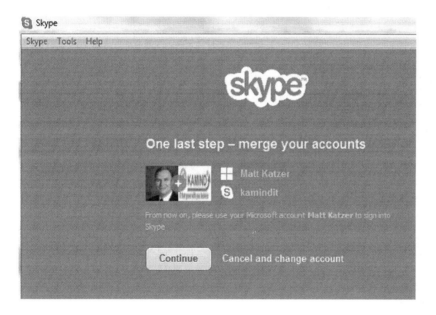

Figure 2-70. Merging the accounts

At this point, select continue to merge the accounts. The wizard will request you to update your profile and you are done. From now on when you call a Lync user, the user's address will appear in the format mjones(company.com)@msn.com.

Lync: Using Skype to Call Lync

Office 365 is integrated with Skype. But how do Skype users talk to Lync? You have already changed your Skype login ID to use a Microsoft account; you are ready to speak to Lync users (Figure 2-71). Once you have logged in, the setup screen looks similar to the one shown in Figure 2-71. (Make sure you have the latest Skype installed!)

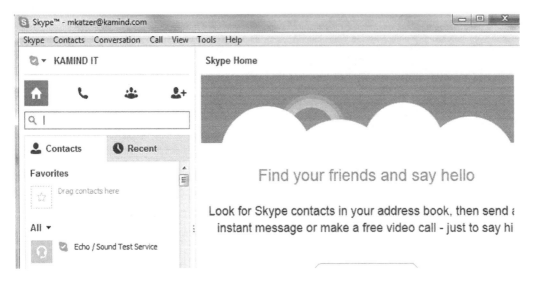

Figure 2-71. *Skype setup main dashboard with Microsoft account integration*

Just add the email address of the Lync user (Figure 2-72), and they will show up on the Skype dashboard.

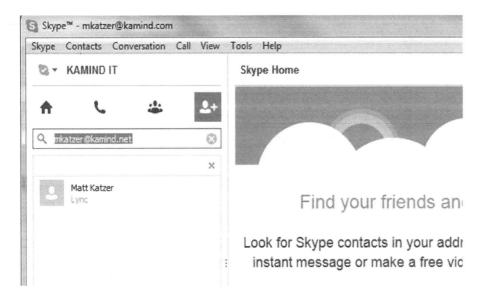

Figure 2-72. *Adding a new contact from Lync*

The Lync user will show up based on the settings on the Office 365 Lync Administration and the user's personal preferences. (Lync users can say no to adding the Skype users contact information.) Just select the user and add the contact to Skype. At this point you can call the Lync user. Your Skype address on Lync will be in the format "mjones(company.com)@msn.com" using the Microsoft account.

Lync: Troubleshooting

SITUATION: Microsoft Lync is set to autoconfigure, but sometimes Lync will not configure to the desktop correctly. To correct this problem, you need to configure the manual server connections by following these steps:

1. Start Lync

2. Select Gear (right-hand side: Figure 2-73)

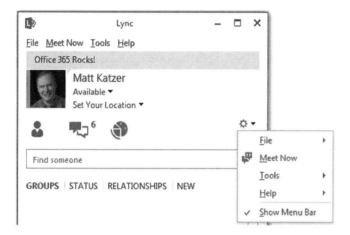

Figure 2-73. *Lync configuration options*

3. Enable "Show Menu Bar" (Figure 2-73)

4. Select Options (Figure 2-73)

5. Sign in (Figure 2-74)

Figure 2-74. *Lync startup screen*

6. Select Advance (Figure 2-75)

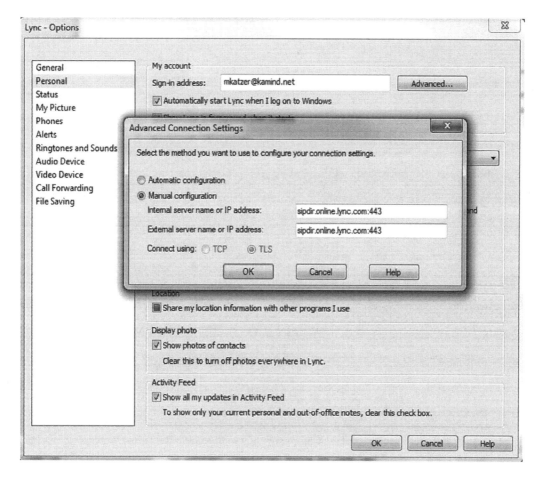

Figure 2-75. *Lync: adding the manual server addresses*

    7.   Enter `sipdir.online.lync.com`:443 as the web address for both internal and external servers

Lync: Firewall Port Configuration

Lync uses port 443 for incoming and outgoing TCP IP traffic. In addition to the TCP ports, the UDP ports that are required to support link are outgoing ports 3478 and 50000–59999. Any changes in this setup must be completed by your administrator.

Reference Links

There is a lot of information about Office 365 on the web, but the issue is finding the right site. The information contained in this chapter is a combination of our experiences in doing deployments and knowledge of support information that has been published by third parties.

    Office 365 Learning Center

`http://office.microsoft.com/en-us/office-home-for-office-365-FX102821134.aspx`

Office 365 Documents and Training Videos

http://getoffice365now.com/Pages/doc.aspx

Using Office 365 SkyDrive Pro

http://www.youtube.com/watch?v=c740qwWR-cs

Adding SkyDrive Pro for Office 2010 and 2007

http://www.microsoft.com/en-US/download/details.aspx?id=39050

Update information from Office 365: Migrating and managing your business in the cloud

http://getoffice365now.com

Next Steps

Your basic Office 365 systems have been set up and configured. At this point you understand the features of Office 365 and are ready to move forward. However, your work is not yet complete. There is more to do depending on your Office 365 configuration. It is recommended that you review Chapters 3, 4, 6, and 8 in preparation for deployment.

- *Chapter 3:* Office 365 Planning and Purchase

  - The key to a successful Office 365 migration is the planning and purchase process. There are three different categories of plans you may purchase from, but the secret to a successful migration to Office 365 is picking the correct plan that supports your business. Once you pick the plan, it is about planning the migration to Office 365 to ensure that the process is seamless for your organization. This chapter describes the basic purchase information and details the choices.

- *Chapter 4:* Office 365 Setup and Migration

  - Once you have selected your Office 365 plan, there are two different ways you can migrate to Office 365: via "cut-over" migration or federation. This chapter covers the most common approach to Office 365 migration.

- *Chapter 6:* Building Your Web Site

  - Office 365 includes a public-facing web site and the necessary developer's tools to build out the web site. This chapter takes you from the basic Office 365 site to a fully functioning web site. Office 365 public-facing web sites fulfill basic web needs for 90 percent of businesses on Office 365. This chapter describes how to configure and build the public-facing web site for your business using the integrated Office 365 web site tools and SharePoint Designer: a design tool that is included with your Office 365 subscription.

- *Chapter 8:* Office 365 Administration

  - This chapter describes the different administration centers in Office 365 and the most common tools that you would use to administer your Office 365 company. Depending on your Office 365 services, there are five possible administration tools. This chapter focuses on the Office 365, Exchange, and Lync administration centers. The SharePoint and Windows Intune administration centers are described in their own chapters. We close the chapter with a guide to using PowerShell to manage your Office 365 environment.

CHAPTER 3

▪ ▪ ▪

Office 365 Planning and Purchase

Office 365 is a family of products grouped under a common name: Office 365. When we walk into a grocery store and down the soup aisle, we may see cans of Campbell's and Progresso soups. Each company offers a set of different products under its label. They both produce similar but different cream of mushroom and chicken noodle soups. Microsoft and Google are comparable to different soup manufacturers; they offer different hosted services. Microsoft Office 365 is the brand of a suite of products composed of Office 365 ProPlus (installed Office), Exchange Online, SharePoint Online, and Lync Online voice communications (see Figure 3-1).

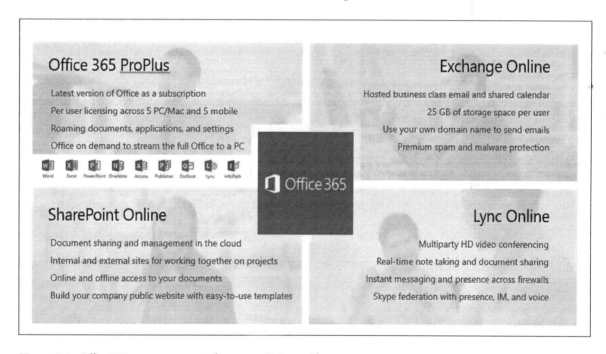

Figure 3-1. *Office 365 component parts (courtesy of Microsoft)*

One major advantage of Office 365 is that Microsoft administers and maintains all of the back-end servers; operating systems; Exchange, SharePoint, and Lync server software; interconnects; geo-redundancy; and network structure. This represents a cost savings compared to having to pay to plan, get the correct capacities, buy and maintain the correct hardware and software, perform software updates, build a second data center, and assume all of the other costs related to owning your own systems. The second advantage is that because Microsoft maintains your e-mail and SharePoint data in the cloud, "business continuity" is provided by going to the premises of any vendor that has an Internet connection!

Purchasing Office 365 is a bit more complicated than purchasing soup. *Be sure to review* "Step 1: Purchase Your Subscription(s)" (in the following "Pre-deployment" section) *before* you purchase your Office 365 licenses.

In Chapter 2, our hypothetical IT manager explored Microsoft Office 365 as a business solution. Reviewing the functionality is only part of the story. A successful Office 365 implementation is based on a planned deployment, which we'll cover in this chapter.

As Microsoft Office 365 partners, we have migrated a significant number of Office 365 organizations to the cloud. The common thread of all of our successful migrations is planning. Planning begins with the selection of the Office 365 subscription plan.

Office 365 Subscription Plans

There are three Office 365 subscriptions plans:

- Small Business

- Midsize Business

- Enterprise

As a shortcut, we refer to the Small Business plans (Small Business and Small Business Premium) as P plans (the name under which they were first introduced) and Midsize Business as the M plan (although Microsoft does not like to call it an M plan, it just is easier to do so).

The most important point about these plans is that you cannot mix the services you choose among subscription plans. For example, if you purchased a Midsize Business plan, you cannot add an Exchange Online e-mail account. Exchange is an Enterprise plan service and can only be used with E1, E3, E4, and Kiosk subscriptions. Frequently, it is less expensive to purchase the Enterprise plan, because you can have different services with different prices. For example, the Midsize Business plan requires everyone to pay for Office 365 ProPlus (Office installed on your computer).

With Office 365 subscriptions (as released in October 2013), you must start a new subscription and do another full migration to change from Small Business Premium or Midsize Business to Enterprise. For this reason, it is important to pick the subscription that makes sense for your business. (See Figure 3-2.)

		Office 365 Small Business Premium	Office 365 Midsize Business	Office 365 Enterprise (E1/2)	Office 365 Enterprise (E3)
Advanced Services	Voicemail, Archiving, Data Loss Prevention				●
	Rights Management, Excel/Visio/Access svcs				●
	Active Directory®		●	●	●
Office	Full Office	●	●		●
	Click to Run Deployment	Pull	Pull		Push
	Office Web Applications	●	●	●	●
Standard Services	Support	Basic	Expanded	Full	Full
	IT Administration Console	Basic	Expanded	Full	Full
	IM, Collaboration, Storage, Email	●	●	●	●

Figure 3-2. *Office 365 subscription plans (courtesy of Microsoft)*

A Microsoft Tier 1 Champion Partner can help you through this decision process and help save your organization considerable time and expense.

Each Office 365 plan includes one or more parts of the Office 365 Suite, as follows:

- Hosted Exchange
- Lync
- Hosted SharePoint (Team Site and "My Site" personal SharePoint storage)

Figure 3-2 and Figure 3-3 show comparisons of the features of Office 365. Early in Chapter 2, we explored the features of Office 365 and how you could use those services in your business.

Office 365 Feature Comparison

	Exchange Online Plans			Office 365 Plans						
				Small Businesses	Midsize Businesses	Enterprise Businesses			Kiosk	
	Kiosk	Plan 1	Plan 2	P	M1	E1	E3	E4	K1	K2
	$2 (per user/ per month)	$4 (per user/ per month)	$8 (per user/ per month)	$6 (per user/ per month)	$15 (per user/ per month)	$8 (per user/ per month)	$20 (per user/ per month)	$22 (per user/ per month)	$4 (per user/ per month)	$4 (per user/ per month)
Anywhere Access, Compatibility & Security										
Each user receives an email account, individual calendar, and contact list	●	●	●	●	●	●	●	●	●	●
Send and receive email from a custom domain	●	●	●	●	●	●	●	●	●	●
Web browser access to Outlook Web App for email, calendar and contacts	●	●	●	●	●	●	●	●	●	●
Access to email, calendars, and contacts from phones capable of receiving email	●	●	●	●	●	●	●	●	●	●
Connect to Microsoft Outlook 2007 and newer versions of Outlook		●	●	●	●	●	●	●		
25 MB maximum attachment size	●	●	●	●	●	●	●	●	●	●
Premium anti-spam and antivirus filtering	●	●	●	●	●	●	●	●	●	●
Configurable anti-spam filtering	●	●	●		●	●	●	●	●	●
Legal hold capabilities for deleted and edited mail			●				●	●		
Storage & Support										
Email storage per user	1 GB	25 GB	unlimited	25 GB	25 GB	25 GB	unlimited	unlimited	1 GB	1 GB
Microsoft community support (online)	●	●	●	●	●	●	●	●	●	●
Live 24 x 7 IT customer phone support	●	●	●		●	●	●	●	●	●
					Office		Office	Office		

Figure 3-3. *Office 365 plans (courtesy of Microsoft)*

Figure 3-3 shows present commercial pricing. There are other pricing packages. Not-for-profit (valid 501c3) organizations can purchase the E3 service for $4.50 per person per month. Prices for educational institutions start at $2.50 per person per month for the equivalent of the E3 service. There is also special pricing for government institutions, as well as for large corporations. Contact your Microsoft Partner for details.

The Enterprise plan allows you to mix and match different subscriptions, based on your business needs. As listed in Figure 3-3, the Enterprise plan includes:

- Kiosk, Exchange Online Plan 1 and Plan 2 subscriptions (e-mail only)

- E1, E3 and E4 Suites

- Kiosk K1 and Kiosk K2 (e-mail plus SharePoint). (K1 and K2 are now the same.)

There are also suite components, applications and services such as Office 365 ProPlus, many versions of CRM, Project, Lync, and SharePoint Only; Azure Active Directory, Visio, Yammer Enterprise, and more.

CRM plans are the only options in the Midsize Business plan. There are no separately priced services in the Small Business plans. Contact your Microsoft Partner for details and pricing.

The Office 365 plan options can be daunting. We always recommend the Enterprise plan for its flexibility in services and pricing. As an example, if you are providing e-mail services for a nursing station or a warehouse user, a Kiosk subscription (at $2 per person per month) may make sense. If you have already purchased Office 2010, you may choose to purchase an E1 for some people and E3 for those who may require the additional features of Office 2013. You may also choose E3 for Mac or Office 2007 users, to provide them the latest version of Office.

Note that there are additional limits (to go with the lower prices) in the Enterprise Kiosk plans. The Kiosk Exchange Online, Plan Kiosk 1, and Plan Kiosk 2 include the following:

- Outlook Web App for e-mail (not Outlook)

- Maximum of 2GB mailbox storage

- Exchange ActiveSync support (for smartphones)

- Premium anti-malware protection and anti-spam filtering

- POP mail support

- Viewing Microsoft Visio diagrams, visiting Access-based web pages, viewing embedded Excel graphs, and filling in and submitting InfoPath forms

The Kiosk Exchange Online, Plan Kiosk 1, and Plan Kiosk 2 do *not* include the following:

- Additional storage to Team Site (SharePoint) (E1, E3, and E4 add 500MB for each user)

- "My Sites" (personal SharePoint sites)

Additionally, the Kiosk Exchange Online does not include:

- Office Web Apps (no SharePoint)

The Plan Kiosk 1 and Plan Kiosk 2 (the features have been combined, and they are now priced the same) do include:

- Office Web Apps: View and Edit

There is a lot of Office 365 information online. We included the reference links at the end of this chapter. Note that these limits are often changing! The maximum Kiosk mailbox size has doubled twice since Office 365 was introduced. Also, there are additional limits for external users availing themselves of SharePoint (see Chapter 5).

Planning and Purchase Chapter Structure

There are many choices in Office 365: how you purchase, how you deploy, and what is involved in an Office 365 migration project. The purpose of this chapter is to help you through the planning process. At this point, we assume that you have made a decision to use Office 365 and are at the point of "what to do next."

There are three planning areas that we have found that will help you through the process of deploying Office 365. These planning areas are:

- Pre-deployment planning and purchase

- Deployment

- Post-deployment

You can mix these areas (see Table 3-1), depending on your business needs and the complexity of your organization, but in general (for the 90% of us), these are the tasks that we have found useful in deployment of Office 365.

Table 3-1. *Office 365 Planning Areas*

Deployment Task	Description
Pre-deployment	This is your preplanning and purchase step. You are collecting information for the deployment and post-deployment phases.
Deployment	You are deploying Office 365. We review the planning areas of an Office 365 deployment and what you need to consider as you manage your project. Typically, this is Lync (voice) and Exchange (e-mail) services.
Post-deployment	You have finished moving your business e-mail to the cloud. You are now moving other business critical functions (such as SharePoint) to Office 365.

We will review each of these planning areas in detail to help you through your Office 365 deployment. In each of these areas, we will reference the chapters in the book to assist you with additional information about Office 365.

Pre-deployment

Purchasing Office 365 is the first step in your Office 365 migration. We talk about the purchase process first, because we have found that many people just want to get started (me included) and tend to read anything called "planning" later. The pre-deployment planning areas cover these topics, shown in Table 3-2.

Table 3-2. *Pre-deployment Planning Grid*

Steps	Action/Component	Notes or Effect
Step 1	Purchase Your Subscription (s) (or Start a Trial)	• Use a sign-up link from your Microsoft Partner. • Choose your Microsoft domain name: the "xxx" of xxx.onmicrosoft.com (this cannot be changed; this is also the basis of your SharePoint site URL). • Consider your branding. • Choose the correct plan. We always recommend Enterprise for price and flexibility (see preceding Figure 3-3). • You cannot move your xxx.onmicrosoft.com brand to another plan (easily). • Buy the licenses that you need. • Combine/Purchase link: Windows Intune and Office 365.
Step 2	Choose Your Sign-on Method	• Office 365 sign-on • DirSync with passwords • AD FS/single sign-on • AD FS/SSO with Exchange Federation

(continued)

Table 3-2. (*continued*)

Steps	Action/Component	Notes or Effect
Step 3	Collect Your Information	• Domain names and DNS • Where are your people located? Home? On the road? • Users and administrators • Distribution groups, security groups • Resources and conference rooms • "Public" external contacts • E-mail sending copiers • E-mail accounts: aliases and special e-mail address (such as info@xxx.com from your web site) • Use of Exchange public folders • Internet speeds • Software and hardware inventory; PC updates • Hardware/software upgrades • Verify version minimums • Phone/voicemail interactions • Compliance archive requirements
Step 4	Define Your Migration Plan and Schedule	• Define migration plan and schedule. • Validate custom domain before user load and Lync setup. • Pilot considerations • Software deployment • Exchange Federation considerations
Step 5	Microsoft Account and Organizational Account	• Microsoft account is one of: hotmail.com, outlook.com, live.com • Organizational ID is an Office 365 login • Windows 8 login • Effects in SkyDrive and SkyDrive Pro • Effects in external sharing
Step 6	SkyDrive and SkyDrive Pro	• Microsoft account/Organizational ID • Limits and limitations
Step 7	Windows Intune	• Initial configuration • User load • User installation • Support for pilot and implementation • Windows Intune Administration (See Chapter 7)

"Step 1: Purchase Your Subscription(s)" is the most important step in starting Office 365. If you do not purchase correctly, you must start over. Many of the decisions that you make at the time of initial purchase cannot be changed later.

Step 1: Purchase Your Subscription(s)

There are four important steps to be followed when purchasing Office 365 and Windows Intune (or starting an Office 365 trial). They are important because they cannot be changed later. It is good to have a Microsoft Tier 1 Cloud Accelerate Partner to help you with this process.

There are many different plans. We recommend that you purchase an Enterprise plan for its flexibility, in particular the ability to have a mixture of licenses at different prices, from $2 to $22. The other plans do not have the range of choices. You generally save money because of the varying prices that are available to meet your needs. See the preceding section "Office 365 Subscription Plans."

To purchase (or begin a trial subscription), follow these steps:

1. Open the purchase or trial link (in a browser) that your Microsoft Partner has sent or navigate to www.office365.com and find "Try now" or "Buy now" for the plan that you are interested in. Note: Pick an Enterprise plan, such as E3 (see the section "Office 365 Subscription Plans").

2. If you have an existing Office 365 or Windows Intune account, click "sign in to add this subscription to your current account" (see Figure 3-4). This will connect your accounts with a common set of users.

Figure 3-4. *Adding a new subscription. (This form may vary, depending on your subscription type.)*

3. Fill out the information in the subscription form.

4. At "create your new user ID" (see Figure 3-5)

Figure 3-5. Purchase Office 365

    a.   Enter something such as "Admin" or "ContosoAdmin" in the area marked "1."
Your first account should not be the name of an actual person.

    b.   Enter your Microsoft internal domain name (e.g., mycompany.onmicrosoft.com)
in the area marked "2." It will also be your name at SharePoint:
e.g., mycompany.sharepoint.com.

    c.   Carefully consider your internal domain name, as it may be important for your
branding. *IT CANNOT BE CHANGED LATER!*

5.   Set a password for this admin account. Verify that you are not a robot. Continue/accept
terms and conditions.

6.   Sign on as the newly added administrator and add yourself as a global admin account
(using your normal e-mail address).

OFFICE 365 PURCHASE NOTES

1.   At the moment, you cannot change from one plan to another (i.e., from M to E) without
(another) e-mail migration. (Microsoft has announced this feature, but there is no information
currently available on this.) In addition,

- You cannot mix licenses among plans.

- You can only mix licenses types on the Office 365 Enterprise plan.

2. It is often less expensive to use the Enterprise plan and much more flexible. You have to run the numbers and look at the license mix. Your Office 365 and Windows Intune accounts should be linked.

   - Linking your accounts allows the same set of user logins on both sides.

   - Even if you decide not to use Windows Intune, add a trial and link the service. This will save you many headaches later on.

3. Your first/admin account is the basis of your Office 365 tenant.

   - It must not be deleted!

   - It will not require an Office 365 license.

4. Your ".onmicrosoft.com" Microsoft internal domain name cannot be changed. This Microsoft domain is the basis of your SharePoint Online and Newsfeed URLs:

   - xxxx.sharepoint.com (SharePoint Online)

   - xxxx-my.sharepoint.com (Newsfeed/SkyDrive Pro site)

Changing this name requires another e-mail migration or waiting 120 days. You will have to disconnect and reconnect your custom domain (DNS) name; there will be downtime.

Step 2: Choose Your Sign-On Method

This is a "Major Fork," because the choice you make here is based on the needs of your organization and will affect your Office 365 implementation and environment. For most organizations (even up to 500 users), the Office 365 sign-on is appropriate. There are several methods of user sign-on to Office 365 and any local servers.

- Office 365 Sign-On

- DirSync with Password Sync

- AD FS/Single Sign-On

- AD FS/Single Sign-On with Exchange Federation

Office 365 Sign-On

This is the standard Office 365 sign-on (through office.com or portal.microsoftonline.com; see Figure 3-6). This is the simplest method. Users sign on with their e-mail addresses and passwords. Their login and assigned Office 365 licenses determine the features that are available (e.g., Lync, SharePoint, or Office 365 ProPlus). There is no connection to any on-premises Active Directory. This is perfect for organizations with no on-premises servers.

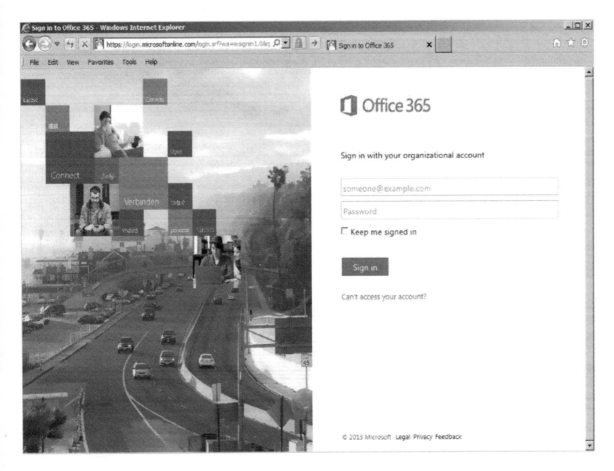

Figure 3-6. *Office 365 sign-in screen*

Passwords are managed by users. The default is that a user must change his or her password every 90 days. (This can be modified.) If there is an on-premises Active Directory environment (for access to other servers), the user passwords for Office 365 and on-premises servers are not synchronized.

This is a valid choice even if you have an established Active Directory environment, if your Active Directory is only used for Exchange (and you are planning to uninstall on-premises Exchange), or if your Active Directory is used to secure on-premises servers to a relatively small number of users. (These users would have an on-premises account and an Office 365 account; most users would only need the Office 365 account.)

DirSync with Password Sync

The DirSync server role adds the ability to synchronize on-premises Active Directory to the Office 365 accounts. This includes users, distribution groups, security groups, meeting rooms, and now user passwords. Passwords must be changed in the on-premises Active Directory; synchronization is one way. All Active Directory actions (adding users, distribution groups, etc.) are done on premises; you can no longer manage Office 365 accounts in the Office 365 management portal. The organization will have to install a DirSync server. (See Chapter 11.)

Active Directory Federation Services (AD FS)/Single Sign-On

This method provides complete federation between your Office 365 accounts and your on-premises Active Directory. Office 365 users who sign in using their e-mail address at office.com or portal.microsoftonline.com are redirected to on-premises sign-on servers. For this reason, Microsoft recommends a primary and backup login server for on-premises logins and a primary and backup proxy server for people signing on from outside your organization. This implies four additional servers (plus the DirSync server). For more on this topic, see Chapter 11.

AD FS/Single Sign-On with Exchange Federation

This method adds Exchange Federation to AD FS/single sign-on. This allows the organization to move Exchange mailboxes between an on-premises Exchange server (there are minimum version requirements) and the Office 365 Hosted Exchange server. This can be used as a migration method to move your on-premises e-mail users to the Office 365 cloud without disruption. (See Chapter 11.)

DirSync and SSO/AD FS Caution

Once you *enable* Microsoft's Active Directory, you *cannot* go back. You can turn off Active Directory Synchronization, but you cannot remove the synced objects. You cannot delete the Office 365 tenant; you can only remove the verified domain. Verified domains take up to seven days to be removed from Exchange Online Protection (EOP). When DirSync is enabled, synced objects mailboxes are not created when an Office 365 license is assigned. A mailbox is only created as part of the Microsoft migration process.

Active Directory integration will require you to use Microsoft conversion tools, or to use Exchange Server Federation mailbox moves. If you choose to use the cutover approach, you can only use Microsoft tools. The Microsoft tools, along with Exchange Federation remote mailbox moves, create the mailbox in Office 365. If you choose to use cutover (after DirSync is enabled), you can only use Microsoft mailbox migration tools and are limited to a maximum of 1,000 mailboxes. Mailbox migrations with more than 1,000 mailboxes must use Exchange Federation remote mailbox move.

Step 3: Collect Your Information

Planning for an Office 365 implementation starts with a complete description of your environment. We normally use a spreadsheet to keep track of these details.

- Domain names

- DNS information (login, owner, other IP addresses)

- Users and administrators

- Distribution groups

- Security groups

- Resources and conference rooms

- "Public" external contacts

- Do you have any e-mail sending copiers?

- Email accounts: Aliases and special e-mail addresses (e-mail accounts that collect e-mail but are not necessarily connected to a person, such as info@xxx.com from your web site or sales@xxx.com)

- Use of Exchange public folders (requires Outlook 2013)

- Internet speeds to your locations

- Software and hardware inventory (computer types and locations)

- Verify version minimums (e.g., Windows 7, web browsers, etc.)

- PC updates: All PCs should have all Windows Updates applied

- Phone types, type of synchronization required (voice mail)

Domains and Domain Information

This subject includes which domains you wish to include in Office 365 and who "owns" your DNS setup (who has the login; whether there is a secondary DNS?). Keep in mind other locations. Do you have an off-premises Exchange server or other special needs for remote locations, such as branch offices or people working from home or hotel rooms? See the section "Step 8: Domain Name Service."

Users and Resources

This is the list of some of the items that you have to track. Many of these items may be part of your Active Directory environment. (Depending on your migration scheme, many of these items can be loaded from your existing Active Directory).

- Users and administrators (who will be which level of administrator)

- Distribution groups (for e-mail)

- Security groups (for SharePoint)

- Resources and conference rooms

- "Public" external contacts and calendar (if you have thousands of contacts that are shared across your organization, you may wish to have a Shared Exchange-Only e-mail account for this purpose)

- Do you have any e-mail sending copiers?

- E-mail accounts: Aliases and special e-mail addresses (e-mail accounts that collect e-mail but are not necessarily connected to a person, such as info@xxx.com from your web site or sales@xxx.com)

Security Groups

Security groups are useful in controlling access in your SharePoint (Team Site) environment. You can set up a security group in your Office 365 portal, or a security group will be synced from your local Active Directory if you use a DirSync method. Carefully consider naming standards. See Chapter 5 for more on security groups.

Special E-mail Addresses: Distribution Groups and Aliases

Special e-mail addresses are those that may not relate to a person (or login). For example, many organizations have external e-mail addresses, such as info@xxx.com. This address may be sent to a single person (as an alias) or to a group of people using a distribution group. You also may have internal distribution groups, such as salesforce@xxx.com or manufacturing@xxx.com. Distribution groups and aliases are free. You may also choose to have an Office 365 licensed account, to have the ability to allow multiple people to use the features of Outlook to manage e-mail (and to send e-mail under that ID). An example might begin orders@.

If you are not using a DirSync migration technique, you will have to build your distribution groups (lists of users who can be referred to with one e-mail address). These lists can be internal (only available within your organization) or external (available to the world). Details on how to set up distribution groups and aliases are in Chapter 8.

Exchange Public Folders

Exchange public folders are again supported in Office 365. You may choose to use SharePoint folders or to migrate your existing public folders to Office 365. Using public folders requires Outlook 2013.

Internet, Hardware, and Software

In general, your Internet speed should be adequate (including your firewall!), and your hardware and software must be up to date. These planning elements include:

- Internet speeds up and down by location; backup requirements (speed upgrades needed?)

- Is your Internet firewall up to date (as fast as your Internet speed)?

- Software and hardware inventory, i.e., computer types and locations (see Chapter 7)

- Macs? Versions of Outlook and Office?

- Phone types, type of synchronization required (consider how voice mail is delivered and deleted)

Perform Any Required Updates and Software or Hardware Upgrades

This may seem obvious, but it is important to have all of your workstations fully updated (Windows Update). This can be accomplished by installing and using Windows Intune. It may also be time to look at upgrading workstations or laptops.

- Any required updates and software or hardware upgrades?

- PC updates: All PCs should have all (even optional) Windows updates applied!

- Verify version minimums (e.g., Windows 7, web browsers, etc.).

There are also minimums on the version of the operating system and browsers. See http://office.microsoft.com/en-us/office365-suite-help/software-requirements-for-office-365-for-business-HA102817357.aspx.

Compliance Archive Requirements

This subject deserves a whole discussion. Check with your Microsoft Partner. If your organization is under litigation, or might be, it is important to consider the needs of your compliance archives. If you are moving an archive from another vendor or just setting one up now, you will want to understand the choices.

See Chapter 9 for additional information. You also should consider your organization's retention policies, or whether they need to be determined.

Step 4: Define Your Migration Plan and Schedule

This is one of the items that you will want to work on in parallel with the other planning steps. This schedule will no doubt have to be updated during the project.

At first, we will introduce some concepts that you should understand to help you set your schedule. Following is a sample schedule. Many of the details depend on your specific organization's needs.

- E-mail flow

- Controlling mail flow (MX record) for Office 365 migration options

- Mail flow options based on organization size

- Implementation notes

- Software distribution options (e.g., Windows Intune, Group Policy, etc.)

- Sample migration plan and schedule

E-mail Flow

E-mail flow is how e-mail is processed in the cloud with your existing e-mail services. In all Office 365 migrations, you should never be without e-mail, and you should not lose e-mail. The information described here is used in Chapter 4.

E-mail flow is simple. The person (program) sending you an e-mail looks up the address of your mail server (using the Domain Name Service [DNS] record known as an MX record). The program then sends the mail to the address (domain) in the MX record. All that is involved in migration is the need to forward mail from one server (where the MX record points) to the new server (where it will point), until the records are "cut over" (the MX record is set to point to the new Microsoft Office 365 Exchange server). This is mail flow. It is important to perform the required steps in sequence, so that no e-mail is lost during the migration.

An example of a risk of losing e-mail is during a cutover migration (see the following list) with a small organization that has been using a POP e-mail server. Since POP servers typically store only recent e-mail on the server, the bulk of an organization's e-mail is in Outlook files on the individual workstations. (Another reason to use Office 365: your e-mail is backed up!) Because the e-mail is only in Outlook, the simplest way to move historic e-mail is with PST export/import (see Chapter 4 for migration details). The failure scenario is:

1. You change the DNS MX record to point to Office 365.

2. An e-mail sender will look up the MX record to the domain and get the old POP server, because the MX record change has not yet propagated to the sender's location.

3. The PST file is exported before the mail arrives into Outlook, so the PST file does not contain the new e-mail.

Mitigation of this failure scenario is simple.

1. Change the MX record to Office 365 some hours before exporting the PSTs, to allow MX record propagation.

2. Be sure to update the local Outlook e-mail files (from the POP server: Outlook F9 key) before starting the PST export.

Controlling Mail Flow for Office 365 Migration Options

There are three methods of controlling e-mail flow (setting the MX record) related to implementing Office 365:

1. 100% cutover: Office 365 receives all e-mail (after the the MX record is cut over).

2. Simple coexistence: E-mail is forwarded from the "old" e-mail servers to Office 365 (normally only for the duration of the e-mail migration). After migration, the MX record is set to point to the Office 365 Exchange servers.

3. Hybrid coexistence: On-premises and cloud operate in tandem. This may be a long-term solution.

Cutover Mail Flow

For small organizations, we recommend a 100% cutover at a particular date and time. The users are loaded onto Office 365; the DNS mail (MX) record is pointed to Office 365; and historical e-mail will be moved after the cutover. This is the simplest and the most cost-effective method. The organization should be simple enough that the "test group" is the implementer, just to prove functions and timing.

Simple coexistence mail flow

Simple coexistence is for organizations that would benefit from having a test group—a group that will learn about Office 365, become advocates, and be able to help the next wave(s) of new users. Depending on the tool, historical e-mail will be moved after each group is cut over.

In simple coexistence, the users are loaded onto Office 365 in groups. The DNS mail (MX) record is *not* changed (until the end of the process). E-mail is still sent to the existing e-mail server, and the existing mail server is set to forward (without saving a copy!) new e-mail to the appropriate Office 365 account. This type of forward ensures that no duplicate e-mails are created. In the Office 365 Exchange management console, we mark the domain as "Internal Relay."

Internal Relay means that when a user who already has an Office 365 account sends an e-mail, one of the two following scenarios occurs:

- If the recipient also has an Office 365 account, the e-mail is kept within Office 365.

- If the user has *not* been loaded (or has no Office 365 license assigned), the e-mail is sent according to the MX record (back to the organization's e-mail server, because the MX record has not been changed yet).

See Chapter 4 for details on how to set Internal Relay.

Hybrid Coexistence Mail Flow

Hybrid coexistence is designed for large organizations that require a single sign-on and that may continue to retain an on-premises Exchange server. Large organizations may have the need to move users to and back from the cloud, such as if you have a legacy application that is not cloud-enabled. This requires an on-premises Exchange management server and knowledge of Federation. We discuss directory syncing (DirSync) and Federation in detail in Chapter 11.

Mail Flow Options Based on Organization Size

Table 3-3 shows different Office 365 deployment options, based on organization size and e-mail flow choice. Our focus here is on the cutover or simple coexistence methods, rather than on hybrid coexistence. See Chapter 11 for more details on hybrid coexistence, including why you may need four more servers.

Table 3-3. *Mail Flow Options*

Organization Size	E-mail Flow Coexistence	Intune	DirSync	AD FS Single Sign-On	Test Group
40 or less	Cutover	Yes	No	No	KAMIND demo account
20–70	Simple	Yes	No	No	Test group (2–4 Users)
70–500	Simple (no exchange)	Yes	Yes	Optional	Single test group, phased
200–2,000	Simple (no exchange)	Yes	Yes	Yes	Test group(s), phased plan

(continued)

Table 3-3. (*continued*)

Organization Size	E-mail Flow Coexistence	Intune	DirSync	AD FS Single Sign-On	Test Group
200–600	Hybrid (exchange)	Yes	Yes	Yes	Test group(s), phased plan
400–2,400	Hybrid (exchange)	Yes	Yes	Yes	Multiple test/deployment
2,400 or more	Hybrid (exchange)	Yes	Yes	Yes	Multiple test/deployment

These mail flow options all recommend a pilot or test group. These test group individuals should be selected to help lead the organization to a fast acceptance of Office 365. If the test groups are chosen correctly, the deployment goes very quickly.

IMPLEMENTATION NOTES

There are a few details that are mentioned elsewhere but deserve to be repeated (and included in your plan).

1. Validate custom domains *before* initial user load and Lync setup.

2. Use Windows Intune to gather hardware and software inventory.

3. Use the information that you gathered in the section "Step 3: Collect Your Information."

Sample Migration Plan

The plans we implement are broken down into six phases, summarized as follows:

Phase I: Plan—work with organization administrator(s) to define migration deliverables.

Phase II: Set up Office 365.

Phase III: Pilot with test groups (recommended for more than 20 users; this will reduce support).

Phase IV: E-mail migration with tool: validate and configure Active Directory.

Phase V: Clean up the environment (depends upon organization's objectives).

Phase VI: Training.

Feel free to adjust the plan task owners and due dates, as appropriate.

REMEMBER: FOLLOW THE PATH BASED ON MIGRATION STRATEGY

1. Cutover (without DirSync)

2. Simple Coexistence (without DirSync)

3. Hybrid Coexistence: DirSync and/or AD FS

4. See Chapter 11 for more details regarding DirSync, AD FS, Single Sign-On, and Exchange Federation

The details of the six phases are described in the following six tables (Tables 3-4 through 3-9).

Table 3-4. *Phase I: Work with Organization Administrator(s) to Define Migration Deliverables*

Due Date	Owner	Task
		a. Define Office 365 product mix based on client's needs.
		b. Define domains to be converted (note existing web sites and subsites, purchase sites).
		c. Determine DNS host username and password.
		d. Determine DNS issues (secondary DNS, owners, SRV issues, other vendors' helpfulness); verify your domain(s) (to Microsoft) as soon as you can.
		e. Determine e-mail migration: cutover, simple coexistence, DirSync and/or AD FS.
		f. Define users (e-mail addresses), plus mailboxes that require storage.
		g. Define e-mail aliases (if required; e.g., info@xxx.com) and who they point to.
		h. Determine e-mail that needs to be migrated and mechanism (distribution groups).
		i. Define security groups and users in those groups (for SharePoint).
		j. Define the scope of the shutdown/conversion of old environment.
		k. Run Active Directory Validation Tool.
		l. Run Exchange Test Connector Validation Tool.

Table 3-5. *Phase II: Set Up Office 365*

Due Date	Owner	Task
		a. Verify your domain(s) with Microsoft! Set up DNS records with domain hosting company (retain existing web sites at existing web service providers). Time highly depends on DNS environment.
		b. Finish Office 365 setups: configure Lync, etc.
		c. Set up your Office 365 SharePoint Team Site with basic Read permissions.
		d. Provide instruction to load proper software for each user's PC (specifically, connector and Lync; on-site activities performed by/at direction of organization administrator). There may be additional time in this task depending upon the available skill set.
		e. Documentation to set up smartphones.
		f. Documentation to use Office 365 (end-user documentation).

Table 3-6. *Phase III: Pilot with Test Groups*

Due Date	Owner	Task
		a. Define the pilot objectives with organization administrator (go/no-go criteria).
		b. Continue to refine this deployment schedule.
		c. Define test group members.
		d. Deploy Intune to all pilot users.
		e. Consider setting up an Office 365 SharePoint and a project site with basic permissions for pilot users (and the project itself). Provide documentation for users to load their files into SharePoint.
		f. Test and evaluate deployment against the go/no-go criteria.
		g. Work issues against the go/no-go criteria.

Table 3-7. *Phase IV: E-mail Migration with Tool—Validate and Configure Active Directory*

Due Date	Owner	Task
		a. Validate the Active Directory domain (to ensure that data will transfer).
		b. Load test group users.
		c. Assign Office 365 licenses (for this test group).
		d. Change domain to "Internal Relay."
		e. Set up e-mail forwarding for existing users, from on-site Exchange server to long-name Office 365 (depends upon implementation plan).
		f. Pre-migrate e-mail, if possible.
		g. Migrate (test or final) e-mail via a properly set-up OWA with your on-premises admin username and password or with username and password for each e-mail user to be migrated.
		h. Migrate each test group (0, n, last).
		i. Validate conference room(s).
		j. Users access e-mail via Outlook Web App (until Outlook is installed and configured).
		k. Per workstation: Install Workstation SW—Lync, Office 365 ProPlus, "Set up and configure your Office Desktop apps"; Special for Office 2010; configure Outlook (new profile); resolve any issues.
		l. When all users have been migrated, proceed with the following:
		m. Build DirSync server, install DirSync.
		n. Run DirSync to "soft match" loaded users.

Table 3-8. *Phase V: Clean Up Environment (Depends on Organization's Objectives)*

Due Date	Owner	Task
		a. Shut down Exchange server (cleanly).
		b. Disconnect the Exchange server part of a small business server.
		c. Build a more detailed or customer designed SharePoint site.
		d. Implement other projects as required (link upgrade speeds, firewall upgrades, etc.).
		e. Clean up and verify licensing.

Table 3-9. *Phase VI: Training*

Due Date	Owner	Task
		As required, timing to be determined

Step 5: Microsoft Account and Organizational Account

There are two types of "login" accounts associated with Microsoft. One is the "Microsoft account." This is the new name for a Live ID (live.com). It also includes accounts at hotmail.com, outlook.com, Xbox Live, and SkyDrive. This is the consumer account. It is this type of account that Windows 8 wants to have you use to synchronize your desktop and other features through SkyDrive. To create a Microsoft account with your e-mail address, go to http://outlook.com and "Sign Up Now" to create a new account.

A Microsoft account can be the same "text" as your organization e-mail; that is, dcrawford@kamind.net can be both a Microsoft account and an Organizational account. You can create a Microsoft account from your Organization ID or from your other e-mail accounts, such as Gmail and Yahoo. This can be confusing, because your passwords may not be synchronized—you will have to determine where you are trying to log in to be sure to use the password for that type of account.

The other type is an "Organizational account" or "Organizational ID." This is an Office 365 login for any organization using Office 365. This is the business account. This is an account that you would use to sign on to Office 365.

If the software is not sure which account you mean, you will see a "We Need a Little More Help" screen, as shown in Figure 3-7.

Figure 3-7. *"We Need a Little More Help" screen*

A side note: Either of these accounts can be used by SharePoint when sharing with external users.

▨ **Note**   To add an external user to your Office 365 SharePoint site, you send him or her an invitation. He or she will require either an Office 365 "Organizational account" or a "Microsoft account" to access your shared data.

Step 6: SkyDrive and SkyDrive Pro

SkyDrive and SkyDrive Pro have similar names. Both are Microsoft data storage services. Their implementation is radically different (see Figure 3-8). SkyDrive (not Pro) is the consumer service. The data storage is hosted on a set of servers completely separate from Office 365. The sign-on for SkyDrive is a "Microsoft account" (see section "Step 5: Microsoft Account and Organizational Account"). SkyDrive will take any type of file.

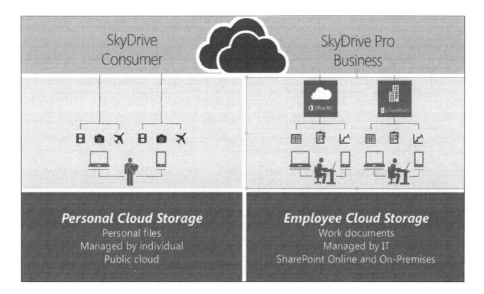

Figure 3-8. *SkyDrive and SkyDrive Pro (courtesy of Microsoft)*

SkyDrive Pro is the business service. The data storage is hosted by the same Office 365 SharePoint servers as the rest of your Team Site. SkyDrive Pro uses the same permissions structure as any other part of SharePoint.

SkyDrive Pro has limits on the number of files, the type of file (you cannot store .exe files, for example), and the maximum size of the amount of data that can be synchronized. These limitations exist because SkyDrive Pro is based on SharePoint. The limitations are continuing to be reduced as Office 365 improves. For example, SkyDrive Pro now allows 20,000 items in a list (the old limit was 5,000 items).

Syncing is performed by a SkyDrive Pro tool (or SharePoint Workspace for Office 2010 Professional users). See Chapter 2 for more information on using SkyDrive Pro.

Step 7: Windows Intune

Windows Intune is a powerful device-management tool that includes anti-malware scanning, anti-spam processing, hardware and software inventory features, a user help feature, and more. We like to use Windows Intune to determine hardware and software in the environment. We recommend installing Windows Intune early in the migration process, both for its inventory capabilities and the ability to install software remotely. See Chapter 7 for installation details and more information.

Deployment

We have completed the planning for your Office 365 deployment. At this point, you have collected the required information and are ready to deploy. Before we start this process, let us discuss the project and how the deployment process will work. This way, when you begin to deploy (as described in Chapter 4), you will have already made the necessary decisions (see Table 3-10).

Table 3-10. Office 365 Deployment Planning Grid

Steps	Action/Component	Notes or Effect
Step 1	Verify Your Environment	• Verify your Active Directory and Exchange Server Readiness.
Step 2	Add Domain Name Service (DNS) Information	• Who has control? • Custom domain: validate your domain. • Validate all of your domains? • Autodiscover and SRV records • IP addresses you need to keep
Step 3	Configure Lync	• Initial user load • Federation settings • Pilot and mail flow considerations • Migration team meetings
Step 4	Initial User Load	• Administrators • Pilot considerations
Step 5	Pilot/Test Group	• Required for a successful migration • Find your raving fans! • Resolve naysayers. • Set criteria for pilot acceptance. • Set deployment schedule. • Verify/resolve any odd things. • There are two types of pilot: • Microsoft pilot using your xxx.onmicrosoft.com names • Preproduction pilot using your custom domain name • Use Windows Intune. • Set up a SharePoint project site. • Missing: GAL, calendar free/busy, distribution groups
Step 6	Inform Your Users	• Inform: what is happening and why? • Planned cutover date • Delete unneeded e-mail (spam, deleted items, etc.) to improve migration time.
Step 7	Train Your Users	• Outlook Web App • Workstation setup (if required) • Lync Sign-On • Smartphone setup
Step 8	E-mail Migration	• Method choices • Global address List • Pilot considerations
Step 9	Set Up Workstations	• Requires admin rights and user password • Ensure all updates have been done! • Install Office 365 ProPlus. • New Outlook profile?
Step 10	Configure External Devices	• Configure external printers and copiers to send to Office 365. See Chapter 10 for detailed information.
Step 11	Cutover	• Change MX; add SPF records. • Finish e-mail migration.

At KAMIND, we have a few sayings, including: "Don't do it" and "Just get started." For example, you may be thinking, "I want to save a buck and get the 'Small Business' plan." Don't do it. The savings are tiny, and the limitations are huge. There are even more limits with Midsize Business (no Exchange-Only, no Kiosk). Just buy Enterprise. For more details, see the discussion in the section "Office 365 Subscription Plans."

"Just get started" basically means don't over-plan. Planning, like most things in life, requires balance. This is especially true when you are implementing Office 365 for the first time and migrating your e-mail.

Granted, you can mix these areas, depending on your business needs and the complexity of the organization, but in general (for the 90% of us), these next steps are the steps that we have found important in our deployment of Office 365 for our customers.

Step 1: Verify Your Environment

Microsoft provides a tool to verify various parts of your environment, including Active Directory. Figure 3-9 shows the screen after the completion of the test. This tool is described in Chapter 4.

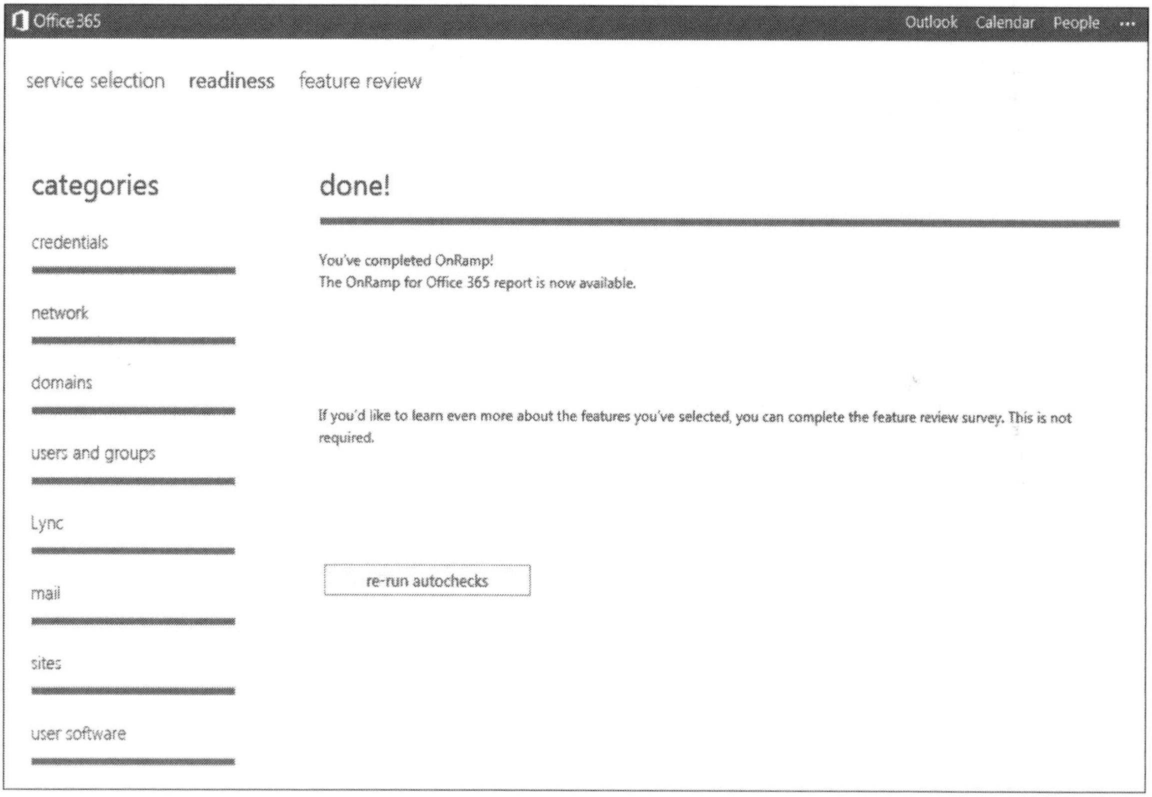

Figure 3-9. *Readiness tool results*

Step 2: Add Domain Name Service (DNS) Information

Domain Name Service (DNS) is the set of data that is used by services in the Internet to find, manage, and secure domain names, such as getoffice365now.com. Security for a domain is provided by services (domain registrars, such as GoDaddy, eNom, and Network Solutions) that require you to have a username and password in order to change information about the domain.

If your domain provider does not supply all of the necessary DNS records required to support Office 365, you will have to change providers. The most common missing records support are the service records (SRV), which are key for Lync VOIP support and Lync Federation. The information that you collected for the DNS will be used in Chapter 4 sections "Step 1: Validate Your Domain(s) to Microsoft" and "Step 2: Add Additional Domain Name Service (DNS) Information." Microsoft uses your ability to add records to your domain information to verify that you can edit and, therefore, "own" the domain.

PLANNING TASKS

1. Determine *all* of the domains (remember `.com`, `.org`, `.net`, etc.) that you wish to include in your Office 365 subscription.

2. Verify the domain registrar, username, and password for each domain. (Hopefully, they are all with the same registrar!)

3. Verify that you can edit the DNS records.

4. Specifically, verify that you can add SRV records at your hosting service.

5. Because of the lead time, now is a good time to start "Step 1: Validate Your Domain(s) to Microsoft," even though this is the planning section. (Do *not* move your MX record.) Return here (to planning) while you are waiting for DNS propagation.

A common problem with DNS service occurs when another provider (perhaps the vendor hosting your web site) has added a "secondary domain server." This is normally a check box and the name of the server(s) in your primary domain registrar. If you cannot add the records that are required (Office 365 requires records, such as Autodiscover, SRV, and TXT), you may have to delete the secondary domain server to get control of your domain(s). In some cases, when you remove the DNS record, the hosting provider may delete your web site. However, if your web hosting provider provided an IP address for your web site, you are in good shape. BE SURE TO RECORD THE FIXED IP ADDRESS OF YOUR WEB (and FTP) SITES. You will have to readd this information again as the "www" record at the primary registrar, as we make changes to support Office 365.

Typically, you use the registrar's DNS (the registrar is the place you purchased the domain name) to manage the services (or address pointers) to the web-hosting, e-mail, and other services. As an example, in the United States, the majority of domains are purchased from GoDaddy, eNom, or Network Solutions. There are secondary domain suppliers, but in essence, those are only front ends to these primary domain suppliers.

Some secondary domain suppliers (such as some web-hosting companies) want to control the DNS: they want to control your pointers to mail, web, and other services. These companies can be inflexible on any changes to DNS. They want to lock you into receiving all services with them, because they know that once you start using these services, it will be too costly for you to change them.

Office 365 does not care who the primary DNS supplier is, or the secondary, for that matter. All Office 365 cares about is that you have the ability to directly change your DNS records.

▓ **Note** Some DNS providers do not want customers to control the DNS. If this is true in your case, you will have to find a new domain service provider.

Autodiscover

One of the records that you will want to insert into DNS is Autodiscover. Autodiscover is the ability of an Outlook client (including your laptop and your smartphone) to discover the location of the Office 365 Exchange e-mail server and to automatically connect to that server (see Figure 3-10). The process of verifying your domain(s) will describe the records that you need to add.

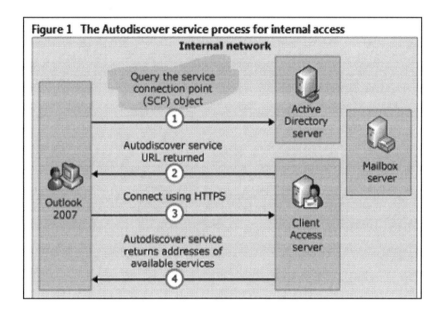

Figure 3-10. Exchange Autodiscover process (courtesy of Microsoft)

If you are on-site, and you are trying to connect to the Office 365 Exchange server, the Outlook client will use the Exchange service control point connection object to attach to the local Exchange server and bypass the external Autodiscover lookup. You may need a registry tweak. (See Chapter 4 for more details.)

SRV Records

SRV are service records. Lync uses these records to support Voice (VOIP) communications. After you verify the domain, you will have to change the SRV records. If your DNS supplier does not support service records, you will have to change suppliers. If you have no desire to use Lync, then these records do not matter.

Step 3: Configure Lync

Lync is a very powerful communications and collaboration tool that is available in Enterprise plans E1 and up. Following are a few setup options that you may choose to implement.

We highly recommend using Lync for your pilot and implementation project, for both your project meetings and user support, as well as for general use throughout your organization.

Lync requires DNS SRV records to be defined, as described previously. If you have local DNS (most sites with servers will), you may also have to add these SRV records to your local DNS.

Lync also has the following general setup options:

- General (Figure 3-11): Presence privacy mode (two options)
  - Automatically display presence information (we recommend this option)

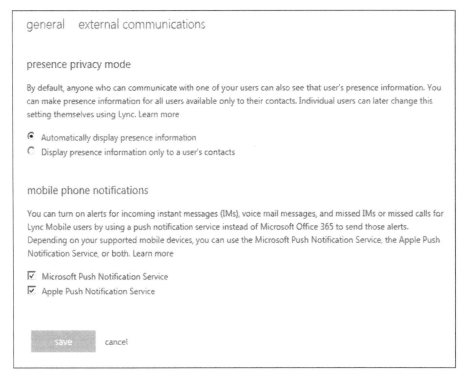

Figure 3-11. *Lync general settings*

- Display presence information only to a user's contactGeneral (Figure 3-11): Mobile phone notifications (two options)
  - Microsoft Push Notification Service
  - Apple Push Notification Service

We recommend that both be checked.

- External communications (Figure 3-12): External Access: Domain Federation (three options)

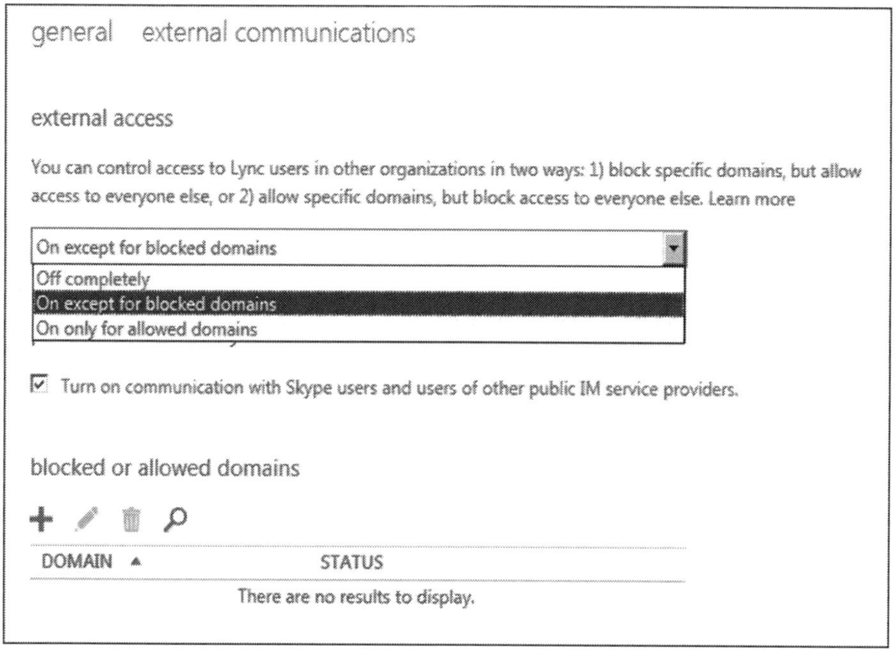

general   external communications

external access

You can control access to Lync users in other organizations in two ways: 1) block specific domains, but allow access to everyone else, or 2) allow specific domains, but block access to everyone else. Learn more

On except for blocked domains

Off completely
On except for blocked domains
On only for allowed domains

☑ Turn on communication with Skype users and users of other public IM service providers.

blocked or allowed domains

✚ ✎ 🗑 🔍

DOMAIN ▲   STATUS

There are no results to display.

Figure 3-12. *Lync external communications settings*

- Off completely

- On except for blocked domains (we recommend this option)

- On only for allowed domains

- External communications (Figure 3-12): Public IM connectivity (and Skype) off or on; we recommend on (checked)

You can specifically include or exclude domains (depending on the setting above). Click "+" to add, or the pencil to edit.

You may also choose to use a third-party conferencing vendor, "Dial-in Conferencing," in order to use regular phone numbers (POTS) in your Lync conference calls.

It is also possible to customize your Lync meeting invitation with your own logo and a Help URL, a Legal URL, and Footer text. See the section "Lync Administration" in Chapter 8 for more information.

It is a good idea to set these options (and to have your domain validated) before loading users. These are the default values that will be copied to individual users. Otherwise, you may have to go to each user to set the appropriate values. See Chapter 4 for details on how to configure these settings.

Step 4: Initial User Load

Define your test groups. Load your e-mail accounts (users), set administrators, assign your Enterprise plan licenses, and assign locations. Determine who will be migrated. Details are important! An accurate list of who and what is to be migrated and how your business processes might have changed improves the odds of an easy and successful migration.

You started collecting this information in "Step 2: Collect Your Information."

Details are important! Following are some of the details that have been missed:

- Are there people that have left the organization?
- On which services or servers is their e-mail?
- Are there name or e-mail address changes?
- Who will be an Office 365 administrator? (There are several levels available.)
- Which Office 365 subscription plan should be used for each user? (Mix and match.)
- Where are the user locations (cities, states, or countries)?
- Will there be meeting rooms (and calendars)?
- Will there be test groups, and who will be in them? (Who is migrated first?)

Users can be loaded, as follows:

- One at a time "by hand," using the Office 365 administrator portal
- Using a .csv spreadsheet
- As part of DirSync processing

When you are building your pilot/test group, it is important to load only the users for that test group (or to be sure that the extra users do not have Office 365 licenses assigned). If the users are loaded, e-mail will be directed to the online account from anyone else with an Office 365 account, not back to the on-premises Exchange server. See Chapter 4 for more information.

Step 5: Pilot/Test Group

KAMIND stresses the use of a test group and a project plan. For organizations with fewer than 100 users, the deployment plans are simpler. Once you reach 100 users, you have to look at phased deployment based on the ability of the organization to absorb the changes. Automated mechanisms to push software updates to the users are more important.

MULTIPLE PURPOSES FOR TEST GROUPS

1. Evaluate Office 365 features.
2. Build a team that knows Office 365.
3. Build a team to become Office 365 advocates.
4. Build a team that can help the next wave(s) of new users.
5. Find your raving fans!
6. Resolve naysayers.
7. Train support staff.

There are two types of pilot:

- Microsoft pilot using your xxx.onmicrosoft.com names

  - The difficulty with this type of pilot is that the user login and Lync configuration will have to be re-done. Use this type of pilot only for a very small number of people, where you are trying the products (for example, Lync). We do not recommend this approach, because of the additional work to undo the pilot.

- Preproduction pilot using your custom domain name

  - This is the type of pilot that we recommend. You are moving toward implementation without having to re-do configurations.

  - Note that with this type of pilot, because you are building real accounts in Office 365 in an environment separate from your on-premises Exchange server, you will not have the following:

    - Access to the on-premises global address list

    - Calendar free/busy information

    - On-premises distribution groups. You can build these, but they are separate.

Take advantage of the tools at hand.

- Use Windows Intune.

- Set up a SharePoint project site.

KAMIND's philosophy includes the design of implementation success criteria for the test groups and the deployment process. Success criteria are Go/NoGo decision points. As examples, Go/NoGo criteria could be

- the successful configuration of the desktop and Outlook for all users

- the installation of Windows Intune for data collection

- completion of Outlook Web App training sessions

- completion of Lync training sessions

At the end of a test group deployment, you must review your criteria and evaluate the success of the process. If the test group deployment is successful, then move to the next step. If the test group does not deploy successfully, then stop, evaluate the failure(s), and make a decision on the deployment of the next test group.

■ **Note**   If the test group has not met the success criteria, fix the problem. Verify and resolve any odd things. Do not proceed until the test group is 100% successful!

Step 6: Inform Your Users

Keep your users up to date.

- Who is involved?

- What are you trying to accomplish?

- Why? Saving money?

- Why? Better service?

- Where? A particular facility or group?

- When? What is the schedule?

Step 7: Train Your Users

This seems obvious as well. The good news is that Outlook is the same (unless you are taking the opportunity to move to a new version). Lync is cool. Everyone loves it. SharePoint may be new, but a good implementation is pretty seamless for your users. For example, explain the similarities and differences between "installed on your computer" Outlook and Outlook Web App (through a web browser on the blue ribbon). The e-mail data is the same, just different front ends. See Chapter 2 for more information.

Step 8: E-mail Migration—Moving Historical E-mail (Migration) Options

Migrating e-mail is the process of copying historical e-mail (and calendars, tasks, contacts, and folders) from an existing on-premises Exchange server or e-mail service into Office 365. After migration, your old e-mail will be available in the users' Outlook(s), Outlook Web App (through a web browser), and their smartphones.

■ **Tip**   When you move historic e-mail, you do not have to move all users' e-mail at once. What we have found is that it is best to move the calendars, tasks, contacts, folders, and at least 100–200 e-mails for each user. This is quick and allows the organization to function. The remainder of the older e-mail is migrated, based on the organization priority list.

Outlook (on all of the users' devices) may also cache the information on the hard drive of the desktop/laptop. Smartphones also cache data locally. This allows a user to review sent or historical e-mail even when disconnected from the Internet.

■ **Note**   The planning task for this section is to consider your migration method(s). You may choose any method for a particular user. You do not have to use the same method for all users: different users may have different requirements. Some users may not require history at all.

There are more details on the pros and cons of each type of migration and specific usage information for each type in Chapter 4, section "Step 9: Migrate Historical E-mail."

There are four types of migration:

1.   Do not move anything.

2.   A third-party tool, such as MigrationWiz

3.   Office 365 tools with DirSync

4.   PST: Export from the local Outlook to a .pst file and import it to Office 365.

Do Nothing

The easiest is to move nothing. Some people have actually chosen this option! This is not normally a choice, but there may be some users who do not need e-mail history. In this do-nothing case, you just cut over all services to Office 365. New mail will flow to the accounts.

Third-Party Tools

The third-party tool that we prefer to use is the data-migration tool MigrationWiz from www.migrationwiz.com. This tool is the simplest to set up and use and requires little oversight; it just runs. MigrationWiz moves e-mail, tasks, contacts, and calendar entries. MigrationWiz also migrates data from many types of e-mail services. The added benefit is that you can start and stop migrations, so you can allow the user accounts to be built and follow up with historical e-mail.

MigrationWiz can only be used if you *do not use* the active directory synchronization tool (DirSync). If you use Microsoft DirSync tool, you will have to use Microsoft's Exchange migration tools.

There are also migration tools available through your Microsoft Partner.

Office 365 with DirSync

Office 365 is supplied with a number of migration tools for moving from on-premises equipment to the cloud. You must use these tools if you use DirSync. The on-cloud mailboxes are only created with Microsoft tools. Directory synchronization is discussed in Chapter 11.

PST Export/Import

The fourth method is to use the .pst file export/import within Outlook. PST migration brings over e-mail, tasks, contacts, and calendar entries data but will not bring over the complete e-mail addresses when the data is imported. As an example, when you try to reply to an e-mail in a PST import, the e-mail address may not be complete.

Typically, we use this method with POP e-mail accounts. In this case, there is not very much (if any) e-mail on the POP e-mail server, so historical e-mail is only stored locally in the user's Outlook files.

It is also important not to try to restart a PST export or import; start over from the beginning, that is, re-do the export, then the import.

▓ **Note**   If the source server is an Exchange server, use MigrationWiz.

PST migration is easy to use. You simply export the cached data in the user's Outlook to a .pst file then import the .pst file to the Office 365 root directory, and the data is uploaded to Office 365. There are two ways to do a PST import:

1. Manually (export files as an archive and import them to Office 365)

2. Using the Microsoft PST capture tool (free download)

See Chapter 4 for details.

Step 9: Set Up Workstations

Workstation setup is now usually "self-service" by the user—that is, the user now does his or her own installation of Office and other components. The user will need his or her Office 365 login and password and Administrative rights to his or her computer. See Chapter 2 for more details.

Step 10: Configure External Devices

One of the areas that is frequently forgotten in deployment and planning is external devices and how those devices are configured to use Office 365 services. Office 365 supports receiving e-mail from trusted and untrusted senders. The actual connection of these devices uses the concept of "connectors." You have to add a trusted connector to Office 365 that allows the device (such as a scanner or copier) to send to Office 365 and have the e-mail sent to both internal and external users.

Step 11: Cutover

This is the step where the MX record is re-pointed to Office 365 and the SPF record is added to your registrar's DNS.

- Change MX; add SPF record.

- Finish e-mail migration.

If you used a third-party migration tool, this is also the time to start DirSync (if you are planning to use it) to get a "soft match" between your on-premises Active Directory and Office 365.

Post-deployment

At this point, we have completed the migration of e-mail services to Office 365 and the implementation of Lync. –Next, we have to address post-deployment activities, including SharePoint deployment and migration (see Table 3-11). We separate this into post-deployment, because the key migration for a business is normally e-mail and voice services. These are business- critical services. SharePoint is business-critical as well, but you can deploy to Office 365 and have a separate project that migrates the SharePoint services to Office 365.

Table 3-11. *Office 365 Post-deployment Planning Grid*

Steps	Action/Component	Notes or Effect
Step 1	Hosted SharePoint Domain Name	• xxx.onmicrosoft name is your Team Site name: xxx.sharepoint.com (chosen when you purchased)
Step 2	Hosted SharePoint Initial Configuration	There are a few settings that you should verify in SharePoint after you first purchase an Office 365 subscription. See Chapter 5, sections "SharePoint Admin Center" and "Initial SharePoint Setup."
Step 3	Hosted SharePoint Planning	See Chapter 5 for additional points about SharePoint planning (best practices) including: • Governance • Administrators • Use simple structures and permissions • Security groups (security structure) • Navigation • External sharing (interaction with security and permissions)
Step 4	Hosted SharePoint Personal Sites	• 25GB (to 100GB) of storage per login • Personal information • Shared and not shared • Part of eDiscovery

(continued)

Table 3-11. (*continued*)

Steps	Action/Component	Notes or Effect
Step 5	Office 365 Hosted Web Site	• See Chapter 6. • Microsoft can host your web site.
Step 6	Exchange Online Protection	• The Exchange Online Protection (EOP) service is the front end of the Office 365 that handles all of the external e-mail front-end processing and filtering. If you have smart devices that e-mail to Office 365, you will use EOP to manage the interaction. • See Chapter 10, which describes initial setup steps that may be important for your organization.
Step 7	Data Loss Prevention	• See Chapter 9
Step 8	Compliance: eDiscovery, Search Center	• See Chapter 9
Step 9	Cleanup	• This includes tasks such as the scheduled shutdown of your Exchange server

Step 1: Hosted SharePoint Domain Name

The domain name for your SharePoint Team Site is `xxx.sharepoint.com` (where xxx is the `.onmicrosoft.com` name that you used when you purchased Office 365). The personal sites are `xxx-my.sharepoint.com`. SharePoint is only a web service; you can use any browser and type in the URL for the page that you wish to see. You can set up favorites in your web browser. See Chapter 5 for more information.

Step 2: Hosted SharePoint Initial Configuration

There are a few settings that you should verify in SharePoint after you first purchase an Office 365 subscription. See Chapter 5, sections "SharePoint Admin Center" and "Initial SharePoint Setup."

Step 3: Hosted SharePoint Planning

SharePoint licensing is included in the Small Business, Small Business Premium, Midsize Business, and Enterprise Business E1, E3, and E4 plans (and to a limited extent, in some of the Kiosk plans). The concepts discussed in this chapter generally apply to all of these versions of Office 365 SharePoint, but these configurations have only been tested with the Enterprise version.

What Is SharePoint?

SharePoint is Microsoft's document-storage and content-management tool. SharePoint was first released in 2001. Originally, SharePoint was used as an enterprise's on-premises "Intranet." SharePoint was included in Small Business Server and in the original Microsoft cloud offering: BPOS. The version with Office 365 is SharePoint Online.

SharePoint is fundamentally a web server that presents web pages to your browser (Internet Explorer, FireFox, Chrome, Safari, etc.). The SharePoint data (structure, permissions, sites, your documents, etc.) is hosted on SQL servers that are maintained by Microsoft within their secure environment.

■ **Note**   Because your data is presented as a URL, you can set a bookmark or favorite to go to a particular
SharePoint page.

This allows people to read, edit, create pages and sites, and control administrative settings, depending on their
permissions. Chapter 2 includes descriptions of capabilities that everyone will normally use (adding documents to
SharePoint, creating and editing documents locally or in the cloud). This chapter includes descriptions of how to
create sites and site features up to full site collection administration ones.

Microsoft has a stated and executed intention of "cloud first." This means that the SharePoint that is available
with Office 365 (Wave 15) is SharePoint 2013 with more extensions and features. There are only a couple of functions
of SharePoint that are in the on-premises version that are not in the Office 365 version. When you include the feature
that you can be up and running in SharePoint Online (the very latest version) in one day, your SharePoint Online
version might be three to six years ahead of your on-premises functionality!

The Two Sides of Permissions: Sites and Groups

Permissions are set as the combination of

- Sites (where)

- Groups that contain people (who)

- What can be done (read, edit, etc.)

See Chapter 5 for additional points about SharePoint planning (best practices), including the following:

- Governance

- Administrators

- Use simple structures and permissions

- Security groups (security structure)

- Navigation

- External Sharing (interaction with security and permissions)

Step 4: Hosted SharePoint Personal Sites

A personal SharePoint site is created for each plan E1 (or above) or SharePoint plan 1 (or above) user. The space
allocated is separate from your other SharePoint space. It is intended for use by that user. The user can decide how
to share his or her data and with whom. The personal sites are xxx-my.sharepoint.com. See Chapter 2 for more on
this topic.

Step 5: Office 365 Hosted Web Site

Office 365 includes the option of a public facing web site hosted by Microsoft (for no additional charge for storage or
bandwidth). There are limitations; see Chapter 6 for details.

Your SharePoint team or personal site is also available for external access (with proper authority). Access
depends on the permissions granted. See Chapter 5 for details.

Step 6: Exchange Online Protection

The Exchange Online Protection (EOP) service is the front end of Office 365 that handles all of the external e-mail front-end processing and filtering. If you have smart devices that e-mail to Office 365, you will use EOP to manage the interaction. See Chapter 10 for more information and a description of the initial setup steps that may be important for your organization.

Step 7: Data Loss Prevention

Data loss prevention in the configuration of services that will process the e-mail communications helps ensure that confidential company information and/or personal information is not e-mailed improperly. The DLP service keeps your business safe (as much as possible) from people making simple mistakes in sending out information in e-mail that they should not have distributed. Please See Chapter 9 for details.

Step 8: Compliance: eDiscovery, Search Center

Office 365 supports a full eDiscovery and compliance center for e-mail communications and access to documents on your SharePoint services. The new compliance center allows you to perform eDiscovery services on Office 365 in response to an external request for judicial or compliance review. See Chapter 9 for details.

Step 9: Cleanup

It is important to "de-provision" your Exchange and SharePoint servers. It is easy to assume that you can just "turn them off" and scrap them. This will lead to problems! You have to plan for the removal of the equipment by uninstalling the server software and removing it from your Active Directory. The general practice is to uninstall the role or server software. See Chapter 4 for the details to complete your migration.

Summary

There is a lot to think about in the planning of an Office 365 deployment. We have tried to address most of the issues that you will face and have provided a plan to address them. As you move forward with your Office 365 deployment, please refer to the next chapters to address your questions related to specific areas of your business.

Reference Links

There is a large amount of information about Office 365 on the Web. The difficulty lies in finding the right information. The information contained in this chapter derives from a combination of our experiences in executing deployments and support information that has been published by third parties.

Office 365 Trial Subscription

http://getoffice365now.com/Pages/default.aspx

Windows Intune Trial Subscription

www.microsoft.com/en-us/windows/windowsintune/try.aspx

Office 365 and Windows Intune Trust Center

www.microsoft.com/online/legal/v2/?docid=36&langid=en-us

Create Microsoft Account Alias to Your Personal E-mail Address

http://account.outlook.com

Office 365 Planning and Migration Spreadsheet

http://getoffice365now.com/Pages/default.aspx

Office 365 Fast Track Migration Tools

http://fasttrack.office.com/

Software Requirements for Office 365

http://office.microsoft.com/en-us/office365-suite-help/software-requirements-for-office-365-for-business-HA102817357.aspx

Next Steps

You have reviewed and performed the required parts of the planning process. You have a migration plan. See Chapter 4 for the details to complete your migration, and along with Chapter 4, here is a list of chapters you may want to read next:

- **Chapter 4**: "Office 365 Setup and Migration"

    - Once you have selected your Office 365 plan and completed the planning process, the next step is the migration process. There are different ways you can migrate to Office 365 and different migration techniques, using cutover migration or federation. This chapter covers the most common approach to Office 365 migration, in a non-federated environment.

- **Chapter 6**: "Building Your Web Site"

    - Office 365 includes a public-facing web site, and the necessary developer's tools to build out the web site. This chapter takes you from the basic Office 365 site to a fully functioning web site. The Office 365 public facing web sites fulfills the basic web needs of 90% of the businesses on Office 365. This chapter describes how to configure and build the public-facing web site for your business, using the integrated Office 365 web site tools and SharePoint Designer—a design tool that is included with your Office 365 subscription.

- **Chapter 7**: "Windows Intune Administration"

    - The secret to an optimal Office 365 site is the management of the desktop, to ensure that updates are current and the user antivirus is functioning. Windows Intune is a desktop-management tool that addresses these issues and reduces the administrators' efforts in desktop management and improves the user's experience.

- **Chapter 8**: "Office 365 Administration"

  - This chapter describes the different administration centers in Office 365 and the most common tools that you would use to administrate your Office 365 company. Depending on your Office 365 services, there are five possible administration tools. This chapter focuses on the Office 365, Exchange, and Lync administration centers. The SharePoint and Windows Intune administration centers are described in their own chapters. We close the chapter with using PowerShell to manage your Office 365 environment.

- **Chapter 9**: "Compliance and Data Loss Prevention"

  - Businesses must adapt their mail document storage systems to correctly process the electronic communications, based on regulatory oversight. The compliance and data loss prevention (DLP) provides this capability to allow businesses to manage their communications and protect from simple mistakes in their electronic communications. Office 365 includes integrated discovery that supports legal discovery and audit requirements.

- **Chapter 10**: "Exchange Online Protection Administration"

  - Office 365 is composed of a set of services. The Exchange Online Protection (EOP) service is the front end of Office 365 that handles all of the external e-mail front-end processing and filtering. If you have smart devices that e-mail to Office 365, you will use EOP to manage the interaction.

CHAPTER 4

■ ■ ■

Setup and Migration Guide

In the previous chapters, we have walked through the Office 365 features and spent a lot of time reviewing the planning requirements for moving your business to the cloud. The focus here is on the setup and migration. There are two points that we have raised in the previous chapters. These are 1) planning and 2) purchasing the correct subscription for your business. Successful migrations are about planning. When you move into production, the production side should be very mechanical - no surprises. The focus on this chapter is to extend the planning chapter with the "how to" approach in moving your business to the cloud. Included in this chapter is the 10-step migration process, along with separate sections covering onboarding users and e-mail to Office 365.

There are three versions of Office 365: Professional, Mid-Size Business, and Enterprise. The Professional version of Office 365 and the Mid-Size Business versions are preconfigured based on focus group feedback for a target market, with a one-size-fits-all approach and no subscription mixing options. The Enterprise version (Figure 4-1) provides full flexibility, which allows you to select the subscription based on the roles in the organization and controlling the overall deployment costs.

Figure 4-1. *Office 365 Login Page (portal.microsoftonline.com)*

The Enterprise version also provides a complete set of tools that are normally found in large corporations, but are needed for businesses of all sizes to control operating costs and to improve productivity. One of the nice features of the Enterprise version is the access to all of the software components for Microsoft Office desktop client suites (see Figure 4-2).

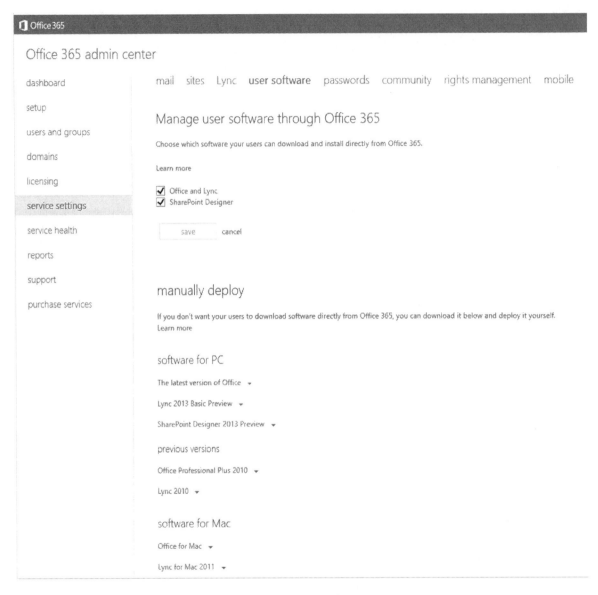

Figure 4-2. Office 365 Service Administration - Software download

We do not recommend the Mid-Market version (M Plans) or Small Business Version (P Plans), unless your business fits into that target configuration. We have found that the overall subscription costs are lower due to the role matching of licenses to the business. The Office 365 Enterprise version includes unlimited administrative support. The Small Business and Mid-Size Business versions have limitations on the support, and in some cases, you are required to pay for support to resolve service issues.

Figure 4-3 shows the planning and deployment overview for moving to Office 365. We contrasted that with the information from Chapter 3, so you can see how we use the information from the planning phase for the deployment to Office 365. There are various paths you use to move your users to Office 365 – either manually or using Active Directory. If you are using Active Directory, you can use Directory Synchronization to move your Active Directory objects to Office 365. The migration steps that you follow to move to Office 365 are outlined in this chapter.

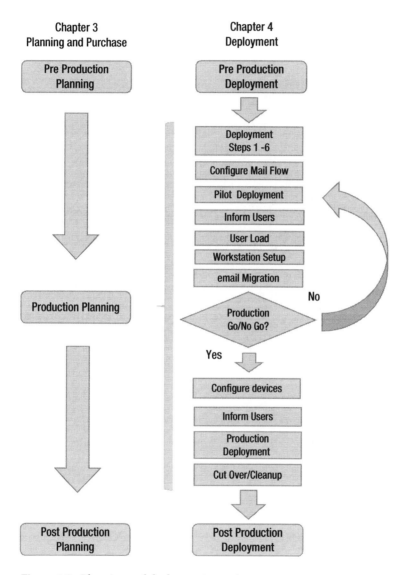

Figure 4-3. *Planning and deployment overview*

■ **Note**   You must have control over your DNS. If you do not have control over your DNS, you either cannot move to the cloud, or the process will be very time consuming.

Once you deploy Office 365 and Windows Intune, you'll find that the service is very cost effective and is a powerful tool to improve productivity. Office 365 includes many different services (Figure 4-4) that can be customized for your business and are configurable:

- Hosted Exchange

- Hosted SharePoint (Team Site)

- Lync

- Data Loss Prevention (DLP) (please refer to Chapter 9)

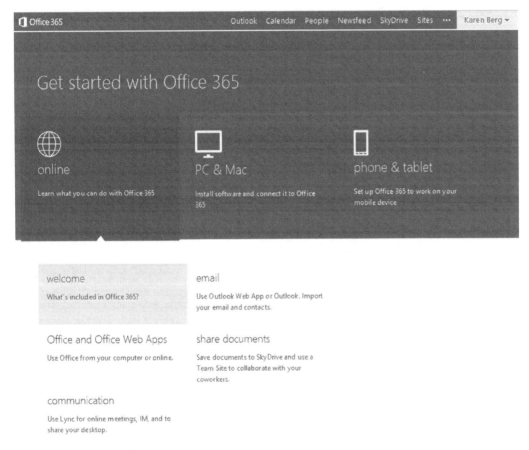

Figure 4-4. *User portal to Office 365*

Configuring Office 365

Office 365 is simple to configure, as long as you have a plan in place that answers two questions:

1. How do you plan to deploy the clients?

2. How do you plan to move historical e-mail to Microsoft Online services?

    a. The simplest migration is a Cut Over Migration

    b. The middle choice is Simple Coexistence

    c. The most complex is Hybrid Coexistence

If you are planning to use Directory Synchronization (DirSync), please review Chapter 11 before you proceed further. The Directory Synchronization tool copies the user accounts from the on-site Active Directory and creates the accounts in Office 365. If you use the Directory Synchronization approach, you cannot manually add accounts. The process that we are describing below is a manual process for the creation of accounts.

This section describes a 10-step plan that you can complete in an evening or over a number of days. If you are using Directory Synchronization (DirSync) or Single Sign On (ADFS) then read Chapter 11 before proceeding.

1. Validate your domain(s) to Microsoft

2. Add additional Domain Name Service (DNS) Information

3. Configure Lync

4. Install PowerShell

5. Load users and assign licenses

6. Migrate e-mail

7. Set mail flow

8. Configure mobile services

9. Configure external devices (copiers, scanners)

10. Clean up

■ **Note** Are you using Single Sign-on? If you are planning to implement Single Sign-on with Active Directory Federation Services (ADFS), see Chapter 11 before you enable Single Sign-On or Directory Synchronization.

Step 1: Validate Your Domain(s) to Microsoft

This step is required to show Microsoft that you control your domain name. Log in as an administrator (or your original SUPER ADMIN/ROOT account). You can sign in at office.microsoft.com or http://portal.microsoftonline.com. Click "Admin" (at the right next to your name). You are at the Office 365 Dashboard. On the left-hand side (See Figure 4-5), select "domains," then select "Add a domain" to start the process of adding your domain to the Microsoft Online environment.

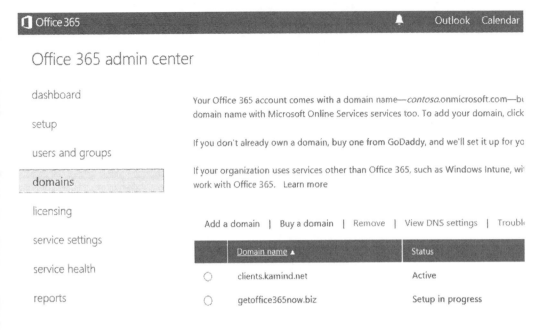

Figure 4-5. *Add a domain in Office 365*

Click on "Specify a domain name and confirm ownership" (see Figure 4-6). In Figure 4-7, enter your Domain Name (getoffice365now.biz in this example) and click "next". Office 365 will show Domain Confirmation information. Click Next.

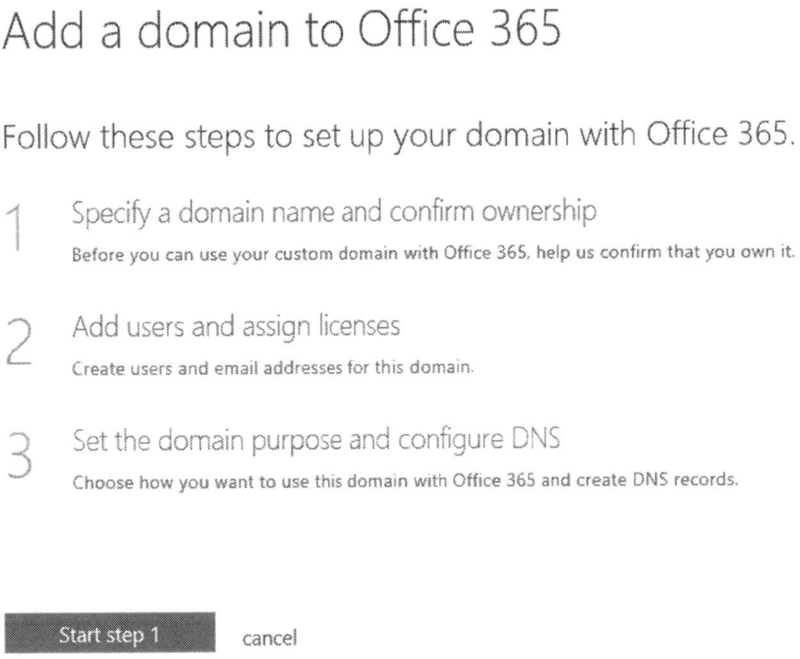

Add a domain to Office 365

Follow these steps to set up your domain with Office 365.

1 Specify a domain name and confirm ownership
   Before you can use your custom domain with Office 365, help us confirm that you own it.

2 Add users and assign licenses
   Create users and email addresses for this domain.

3 Set the domain purpose and configure DNS
   Choose how you want to use this domain with Office 365 and create DNS records.

Start step 1   cancel

Figure 4-6. *Add a Domain – Step 1*

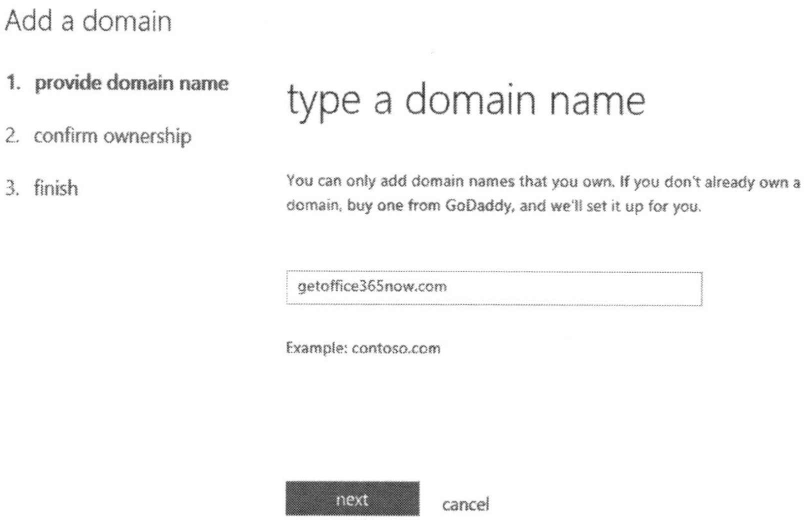

Add a domain

1. **provide domain name**

2. confirm ownership

3. finish

type a domain name

You can only add domain names that you own. If you don't already own a domain, buy one from GoDaddy, and we'll set it up for you.

> getoffice365now.com

Example: contoso.com

[next] cancel

Figure 4-7. *Enter the Domain Name*

Office 365 will examine your domain and provide you an automated way to set up your domain. In Figure 4-7, Office 365 detected that the domain we want to verify is on Go Daddy, so it has promoted us to use an automatic configuration of the domain and DNS records.

The Office 365 Domain Wizard will prompt you to select the service for verification. We normally select "general instructions." However, you can pick the service, and the Office 365 service will provide instructions on verification of that domain to that service (Figure 4-8).

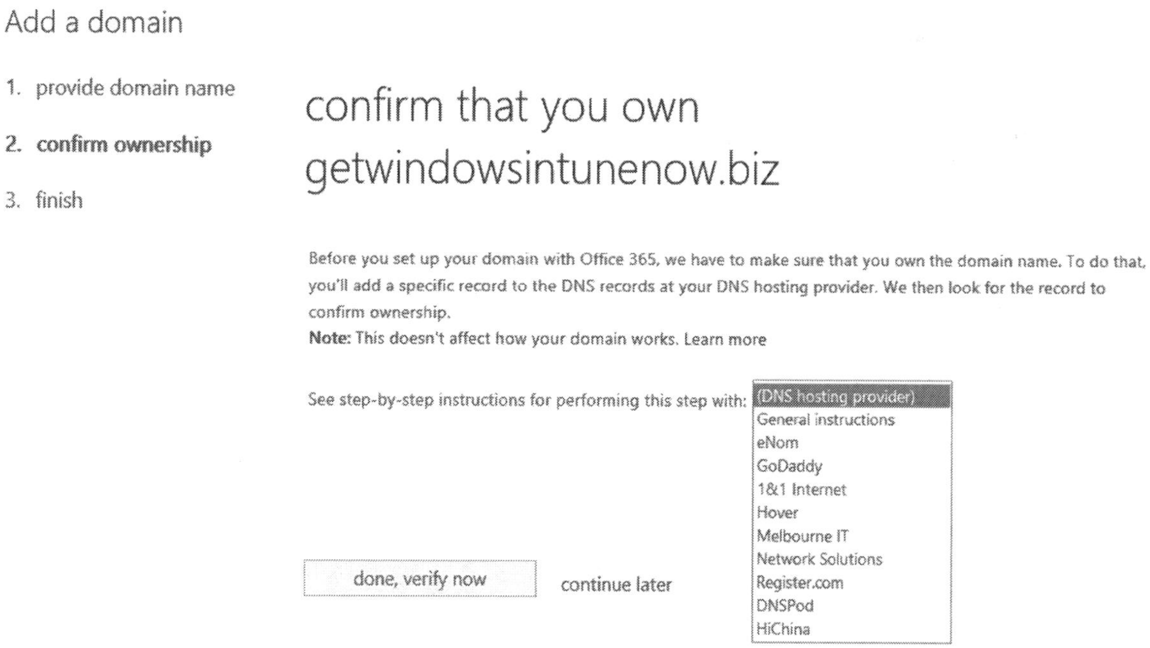

Add a domain

1. provide domain name

2. **confirm ownership**

3. finish

confirm that you own getwindowsintunenow.biz

Before you set up your domain with Office 365, we have to make sure that you own the domain name. To do that, you'll add a specific record to the DNS records at your DNS hosting provider. We then look for the record to confirm ownership.

Note: This doesn't affect how your domain works. Learn more

See step-by-step instructions for performing this step with:

(DNS hosting provider)
General instructions
eNom
GoDaddy
1&1 Internet
Hover
Melbourne IT
Network Solutions
Register.com
DNSPod
HiChina

[done, verify now]   continue later

Figure 4-8. *Selecting a method for domain verification*

Once you select the DNS provider (or general instructions in our case), you can choose which method used to "verify" your domain (Figure 4-9). Normally you can use the TXT record method. Follow the directions on the screen: sign in to your Domain Registrar and add the TXT (or MX) record as specified on this screen. Figure 4-10 shows a Go Daddy TXT record and Figure 4-11 shows a TXT records at Network Solutions.

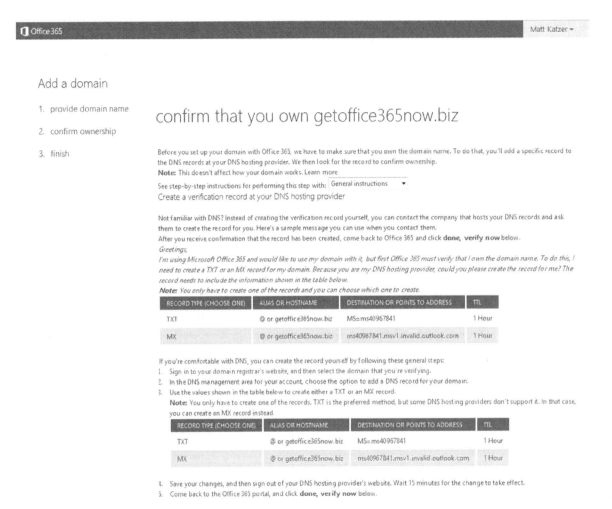

Figure 4-9. *Add Domain Verification*

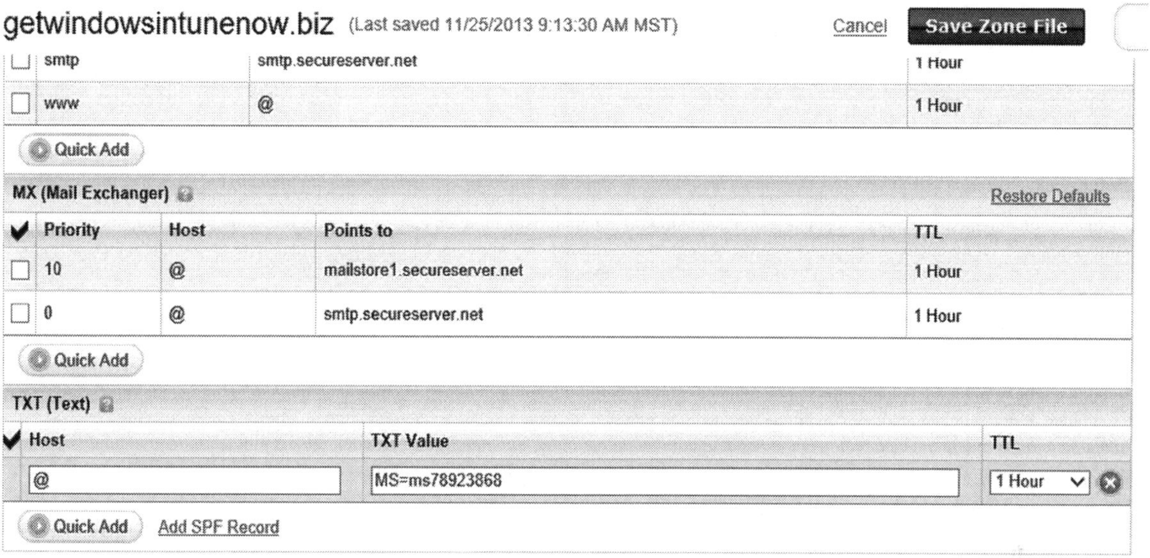

getwindowsintunenow.biz (Last saved 11/25/2013 9:13:30 AM MST)   Cancel   **Save Zone File**

☐ smtp	smtp.secureserver.net		1 Hour
☐ www	@		1 Hour

○ Quick Add

MX (Mail Exchanger) ▣   Restore Defaults

✔ Priority	Host	Points to	TTL
☐ 10	@	mailstore1.secureserver.net	1 Hour
☐ 0	@	smtp.secureserver.net	1 Hour

○ Quick Add

TXT (Text) ▣

✔ Host	TXT Value	TTL
@	MS=ms78923868	1 Hour ⌄ ✖

○ Quick Add   Add SPF Record

Figure 4-10. *Go Daddy TXT Record Configuration*

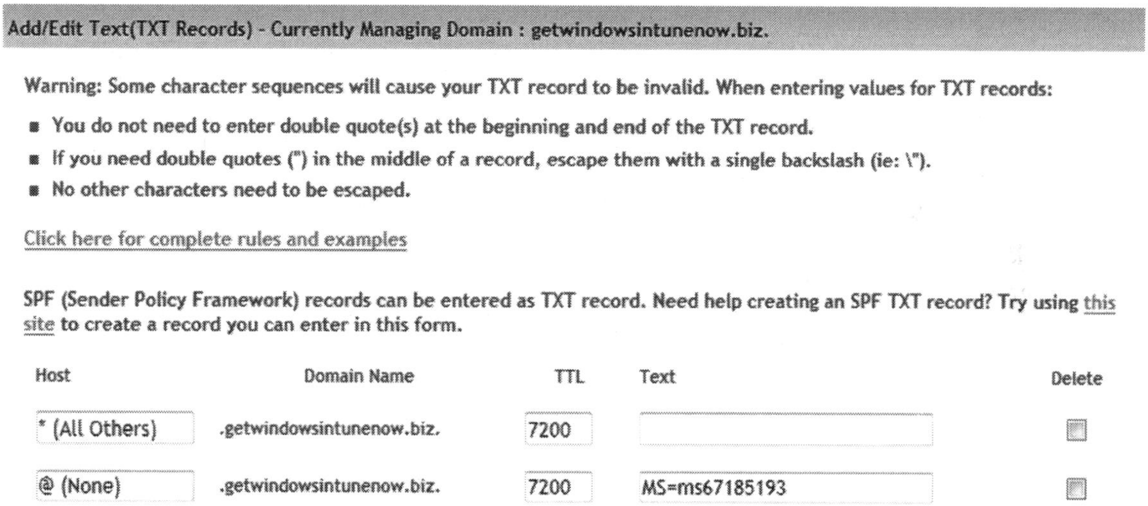

Add/Edit Text(TXT Records) - Currently Managing Domain : getwindowsintunenow.biz.

Warning: Some character sequences will cause your TXT record to be invalid. When entering values for TXT records:

- You do not need to enter double quote(s) at the beginning and end of the TXT record.
- If you need double quotes (") in the middle of a record, escape them with a single backslash (ie: \").
- No other characters need to be escaped.

Click here for complete rules and examples

SPF (Sender Policy Framework) records can be entered as TXT record. Need help creating an SPF TXT record? Try using this site to create a record you can enter in this form.

Host	Domain Name	TTL	Text	Delete
* (All Others)	.getwindowsintunenow.biz.	7200		▣
@ (None)	.getwindowsintunenow.biz.	7200	MS=ms67185193	▣

Figure 4-11. *Network Solutions TXT record – domain verification*

■ **Note**   Typically it takes about 15 minutes for your changes to take effect. However, it can take up to 72 hours for the record that you created to propagate through the DNS system.

Each domain supplier has different tools and processes to add a domain record. You can only add domain records if the domain is managed by the domain supplier. In the Go Daddy case, the name servers are at Go Daddy, so we are adding records in the Go Daddy servers. This is also the case for Network Solutions.

After you have configured the domain for validation, if the domain does not verify, use `http://www.mxtoolbox.com` to verify that the TXT records have propagated. Once the TXT records show up in `mxtoolbox.com`, you can validate the domain in Office 365. In Figure 4-11 we verify the record on `mxtoolbox.com`. The purpose is to check to see if the changed record in the DNS has replicated to the other World Wide Web DNS servers. These records will also replicate to Office 365. In our example, we are looking for the TXT record that we inserted into our DNS earlier. At MX toolbox we enter the command "`txt:kamind.biz`". When the record shows up (see Figure 4-12), we can verify the DNS record in Office 365 and validate the domain. After the domain shows up on mxtoolbox, it should validate within an hour. If it does not validate, you will need to submit a ticket to Microsoft Online Services or contact a partner to help resolve the issue.

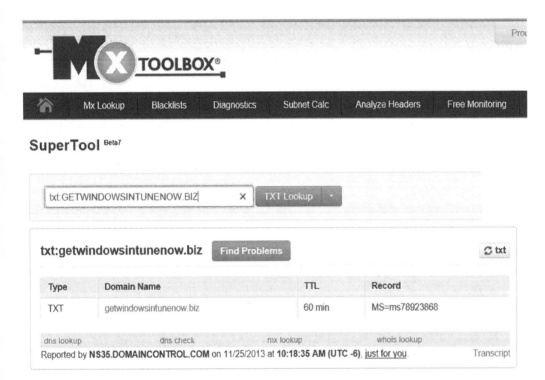

Figure 4-12. *MXToolbox TXT Record Validation*

Once you have the record in the MX toolbox, then select "verify" in Office 365 (see Figure 4-12). If the domain verifies correctly, you will be provided with an acknowledgement that your domain is valid (Figure 4-13).

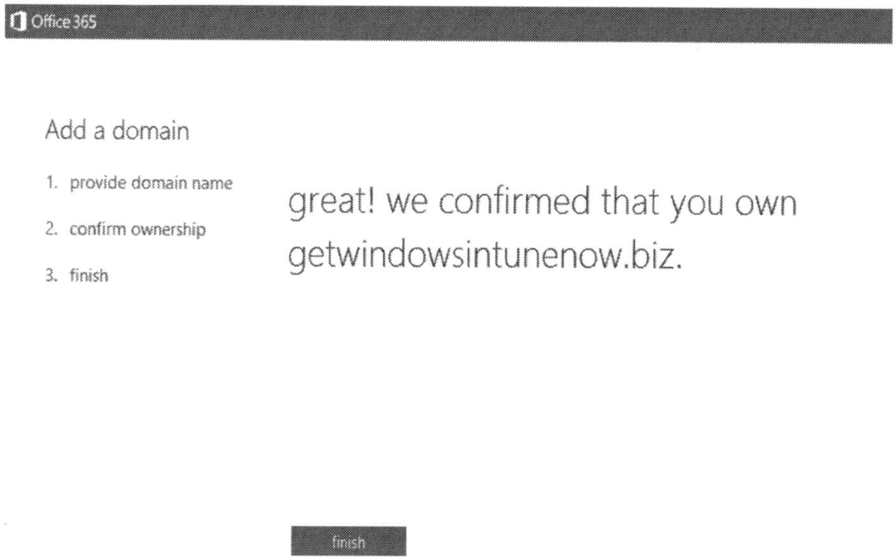

❚ Office 365

Add a domain

1. provide domain name
2. confirm ownership
3. finish

great! we confirmed that you own
getwindowsintunenow.biz.

finish

Figure 4-13. *Domain Validated – Proof of Ownership*

The next step (according to Microsoft) is to add users and assign licenses. We have found that it is better to complete the domain configuration (with the exception of changing the MX records) and add users after you have defined the domain Intune. After you click "finish" in Figure 4-13 , select "assign users," then select the radio button "I do not want to assign users right now" – Figure 4.14).

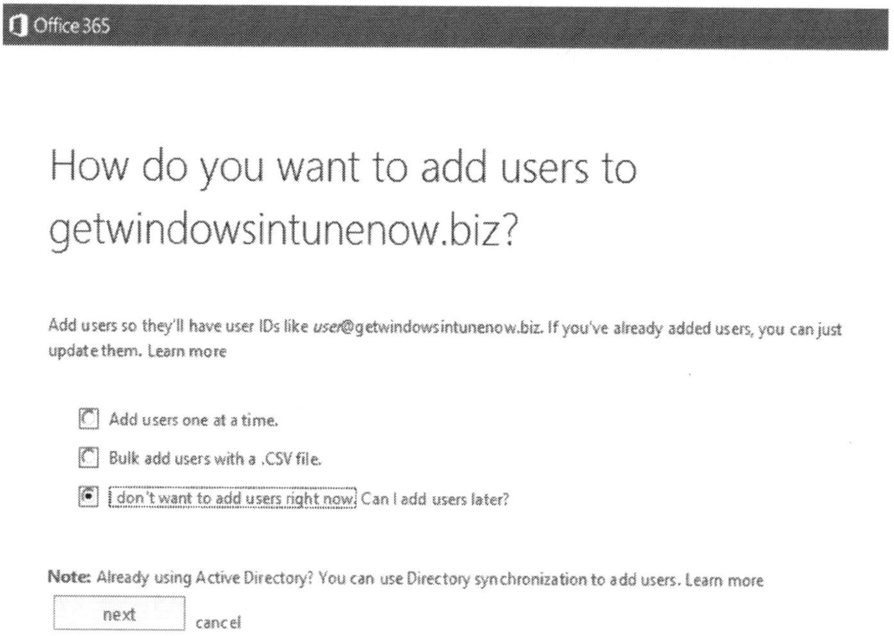

❚ Office 365

How do you want to add users to getwindowsintunenow.biz?

Add users so they'll have user IDs like *user*@getwindowsintunenow.biz. If you've already added users, you can just update them. Learn more

- ◯ Add users one at a time.
- ◯ Bulk add users with a .CSV file.
- ◉ I don't want to add users right now. Can I add users later?

Note: Already using Active Directory? You can use Directory synchronization to add users. Learn more

    next   cancel

Figure 4-14. *Select the Assign Users "later" option*

After you select Next, select the domain purpose (Figure 4-15) - item #3 – to set domain intent.

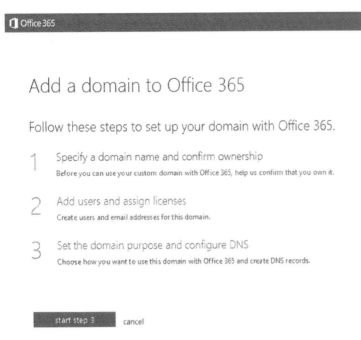

Figure 4-15. *Set the domain purpose*

Specifying the domain services is an important step (Figure 4-16). You are letting Office 365 know how you are planning to use the domain that you just validated. Normally you will choose Exchange Online. You will choose Lync Online if you have Lync in your plan (E1 or above) and you have set up this domain with the correct SRV records.

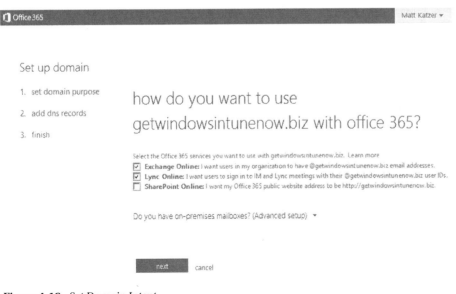

Figure 4-16. *Set Domain Intent*

■ **Note**   "SharePoint Online" actually refers to the public facing web site that is included in Office 365 Plan E1 or above.

After you complete the configuration of the domain intent, you will have an option to automatically configure Office 365 (and skip Step 2). Automatic configuration (Figure 4-17) only works if you are using a cutover migration. The MX records are changed using the automatic setup. We recommend the manual setup (see Step 2).

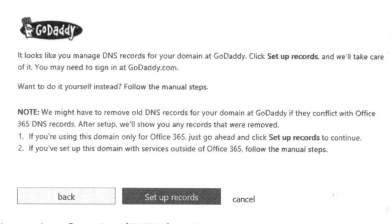

Set up domain

1. set domain purpose

2. **add dns records**

3. finish

add these dns records for getoffice365now.com at your dns hosting provider.

Figure 4-17. *Go Daddy Automatic configuration of DNS information*

Step 2: Add Additional Domain Name Service (DNS) Information

After your domain has been validated, it is time to add additional DNS information. You have chosen to bypass automatic setup, and manually set up the records. You need to add all of the records listed in Figure 4-18. In this step you are adding DNS records as follows:

- CNAME (alias or canonical name) records. These records are used to provide standard names to other Microsoft web services forOffice 365. You will be adding:

  - "autodiscover" "autodiscover.outlook.com" to enable Outlook autodiscover

  - " lyncdiscover" "webdir.online.lync.com"

  - "sip" "sipdir.online.lync.com"

- SPF (sender policy framework) record (a TXT @ record with text "v=spf1 include:outlook.com ~all"). This record is part of an e-mail validation system designed to help prevent e-mail spoofing and phishing. This record will help prevent your outgoing e-mail from being considered "spam."

- SRV (service record) records. These records specify information about available services. SRV records are used by Microsoft Lync Online to coordinate the flow of information between Office 365 services.

add these dns records for getwindowsintunenow.biz at your dns hosting provider.

Need help adding the records? See step-by-step instructions for creating these records at popular DNS hosting providers.

Exchange Online

TYPE	PRIORITY	HOST NAME	POINTS TO ADDRESS	TTL
MX	0	@	getwindowsintunenow-biz.mail.protection.outlook.com	1 Hour
CNAME	-	autodiscover	autodiscover.outlook.com	1 Hour

TYPE	TXT NAME	TXT VALUE	TTL
TXT	@	v=spf1 include:spf.protection.outlook.com -all	1 Hour

Lync Online

TYPE	SERVICE	PROTOCOL	PORT	WEIGHT	PRIORITY	TTL	NAME	TARGET
SRV	_sip	_tls	443	1	100	1 Hour	getwindowsintunenow.biz	sipdir.online.lync.com
SRV	_sipfederationtls	_tcp	5061	1	100	1 Hour	getwindowsintunenow.biz	sipfed.online.lync.com

TYPE	HOST NAME	POINTS TO ADDRESS	TTL
CNAME	sip.getwindowsintunenow.biz	sipdir.online.lync.com	1 Hour
CNAME	lyncdiscover.getwindowsintunenow.biz	webdir.online.lync.com	1 Hour

Figure 4-18. *Complete Domain Records*

Depending upon the services you are supporting, you may need to delete the older DNS records.

■ **Note**   Do NOT change your DNS MX records or Autodiscover records at this time. When you change your MX records, you will stop the mail flow to your existing e-mail server. When you change Autodiscover, the Outlook clients will go directly to Office 365 for e-mail. We will change mail flow in Step 6 after we have added the users.

Do not add the MX or e-mail Autodiscover records to your DNS - do this in Step 6.

After you have added the rest of the DNS records you will need to validate these records. Select the domain (see Figure 4-19), then select "troubleshoot." On the next screen select "more than 72 hours" then "next" to verify the DNS records. If your DNS is valid, all check marks will be green. If there are errors there will be red Xs. Fix the errors until you have green check marks. You may run into a situation where the DNS cannot be fixed. If this is the case, you will need to move your DNS to a new provider. Once the records have been validated, you can change the primary domain to the user account domain and add the necessary users to the account.

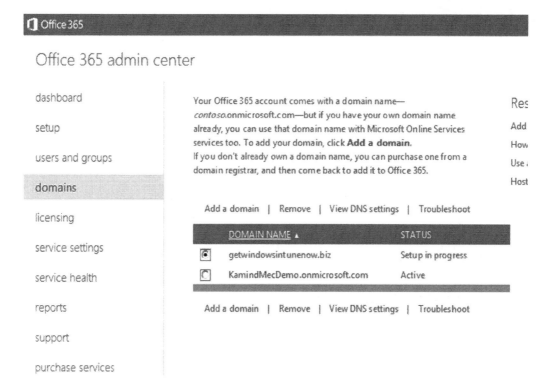

Figure 4-19. *Troubleshooting Domain*

■ **Note**   If you are using Windows Intune, you will need to add the CNAME "enterpriseenrollment" to your DNS.
See Chapter 7.

Use the trouble shooting tools to correct the DNS problems. Always select more than 72 hours, so the automated tool provides useful information (see Figure 4.20). If you have red check marks, then correct those problems. The only red check marks you should have are for the mail records.

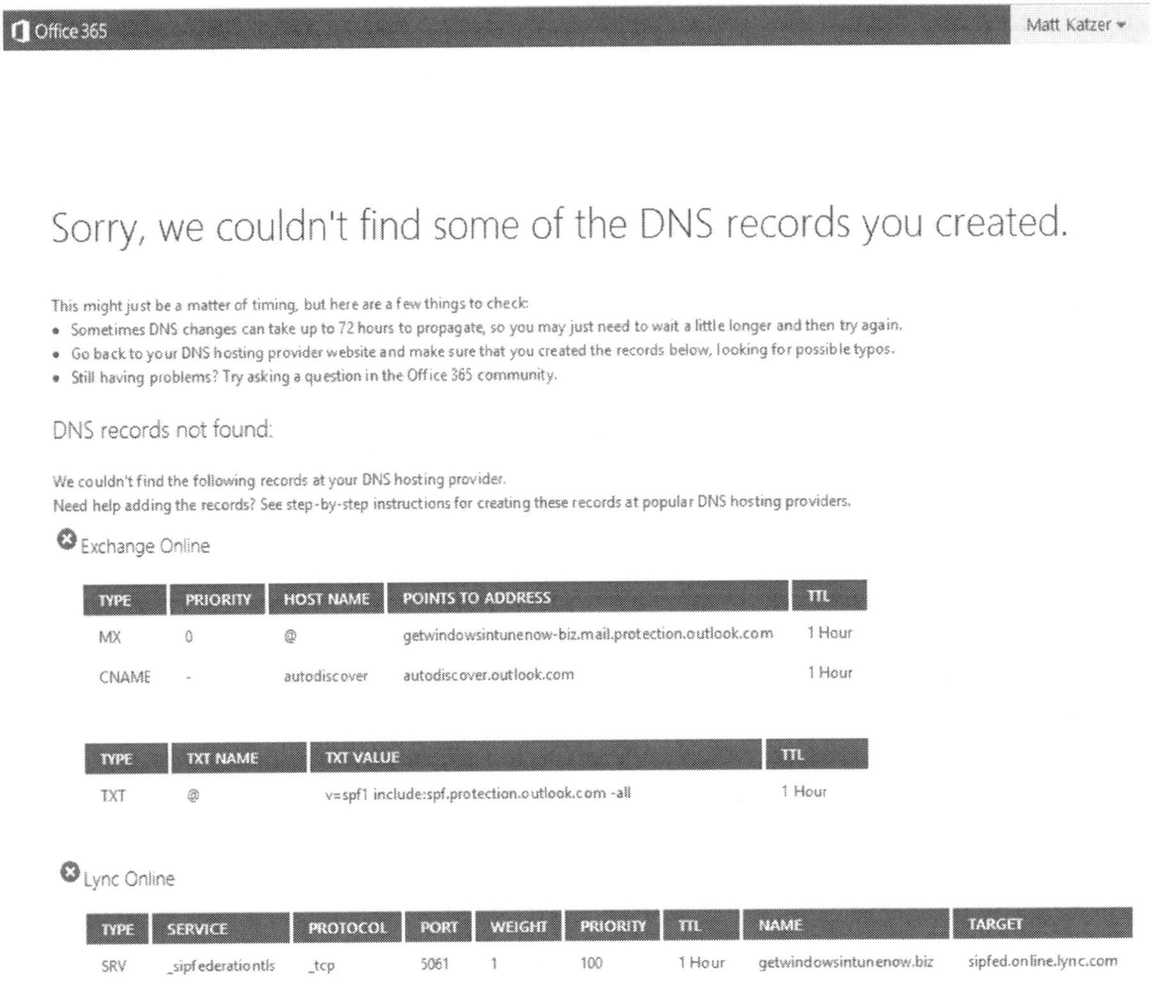

Sorry, we couldn't find some of the DNS records you created.

This might just be a matter of timing, but here are a few things to check:

- Sometimes DNS changes can take up to 72 hours to propagate, so you may just need to wait a little longer and then try again.
- Go back to your DNS hosting provider website and make sure that you created the records below, looking for possible typos.
- Still having problems? Try asking a question in the Office 365 community.

DNS records not found:

We couldn't find the following records at your DNS hosting provider.
Need help adding the records? See step-by-step instructions for creating these records at popular DNS hosting providers.

⊗ Exchange Online

TYPE	PRIORITY	HOST NAME	POINTS TO ADDRESS	TTL
MX	0	@	getwindowsintunenow-biz.mail.protection.outlook.com	1 Hour
CNAME	-	autodiscover	autodiscover.outlook.com	1 Hour

TYPE	TXT NAME	TXT VALUE	TTL
TXT	@	v=spf1 include:spf.protection.outlook.com -all	1 Hour

⊗ Lync Online

TYPE	SERVICE	PROTOCOL	PORT	WEIGHT	PRIORITY	TTL	NAME	TARGET
SRV	_sipfederationtls	_tcp	5061	1	100	1 Hour	getwindowsintunenow.biz	sipfed.online.lync.com

Figure 4-20. *Validated DNS records – Red checks*

■ **Note**   The Office 365 automatic DNS tool will build the complete DNS records to match the Office 365 suggested configuration. This only works if you have loaded all of the users in step 2. The automated tool will set your MX record to Office 365. If you are using any other migration than a pure cut over, your mail flow will stop. We recommend that you load users as a manual process. If you have Active Directory (and Exchange 2007 or later) use Directory Sync to move your user objects.

Step 3: Configure Lync

When your Office 365 site is created, Lync is ready to operate within your intranet. As an administrator you need to decide if you want to open up Lync communications, federate the domain, and allow public instant messaging.

Lync "Domain Federation" allows your intranet to interact with other Office 365 customers and non-Office 365 e-mail addresses that support Microsoft Federation services. For example "Domain Federation" allows your users to see the presence of external vendors (see Figure 4-21).

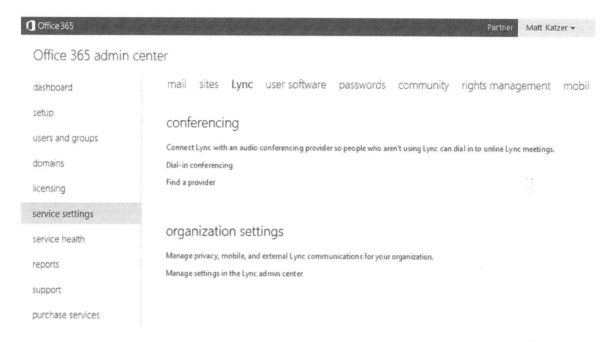

Figure 4-21. *Admin screen - Lync setup*

The public instant messaging interface allows you to communicate within your intranet, with other Office 365 organizations that have federated with Office 365, and Live Messenger. Public IM connectivity is supported with Skype. At this time AOL and Yahoo messengers are not supported.

To enable these services, in the main admin dashboard, select "Lync" (figure 4-20), then select "organization settings" and the link "Manage Settings in the Lync Admin Center."

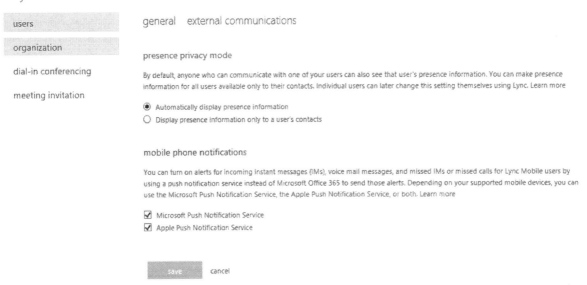

Figure 4-22. Lync Control Panel

In the Lync Control Panel (Figure 4-23) select "external communications." Enable "Public IM," and set "on except for blocked domains." This action enables these services. "Enabled" is the recommended setting for both services. The default is off (disable).

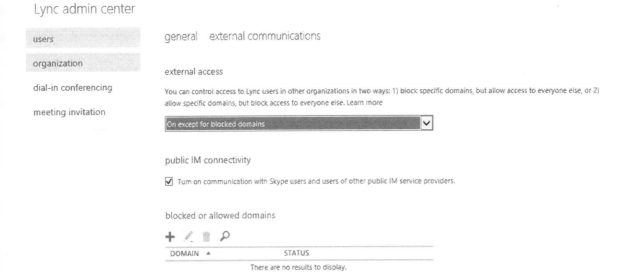

Figure 4-23. Enabling Lync Domain Federation

Step 4: Install PowerShell

Earlier we briefly discussed PowerShell and the capabilities that it provides to you. This step is an optional step and it depends if you need the capability for your management of Office 365. The simplest way to install the latest version of PowerShell is to select Single Sign-on (see Figure 4-24) option.

Figure 4-24. *selecting Single Sign-on to Install PowerShell*

Select step 3, "Install PowerShell" (See Figure 4-25). The PowerShell installation will verify the updates required to support the Windows Azure PowerShell. You are welcome to review step 1 and 2. However, the only option we are interested in is the installation of PowerShell on your desktop systems. Select the correct version (32 bit or 64 bit) for your system.

Set up and manage single sign-on

When you set up single sign-on (also known as identity federation), your users can sign in with their corporate credentials to access the services in Microsoft Office 365 for enterprises. As part of setting up single sign-on, you must also set up directory synchronization. Together, these features integrate your on-premises and cloud directories.

1 Prepare for single sign-on

Learn about the benefits of single sign-on and make sure you meet the requirements before you set it up.
Learn how to prepare for single sign-on

2 Plan for and deploy Active Directory Federation Services 2.0

Work through the in-depth documentation to deploy and configure AD FS 2.0.
Follow instructions for planning and deploying AD FS 2.0 for single sign-on

3 Install the Windows Azure Active Directory Module for Windows PowerShell

Download the Windows Azure Active Directory Module for Windows PowerShell, which includes cmdlets to establish the trust relationship between your AD FS 2.0 server and Office 365 for each of your domains that use single sign-on.
Learn about installing and configuring the Windows Azure Active Directory Module for Windows PowerShell

- ⦿ Windows 32-bit version
- ○ Windows 64-bit version

> Download

Figure 4-25. *Installing Office 365 PowerShell*

Typically, we recommend that if your organization has more than 20 accounts, you may find it more convenient to use PowerShell. This is a command interface in Office 365. In Chapter 8 we have offered additional troubleshooting steps and configuration options (such as shared mailboxes) using PowerShell. The account that you will use for PowerShell management is the Global Administrator user account. Users without global administrative privileges will not be able to use this feature.

Once you have install Office 365 PowerShell, launch the PowerShell module and enter the following commands:

```
Set-ExecutionPolicy RemoteSigned
$LiveCred = Get-Credential
Import-module msonline
Connect-MSOLService - Credential $LiveCred - Verbose
Get-MsolGroup
```

The results of running theses commands should be similar to Figure 4-26.

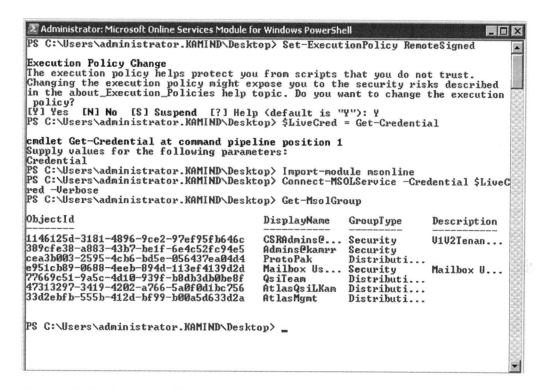

Figure 4-26. *Validating PowerShell Commands*

You have completed the base PowerShell setup, now use the above command to validate the installation. If the command above does not work, you have either installed the PowerShell GUI incorrectly, there is a lack of permissions, or you have not installed the desktop connector for Office 365. Using PowerShell requires administrative privileges.

Step 5: Load Users and Assign Licenses

We are ready to start loading or enabling users into Office 365. As part of the loading user process, we have decided that we will either push the software out to the clients (using Windows Intune deployment), or we will request that the clients download the new software from the Office 365 site. If you are using a test group, you will repeat this step until you are ready for production. Test groups are iterative; by this we mean that you will add additional users to the test group as you reach the production decision point. If the organization is small, you will cut over to Office 365. If the organization is large, then run the test group and resolve deployment issues.

The purpose of the test group is to validate deployment. Once you have validated the business goals of the test group, you will continue your Office 365 migration. Step 5 (and some follow-on steps) can be repeated until you are ready to cut over to production (see Figure 4-27).

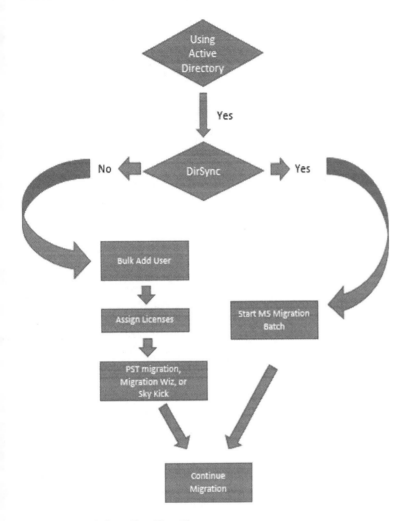

Figure 4-27. *Onboarding Flow Chart*

Let's review what we have completed at this point:

1. The domain(s) that we want to use have been validated.

2. Lync DNS has been configured.

3. We have collected our users, security groups, test groups, etc. (see Deployment Options).

4. If we are using DirSync, the disabled user accounts are loaded in Office 365.

5. We have communicated with the test groups that are being deployed (scheduled).

6. We have pushed out software to the clients or we have instructed users how to download the applications themselves.

Now we load/enable the first batch, or nth batch users into Office 365. There is no technical limit on how many users we can deploy. The deployment group size is a function of support, and how many support calls that you wish to tender, or to avoid because you had a good business process for deployment.

■ **Note**   If you choose to use directory Synchronization for loading users' accounts (and the appropriate migration method), you configure the service at this point. See Chapter 11 for the steps to configure Directory Synchronization.

THERE ARE THREE METHODS TO LOAD USERS

1. Add each user (See "Onboarding Users" later in this chapter). This method is appropriate for a few users or a test group.

2. Bulk-add users, using a specially formatted CSV spreadsheet with the user information. Use the bulk import option to load the information into Office 365. (See "Onboarding Users" later in this chapter).

3. Enable Directory Synchronized users for access to Office 365 (See "Onboarding Users" later in this chapter).

Pick your method to load users to Office 365. Once you have selected your method (manual or using Directory Synchronization), you are ready to begin moving user data to Office 365. If you choose Directory Synchronization, you are restricted to use Microsoft Migration tools (if you have an exchange server in your Active Directory). After you have selected your loading-user approach, then you can begin the mail migration process.

■ **Note**   The different user loading processes are described later in this chapter, in the "Onbarding Users" section.

License Assignment

If you selected DirSync (option 3 above), you do not need to assign licenses until you begin the migration. Directory Synchronized objects from the on-site Active Directory appear as disabled users in Office 365 and no mailbox is created. Once the users object is in Office 365, you can manually assign licenses or bulk assign them with PowerShell. If you selected manual loading (option 1 or 2), you need to purchase licenses to create the mailbox for the user. It is not possible to load users as a disabled user in Office 365, if you use a manual process (option 1 or 2).

■ **Note**   If you are using a test group, Step 5 through 8 will be repeated in the test group evaluation. After you completed the test group, return back to Step 5 to begin the deployment of Office 365.

Step 6: Migrate E-mail

In Step 5, our method of loading users defines the toolset we should use for copying e-mail to Office 365 (this moving of e-mail is called migration). Depending on the method you selected, you can use Microsoft tools or external tools. The key decision factor in the toolset you use is based on Directory Sync integration (see Figure 4-28). If you use Directory Sync (DirSync), and there is an on-premises exchange server, you are required to use Microsoft migration tools. There are cases where you can use Microsoft DirSync and external tools, but we recommend that you consult a Microsoft partner if you use this approach.

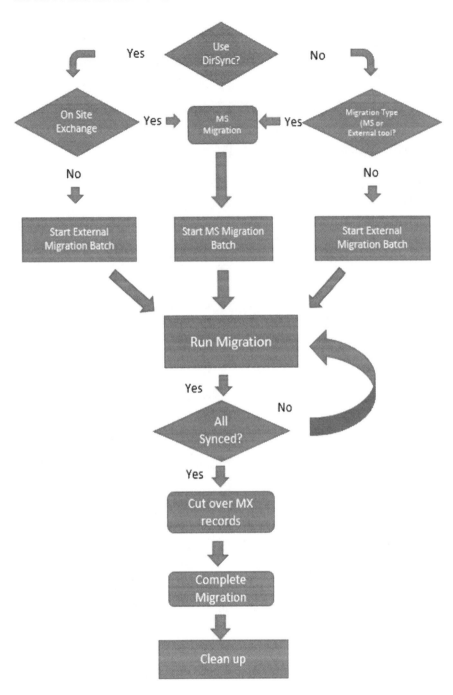

Figure 4-28. *E-mail Migration*

Test Group or Staged Migration

Test groups are nothing more than a stage migration. Stage migrations take a lot of work and should only be used for a limited time and for a small number of users. When we discuss test groups, we are using those users to test our deployment processes. A test group is nothing more than placing a group of users on a different mail server that is separate from the existing organization. A test group will not have access to a common calendar or a common address list. It is for these two reasons that you want to use test groups for a very limited time with a definite set of objectives. A stage migration is nothing more than a test group.

■ **Note**   If the user accounts are POP or IMAP, stage migration is a viable option because there are no common shared resources (like calendar and address lists).

Client Configuration Changes for Test Group

If you are using a test group with an on-premises Exchange Server, you will encounter two problems: AutoDiscover (for outlook client) and the presence of the Exchange Server in the Active Directory. There are only manual workarounds to enable the clients to find the Office 365 mail server. Once you have deployed, you need to remove these "enhancements" to eliminate a future support problem in using Office 365. If you choose to manually configure outlook, you will still need to make these changes, since outlook will verify the connection via autodisocver everytime itis started.

These are the client steps required to support a test group if there is an on-premises exchange server:

1. Add the Autodiscover record in the host file, located at `<drive:>windows/systems32/drivers/etc`

    a. Ping `Auotdiscover.outlook.com`.

    b. Add the record "autodiscover" with the address discovered above.

    c. Open up a command prompt and enter "ping autodiscover." This should display the IP address you just entered.

2. Add the registry fixes to ignore the Exchange server – Service Control Point. The registry entries required to be modified for the clients are listed below (see Microsoft KB article – 2612922).

    a. Navigate to the following registry key: `HKEY_CURRENT_USER\Software\Microsoft\Office\12.0\Outlook\AutoDiscover`

    b. Set the following values for the Value Names listed below:

    ```
    "PreferLocalXML"=dword:1
    "ExcludeHttpRedirect"=dword:0
    "ExcludeHttpsAutodiscoverDomain"=dword:1
    "ExcludeHttpsRootDomain"=dword:1
    "ExcludeScpLookup"=dword:1
    "ExcludeSrvLookup"=dword:1
    "ExcludeSrvRecord"=dword:1
    ```

Test Group Mail Flow

Mail flow in a test group uses a combination of forwarders from the on-site server to Office 365. The on-site server will use the onmicrosoft.com as the forwarding address (see Figure 4-29). This approach works, and is useful for testing, but not a recommend practice. Test groups are not integrated into the on-premises exchange server.

When you add the users to Office 365 these users have an active e-mail address. This means that:

1. E-mail that is sent to one of these new Office 365 e-mail accounts from outside Office 365 or from other Office 365 tenants will NOT be received until your MX records are configured and verified by Office 365.

2. Any e-mail sent from one of these new accounts will be routed to your other new accounts. (E-mail to outside addresses will route as expected.)

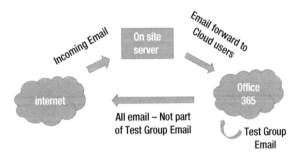

Figure 4-29. Test Group Mail Flow

We recommend that you configure mail routing as follows:

1. Only load users that are using Office 365 (during test or evaluation).

2. If you are using both the Office 365 service and an on-site Exchange Server you need to set your email Domain Type to "Internal." You should have e-mail for these Office 365 users forwarded from the on-site Exchange Server to the Office 365 e-mail accounts using the "long" address user@<domain>.onmicrosoft.com.

E-mail Migration

E-mail Migration is nothing more than copying the e-mail from the old mail server to the new mail server. The mail is not destroyed in the process. We are just copying the e-mail messages (and other mailbox information) over to Office 365. There are different approaches to moving the e-mail to Office 365. Depending upon the approach you are using for migration, you may choose to "cut over the mail records before you move e-mail" or move e-mail, then cut over records. Typically the decision is based more on the source of the mail server and the size of the organization. There is no hard or fast rule on the migration of e-mail, with one exception: if you are running some type of coexistence (such as a stage migration), then place a mail forwarder (to the "long" name) in the older mail system before you start the migration. Once the MX records are moved there is no need to add a forwarder.

■ **Note**　Our policy on e-mail migration is to move at least the first 200 e-mail messages for each user (1 – 2 weeks), along with the contacts, calendars and folder structure into the new mailbox. The older e-mails can come later. We use Migration Wiz to move historical e-mail as our first choice in tools.

There are four tools that you can use for e-mail migration. These are PST export/import, Third Party external tools (such as Migration Wiz), the Microsoft Office 365 Migration Tool, or moving mailboxes with Exchange Federation. Each tool has its fans and critics (see Table 4-1).

Table 4-1. *Different Migration Methods*

Description	Pros	Cons
PST Migration	Simple	Email addresses are not complete
	Free	Requires execution at a workstation
		Network bandwidth (copy up, and copy down)
Migration Wiz	Simple	Costs $12 per mailbox to migrate
Office 365	Free	Complex to use (1 mailbox at a time)
Exchange 2010/2013	License	Requires AFDS and Exchange Federation (not supported with exchange 2007 or 2003)

There are different deployment methods that you can use depending on how your data is kept. As an example, if you have been using POP mail, and all of your data is stored in PST, then you can only use a PST migration. There are no other options. If you mail is stored on a web server (such as on an Exchange Server), you can use the other tools for mailbox migration. We typically use Migration Wiz then use the Microsoft internal migration tool as a backup. If you have chosen to use Exchange Federation, you can only use the mailbox move for DirSync'ed accounts.

▓ **Note**   To see the different steps in the migration, see section "Onboarding E-mail" later in this chapter.

We discuss the process for each of these approaches later in this chapter under "Onboarding E-mail." The onboarding process will be similar to Figure 4-30.

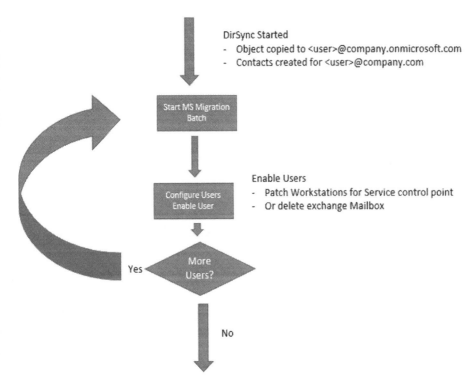

DirSync Started
- Object copied to <user>@company.onmicrosoft.com
- Contacts created for <user>@company.com

Enable Users
- Patch Workstations for Service control point
- Or delete exchange Mailbox

Figure 4-30. *DirSync Migration Approach*

Exchange Server – Mailbox changes

When you use the Microsoft migration tools, what the Microsoft tools do at the end of the data sync step is to convert the mailbox from an "Exchange Mailbox" to a Mail Enabled Users. What is really happening is that the exchange mailbox is converted to a contact and the existing mailbox is placed in a disabled state. When e-mail is received by the on-premises exchange server, the server looks up the contact and sends the e-mail to the destination. The contact for the user of the on-site exchange server contains the Office 365 long address (user@company.onmicrosoft.com).

Step 7: Set Mail Flow

At this point we are ready to set the mail flow based on our migration strategy. If you chose to cut over all users at one time (Cut over Migration), the Office 365 Global Address List (GAL) will contain all of the new user accounts. This limited GAL also applies to sharing calendars and free-busy status. If you choose to move users in groups (Simple Coexistence), the GAL will only contain those users that have been moved.

In our planning discussion, there are three possible migration plans:

1. *Cutover Migration:* All users are loaded, MX and Auto Discover records are changed and Office 365 receives all e-mail.

2. *Simple Coexistence:* Some users are loaded; e-mail is forwarded from on-premises servers to Office 365 (temporary).

3. *Hybrid Coexistence:* On premises and Office 365 operate in tandem.

The Hybrid Coexistence migration is a complex migration and is addressed in Chapter 11. Hybrid Coexistence requires an IT migration specialist assist you in the migration to Office 365. The other two methods are described below.

Cutover Migration

This is also called a 100% conversion. Cutover means that you have loaded up the users, and you point the e-mail records to Office 365 servers. All historical e-mail is brought over in a post-migration process. This is the most common and simplest e-mail migration.

▓ **Note**   If you have completed loading the users, you can change the DNS records to point to Office 365 services. These MX records are described in Figure 4-12.

Simple Coexistence

This is an iterative migration. Cutover migration will happen at the point that all users are moved to the cloud. Simple Coexistence is used to train IT staff and to build experience using Office 365. In Simple Coexistence, a "test group" of users are migrated to Office 365, and those users that migrate do not have access to the Global Address list, and shared calendars of the other users who have not migrated. E-mail for converted users is forwarded from the on-premises or hosted e-mail server to their "long" e-mail address (discussed below) in the cloud. The iterative approach requires that only a portion of the users are loaded in Step 5, and the Domain Type is set to "Internal Relay" (see Figure 4-31).

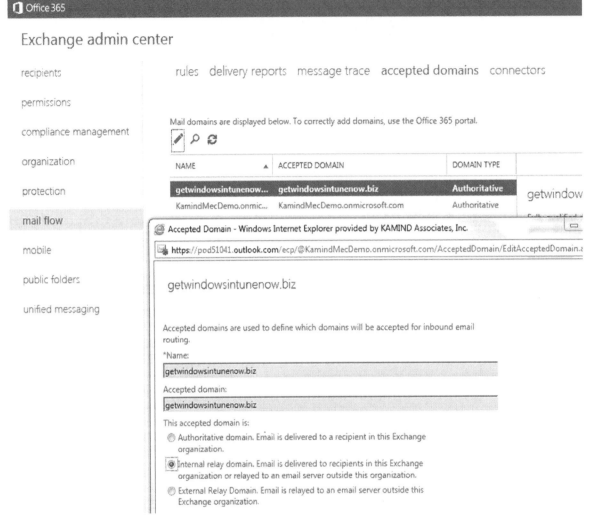

Figure 4-31. *Setting a Domain as a shared domain (some users are on an external server)*

To set the mail flow, you need to access the Exchange control panel access. To access the Exchange control panel select the following:

1. Select "Office 365 in the admin center.

2. Select "service settings."

3. Select "Mail option," then select "don't see what you are looking for... ," and the "Manage Additional settings in the exchange admin center."

The Domain Type is set to "Internal relay" (see Figure 4-31) until all of the users have been migrated. When the user migration has been completed, the domain is changed to "Hosted" and the MX records are changed to point to Office 365.

■ **Note**   If the domain is not set to Internal Relay, e-mail will not be forwarded from Office 365 to the on-premises mail server.

Coexistence E-mail Flow

When you initially purchase Office 365, one of the items created is the sub-domain "yourdomain.onmicrosoft.com." This is a valid e-mail domain, and is the "long" e-mail address. You can e-mail to <user>@<yourdomain.onmicrosoft.com> and your e-mail will be delivered into your e-mail box. When you validate a domain and add a user account, the user account is created with two e-mail addresses: <user>@<yourdomain.onmicrosoft.com> and <user>@<yourdomain.com>.
Simple coexistence works as follows:

- E-mail is forwarded from the on-premises domain or other hosted e-mail address to your Office 365 "long" address (i.e. @yourdomain.onmicrosoft.com).

- When e-mail is sent from inside Office 365, Office 365 looks to see if the e-mail needs to be delivered to a migrated user (i.e. @yourdomain.com). If not, the e-mail is forwarded to the real e-mail domain (via the DNS MX records).

■ **Note**   After you have moved all of the users into Office 365 and changed the DNS so the MX records point to Office 365, change the domain from "Internal Relay" to "Authoritative" (see Figure 4-29). At this point your e-mail is 100% on Office 365.

Once you have moved all of the e-mail addresses to Office 365, the MX records are changed to point to Office 365 (see Step 2). When the MX records are changed, coexistence mode is completed, and you have implemented your cutover migration. That is all that is really needed to move users to Office 365 for mail flow.

Step 8: Configure Desktop and Mobile devices

The desktop configuration for mobile devices and user desktop is in Chapter 2: Using Office 365 and Windows Intune. There are different philosophies on when to configure these services. However, unless you want to manually configure these services, you cannot add them until you have changed the MX and auto discover records. Desktop services (outlook) require the auto discover record to be changed. Most mobile devices use the MX record to find the Office 365 mail server.

Configure desktop services

Depending upon the subscription (see Figure 4-32), the user will need to log into Office 365 and download the Office professional Plus software (located under the gear and "office 365 settings") after you log into Office 365.

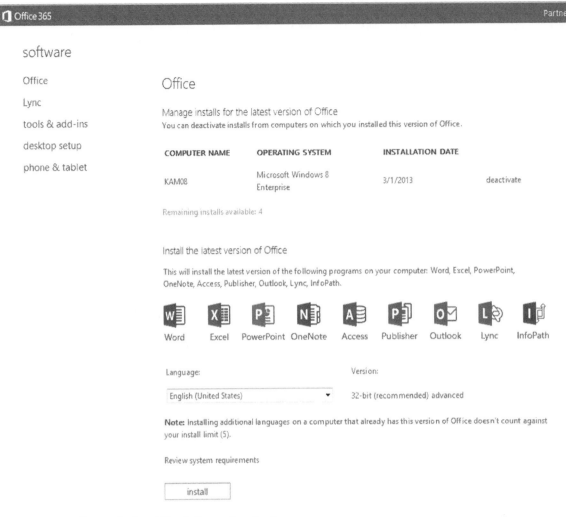

Figure 4-32. *Office Professional Plus Software download*

The installation process can be managed by any end user. The workstation setup guide is contained in Chapter 2. We designed chapter 2 to contain all of the Office 365 end user configuration in one location.

Mobile Device Configuration

The Office 365 supports different mobile devices. The software can be installed at any time, and is user driven (See Figure 4-33). To install the Office apps on your smart phone, go to the Office 365 web site, login, select the "software option" – under Office 365 settings), and install. You will receive a link in the e-mail on where you can download the information to your smartphone and configure the mobile device.

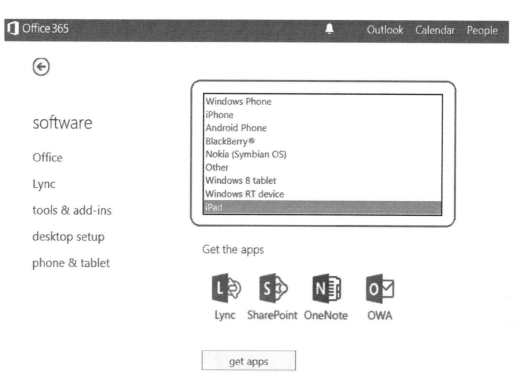

Figure 4-33. *Adding application support for your smart phone*

Complete information for end users to configure the device is in Chapter 2.

Step 9: Configure External Devices

External devices need to be configured (if there are any devices on your network). There are different ways that you can configure your devices to send e-mail to Office 365, either directly or through a SMTP server in your network. Chapter 10 has detailed instructions on device configuration for Office 365.

Step 10: Cleanup

The cleanup operation depends on what mail systems you have migrated to Office 365. If you are using a hosted e-mail system, or a non-exchange e-mail system, you need to contact the software supplier to determine if there is any special process needed to remove the third party mail server. Unless the e-mail server is integrated into Microsoft local active directory, usually there is no shut down sequence. This is not the case with an Exchange Server. An Exchange Server must be decommissioned to remove it from your local environment. To remove the Exchange Server, you simply uninstall the server. Seems simple, but to uninstall the server, you need to remove all users and delete public folders. The uninstallation wizard will walk you through the steps until the Exchange Server is removed; it is uninstalled.

■ **Note**   Do not power off the Exchange server once you have migrated to Office 365. The Exchange server must be uninstalled from the Exchange Server setup media. You must uninstall the Exchange Server software.

Final Check List

Your Office 365 is ready to be used. At this point verify the following:

1. If you have Outlook clients that you have not installed Office 2013 or run the desktop upgrade for outlook 2007/2010, complete that task now. If you do not do this, outlook will stop working.

2. Run the domain trouble shooting in Office 365 (select more than 72 hours) and make sure you have all green check marks. (See Figure 4-15). Correct the areas where you do not have green checkmarks.

3. Verify that your Office 365 domain is set to Authoritative, and not shared (see Figure 4-31).

4. Verify that you have placed a local DNS record in you on premise DNS server. You will need to add an "AutoDiscover" CNAME to your internal DNS, which points to `autodiscover.outlook.com`.

5. Extend the 14-day delete holding time to 30-day delete holding time. Run the PowerShell command (see the administration chapter 8 for information on how to run this command).

   a. Extend 30-day delete for a mailbox

      ```
      Set-mailbox user@contoso.com –retaindeleteditemsfor 30
      ```

   b. Extend 30-day delete for the Organization

      ```
      Get-mailbox | Set-mailbox –retaindeleteditemsfor 30
      ```

6. The default retention policies are not enabled until the archive is enabled. If you enable the archive on a user mailbox, the retention polices will begin to execute. Review the chapter on retention polices before you enable the archive.

7. Verify that you configured Yammer to replace Office 365 newsfeeds for your company internal social site.

Congratulations! You are all set up for Office 365!

DNS Trouble Shooting

One of the problems associated with the DNS records are who is managing them. In some cases, this may be a web developer who is no longer in business. You may also have it registered with an e-mail address that you no longer use (or can remember). If you cannot access the DNS, how do you find out the records?

We use a site at "`http://who.is`." This service will give you a good snapshot of the DNS records for the domain that you are moving (see Figure 4-34). We use this tool in conjunction with `mxtoolbox.com`. If you do not have access to the actual DNS zone file before you move, you need to use tools like "who.is" to collect the information before you move the service to a new registrar.

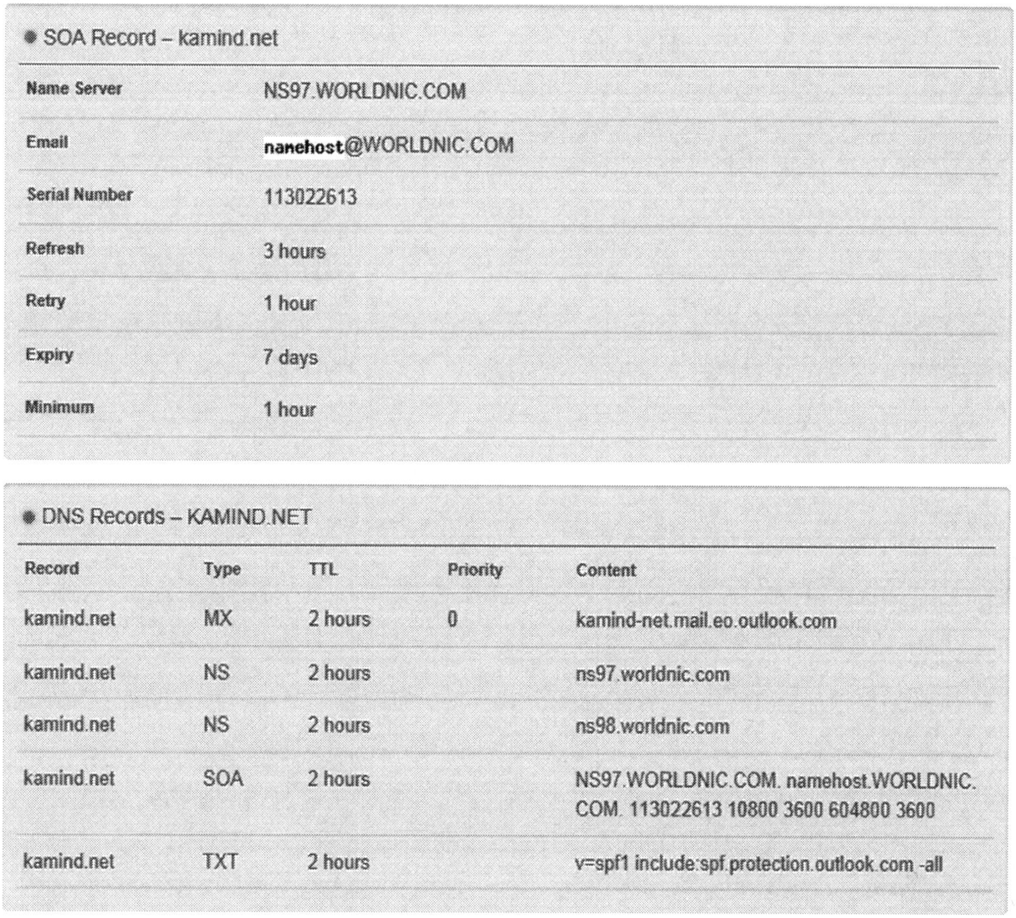

● SOA Record – kamind.net

Name Server	NS97.WORLDNIC.COM
Email	namehost@WORLDNIC.COM
Serial Number	113022613
Refresh	3 hours
Retry	1 hour
Expiry	7 days
Minimum	1 hour

● DNS Records – KAMIND.NET

Record	Type	TTL	Priority	Content
kamind.net	MX	2 hours	0	kamind-net.mail.eo.outlook.com
kamind.net	NS	2 hours		ns97.worldnic.com
kamind.net	NS	2 hours		ns98.worldnic.com
kamind.net	SOA	2 hours		NS97.WORLDNIC.COM. namehost.WORLDNIC. COM. 113022613 10800 3600 604800 3600
kamind.net	TXT	2 hours		v=spf1 include:spf.protection.outlook.com -all

Figure 4-34. DNS records form who.is for kamind.net

■ **Caution**   If you move the DNS from some suppliers, the web site may go offline.

Onboarding Users

There are three ways to load users: 1) Directory Synchronization, 2) the Office 365 Graphical User Interface or 3) using the bulk load process. The GUI is great for maintenance and small numbers of user accounts, but is not an effective tool for loading a large number of user accounts. If you chose to use Directory Sync and you have an on-premises Exchange server, you will need to use the Office 365 migration tools.

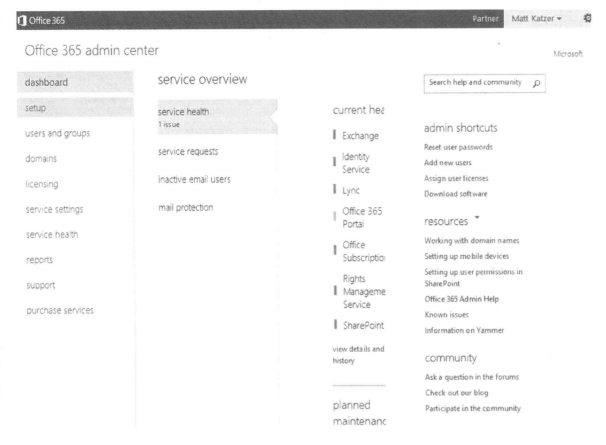

Figure 4-35. *Office 365 administration screen*

Bulk Loading Users through DirSync

DirSync links your on-premises Active Directory to Office 365. This allows you to import the existing e-mail addresses, contacts, and distribution list into Office 365, through a process called Directory Synchronization.

Figure 4-36 shows two types of objects: manually created objects "in Cloud" and DirSync objects from the on-premises server. There is no loading of users with Directory Synchronization.

Figure 4-36. *Directory Sync Objects - "Synced with Active Directory"*

Manually Bulk-Loading Users

There are two ways to manually load users: with the Office 365 Graphical User Interface or using the bulk load process. The GUI (Figure 4-37) is great for maintenance and small numbers of user accounts, but is not an effective tool for loading a large number of user accounts. The "single user add" process is explained in Chapter 10. The process that we will use below is the "Bulk add users" process.

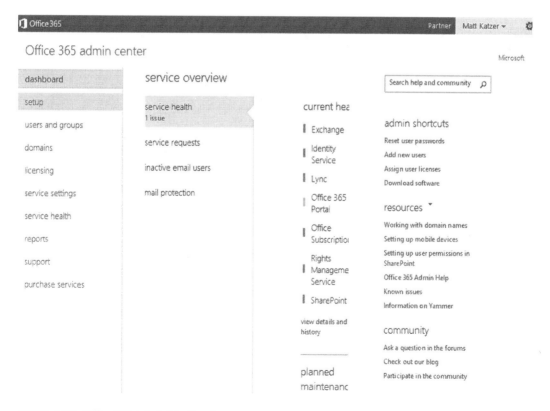

Figure 4-37. *Office 365 Administration Screen*

Log in as an administrator (at http://office.microsoft.com or http://portal.microsoftonline.com), then select "users and Groups" (under dashboard, click the drop down "New," and select "Bulk add"). The menu (Figure 4-38) has two options: add a single user, or "Bulk add users."

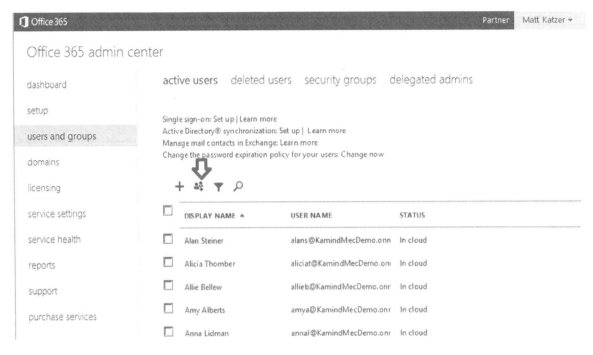

Figure 4-38. *Admin manage users; bulk add users*

The first step is to build, then select the CSV file with the appropriate users to be added. Download a blank CSV file to get the format. You can open this file in Excel (be sure to save it as a CSV file, without extra lines or columns), or edit it with the text editor.

We recommend that you use the optional fields and enter all of the data possible. If you are accurate at this step, it significantly reduces the amount of work necessary to manually fix user profiles.

After you have built the CSV file "Browse . . ." to it, find the file that you created and open it. Click "next" (see Figure 4-39).

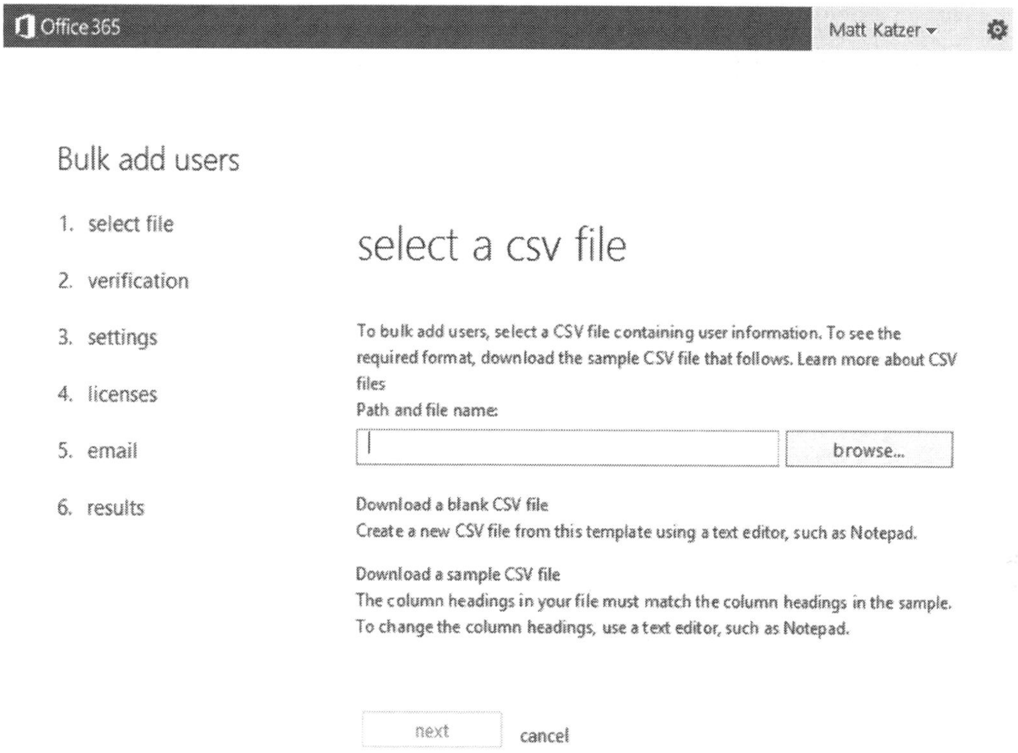

 Office 365   Matt Katzer ▾   ⚙

Bulk add users

1. select file
2. verification
3. settings
4. licenses
5. email
6. results

select a csv file

To bulk add users, select a CSV file containing user information. To see the
required format, download the sample CSV file that follows. Learn more about CSV
files
Path and file name:

| | | browse... |

Download a blank CSV file
Create a new CSV file from this template using a text editor, such as Notepad.

Download a sample CSV file
The column headings in your file must match the column headings in the sample.
To change the column headings, use a text editor, such as Notepad.

next   cancel

Figure 4-39. *Bulk add users – page 1 select CSV file*

The users should pass verification. If not, repair the CSV file and try again (Figure 4-40). Click "next."

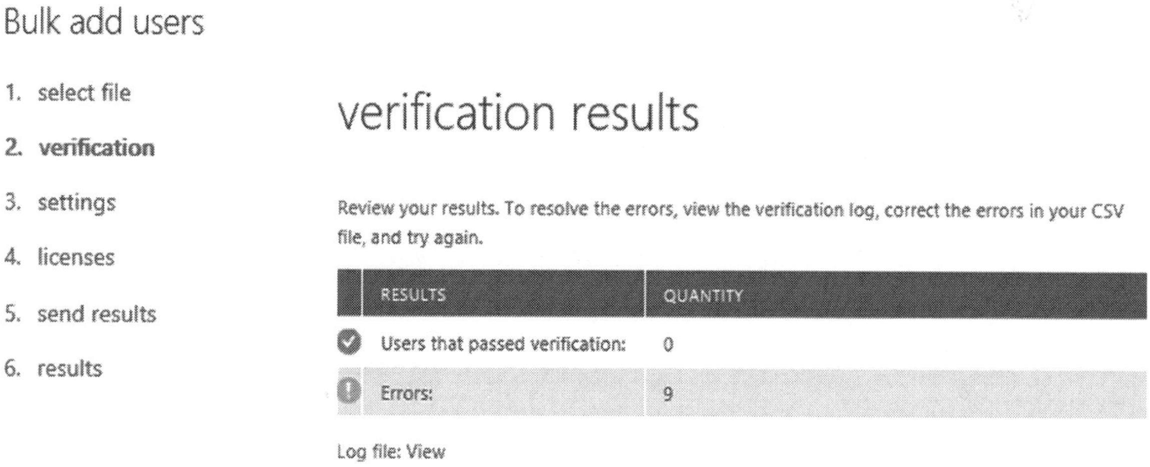

Bulk add users

1. select file
2. **verification**
3. settings
4. licenses
5. send results
6. results

verification results

Review your results. To resolve the errors, view the verification log, correct the errors in your CSV
file, and try again.

RESULTS	QUANTITY
✔ Users that passed verification:	0
❗ Errors:	9

Log file: View

Figure 4-40. *Bulk add users - page 2 verification*

Set sign-in status and set the user location (for all of the users being added - Figure 4-41). Click "next."

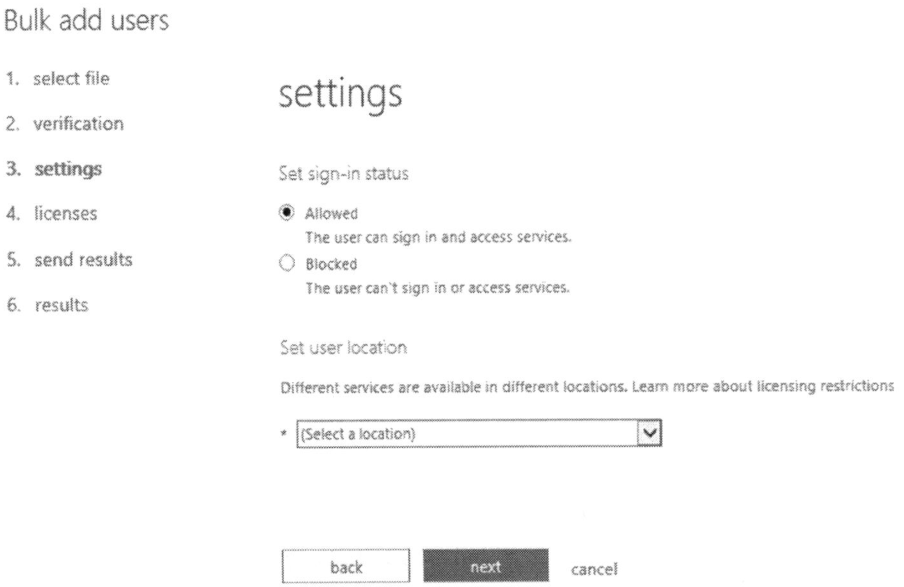

Bulk add users

1. select file
2. verification
3. **settings**
4. licenses
5. send results
6. results

settings

Set sign-in status

◉ Allowed
   The user can sign in and access services.
○ Blocked
   The user can't sign in or access services.

Set user location

Different services are available in different locations. Learn more about licensing restrictions

* [(Select a location)] ▽

[back]   [next]   cancel

Figure 4-41. Bulk add users - page 3 settings

Assign licenses (Figure 4-42). If you do not have enough licenses for the users you are loading, those users will not be loaded and will show up as an error. License assignment can be tricky if you are using different Office 365 Plans. It is best to load a small number of users to verify how the licenses are assigned. Assign licenses as required then load the next batch. Click "next."

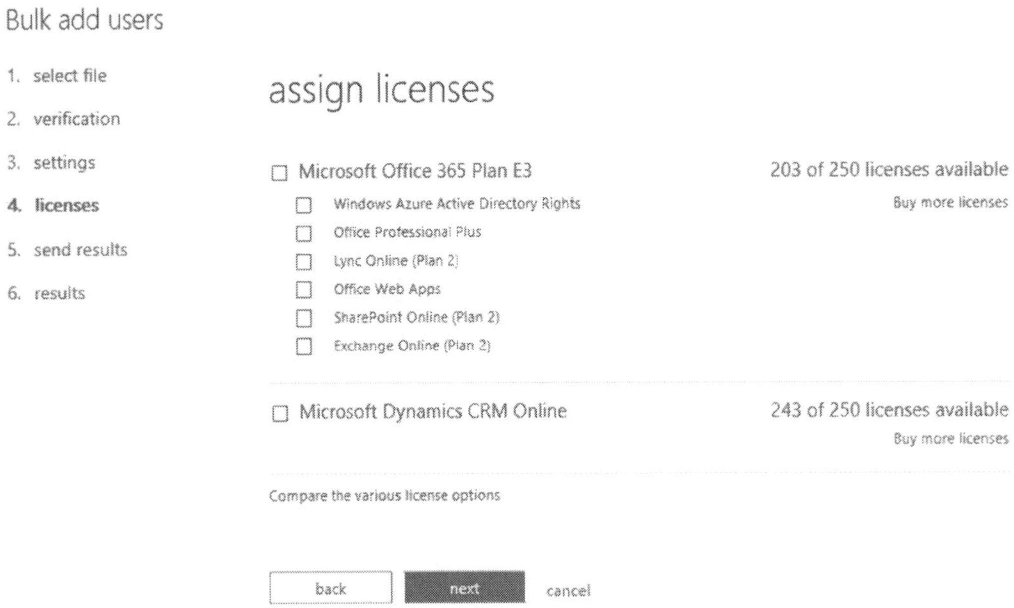

Bulk add users

1. select file
2. verification
3. settings
4. **licenses**
5. send results
6. results

assign licenses

☐ Microsoft Office 365 Plan E3   203 of 250 licenses available
                                                                         Buy more licenses
   ☐ Windows Azure Active Directory Rights
   ☐ Office Professional Plus
   ☐ Lync Online (Plan 2)
   ☐ Office Web Apps
   ☐ SharePoint Online (Plan 2)
   ☐ Exchange Online (Plan 2)

☐ Microsoft Dynamics CRM Online   243 of 250 licenses available
                                                                         Buy more licenses

Compare the various license options

[back]   [next]   cancel

Figure 4-42. Bulk add users - page 4 assign licenses

Bulk add users

1. select file
2. verification
3. settings
4. licenses
5. **send results**
6. results

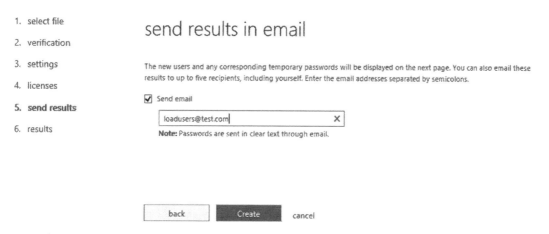

send results in email

The new users and any corresponding temporary passwords will be displayed on the next page. You can also email these results to up to five recipients, including yourself. Enter the email addresses separated by semicolons.

☑ Send email

| loadusers@test.com | ✕ |

Note: Passwords are sent in clear text through email.

back   Create   cancel

Figure 4-43. *Bulk add users - page 5 e-mail*

Change the send e-mail to whateveryouchoose@yourdomain.com to document the users' creation. This is a complete list and comes in handy if you need to bulk sign on the users and present the passwords. Click "create."

Copy the temporary passwords back into your users spreadsheet (see Figure 4-44). You will need them to notify your users. Click "close."

Bulk add users

1. select file
2. verification
3. settings
4. licenses
5. send results
6. **results**

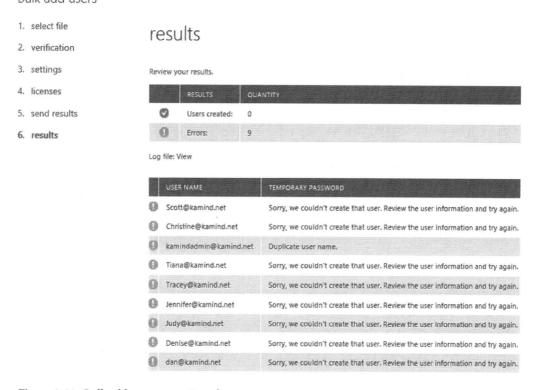

results

Review your results.

	RESULTS	QUANTITY
✔	Users created:	0
!	Errors:	9

Log file: View

	USER NAME	TEMPORARY PASSWORD
!	Scott@kamind.net	Sorry, we couldn't create that user. Review the user information and try again.
!	Christine@kamind.net	Sorry, we couldn't create that user. Review the user information and try again.
!	kamindadmin@kamind.net	Duplicate user name.
!	Tiana@kamind.net	Sorry, we couldn't create that user. Review the user information and try again.
!	Tracey@kamind.net	Sorry, we couldn't create that user. Review the user information and try again.
!	Jennifer@kamind.net	Sorry, we couldn't create that user. Review the user information and try again.
!	Judy@kamind.net	Sorry, we couldn't create that user. Review the user information and try again.
!	Denise@kamind.net	Sorry, we couldn't create that user. Review the user information and try again.
!	dan@kamind.net	Sorry, we couldn't create that user. Review the user information and try again.

Figure 4-44. *Bulk add users - page 6 results*

Onboarding E-mail

After you have loaded the user account to Office 365, you need to copy the e-mail from the current mail servers to Office 365. There are different ways to do this depending on the method you used for loading users. As an example, if you have an on-premises exchange server and have enabled DirSync, your only option is to sue the Microsoft migration tools. If you do not have an existing exchange server, you can use different migration tools to move mail to Office 365. The three methods discussed here are 1) PST migration, 2) third party tool migration and 3) using Microsoft Office 365 migration tools.

PST Mail Migration to Office 365

PST migration is the importing of the existing PST file into your Office 365 mailbox. A PST Export/Import is performed at each user's workstation, with data from their Outlook. PST migrations are the simplest, but should be used as a last resort. When you migrate PST data, you need to export the old mailbox at the root, and import the data into Office 365 at the root. If the PST data already exists, then import the data at the level that you wish to see the data in Office 365.

■ **Note**   If you start a PST migration, you need to complete it. There is no real error checking on data import or duplicates. If you stop and restart a PST migration, you will have duplicate data.

Typical user data in a PST contains all of the information in the mailbox, including e-mails, folders and subfolders, calendar, and contacts. To install the calendar and contacts into Office 365, you can either copy it manually over to Office 365 (drag ann drop), or overlay the Office 365 calendar and contract information using an export and an import data command, specifying the root inbox. Below are the two options for this command.

Export Outlook 2010 or 2013 Mailbox Information

Follow these steps below on exporting the PST data into your outlook. If you already have your PST files as an archive, refer to the import. When you export outlook information into a PST for import into Office 365, you must export the root mailbox.

1.   Start Outlook (Outlook 2010 or 2013). Use your on-premises Exchange Server Outlook profile (probably your default profile) for the export of PST mailbox information (Figure 4-45).

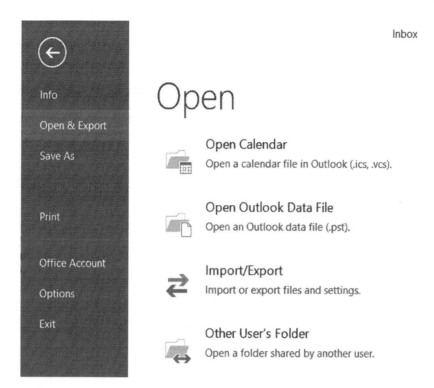

Inbox

Figure 4-45. *Outlook 2013 - exporting files to a PST*

2.   In Outlook 2013: Click "File ➤ Open ➤ Import" (this includes file export as well).

3.   Select "Export to a file," then "Outlook Data File (.pst)" as shown in Figure 4-46.

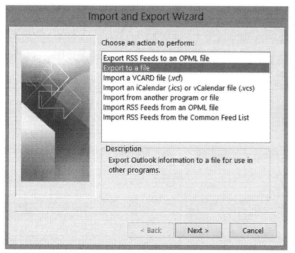
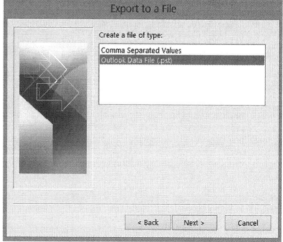

Figure 4-46. *Exporting Outlook files as a PST*

4.   Select the Mail location to export (normally you want to select the very top item: the mailbox account), and export options: a file name and normally "Replace duplicates with items exported" (Figure 4-47).

Figure 4-47. Selecting Outlook mail and file save location

5.   Once you have exported the documents, write down the location where the PST file is located (Figure 4-47). The next step is to import the PST file.

Import Outlook 2010 or 2013 Mailbox Information

Follow the steps below to import your exported PST e-mail data into your Office 365 e-mail account. This is done by loading the existing mailbox on top of the Office 365 mailbox.

1.   Exit Outlook.

2.   Sign in to the user's Office 365 account.

3.   Start Outlook with either a new profile or with the user's Office 365 profile. (We normally call the new profile "O365" to distinguish it.)

4.   In Outlook 2010 (or 2013) Click "File ➤ Open ➤ Import".

5.   Select "Import from another program or file".

6.   Select "Outlook Data File (.pst)" (or it may say "Personal Folder File (.pst)" as shown in Figure 4-48.

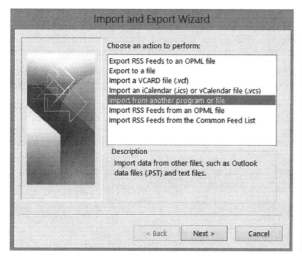
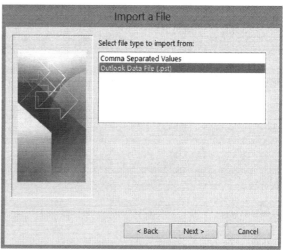

Figure 4-48. *Importing PST archives into Office 365*

7. Browse to the file to be imported (the one you exported above). Select "Do not import duplicates." You will want to import the PST folder into the same structure as the export. As an example, if you export the .pst file as the root mailbox, you need to import it as a root mailbox (shown in Figure 4-49). You may import the e-mail account to a lower level (for example, if you are importing several e-mail accounts into one e-mail account).

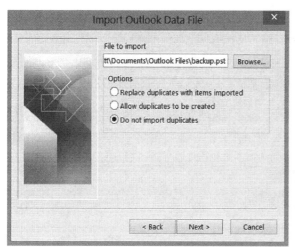
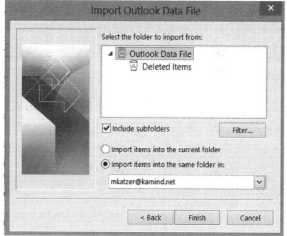

Figure 4-49. *Importing PST archives into Office 365*

The import process uploads the Outlook PST data to the Microsoft Office 365 Exchange Server. Your data will then be replicated down to your Outlook 2010. It is best that you import data using a high-speed data link, since the data will travel twice: up to Office 365 and back down to your Outlook local cache.

Third Party tool – Migration Wiz

Migration Wiz (www.migrationwiz.com) is the tool (Figure 4-50) that is used for most of the migration from either on premises or another hosted provider to Office 365. The tool is easy to use and allows thousands of mailboxes to move simultaneously. We recommend that you purchase the premium mailbox, which allow multiple error retries. The factor in how fast you can migrate is a function of the source speed of the server where data is being pulled from. As an example, if you are migrating form a Small Business server 2003 R2, we have found that you can only pull one or two mailboxes at a time.

Mailbox Migration Overview

Status	Success
Progress	182 of 185 folders complete
Migration Type	Premium Mailbox Migration
Submissions	5 submissions
Passes Used	4 passes used
Currently Migrating Source Folder	N/A
Currently Migrating Destination Folder	N/A

Last Started	November 23, 2013 7:48 AM
Last Completed	November 23, 2013 7:56 AM
Last Updated	November 23, 2013 7:56 AM
Total Duration	8 minutes

Migrated Items Count

TYPE	SUCCESS COUNT	SUCCESS SIZE	ERROR COUNT	ERROR SIZE
Folders	175	0 bytes	0	0 bytes
Calendars	0	0 bytes	0	0 bytes
Contacts	289	62.87 KB	0	0 bytes
Mail	7086	1.28 GB	0	0 bytes
Tasks	0	0 bytes	0	0 bytes
Notes	0	0 bytes	0	0 bytes
Journals	0	0 bytes	0	0 bytes
Rules	0	0 bytes	0	0 bytes
Total	7550	1.28 GB	0	0 bytes

Duration & Speed

STATISTIC	SOURCE	DESTINATION
Active Duration	56 minutes	2 hours and 34 minutes
Passive Duration	1 hour and 52 minutes	32 minutes
Data Speed	1386.7 MB/hour	511.6 MB/hour
Item Speed	7958 items/hour	2936 items/hour

Figure 4-50. *Migration Wiz Summary screen*

Figure 4-51 shows the typical Migration speeds from a hosted service to Office 365.

Charts

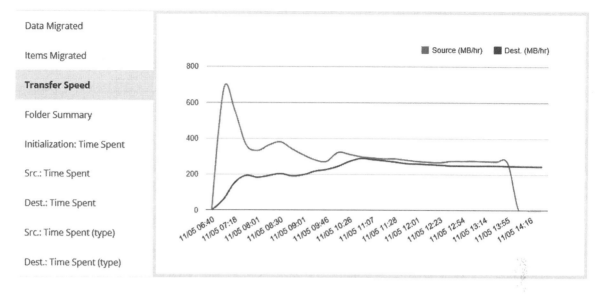

Data Migrated

Items Migrated

Transfer Speed

Folder Summary

Initialization: Time Spent

Src.: Time Spent

Dest.: Time Spent

Src.: Time Spent (type)

Dest.: Time Spent (type)

Figure 4-51. *Migration Wiz transfer speed*

Using the Migration Wiz tool is pretty easy. All you need to use the tool is the administrator privileges to the source mail account (in some cases you will need the user login and passwords) and the Office 365 administrative credentials (you need to be a global admin). Migration Wiz provides you with statistics so that you can gauge the speed of your mgiration (see Figure 4-51). The most difficult portion in using Migration Wizard is the configuration of the mailbox with the correct passwords. Remember that in Office 365 the user e-mail address and login are the same.

If you are using Migration Wiz with an on-premises Exchange Server, you will need to install either the registry changes to block service control point (SCP) lookup, or convert the mailbox to a mail-enabled user (MEU). The registry entries required to be modified for the clients are listed below (see Microsoft KB article – 2612922).

Office 365 Migration Tool

The Office 365 migration tool is designed to migrate up to 10 mailboxes at a time. Follow the steps below to access the admin screen to use the tool:

1. Select "Office 365" in the admin center.

2. Select "service settings."

3. Select "mail" option, then select "don't see what you are looking for… ," and the "Manage Additional settings in the Exchange admin center."

Once you have selected this, you will see the screen in Figure 4-52. Select "Migration" then click the "+" sign, and select "Migrate to Exchange Online." When a mailbox is migrated, the on-premises mailbox is converted to a mail enabled unit.

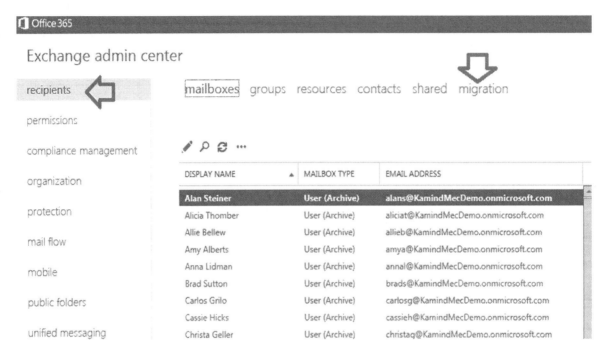

Figure 4-52. *Selecting the Office 365 Migration Tool*

Your options with the Office 365 tool are limited to Exchange Servers (2003, 2007 and 2010) and IMAP. POP mail is problematic, since POP e-mail has just the e-mail and no folders. Typically, if you are using POP mail, you will most likely use a PST export/import, because the POP e-mail is stored locally. We always recommend that you use Migration Wiz as the first option. It is simpler to use. In our example, we are going to use the IMAP to import mail from a non-Exchange server, and we will need to build a CSV file for the usernames and passwords. To import using IMAP, select the IMAP option (Figure 4-53).

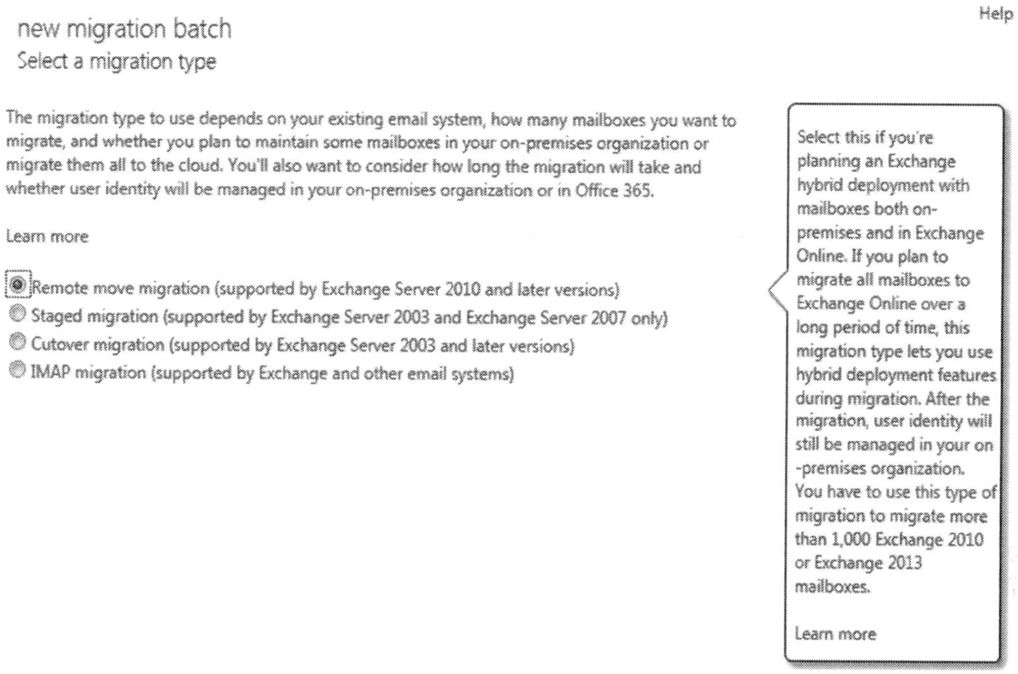

new migration batch
Select a migration type

The migration type to use depends on your existing email system, how many mailboxes you want to migrate, and whether you plan to maintain some mailboxes in your on-premises organization or migrate them all to the cloud. You'll also want to consider how long the migration will take and whether user identity will be managed in your on-premises organization or in Office 365.

Learn more

⦿ Remote move migration (supported by Exchange Server 2010 and later versions)
◯ Staged migration (supported by Exchange Server 2003 and Exchange Server 2007 only)
◯ Cutover migration (supported by Exchange Server 2003 and later versions)
◯ IMAP migration (supported by Exchange and other email systems)

Help

Select this if you're planning an Exchange hybrid deployment with mailboxes both on-premises and in Exchange Online. If you plan to migrate all mailboxes to Exchange Online over a long period of time, this migration type lets you use hybrid deployment features during migration. After the migration, user identity will still be managed in your on-premises organization. You have to use this type of migration to migrate more than 1,000 Exchange 2010 or Exchange 2013 mailboxes.

Learn more

Figure 4-53. *Migrating e-mail using Office 365 e-mail migration*

■ **Note** If you do not have a third-party certificate, do not use the Microsoft Mail Migration tool. Use the Migration Wiz.

Provide the credentials to import the user accounts into Office 365, and create a CSV file to load the users from the source server into Office 365 (Figure 4-54). The wizard assumes that the e-mail address of the source server is the destination e-mail address on Office 365. You will need to be a global administrator to use this tool.

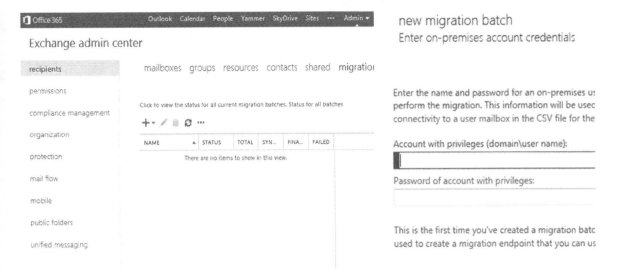

Figure 4-54. *Office 365 e-mail migration*

After you have selected "run," Office 365 will monitor the status and send you an e-mail when the migration is completed and will list the batch status (Figure 4-55).

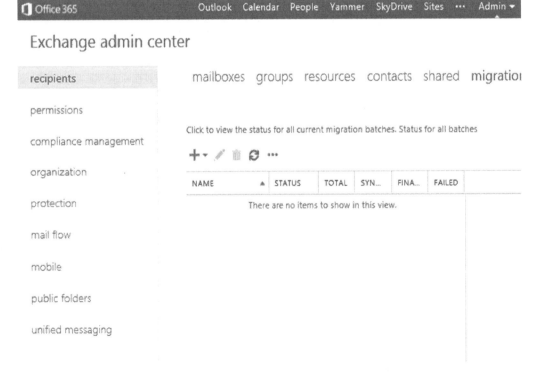

Figure 4-55. *Migration status using Office 365 migration*

After you have started the migrations, the next step is to install PowerShell. In some cases, you may need to install PowerShell early on if you have any problems with domain validation. In most instances, you will be using PowerShell under the guidance of the Office 365 support staff.

Outlook Manual Configuration

Chapter 2 contains the information necessary for the automatic configuration of Outlook. However, there are cases where this will not work and you will need to manually configure the Outlook desktop client. Office 365 uses Microsoft Exchange 2013 and no longer uses RPC or SSL (HTTPS) to connect to the exchange server through the client access server. The new structure uses exchangeGUID@<compnay.com> to connect e-mail services. Since there are no longer any mail servers to configure, you need to determine the ExchangeGuid ID as the server, and create the Exchange server name to manually configure the Outlook client. To manually configure the outlook client, follow the instructions below.

■ **Note**   At this point, we assume that you have downloaded Office 2013, and Outlook is configured to prompt for profile. You have tried to connect Outlook to Office 365 and it has failed to automatically connect. This manual process should only be used if you failed the automatic connection to Office 365.

Step1: Run the PowerShell command to retrieve the ExchangeGuid

Open up a PowerShell command session and run the following command for the users who cannot connect to Office 365. If you need instructions on the configuration of PowerShell, please refer to Chapter 8: Office 365 Administrator Guide. Use the results of this command to build the server name for each user in the format "exchangeGuid@company.com:"

```
Set-ExecutionPolicy RemoteSigned
$LiveCred = Get-Credential
Import-module msonline
Connect-MSOLService-Credential $LiveCred-Verbose
$Session = New-PSSession-ConfigurationName Microsoft.Exchange-ConnectionUri
https://ps.outlook.com/powershell/-Credential $LiveCred-Authentication Basic-AllowRedirection
Import-PSSession $Session-AllowClobber
Get-Recipient | fl name, exchangeguid
Remove-PSSession $Session
```

Step 2: Configuration of Outlook

Change your Outlook profile to prompt for profile (see the section at the end of this note). At this point you have tried the automatic configuration (and verified that the auto discover records were setup correctly). The only option left is the manual configuration of Office 2013. To begin the manual configuration, start Outlook, and select "new" (Figure 4-56) to create a new profile.

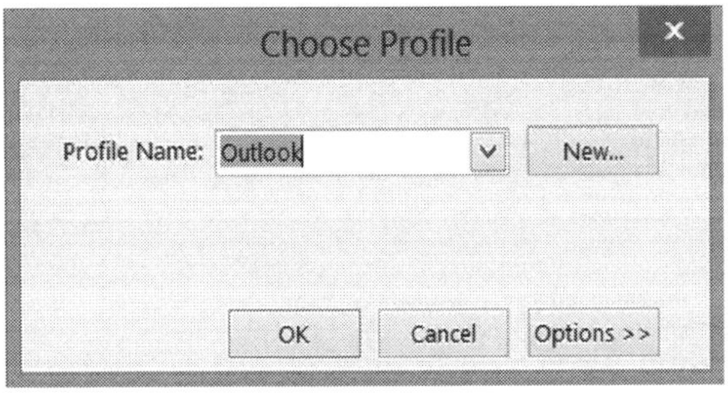

Figure 4-56. Outlook New Profile

If you wish to speed up the configuration of Outlook, log in to the web site `http://office.microsoft.com` before you start the manual connection process. Outlook uses a secured HTTPS connection, and will use the same connection that you enter for your browser. If the automatic configuration fails, create a new profile and select the "manual" button. In Figure 4-57, select "manual."

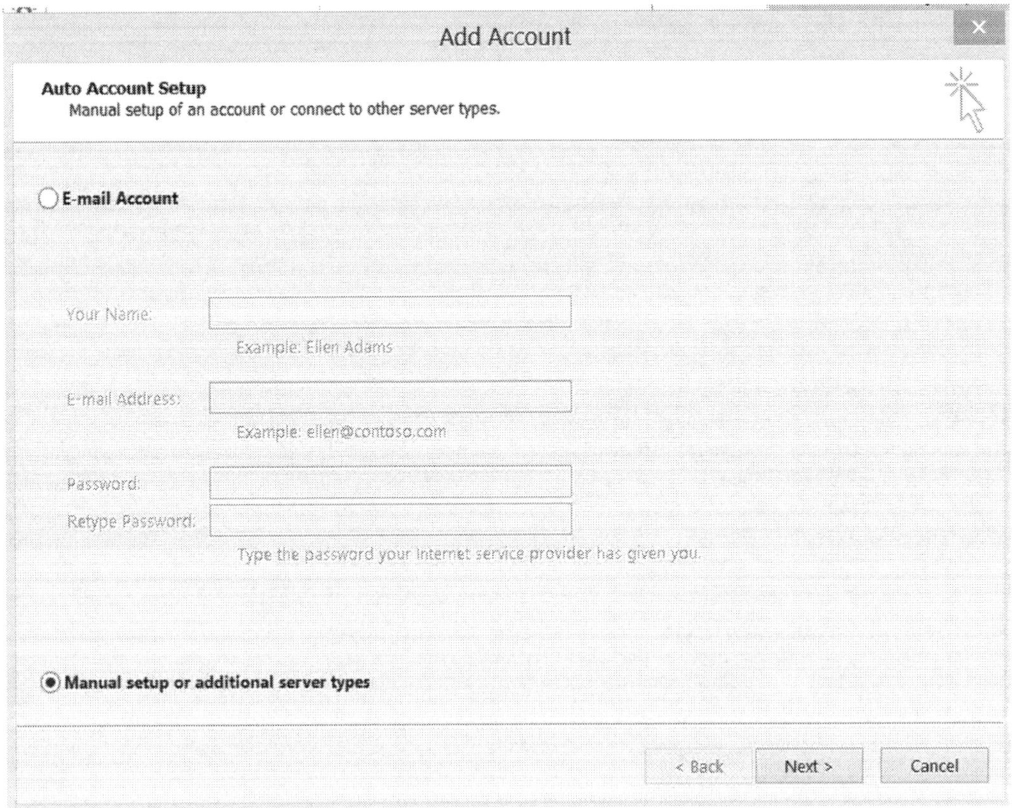

Figure 4-57. Outlook Setup

In Figure 4-58, select "Microsoft Exchange server or compatible service," then "Next."

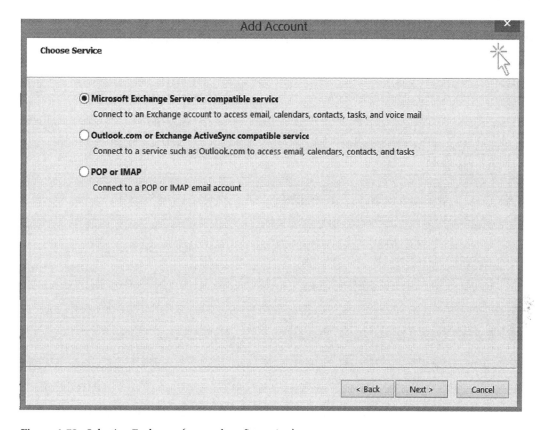

Figure 4-58. Selecting Exchange (manual configuration)

In Step 1 above, we ran the PowerShell script to retrieve the ExchangeGuid. We appended the domain name after the ExchangeGuid to build the server name (in this format ExchangeGuid@company.com). As an example, using the domain KAMIND.com, the server name would look like: c29c8a0e-26c0-7d4f-8cd2-df1658f1f421@kamind.com. Enter this: exchangeGuid@company.com for the server (Figure 4-59). The user name for Office 365 is the user e-mail address (the user Principal Name should be the same for Office 365). Select "More Settings" to enter the extended parameters of the connection to Office 365. Do not select "check name."

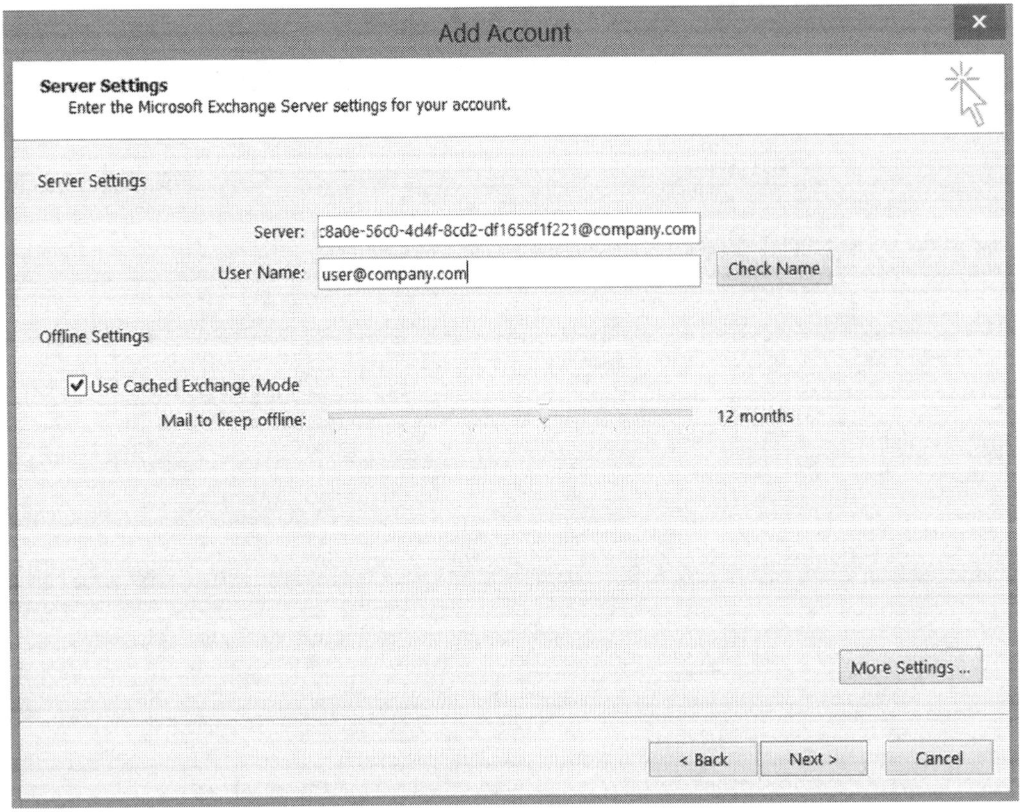

Figure 4-59. Entering the server name (exchangeGuid) and the user e-mail address (for user name)

After you have selected "More Settings," select the "Security" tab (see Figure 4-60), and clear the "Encrypt data between Microsoft Outlook and Microsoft Exchange" (you are using an SSL connection to access Office 365, so unchecking this does not expose you to risk since your data is encrypted via SSL). In the "Logon network security," section select "Anonymous Authentication."

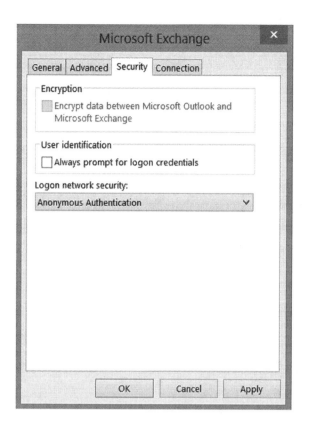

Figure 4-60. *Remove the encryption check mark, and set to anonymous settings*

Set the security to the proper values. Then select the "Connection" tab, and check the "Connect to Microsoft Exchange using HTTP." Select "Exchange Proxy Settings" (see Figure 4-61) to set the connection properties.

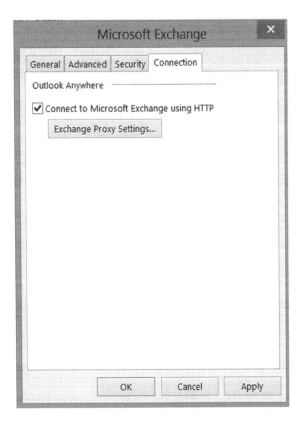

Figure 4-61. *Selecting the Exchange server proxy*

Next, select the Exchange server proxy settings. Enter the following settings for Office 365 Exchange server (see Figure 4-62 and Table 4-2):

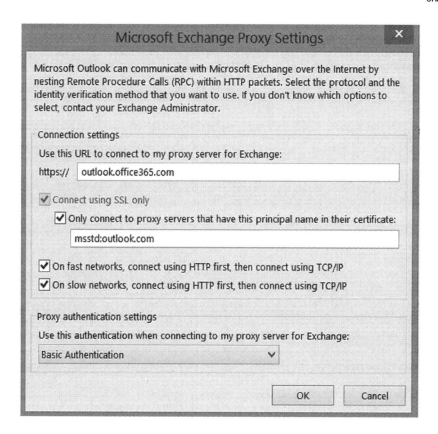

Figure 4-62. *Manual configuration of HTTPS proxy settings*

The parameters that you have changed are listed in Table 4-2.

Table 4-2. *Correct setting for HTTPS connection to sever*

Field	Value
Proxy server	`http://outlook.office365.com`
Principal name	`msstd:outlook.com`
Connected Fast/Slow	Check both check boxes (see Figure 4-7)
Authentication	Basic

Select "Apply," then "OK." Enter the password when prompted. You will need to restart Outlook and then it should connect to Office 365. You will be requested to login to Office 365. Restart Outlook and select the new profile that you just created. You should see Outlook connect to Office 365 and download your profile.

If Outlook does not connect up, verify the parameters used in the manual connection. Usually the problem is that the server name is incorrect or that the user name is wrong. Verify the parameters and try again.

Reference Links

Office 365 seem simple, but they are complex. There are many different areas to retrieve information about how to migrate to Office 365. Listed below are the important links for migration.

Onboarding Checking tool

http://onboard.office365.com

Office 365 Migration videos

http://technet.microsoft.com/en-jm/video/office-365-jump-start-01-microsoft-office-365-overview-for-it-pros

Conversion of on-site user to mail enable user

http://community.office365.com/en-us/blogs/office_365_community_blog/archive/2011/12/02/convert-exchange-2007-mailboxes-to-mail-enabled-users-after-a-staged-exchange-migration.aspx

Office 365 Migratign and Managing your business in the cloud - Update

http://getoffice365now.com

Next steps

Your basic Office 365 systems have been set up and configured. At this point you are 100% functional and ready to move to the next steps. However, your work is not yet complete. There is much more to do depending on your Office 365 configuration. The key chapters that you need to review for your Office 365 deployment are:

- **Chapter 5** – SharePoint Administration

  - There are a lot of different features in Office 365 that the user can configure, which do not require support from the systems administrator. This chapter discusses how the administrator sets up the collaboration environment for Office 365 users.

- **Chapter 7** –Windows Intune Administration

  - The secret to an optimal Office 365 site is the management of the desktop to ensure that updates are current, and the user antivirus is functioning. Windows Intune is a desktop management tool that addresses these issues and reduces the administrators' effort in desktop management, and improves the user's experience.

- **Chapter 8** – Office 365 Administration

  - The administrator's job is never complete. This chapter contains information for common tasks such as configuring SharePoint permissions, using different types of PowerShell scripts for configuration of the Office 365 sites and other tips and tracks what we use to make Office 365 work without any support calls.

- **Chapter 11** – ADFS/Single Sign-On, Password Sync and Federation

  - Federation Services is the integration of the Office 365 Exchange servers with on-site Exchange servers. Federation places the security and control in the hands of the on-site administrators and equipment. Integration requires on-site equipment to manage the cloud security.

CHAPTER 5

■ ■ ■

SharePoint Administration Guide

This chapter introduces SharePoint Online concepts and describes many of the methods that SharePoint Administrators may use to control and modify their site collections and sites. The information in this chapter will allow you to create sites and control access, and to use settings that control various features of SharePoint. We will take you through creating a sample site with designed permissions.

Note that the control by SharePoint Administrators (and delegates) only applies to the features and structure of SharePoint. There are separate Administrators for other Office 365 components.

This is not a chapter on using SharePoint. The "user" SharePoint features that are generally available to people using the system are described in Chapter 2.

SharePoint Administration Chapter Structure

Not every feature of SharePoint Online is described here. Our goal is to provide an overview of the key terms and features that a SharePoint Administrator will need to configure and control their site. SharePoint is a very large topic. There are numerous books written about SharePoint. There is also quite a bit of information in the Office 365 community and on the Web in general.

This overview section covers the following topics:

- Introduction to Office 365 SharePoint

- Description of SharePoint (what it is and is not)

- SharePoint definitions

The rest of this chapter is in three parts:

- The "Planning, Governance, and Initial Setup" section introduces planning for a SharePoint implementation and additional definitions (such as types of Administrators)

- Site-related Administration functions

- Site and Site Collection Administrator functions

The SharePoint site-related Administration functions may be used by the associated Site Administrator or delegated to a user with permissions. This section has further subsections.

- "Building Your SharePoint Structure"

- "SharePoint Permissions and Groups"

- "Site Editing"

- "Creating a Project Site"

179

The following sections are for Site and Site Collection Administrators:

- "SharePoint Admin Center"
- "Additional Administrator Concepts and Tools"
- "Initial SharePoint Setup"

The information contained in this chapter is based on the most common questions that we have been asked about Office 365 SharePoint in our deployments.

Introduction to Office 365 SharePoint

Office 365 Hosted SharePoint (SharePoint Online) is a part of a set of three product families: Small Business, Midsize Business, and Enterprise Business/Exchange Online/Kiosk (see Figure 5-1). Office 365 Hosted SharePoint is Microsoft SharePoint. The major difference is that Microsoft administers and maintains all of the back-end servers, operating systems, SharePoint Server software, interconnects, geo-redundancy, and network structure. SharePoint licensing is included in the Small Business, Midsize Business, and Enterprise Business E1, E3, and E4 plans (and to a limited extent in some of the Kiosk plans). The concepts discussed in this chapter generally apply to all of these versions of Office 365 SharePoint, but these configurations have only been tested with the Enterprise version.

SharePoint Online and Office 365 Feature Comparison

	SharePoint Online Plans		Office 365 Plans								Features external users can access
			Small Businesses	Midsize Businesses	Enterprise Businesses			Kiosk		
	Plan 1	Plan 2	P	M1	E1	E3	E4	K1	K2	
Cost (per user/per month)	$3	$7	$6	$15	$8	$20	$22	$4	$4	
Access a team intranet site	●	●	●	●	●	●	●	●	●	When invited
Create a team intranet site	●	●	●	●	●	●	●			
Incremental team storage beyond 10 GB	500 MB per user	500 MB per user	500 MB per user	500 MB per user	500 MB per user	500 MB per user	500 MB per user	0	0	
Maximum storage per subscription	Up to 25 TB	Up to 25 TB	Up to 35 GB	Up to 25 TB	Up to 25 TB	Up to 25 TB	Up to 25 TB	0	0	
My Sites personal storage and file sharing (additional 500MB per user)	●	●		●	●	●	●			
View Office docs online	●	●	●	●	●	●	●	●	●	
Edit Office docs online*	+$2	+$2	●	●	●	●	●	●	●	
View Access-based web pages		●	●			●	●	●	●	●
Publish Access-based web pages (requires a copy of Access 2010)		●	●			●	●			●
View build and publish Visio diagrams, external lists, embedded Excel graphs and InfoPath forms		●				●	●			●
Office 365 community support	●	●	●	●	●	●	●	●	●	
Live 24 x 7 IT customer phone support	●	●		●	●	●	●			

Figure 5-1. *SharePoint plans (courtesy of Microsoft)*

There are several notes with Figure 5-1:

1. SharePoint Plan 1 and Plan 2 and Kiosk K1 and K2 are part of Enterprise.

2. The first license creates a 10GB Team Site. Additional licensed users (except K1 and K2) add 500MB each to the Team Site storage allocation (you can buy more, up to 25TB).

3. SkyDrive Pro sites are 25 to 100GB per license. SkyDrive Pro is a type of SharePoint site, allocated and controlled by a particular user.

4. Web editing is allowed for SharePoint Plan 1 and 2 for an additional $2/month.

What is SharePoint?

SharePoint is Microsoft's document storage and content management tool. SharePoint was first released in 2001. Originally, SharePoint was used as an enterprise's on-premises "intranet." SharePoint was included in Small Business Server and in the original Microsoft Cloud offering, BPOS. The version with Office 365 is SharePoint Online.

SharePoint is fundamentally a web server that presents web pages to your browser (Internet Explorer, Firefox, Chrome, Safari, etc.). The SharePoint data (structure, permissions, sites, your documents, etc.) is hosted on SQL servers that are maintained by Microsoft within their secure environment.

This allows people to read, edit, and create pages and sites and to control administrative settings depending upon their permissions. Chapter 2 includes descriptions of tasks that everyone will normally do (add documents to SharePoint, create and edit documents locally or in the cloud). This chapter includes descriptions of how to create sites, site features, and up to full site collection Administration features.

■ **Note** Because your data is present through a URL, you can set a Bookmark or Favorites to go to a particular SharePoint page.

Microsoft has a stated and executed intention of Cloud First. This means that the SharePoint that is available with Office 365 (Wave 15) is SharePoint 2013 Enterprise with more extensions and features. The limits of SharePoint Online (compared to the on-premises Enterprise version) are related to the fact that the Online version shares the SharePoint farm with other users (shared tenancy). Two examples are limited control of searching (to limit resource consumption) and Sandbox only (no full-trust solutions).

When you add in the feature that you can be up and running in SharePoint Online (in the very latest version) in one day, your SharePoint Online version might be three to six years ahead of your on-premises functionality!

With SharePoint Online:

- Your data is stored and organized in one place.

- Your data is available from anywhere you choose.

- Microsoft takes care of operating details such as sizing the equipment, backups, geo-redundancy, equipment upgrades, equipment failures, software and network failures, software patches, etc.

SharePoint Online provides:

- Tools for collaboration, synchronization, projects, and robust searching.

- Tools to maintain the one version of your document, and to make it easy to find and share; no long do you have to chase down who has the latest version of your document.

- Tools to share your documents and build your team; share your company picnic pictures, your company calendar; engage your employees! Create and share your best practices within your enterprise, or with your suppliers and customers.

- Tools to build internal web (intranet) portals and public-facing web sites.

- Familiar Office tools to create and edit your SharePoint documents from anywhere on any device.

SharePoint Online benefits include:

- Helping your Sales and Marketing teams work together to share ideas and improve your processes.

- Using SharePoint and Excel Web App to share your spreadsheets so you can work together at one time to create your budgets and reports.

- Improving your in-house support services such as IT: searchable best practices and known bugs, track requests, even remote support with tools such as Lync and Windows Intune.

- Support for project planning and reporting; creating tasks, setting priorities, watching for missed milestones. SharePoint is the data storage for huge projects that you may manage with Microsoft Project Professional.

- Search! Save time and find what you need.

- Allowing for the controlled combination of security and empowering employees.

- Dashboards: Data, Power Pivot, and Power View.

- Workflows for automatic routing of business processes, such as training a new employee: you can use your existing forms, your employee handbook, training videos, contacts to bring new employees up to speed.

- Using SharePoint and your other Office 365 tools such as eDiscovery to manage, protect, and control access to your critical data. You can create retention schedules. It also supports audits and discovery requests at the lowest cost.

What is SharePoint Not?

SharePoint is a place to store documents and files. SharePoint documents are indexed, backed up, and maintained according to the Office 365 service-level agreement (SLA). You do not use SharePoint for the following:

1. **Do not** use SharePoint as a place to put backups (there are size and file type limits).

2. **Do not** place huge working files that have to be moved to edit (SharePoint is a good place for archiving your larger files).

3. There is presently a limit of 5,000 items in a single list or document library view.

SharePoint Definitions

These words are used throughout this chapter and throughout SharePoint documentation in general. Here are summarized definitions:

- *URL*: Universal Resource Locator. The specific universal address for a web page. It is essentially a specific location within a domain within the World Wide Web. This doesn't necessarily mean that you can see it from anywhere; there can be security restrictions. For example, https://kamind.sharepoint.com or http://getoffice365now.com.

- *Tenant*: This is your Office 365 account including Hosted Exchange, Lync, SharePoint, and your Office 365 Active Directory. The first account that you create when you first purchase Office 365 is the "owner" of your tenant. This account should be an admin account, not a person. This account does not normally need an Office 365 license. Relating to SharePoint, all of your site collections are within your tenant. You can have any number of domains within your tenant (with e-mail accounts) but you will have only one root SharePoint URL: `https://xxxx.sharepoint.com`. See "Planning, Design, and Governance" for planning notes.

- *Site Collection*: This is a collection of sites. With the Enterprise Plan you may have multiple site collections within your tenant. Site collections have sets of properties that are the same for all sites within a site collection, which may be different between site collections.

- *Site*: A SharePoint site is a collection of SharePoint "apps" and "Web Parts" (components) such as document libraries, lists, tasks, blogs, pictures, templates, and text that are presented to a user at a particular URL as a page. A site is within a particular site collection. An example is a project site.

- *Subsite*: A subsite is just a site under (within) a site. You can nest sites until you confuse yourself.

- *Page*: A page is what you see with your web browser. You can have multiple pages within a site. Generally, a site presents a default page that the users will think of as "the site."

- *Web Part*: Components that can be inserted into a page (part of a site). Web Parts are very powerful and can interact with other sites and data outside of SharePoint.

- *App*: A component of a site, such as a document library or list. A type of Web Part.

- *List*: A set of items within a site. You can think of a list as a bunch of rows and columns with potentially a data value at the intersection, like a spreadsheet. There are specialized lists that have special properties. A list is separate from a page, but usually is displayed on a page. When you select and display a specific list, the page ribbon shows actions that can be performed on the list or items in it, such as set permissions or delete an item. Special list types include task list or calendar list.

- *Document Library*: A set of documents within a site. In many ways a document library is a specialized list that contains the document and associated metadata. A document library is separate from a page, but usually is displayed on a page. When you select and display a specific document library, the page ribbon shows actions that can be performed on the document library or folders and documents within it, such as set permissions or delete an item. A document library may contain folders and documents.

- *Folder*: Similar to a folder on your PC. Part of a SharePoint document library. Folders may have independent permissions. A folder contains documents.

- *Document*: A Word, Excel, PowerPoint, or other type of file within a document library. A document may have independent permissions.

- *Metadata*: Additional data stored about/with an item, such as the date and author of a document. The data is searchable.

- *Permissions*: The "who can do it" part of SharePoint. Permissions are set on a site, list, document library, etc. Permission levels include None, Read, View, Contribute (Read and Write), and more. A particular user must have the "permission" to do that activity on that item. For example, to be able to update the item.

- *Site Contents*: Contents of a site. The Site Contents page shows lists, libraries, and other apps and subsites that are associated with this site. This page is a helpful reference to your site structure. Access to this screen appears as a link on a site page, or as a drop-down choice under the Gear icon at the top right of the screen. Only items that you have permission to see will show.

- *Document Set*: Document sets are a feature in SharePoint Server 2013 that enables an organization to manage a single deliverable, or work product, which can include multiple documents or files. A document set is a special kind of folder that combines unique document set attributes, the attributes and behaviors of folders and documents, and provides a user interface (UI), metadata, and object model elements to help manage all aspects of the work product. See the Reference Links page.

- *Content Type*: A content type defines the attributes of a list item, a document, or a folder. There is a content type per site collection. It could be considered as a "collection of columns for re-use" in other lists or document libraries. Content types are inherited. See the Reference Links page.

- *Web site*: A SharePoint web site is a specialized site collection that can be seen by the outside world (public facing) through a standard URL (such as http://getoffice365now.com). You may only have one web site within your tenant.

SharePoint Planning, Governance, and Initial Setup

SharePoint is a very powerful system. With power comes opportunity and the opportunity for confusion. Thank you for being a person that wants to read about planning! To reward you, this is a short section. One could consider many of these "Best Practices." Some are just warnings!

The key points are as follows:

1. Your xxxx.onmicrosoft.com name is your SharePoint site name: xxxx.sharepoint.com. This "xxxx" name was (or will be, if you are reading this in advance) picked at the time you signed up for Office 365. It cannot be changed. (You can get a different name, but you have to migrate your old data to the new tenant. It is not clear that you will even be able to keep your old .onmicrosoft name if you move to a different plan family (Small Business to Midsize or to Enterprise) even though Microsoft has indicated that you will be able to change your plan family. See point 2.

2. At KAMIND we have a few sayings including "Don't do it" and "Just get started." For example: "I want to save a buck and get the 'Small Business' plan." Don't do it. The savings are tiny and the limitations are large. There are even more limits with Midsize Business (no Exchange Only, no Kiosk). Just buy an Enterprise Plan. See the discussion in Chapter 3's "Office 365 Subscription Plans" section. "Just get started" basically means don't over-plan. This is especially true when you are implementing Office 365 for the first time and migrating your e-mail; see Chapter 4.

3. Keep your SharePoint structures and permissions as simple as you can. Set permissions at the site level, not at the document library, list, or folder level.

4. There is no included tool that will give you a comprehensive permissions structure. It is important to build a plan (as simple as possible) of who gets to go where and to document it so you don't accidently create exceptions.

5. Sub-sub-sub...subsites are confusing. Build a structure plan (as simple as possible) of how you want to keep your data and document it so you don't accidently create exceptions.

6. There is a strong push within the SharePoint community to use Search rather than a folder structure to organize documents. Consider this.

7. One of the nice features of SharePoint is the site-to-site (page-to-page) navigation (this is what shows at the top and side of each page). This is an optional feature of a site collection that has SharePoint Server Publishing Infrastructure activated. This site collection feature "provides centralized libraries, content types, master pages, and page layouts, and enables page scheduling and other publishing functionality for a site collection." It also allows this form of navigation. This is a planning item because there is no nice way to turn this feature on after you have built a ton of sites. (You have to go back to each site and adjust the settings for that site.) Set this feature when you create a site collection (or on your first or only site collection). See the "SharePoint Admin Center" section.

8. External sharing (sharing a site or other entity with accounts outside of your Office 365 tenant) is very powerful, and a great feature, but it has limitations. These limitations include the following:

   a. Permissions for these external users must be built within SharePoint. That is, you cannot add an external user to an Active Directory group (if you are using DirSync or ADFS) nor to an Office 365 portal Security Group. You must add the outside user to a SharePoint group (or to an individual site, document library, folder, or file if you like living on the edge).

   b. You cannot add these external users to Distribution Groups (you cannot e-mail to them as a group). As an aside, they cannot receive alerts (if an item on alert changes).

   c. Because it is now easier to inadvertently incorrectly share a site, it may be worth having a completely separate site collection to be used for external users.

   d. There is a bit of activity that the external user has to perform to be able to see your shared data. They must have either an Office 365 account (by far the easiest, and a great reason to get your friends and suppliers and customers on Office 365) or a Microsoft ID (which used to be called a Live ID). A Microsoft ID includes hotmail.com and outlook.com addresses. They can convert any e-mail address (including Gmail, Yahoo, or any corporate account) into a Microsoft ID. When a site is shared, the external user receives an e-mail and they must sign in with their Office 365 or Microsoft ID. The point is that setting up a Microsoft ID might be more pain than it is worth for some of your external users.

   e. Consider using a SharePoint Only license (the Plan 1 license is just $3 per month, Enterprise plan; see point 2 above) to share externally if you have a less-than-simple environment. Since it is a regular license within your tenant, you can set the login name, password, and permissions just with any other internal user. You can delete the user and downgrade your license count when the project ends.

   f. See the section "SharePoint Admin Center" to set up external sharing and Chapter 2 to use sharing and external sharing.

Governance

"Governance" is a fancy word to describe the planning associated with who does what and who can do what. For example, who is in charge of adding a site? Is it a specific individual within a department? Or is it anyone in the department? Just IT people for everyone? This is usually a trade-off between control and free market (and to some extent how much training an organization wants to do; in reality, it is not that hard and the training is straightforward).

Permissions may need to be better controlled. If you are storing important, sensitive information (as you should; this is one of the things that SharePoint Online is great for) you may want a security-oriented person to think about the consequences of your permissions structure. SharePoint provides a great deal of granularity in access control. (Do resist the urge to make it too complicated.)

A core governance issue is how Administrator roles are assigned. Various administrators can set permissions for users that control what they can see and edit.

In larger organizations it is very proper to create a site collection with a Site Collection Administrator for a particular department or entity. This allows that group to have complete control over their part of your SharePoint Online. See the sections "SharePoint Administrators" (next) and "SharePoint Admin Center."

SharePoint Administrators

One of the basic concepts of SharePoint is that control and access are based on a role that you have been assigned. Microsoft creates and maintains the SharePoint Farm in their data centers and retains control of Central Administration (see Figure 5-2). When you buy an Office 365 Subscription, the first account is the root Global Administrator, which is also the first SharePoint tenant Administrator (called a SharePoint Online Administrator).

Figure 5-2. Microsoft Admin structure (courtesy of Microsoft)

Table 5-1 shows a summary of the capabilities of a SharePoint Online Administrator, a Site Collection Administrator, and a Site Level Owner.

Table 5-1. *SharePoint Administration Roles*

SharePoint Online Administrator	Site Collection Administrator	Site Level Owner
• Create and manage site collections • Site Delete and Undo (Recycle Bin) • Review site properties • Designate Site Collection Administrators • Set site sharing options • Manage settings including site quotas • Configure web site domains • Manage InfoPath, user profiles, BCS, term store, records management, search, apps • Manage tenant settings	• Manage site collection features (this site only) • Add more Site Collection Administrator s • Create new subsites, new document libraries and lists • Manage permissions and groups • Manage the look and feel (title, navigation, theme, master pages) • Save site as template • Manage site columns and site content types • Site deletion • Manage user alerts, RSS settings • Adjust default regional and language settings • Invite internal or external groups/users via e-mail to share your site	• Settings that only affect the single site they own (no cross-site actions) • Manage site features • Save site as template • Manage site columns and site content types • Site deletion • Manage user alerts, RSS settings • Adjust default regional and language settings • And more...

The general roles include types of Administrator and permissions that can be assigned. There are three types of Administrators in Office 365 and a category of User with Permissions:

- *Global Administrator*: This is an Office 365 administrator role. A Global Administrator manages users and (Office 365) groups, service licenses, and domains. Chapter 8 describes these functions. The Global Administrator also manages Exchange and Lync. A Global Administrator is also a SharePoint Online Administrator.

- *SharePoint Online Administrator*: Uses the SharePoint Online Administration Center to create and manage site collections, designate Site Collection Administrator s, and configure InfoPath, user profiles, BCS, term store, records management, search, secure store, and apps. See the section "SharePoint Admin Center." Note that you MUST be an Office 365 Global Administrator to be a SharePoint Online Administrator (no lower Office 365 administrator role levels work).

- *Site Collection Administrator*: A user with a role assigned by a SharePoint Online Administrator has permissions to manage a site collection, including setting permissions for other users within the site collection. There is one Primary Site Collection Administrator. There can be many Site Collection Administrators.

- *User with Permissions (Site Level Owners)*: There are a variety of permissions that can be assigned to a user through their group membership (see the section "SharePoint Permissions and Groups").

Site Collection Administrator Permissions

Table 5-2 shows the permissions given to a Site Collection Administrator.

Table 5-2. *SharePoint Site Collection Administrator Permissions*

Permission	Description
Manage Permissions	Create and change permission levels on the web site and assign permissions to users and groups.
View Web Analytics Data	View reports on web site usage.
Create Subsites	Create subsites such as team sites, Meeting Workspace sites, and Document Workspace sites.
Manage Web Site	Grants the ability to perform all administration tasks for the web site as well as manage content.
Add and Customize Pages	Add, change, or delete HTML pages or Web Part Pages, and edit the web site using a Microsoft SharePoint Foundation-compatible editor.
Manage Lists	Create and delete lists, add or remove columns in a list, and add or remove public views of a list.
Apply Themes and Borders	Apply a theme or borders to the entire web site.
Apply Style Sheets	Apply a style sheet (.CSS file) to the web site.
Override List Behaviors	Discard or check in a document that is checked out to another user, and change or override settings that allow users to read/edit only their own items
Manage Personal Views	Create, change, and delete personal views of lists.
Add/Remove Personal Web Parts	Add or remove personal Web Parts on a Web Part Page.
Update Personal Web Parts	Update Web Parts to display personalized information.
Add Items	Add items to lists and add documents to document libraries.
Edit Items	Edit items in lists, edit documents in document libraries, and customize Web Part Pages in document libraries.
Delete Items	Delete items from a list and documents from a document library.
Create Groups	Create a group of users that can be used anywhere within the site collection.
Browse Directories	Enumerate files and folders in a web site using SharePoint Designer and Web DAV interfaces.
Approve Items	Approve a minor version of a list item or document.
Enumerate Permissions	Enumerate permissions on the web site, list, folder, document, or list item.
Delete Versions	Delete past versions of a list item or document.
Manage Alerts	Manage alerts for all users of the web site.
Edit Personal User Information	Allow a user to change his or her own user information, such as adding a picture.

Building Your SharePoint Structure

Now that you have read a bit about SharePoint planning, including SharePoint definitions, let's build something. This section is designed for people that will be building sites and other structures.

In this section, you are building the Procedures site (one of four sites in your sample small company SharePoint setup) within a site collection with a page, a document library, and in one case a calendar list. Let's assume that you are using the default (initial) site collection, or that the SharePoint Online Administrator has built a site collection for you. You will also assume that the site collection feature of SharePoint Server Publishing Infrastructure has been activated (see the section "SharePoint Admin Center").

You will start by defining a sample set of sites with initial permissions for users for your small company. You will also take a look at site navigation.

Tasks (such as site creation and setting permissions) in this section can be performed by anyone with permissions. Again, Chapter 2 contains information aimed at using the sites that you are creating in this section.

Design Your Site and Security Structure

A way to approach SharePoint configuration is to look at your information and organize it based on user roles: what storage locations do you have and who should be able to do what? For the example in this chapter you have a set of sites and a set of roles. Table 5-3 defines who (which roles) should have what access capability (rights) to the sites (where).

Table 5-3. *SharePoint Sites Company Example*

Roles	Procedures	Operations	Board	Customers
SP_Senior_Team	RW	RW	RW	RW
SP_Management	RW	RW	None	RO
SP_Human_Resources	RW	None	None	RO
SP_Manufacturing	RO	RO	None	RO
SP_Customer_Support	RO	None	None	RW
		Subsite: Turnover; same permissions as Operations		

There are a number of ways to organize your security structure. A common way is to separate access to your sites by organizational role. You might have a group like SP_Senior_Team that is the CEO, COO, CFO, etc. Generally this team will have at least Read access to everything (although perhaps not Edit). We recommend that you prefix your SharePoint Groups with "SP_". As your organization grows, you might end up with groups from the Office 365 Portal or from Active Directory (which might have the prefix SG_). This will help you keep track of how permissions flow (see "SharePoint Permissions and Groups").

In Table 5-3, RW represents Read-Write (SharePoint Contribute) access, RO represents Read Only, and None represents no access. Each site will have its own document library.

For example, people in the group SP_Human_Resources can create, delete, and update documents in the Procedures site, see information in the Customers site, but won't even see the Operations and Board sites. The SP_Senior_Team group has all access to all four sites.

You will implement permissions as discussed in the section "SharePoint Permissions and Groups." It is a good idea to read both sections before you start building a production site. (Try things as you like; it is easy to delete and start over. This falls in the "just get started" category.)

Initial Site Collection: Top-Level Site

Figure 5-3 shows your top-level site. In this case, it is in a new site collection, but it will look similar if you are using the default first site xxxx.sharepoint.com that is created when you first purchase Office 365.

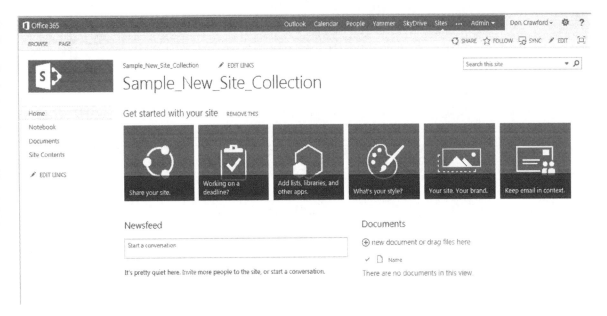

Figure 5-3. *New site collection top-level site*

You will modify this site to add the structure described in Table 5-3.

Gear Icon Options

Let's take a look at the most important icon in SharePoint, the Gear icon. This menu will vary depending upon your permissions. Click the Gear icon at the top right; this will bring up the top level action menu (see Figure 5-4).

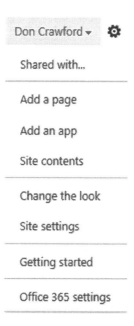

Figure 5-4. *SharePoint Gear icon options*

Site Settings

One of the important functions in the Gear list is site settings (see Figure 5-5). This is a screen of additional links to site-related settings. The list varies based on your permissions and where you are in the structure. For a person with only Read access to a site, this entry does not appear in the Gear list. For a person with Edit permission to the site, the list is reduced.

Sample_New_Site_Collection   Operations   ▾   Procedures

Site Settings

Look and Feel	Site Administration
Import Design Package	Site libraries and lists
Navigation	Content and structure

Figure 5-5. *Site Settings - Edit Permissions*

Even if a link is present, the person may not have permissions to edit the item.

Site Settings: The Subsite List

The site settings for a person with full control viewing a subsite refers to this subsite (see Figure 5-6). There is a link to the site collection-level site settings. Click this link to go to the top-level site collection settings.

Sample_New_Site_Collection   Operations   ▾   Procedures

Site Settings

Users and Permissions	Look and Feel
People and groups	Design Manager
Site permissions	Title, description, and logo
Site app permissions	Device Channels
	Tree view
	Change the look
Web Designer Galleries	Import Design Package
Site columns	Navigation
Site content types	
Master pages	
Composed looks	**Site Actions**
	Manage site features
	Save site as template
Site Administration	Enable search configuration export
Regional settings	Reset to site definition
Language settings	Delete this site
Site libraries and lists	
User alerts	
RSS	**Site Collection Administration**
Sites and workspaces	Go to top level site settings
Workflow settings	
Site Closure and Deletion	
Popularity Trends	
Term store management	
Content and structure	
Content and structure logs	
Translation Status	

Search
Result Sources
Result Types
Query Rules
Schema
Search Settings
Searchable columns
Search and offline availability
Configuration Import
Configuration Export

Figure 5-6. *Site settings: subsite*

Site Settings: The Full List

Figure 5-7 shows the full set of site settings, for the top level site and the site collection. The full list only appears for Site Collection Administrators.

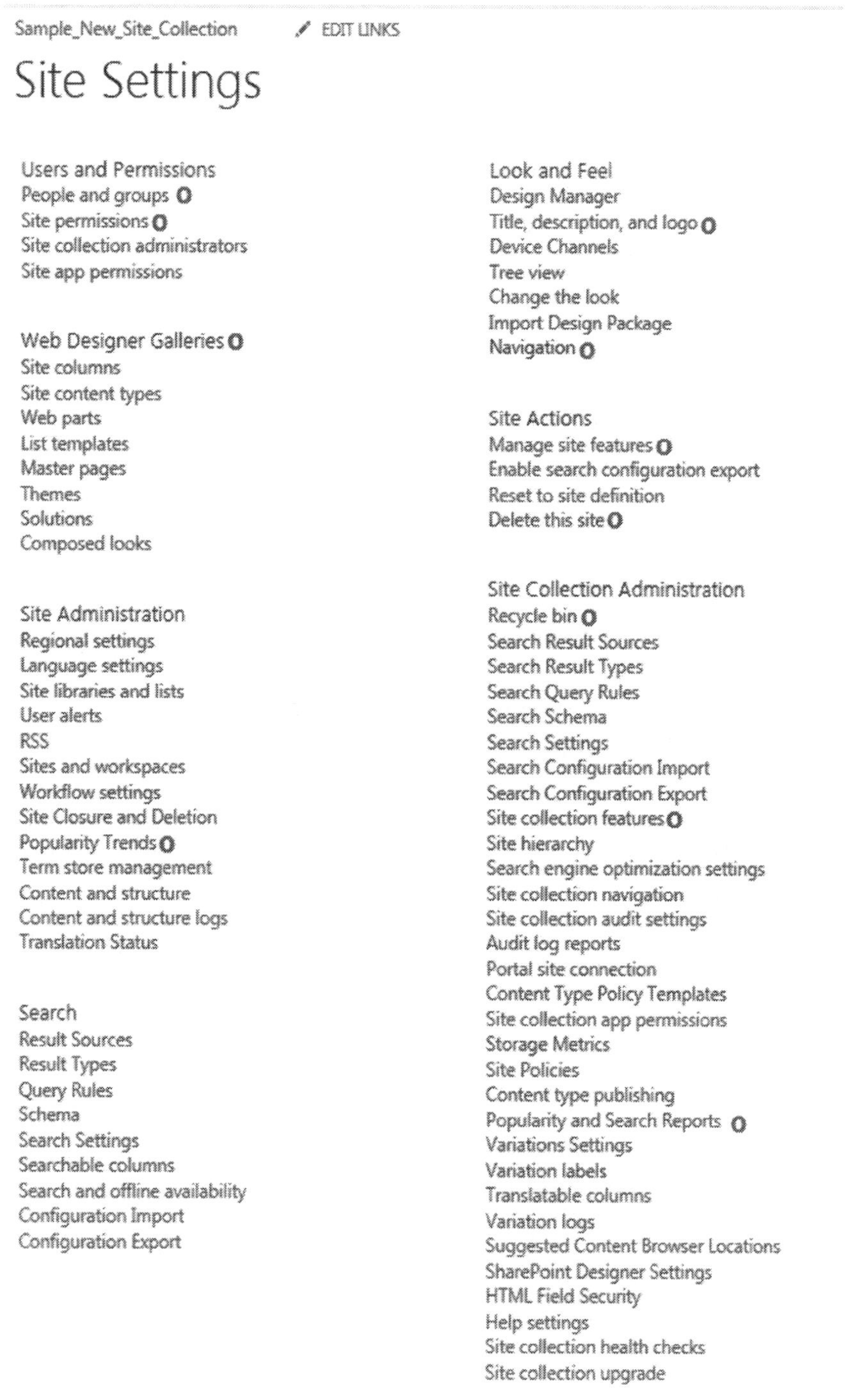

Sample_New_Site_Collection   ✎ EDIT LINKS

Site Settings

Users and Permissions
People and groups ○
Site permissions ○
Site collection administrators
Site app permissions

Web Designer Galleries ○
Site columns
Site content types
Web parts
List templates
Master pages
Themes
Solutions
Composed looks

Site Administration
Regional settings
Language settings
Site libraries and lists
User alerts
RSS
Sites and workspaces
Workflow settings
Site Closure and Deletion
Popularity Trends ○
Term store management
Content and structure
Content and structure logs
Translation Status

Search
Result Sources
Result Types
Query Rules
Schema
Search Settings
Searchable columns
Search and offline availability
Configuration Import
Configuration Export

Look and Feel
Design Manager
Title, description, and logo ○
Device Channels
Tree view
Change the look
Import Design Package
Navigation ○

Site Actions
Manage site features ○
Enable search configuration export
Reset to site definition
Delete this site ○

Site Collection Administration
Recycle bin ○
Search Result Sources
Search Result Types
Search Query Rules
Search Schema
Search Settings
Search Configuration Import
Search Configuration Export
Site collection features ○
Site hierarchy
Search engine optimization settings
Site collection navigation
Site collection audit settings
Audit log reports
Portal site connection
Content Type Policy Templates
Site collection app permissions
Storage Metrics
Site Policies
Content type publishing
Popularity and Search Reports ○
Variations Settings
Variation labels
Translatable columns
Variation logs
Suggested Content Browser Locations
SharePoint Designer Settings
HTML Field Security
Help settings
Site collection health checks
Site collection upgrade

Figure 5-7. *Full site settings*

Some interesting links are marked in Figure 5-7, such as:

- Users and Permissions
  - People and Groups: Manage Groups: This is used in permissions
  - Site Permissions: Manage the site: This is used for permissions
- Web Designer Galleries: More detailed site control links
- Site Administration
  - Popularity Trends: A chart of usage for this site
- Look and Feel
  - Title, description, and logo: Site logo for top left of screen
  - Navigation: Manage Top Links and Quick Links; see below
- Site Actions
  - Manage site features: See the section "SharePoint Admin Center"
  - Delete this site
- Site Collection Administration
  - Recycle bin (for the site collection): Includes documents, folders, etc.
  - Site Collection Features: See the section "SharePoint Admin Center"
  - Popularity and Search Reports: A wide variety of reports

Site Contents

Before you create the Procedures subsite, let's take a look at what is in your new or default site in your site collection. Click the Gear icon at the top right, then Site Contents or the Site Contents link at the left of the screen. You will see the Site Contents page, as shown in Figure 5-8.

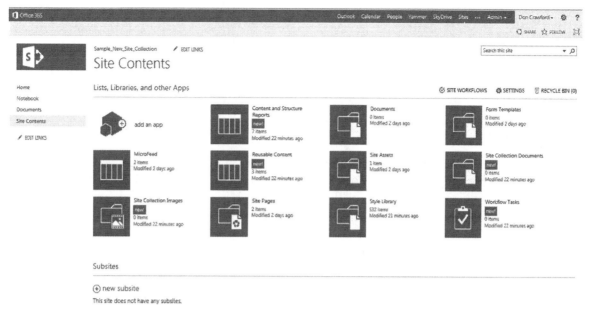

Figure 5-8. *Site contents*

There are a number of interesting things on Site Contents page, including the following:

- Share, Follow and Full Screen: These links are on most every page. Share is a way to share this site (also a way to expand permissions to more people), Follow is connected to Newsfeed and is a way to link something interesting for yourself.

- Search this site.

- Top Link Bar: Not yet filled out.

- Quick Links: Links at the left edge, with an EDIT LINKS option.

- Site Workflows, Settings, and the Site Recycle Bin: See below for Site Settings page description.

- Each blue square item also includes an item count and a modified date/time.

- "add an app": The new-with-SharePoint 2013 model for adding parts to a web page.

- Documents: Created by default for a new team site. This is the default site document library.

- Form Templates, MicroFeed, Site Assets, Site Pages and Style Library: Created by default for a new team site.

- The items marked "new!" in green were created by activating the SharePoint Server Publishing Infrastructure.

- Subsites: A list of subsites and the + icon to create a new subsite. You will use this button.

Create the Site Structure Defined Above

Follow these steps to create the structure defined above. Reference information is interspersed with the steps.

Step 1: Create the Subsite Procedures

Let's create your first subsite. Click the Site Contents option (or the Gear icon and then Site Contents). Click "New subsite" (see Figure 5-9).

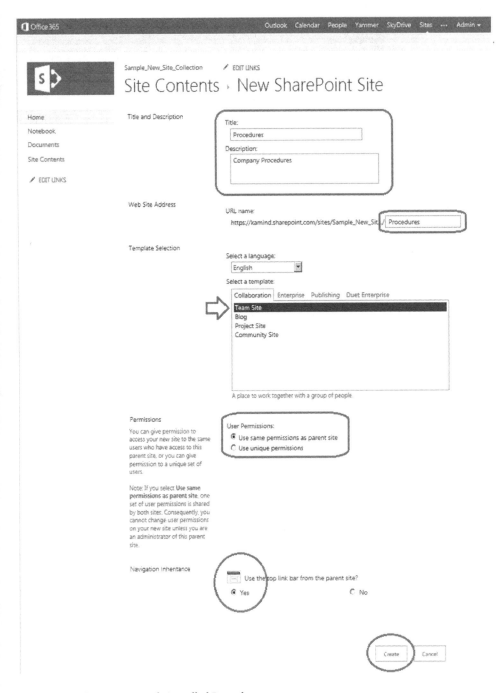

Figure 5-9. *Create a new subsite called Procedures*

You will name this subsite Procedures and give it a description. You will also give the URL name Procedures. Since this web site address is a URL, spaces will be replaced with %20 (hex for the space character). Since this is ugly, it is common to replace the spaces in the title with underscores ("_"). It is possible to change both the title and site URL later.

Pick your language. Template Team Site is fine. The pick "Use same Permissions as Parent" (you will change this in the next section). This is a change from the default: Click Yes for "Use the top link bar from the parent site?" This will, guess what, use the top link bar from the parent site. Unless you are building a very separate site, or you have specific reasons to hide the navigation or create a specialized navigation, it is usually simpler for the user to see the same top link bar on the various pages. This kind of consistency is less likely to confuse your users. (You can change this later if needed.) Click Create.

You will note that the new site does not show up automatically in your top link bar or Quick Links. Let's set navigation to show your new site.

Site Settings: Navigation

Site settings is a rather jumbled list of tasks and settings for this site. At this moment you are going to start by looking at Navigation under Look and Feel to set up the "mother" site to show your new subsite. Navigate to your mother site; in this case it is Sample_New_Site_Collection. Click Gear ➤ Site Settings (Figure 5-10).

Figure 5-10. *Site settings subset*

Click Navigation. This will bring up the Navigation Settings screen for this particular site (see Figure 5-11). As you recall, Navigation only appears as part of Site Collection Features ➤ SharePoint Server Publishing Infrastructure, which was listed as an assumption for this site collection. If there is no Navigation link, check with your Site Collection Administrator.

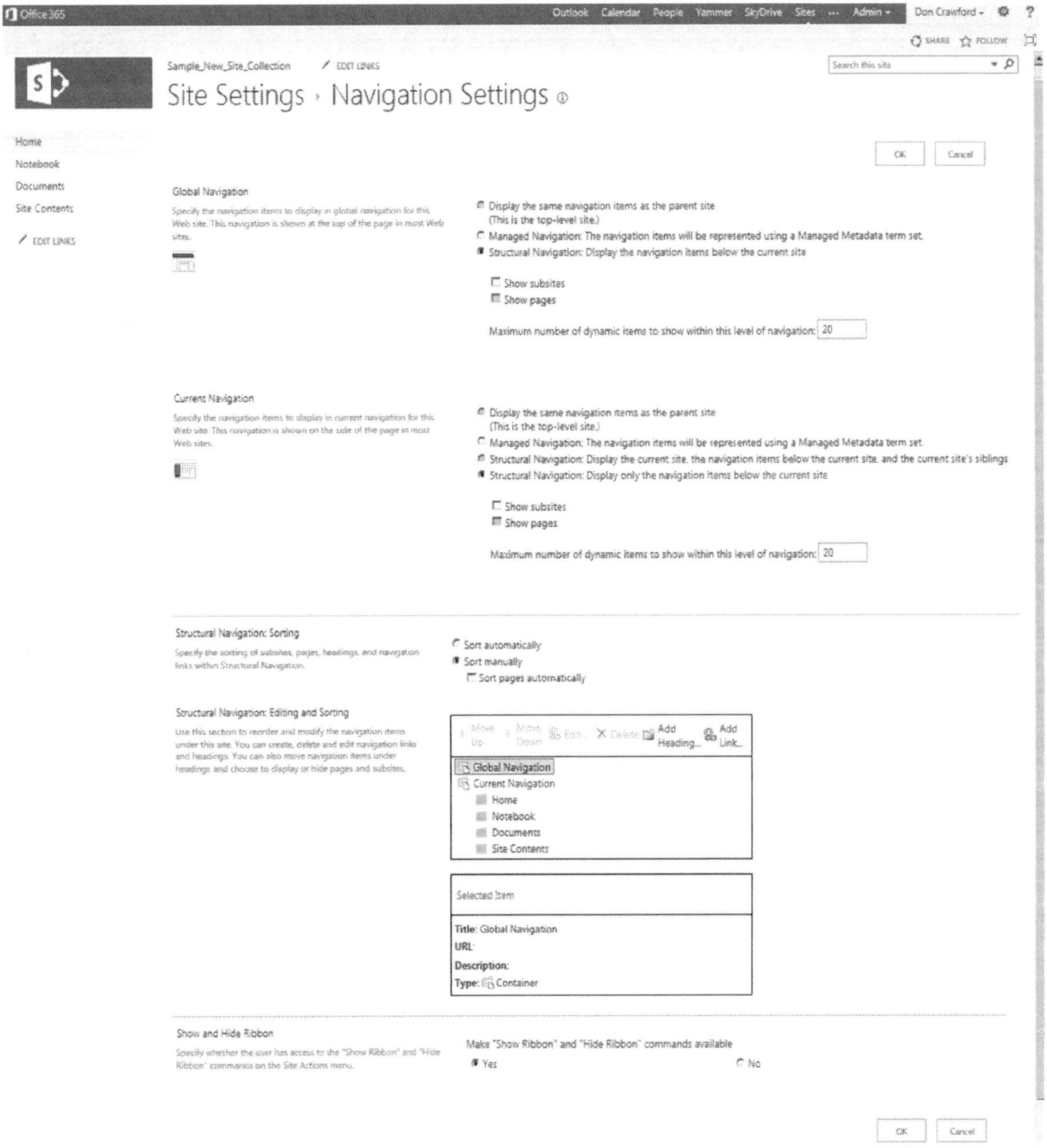

Figure 5-11. *Navigation settings*

■ **Note** It is easy to lose track of which site that you are editing; to see, hover over the Web Browser tab to see exactly what you are editing.

Step 2: Edit Top Level Navigation

Now you will continue to set navigation for your top-level site.

Select your top-level site (Sample_New_Site_Collection) and click Gear ➤ Site Settings ➤ Navigation.

- Under Global Navigation, click "Structural Navigation: Display the navigation items below the current site" and then check the "Show subsites" option.

- Under Current Navigation, click "Structural Navigation: Display only the navigation items below the current site" and then check the "Show subsites" option (see Figure 5-12).

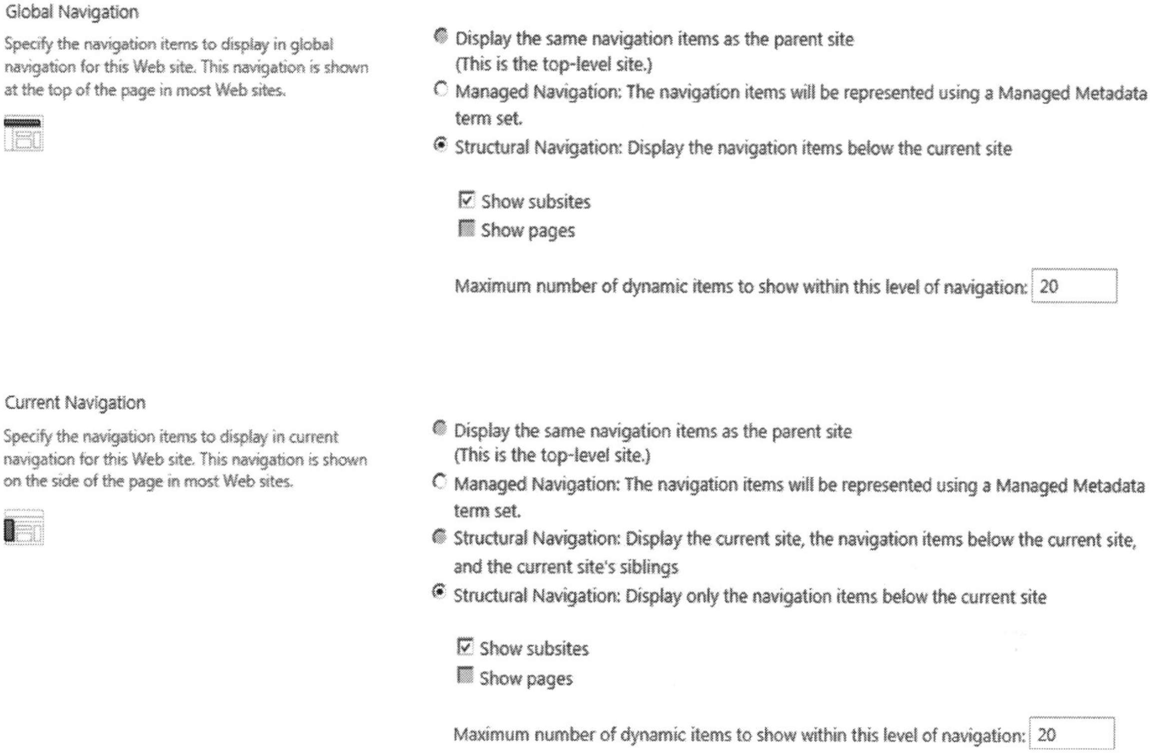

Global Navigation

Specify the navigation items to display in global navigation for this Web site. This navigation is shown at the top of the page in most Web sites.

- ○ Display the same navigation items as the parent site (This is the top-level site.)
- ○ Managed Navigation: The navigation items will be represented using a Managed Metadata term set.
- ● Structural Navigation: Display the navigation items below the current site

  ☑ Show subsites
  ☐ Show pages

  Maximum number of dynamic items to show within this level of navigation: 20

Current Navigation

Specify the navigation items to display in current navigation for this Web site. This navigation is shown on the side of the page in most Web sites.

- ○ Display the same navigation items as the parent site (This is the top-level site.)
- ○ Managed Navigation: The navigation items will be represented using a Managed Metadata term set.
- ● Structural Navigation: Display the current site, the navigation items below the current site, and the current site's siblings
- ● Structural Navigation: Display only the navigation items below the current site

  ☑ Show subsites
  ☐ Show pages

  Maximum number of dynamic items to show within this level of navigation: 20

Figure 5-12. *Top-level site navigation*

Step 3: Edit Subsite Navigation for Procedures

Now you will set navigation for your subsite procedures. Select your new site Procedures and click Gear ➤ Site Settings ➤ Navigation.

- Under Global Navigation, click "Display the same navigation items as the parent site" should be set (from the Site Creation screen)" and check the "Show subsites" option.

- Under Current Navigation, click "Structural Navigation: Display the current site, the navigation items below the current site, and the current site's siblings" and then check the "Show subsites" option (see Figure 5-13).

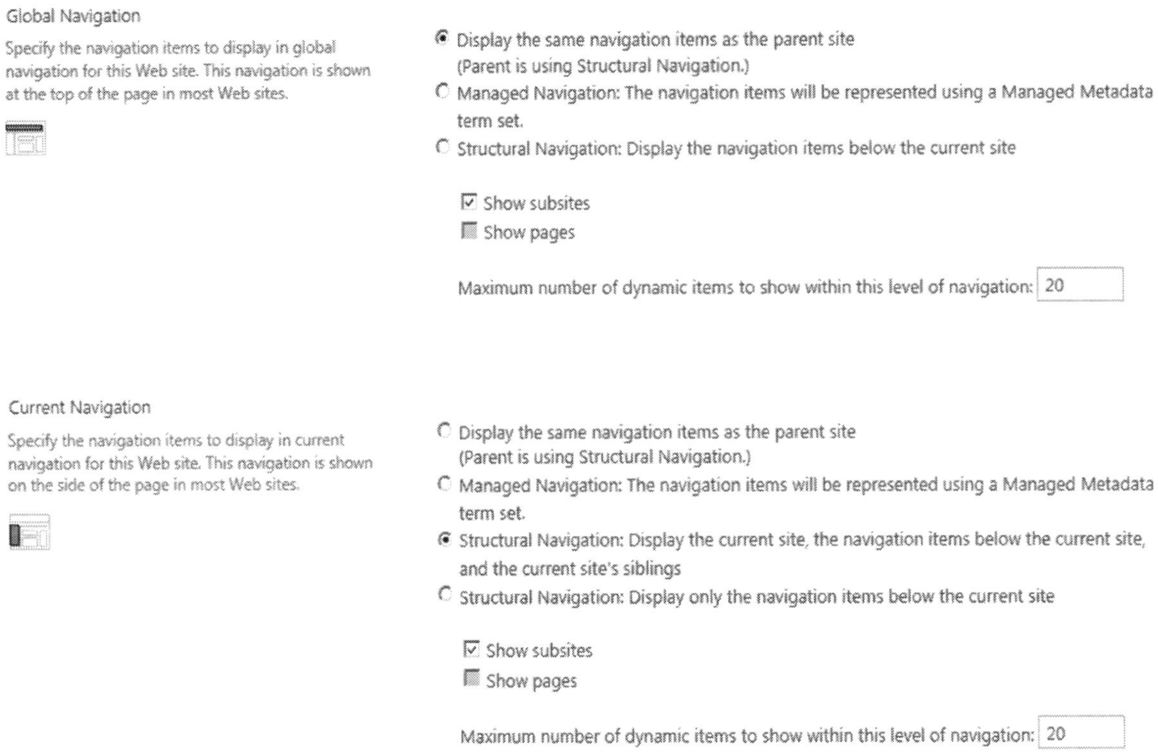

Global Navigation

Specify the navigation items to display in global navigation for this Web site. This navigation is shown at the top of the page in most Web sites.

◉ Display the same navigation items as the parent site
(Parent is using Structural Navigation.)

○ Managed Navigation: The navigation items will be represented using a Managed Metadata term set.

○ Structural Navigation: Display the navigation items below the current site

☑ Show subsites
☐ Show pages

Maximum number of dynamic items to show within this level of navigation: 20

Current Navigation

Specify the navigation items to display in current navigation for this Web site. This navigation is shown on the side of the page in most Web sites.

○ Display the same navigation items as the parent site
(Parent is using Structural Navigation.)

○ Managed Navigation: The navigation items will be represented using a Managed Metadata term set.

◉ Structural Navigation: Display the current site, the navigation items below the current site, and the current site's siblings

○ Structural Navigation: Display only the navigation items below the current site

☑ Show subsites
☐ Show pages

Maximum number of dynamic items to show within this level of navigation: 20

Figure 5-13. *Next level site navigation*

Step 4: Create the Subsite Operations

Create the subsite operations. To do so, see Step 1, with title and URL operations.

Step 5: Edit Subsite Navigation for Operations

Edit the navigation for the subsite operations by referring to Step 3.

Step 6: Add a Sub-Subsite Turnover

Navigate to Site Operations ➤ Site Contents ➤ New site. See Step 1, with title and URL turnover. This will create a subsite turnover under the subsite operations. You will next adjust the navigation to show Turnover under Operations on the top-level menu.

Step 7: Edit Sub-Subsite Navigation for Operations/Turnover

Edit navigation for sub-subsite operations/turnover. Navigate to Operations ➤ Turnover. See Step 3 to set Navigation options.

Step 8: Verify Your Structure

If all of the steps above have been performed, you should see a top-level web site as shown in Figure 5-14.

Figure 5-14. *Structure verification*

On the top link bar are the two subsites that you have created: Operations and Procedures; they're also shown in the Quick Links at the left. The site Turnover that is a subsite of Operations is indented at the left and as a drop-down under the small triangle at the top (Figure 5-14).

The Board and Customer sites for your company example can be created in the same manner. In the next section, we will discuss permissions and groups, and you'll set permissions for your company example. Later, you will edit the pages and the links.

SharePoint Permissions and Groups

In this section, we are going to cover the basics of creating and using SharePoint permissions. You will continue to work on your example structure: you will set permissions per the company example. You will start with basics about permissions and groups and inheritance, Active Directory and Office 365 Security Groups, SharePoint Groups, and inheritance. Next are sections about setting permissions.

The general flow of this section is that we will introduce concepts and then intermix activities to accomplish a goal. We hope that you, as the reader, will extrapolate a particular action from one of these examples to the problem that you are trying to solve. At least you should see that certain functions and screens exist!

As mentioned above in "Planning, Governance and Initial Setup" it is easiest (and least likely to confuse people in the future) to set unique permissions at Site (or subsite) level (instead of the document library, folder, or document level).

■ **Note** Interactions with SharePoint, including setting permissions, are done through a web browser. This means that you can set Bookmarks/Favorites for both locations (a page or site) and commands (an action). You can also edit the URL to change locations or to open a command for a new site.

Permissions Basics and Groups

Permissions are essentially defined for each individual login. The effective permissions for an individual account are the least restrictive of any permissions that an individual has for a site, page, document library, list, folder, document, etc. This means that you should consider how to test the permissions that you assign.

It is too cumbersome to assign more than one or two individuals to all of the proper items that they should have access to, so the answer is groups. There are several types of groups available to set SharePoint permissions. These include the following:

- Without DirSync: Office 365 security groups created in the Office 365 Portal

- With DirSync: These groups appear in the Office 365 Portal as groups, but cannot be edited in Office 365.

  - Active Directory security groups

  - Active Directory mail-enabled security groups

  - Active Directory distribution groups are NOT eligible to be used.

- SharePoint groups

For discussion about creating and maintaining Office 365 security groups and Active Directory synchronization, please see Chapters 8 and 11.

There are tradeoffs between using Office 365/AD security groups and SharePoint groups. The differences between the types of groups are explained below.

- Office 365/Active Directory Synchronized Security Groups:

  - Generally more closely tied to business processes such as adding and changing user accounts (logins); the account management people that deal with logins can add or change their group membership at the same time in the same place.

  - For Active Directory (DirSync'ed) groups the same security information is consistent across the whole organization.

  - An Active Directory security group can contain a security group.

  - CANNOT contain externally shared user logins; see the section "Planning, Governance and Initial Setup" item "External Sharing."

  - You cannot see the members of an Office 365/Active Directory group from within SharePoint (without using PowerShell). That is, if an Office 365/Active Directory group is a member of a SharePoint group, you cannot see the members when viewing through People and Groups. (Check if permissions are still accurate.)

- SharePoint Groups:

  - More closely tied to SharePoint operation (part of SharePoint); the contents of Office 365/AD groups are synchronized with a slight time delay.

  - Editing of permissions can be done entirely by local SharePoint site owners without editing Office 365 Portal security groups or Active Directory.

  - Can contain externally shared userids (see the section "Planning, Governance and Initial Setup").

  - Can contain Office 365, AD security groups, and AD mail-enabled security groups.

  - A SharePoint group cannot contain another SharePoint group.

There are no out-of-the-box SharePoint tools to review permissions. (There are outside vendors that supply such tools.)

The closest things to reports are:

- Site Settings/People and Groups (see SharePoint "People and Groups" Tasks/ Settings: View Group Permissions")

- Check Permissions (one person at a time)

It is important to plan and document your permissions structure!

With SharePoint 2013 there are SharePoint groups that are automatically created, specifically Owners, Members, and Visitors Groups for each site collection that is created, and for each site (or other entity) that has permission inheritance removed. This can help you keep track of where to place users needing permissions.

Permissions Inheritance

In SharePoint, permissions are inherited from the parent site. This is normally what you want. For your company example, the various sites have different permissions needs. You will "break inheritance" to meet these needs.

■ **Note**   It is easy to lose track of where you are setting permissions. To see this, hover over the Web Browser tab, or check the URL to see exactly where you are editing.

The Two Sides of Permissions: Sites and Groups

Permissions are set as the combination of:

- Sites (where)

- Groups, which contain people (who)

- What can be done (Read, Edit, etc.)

The two different screens that deal with the two sides are summarized in Table 5-4.

Table 5-4. *SharePoint Permissions: Sites and Groups Summary*

Title	Site Permissions	People and Groups
Section Title	Permissions: Site Settings	Permissions: People and Groups
Gear, Site Settings Link	Site Settings/Site Permissions	Site Settings/People and Groups
Screen Figure	Figure 5-16	Figure 5-25
Refers to	Specific site	Entire site collection
Special Actions	<ul><li>Create Group</li><li>Check Permissions (for a person at this site via which groups)</li><li>Change Permissions for an existing Group (see Icon 4, Edit User Permissions for Existing Group)</li></ul>	<ul><li>New Group (same as Create Group)</li><li>Settings ➤ View Group Permissions (sites for which this group has what level of permissions)</li><li>Change Group Settings (such as Name and Group Owner, other than Permissions levels)</li></ul>

(continued)

Table 5-4. (*continued*)

Title	Site Permissions	People and Groups
URL Suffix (add to a site URL)	_layouts/15/start.aspx#/_layouts/15/user.aspx	_layouts/15/start.aspx#/_layouts/15/groups.aspx, _layouts/15/start.aspx#/_layouts/15/people.aspx
All people in site collection URL		_layouts/15/start.aspx#/_layouts/15/people.aspx?MembershipGroupId=0

Permissions: Site Permissions

This section describes the key steps to set permissions for a site (for other entities see "Set document library Permissions" and "Set a Document's Permissions" below). Permissions are set for a site by:

- Adding users to new or existing SharePoint groups associated with the site.

- Adding Office 365 Portal/AD groups to new or existing SharePoint groups associated with the site.

- Adding users directly to the site permissions (not recommended).

To set permissions, follow these steps:

1. Navigate to the site.

2. Click Gear ➤ Site Settings.

3. Click Site Permissions (see Figure 5-15).

Figure 5-15. *Site Settings ➤ Site Permissions*

4. See the Site Permissions screen (Figure 5-16).

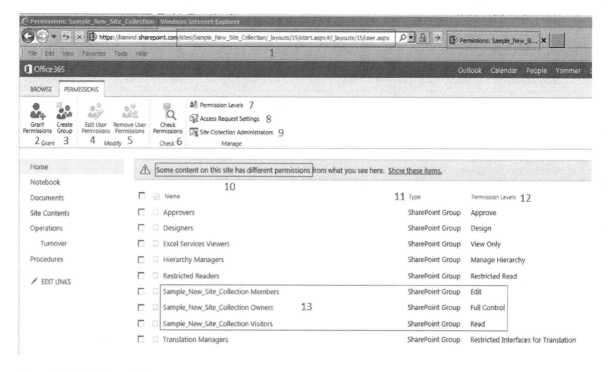

Figure 5-16. *Site Permissions screen*

5. Perform one of the sets of Permissions Actions described below, based on your needs.

Click "Site permissions" for the next screen (Figure 5-16).

The Site Permission screen is a main control point for setting permissions. There is a similar screen for document libraries, folders, documents, etc. Note that this screen is slightly different if the site inherits permissions from its parent: item 2 will say "Manage Parent" (to go to where the permissions are set) and items 7, 8, 9, and 10 do not appear.

The following is a description of Permissions Screen by number.

1. "Where you are" information: In the title bar, the URL and the tab itself ("Permissions: Sample...") and if you hover over the tab. It is very easy to be in the wrong place. It is always a good idea to glance up to see where you are.

2. Icon Grant Permissions: Add permissions for a user or group to this list (add permissions to "where you are").

3. Icon Create Group: You can create a SharePoint group.

4. Icon Edit User Permissions.

5. Icon Remove User Permissions.

6. Icon Check Permissions.

7. Link Manage: Permission Levels.

8. Link Manage: Access Request Settings.

9. Link Manage: Site Collection Administrators.

10. Link "Some content on this site has different permissions": This warning is generally because of SharePoint structure (see Figure 5-17).

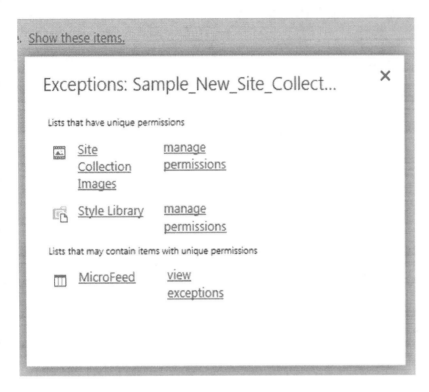

Figure 5-17. *Permissions screen for different permissions*

11. Type: SharePoint Group, User, Domain Group

12. Permission Levels: Edit, Full Control, Read are normally used.

13. Automatic SharePoint Groups: Members (Edit), Owners (Full Control) and Visitors (Read) for the (top level) Site Sample_New_Site_Collection were created when the site was created.

■ **Note**   Click the hyperlink that is the name of a group to get to the permissions: People and Groups screen for that group. Also, click "Browse" to see the top link bar again.

Icon 2: Grant Permissions

This is the core activity of permissions: to give someone or some group access. In general, you will add an individual to a group on this page (such as one of the groups highlighted in Item 13 in Figure 5-16). You can also add a user or SharePoint Group or Office 365 group with a specific permission level directly to this list. This is an example of power and confusion. It is best for you to pick a mechanism, document it, and use it consistently. Here are your choices:

1. Add the user or group to an existing "standard" group (those ending in Members, Owners, and Visitors). These SharePoint groups have predefined permission levels (Edit, Full Control, and Read, respectively) and are automatically created when the Site is created (or optionally when inheritance is broken; see "Breaking Inheritance" below).

2. Use Office 365 Portal/Active Directory Groups. Add them directly to the list with the appropriate permission level.

3. Use the SharePoint groups that you have created. Add them directly to the list with the appropriate permission level.

4. Add individual users directly to this list. Someone will hate you for this in the future. Because there is no easy permissions cross reference, someone will have to check each site to see where someone has permissions.

There is a new "sharing" mechanism that sets permissions. Share shows up as a user-level function. See Chapter 2 and also the "Set Document Library Permissions" section below.

Icon 3: Create Group

You can create a SharePoint group on a Site Settings screen or a People and Groups screen. The groups are global to the site collection. That is, once created, they can be used anywhere within the site collection. You don't create a group just for this site, but for all sites in the site collection.

To create a group from a Site Settings screen, follow these steps:

1. Navigate to a site in the proper site collection.

2. Click Gear ➤ Site Settings.

3. Click Site Permissions (see Figure 5-18).

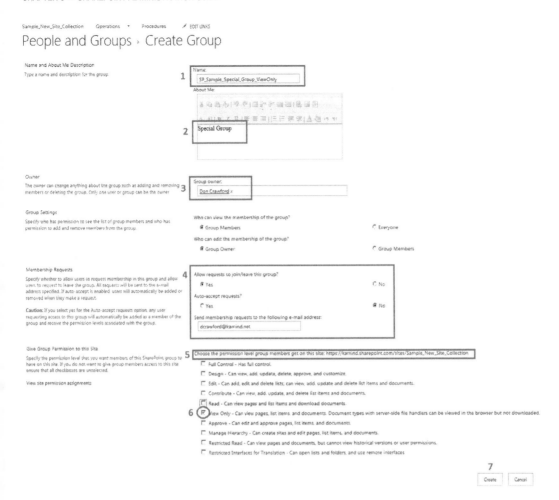

Figure 5-18. *Permissions Ribbon Create Group*

4. Click the Create Group icon.

5. On the next screen, fill in the fields as described.

6. Click Create.

To create group notes, follow these steps.

1. Give your new group a name. It is a good convention to start SharePoint groups with "SP_". You will appreciate this when you have an environment of mixed SharePoint and Office 365/AD security groups. It helps to know where to look to edit the members. Good luck on getting the editors of the other groups to adopt a standard! (Usually these things have been going on for years and there have been several different people that have an idea of the correct standard.) Underscores are not important here, but you might want to be consistent; either use them or not. The auto-generated group names will have a space before "Members" and such.

2. Document this group's usage.

3. The group owner defaults to the creator.

4. Do you want to allow requests to join/leave the group? Generally you want to know if you have left someone out (or a new person has joined the firm but has not been added to all of the proper groups). This sends an e-mail to you (or whoever you designate) saying that this person would like access. They can give you a reason. Generally you don't want auto-accept, except perhaps for a company calendar or some such.

5. Since groups are created in a site collection, this item tells you the site collection in which you are creating the group.

6. Select the permission level(s). We selected "View Only" in this case. These values can be changed; see "Icon 4: Edit User Permissions for Existing Group." Some selections are redundant. These permissions belong to the group; when you add a group to a site, the members of this group will have these permissions at that site. Having unique permissions on the site does not affect this relationship.

7. Click Create.

Icon 4: Edit User Permissions for Existing Group

Since you have a nice list of groups, the SharePoint designers decided to put "Edit the Permissions of an existing group" here; see Figure 5-19. (This function is in Site Permissions rather than People and Groups.)

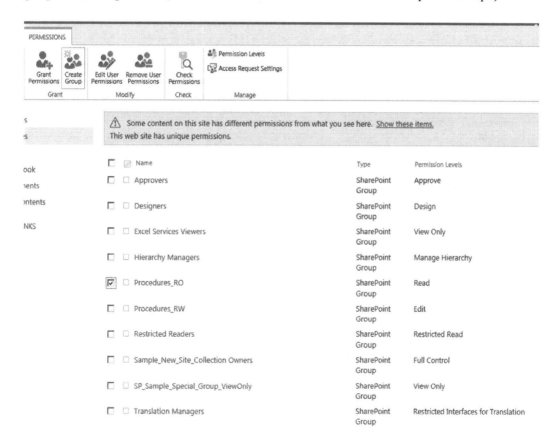

Figure 5-19. *Edit permissions level for existing group*

To change the permissions for an existing group, follow these steps:

1. Navigate to a site that uses the group.

2. Click Gear ➤ Site Settings.

3. Click Site Permissions (see Figure 5-19).

4. Select the group by marking the checkbox to the left.

5. Click the Edit User Permissions icon.

6. On the next screen, check and uncheck permissions as you desire (see Figure 5-20).

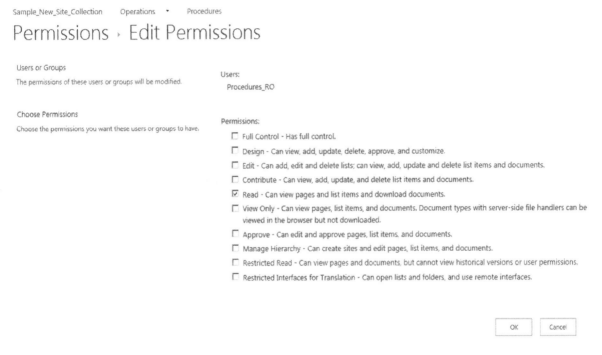

Figure 5-20. *Set group permissions*

7. Click OK.

Icon 5: Remove User Permissions

You can remove permissions for one or more users or groups by following these steps.

1. Navigate to the site (or item) from which you wish to remove permissions.

2. Click Gear ➤ Site Settings.

3. Click Site Permissions.

4. Verify that you are in the right place!

5. Mark the items (see Figure 5-21).

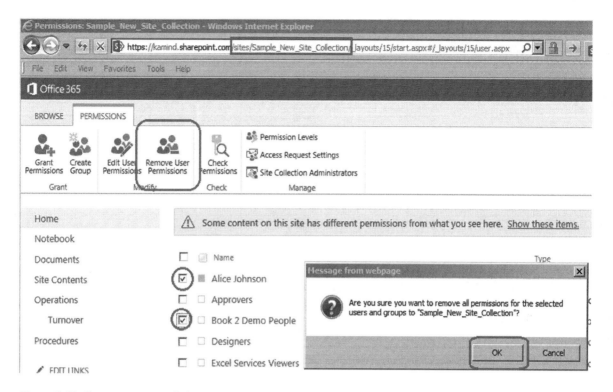

Figure 5-21. *Remove user permissions*

6. Click the Remove User Permissions icon.

7. Click OK on the warning message.

Icon 6: Check Permissions

Check permissions for a person at this site. See "Check Company Permissions" below for a usage example.

Link 7: Manage Permission Levels

This link documents the particular permission levels. Clicking a link at left shows the exact details.

Link 8: Manage Access Request Settings

Figure 5-22 shows the way to set the e-mail address that will receive requests to access this site.

Figure 5-22. *Manage Access Request Settings*

Link 9: Manage Site Collection Administrators

This is another way to be able to edit the list of Site Collection Administrators. This link only appears when you are on the top site of a site collection and you are a Site Collection Administrator (Figure 5-23).

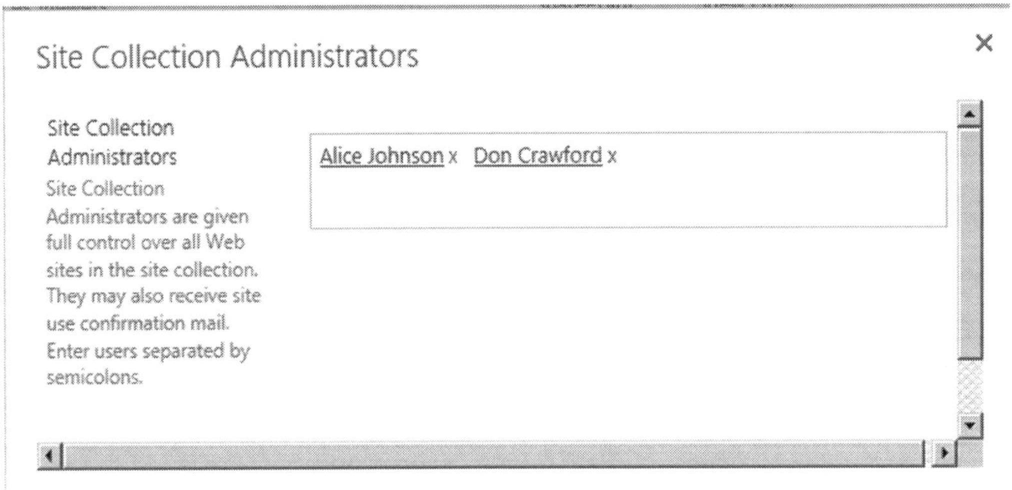

Figure 5-23. *Edit Site Collection Administrators*

Permissions: People and Groups

The People and Groups screen describe access to the SharePoint groups for a particular site collection (Figure 5-24).

Sample_New_Site_Collection   ✎ EDIT LINKS

Site Settings

Home

Notebook

Documents

Site Contents

✎ EDIT LINKS

Users and Permissions
People and groups
Site permissions
Site collection administrators
Site app permissions

Web Designer Galleries
Site columns

Look and Feel
Design Manager
Title, description, and logo
Device Channels
Tree view
Change the look
Import Design Package
Navigation

Figure 5-24. *Site Settings ➤ People and Groups*

Click "People and groups" for the next screen (Figure 5-25).

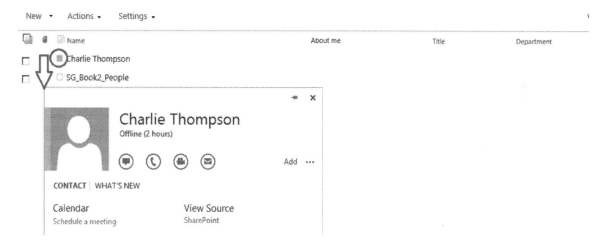

Sample_New_Site_Collection   Operations ▾   Procedures

People and Groups › Sample_New_Site_Collection Members ⓘ

New ▾   Actions ▾   Settings ▾

☐ 📎 ☐ Name   About me   Title   Department

☐   ☐ Charlie Thompson

☐   ☐ SG_Book2_People

Charlie Thompson
Offline (2 hours)

CONTACT | WHAT'S NEW

Calendar   View Source
Schedule a meeting   SharePoint

Figure 5-25. *Permissions: People and Groups*

A nice feature of the People and Groups/specific group screen (Figure 5-26) is that if you hover over the small presence indicator (by the name) a floating menu with a link for a contact card appears.

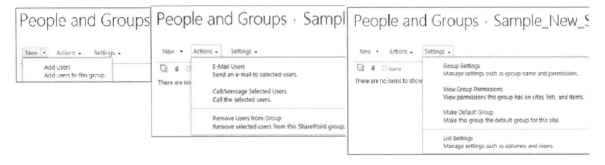

Figure 5-26. *SharePoint People and Groups menus*

To perform "People and Groups" tasks, follow these steps:

1. Navigate to any site in the appropriate site collection.

2. Click Gear ➤ Site Settings.

3. Click "People and Groups" (see Figure 5-24).

4. If you do not select a specific group, you have these tasks (or select "Groups" at the top left):

   a. New ➤ New Group ➤ Create a New SharePoint Group: This is the same as Icon 3: Create Group (see Figure 5-18).

   b. Settings ➤ Edit Group Quick Launch: Edit list of groups that appear at the left edge.

   c. You can edit many things about a group (except the permissions) with the small Edit icon in the Edit column. (To edit an existing group's permissions, see "Icon 4: Edit User Permissions for Existing Group").

5. If you wish to work with a specific group, at the left edge, click a group (click More to see more groups). Once you have selected a group you have a choice of several tasks.

   a. New: Add Users (to this group).

   b. Actions: E-Mail Users.

   c. Actions: Call/Message Selected Users (Lync Message/Call).

   d. Actions: Remove Users from Group.

   e. Actions: Leave Group (remove yourself from the group).

   f. Settings: Group Settings (manage settings such as group name and permissions).

   g. Settings: View Group Permissions (view permissions this group has on sites, lists, and items).

   h. Settings: Make Default Group (make this group the default group for this site).

   i. Settings: List Settings (manage settings such as columns and views).

Next are the descriptions of these tasks.

New: Add Users

This task adds a person (user), or an Office 365/Active Directory security group to the selected SharePoint group. The new person or group will have immediate permissions wherever this group is used.

To add a User or Office 365/Active Directory security group, follow these steps:

1. Select the group.

2. Click New ➤ Add Users (the only choice).

3. In the menu box, verify that you are in the group that you intended. Note that the title is "Share ...". In this case you are adding a user, but the effect is that the new user will have access to wherever the group is used. (See "Settings: View Group Permissions" below.)

4. Enter names, e-mail addresses, or "Everyone" into the box. As you start typing a name or e-mail address, the system looks for matches. Select a name from the drop-down list. Type the next name.

5. Click SHOW OPTIONS; if you wish to send e-mail to the new members leave the "Send an e-mail invitation" box checked.

6. Enter a custom message if you wish.

7. Click Share (see Figure 5-27).

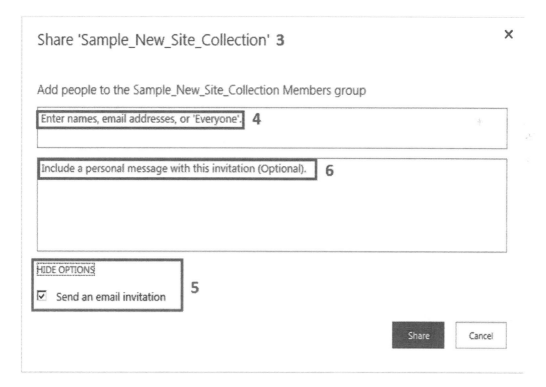

Figure 5-27. *Add users to a group/share a site*

Actions: E-Mail Users

Open an Outlook window to build an e-mail to the names that you select.

Actions: Call/Message Selected Users

Open a Lync communication with the names that you select.

Actions: Remove Users from Group

Remove the names you select from the Group.

Settings: Group Settings

Change this group's settings including name, About Me, group owner, etc. You might wish to set an e-mail address if you wish to accept member ship requests to the group (see Figure 5-28).

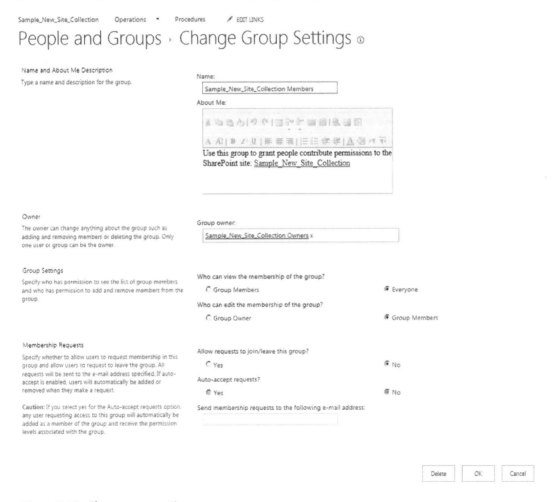

Figure 5-28. *Change group settings*

Settings: View Group Permissions

This People and Groups ➤ Settings: View Group Permissions option is a hidden gem (see Figure 5-29).

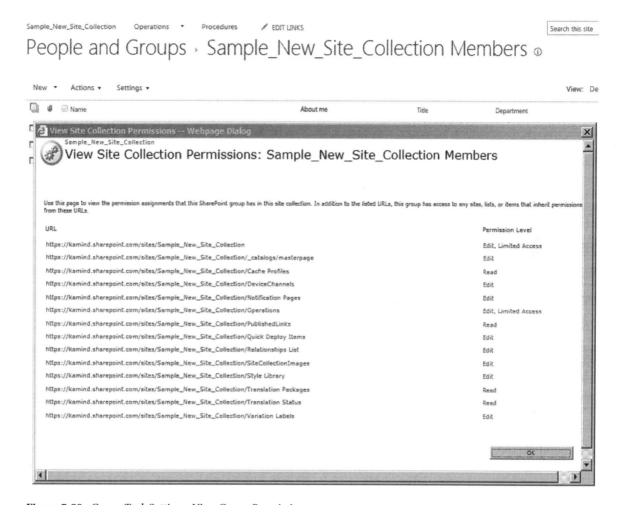

Figure 5-29. Group Task Settings: View Group Permissions

Note the note: "Use this page to view the permission assignments that this SharePoint group has in this site collection. In addition to the listed URLs, this group has access to any sites, lists, or items that inherit permissions from these URLs."

The resulting web page dialog box shows the name of the group and each URL (site) to which the group has been assigned and the permission level. (The second part of the note is a warning that all subsites that inherit from these sites also have the same permissions.)

The URLs are hyperlinks to the sites. Click OK to exit.

Settings: Make Default Group

Click to make this group the default group.

Settings: List Settings

Set the settings for the User Information List (Figure 5-30).

Sample_New_Site_Collection   Operations ▾   Procedures   ✎ EDIT LINKS

User Information List › Settings

List Information

Name: User Information List
Web Address: https://kamind.sharepoint.com/sites/Sample_New_Site_Collection/_layouts/15/people.aspx
Description: All people.

General Settings	Permissions and Management	Communications
▫ List name, description and navigation	▫ Permissions for this list	▫ RSS settings
▫ Advanced settings	▫ Workflow Settings	
▫ Validation settings	▫ Generate file plan report	
▫ Audience targeting settings	▫ Enterprise Metadata and Keywords Settings	
▫ Rating settings	▫ Information management policy settings	
▫ Form settings		

Columns

A column stores information about each item in the list. The following columns are currently available in this list:

Column (click to edit)	Type	Required
Modified	Date and Time	
Created	Date and Time	
Created By	Person or Group	
Modified By	Person or Group	

▫ Create column
▫ Add from existing site columns
▫ Column ordering
▫ Indexed columns

Views

A view of a list allows you to see a particular selection of items or to see the items sorted in a particular order. Views currently configured for this list:

View (click to edit)	Default View	Mobile View	Default Mobile View
Detail View	✓		
List View			

▫ Create view

Figure 5-30. *User Information List* ➤ *Settings*

Set Top Level Permissions to Read Only

When a site collection is created, no one is given permission, but default SharePoint groups are created. You will add Read Only for all users to allow everyone to see the top-level site. This will allow a safe landing space for users that click Team Site. This permission will be inherited for subsites (unless they have unique permissions).

Here you will set the default permission to Read. With Read, users can view pages and list items and download documents. Follow these steps.

1. Navigate to the top level site, such as Sample_New_Site_Collection.

2. Click Gear ➤ Site Settings.

3. Click Site Permissions (see Figure 5-15).

4. Click Sample_New_Site_Collection Visitors or your Visitors group (see Figure 5-16, item 13).

5. Type "every" into the "Add people" box; pick one of the Everyone options depending upon your needs.

6. Click SHOW OPTIONS; you probably want to turn off "Send an e-mail to everyone."

7. Click Share. This will add everyone to the group Visitors with permissions Read.

8. Check Permissions (see Figure 5-31).

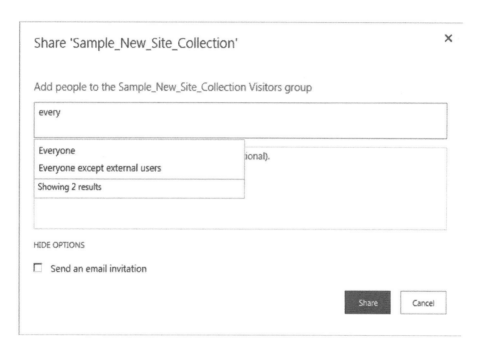

Figure 5-31. *Set top-level permissions to Read Only*

Set Document Library Permissions

We recommended above to use sites as your basic level of special permissions. In this method, the document libraries within a site would inherit these special permissions. In some cases it is appropriate to set unique permissions for a document library. You will use the document library that is part of the top level site as an sample.

To set unique permissions for a document library, follow these steps:

1. Navigate to the site.

2. Click the title part of the documents (Figure 5-32).

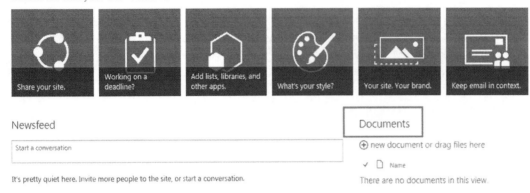

Figure 5-32. *Set unique document library permissions part 1*

3. Click Library on the Ribbon bar to open the Library ribbon (Figure 5-33).

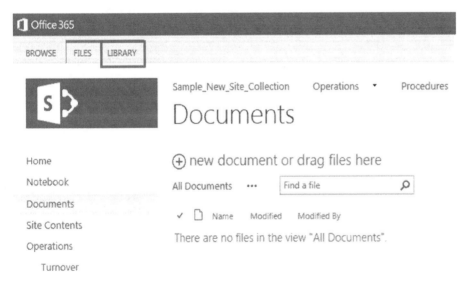

Figure 5-33. *Set unique document library permissions part 2*

4. Click Library Settings on the open Library ribbon to show options (Figure 5-34).

Figure 5-34. *Set unique document library permissions part 3*

5. In Documents ➤ Settings, click "Permissions for this document library" (Figure 5-35).

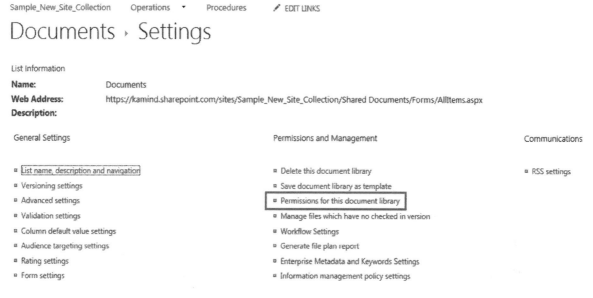

Figure 5-35. *Set unique document library permissions part 4*

6. Click "Stop Inheriting Permissions" (Figure 5-36).

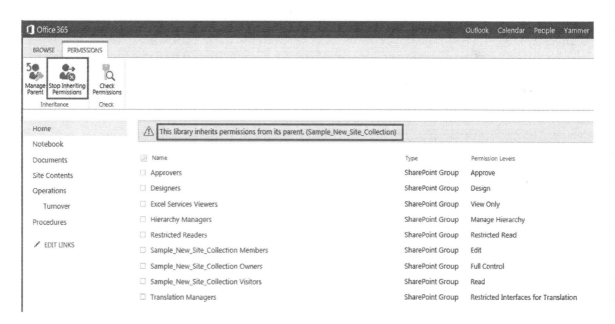

Figure 5-36. *Set unique document library permissions part 5*

7.   Accept the message (Figure 5-37).

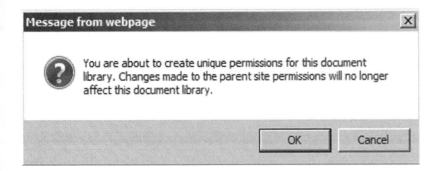

Figure 5-37. *Set unique document library permissions part 6*

8.   Delete any extra SharePoint groups; add any required groups (grant permissions); undo unique permissions by clicking "Delete unique permissions" (Figure 5-38).

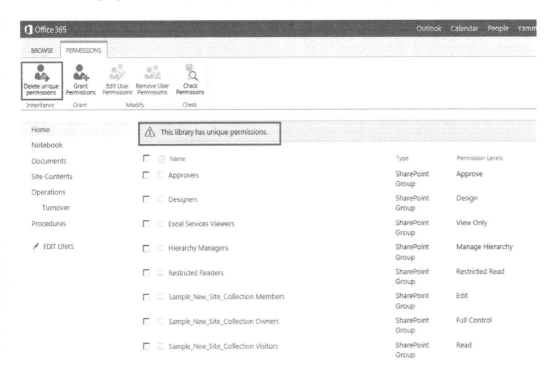

Figure 5-38. *Set unique document library permissions part 7*

As you can see, there are quite a few steps.

It is important, if you use unique permissions for a document library, that you recognize that Site Settings ➤ Site Permissions work on the SITE, not the document library that you are looking at when you click the Gear icon. You must use most of the steps above to change permissions for a document library.

Click "Documents" to open the next screen.

Click LIBRARY to open the ribbon (Figure 5-34).

Click "Library Settings" to open the next screen.

Click "Permissions for this document library" to open the next screen (Figure 5-36).
Click "Stop Inheriting Permissions." You will have the message box in Figure 5-37.
Click OK to accept the warning and to open the next screen (Figure 5-38).

Set a Document's Permissions

We recommended above to use sites as your basic level of special permissions. In this method, the documents within libraries within a site would inherit these special permissions. In some cases, it is appropriate to set unique permissions for a document. You will use the document that is part of the document library of the site Operations/Turnover as an example.

To set unique permissions for a document, follow these steps:

1. Navigate to the document.

2. Click the "..." beside the document (Figure 5-39).

Figure 5-39. Set unique document permissions part 1

3. A preview of the document shows. Click the "..." at the bottom of the pop-up (Figure 5-40).

Figure 5-40. Set unique document permissions part 2

4. Click "Shared with" (Figure 5-41).

Figure 5-41. *Set unique document permissions part 3*

5. Click ADVANCED (Figure 5-42).

Shared With   ✕

Alice Johnson

Don Crawford
Partner

Everyone

INVITE PEOPLE   EMAIL EVERYONE   ADVANCED

Close

Figure 5-42. *Set unique document permissions part 4*

> 6. Click "Stop Inheriting Permissions" (Figure 5-43).

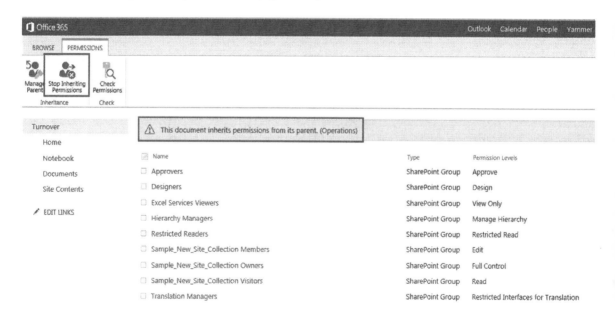

Figure 5-43. *Set unique document permissions part 5*

7.   Accept the message.

8.   Delete any extra SharePoint groups; add any required groups (grant permissions); undo
     unique permissions by clicking "Delete unique permissions" (Figure 5-43).

As you can see, there are quite a few steps.

It is important, if you use unique permissions for a document (or folder), that you recognize that Site Settings ➤
Site Permissions work on the SITE, not the document or document library that you are looking at when you click the
Gear icon. You must use most of the steps above to change permissions for a document (or folder).

Click the ellipses to open the next screen.

Click the ellipses to open the next screen.

Click "Shared With" to open the next screen (Figure 5-42).

Click "ADVANCED" to open the next screen (Figure 5-43).

Click "Stop Inheriting Permissions" to stop using the permissions of the parent for this document.

Setting Permissions for Your Company Example

We discussed your objectives for this simple company site with specialized permissions above. You are now ready
to set the permissions for the sites that you created above. Here are your permissions objectives from Table 5-3
(reproduced here as Table 5-5).

Table 5-5. *SharePoint Sites Company Example*

Roles	Procedures	Operations	Board	Customers
		Sites		
SP_Senior_Team	RW	RW	RW	RW
SP_Management	RW	RW	None	RO
SP_Human_Resources	RW	None	None	RO
SP_Manufacturing	RO	RO	None	RO
SP_Customer_Support	RO	None	None	RW
		Subsite: Turnover; same permissions as Operations		

To implement the permissions designed above, for each site you will:

•   Navigate to the site.

•   Select Gear ➤ Site Settings ➤ Site Permissions.

•   Click "Stop Inheriting Permissions" (see Figure 5-44).

Figure 5-44. *Stop inheriting permissions*

- This will automatically create new SharePoint groups (see Figure 5-46).

- Fill the new groups with the Roles SP_ groups from Table 5-5.

Stop Inheriting Permissions

As discussed above, a site or library by default inherits permissions from its parent. In this security model, you stop inheriting permissions to be able to cleanly start over with specific security groups that have Read Only or Read/Write permission. This model makes it simple to add new users to the correct groups, and minimizes incorrect permission risks.

To stop inheriting permissions, follow these steps:

1. Navigate to the site.

2. Click Gear ➤ Site Settings ➤ Site Permissions.

3. Note the warning that "This library inherits permissions from its parent." Click "Stop Inheriting Permissions" (see Figure 5-44).

4. Click OK to accept the warning (Figure 5-45).

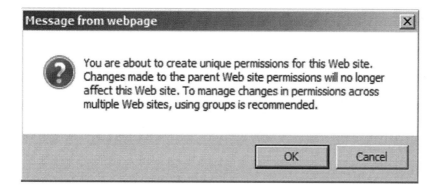

Figure 5-45. *Accept unique permissions*

5. SharePoint automatically gives you the chance to make new groups for your newly un-inheriting site! It wants to build three types of groups: [*name*] Visitors for people that will have Read Only, [*name*] Members for Read-Write access, and [*name*] Owners that have full control, including who will have the ability to add more members to these groups (see Figure 5-46).

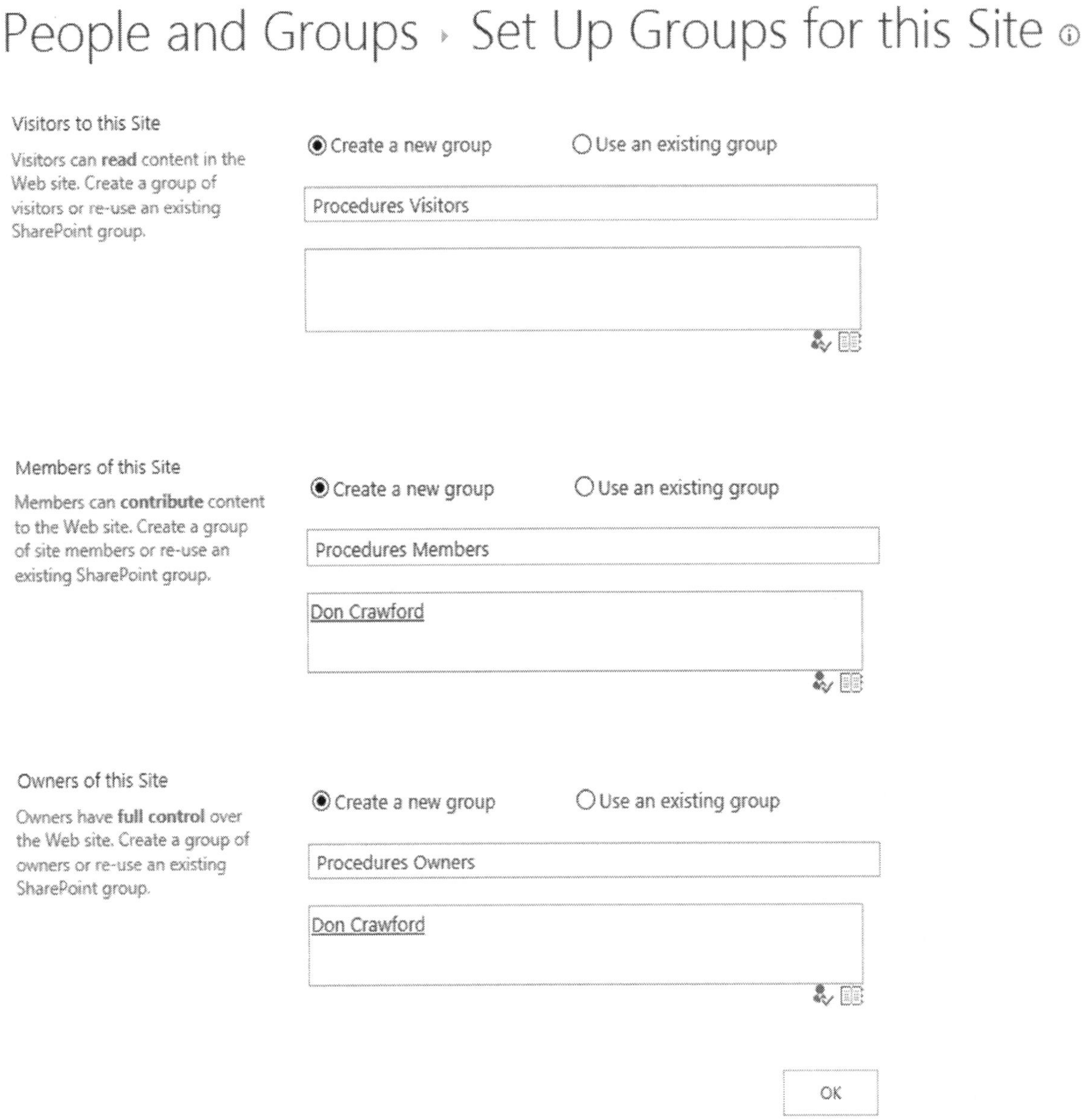

People and Groups › Set Up Groups for this Site ⓘ

Visitors to this Site

Visitors can **read** content in the Web site. Create a group of visitors or re-use an existing SharePoint group.

◉ Create a new group   ○ Use an existing group

Procedures Visitors

Members of this Site

Members can **contribute** content to the Web site. Create a group of site members or re-use an existing SharePoint group.

◉ Create a new group   ○ Use an existing group

Procedures Members

Don Crawford

Owners of this Site

Owners have **full control** over the Web site. Create a group of owners or re-use an existing SharePoint group.

◉ Create a new group   ○ Use an existing group

Procedures Owners

Don Crawford

OK

Figure 5-46. New company groups

6. You will create the standard groups for this site: Procedures Visitors, Procedures Members, and Procedures Owners. You can, using the radio buttons, use other existing groups. Commonly the proper Owners group will already exist; in this case, for example, you might want the same Owners group for all of the sites (the same owners for Procedures, Operations, Board, and Customers). By default the group's creator name is added to Members and Owners.

7. Click OK to create the groups.

8. You now add the defined SharePoint groups to the proper groups that you just created. As an alternative, you can add the proper people to each of the groups that you just created. It is more about consistency and your long-term plan.

9. Return to the site (Procedures) and select Gear ➤ Site Settings ➤ Site Permissions.

10. As discussed above, you probably want to delete the extra groups, such as Sample_ New_Site_Collection Members and Sample_New_Site_Collection Visitors. Leave just Procedures Visitors, Procedures Members, and Procedures Owners.

11. Populate the new groups with the security groups

    a. Add SP_Senior_Team, SP_Management and SP_Human_Resources to Procedures Members (for RW access).

    b. Add SP_Manufacturing and SP_Customer_Support to Procedures Visitors (for RO access).

12. At some point, fill the SP_ groups with the appropriate people (or other groups).

13. Repeat for the other three sites: Operations, Board, and Customers.

Check Company Permissions

While most people do everything carefully and correctly, it is always a good idea to check. In this procedure you will check the permissions for one of your users, John Q. Demo. He should have Read/Write access to the Procedures document library (from your company security design above).

To check permissions, follow these steps:

1. Navigate to the site (Procedures, in this case).

2. Go to Gear ➤ Site Settings ➤ Site Permissions.

3. Click "Check Permissions" in the Permission Tools ribbon.

4. Enter part of the name, let it autofill, and click the result (see Figure 5-47)

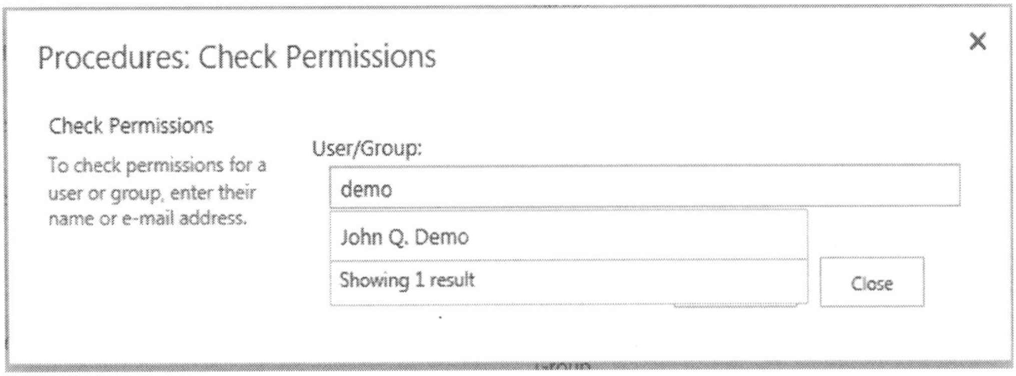

Procedures: Check Permissions ✕

Check Permissions

To check permissions for a user or group, enter their name or e-mail address.

User/Group:

demo

John Q. Demo

Showing 1 result

Close

Figure 5-47. *Check document library permissions part 1*

5. Click Check Now.

6. Check results (see Figure 5-48). Note that John Q has permissions via two other groups. They are not higher permissions, so it doesn't matter. It is good to delete John from these two other groups. (You see that we checked Permissions before we deleted the extra groups in Step 10 above).

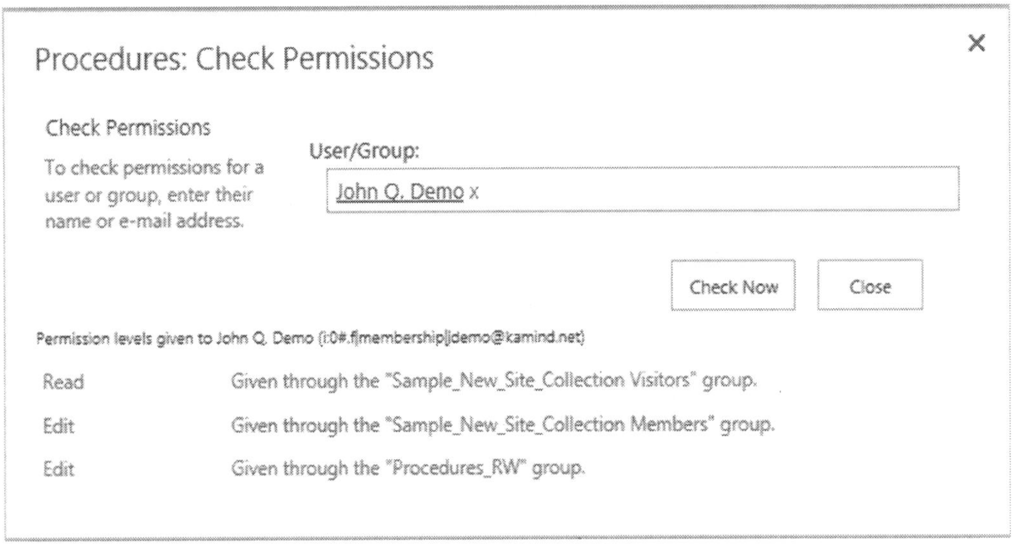

Procedures: Check Permissions ✕

Check Permissions

To check permissions for a user or group, enter their name or e-mail address.

User/Group:

John Q. Demo ✕

Check Now   Close

Permission levels given to John Q. Demo (i:0#.f|membership|jdemo@kamind.net)

Read   Given through the "Sample_New_Site_Collection Visitors" group.

Edit   Given through the "Sample_New_Site_Collection Members" group.

Edit   Given through the "Procedures_RW" group.

Figure 5-48. *Check document library permissions part 2*

7. Check the permissions for the other people.

After you find the person or group that you wish to check permissions for, click Check Now. The next screen shows the results of the check: John Q. Demo the listed permission on this site as given by the listed groups.

Site Editing

This is a brief introduction to page (site) editing. It is really not too complicated. One important point to note is that when you save your work, it is live to your users!

Edit Your Site Page

You can change the look of the pages that are displayed through the web browser. You will edit the default page for the top-level site in your new site collection. Follow these steps:

1. Navigate to the page that you wish to edit. (You will need permission.)

2. You may choose to remove the "Get started with your site" by clicking REMOVE THIS. You can also use it to add your first app or to make the other changes listed. It is a good introduction to the new SharePoint 2013 features.

3. Click Page to show the Edit ribbon.

4. Click Edit (1) or Check Out (2), then Edit (Figure 5-49).

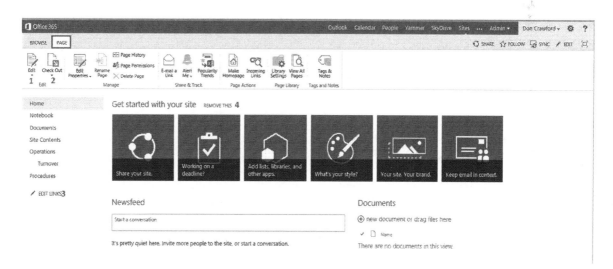

Figure 5-49. *Prepare to edit a page*

5. Your page becomes editable (Figure 5-50). This page is pretty self-explanatory, but here are a few points.

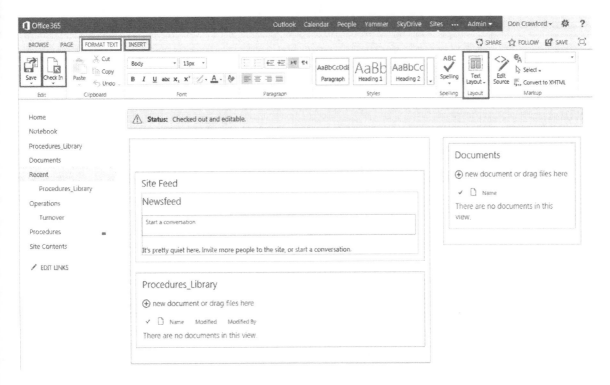

Figure 5-50. *Edit Page overview*

a. Save and Check In when you are done.

b. This is the FORMAT TEXT Ribbon; click INSERT for the Insert ribbon (see Figure 5-50).

c. The text layout (Figure 5-51) changes the overall look, such as the number of columns and headers, etc.

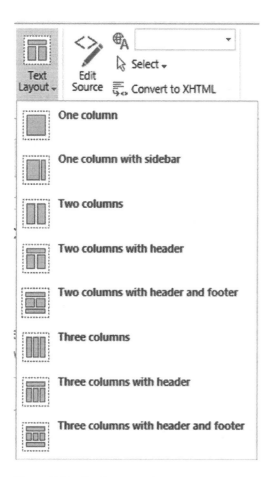

Figure 5-51. Text layout options

    d.   Click on a part of the screen and start editing!

    e.   You might want to practice on a test site.

  6.   Review the INSERT ribbon (Figure 5-52).

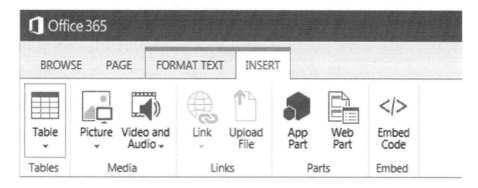

Figure 5-52. Edit Page Insert ribbon

a. You can insert the various items listed onto your page such as a table, picture, video and audio, a hyperlink, a file, an app, a Web Part, or direct code. These are all pretty straightforward except the app part.

b. The Insert an App part has two steps.

    i. See "Add an App" below for the first step.

    ii. Determine where (on the screen) your app should go.

    iii. Click (INSERT) App Part (see Figure 5-51).

    iv. Find the app that you added previously (Procedures_Library in this case) and click Add. The app will be added to the place that you selected on the screen (see Figure 5-53).

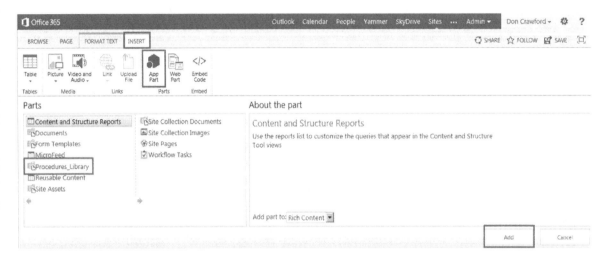

Figure 5-53. *Edit page for the Add an App part*

7. Click Save and Check In when you are done; your page is immediately published.

Click PAGE to open the Edit ribbon.
There are various controls on the ribbon. Click "Text Layout" for the Text Layout menu.
Click the INSERT tab for the Insert ribbon.
Click "App Part" for the Apps submenu. Select the app that you wish, "Procedures_Library" in this case.
Click Add.

Add an App

The new SharePoint 2013 model has added "Add an App" in addition to Web Parts. You now add an app first, and then add it to a web (site) page.

To create an app to be added, follow these steps.

1. Go to Gear ➤ Add an App (Figure 5-54). Click the document library app. This is the type of the app; you actually name it to add it as an app later (above).

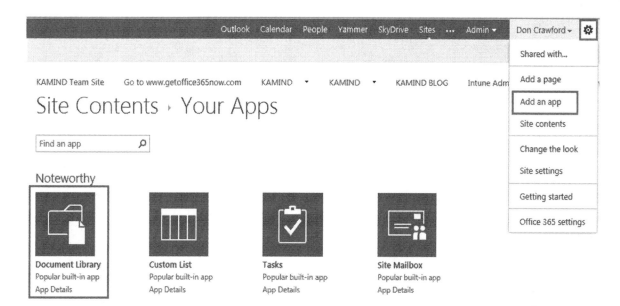

Figure 5-54. *Add an app part 1*

2. Name your app (Figure 5-55).

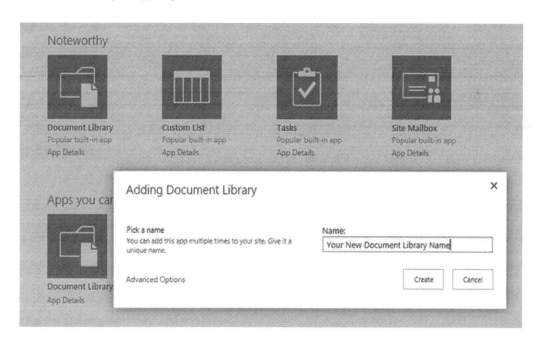

Figure 5-55. *Add an app part 2*

3. Your app is added (Figure 5-56). You can add it to your page now.

Figure 5-56. *Add an app part 3*

Click Gear ➤ Add an app, then select the Document Library ➤ Adding document library option.

Enter the name of your new document library, then click Create. Your new document library has been added to your site.

Edit Links: Edit the Top link Bar

The top link bar is designed for easy access to other parts of your system. You can add a link to another page that will be propagated to other pages (when you have a top link bar in lower sites).

Navigate to your top site. Click EDIT LINKS to edit the links. You can move them around and add a link to any URL (such as your web site). Be sure to click Save when you are done (Figure 5-57).

Figure 5-57. *Edit the top link bar*

Edit Links: Edit the Quick Links Bar

This editing is the same as the top link bar. Click EDIT LINKS to edit the links. You also may wish to edit the links in Gear, Site Settings, and Navigation. This allows you to change the order of the Quick Links in a different way.

Create a Project Site

This section describes how to create a SharePoint project site in your SharePoint Online site collection. This is simply another example of a site that can be created.

Office 365 offers several levels of projects, including a hosted project server and an individual project subscription. Data for these services is stored in SharePoint. SharePoint also offers a simple project site with documents, tasks, calendar, and e-mail specific to the project site. The steps to create this simple site are described below. There is also can be a Project Web App in the SharePoint admin center (see Figure 5-58).

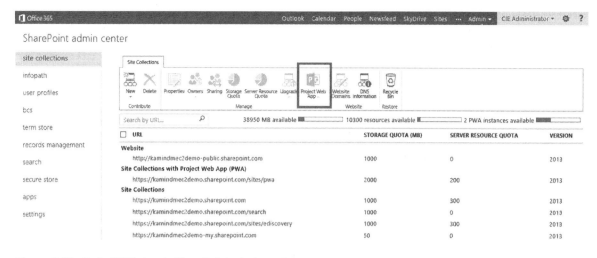

Figure 5-58. *Project Web App in SharePoint admin center*

Step 1: Sign On to Your SharePoint Site

You must sign on as a user with full control for the parent site to be able to create a site. Go to
`https://portal.microsoft.com` ➤ Sites ➤ Team Site. As a shortcut you can use your "onmicrosoft" name;
for example, for us it is `kamind.sharepoint.com`.

Step 2: Navigate to "Parent" of Where You Want to Create Your Project Site

Choose where you want your new project site.

Step 3: Create a Project Subsite

Click Gear ➤ Site Contents (see Figure 5-59).

Figure 5-59. *Gear ➤ Site Contents*

At the bottom of the Site Contents screen, click "new subsite" (see Figure 5-60).

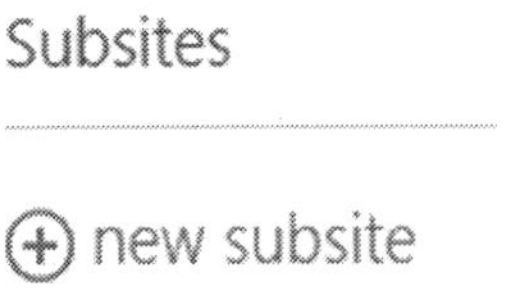

Subsites

⊕ new subsite

Figure 5-60. *New subsite*

You will see the New SharePoint Site screen (see Figure 5-61).

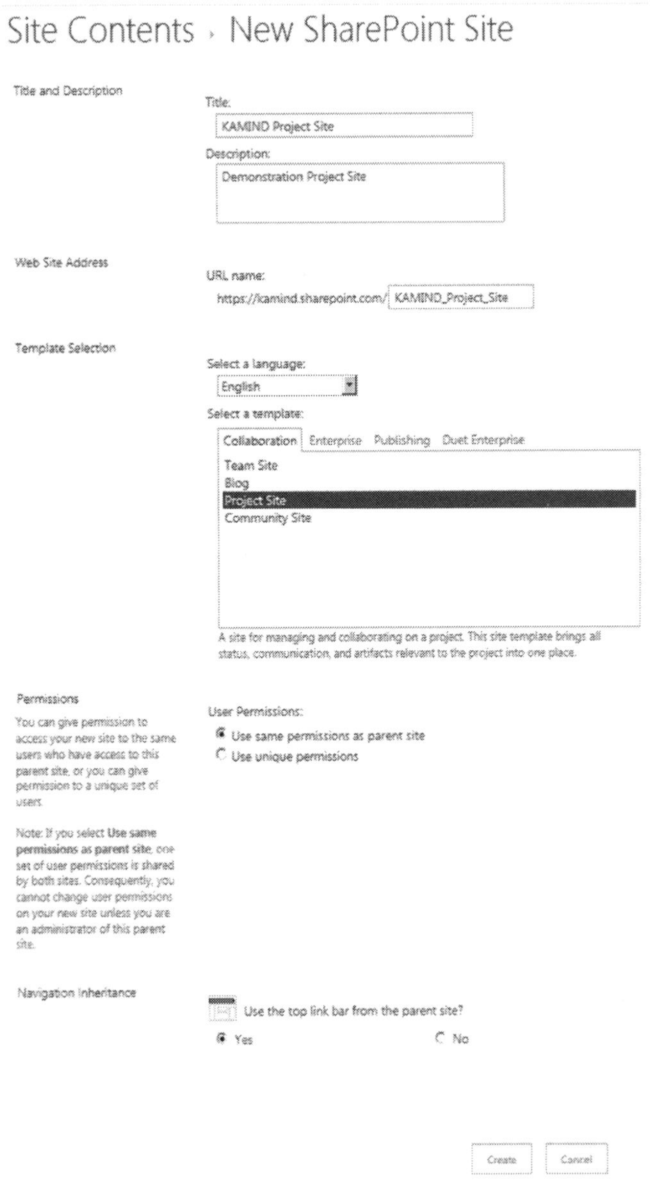

Site Contents › New SharePoint Site

Title and Description

Title:

KAMIND Project Site

Description:

Demonstration Project Site

Web Site Address

URL name:

https://kamind.sharepoint.com/ KAMIND_Project_Site

Template Selection

Select a language:

English

Select a template:

Collaboration   Enterprise   Publishing   Duet Enterprise

Team Site
Blog
Project Site
Community Site

A site for managing and collaborating on a project. This site template brings all
status, communication, and artifacts relevant to the project into one place.

Permissions

You can give permission to
access your new site to the same
users who have access to this
parent site, or you can give
permission to a unique set of
users.

Note: If you select **Use same
permissions as parent site**, one
set of user permissions is shared
by both sites. Consequently, you
cannot change user permissions
on your new site unless you are
an administrator of this parent
site.

User Permissions:

◉ Use same permissions as parent site
○ Use unique permissions

Navigation Inheritance

☐ Use the top link bar from the parent site?

◉ Yes   ○ No

[Create]   [Cancel]

Figure 5-61. *Create New Project screen*

Set title, description, URL, and language. Since spaces are translated as %20 in the URL, it is common to use "_" in place of spaces. This is much prettier, as mentioned before.

Select a template: click Collaboration, Team Site, or use a template that you have saved before. Click the Custom tab (there will be a Custom tab if you have any saved templates).

Choose permissions: "Use same permissions as parent site" or "Use unique permissions." If you choose "Use unique permissions" you will have a chance to create SharePoint groups unique for this site.

Choose Yes or No for "Use the top link bar from the parent site?" Normally you will have set up navigation and you will want to choose Yes. Click Create.

Step 4: Alter Your Site

Your initial project site can now be altered to fit your needs (see Figure 5-62).

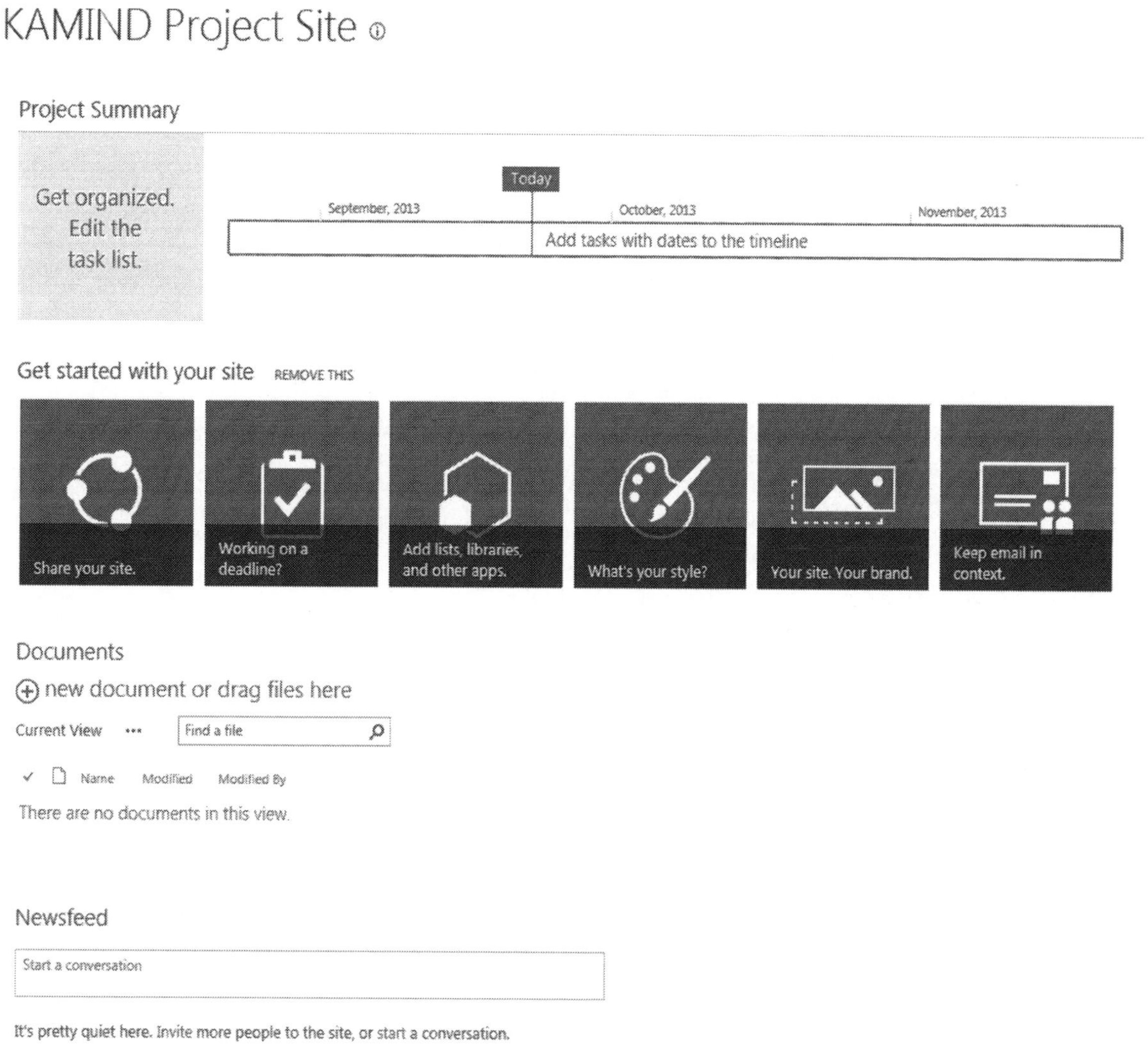

Figure 5-62. Initial SharePoint project site

If you are planning to use a similar project site setup in the future, you probably want to set your style (or use the default) and your logo before you save the template (see Figure 5-63).

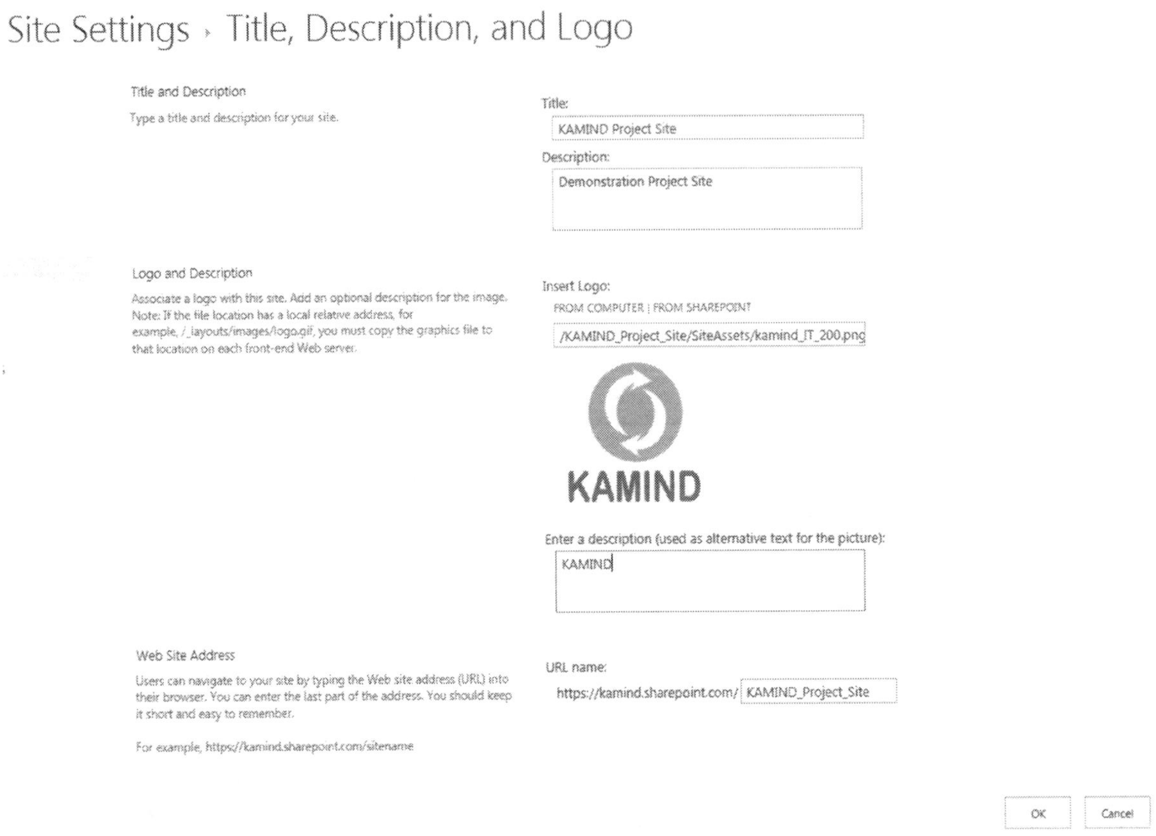

Figure 5-63. *Set title, description, and logo*

Your logo can be referenced either from your local computer (a copy will be made in SharePoint) or from another SharePoint location. You can also use this screen to change the title, etc. that you set when you created the site. Quick navigation: Gear ➤ Site Settings ➤Title, Description, and Logo under Look and Feel.

Step 5: Save Your Project Site Template

If you will create more (similar) sites, now would be a good time to save the project site as a template.

▨ **Note** Save as a template BEFORE adding any project specific tasks or calendar entries!

Click Gear ➤ Site Settings ➤ Save site as template (see Figure 5-64).

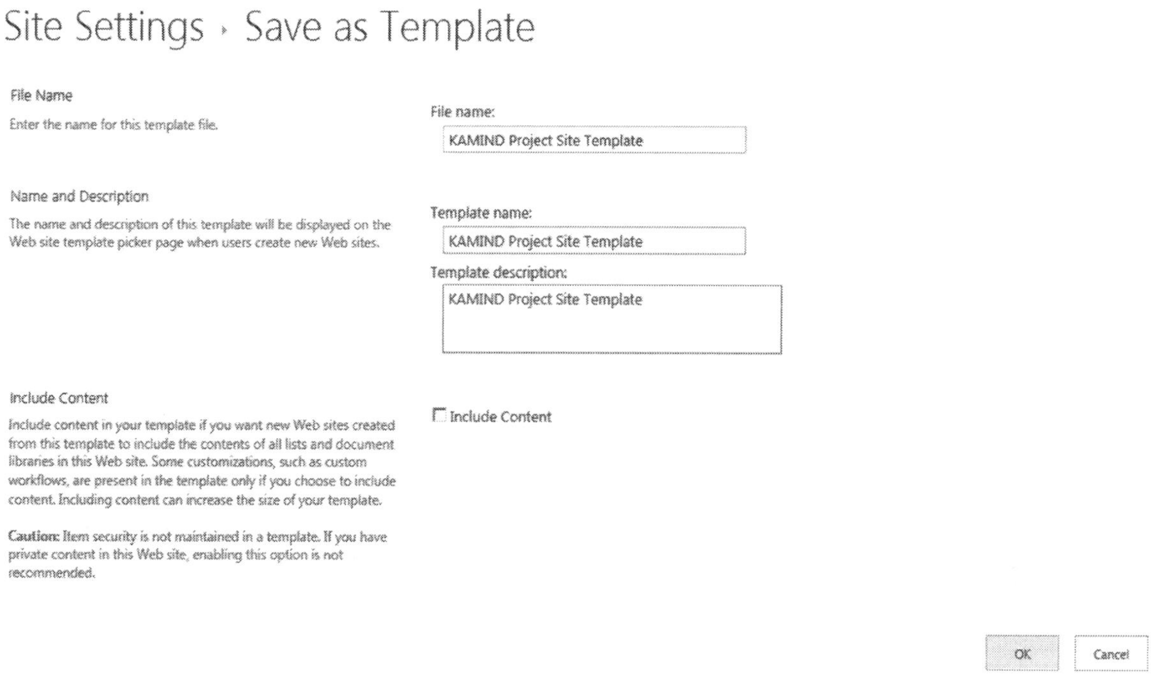

Site Settings › Save as Template

File Name

Enter the name for this template file.

File name:

KAMIND Project Site Template

Name and Description

The name and description of this template will be displayed on the Web site template picker page when users create new Web sites.

Template name:

KAMIND Project Site Template

Template description:

KAMIND Project Site Template

Include Content

Include content in your template if you want new Web sites created from this template to include the contents of all lists and document libraries in this Web site. Some customizations, such as custom workflows, are present in the template only if you choose to include content. Including content can increase the size of your template.

Caution: Item security is not maintained in a template. If you have private content in this Web site, enabling this option is not recommended.

☐ Include Content

[OK] [Cancel]

Figure 5-64. *Save as Template screen*

Pick a name for your template and fill in the other fields. Pick a very descriptive name, perhaps even with a version number. You will have to recognize it the next time that you create a site.

The logo is included in the template (if you specify "Include Content"). See the note relating to "Include Content." Click OK. You will get an "Operation Completed Successfully" message. Your template is now available as a custom template the next time that you wish to create a site.

Step 6: Clean Up Your Site and Add Apps as Appropriate

Return to your new site. Now it is time to adjust it to your specific needs for this project. In the center of the site are some editing buttons (unless you have removed them already); see Figure 5-65.

Get started with your site   REMOVE THIS

Figure 5-65. *Site Edit buttons*

A very common addition is project E-mail. This creates a special Exchange Mailbox just for this project, with a special e-mail address. E-mail copied to this address will appear in the site (project) mailbox. This allows you to keep all project e-mail together in one place, along with documents, calendar entries, and the task list.

To create a project site mailbox (or actually for any kind of site), click the "Keep e-mail in context" button at the right of Figure 5-65. You will see a screen to add a site mailbox; click ADD IT. It may take up to 30 minutes for the mailbox to be provisioned. This mailbox is unique to this site. The email address will be SMO- plus the name of the `Site` plus `@yoursite.com/net/org`. The KAMIND project site mailbox is `SMO-KAMINDProjectSite@kamind.net` in this example.

This action will create a Site Mailbox app. You may wish to add this app to the links at left. This action is the same as adding a Mailbox app. Quick navigation: Gear ➤ Site Contents ➤ add an app (upper left).

"Share our site" is the same as the SHARE button at the top right. See Chapter 2 for more information.

"Working on a deadline?" is a chance to add more calendar and task list apps. "Add lists, libraries and other apps" adds apps. You can do both of these later with "Add an App."

You probably set your style and your brand before you created a template. You can alter them again if you wish. Most people remove the "Get started with your site" buttons (click the REMOVE THIS button in Figure 5-65).

You may also wish to edit links (at left) to match your design (in addition to adding the Site Mailbox app). Quick navigation: Gear ➤ Site Contents ➤ Edit Link, and then drag any apps (including Site Mailbox) into the Links area. You can edit the site for any other customization that you wish. (You may want to customize before creating a template, or create another template.)

Step 7: Set Permissions

Depending upon your needs, you may wish to have special permissions for your project site. If you are planning to share your entire site with internal or external users (outside of your organization), you have a choice of Read Only or Edit. If you have documents or other apps that you do NOT wish to share with others, you can create a subsite (in this site or another site) with unique permissions that are not visible to others.

You had a chance to create unique permissions when the site was created; you can also change permissions later. You can create unique permissions for a site. See "Permissions: People and Groups" for more details.

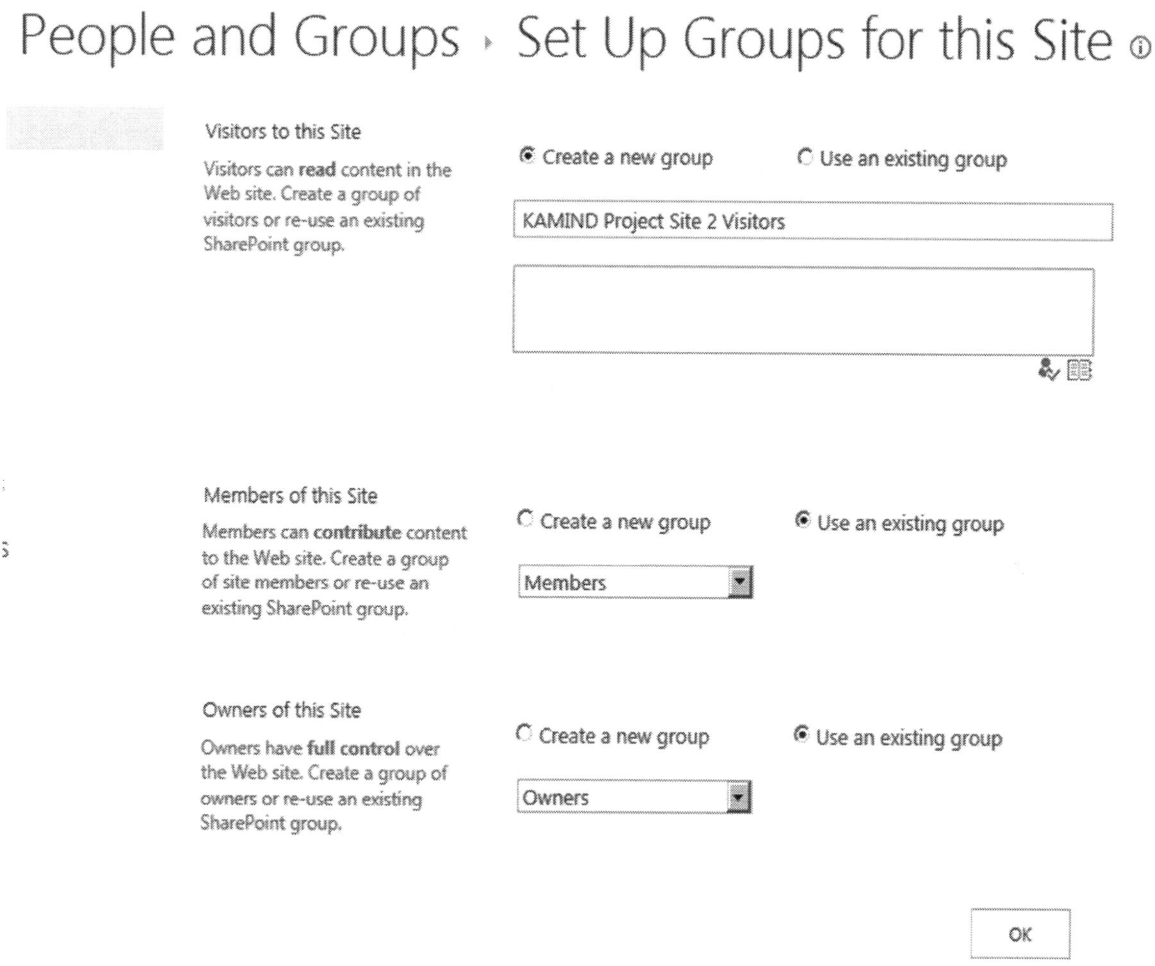

People and Groups › Set Up Groups for this Site ⓘ

Visitors to this Site

Visitors can **read** content in the Web site. Create a group of visitors or re-use an existing SharePoint group.

◉ Create a new group   ○ Use an existing group

KAMIND Project Site 2 Visitors

Members of this Site

Members can **contribute** content to the Web site. Create a group of site members or re-use an existing SharePoint group.

○ Create a new group   ◉ Use an existing group

Members ▾

Owners of this Site

Owners have **full control** over the Web site. Create a group of owners or re-use an existing SharePoint group.

○ Create a new group   ◉ Use an existing group

Owners ▾

OK

Figure 5-66. *Set up groups for this site*

Step 8: Using Your Project Site

Your site can now be used by people with Read or Edit (Contribute) permissions to your site. You can control whether others can upload and edit documents, calendar entries, or tasks with permissions.

Using Project E-mail

If you created a site mailbox (see above), you can use it to keep e-mail about your project. This is a great way to keep e-mail about your project in one place.

The e-mail address for your site will be SMO- plus the name of the site plus @yoursite.com/net/org. The KAMIND Project Site mailbox is SMO-KAMINDProjectSite@kamind.net in this example (Figure 5-67). Anyone on the Internet can send to this address. If you reply to a message in the project inbox, the e-mail will be sent from your email (your Office 365 login address). Send a copy to your project e-mail address.

Figure 5-67. *Outlook Web App site mailbox*

When you click on the Mailbox link, you will start Outlook Web App. This is the same app that you use to process your personal e-mail on the Web. The first time that you use Outlook Web App, you will need to set your language and time zone. The first e-mail contains a link describing how to use your site mailbox.

You may wish to change from CONVERSATIONS BY DATE to ITEMS BY DATE (click the item above the inbox list).

Uploading and Creating Documents

The project site, by default, has a document library. Just drag a file from Windows Explorer onto "drag files here" to upload one or more documents. Click "+ new document" to create a new Word, Excel, PowerPoint document or OneNote notebook, or a new folder. You can also choose to UPLOAD EXISTING FILE, which gives you the opportunity to browse to a file on your computer that you want to upload.

You can view or edit documents with the appropriate web app or with a locally installed version of Word, Excel, etc. Just click on the document name. See Chapter 2 for more information.

Add Tasks and Task Management

The project site automatically includes a Tasks app. Click Edit in the "Get organized" box (see Figure 5-68) or Tasks on the left links. You can then add tasks (task name, due date, assigned to) and add columns (such as comment).

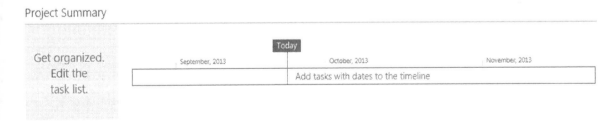

Figure 5-68. *Task list to get organized*

A task is a line in a SharePoint list, with all of that flexibility. The list can also be shown as a calendar or Gantt chart (click Tasks, then "..." just to the left of the "Find and item" box to see the choices). You can show completed or late tasks. See Figure 5-69 for choices and below for sample screens.

new task or edit this list
All Tasks
Calendar
Completed
...
Find an item
Task Name
Date
Assigned To
Comment
Order the T Shirts
ays ago
Don Crawford
This is important!
Have a Kick Off Me
rsday
Don Crawford
Gantt Chart
Late Tasks
My Tasks
Upcoming
Modify this View
Create View

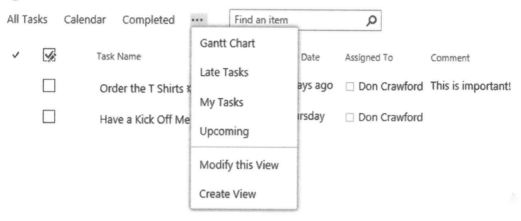

Figure 5-69. *View choices*

After you have added some task, the project summary will have more information (see Figure 5-70). You now have the + ADD TASK and EDIT LIST links.

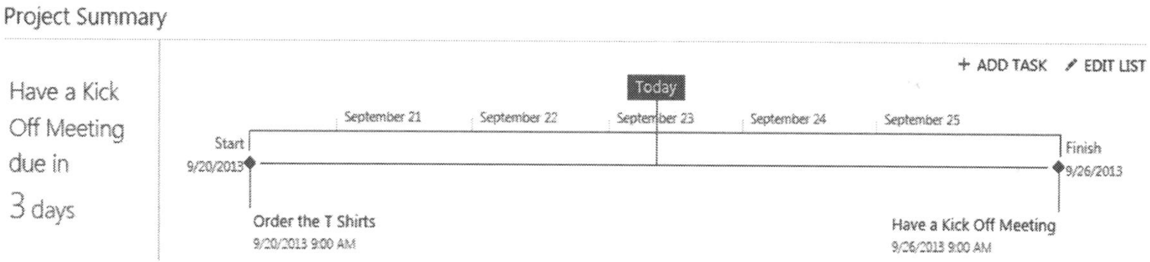

Project Summary
Have a Kick Off Meeting due in 3 days
+ ADD TASK
EDIT LIST
Today
September 21
September 22
September 23
September 24
September 25
Start
9/20/2013
Finish
9/26/2013
Order the T Shirts
9/20/2013 9:00 AM
Have a Kick Off Meeting
9/26/2013 9:00 AM

Figure 5-70. *Project Summary timeline*

To add a task, click "+ ADD TASK" on the project home page or click Tasks at left, then "+ new task" to get to the new task screen (see Figure 5-71. Note that this figure is after clicking SHOW MORE to see the additional fields, including % Complete, Description, Predecessors, Priority, Task Status and the one that we added called Comment).

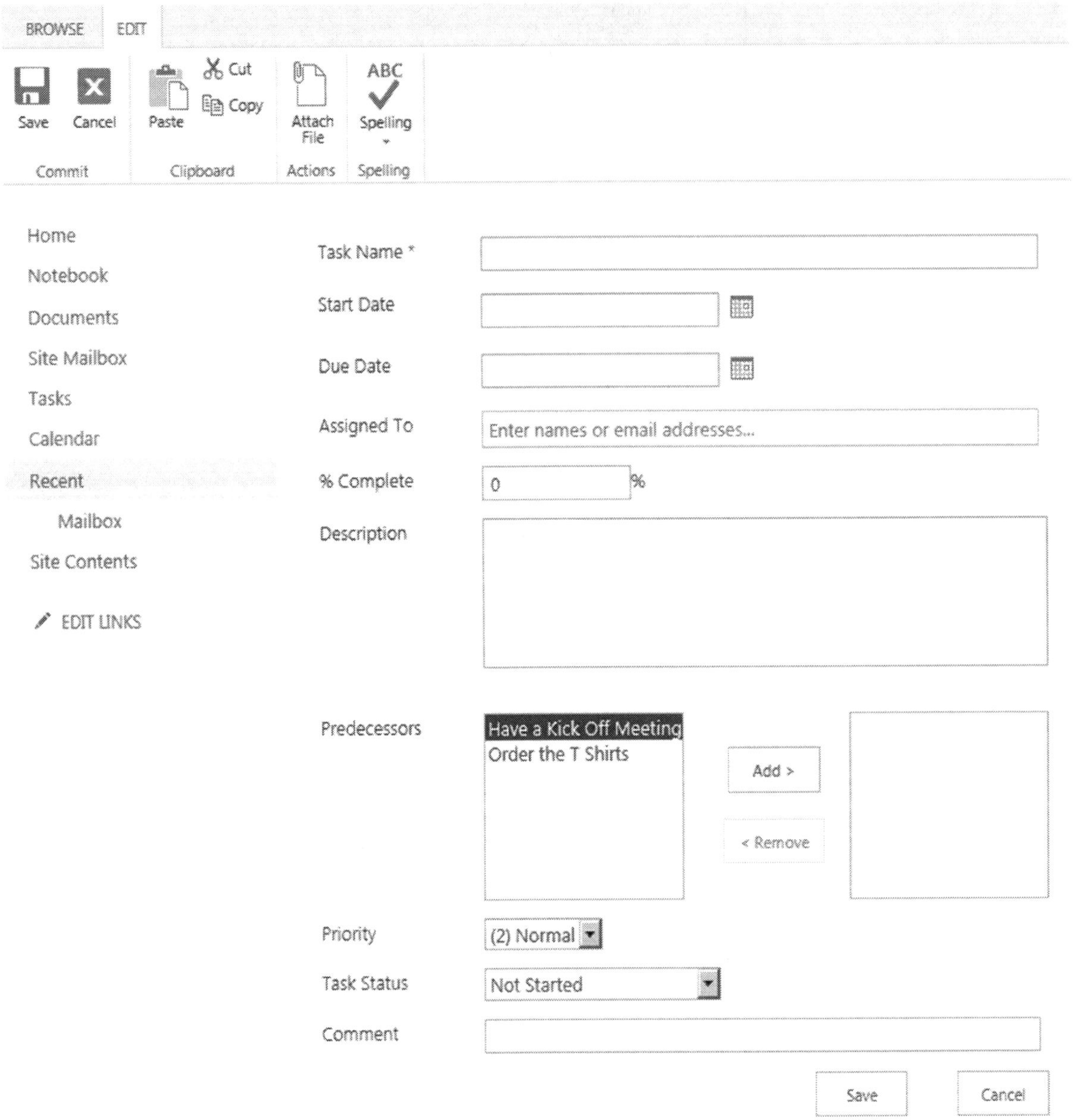

Figure 5-71. *Add a task*

Enter values in the fields as required and click Save. Note that "Assigned to" will be an e-mail address. You can use the small calendar to set a date. If you wish to set a date and time use the format "9/23/13 9:00am". You may also wish to alter the date format (see Figure 5-72). Note the tabs such as BROWSE, TASKS, LIST, and TIMELINE that show depending upon what you have selected.

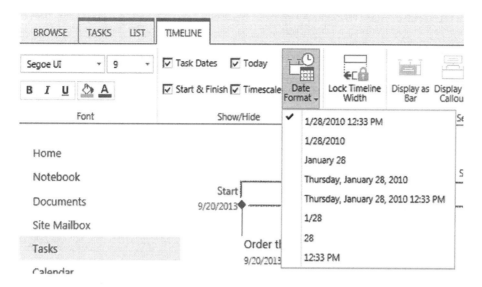

Figure 5-72. Set timeline date format

Note that after you add a task, you must click the ellipses by the item to ADD TO TIMELINE (you can also remove tasks to simplify your timeline). The ellipses also allow you to perform additional tasks including Edit Item, Alert me, and Delete Item (see Figure 5-73).

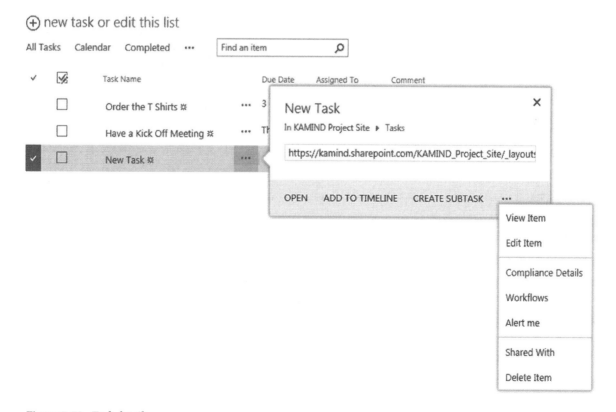

Figure 5-73. Task details

Click the checkbox to mark a task complete. The small green star shows new tasks. As mentioned above (see Figure 5-69), there are other standard views including

- Calendar (see Figure 5-74)

Figure 5-74. *Task Calendar*

- Gantt Chart (see Figure 5-75)

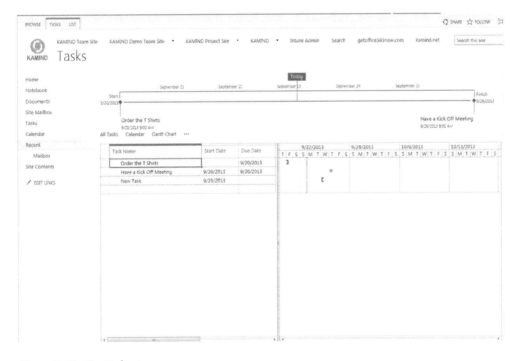

Figure 5-75. *Gantt chart*

All tasks show, even if they are not on the timeline.

You can create any number of specialized SharePoint views (see Figure 5-76).

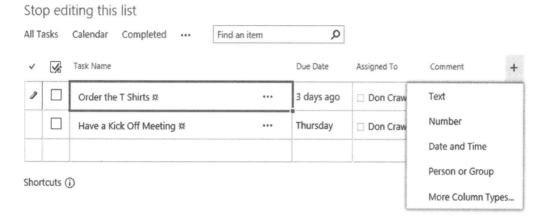

Figure 5-76. Add a Task list column

Figure 5-75 is an example of a Gantt chart, set as described above.

To add a column to your Tasks list, click the EDIT LIST link on the project home page or Tasks then "edit this list." (see Figure 5-76). Click the + at right of the columns. This will show the types of columns that you can create.

Because the Task list is a SharePoint list you have all of the power of SharePoint, including creating new views. See Figure 5-77 for the SharePoint List ribbon.

Figure 5-77. SharePoint List ribbon

Add Calendar Entries

The calendar that is added to the project site by default is a standard SharePoint calendar. It is not linked to the Tasks calendar that you saw previously; see Figure 5-78. Click New Event to add an event to the calendar. The CALENDAR tab allows you to change the calendar formatting and other connection activities.

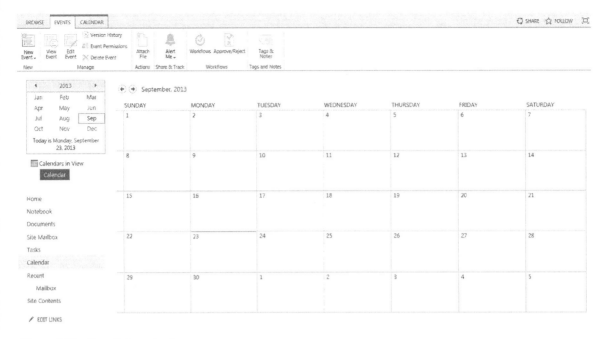

Figure 5-78. *SharePoint calendar*

One Note Notebook

A One Note notebook is created by default. Click the link at left to open the One Note Web App.

Start a Newsfeed Conversation

A newsfeed conversation helps you share information about your project. See Chapter 2.

Share Your Project Site

You may choose to share your project site with others in your organization, or with people outside your organization. See k02_07v01_KAMIND_Office_365_SharePoint_Sharing or the appropriate section in Chapter 2.

Sync Your Site with SkyDrive Pro

You may sync the document libraries in your project site with SkyDrive Pro. See k02_04_v05_KAMIND_Office_365_Using_SkydrivePro or the appropriate section in Chapter 2.

SharePoint Admin Center

This section describes tasks and settings that are normally executed by your (top level) SharePoint Online Administrator(s). Site Collection Features are available to a Site Collection Administrator; Site Features are available to User with Full Control.

We will describe settings and actions in

- SharePoint admin center: Site Collections ribbon

- SharePoint admin center: Other menus (InfoPath, etc.)

- SharePoint admin center: Settings

- Site Collection Features settings (settings for a site collection)

- Site Feature settings (settings for a site)

- Initial SharePoint Setup

A few of these settings will need to be checked or changed for a newly purchased Office 365 tenant (see Table 5-7) since the initial defaults may not match your needs. See the "Initial SharePoint Setup" section below.

Not all settings and features are described in this section. Again, this is a chapter, not a book! There are links to additional information in the Links section. There are a large number of books that are entirely dedicated to the details of SharePoint.

SharePoint Admin Center

The SharePoint admin center is the "home page" for SharePoint Administration. To access your SharePoint admin center, sign on as an Office 365 Global Administrator. Select the Admin drop-down, then SharePoint (Figure 5-79).

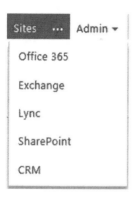

Figure 5-79. *Admin drop-down list*

The SharePoint Admin Center (Figure 5-80) includes the following submenus with functions:

- Site Collections ribbon (New, Delete, Properties, Owners, Sharing, Quotas, etc.)

- SkyDrive Pro settings

- InfoPath (InfoPath configuration options)

- User profiles (settings for People, Organizations, and My Sites)

- BCS (Business Connectivity Services): manage connectivity to other data sources)

- Term store (define and configure your metadata taxonomy)

- Records management (Send To Connections – Content Organizer configuration)

- Search (search administration: schema, dictionaries, reports, etc.)

- Secure store (configure a secure store target application)

- Apps (configure apps: catalog, purchase, licenses, permissions, etc.)

- Settings (Enterprise Social Collaboration, External Sharing, Global Experience Version Settings, Information Rights Management (IRM), Start a Site, Office on Demand, Preview Features)

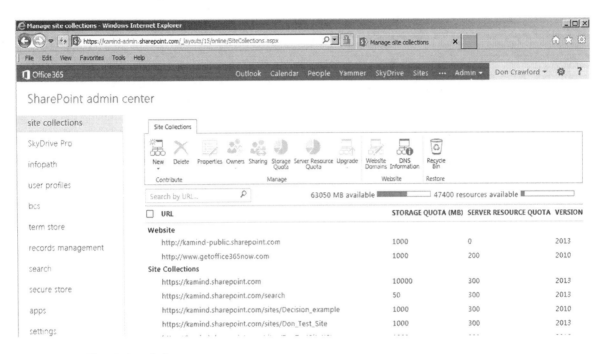

Figure 5-80. *SharePoint admin center*

If you get the "Sorry, something went wrong" error message shown in Figure 5-81, it generally means that your permissions for the SharePoint admin center page has timed out. Return to the SharePoint admin center, click Refresh, and try again.

site collection properties

Sorry, something went wrong

The security validation for this page has timed out. Click Back in your Web browser, refresh the page, and try your operation again.

TECHNICAL DETAILS

GO BACK TO SITE

Figure 5-81. *Sorry, something went wrong*

SharePoint Admin Center Site Collections Ribbon

Click "Site Collections" in SharePoint Admin Center to manage site collections. The Site Collections Ribbon (Figure 5-82) will display, along with your list of site collections. Select one (or more, depending upon the action that you wish to perform) to activate the Ribbon icons. These icons are described below.

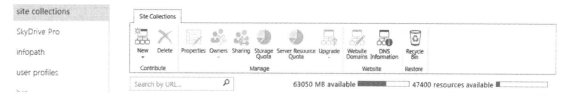

Figure 5-82. *SharePoint Admin Center Site Collections ribbon*

The Site Collection icons include the following:

1. New: Create a new site collection or public web site.

2. Delete: One or more site collections (select a site collection to activate icon).

3. Properties: Show properties of one site collection.

4. Owners: Set owners ("Manage Administrators" and "Add Support Partner") for one or more site collections.

5. Sharing: Set external sharing options on one or more site collections.

6. Storage Quota: Set quantity and a notification e-mail at limit.

7. Server Resource Quota: Set quantity and a notification e-mail at limit.

8. Upgrade: Site collection upgrade settings (for one site) and upgrade notifications.

9. Website: Settings for public-facing web site.

10. Recycle Bin: site collections in the Recycle Bin.

Icon 1: New

sCreate private site collection or a public web site. There can only be one public web site, which is created by default, so the public web site will be grayed out. Select "Private Site Collection" (Figure 5-83).

Figure 5-83. *Create new site collection*

Title your new site collection as you choose (see Figure 5-84). It is a good idea to use the same title as the web site address. This will be less confusing in the future. Since the web site address is a URL, spaces will be replaced with %20 (hex for the space character). Since this is ugly, it is common to replace the spaces in the title with underscores ("_"). It is easy to change the title for the top site in a site collection: navigate to the Site ➤ Gear ➤ Site Settings ➤ Title, Description, and Logo, but to change the web address you must create the new address and copy your data to it.

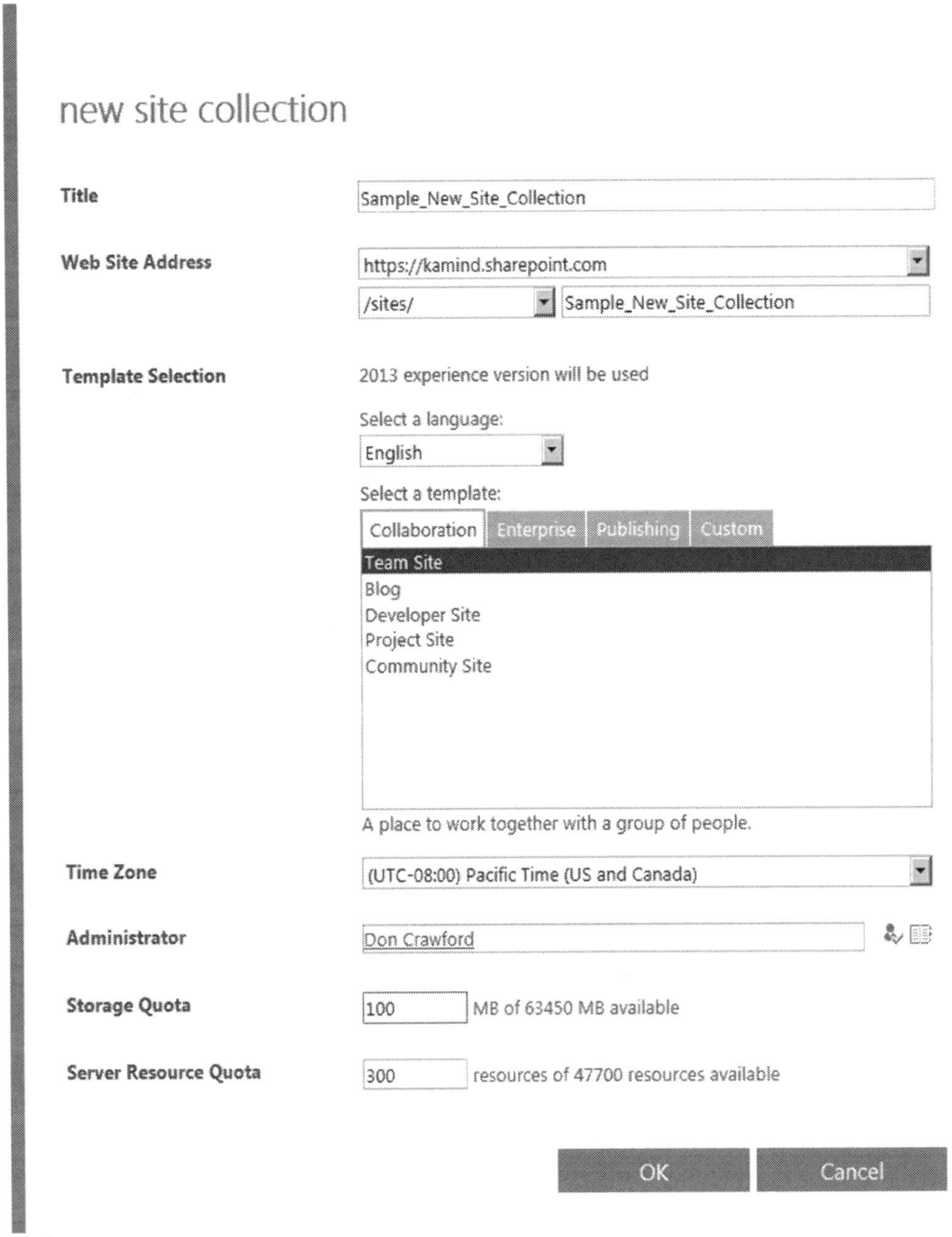

×

new site collection

Title

Sample_New_Site_Collection

Web Site Address

https://kamind.sharepoint.com

/sites/ Sample_New_Site_Collection

Template Selection

2013 experience version will be used

Select a language:

English

Select a template:

| Collaboration | Enterprise | Publishing | Custom |

Team Site
Blog
Developer Site
Project Site
Community Site

A place to work together with a group of people.

Time Zone

(UTC-08:00) Pacific Time (US and Canada)

Administrator

Don Crawford

Storage Quota

100   MB of 63450 MB available

Server Resource Quota

300   resources of 47700 resources available

OK   Cancel

Figure 5-84. *New site collection screen*

Template Selection: Normally you will only have 2013 experience as a version (until the next time!). Select a language for your site. Select a site collection template. "Team Site" is fine; you can change this later. This is the template for the first site created in your new site collection. Figure 5-85 shows alternate templates.

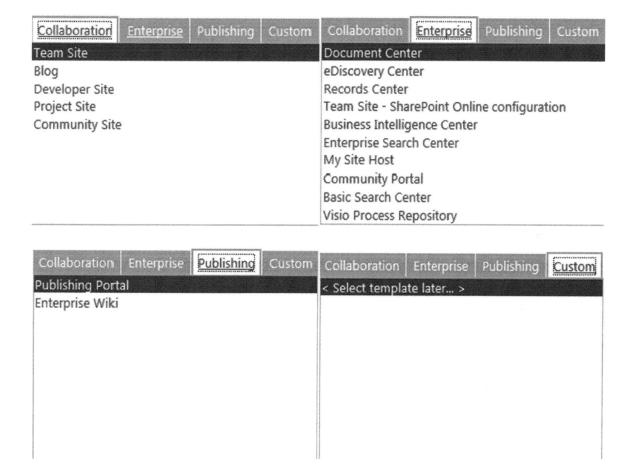

Figure 5-85. *New site collection templates*

Select a time zone. You can change this later in site collection Settings/Regional Settings. Set your Site Collection Administrator. You can add more administrators later. Set the storage quota and resource quota (you can change these later, and it is a good idea to set an e-mail notification when you are approaching the limit). Click OK.

Your new site collection will take a few minutes to be configured. You will have a site (of the template that you selected above). You can edit your new site page as described in the section "Building Your SharePoint Structure."

Icon 2: Delete

You can delete a selected site collection by clicking the Delete icon. There is a confirmation screen. You can recover a deleted site collection within 30 days (see "Icon Recycle Bin" below).

Icon 3: Properties

Double-click a site collection or select a site and click Properties to see properties for the site (Figure 5-86). You can click the web site address hot link to go to the actual site.

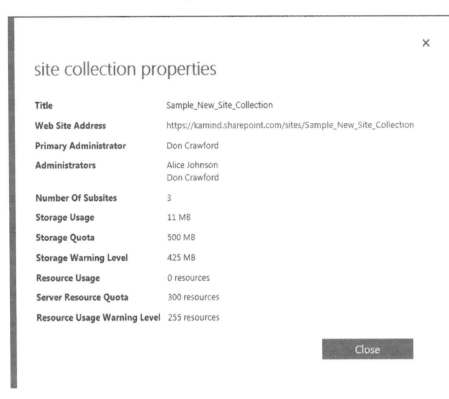

Figure 5-86. *Site collection properties*

Icon 4: Owners

The Owners icon is used to manage Site Administrators and to set a support partner for a site collection (see Figure 5-87).

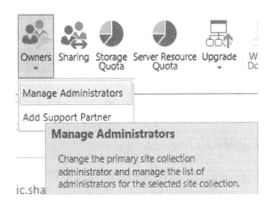

Figure 5-87. *Site Collection ribbon ➤ Owners*

Click Owners ➤ Manage Administrators to see the screen shown in Figure 5-88.

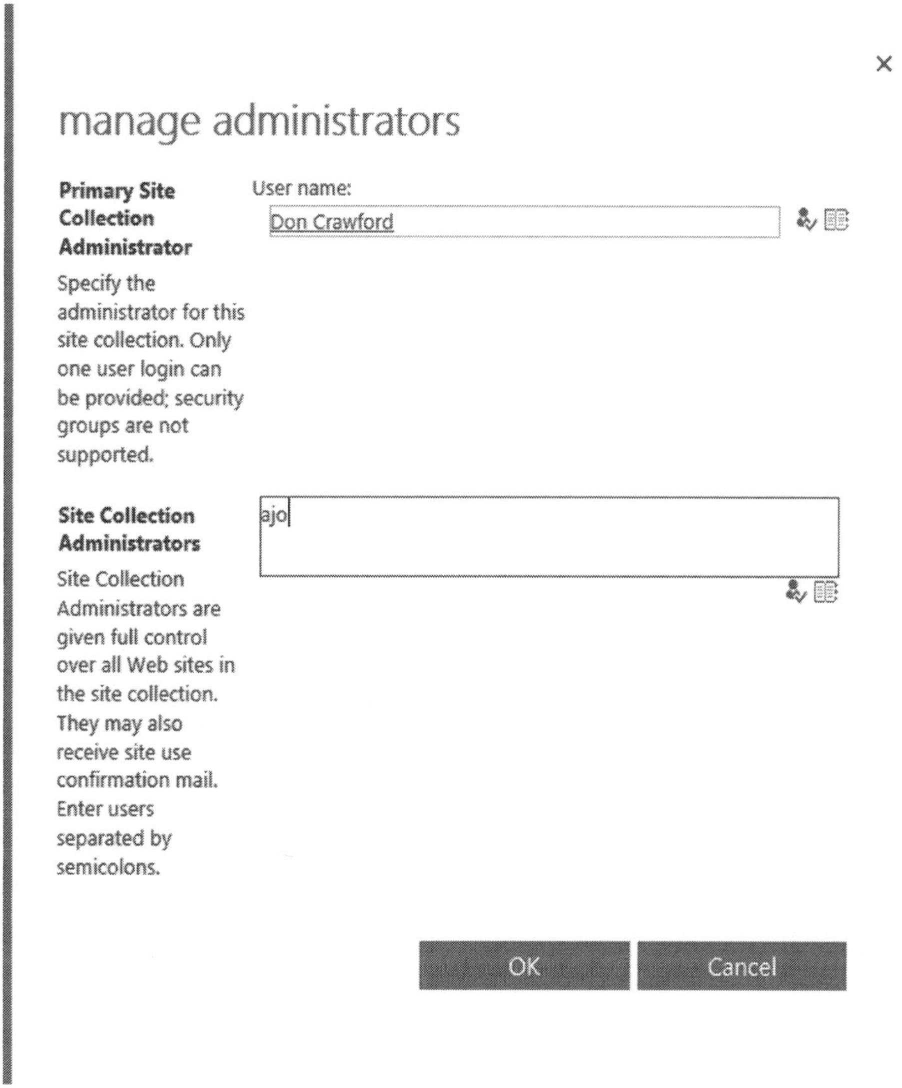

manage administrators

Primary Site Collection Administrator

Specify the administrator for this site collection. Only one user login can be provided; security groups are not supported.

User name:

Don Crawford

Site Collection Administrators

Site Collection Administrators are given full control over all Web sites in the site collection. They may also receive site use confirmation mail. Enter users separated by semicolons.

ajo

OK   Cancel

Figure 5-88. *Manage administrators*

The primary Site Collection Administrator was set when the site collection was created. You can add other Site Collection Administrators. Type the first part of their name, or log in and click People Finder, or select from the Browse "select people and groups." Click OK.

The second icon choice of "Add Support Partner" is to add support partner privileges for a Microsoft representative or your Office 365 License Advisor.

Icon 5: Sharing (External Sharing)

The Sharing icon is used to set sharing options for one or more site collections. Select a site collections(s) and click Sharing (Figure 5-89).

Figure 5-89. Site Collection ribbon ➤ Sharing

There are two classes of sharing: internal (within your tenant) and external (outside your Office 365 tenant).

Internal sharing is controlled by permissions. If a user has a link (URL) to a page but does not have permission to view the page, it cannot be seen.

External sharing is very powerful, and a great feature, but has limitations. Please see the item "External sharing" in the section "Planning, Governance, and Initial Setup" for limitations. A Site Collection Administrator must enable external sharing within "Settings" (see below) and external sharing for each appropriate site collection. It can take a few minutes for changes in menu settings to take effect (see Figures 5-90 and 5-91).

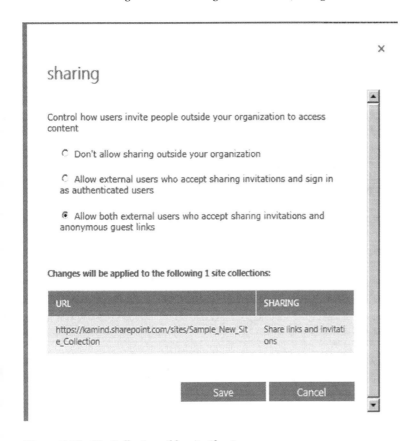

Figure 5-90. Site Collection ribbon ➤ Sharing

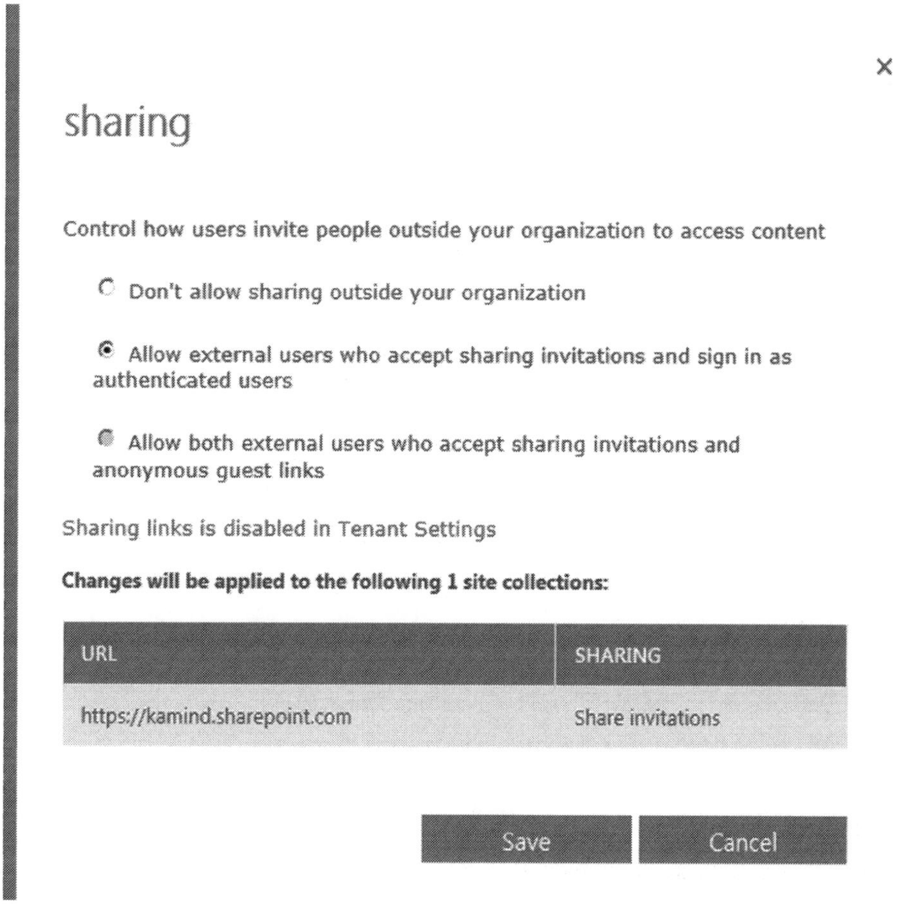

Figure 5-91. *Site Collection ribbon ➤ Sharing screen with error*

The external sharing choices include the following parameters:

- Don't allow sharing outside your organization,

- Allow external users who accept sharing invitations and sign in as authenticated users.

- Allow both external users who accept sharing invitations and anonymous guest links. You usually want this third choice.

Icon 6: Storage Quota

Generally it is a good idea to set "Send e-mail to site collection administrators when a site collection's storage" and to set the "reaches:" percent to 85 or so. This will warn you before you run out of allocated (or available) space (Figures 5-92 and 5-93).

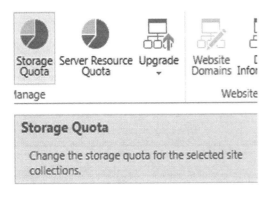

Storage Quota

Change the storage quota for the selected site collections.

Figure 5-92. *Site Collection ribbon* ➤ *Storage Quota*

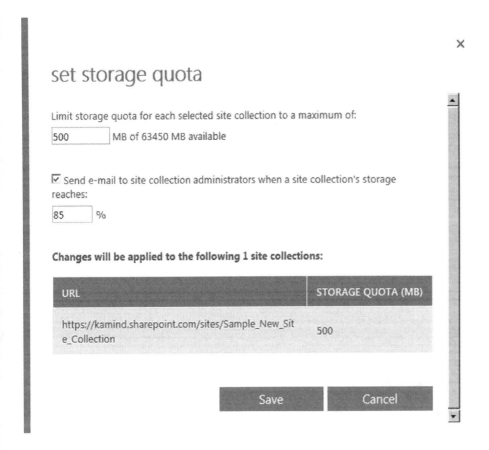

Figure 5-93. *Set storage quota values*

Icon 7: Server Resource Quota

Generally it is a good idea to set "Send e-mail when each selected site collection resource usage reaches warning level at:" and to set the "reaches:" percent to 85 or so. This will warn you before you run out of resources (Figures 5-94 and 5-95).

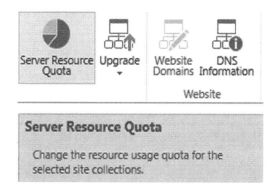

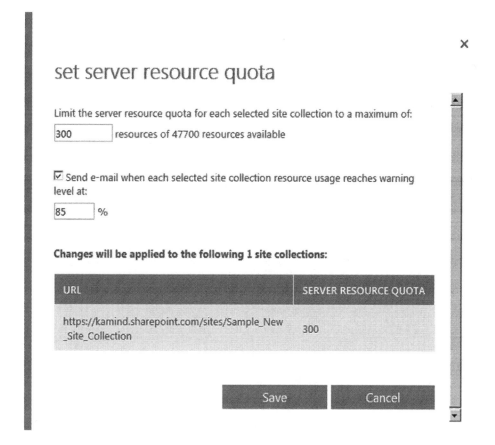

Figure 5-94. Site Collection ribbon ➤ Server Resource Quota

Figure 5-95. Set server resource quota values

Icon 8: Upgrade

Normally your site collections will be created in the SharePoint 2013 version. If not, you may wish to force site upgrades. This button really only applies when Microsoft is doing a major change, as from Wave 14 to Wave 15. You can see the version of your site collections on the SharePoint admin center (see Figure 5-79).

Icon 9: Web Site

The information for your public-facing web site is set here. See Chapter 6 for the specific details.

Icon 10: Recycle Bin/Deleted Item Recovery

SharePoint Online users have a Recycle Bin where deleted content is stored. This Recycle Bin contains site collections that can be recovered. Items in the Recycle Bin are retained for 30 days.

The following data types are captured by the various Recycle Bins:

- Site collections (this Recycle Bin)
- Sites
- Lists
- Libraries
- Folders
- List items
- Documents
- Web Part pages

SharePoint Admin Center Menus

There are additional menus to control more of the features of SharePoint at the left of the SharePoint admin center page:

- InfoPath (InfoPath configuration options)
- SkyDrive Pro settings
- User profiles (settings for People, Organizations, and My Sites)
- BCS (manage connectivity to other data sources)
- Term store (define and configure your metadata taxonomy)
- Records management (Send To Connections – Content Organizer configuration)
- Search (search administration: schema, dictionaries, reports, etc.)
- Secure store (configure Secure Store Target Applications)
- Apps (configure apps: catalog, purchase, licenses, permissions, etc.)
- Settings (Enterprise Social Collaboration, External Sharing, Global Experience Version Settings, Information Rights Management (IRM), Start a Site, Office on Demand, Preview Features)

InfoPath

Configure InfoPath options. This is outside the scope of this chapter.

SkyDrive Pro Settings

This screen controls adding additional SkyDrive Pro (personal SharePoint storage) to particular users (see Figure 5-96). Choose particular logins and set them all to 25GB, 50GB, or 100GB storage limit.

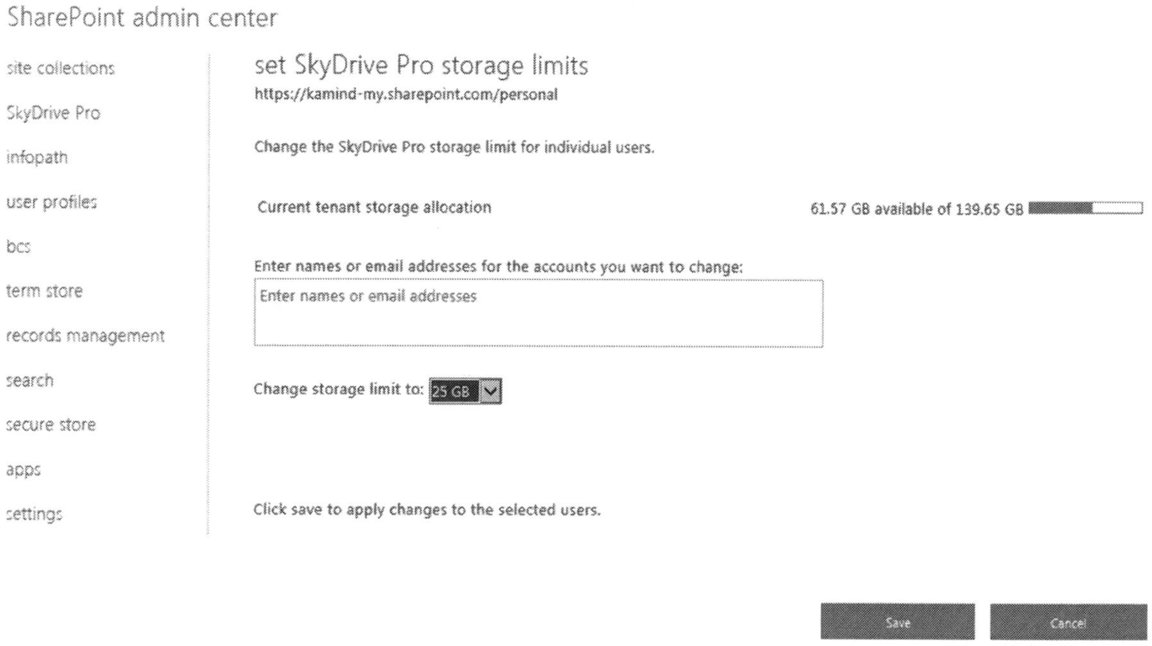

Figure 5-96. SkyDrive Pro settings

User Profiles

User profiles are used to preset values for your users, and include promoted sites.

BCS

Manage Business Connectivity Services. This is outside the scope of this chapter.

Term Store

Term store is global for entire SharePoint tenant. Term Store values are used in metadata fields. This is outside the scope of this chapter.

Records Management

Manage features associated with Content Organizer.

Search

Manage Search parameters.

Settings

Settings includes a selection of global settings (for all of your SharePoint Office 365 tenants) including (see Figure 5-97) the following:

- Enterprise Social Collaboration (Yammer or Newsfeed)

- External sharing (control how users invite people outside your organization to access content)

- Global Experience version settings (control which version of site collections can be created)

- Information Rights Management (IRM) (set IRM capabilities for SharePoint)

- Start a Site (give users a shortcut to create new team sites at a defined location)

- Office on Demand (enable/disable links to launch Office On Demand)

- Preview Features (enable/disable; see item for list of features)

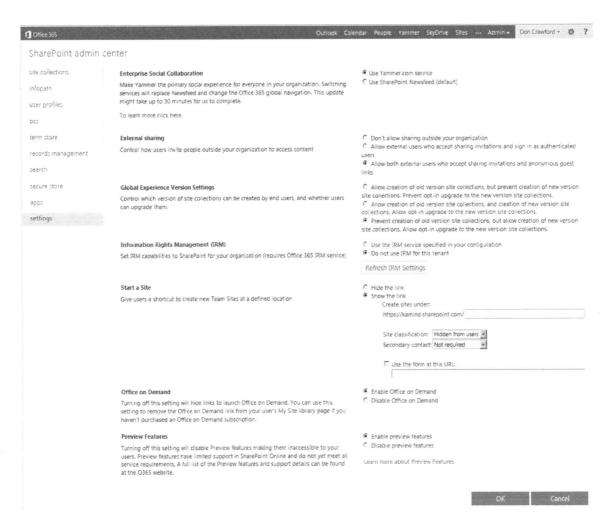

Figure 5-97. *SharePoint Admin Center Menu settings*

Site Collection Settings: Site Collection Features

Site Collection settings, as you might presume, apply to an entire site collection. You must be a Site Collection Administrator for the specific site (or an Office 365 Global Administrator/ SharePoint Online Administrator) to edit these features.

There are many, many features for a site collection. They are listed alphabetically, by titles that were made up by people with a specific idea of what the feature includes. Figures 5-98 through 5-100 show the default values when a site collection is created. We will discuss some (not all!) of the important site collection features. Click Activate/ Deactivate to change the status of a feature. Some features take a while to activate.

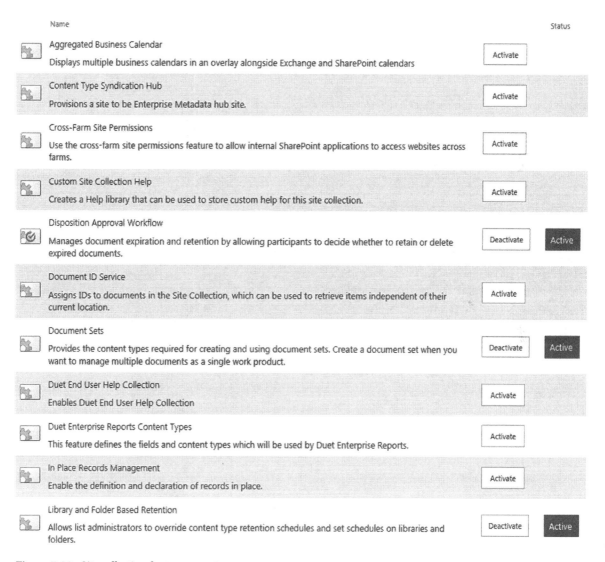

Figure 5-98. *Site collection features part 1*

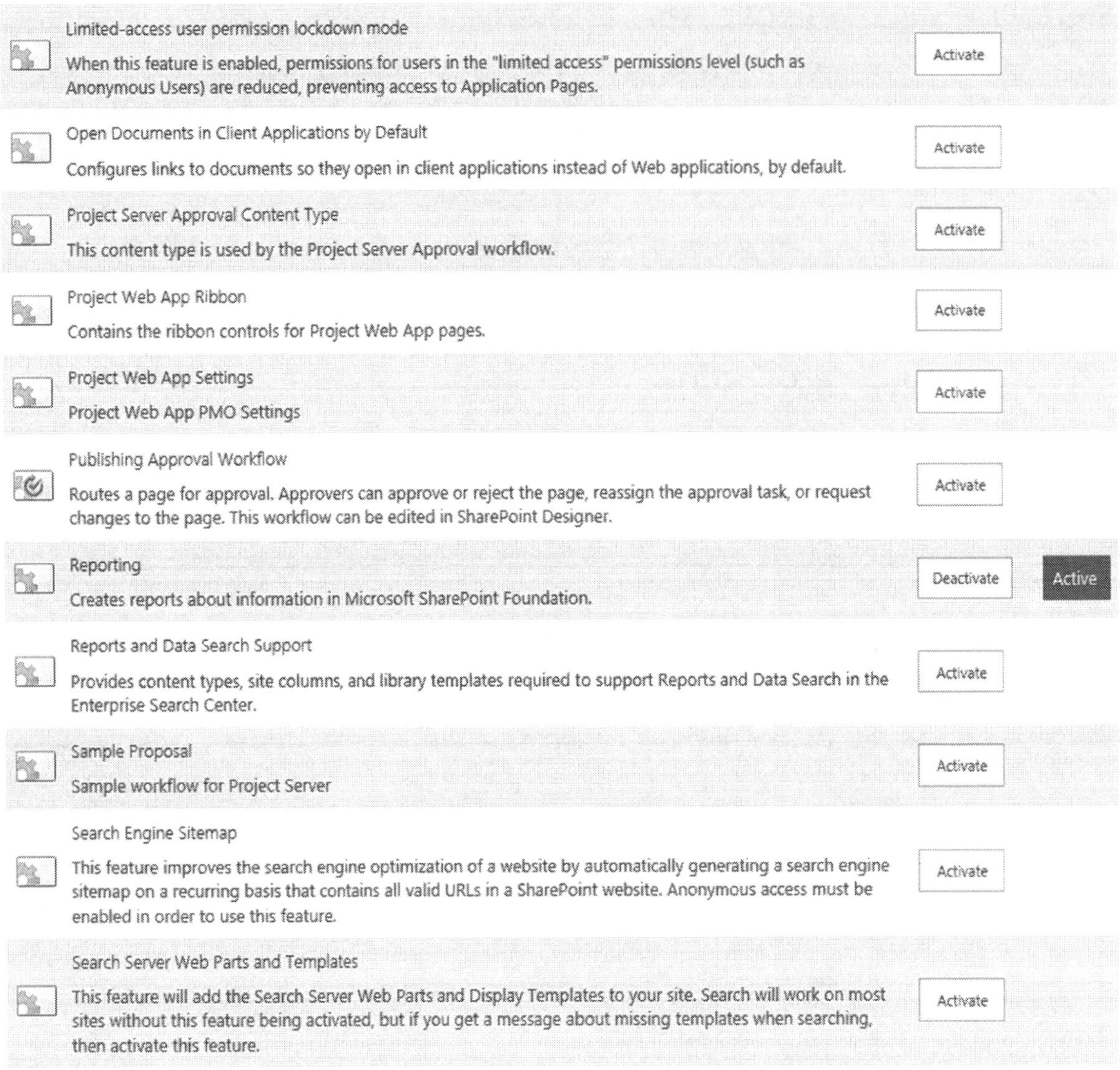

Limited-access user permission lockdown mode When this feature is enabled, permissions for users in the "limited access" permissions level (such as Anonymous Users) are reduced, preventing access to Application Pages.	Activate	
Open Documents in Client Applications by Default Configures links to documents so they open in client applications instead of Web applications, by default.	Activate	
Project Server Approval Content Type This content type is used by the Project Server Approval workflow.	Activate	
Project Web App Ribbon Contains the ribbon controls for Project Web App pages.	Activate	
Project Web App Settings Project Web App PMO Settings	Activate	
Publishing Approval Workflow Routes a page for approval. Approvers can approve or reject the page, reassign the approval task, or request changes to the page. This workflow can be edited in SharePoint Designer.	Activate	
Reporting Creates reports about information in Microsoft SharePoint Foundation.	Deactivate	Active
Reports and Data Search Support Provides content types, site columns, and library templates required to support Reports and Data Search in the Enterprise Search Center.	Activate	
Sample Proposal Sample workflow for Project Server	Activate	
Search Engine Sitemap This feature improves the search engine optimization of a website by automatically generating a search engine sitemap on a recurring basis that contains all valid URLs in a SharePoint website. Anonymous access must be enabled in order to use this feature.	Activate	
Search Server Web Parts and Templates This feature will add the Search Server Web Parts and Display Templates to your site. Search will work on most sites without this feature being activated, but if you get a message about missing templates when searching, then activate this feature.	Activate	

Figure 5-99. *Site collection features part 2*

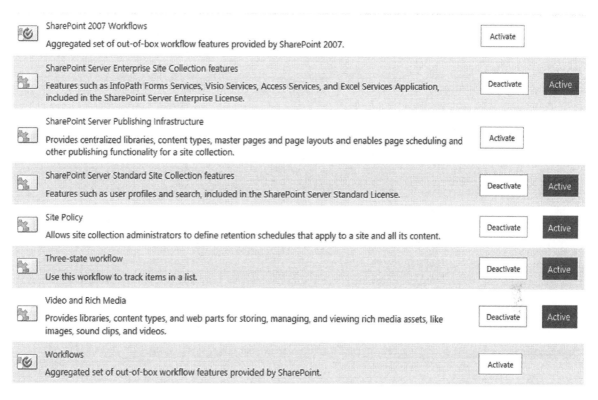

Figure 5-100. *Site collection features part 3*

Important Site Collection Settings: Site Collection Features

This list is somewhat arbitrary (Table 5-6). Some features depend upon what you are intending to accomplish in your site collection. See Reference Links for a link to other descriptive material.

Table 5-6. *Site Collection Settings*

Name	Description	Usage/Notes
Aggregated Business Calendar	Displays multiple business calendars in an overlay alongside Exchange and SharePoint calendars.	
Document ID Service	Assigns IDs to documents in the site collection, which can be used to retrieve items independent of their current location.	
Document Sets	Provides the content types required for creating and using document sets. Creates a document set when you want to manage multiple documents as a single work product.	Active by default.
Library and Folder Based Retention	Allows list administrators to override content type retention schedules and set schedules on libraries and folders.	Active by default.
Limited-access user permission lockdown mode	When this feature is enabled, permissions for users in the "limited access" permissions level (such as anonymous users) are reduced, preventing access to application pages.	Active by default.

(continued)

Table 5-8. (*continued*)

Name	Description	Usage/Notes
Open Documents in Client Applications by Default	Configures links to documents so they open in client applications instead of web applications, by default.	Not active by default.
Various "Project" Related Features, Sample Proposal		As required (related to Projects and Project Server)
Publishing Approval Workflow	Routes a page for approval. Approvers can approve or reject the page, reassign the approval task, or request changes to the page. This workflow can be edited in SharePoint Designer.	
Reporting	Creates reports about information in Microsoft SharePoint Foundation.	Active by default.
SharePoint 2007 Workflows	Aggregated set of out-of-box workflow features provided by SharePoint 2007.	
SharePoint Server Enterprise site collection features	Features such as InfoPath Forms Services, Visio Services, Access Services, and Excel Services Application, included in the SharePoint Server Enterprise License.	Active by default.
SharePoint Server Publishing Infrastructure	Provides centralized libraries, content types, master pages, and page layouts and enables page scheduling and other publishing functionality for a site collection.	Hidden gem. Not active by default. Includes "Navigation" features.
SharePoint Server Standard site collection features	Features such as user profiles and search, included in the SharePoint Server Standard License.	Active by default.
Site Policy	Allows Site Collection Administrators to define retention schedules that apply to a site and all its content.	Active by default.
Three-state workflow	Use this workflow to track items in a list.	Active by default.
Video and Rich Media	Provides libraries, content types, and Web Parts for storing, managing, and viewing rich media assets, like images, sound clips, and videos.	Active by default.
Workflows	Aggregated set of out-of-box workflow features provided by SharePoint.	

Site Settings: Site Features

Site settings, as you might presume, apply to a specific site. You must be a Site Collection Administrator for the specific site (or an Office 365 Global Administrator/SharePoint Online Administrator) or have full control permission on the site to edit these features.

There are many, many features for a site. They are listed alphabetically, by titles that were made up by people with a specific idea of what the feature includes. Figures 5-101 through 5-103 show the default values when a Site is created. We will discuss some (not all!) of the important site features. Click Activate/Deactivate to change the status of a feature. Some features take a while to activate.

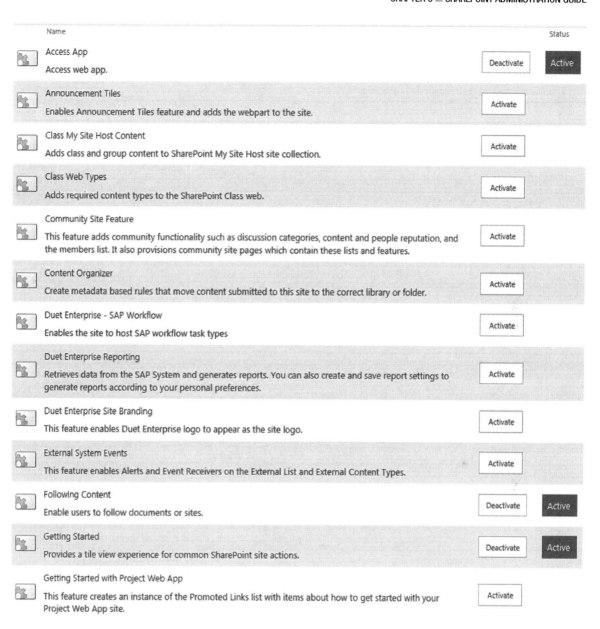

Name		Status
Access App Access web app.	Deactivate	Active
Announcement Tiles Enables Announcement Tiles feature and adds the webpart to the site.	Activate	
Class My Site Host Content Adds class and group content to SharePoint My Site Host site collection.	Activate	
Class Web Types Adds required content types to the SharePoint Class web.	Activate	
Community Site Feature This feature adds community functionality such as discussion categories, content and people reputation, and the members list. It also provisions community site pages which contain these lists and features.	Activate	
Content Organizer Create metadata based rules that move content submitted to this site to the correct library or folder.	Activate	
Duet Enterprise - SAP Workflow Enables the site to host SAP workflow task types	Activate	
Duet Enterprise Reporting Retrieves data from the SAP System and generates reports. You can also create and save report settings to generate reports according to your personal preferences.	Activate	
Duet Enterprise Site Branding This feature enables Duet Enterprise logo to appear as the site logo.	Activate	
External System Events This feature enables Alerts and Event Receivers on the External List and External Content Types.	Activate	
Following Content Enable users to follow documents or sites.	Deactivate	Active
Getting Started Provides a tile view experience for common SharePoint site actions.	Deactivate	Active
Getting Started with Project Web App This feature creates an instance of the Promoted Links list with items about how to get started with your Project Web App site.	Activate	

Figure 5-101. *Site features part 1*

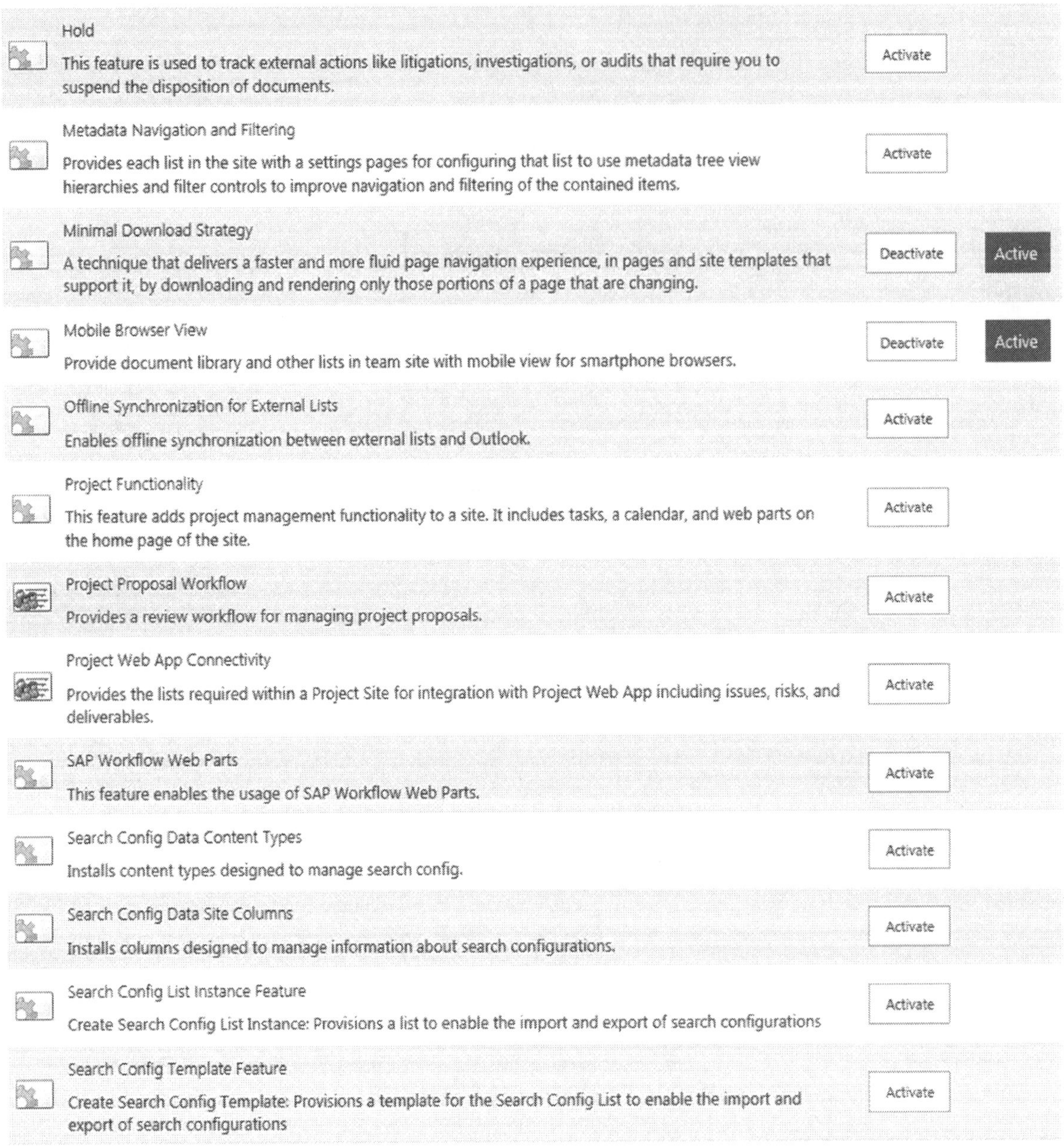

Hold This feature is used to track external actions like litigations, investigations, or audits that require you to suspend the disposition of documents.	Activate		
Metadata Navigation and Filtering Provides each list in the site with a settings pages for configuring that list to use metadata tree view hierarchies and filter controls to improve navigation and filtering of the contained items.	Activate		
Minimal Download Strategy A technique that delivers a faster and more fluid page navigation experience, in pages and site templates that support it, by downloading and rendering only those portions of a page that are changing.	Deactivate	Active
Mobile Browser View Provide document library and other lists in team site with mobile view for smartphone browsers.	Deactivate	Active
Offline Synchronization for External Lists Enables offline synchronization between external lists and Outlook.	Activate		
Project Functionality This feature adds project management functionality to a site. It includes tasks, a calendar, and web parts on the home page of the site.	Activate		
Project Proposal Workflow Provides a review workflow for managing project proposals.	Activate		
Project Web App Connectivity Provides the lists required within a Project Site for integration with Project Web App including issues, risks, and deliverables.	Activate		
SAP Workflow Web Parts This feature enables the usage of SAP Workflow Web Parts.	Activate		
Search Config Data Content Types Installs content types designed to manage search config.	Activate		
Search Config Data Site Columns Installs columns designed to manage information about search configurations.	Activate		
Search Config List Instance Feature Create Search Config List Instance: Provisions a list to enable the import and export of search configurations	Activate		
Search Config Template Feature Create Search Config Template: Provisions a template for the Search Config List to enable the import and export of search configurations	Activate		

Figure 5-102. *Site features part 2*

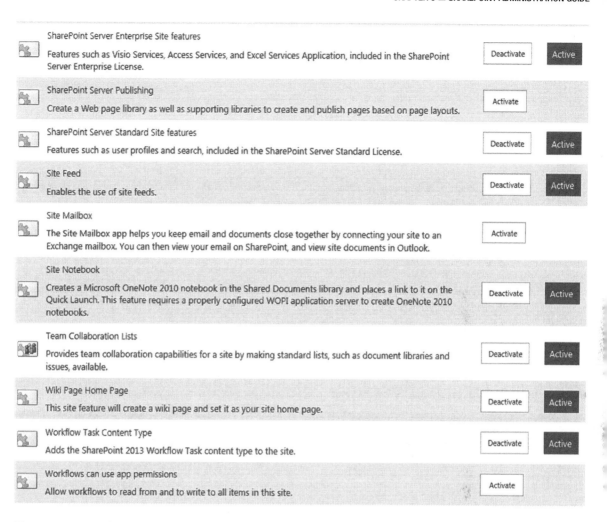

Figure 5-103. *Site features part 3*

Important Site Settings: Site Features

This list is somewhat arbitrary (Table 5-7). Some features depend upon what you are intending to accomplish in your Site. See Reference Links for a link to other descriptive material.

Table 5-7. *SharePoint Site Features*

Name	Description	Usage/Notes
Content Organizer	Create metadata based rules that move content submitted to this site to the correct library or folder	A specialized, but valuable function.
Following Content	Enable users to follow documents or sites.	Defaults to Active
Getting Started	Provides a tile view experience for common SharePoint site actions.	Defaults to Active
Site Mailbox	The Site Mailbox app helps you keep e-mail and documents close together by connecting your site to an Exchange mailbox. You can then view your e-mail on SharePoint, and view site documents in Outlook.	This is very powerful new feature. Defaults to Not Active
Site Notebook	Creates a Microsoft OneNote 2010 notebook in the Shared Documents library and places a link to it on the Quick Launch. This feature requires a properly configured WOPI application server to create OneNote 2010 notebooks.	Defaults to Active. OneNote is a wonderful tool. If people will use these OneNote notebooks this is great.

The Site Features page looks very similar to the Site Collection Features page; be sure that you are on the correct page.

Additional Administrator Concepts and Tools

This section mentions some additional concepts and tools. Detailed descriptions of these items are outside the scope of this chapter.

Document Sets

Document sets are a special kind of library valuable for documentation projects.

Document Versioning

It is possible to configure major and minor versions of documents, and control how many versions are kept. Select a document library and then LIBRARY tab ➤ Library Settings ➤ Versioning Settings.

Workflows

Workflows are processes started by an activity that can perform such functions as getting document approval from multiple people at the same time. Select a document library and then LIBRARY tab ➤ Library Settings ➤ Workflow Settings.

Apps for SharePoint

SharePoint has built-in apps, such as document libraries; it is also possible to build custom apps.

SharePoint Designer 2013

SharePoint Designer 2013 is the screen designer for the visible web pages plus additional features; "the tool of choice for the rapid development of SharePoint applications". You can find more information at the following links:

http://technet.microsoft.com/en-us/library/jj219638%28office.15%29.aspx
http://msdn.microsoft.com/en-us/sharepoint/hh850380

You can also find great information on SharePoint Designer 2013 and the new Workflow architecture at:

http://msdn.microsoft.com/en-us/library/sharepoint/jj163986(v=office.15)

You can find the download of SharePoint Designer 2013 here (be sure to look for updates as well):

http://www.microsoft.com/en-us/download/details.aspx?id=35491

PowerShell for SharePoint Online

There is a set of PowerShell commands for SharePoint Online. Here is more information:

http://search.microsoft.com/en-us/DownloadResults.aspx?rf=sp&q=SharePoint+powershell&x=10&y=10

Initial SharePoint Setup

Initial setup includes setting owners, sharing, storage quota, and server resource quota. These items should be set for the first (initial) site collection. They can also be set for each additional site collection. See Table 5-8.

Table 5-8. *Initial SharePoint Administration Functions*

Task	Description
Initial Setup: Settings (lower left edge)	The default for external sharing is "Allow both external users who accept sharing invitations and anonymous guest links." This is also the default for the sites. This default is normally acceptable.
Initial Setup: set Owners	At SharePoint admin center, select your site collection(s) and select "Owners, manage administrators." Normally the primary Site Collection Administrator will be the first account that you created when you first purchased Office 365. This is why we recommend that this be an Admin account and not a particular person. You may also set additional Site Collection Administrators. These are the people that have full control over all web sites in the site collection. Each site collection can have different Administrators. You (or your License Advisor Partner) may add themselves under "add support partner" as a Foreign Principal to provide additional support.
Initial Setup: set Sharing	Set sharing options for your site collection. You may select multiple site collections. The default is normally acceptable.
Initial Setup: set Storage Quota	Set your storage quotas. It is a good idea to set a limit to get warning emails. 80% or 90% depending upon usage and total size is good. You may select multiple site collections to edit at one time.

(continued)

Table 5-8. (*continued*)

Task	Description
Initial Setup: set Server Resource Quota	Set your server resource quotas. It is a good idea to set a limit to get warning e-mails. You may select multiple site collections to edit at one time. The purpose of this quota is to set a maximum percentage of server resources (such as CPU and RAM) that your site collection should use. The quota helps prevent one site collection from depleting server resources, which might adversely affect performance for all site collections.
Set Permissions for Top Level Site (or new site collection)	The default for a new site collection is that there are no permissions set. Normally you want the top level site to have at least Read Only so users at least have a landing page. See the sections "SharePoint Permissions and Groups" and "Set Top Level Permissions to Read Only."

Reference Links

There is a large amount of information about Office 365 on the Web. The difficulty is finding the right information. The information contained in this chapter is a combination of our experiences in doing deployments and support information that has been published by third parties. There are additional links in the "Additional Administrator Concepts and Tools" section above.

SharePoint Permissions – Best Practices (login required)

www.microsoft.com/en-us/download/details.aspx?id=9030

User Level Permissions in SharePoint

http://technet.microsoft.com/en-us/library/cc721640.aspx

Office 365 Technology Blog

http://blogs.office.com/b/office365tech/archive/2013/09/05/sharepoint-online-improves-limits-and-makes-it-easier-to-restore-documents.aspx

SharePoint Online Planning Guide

http://office.microsoft.com/en-us/office365-sharepoint-online-enterprise-help/sharepoint-online-planning-guide-for-office-365-enterprise-and-midsize-HA101988931.aspx

TechNet – Plan for SharePoint Online

http://technet.microsoft.com/en-us/library/hh852565.aspx

Assigning Administration Roles in SharePoint Online

http://office.microsoft.com/en-us/office365-suite-help/assigning-admin-roles-HA102816050.aspx

Manage External Sharing for Your SharePoint Online Environment

http://office.microsoft.com/en-us/office365-sharepoint-online-enterprise-help/manage-external-sharing-for-your-sharepoint-online-environment-HA102849864.aspx

Next Steps

Your basic Office 365 SharePoint system has been configured. At this point your (first) site collection is 100% functional. You have been introduced to important parts of SharePoint structure, permissions, and other details needed to create and maintain sites and their subparts and permissions. One obvious next step is to read about how to use SharePoint. (These two chapters really need to be read in conjunction.) However, your work is not yet complete. There is much more to do depending on your Office 365 configuration. The key chapters that you need to review for your Office 365 deployment are as follows:

- **Chapter 7** – Windows Intune Administration

  - The secret to an optimal Office 365 site is the management of the desktop to ensure that updates are current, and the user antivirus is functioning. Windows Intune is a desktop management tool that addresses these issues and reduces the administrators' effort in desktop management, and improves the user's experience.

- **Chapter 8** – Office 365 Administration

  - The administrator's job is never complete. This chapter contains information for common tasks such as configuring SharePoint permissions, using different types of PowerShell scripts for configuration of the Office 365 sites and other tips and tracks what we use to make Office 365 work without any support calls.

- **Chapter 9** – Compliance and Data Loss Prevention

  - Businesses must adapt their mail document storage systems to correctly process the electronic communications, based on regulatory oversight. The compliance and data loss prevention (DLP) provides this capability to allow businesses to manage their communications and protect from simple mistakes in their electronic communications. Office 365 includes integrated discovery that supports legal discovery and audit requirements.

CHAPTER 6

■ ■ ■

Web Site Setup and Configuration

All businesses need a web site. The way we solve our web site problem is to use different web hosting companies to manage our web site and different web technologies. One of the less-known features of Office 365 is its web site capabilities. There are three different web technologies that are available to users on Office 365 Enterprise subscriptions. These are the public web site, the SharePoint team site, and Windows Azure. The SharePoint team site is activated as an intranet site (by default). The Office 365 public web site and Windows Azure will need to activated and configured.

Before we dive into building your own web site, let's step back and look at Office 365 user permissions. User permissions and security use Active Directory as the security supervisor. The security supervisor keeps track of the user logins, passwords, and user account information. Microsoft Office 365 uses this account information to link to other cloud services, using a concept of "federation." Federation is simply the linking of different services to a central security supervisor (or Active Directory). When you look at the Office 365 web site capability, there are two different types of services: SharePoint and Azure. The security supervisor manages the Office 365 accounts and provides access to users to these different services. This is where the concept of Office 365 web site is derived. There are two different SharePoint web sites: an intranet and a public web site. Figure 6-1 is an example of an intranet web site.

Figure 6-1. *Private Office 365 intranet (courtesy of Reed Integration)*

Figure 6-2 is an example of an Office 365 public web site. This is your basic web site that is accessible to all users on the Internet. The public web site is fully searchable and is indexed by the search engines, and no login is required to access the site.

Figure 6-2. Public-facing Office 365 Internet web site (courtesy of Viking Mars Missions Preservation and Education Project)

In the preceding two examples, you have two different web site designs and capabilities: an intranet (using traditional SharePoint design tools and workflows) and an external web site (using traditional HTML and the integrated tools). Intranets (Figure 6-1) typically have a more robust capability, because the users are trusted users. A trusted user is a user with an Office 365 account. The trusted users access the SharePoint team site, based on the permission that the SharePoint administrator assigns to the user.

■ **Note** Azure is a PaaS—platform as a service—solution. Windows Azure allows any company to place a line-of-business (LOB) application in a private Microsoft cloud. The server resources are scalable (you pay for what you need), and any operating system (including non-Microsoft) can be hosted on an Azure server. Azure is an optional subscription service that is integrated with Office 365. See `http://account.windowsazure.com`, and log in with your Office 365 global admin account to set up the service.

Azure is a Microsoft hosting service that can support any hosted operating system (even Linux) in the Microsoft cloud. One of the great features of Azure is that it can be linked to the Office 365 user account Active Directory services, providing secured access for your business. The alignment of Azure to Office 365 is a free service with Office 365 Enterprise subscriptions. This is very important, because many web developers are under the misconception that Office 365 restricts your capability to only use Microsoft tools. This is not true with Azure. Azure allows you to build and host any web site. As illustrated in Figure 6-3, you can easily add a WordPress web site with an SQL database support and link that web site to your Office 365 user accounts through federation with Office 365.

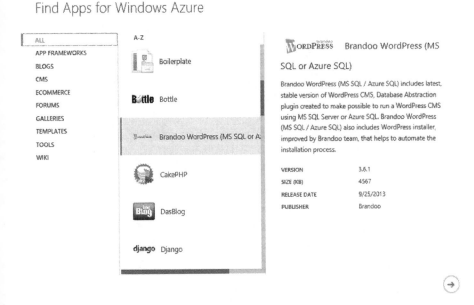

Figure 6-3. *Azure web site linked to Office 365*

We can spend a lot of time talking about Azure services and how to extend your Office 365 capabilities. Our focus in this chapter is on the Office 365 public web site. As your business grows, you want to provide your business with as much flexibility as possible to build your business at the lowest possible costs. The Office 365 public web site is a great starting point for your business. The Microsoft Azure web site is a very powerful option, as you look to expand your business in the cloud.

Office 365 Public Web Site

One of the hidden features of Office 365 is the hosted web site that is included as part of the Office 365 subscription. The configuration is simple, just create the web site, update DNS (allow the www records to point to the Office 365 web site), and configure the template. Office 365 allows one public web site per company subscription. What is really cool about the Office 365 public web site is the integration of the web site with SharePoint. As a company owner of an Office 365 subscription, you can now have a web site with an external interface and have the options to configure the SharePoint template (for intranet access) or use Azure services.

Figure 6-4 is the Office 365 public web site. There are two tools from Microsoft that you can use to configure your public web site. These are the Office 365 integrated editor and Microsoft SharePoint Designer 2013. If you are building an Azure web site, you can use almost all design tools (Microsoft and non-Microsoft tools). Personally, we like to use Visual Studio 2014 for Azure modification or WordPress editor tools for our WordPress web site. We are not going to cover these tools in this section. We will focus on the standard tools that are part of your Office 365 subscription that work with the public web site.

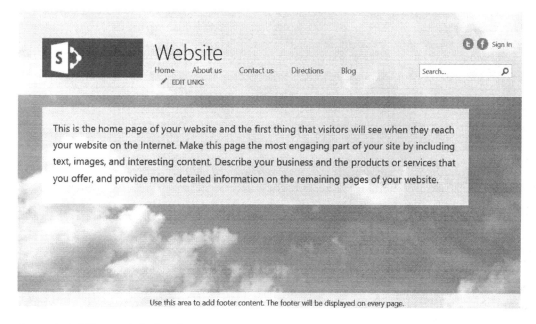

Figure 6-4. Office 365 default web site

Let's get started on building our customer web site. When your Office 365 subscription was created, the Exchange mailbox storage, instant communication (Lync communicator), and the base SharePoint site were also created. We are going to focus on the creation of a SharePoint external web site (a.k.a. public web site). Microsoft supplies two tools (Office 365 integrated editor and SharePoint Designer 2013) that help us to create a SharePoint public web site.

The approach we will use in building the web site is to create a base web design from one of the templates supplied by the Microsoft tools. Once the template has been chosen, and we have some content posted on the site, we will extend the web site, using SharePoint Designer. Each Office 365 subscription has one public-facing web site, and it is created (and blocked from external views) when the subscription is acquired.

■ **Note** The SharePoint public web site has the standard URL `http://< domain>-public.sharepoint.com`, where <domain> is the `onmicrosoft.com` domain. The internal websites <domain>`sharepoint.com` and <domain> `outlook.com` are only access via https://.

How Do You Make an Office 365 Web Site Visible?

Office 365 refers to the public web site as a feature of Office 365. To enable this feature, you must convert the internal URL `http://<domain>-public.sharepoint.com` to an Internet domain (vanity domain accessible without login from the Web). If you have the Small Business version of Office 365, you do not have to configure the web site. The web site is enabled by default. All that you have to do is to configure the "vanity" domain name.

■ **Note** There are three versions of Office 365: Small Business (P plan), Midsize Business (M plan), and Enterprise. The Enterprise plan provides users with greater flexibility over the P or M plans. The web site tools and configuration are some of those differences.

If you are running the Enterprise version of Office 365, you have to convert the generic URL <company name>-public.sharepoint.com to a public-facing URL in the form of www.<companyname>.com, and have it resolved to your newly created web site. It is pretty simple (we will describe this in more detail near the end of the chapter, after we build our web site). The steps to convert the internal domain (and grant permissions for external access) are outlined below.

1. Add a vanity domain (company.com) to your Office 365 plan and verify.

2. Add the subdomain "(www.company.com)" to Office 365 and verify.

3. Select "SharePoint" as the domain intent for the www.subdomain.com.

4. In the SharePoint admin center, convert the <company name>-public.sharepoint.com to the vanity domain (using the menu item "Website Domains").

5. Add the CNAME reference in your DNS servers (at GoDaddy, Network Solutions, or elsewhere).

6. Add the root domain "company.com" as an https-redirector in GoDaddy or Network Solutions.

That is it. There are some restrictions. These are centered on the registration of the domain at Office 365. Microsoft disallows having multiple web sites point to the same site. You have to use a web site redirector service from an external web site. GoDaddy and Network Solutions both offer these services. Other than that, web site hosting and creation is really simple. Let's review the SharePoint admin center in more detail, before we go further in our actual design of the site. The last step of the process is the conversion of the site for access by anyone on the Web.

Quick Tour of SharePoint Administration

Before we start with the public web site, let's take a quick look at the SharePoint admin center. When you log in to Office 365, the admin web site visibility is based on your administrative roles. As an administrator, there are additional functions for which you have responsibility. To begin, let's log in as the site administration user. Afte you login to Office 365, select the "admin" menue (see Figure 6-5), and select sharepoint. This action will direct you to the Sharepoint admin center. The public web site is shown in Figure 6-6. Select "Website" URL to access the public web site.

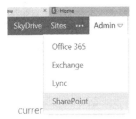

Figure 6-5. *Office 365 Admin*

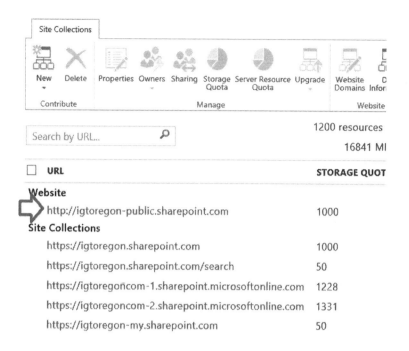

Figure 6-6. *Selection of "Website"*

The public web site will be found under the "Website" category item. If the web site is a private web site, it will have a URL similar to that in Figure 6-6; otherwise, it will have the www reference name. If you have to access the web site, select the pubic web site, then select the URL.

The public web site is different from the other Office 365 SharePoint sites, because the site is preconfigured, and you can only have one public web site per Office 365 organization. The number of SharePoint sites depends on the subscription plan. The Enterprise plan for Office 365 is most flexible in this regard. The only issue that you have with a team site being made public is the permission issues and the security of the rest of your site. Microsoft allows you to invite external e-mail users (via an e-mail address) or to add additional SharePoint users to your Office 365 organization. However, the public web site does not support any membership functions.

The public web site is different from an Office 365 SharePoint site. The public web site can be accessed via SharePoint Designer or the integrated editor; however, the public web site is preconfigured and does not support the standard SharePoint templates. The public web site does not support a private members area for login, and the only person who can modify the public web site is the SharePoint site administrator.

Adding a SharePoint Site Collection Administrator

The first step in accessing the public web site is to add a site collection administrator. All global administrators are members of the "Company Administrator" group, and by default are site collection administrators. However, if you are using a different person from a global administrator, you will have to add them as a site collection administrator for the public web site management. Adding a site administrator is easy. Log in as the global administrator, select the SharePoint site (under the Admin toolbar), then select "Owners" (see Figure 6-7) and enter the user as a site collection administrator (Figure 6-8). Chapter 5 has detailed information about adding users as SharePoint site administrators.

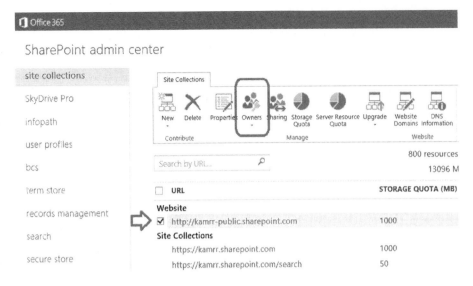

Figure 6-7. Selecting the public web site to add a site collection administrator

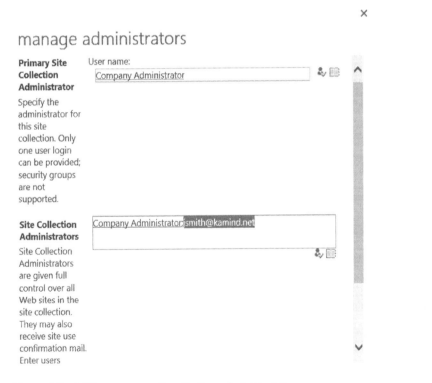

Figure 6-8. Adding user as a site collection administrator

Once you have selected the "Owners," enter the user account as the site collection administrator (see Figure 6-8). Once your add the user account as a site collection administrator, that user can modify and change the public web site with any of the tools that are supported with Office 365. Typically, the tool that is used to make changes to the public web site is the Office 365 integrated web editor.

Office 365 Integrated Web Editor

Office 365 supports two different tools for editing the Office 365 public web site. These are the integrated editor and SharePoint Designer. The simpler tool to use is the Office 365 integrated web editor. We have included information on how to install SharePoint Designer, but that is beyond the scope of this chapter. We recommend that you start with the integrated editor, and if you still have to use SharePoint Designer, purchase a book dedicated to the use of that tool. SharePoint Designer is a complex tool to use, and the primary purpose is to design to build and manage SharePoint team sites.

■ **Note**   SharePoint Designer is an advance SharePoint tool used for the modification and maintenance of SharePoint team sites. The Office 365 public web site is a subset of a SharePoint team site.

Let's walk through an overview of using the Office 365 integrated web-editing tool. Our focus will be on pointing out the key features, to give you a better understanding of the tool's capabilities. Later we will use the tool to build our sample web site with a PayPal payment integration. We deploy a ten-step process (discussed later) in the building of our web site that you can deploy for your own Office 365 public web site.

Getting Started on the Public Web Site

To get started on the public web site, select the public web site link that is located in the SharePoint admin center. The landing page of the public web site should look like Figure 6-9.

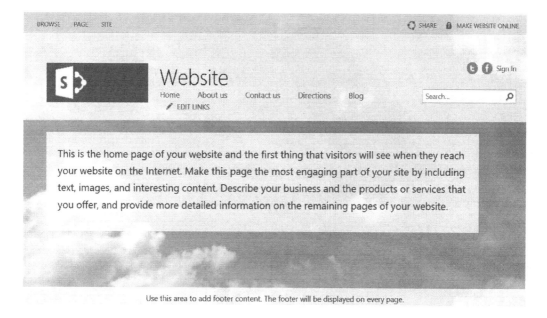

Figure 6-9. Default public web site

The Office 365 public site editing tool uses two controls: "Page" and "Site." The "Page" control is used for content management, and the "Site" control is used for global look changes. This is similar to the SharePoint controls on the Office 365 team site, but different. The public web site controls are optimized for web development and not user permission or library management. The Office 365 SharePoint tools were discussed in detail in Chapter 5.

Accessing the Public Web Site

You can access the public web site in three ways:

1. Access the URL from the SharePoint admin console.

2. Access the URL directly through your browser (in our case the URL is
    http://kamrr-public.sharepoint.com. (If the site is not published, you will be requested
    to log in with your Office 365 account.)

3. Access the URL and select "Sign In" (see Figure 6-9, upper right, above the search
    menu bar).

The Office 365 public web site only supports site collection administrators. There are no private member areas for user access. This may change in a future release, but the date is not known. If you are looking for a member-only web site, you have two options: (1) use the Office 365 team site (assign licenses or external users) or (2) look at hosting a web site in Microsoft Azure.

Using the Page Control

The Page control is used to modify and create new page content (Figure 6-10). Selecting the Page control will expand the different content editing functions. There are two types of edit controls: "Edit," for the content of the page, and "Edit Properties," for the site. The Edit control also allows you to have an internal page and a public page. You can "Save and Publish" and review page history options to revert to an earlier page.

Figure 6-10. *Web site Page controls*

To create new pages, select "New" and enter the page description (see Figure 6-11). As an example, we can create two new pages, "Product" and "Store." These two pages are top-level pages; they will appear on the menus.

Add a page   ✕

Give it a name

Find it at https://kamrr-public.sharepoint.com

Create   Cancel

Figure 6-11. *Adding pages to our web site*

When you select create a page, Office 365 changes the menu to the Page Edit control to build out the web page with content. You can add content into the page as needed. In our example, we will add some basic text content and create our "Store" page, so our customers can purchase products from our company. Once you have added content, select "Save," then "Save and Publish" (or "Unpublish," for an existing page).

■ **Note** Office 365 Page editor allows you to Save (and not publish), Save and Publish, or Unpublish an existing page. The page history contains all of the differnt versions that were publised on the public website. When you unpublish, you are reverting to an earlier version.

Page Control: Edit Content

Once you have content, there are certain basic controls available to modify the page. These are your standard formatting tools (as you would expect in Microsoft Word), including a spell-checker. There are some additional controls; these are for editing the source and converting content to XHTML (Figure 6-12).

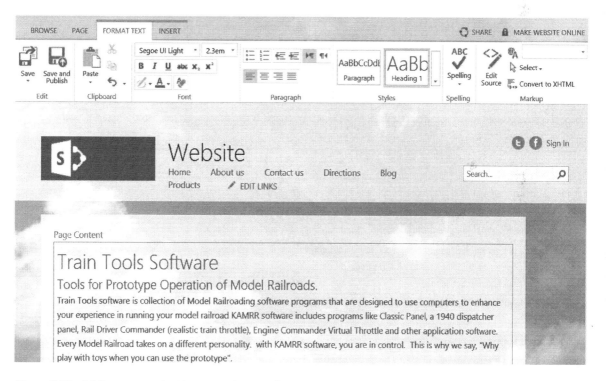

Figure 6-12. *Adding page content to our newly created page*

Insert Options

Once you have selected the edit content, you can now select the page and insert additional elements onto the page. The insert elements are the expected elements (see Figure 6-13), with the exception of three new controls. The standard controls that you will take advantage of in your design are

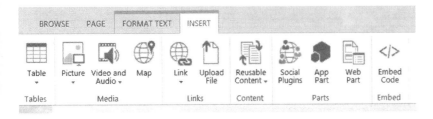

Figure 6-13. *Insert options for page content*

Table, Picture, Video and Audio, Map, Link, and Embed Code. Granted, some of these controls are expected, such as Map, but the interesting controls are the Reusable Content control (for typing data that is used on multiple pages), the Social plug-in, and the Embed Code control. The Embed Code control allows you to do interesting things, such as insert HTML code for a shopping cart (from PayPal) on our web site or add tracking metrics (to see who has visited our site and when).

The control we find the most interesting is the Social plug-in (see Figure 6-14). This control opens the SharePoint Store and allows you to insert different controls and apps into your Office 365 public web site. We're not sure why SharePoint called this "Social"—it seems more akin to a developer toolkit—but whatever the reason, this control is a real gem.

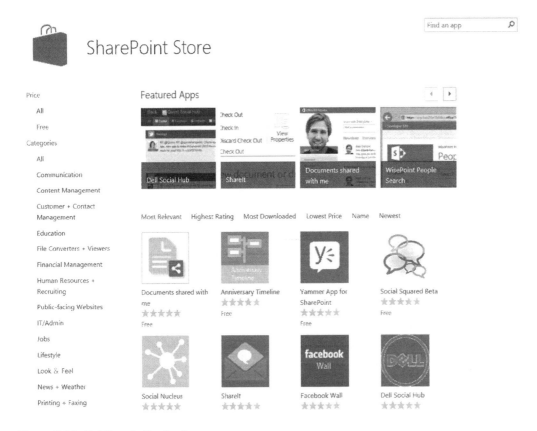

Figure 6-14. *Public web site plug-ins*

Page Control: Edit Properties

Edit Properties is a very important feature in your public web site setup. This control offers two different options: editing properties of the pages on your web site and editing the search engine optimization (SEO) properties that are used by search engines to find your web site, so that you can engage more customers for your product or services.

The SEO interface allows you to rename a page, change the title, change the browser title, give detailed meta-and keyword descriptions, and control the search engine (whether it is allowed to scan or not scan). Typically, an SEO expert will modify the HTML and meta-data directly on your pages. What we have in this case is a tool that will format the SEO characteristics, so that you can use these later on in your Bing and Google ad campaigns to drive leads to your web site for conversion into opportunities and business transactions.

Page: Page History

The most useful control is the Page History. Once you have started to edit a page, select "Page History" to view your changes (see Figure 6-15). Page History allows you to look at different versions and compare the versions to what you have currently published. This feature is extremely useful for ensuring that you do not lose content and have a record of what you've published.

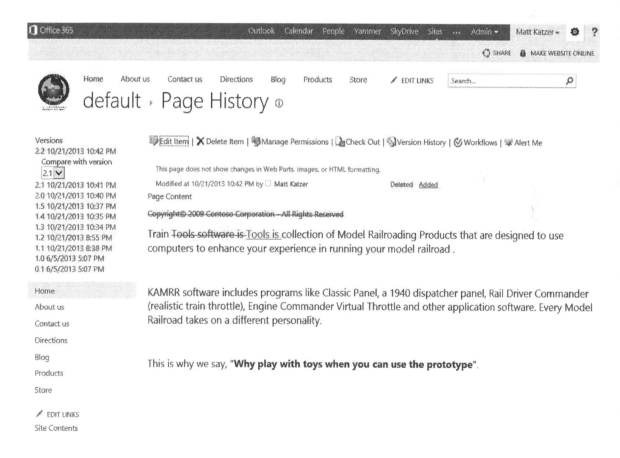

Figure 6-15. *Page History*

Using the Site Control

Earlier, we looked at the Page elements. The "Site" control raises us a level to look at the site in detail (Figure 6-16). The Site control allows you to set the global site characteristics, form, and feel.

Figure 6-16. *Site control options*

With the Site control, you set up the site's look and feel, style sheets, logos, menus, structure, etc. This is how you give your web site personality. As an example, the basic template for all Office 365 web sites is a cloud theme. If you do not like clouds, this is where you change the site.

The preceding was a quick look at the editing tools that you can use to build your web site, but to take advantage of the tools, you must have a plan. To show you how make one, we have created an eight-step process to build your own web site. Our test web site will be about model trains, and we will use the different internal editor tools to build the web site. Our goal is to give you the necessary information, so that you can repeat the process for your own Office 365 public web site.

Build Your Public Web Site in Eight Steps

All web sites need a project focus. In our example, we will build a model train web site that offers model train software products (we are all big kids, so why not make this fun). Before we start building our web site, let's look at why we want to build a web site. We need to put a basic plan in place that will guide our development of the pages for the web site.

We looked at different web site projects that we have been involved with over the years and designed a web site around these four questions. Granted, more complex web sites will have different issues, but for the sake of discussion, we are looking at a simple web site that supports most businesses. We will use these questions to describe our web site www.kamrr.com. Review the questions and answer them in terms of your own web site. Try to be as brief as possible. You want your web site to be focused. That way, you have a clear set of objectives and requirements.

1. What is the purpose of the web site?

    The purpose of www.kamrr.com is to sell model railroad products and services.

2. What problem does the web site solve for the client?

    Visitors come to The Conductor (the name of www.kamrr.com) web site to find information on using computers to control model trains and purchase KAMRR products or services to meet this need.

3. How do we convert a lead (visitor) into an opportunity?

   There are three methods the `www.kamrr.com` web site uses to increase visitor conversions: (1) all material downloaded from the web site is branded with KAMRR contact information; (2) there are purchase options for KAMRR support services for KAMRR products; and (3) an integrated contact mechanism allowing a lead to request more direct information from KAMRR.

4. What is the perception that the customer has when he or she leaves our web site?

   The visitor should leave `www.kamrr.com` with the understanding that KAMRR has the solution for computerized model trains and is capable of solving the customer's problem with KAMRR products.

We want the site to be functional, act as a business card for our products, and support a payment system using PayPal. The default pages that are created by Office 365 are about us, directions, and blog. The assumption is that customers will look at the web site, download product information (perhaps a demo), then come back and purchase product. Let's get started with our Office 365 public web site project.

Step 1: Collect the Content and Images for the Home and About Pages

There are two content items that we have to collect before we begin our web site construction. We need content for the home and about pages. Our home page should have sufficient information about the product or service that we are offering.

When you build your content, look back at the four questions that we asked, and then build your content for the home page (Figure 6-17) and the about page (about your company). In KAMRR's case, we created a capabilities document (PowerPoint form) that describes our skills and accomplishments. The other items that we added to our home page are information about our products and community support (KAMRR has been producing model railroad products since the early 1990s).

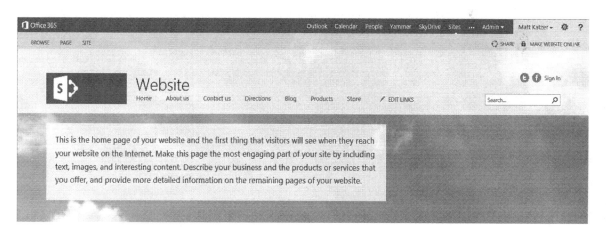

Figure 6-17. *Office 365 default web site*

Step 2: Browse to the Default Site and Select - Sign In

When you see the default web site, the first question becomes how to edit the site. To edit the site, browse to the sign in (see menu item in Figure 6-17) and select sign in. If you have permission, you will be granted access to the site at the appropriate permission level. The admin user who created the site (as we discussed earlier) will have full content control and edit privileges. Log in to the site. If you do not have permission to log in, you will have to see your site collection administrator and have him or her add you as a site collection administrator (discussed earlier in "Adding a SharePoint Site Collection Administrator") to edit the site.

Step 3: Select Home Page and Edit to Change to Edit Controls

After you log in, the next step is to select the page that you wish to change and to edit that page. To see all pages, select view pages (Figure 6-18). The default page (notice default.aspx in the URL) is the home page for your site. Notice thatyou can add pages easily (drag and drop them to "or drag files here." Also, the various pages are HTML documents. You can use your favorite HTML editor to edit the pages, or you can use the Office 365 integrated editing tools. To download the page, select the three ellipses (. . .), then select the three ellipses (. . .) (again) on the share page. Select download to save a local copy. However, be careful about what you change. The format is in an XML as an active server page (aspx). Be careful; it is easy to break the page. It is best that you try to modify the page in the editor, then change the HTML afterward (and keep a copy of the page before you change it).

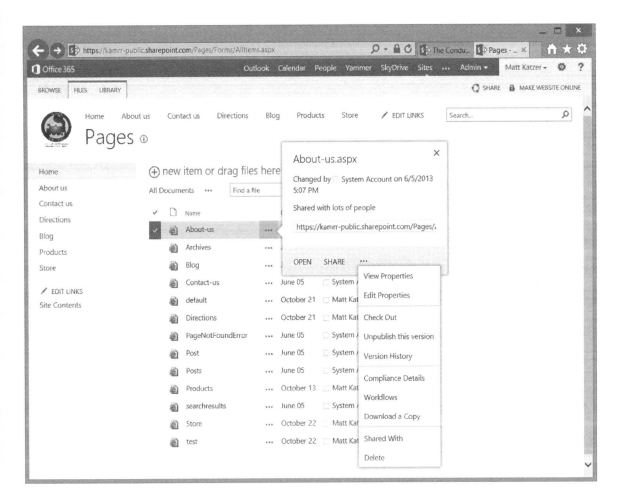

Figure 6-18. *View all pages*

Step 4: Select Home Page, Then Configure Using the Site Controls

The site design mode is where we make the global look and feel changes for our site. We are going to use each of the controls (Figure 6-19) and change the look and feel from those of the default web site (cloud) to our new web site design.

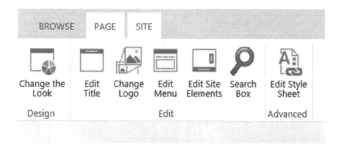

Figure 6-19. *Site controls to be used*

In the design mode, there are three actions you have to complete.

1. Change the look. This is the web site theme and color.

2. Edit the title. Give the web site a name (in this case, "The Conductor").

3. Change the logo. Add your business logo.

Select each of the controls in Figure 6-19, and then select what makes sense for your business. In our case, we selected a black theme with light colored buttons. We wanted a simple, but different, site. When you have completed the above three actions, the site will have a new look, and the title will reflect your business. Remember the four questions we asked earlier about your web site? You will want to refer to these as you continue to build your site and add content. At this stage, we have completed the necessary changes for a consistent look and feel for our new web site. After you complete the above three steps, the site home page will look similar to Figure 6-20 (but with your content).

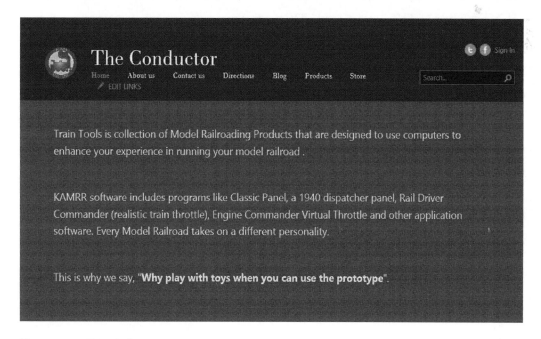

Figure 6-20. *KAMRR home page*

Step 5: Select the Footer Control and Create Your Footer

The next step is to build your footer control and add the necessary legal information (see Figure 6-21). To add the footer, select the "Edit Site Elements" control and add your footer. Save your work and publish the changes.

Figure 6-21. Adding copyright statement to footer

Step 6: Select "Edit Properties" in Site Control to Add Your Keywords

This is where we add the SEO support for the site. We return to the home page and select "Page," then "Edit Properties" (Figure 6-22). Edit SEO Properties allows you to enter the keywords and description for your web site. This will appear as meta-data in the description for the site. Search engines use this information to index the web site. The keywords that you enter should be descriptive and meaningful. To help the search engine locate information on your web site, the document or image that you upload should also be descriptive.

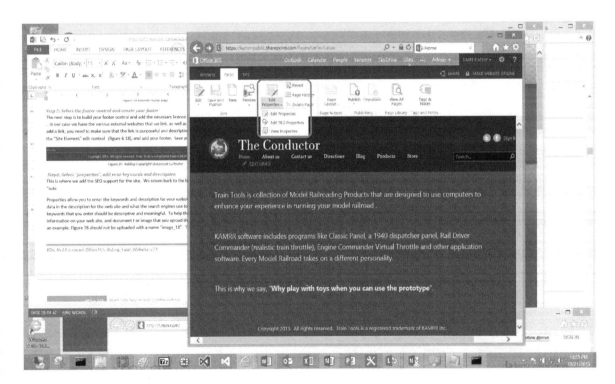

Figure 6-22. Adding SEO properties

■ **Tip** When you add images, assign a descriptive name. Search engines use this name, as well as your content, to place your web page in their search engineers. For example, do not use a generic name like "image_21." Use a descriptive name like "kamrr Inc logo–Run with the prototypes." You will have better search results.

Step 7: Add Content

Once you have defined the content, just add additional pages. In our case, we added a PayPal payment feature (see the "Adding PayPal Online Shopping" section) to our web site. You may have other pages that you want to add. This is a mechanical process: simply fill out the pages with the content and add them to the site. Figure 6-23 shows the online store that we created.

Figure 6-23. *Online store using PayPal*

Step 8: Save the Web Site and Make It Public.

We hope that you have been saving your web site all along. At any point, when you save your web site, it is published (save and publish are your options). There is nothing that you have to do or create. It is a very simple process. Remember that until you make your web site "online," it is not visible to the outside world. Office 365 permission controls restrict the site to those users who have the correct permissions (site collection administrators).

If you have not configured an external www domain and verified it, following is a summary of the steps you must follow. It is very simple process.

1. Add a vanity domain to your Office 365 domain's admin console. (You will add `www.companyname.com` to Office 365 to be verified.)

2. Verify the www domain in the Office 365 admin console.

3. Select "SharePoint" as the domain intent.

4. In the SharePoint admin center, convert the `<company name>-public.sharepoint.com` to the verified domain (using the menu item "Website Domains").

5. Add the CNAME reference in your DNS servers (at GoDaddy, Network Solutions, etc.).

These steps are explained in detail later in the chapter.

■ **Note** The external web site only allows one domain name to be appointed. Additional domain names will result in a 404 error. Office 365 configuration is for one public-facing web site. Services such as GoDaddy allow a domain redirection, which will resolve correctly to the Office 365 public web site.

Adding PayPal Online Shopping

This is not an advertisement for PayPal. You should look at each payment-processing engine and determine which approach works best for your business. We are only looking at PayPal because it offers a preconfigured shopping cart that is easy to add to an Office 365 public web site. To use PayPal, log in with your PayPal account. Our PayPal account is a business account, so we have access to the PayPal merchant services. Once you have verified the account, log in to the PayPal web site and select "Merchant Services" (see Figure 6-24).

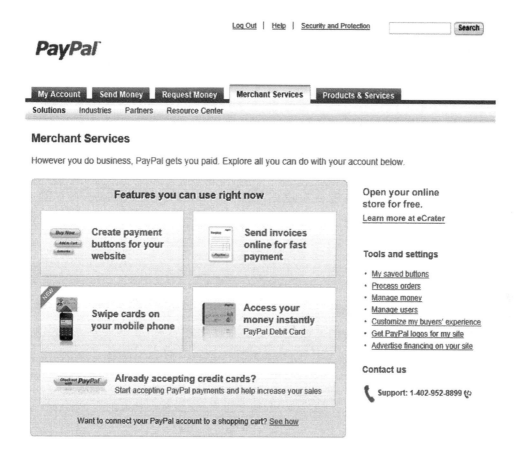

Figure 6-24. *PayPal Merchant Services*

There are different strategies for using the online store. Our store example is a simple one: we have three products to sell, and we will use a shopping cart. The best way to approach PayPal is to determine the customer purchase model that you want to use (see Figure 6-25) and allow PayPal to build the necessary HTML files for the code of the web site add-in.

Figure 6-25. *PayPal Payment processing options*

The next step in the shopping cart is to build your product purchase button. PayPal allows you to have six different product purchase button options, depending on your needs (Figure 6-25). You can mix and match different product purchase button types. We recommend that you use the supplied PayPal shopping cart and allow your customers to purchase items and place them in the cart. Keep your Office 365 public web site simple. This makes it easier to maintain and change.

Fill in the product name and price and enter an inventory code (a code you use to track the products that are ordered; this is a number that you create to help you fulfill your sale. Paypal views the inventory code as the Item ID.). Once you have entered this information, select the "Save Changes" button and allow PayPal to build your shopping cart HTML code (Figure 6-26).

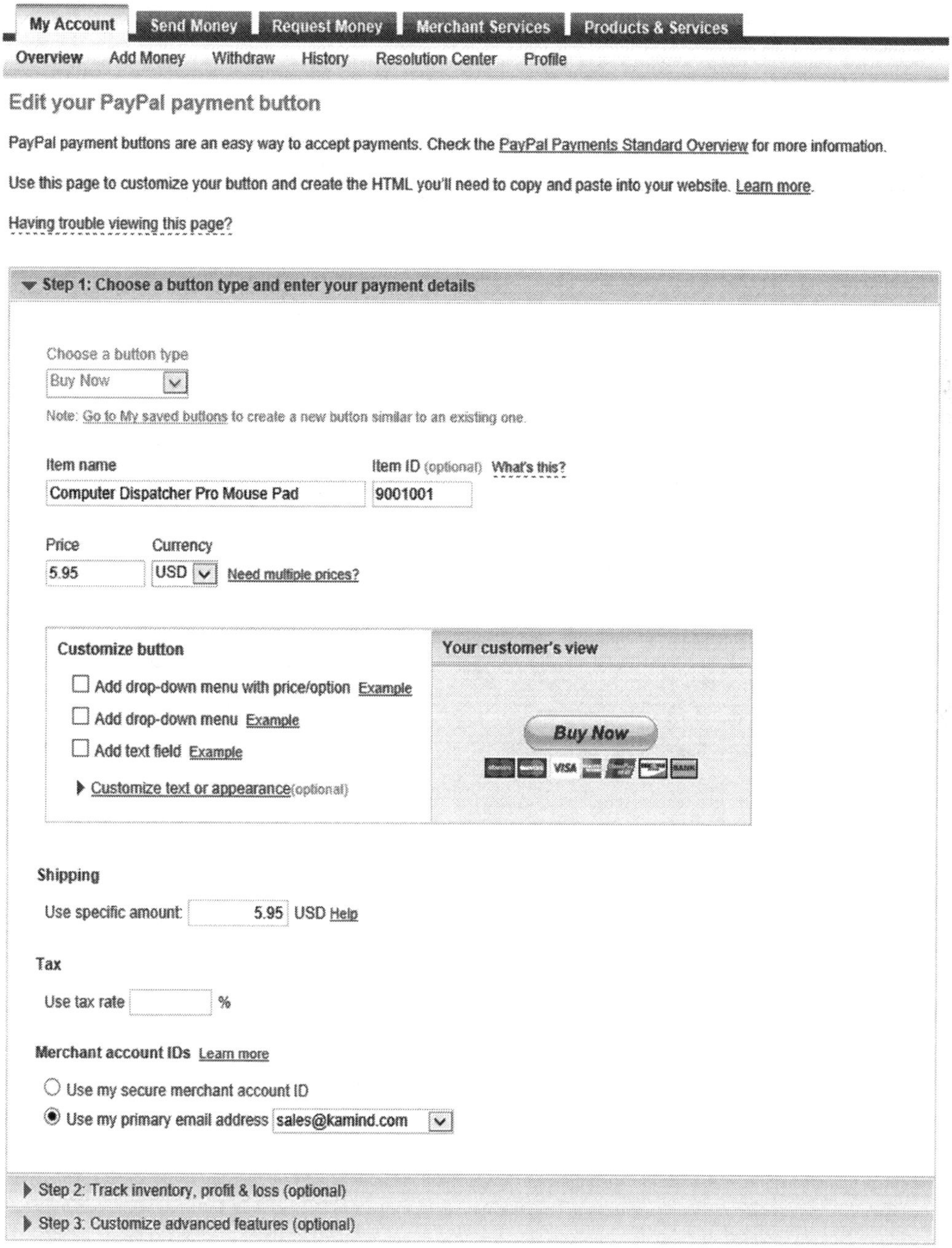

Figure 6-26. *PayPal–add online store Buy Now button for the shopping cart*

Once you build the button, highlight the code and insert it into our HTML online store page.

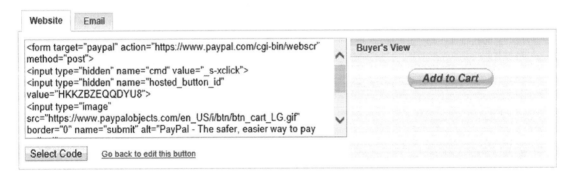

Figure 6-27. *Building PayPal shopping cart*

Online stores can be complex or simple. The easiest way to look at an online store is as a collection of images, descriptions, and buttons. The PayPal approach is a simple store approach, not a good solution for a complex online store. When we complete the button for the cart, we add the button to view the cart. At the bottom of the screen (see Figure 6-28), select "View Cart," to build the HTML code to view the cart.

Create more buttons

Create similar button | Create a new button

Similar: Use the button you just created as a template for another button.
New: Create a completely new button from a blank form.

Create a View Cart button

Give your customers convenient access to their shopping carts while browsing your website. You need just one View Cart button for a website.

Go to My saved buttons

- Edit most characteristics of a button.
- Create a new button that is similar to an existing one.

Figure 6-28. *PayPal View Cart option*

If you are building a web site that that needs more features, the simple PayPal solution will not work for you. Your only alternative is a different hosting company, or use Microsoft Azure. Microsoft Azure allows you to build an environment that is composed of any computing resource needed. Azure is a service that you can add to Office 365.

■ **Note**   Office 365 user accounts can be linked to the Azure Active Directory. Please see `http://account.widnowsazure.com` for more information about Azure services.

Earlier, we built a sample web site with some dummy pages for our PayPal online store integration. The hardest part of adding the PayPal integration is getting the correct buttons to be built on the PayPal site. Once you have the buttons built, all you have to do is add the code to the existing page.

Adding PayPal HTML Code to an Existing Page

Once our web site is created, the next step is to modify the content of a web page. You can make most of your changes using the Office 365 integrated editor. The PayPal code will be inserted into the store page. To add the new content to an existing web page, take the following the steps:

1. Log in to the public web site as a site collection administrator.
2. Select the page to be edited.
3. Edit the page.
4. Add content to the page.
5. Insert the PayPal HTML code.
6. Publish the page.

Step 1: Log In As a Site Collection Administrator

Modification of the Office 365 public web site (or team site) requires you to be a site collection administrator. If you are not a site collection administrator, you cannot log in to the Office 365 non-published public web site. To access the public web site, go to the SharePoint admin center and click the public web site link or enter the link into your browser (`<company name>-public.sharepoint.com`). You will be prompted to log in with your site collection administrator credentials and, after login, will land on the landing page (Figure 6-29).

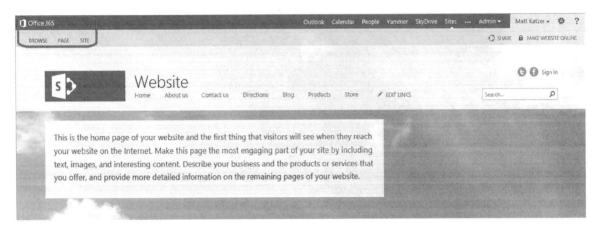

Figure 6-29. *Public web site landing page*

Step 2: Select the Page to Edit

Once you have logged on to the public web site, select the page to edit. To find the correct page, select "Page," then view pages. Our PayPal store is located on the "Store" page. Select "Store" (see number 1, Figure 6-30), then select "Page" (see number 2, Figure 6-30).

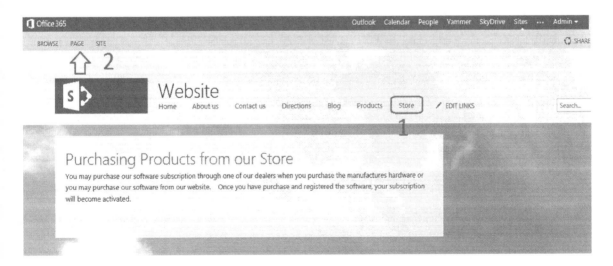

Figure 6-30. *Store landing page*

Step 3: Edit the Page

There are two edit options on the page: site properties and page properties (or content area). We are interested in the content area. Select "Edit" (see Figure 6-31) to extend the content page with the additional fields required for the PayPal order icon and shopping cart.

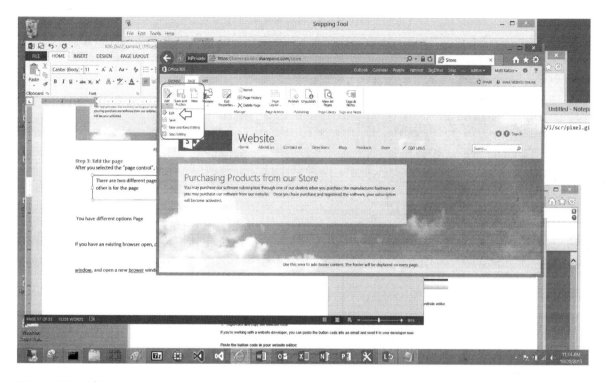

Figure 6-31. *Editing an existing page*

Step 4: Add Content to the Page

Online stores are built around tables. Each row of the table is allocated to a product and ordering button. When you create your PayPal payment engine, you define a number of products that you want your customers to add to their shopping cart. You then add the products in each row. This works well for simple stores but not for more complex stores with lot of products.

To add a table (see Figure 6-32) to the page that we are editing is simple. Follow these steps:

1. Move your mouse to the content page.

2. Enter a heading for the table insert, such as "Product Offering."

3. Select Insert ➤ Table and select the table size.

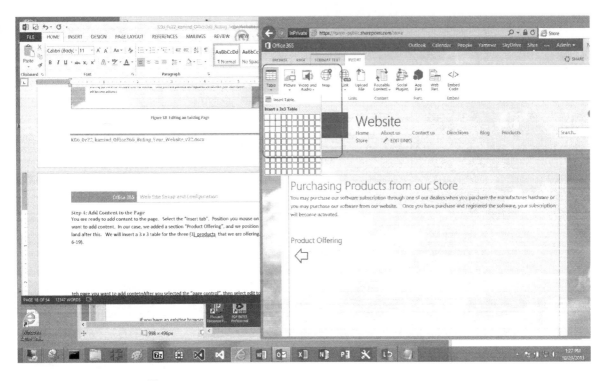

Figure 6-32. *Inserting a table*

Step 5: Insert the PayPal HTML Code

Earlier, we generated two code snippets from the PayPal site. These were "Add to Cart" and "View Cart." In the table that we created in Step 4, select one of the cells (we used the right-most cell in row 2) and embed the PayPal code (see Figure 6-33). Follow the steps outlined below.

1. Select the second row, third column with your mouse.

2. Select "Embed Code."

3. Insert the PayPal "Add to Cart" code.

4. Advance to the next row and insert additional PayPal "Add to Cart," as required.

5. Insert "View Cart" in the last row.

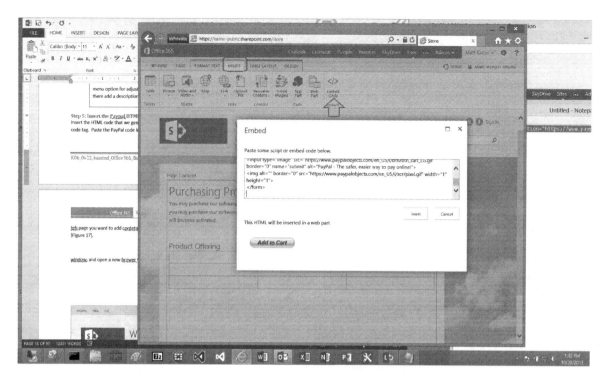

Figure 6-33. *Insert PayPal "Add to Cart" button into the page*

Step 6: Publish the Page

Save and publish the page. Test the add to cart and view shopping cart (see Figure 6-34) and make changes in the PayPal code, as appropriate. You now have a payment engine with PayPal and no responsibility for the payment processing (PCI compliance for credit card information is PayPal responsibility.)

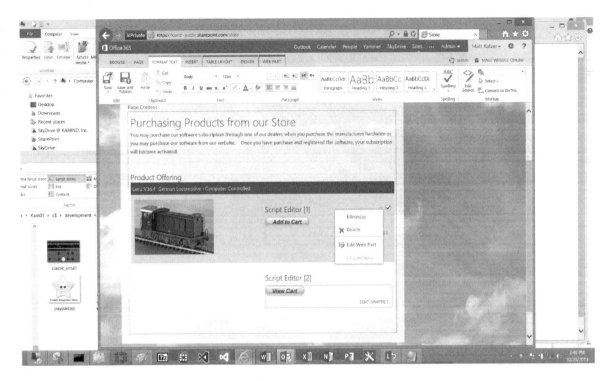

Figure 6-34. *Online store page with "View Cart" button*

Installation of SharePoint Designer

We spent most of this chapter on how to use Office 365 integrated editor. There is another tool that you can use for web site design. This is the SharePoint Designer 2013. SharePoint Designer is a download from the Office 365 site that is free with subscribers who have access to SharePoint team site. To use the tool on an Office 365 site, you must be a global administrator or have rights granted to you as a SharePoint site collection administrator. The different privileges are discussed in Chapter 5.

To download the SharePoint Designer tool, log in to the Office 365 site (`http://office.microsoft.com`) and select the "gear" icon (Tools menu) and Office 365 settings (Figure 6-35).

Figure 6-35. *Selecting "Office 365 settings" from the Tools menu ("gear" icon)*

After you select "Office 365 settings," select "tools & add-ins," then select SharePoint Designer and install the software on your systems (Figure 6-36).

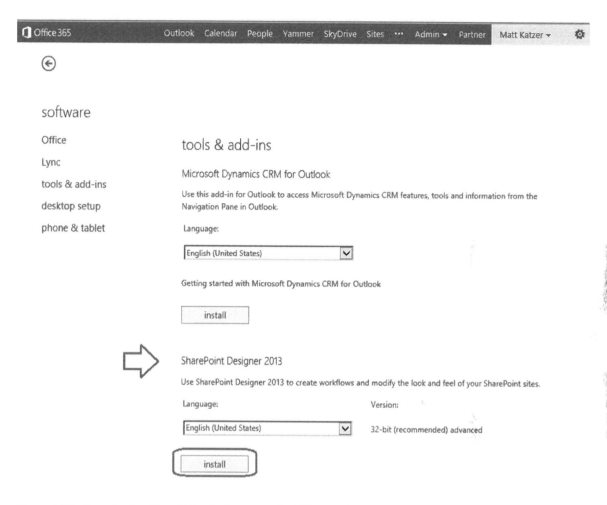

Figure 6-36. Downloading SharePoint Designer 2013 for Office 365 SharePoint

---

■ **Note**   If you have Office 2010 and SharePoint Workspace 2010, you will have to uninstall these tools before you install Office 2013 or SharePoint Designer 2013. If not, you will have conflicts with the 2013 tools, and they may not work properly.

Before you install SharePoint Designer 2013, uninstall Office 2010 and SharePoint 2010. The 2010 software will be in conflict with the 2013 software when you use these advanced features. SharePoint Designer is a streaming download, similar to Office 2013. Once the software has been installed, start up the SharePoint Designer account to match your Office 365 company account. In Chapter 5, we discussed the different permission settings to be used to modify a SharePoint site. To modify the Office 365 public web site, you must be a site collection administrator on the site you are going to modify. Once SharePoint Designer has downloaded, start up SharePoint Designer, then select the account screen and enter your Office 365 credentials (Figure 6-37).

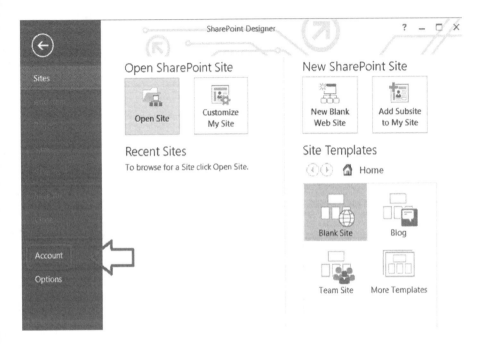

Figure 6-37. *Selecting account screen on SharePoint Designer startup*

Fill in your account information. You want to make sure that the connected services match your Office 365 company (Figure 6-38) and that the account you are using has the site administrator permissions allowing you to actively change the SharePoint public web site. Once you add the account, you can then actively change the SharePoint public web site or team site on Office 365.

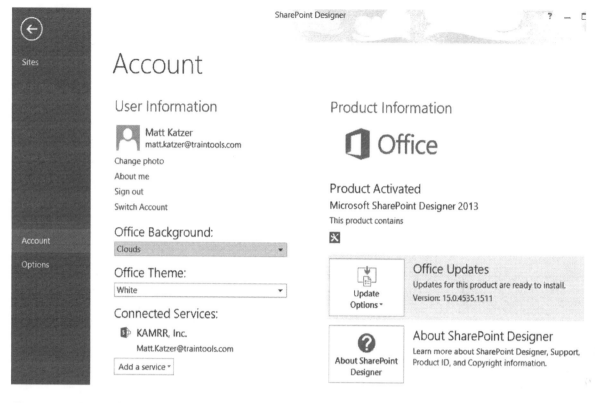

Figure 6-38. Setting the account information to match Connected Services

Public Web Site and Domain Name Configuration

Microsoft Office 365 allows one public web site to be created for your company. A default SharePoint team site and public web site are created with the default domain name that is used when you subscribe to the Office 365 service. For example, if your domain name is "contoso.com", the admin center is created as @contoso.onmicrosoft.com, and the default public web site will have the external public name: http://contoso-public.sharepoint.com. The only real work to make the web site public is to add a www subdomain that will resolve to your public web site. Once you add the "www" subdomain, all that is left is to enable the public website in the Sharepoint admin center.

There is a seven-step process that you must follow in setting up the externally hosted web site on Office 365. The steps are simple.

1. Create the public web site. (Go to the SharePoint admin center.)

2. Validate the www domain, a subdomain of <mycompanyname.com> domain.

3. Change the domain to a SharePoint-only domain.

4. Change the web site internal name (to the public Internet domain name).

    a. Select the check box URL of the public web site.

    b. Select the web site domain (rename your web site button).

    c. Change the URL to the Internet domain name URL, then select OK.

5. Look up the DNS name for the web site.

    a. Select the check box URL on the vanity domain.

    b. Get the DNS name from the SharePoint admin center.

6. Change the hosted DNS and add the CNAME to the DNS registrar.

7. Make web site "online."

The process is very straightforward and simple to do. The primary decision is a simple one. Do you make the web site public "before you are ready, or wait till the content is deployed?" If you want to delay publishing your web site, stop at step 3. This stops the vanity domain from being published, but the web site is still published with a default web domain in the format "domain"-web.sharepoint.com. Step 7 is important, because you have to change the permissions for public access. Until you "Make Website Online," it is only available to your Site Collection Administrator.

Step 1: Create the Public Web Site

You should have your public web site created and tested and ready to go live. The default public web site is <company name>-public.sharepoint.com.

Step 2: Validate the www Domain (or the Subdomain)

Add the full domain name (www) and validate the domain for Office 365 (Figure 6-39). This will be a fast process. Once the domain is verified, step 2, skip setting any users.

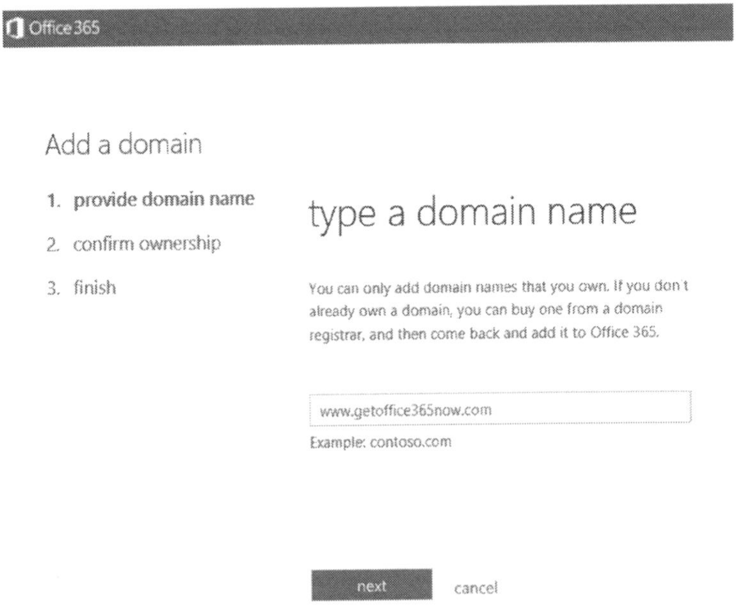

Figure 6-39. Add the www domain to be validated

Step 3: Change the Domain to SharePoint Intent

The next step in the domain validation is setting the domain intent. The domain (www) is being used Sharepoint online (the public website). Figure 6-40 shows setting the domain intent as SharePoint.

Set up domain

1. **set domain purpose**

2. design website

3. make it online

4. change address

5. finish

how do you want to use www.getoffice365now.com with office 365?

Select the Office 365 services you want to use with www.getoffice365now.com. Learn more

☐ **Exchange Online:** I want users in my organization to have @www.getoffice365now.com email addresses.

☐ **Lync Online:** I want users to sign in to IM and Lync meetings with their @www.getoffice365now.com user IDs.

☑ **SharePoint Online:** I want my Office 365 public website address to be http://www.getoffice365now.com.

⚠ When you first set up your domain, you can't use it with SharePoint Online together with Exchange Online and Lync Online. To learn how to work around this restriction, read Use SharePoint Online on a custom domain together with other services.

NOTE: A CRM Online subscription doesn't require any domain set up.

Do you have on-premises mailboxes? (Advanced setup) ▾

next   cancel

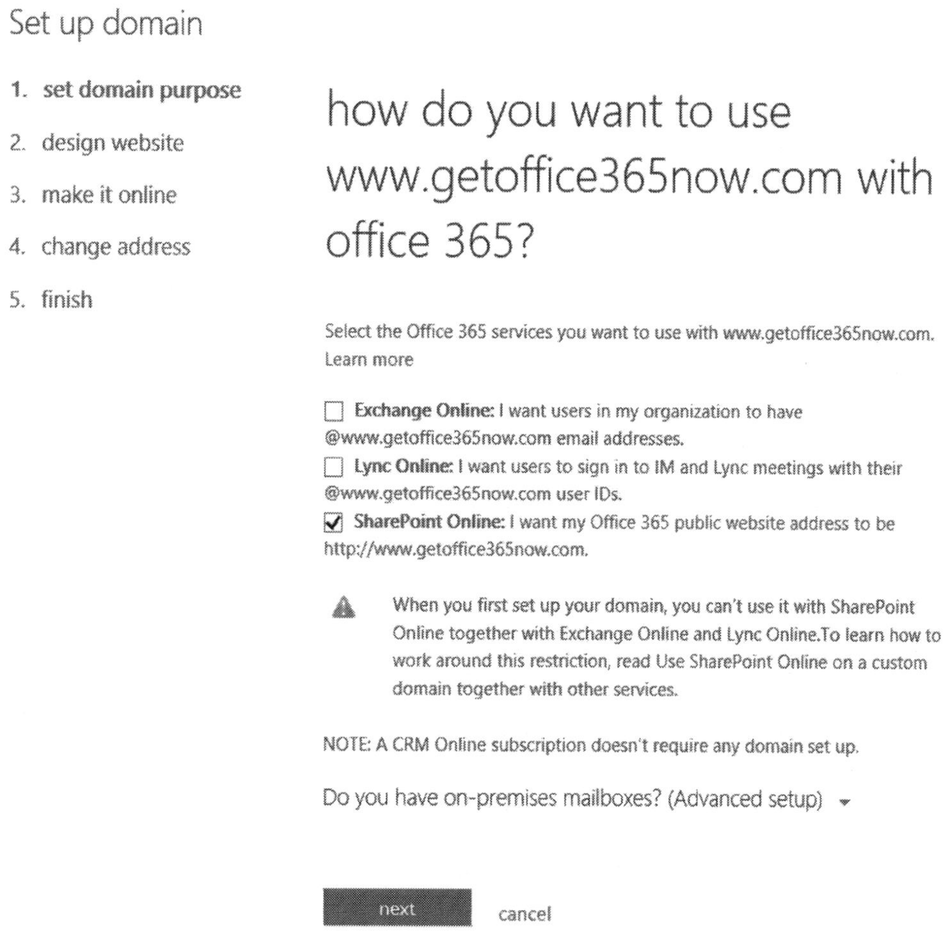

Figure 6-40. *Setting domain intent as SharePoint*

Step 4: Change the Web Site Internal Name

At this step, select the web site domain, to assign the Internet domain to the Office 365 public web site. From the SharePoint admin center, select "Website Domains" (see Figure 6-41).

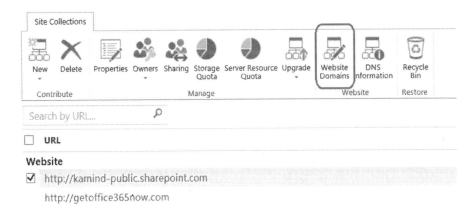

Figure 6-41. *Assign the web site domain to the internal site*

After you select "Website Domains," select the new URL that will replace the current public web site domain name (see Figure 6-42).

Figure 6-42. *Selecting the public Internet address for the web site*

Step 5: Look Up the DNS Name for the Web Site

At this point, the web site has been assigned, all that is needed is to look up the DNS records and have the CNAME assigned at GoDaddy or Network Solutions. In Figure 6-42 (preceding), we see the public web site as http://kamind-public.sharepoint.com. If you select "DNS Information" (Figure 6-43), this will give you the DNS information for the main SharePoint web site, kamind.sharepoint.com. The Office 365 DNS manager will redirect the web traffic to the correct location. After you select the menu item, retrieve the DNS information (Figure 6-44). This is the information you require to add a CNAME in your domain registrar.

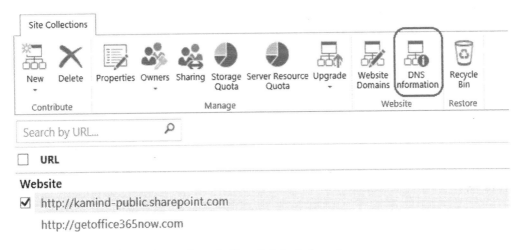

Figure 6-43. Retrieve the DNS name from the SharePoint admin center

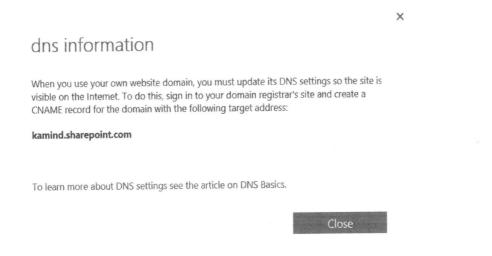

Figure 6-44. DNS information for web site registration

Step 6: Update the DNS Information

You will have to update the DNS information in your local DNS servers and at the domain registrar. This change allows external Internet users to find your web site. Figure 6-45 is an example of the CNAME changes at Network Solutions.

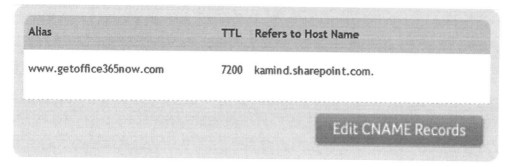

Figure 6-45. *Adding CNAME to SharePoint web site*

Step 7: Make the Web Site Online

Once you have set the public DNS records, you will have to log the public web site, and "Make Website Online." This final step reconfigures the public web site with the correct permissions for access by users from the Internet (see Figure 6-46).

Figure 6-46. *Converting the offline web site to an online web site*

During the conversion process, you will be notified that the draft pages will be offline until you publish them (see Figure 6-47). This is followed by a verification message, to make sure that you intend to make the web site online (Figure 6-48).

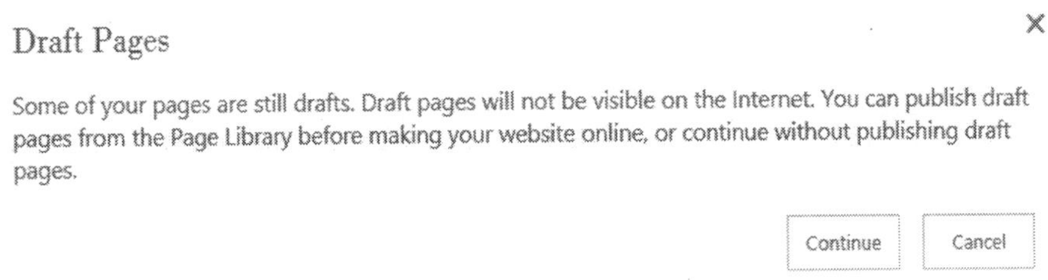

Draft Pages ✕

Some of your pages are still drafts. Draft pages will not be visible on the Internet. You can publish draft pages from the Page Library before making your website online, or continue without publishing draft pages.

Continue | Cancel

Figure 6-47. Verification that the draft pages are not being published

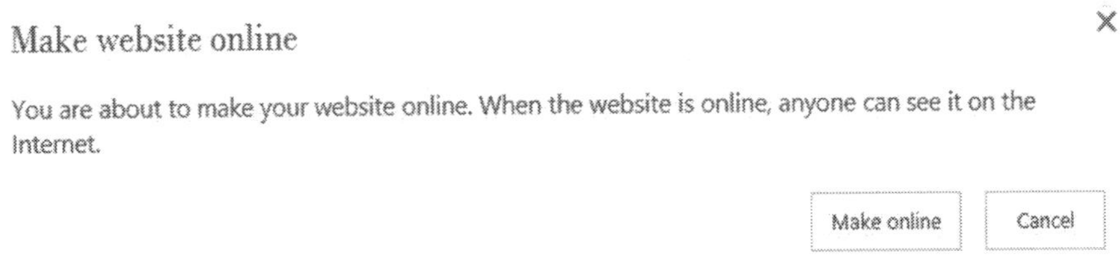

Make website online ✕

You are about to make your website online. When the website is online, anyone can see it on the Internet.

Make online | Cancel

Figure 6-48. Final step before web site is published to the Internet

Once you have selected "Make online," the draft pages that you access as a site collection administrator will have a prompt to publish the web page (see Figure 6-49).

Figure 6-49. Home page with message to site collection administrator to publish

■ **Note** The public web site will repond to either the internal name, kamind-public.sharepoint.com, or kamind. sharepoint.com. The domain intent determines how the Office 365 DNS will respond to an external web request.

Last Thoughts–Office 365 Public Web Sites

We covered a lot of material in this chapter. You should now know how to create a web site with the Enterprise version of Office 365. If you have purchased the Professional or Midsize versions, you will have noticed that a lot of the options we described in this chapter are already configured for you or not present.

That is the main difference between the Professional version and the Enterprise version. The Enterprise version scales across thousands of users, whereas the Professional version can support a maximum of 50. The other difference between the Professional version and the Enterprise version is the level of support. The Professional version uses support groups. The Enterprise version uses online services or direct phone support to give you access to the resources you need to handle support problems. We typically recommend that you find yourself a Microsoft Partner. You need to add the partner to your subscription (see Figure 6-50).

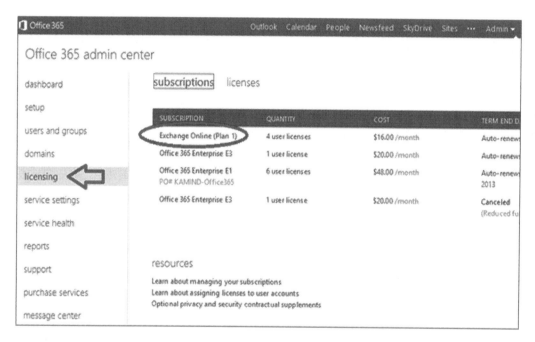

Figure 6-50. *Selecting a Microsoft Partner as a license adviser*

Once that partner is added, you can work with your Microsoft Partner as well as Microsoft online service support personnel to address support issues. When you use the Enterprise version, Microsoft and your partner will team up to find a solution to a problem. In the case of the Professional packages, the service support is only through MS online forums and partners. Any direct support from online services will be paid support.

If you do not have a partner, contact one and ask for his or her partner ID. Select the subscription (Figure 6-51), then edit the partner information. For example, if you selected KAMIND, you would enter the partner ID 598821. Our recommendation is that you contact different Microsoft Partners and interview them to find out what they will offer you as license advisers. Microsoft compensates licenses advisers with adviser fees, to assist you in the management of your Office 365 site. The overall objective of the licenses adviser program is to link you to a Microsoft Partner, so your experience in using Office 365 is a good one, with minimal issues.

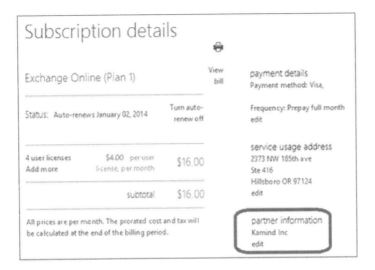

Figure 6-51. Adding KAMIND (partner ID 598821) as a licnese adviser

Reference Links

There is a lot of information about Office 365 on the Web. The point is to find the right site. The information contained in this chapter is a combination of our experiences executing deployments and the support information that has been published by third parties.

Getting Started with the Public Web Site

```
http://office.microsoft.com/en-us/sharepoint-help/get-started-with-the-public-website-HA102801171.
aspx
http://office.microsoft.com/en-us/office365-sharepoint-online-enterprise-help/public-website-help-
for-office-365-HA102891740.aspx
```

Customizing Your Public Web Site

```
http://blogs.office.com/b/microsoft_office_365_blog/archive/2012/05/10/customize-public-website-
office-365--gadgets.aspx
```

Office 365 Two Public Web Sites (Wave 14 and Wave 15)

```
http://office.microsoft.com/en-us/office365-suite-help/work-with-your-two-office-365-public-
websites-HA103148336.aspx
```

Tagging Documents and Pages in the Cloud

```
http://office.microsoft.com/en-us/sharepoint-server-help/add-a-tag-cloud-web-part-to-a-page-
HA101929584.aspx
```

Office 365 SharePoint Online Developers Guide

```
www.microsoft.com/en-us/download/details.aspx?id=17069
```

Next Steps

Your basic Office 365 systems have been set up and configured. At this point, you are 100% functional and ready to move to the next steps. However, your work is not yet complete. There is much more to do, depending on your Office 365 configuration. The key chapters that you have to review for your Office 365 deployment and management are the following:

- **Chapter 5:** SharePoint Administration

  - SharePoint administration and design can be simple or complex, depending on your business needs. This chapter provides you with a basic overview of the configuration necessary to be up and running, using the Office 365 team site. This chapter describes site design and construction issues, as well as the full SharePoint administration functions for Office 365.

- **Chapter 9:** Compliance and Data Loss Prevention

  - Businesses must adapt their mail document storage systems to correctly process electronic communication, based on regulatory oversight. Compliance and data loss prevention (DLP) provides this capability, to allow businesses to manage their communications and protect them from simple mistakes in their electronic communications. Office 365 includes integrated discovery that supports legal discovery and audit requirements.

- **Chapter 10:** Exchange Online Protection Administration

  - Office 365 is composed of a set of services. The Exchange Online Protection (EOP) service is the front end of Office 365 that handles all of the external e-mail front-end processing and filtering. If you have smart devices that e-mail to Office 365, you will use EOP to manage the interaction.

- **Chapter 11:** DirSync, AD FS, Single Sign-On, and Exchange Federation

  - Active Directory Federation Services and Single Sign-On is the integration of the Office 365 Active Directory with on-premises Active Directory. This allows one sign-on (controlled by on-premises servers) to give access to both cloud and on-premises resources. Password Sync can be a simpler implementation that meets many requirements. Federation allows on-premises and cloud Exchange servers to work together.

CHAPTER 7

■ ■ ■

Office 365 – Windows Intune Administration Guide

Office 365 is a suite of technologies delivered as a Software as a Service (SaaS) offering. Office 365 reduces the IT costs for businesses of any size and significantly reduces the need for an IT professional to manage the Office 365 services. Windows Intune is a desktop management SaaS offering, which complements Office 365. Office 365 deployments work better when Windows Intune is deployed for desktop and mobile device management. The change in desktop management has moved from device-centric management to user management (see Figure 7-1). Microsoft extended this management into Microsoft Systems Center and the standardization of a five (5) user licenses model for Windows Intune and Office 365 subscription services. Users can bring their own devices to Office 365, and have those devices managed by Windows Intune.

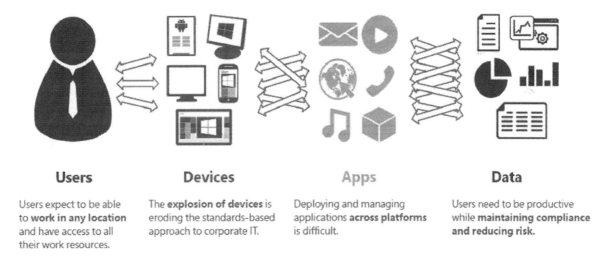

Users

Users expect to be able to **work in any location** and have access to all their work resources.

Devices

The **explosion of devices** is eroding the standards-based approach to corporate IT.

Apps

Deploying and managing applications **across platforms** is difficult.

Data

Users need to be productive while **maintaining compliance and reducing risk.**

Figure 7-1. *Windows Intune focus (courtesy of Microsoft)*

Why would you use Windows Intune to manage devices that use Office365? The simple answer – it just works. Devices that have Windows Intune deployed with Office 365 have less support calls and trouble tickets. Our own experience is that the Windows Intune reduces support calls by 50% when deployed with an Automatic upgrade management and integrated anti-virus scans.

Device management is no longer desktops, you are managing users, devices, applications, and data. Office 365 and Windows Intune are built with a self-service model providing user's access to Microsoft Cloud Services - worldwide. Windows Intune provides consistent experiences for all users and the management of the devices. Users (and IT administrators) can add users to the local Active Directory; either through a workplace join or a traditional Active Directory Add User/Computer. Windows Intune provides consistency of device Management with:

- – Workplace join; allows you to dynamically add a device with second factor authentication

- – Domain joined systems — download and select Windows Intune

- – Consistent opt-in message across all environments

- – Consistent implementation of self-service portals across all environments

Office 365 self-service portal (allows users to install Professional Plus software on demand) is extended with Windows Intune. This trend is forcing the change to the management of devices: application distribution via a company owned application store. As new users enter the workforce, they want to use their own devices, and load the software that they need to use to improve their personal productivity. As an IT manager, you need to figure out how to supply these services, without adding additional support costs. This is where Windows Intune comes into play. Windows Intune solves these problems for users and IT Managers. IT Managers (see Figure 7-2) now have a single view to all the devices in the organization. – including Apple and Android devices. Device Management with integrated Office 365 support - is the power of Windows Intune.

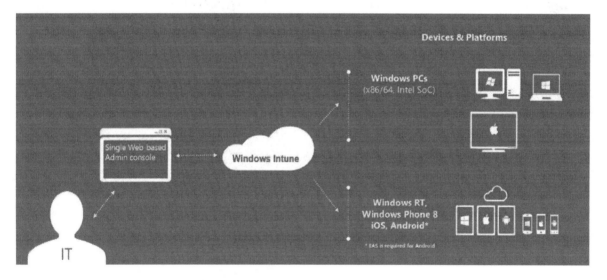

Figure 7-2. *Windows Intune Management Console (courtesy of Microsoft)*

Intune versus System Center

Windows Intune may operate with Microsoft Systems Center or as a standalone Cloud Service. Which service configuration do you use? It depends on the size of the organization. Larger Organization (100 users) use Microsoft Systems Center for desktop and server management. Smaller organization (less than 100 and no servers), use Windows Intune without Systems center. Windows Intune design is scalable for both environments, with the integration into Systems center using the Systems center Configuration Manger (see Figure 7-3). This scalability is a byproduct of Microsoft's cloud services deployment and the security model deployed with Window's Azure Active Directory federation. User's accounts in Office 365, and Windows Intune are linked to a common active directory through Windows Azure Active directory.

Figure 7-3. *Windows Intune Systems Center Comparison (courtesy of Microsoft)*

As Microsoft deploys newer Operating Systems (OS) Software (a.k.a. recent Windows 8.1 and Windows Phone 8 and future releases), these operating systems are shipped with a lightweight management agent integrated into the OS. These management agents simplify the user access in enabling their own devices to be managed by Microsoft Management. These agents are:

- Mobile Device Management – Intune Management (lightweight management)

- Configuration Device Management – Systems Center (Corporate Management: allows download of full management agent from Systems Center)

The difference with the two approaches has to do with the management of the device. Microsoft introduces a new feature in System Center 2012R2 called workplace join. Workplace join allows the end user to enroll their smartphone, laptop, or desktop into a corporate network for secure access too business data. Corporate users who have deployed Microsoft Systems Center have two options: use the workplace join (if deployed Windows Server 2012R2) or use Windows Intune enrollment via the Company Portal. This allows users to self-enroll their devices using the Company Portal in the Window's Intune Center (`http://account.manage.microsoft.com`).

If the organization has deployed Systems Center 2012 R2 or later, the device can be dually enrolled with both Windows Intune and Systems Center. When this happens, the IT department can supply additional services to the client device, and the user can download the company applications on demand form the company portal (Figure 7-4). This approach allows IT departments to permit users to bring their own devices into the company network while protecting the corporate data. When the user leaves the Company, the IT department can selectively wipe portions of the user device and remove all of the company's information. This feature works on Windows devices, iOS devices, and Android devices.

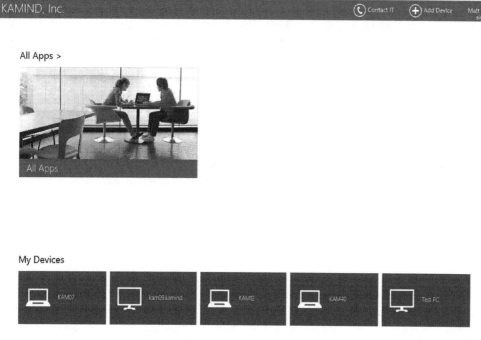

Figure 7-4. *User enrollment using Windows Intune Company Portal*

As an administrator, you need to select the management approach (Microsoft Systems Center 2012 R2 or Windows Intune Administrative console) depending upon your organization. Microsoft Systems center 2012 R2 configuration can be very complex and entire books have been written on this. Our focus in this chapter is on the Windows Intune configuration with Office 365 and how to configure and deploy Windows Intune in your environment.

Windows Intune Purchase Process

The Windows Intune process is a separate purchase process, and it must be manually linked to Office 365. When you purchase Windows Intune, you must be logged out of Office 365. You start the purchase process for Windows Intune then link the subscription to Office 365 using your Office 365 global Administrator account. If you complete the purchase process and do not supply your existing Office 365 account, the Windows Intune site will not be linked to your Office 365 subscription. **There is no workaround if you do this incorrectly.** If you purchase the subscription incorrectly, your only option is to contact your partner and have them contact Microsoft Online services and have your newly created Windows Intune account canceled.

Step 1: Purchasing Intune

Select the purchase link (supplied by your partner) and verify the price and select the Delegated administration option (see Figure 7-5), and then click next. There are two types of access a partner has to an Office 365 (and Windows Intune subscription): a licenses advisor, or a Delegated Administrator. Licenses advisor only gives access to licenses information and no data. Delegated administrator gives your partner access to the Office 365/Windows Intune site as a Global administrator. If your Microsoft Partner is configuring your Windows Intune account, they will need access as a Delegated or a Global Administrator.

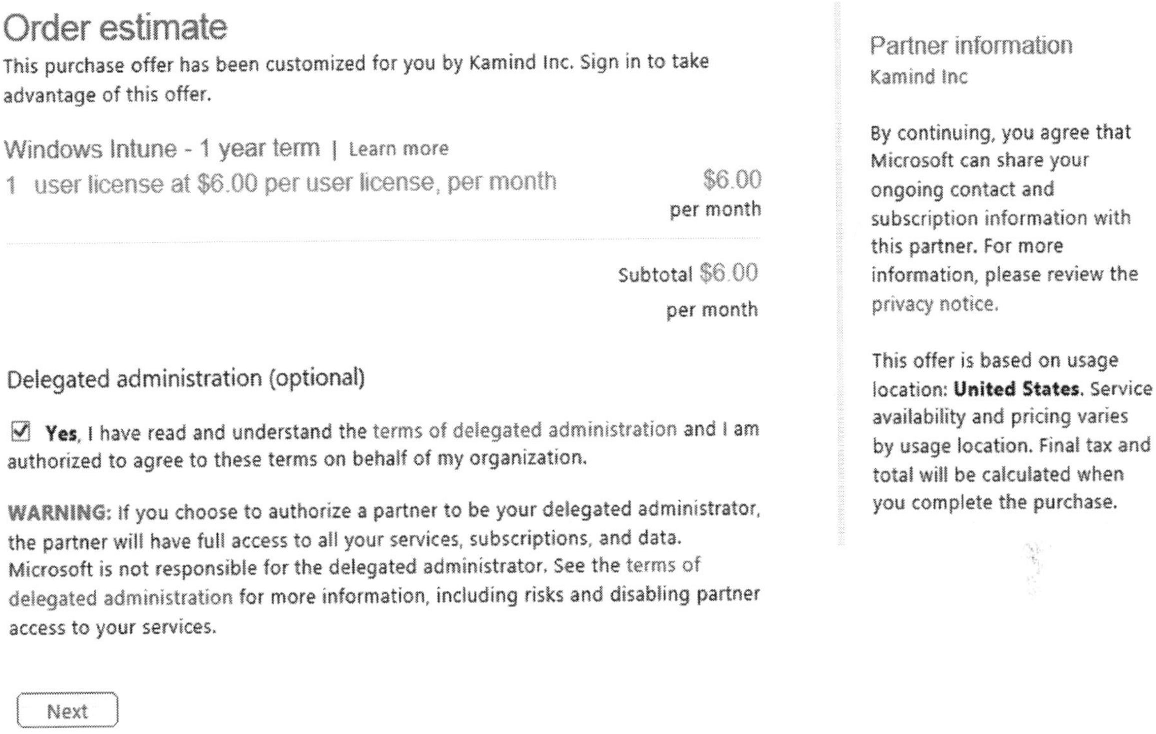

Order estimate

This purchase offer has been customized for you by Kamind Inc. Sign in to take advantage of this offer.

Windows Intune - 1 year term | Learn more

1 user license at $6.00 per user license, per month $6.00

per month

Subtotal $6.00

per month

Delegated administration (optional)

☑ **Yes**, I have read and understand the terms of delegated administration and I am authorized to agree to these terms on behalf of my organization.

WARNING: If you choose to authorize a partner to be your delegated administrator, the partner will have full access to all your services, subscriptions, and data. Microsoft is not responsible for the delegated administrator. See the terms of delegated administration for more information, including risks and disabling partner access to your services.

[Next]

Partner information
Kamind Inc

By continuing, you agree that Microsoft can share your ongoing contact and subscription information with this partner. For more information, please review the privacy notice.

This offer is based on usage location: **United States**. Service availability and pricing varies by usage location. Final tax and total will be calculated when you complete the purchase.

Figure 7-5. *Purchase process with Delegated Administrator*

Why Only One License When I Have 50 users?

Different partners will have different approaches to the purchase process. At KAMIND our policy is to add the licenses based on the business needs, so we start all subscriptions with one user license. This way you can configure your Windows Intune site before you begin your deployment. You add the licenses based on your deployment schedule. It is easy to add licenses, but difficult to remove licenses.

What Is Delegated Administration?

Delegated administration is when you give permission to a partner (KAMIND) to administrate your Office 365 or Windows Intune accounts. A Delegated Administration Partner (DAP) can perform 99 percent of the administration tasks on your Office 365 Windows Intune account. However some tasks (such as content of email, documents, and certain PowerShell commands) require a locally licensed account.

Step 2 Linking Windows Intune to Office 365

If you have an Office 365 account, this is the step where you sign into that account and link the new Windows Intune subscription to your Office 365 account. When you link the accounts, you automatically populate "Windows Intune" with the users from your Office 365 account (this process is transparent and uses Windows Azure Active Directory federation to manage the user accounts).

In Figure 7-6, click "Sign in" and enter the Office 365 global administration account to link the subscription.

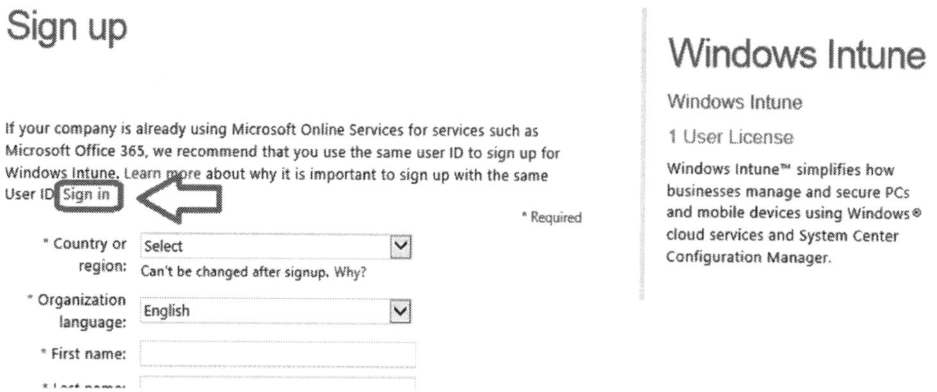

Sign up
If your company is already using Microsoft Online Services for services such as Microsoft Office 365, we recommend that you use the same user ID to sign up for Windows Intune. Learn more about why it is important to sign up with the same User ID Sign in
* Required
* Country or region:
Select
Can't be changed after signup. Why?
* Organization language:
English
* First name:
Windows Intune
Windows Intune
1 User License
Windows Intune™ simplifies how businesses manage and secure PCs and mobile devices using Windows® cloud services and System Center Configuration Manager.

Figure 7-6. *Sign into Office 365*

After you signed into Office 365, complete the payment process. At this point, you need to configure Windows Intune administrator center and begin your deployment.

Configuration of Windows Intune Administration Center

You have completed the purchase Windows Intune and you are ready to go! What do you do next? The first step is to configure the Windows Intune Administration center using the admin console. To access the administrator portal login to `http://Accounts.manage.microsoft.com` and use your Office 365 Global administrator account, select Admin Console (Figure 7-7).

Windows Intune
Home | Company Portal | Admin Console | Admin
KAMIND IT, Inc.
Admin Overview
Setup
Overview
Management
Users
Security Groups
Domains
Subscriptions
Manage
Licenses
Purchase
Software
Support
Overview
Service Requests
Service Health
Start here tasks
1. Add users
2. View Setup overview page
Admin shortcuts
Reset user passwords
Add new users
Assign users
Create a service request

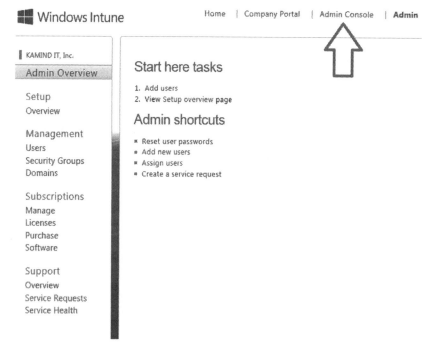

Figure 7-7. *Accessing the Windows Intune Admin Console*

The Windows Intune administration console (Figure 7-8) has four areas for management that need to be configured before you can use the service. These are the Windows Intune configuration for Agent (software that runs on a device), Mobile (governs how to manage mobile devices), Firewall (Windows firewall settings), and Intune Center Settings.

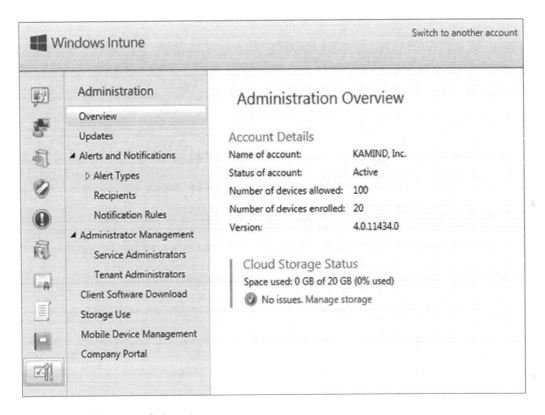

Figure 7-8. *Admin Console Overview*

As an administrator, you have different options on the configuration of Windows Intune. As you become more experienced with Windows Intune, you can adjust the capabilities to meet your desired objectives.

Windows Intune Policy Management

Windows Intune manages devices and users by policy. Policies are applied to the groups and are pushed out to the clients. In the December 2013 release, there are four policies available for Windows Intune. There two different policy configuration options: default (Microsoft chooses) and custom (you choose). Our Windows Intune configuration will walk through the processes we use in the configuration of a Window's Intune center. The Windows Intune policies are listed in Table 7-1 and are configured in the steps listed below.

Table 7-1. *Window Intune Policy Settings*

Policy Name	Step	Policy Description
Agent Settings	3	Controls the antivirus and Windows update settings.
Mobile Security	4	Allows the setting of password, encryption and other security features for mobile devices managed by Windows Intune.
Firewall Settings	5	Controls the setting of the Windows firewall on the device.
Center Settings	6	Publishes the support information to the desktop

We have discovered a very interesting side effect as we have deployed Windows Intune. When we combine an Office 365 subscription with a Windows Intune subscription, our support call load has decreased. There are many different reasons this is the case, but what we have found is that Systems that are managed by Windows Intune with very aggressive updates – the Office 365 integration just works. Cloud solutions require that the desktop devices must have the latest security patches and fixes. Those clients that we have not deployed Windows Intune for have a higher support call load, either internally to their own IT organization or with our post-sales support.

Configuration of Window's Intune consist of the following nine steps

1. Add Administrator Notification

2. Configure Auto Updates

3. Configure Agent Policies

4. Configure Mobile Policies

5. Configure DNS changes for Mobile Devices

6. Configure Device Firewall Policies

7. Configure Intune center Policies

8. Deploy Window's Intune

9. Linking users to Windows Intune Accounts

The nine-step process for deploying Windows Intune is outlined below. All of our initial Window's Intune accounts are configured this way with very aggressive Windows Auto update configuration.

Step 1: Add Administrator Notification

Windows Intune notifies administrators when there is an error event on the device. This is used to inform the administrator list on the necessary corrective actions you need to take to resolve device issues. There are two steps in setting up notifications: adding the user to be notified and adding the notification that you wish the user to receive. When you add a user for notification, you define the rights for access to the Windows Intune Admin console.

1. Login to Account.manage.microsoft.com.

2. Select the Admin Console (see previous Figure 7-7).

3. Select the Administration tab, select Recipients, and then Add. Enter the email address for notification, then click OK (see Figure 7-9).

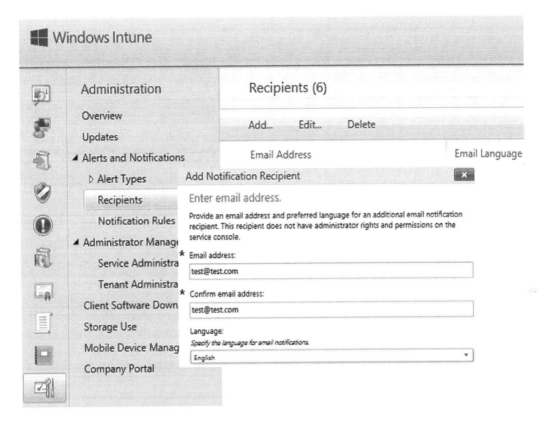

Figure 7-9. *Adding Notification Accounts*

    4. Select the notification rules, assign the recipient to the notification rules, and then click OK (see Figure 7-10).

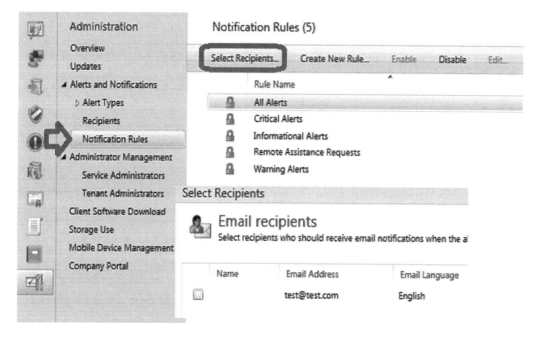

Figure 7-10. *Adding Notification Accounts*

5. Select OK when completed.

Step 2: Configure Auto Updates

After you have set the notification rules, you need to configure the auto updates. There are two philosophies on updates: configure the minimum updates you need, or configure all updates (including optional ones). What we have discovered is that for the clients where we have configured all updates including optional ones), there are less support calls and the Windows desktop runs faster.

1. Select the Update tab then click Configure Automatic Approval Settings (Figure 7-11).

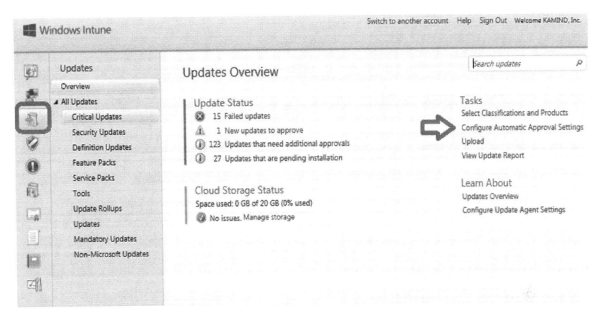

Figure 7-11. *Adding Automatic Updates*

2. Scroll down until you see the Auto Update window and select New (Figure 7-12).

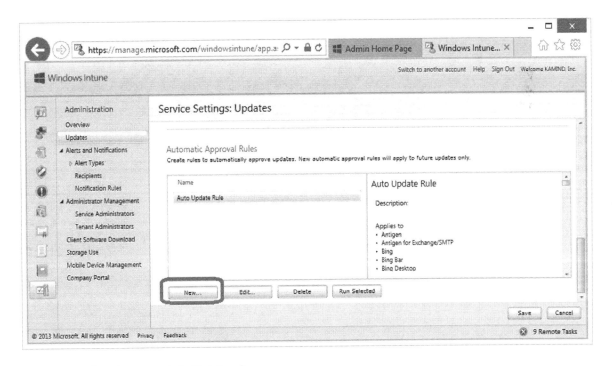

Figure 7-12. *Creating a new Auto Update rule*

3. Name the rule and fill in the description (Figure 7-13). Click "Next" when completed.

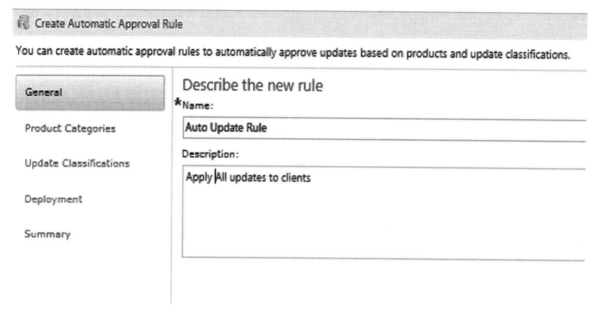

Figure 7-13. Name the Rule

4. Select All Categories (Intune works best if you apply all updates), as shown in Figure 7-14, and then select Next.

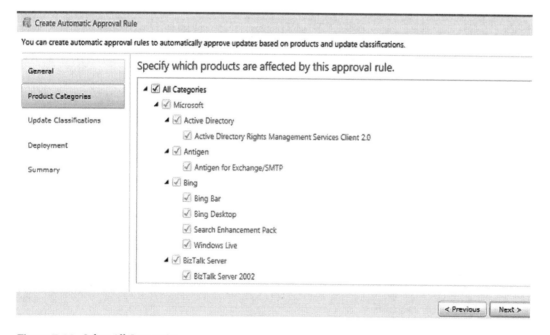

Figure 7-14. Select All Categories

5. Select All Classifications (Figure 7-15), and then select Next.

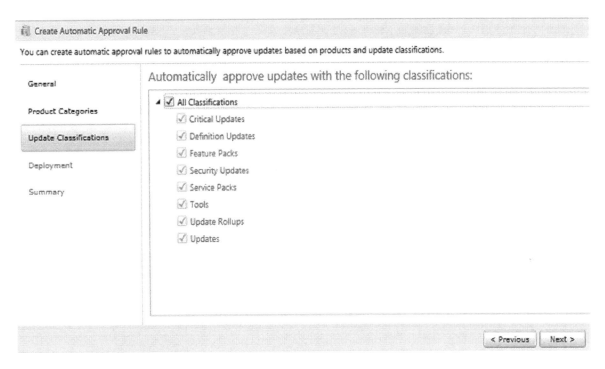

Figure 7-15. *Select All Classifications*

6. Select the deployment. This is extremely important and this is where Windows Intune differs from other update products. Windows Intune will install updates if the user fails to install the update by required deployment date, Window's Intune will install the update and force a systems reboot. Make sure you select All Computers to install updates (Figure 7-16).

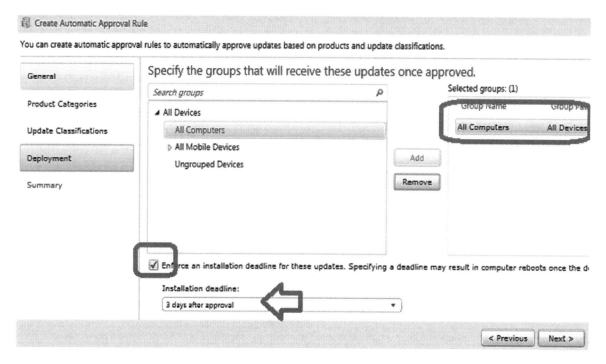

Figure 7-16. *Adding the deployment option for the update rule*

7. Select Next and then Finished. This creates the Automatic installation rule. The rule will execute and force updates to be installed three days after approval. The user can install updates early.

Step 3: Configure Agent Policies

Windows Intune manages desktop and mobile devices based upon Group Policies. There are four policy collections that you need to configure in Windows Intune. These policy collections enforce group policies on the clients that are enrolled in the Windows Intune service. The policy collections that you need to configure are the agent policy, mobile policy, firewall policy, and support policy. The first policy to configure is the agent policy. Select the policy icon (Figure 7-17), and then select Add Policy. Our configuration uses the "Custom Policy". We do not recommend that you use the Default Policy.

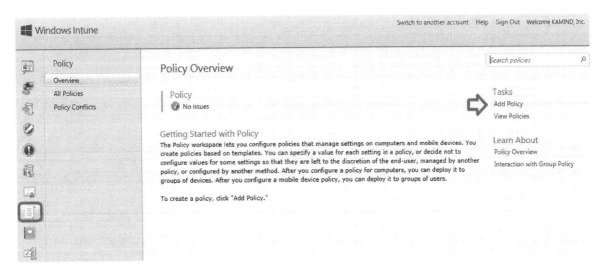

Figure 7-17. *Adding a new policy to Windows Intune*

Select the Windows Intune Agent Policy and Create and Deploy a Custom Policy (see Figure 7-18).

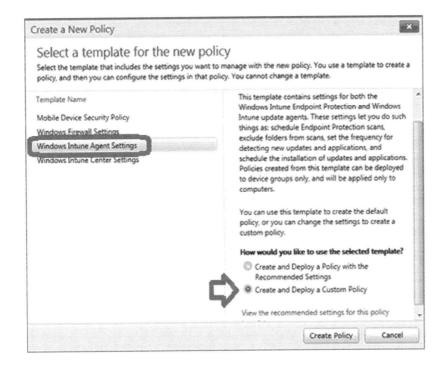

Figure 7-18. *Creating the Agent Policy*

Each policy is different. Depending upon your business needs, you may need to modify the policy settings to meet certain business objectives. Our approach is to identify the policies that we used in our standard deployment. We do not use all policies in the Collection; only a few. The ones we have identified in the following configuration are the important policies for the Windows Intune Operation. Follow the configuration wizard and the item configuration listed below.

1. Name the policy and supply a description (Figure 7-19).

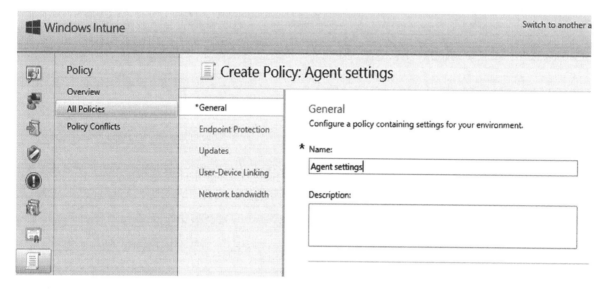

Figure 7-19. *Setting up the Agent Policy*

2. Configure the antivirus settings (Figure 7-20).

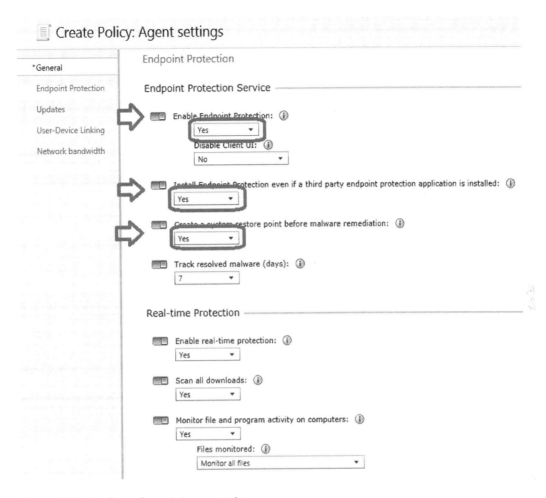

Figure 7-20. *Configure the antivirus protection*

3. Configure the daily and full scans (Figure 7-21). This is an important configuration. Office 365 will filter most viruses out of your environment, but you need to make sure you scan to eliminate the other problem areas.

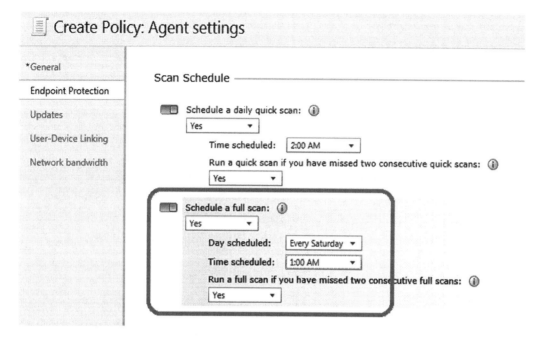

Figure 7-21. *Configure the Scanning behavior*

4. Configure the Quarantine settings (Figure 7-22).

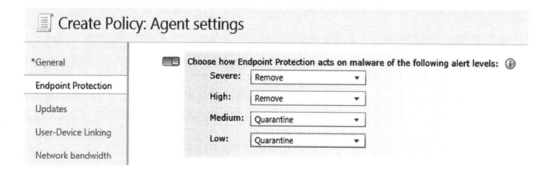

Figure 7-22. *Configure the Quarantine Settings*

5. Configure the update settings and membership in the active protection services. The active protection services coordinate information about known viruses to help the community to address threats (Figure 7-23).

Create Policy: Agent settings

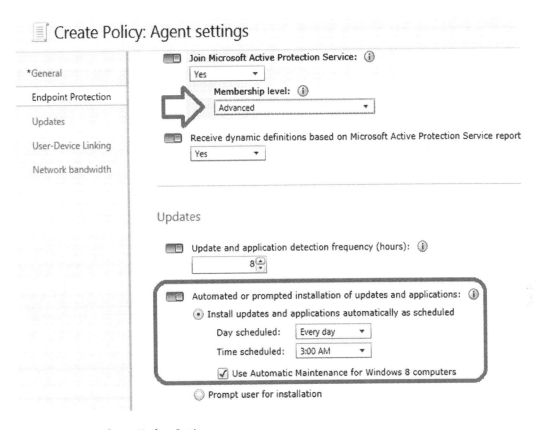

Figure 7-23. *Configure Update Settings*

6. The final steps are the configuration of the data transfer to reduce bandwidth consumption during working hours (Figure 7-24).

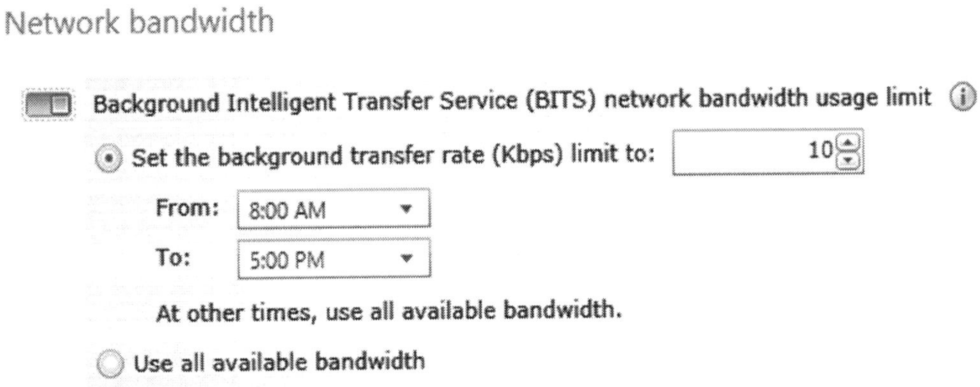

Network bandwidth

Background Intelligent Transfer Service (BITS) network bandwidth usage limit ⓘ

⦿ Set the background transfer rate (Kbps) limit to: `10`

From: `8:00 AM`

To: `5:00 PM`

At other times, use all available bandwidth.

◯ Use all available bandwidth

Figure 7-24. *Configuration of the update loading to reserve bandwidth*

7. Select Save Policy and you have created the first policy. Windows Intune will ask if you want to deploy the policy; select Yes to deploy the policy (Figure 7-25).

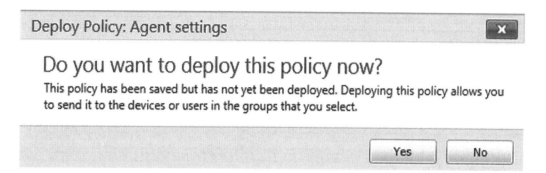

Figure 7-25. *Deploying Windows Intune Agent Policy*

8. Deploy the policies by selecting the group for deployment. The default group is either All Computers or Ungrouped Devices (see Figure 7-26). Just select the group, then click Add, and then click OK. The policy is deployed.

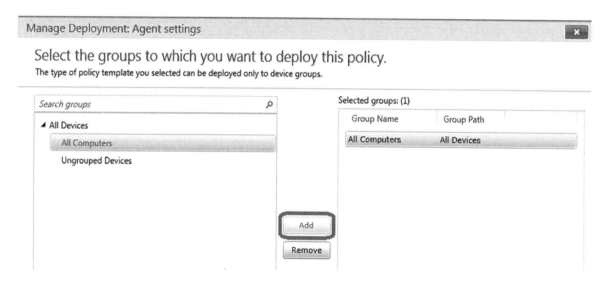

Figure 7-26. *Deploying Policies against a group*

Step 4: Configure Mobile Policies

After you configure the policy for desktop, you need to configure the policies for Mobile Device Management. If the policies are not configured, then the mobile devices will not be allowed to enroll in the Windows Intune management service. Select the Policy icon, and then select Add Policy.

1. Select Mobile Device Security Policy and select Create and Deploy a custom Policy (Figure 7-27).

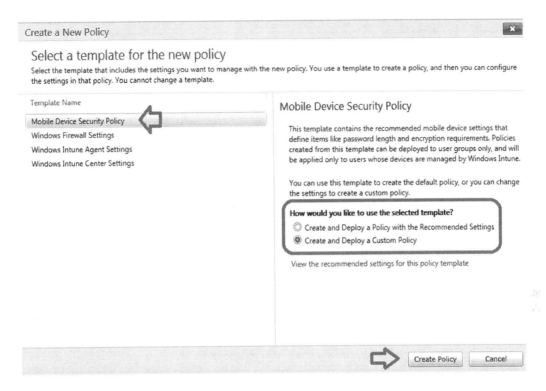

Figure 7-27. *Adding Mobile Device Policies*

2. Enter a policy name for the mobile device policy.

3. Define the password structure for the mobile device and enable the RT passwords (Figure 7-28).

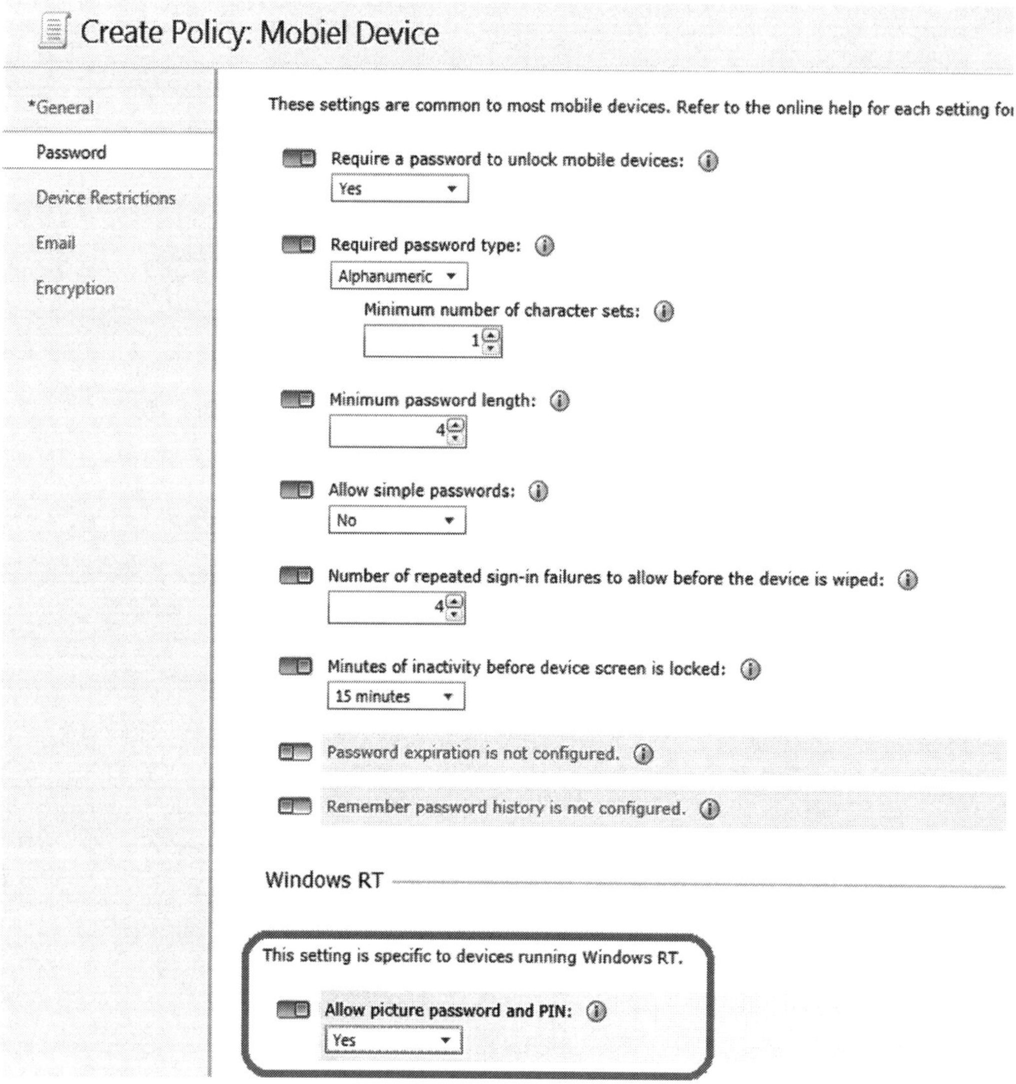

Create Policy: Mobiel Device

*General

Password

Device Restrictions

Email

Encryption

These settings are common to most mobile devices. Refer to the online help for each setting for

Require a password to unlock mobile devices: ⓘ

Yes ▼

Required password type: ⓘ

Alphanumeric ▼

Minimum number of character sets: ⓘ

1

Minimum password length: ⓘ

4

Allow simple passwords: ⓘ

No ▼

Number of repeated sign-in failures to allow before the device is wiped: ⓘ

4

Minutes of inactivity before device screen is locked: ⓘ

15 minutes ▼

Password expiration is not configured. ⓘ

Remember password history is not configured. ⓘ

Windows RT ─────────────────────

This setting is specific to devices running Windows RT.

Allow picture password and PIN: ⓘ

Yes ▼

Figure 7-28. *Device the password security policy*

4. Configure the additional security policies for mobile devices that your organization supports. In this case, the organization does not allow the SharePoint documents to be backed on iCloud, so they are restricted (Figure 7-29).

🗉 Create Policy: Mobiel Device

*General	These settings are common to iOS-based and Android-based devices.
Password	▢▢ Allow camera is not configured. ⓘ
Device Restrictions	▢▢ Allow web browser is not configured. ⓘ
Email	
Encryption	iOS

These settings are specific to iOS-based devices. iCloud is a service mark of Apple Inc., registered in the U.S countries.

▢▢ Allow backup to iCloud® is not configured. ⓘ

▢▢ **Allow document sync to iCloud®:** ⓘ
   No ▾

▢▢ Allow Photo Stream sync to iCloud® is not configured. ⓘ

Email

Exchange ActiveSync

These settings will apply only to devices that have connected to your corporate Exchange servers via Exchan technology.

▢▢ Allow users to download email attachments is not configured. ⓘ

▢▢ Email synchronization period is not configured. ⓘ

▢▢ Allow mobile devices that don't fully support these settings to synchronize with Exchange: ⓘ
   Yes ▾

Figure 7-29. Restricting security on Mobile Devices

5. Select Save Policy and then deploy the policy. When you deploy the policy, you deploy it to users (Figure 7-30). The model is that users bring mobile devices, and are licensed according to Windows Intune. Each user can support up to five devices under one Windows Intune license.

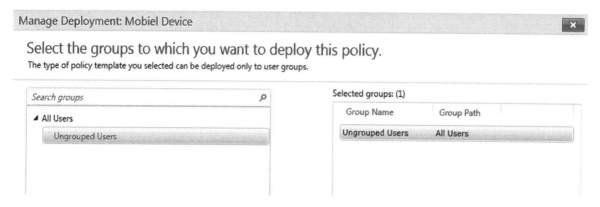

Figure 7-30. *Deploying Mobile Device Policy to the User Group*

Step 5: Configure Mobile Device DNS Enrollment

After you have configured the mobile device policies, you need to configure the DNS changes to allow the mobile devices (such as Windows Phone 8) to find the Windows Intune management service. There are two parts of this configuration: 1) DNS changes and 2) testing the changes with Windows Intune. These are outlined below.

1. Add the following CNAME "enterpriseenrollment" to your DNS. If your domain name was "kamind.biz", you would add the following CNAME shown in Figure 7-31.

TYPE	HOST NAME	POINTS TO ADDRESS	TTL
CNAME	enterpriseenrollment.kamind.biz	enterpriseenrollment.manage.microsoft.com	1 Hour

Figure 7-31. *Adding DNS changes for Windows Device Enrollment*

If you have multiple domain names "verified" in Office 365, you will need to enter a CNAME for all domains in your DNS. Otherwise, the enrollment test validation will fail.

---

2. Enable the Windows Intune device management. Do this only if you are not planning to use Microsoft Systems center 2012. Select the Mobile Device management Option (see Figure 7-32). Windows Intune will verify that you want to make this change. This change cannot be reversed.

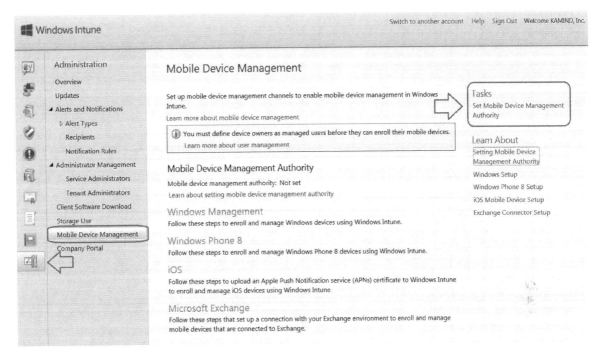

Figure 7-32. Enabling Windows Intune Mobile Device Management

3. Verify the DNS changes in the Windows Intune Administration center. Under the Mobile Device Management Select the Windows management (Figure 7-33).

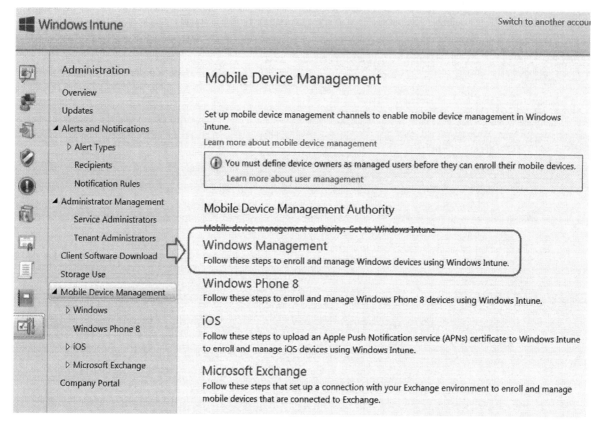

Figure 7-33. *Verify the Windows Management DNS changes*

4. Enter the domain name for verification (Figure 7-34). Click test and verify the domain.

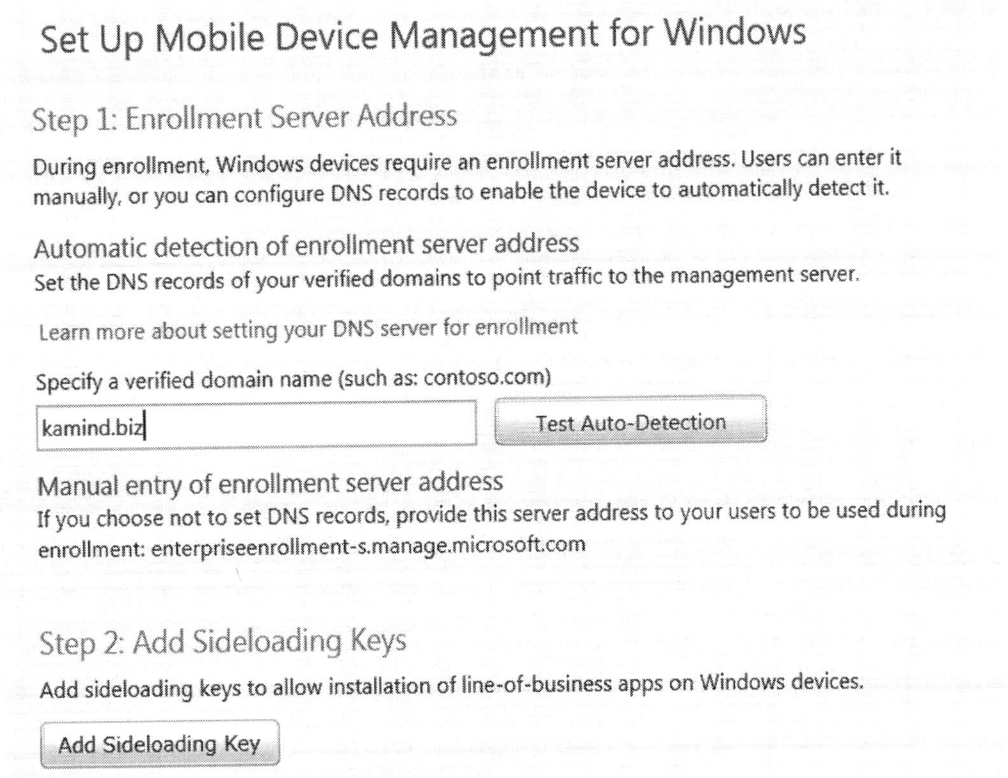

Set Up Mobile Device Management for Windows

Step 1: Enrollment Server Address

During enrollment, Windows devices require an enrollment server address. Users can enter it manually, or you can configure DNS records to enable the device to automatically detect it.

Automatic detection of enrollment server address
Set the DNS records of your verified domains to point traffic to the management server.

Learn more about setting your DNS server for enrollment

Specify a verified domain name (such as: contoso.com)

| kamind.biz | | Test Auto-Detection |

Manual entry of enrollment server address
If you choose not to set DNS records, provide this server address to your users to be used during enrollment: enterpriseenrollment-s.manage.microsoft.com

Step 2: Add Sideloading Keys

Add sideloading keys to allow installation of line-of-business apps on Windows devices.

Add Sideloading Key

Figure 7-34. *Testing Windows Intune Company Portal*

The basic Windows Intune Mobile device management has been setup. There are different steps that you will need to follow to add the mobile device management support. These are company-specific changes. What we covered here was the basic enabling of the Mobile Device Manage services.

Step 6: Configure Firewall Policies

The firewall policies (Figure 7-35) are designed to set up and configure the desktop policies for a firewall: domain, public access, and private network. There are additional configuration parameters set up to manage the branch cache. The normal configuration for these policies is the default. If you have any predefined exceptions, then you enable all of the policies and define the exceptions. After you create the policy, save and deploy the policy.

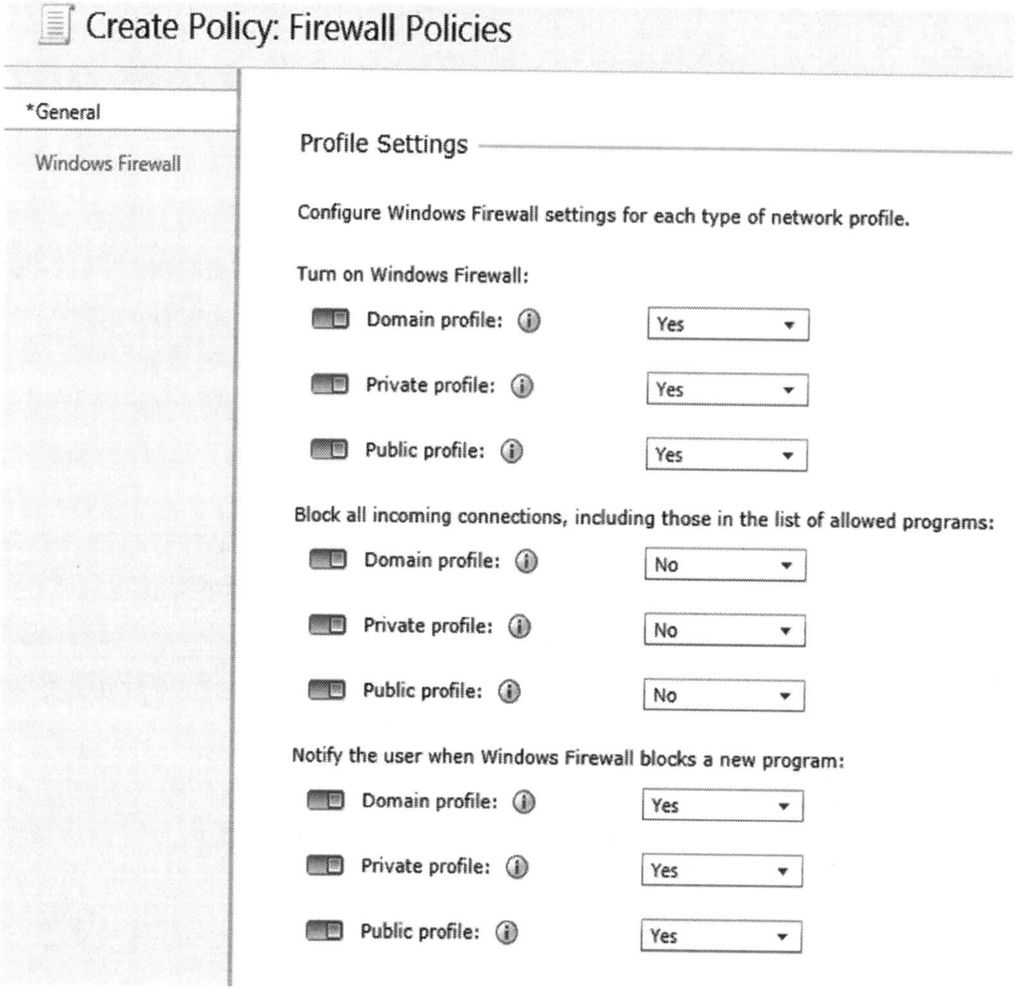

Create Policy: Firewall Policies

*General

Windows Firewall

Profile Settings

Configure Windows Firewall settings for each type of network profile.

Turn on Windows Firewall:

Domain profile: ⓘ   `Yes ▼`

Private profile: ⓘ   `Yes ▼`

Public profile: ⓘ   `Yes ▼`

Block all incoming connections, including those in the list of allowed programs:

Domain profile: ⓘ   `No ▼`

Private profile: ⓘ   `No ▼`

Public profile: ⓘ   `No ▼`

Notify the user when Windows Firewall blocks a new program:

Domain profile: ⓘ   `Yes ▼`

Private profile: ⓘ   `Yes ▼`

Public profile: ⓘ   `Yes ▼`

Figure 7-35. *Firewall Default Policies*

Step 7: Configure Intune Center Policies

After you have created the base policies, you build the desktop support center to allow your user to contact your support services. This is the purpose of the Intune Center policies. Figure 7-36 and Figure 7-37 show the support center for Windows Intune.

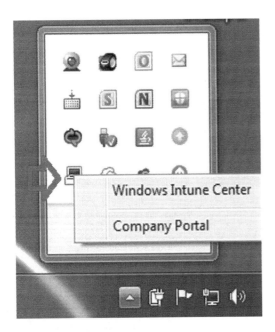

Figure 7-36. *Accessing the IT support help desk from the hidden icons*

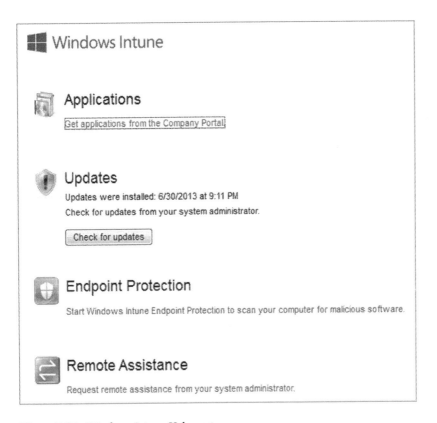

Figure 7-37. *Windows Intune Help center*

To configure the support center, just select the Windows Intune Center and enter the organization support information and deploy the policy (Figure 7-38). The process is identical to the previous policy deployments.

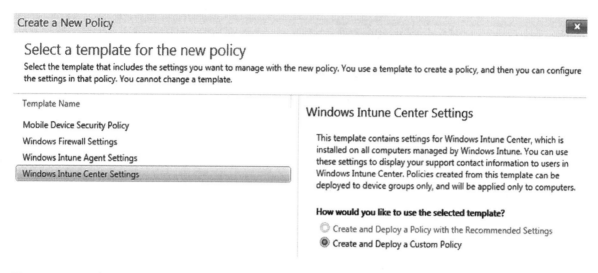

Figure 7-38. *Deploying Custom Support Desk Policy*

Step 8: Deploy Users

At this point you are ready to deploy users to Windows Intune. There are two ways to deploy users: either through the administrative download (Figure 7-39), or by having the user self-enroll using the Company Portal (described later). The enrollment process for each of these steps is outlined in detail later and briefly described below. As an administrator, if you deploy Windows Intune, you need to link the user to the device in the administrative console.

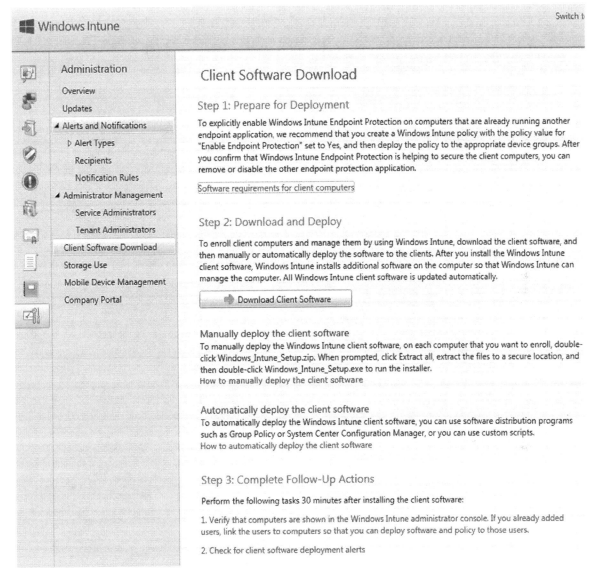

Figure 7-39. *Administrative Deployment of Windows Intune*

Step 9: Linking users

After you have deployed Windows Intune using the administrative deployment, you need to link the user to the device that they use. Earlier we federated Office 365 into Windows Intune. In federation we link the user accounts so the user will have a seamless experience between different environments. This is extremely important, because Mobile devices are linked to user accounts. When you enable a user in Windows Intune, you are allowing the user to access the Windows Intune Company portal to download company applications and to self-enroll Windows Intune on the user's device.

Follow these steps:

1. Select the group icon and then select the number of computers enrolled (Figure 7-40).

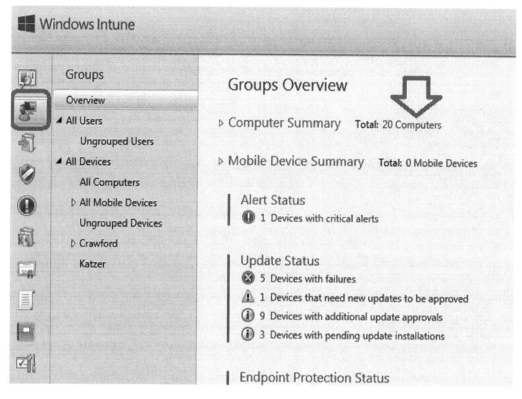

Figure 7-40. Select the Computers under Management

2. Select the computer and then select Link User (Figure 7-41).

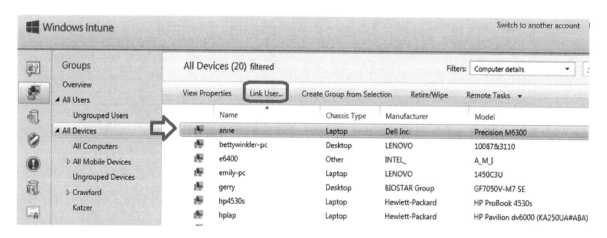

Figure 7-41. Linking users to Computers

3. Select Link User and assign the user to the device. The users listed are those users that have been assigned a Windows Intune license in the administration center (Figure 7-42). After you link the user, then click OK. The user is now linked to the device.

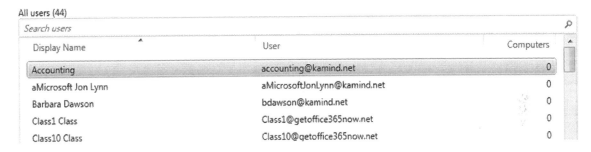

Figure 7-42. *Assigning User to computers - Linking*

If you deployed users via the self-enrollment of the Company Portal, the user accounts will automatically be assigned to the device.

You are finished with the configuration of Windows Intune. At this point you can use Windows Intune for the desktop, user, and device management. The Windows Mobile management, was a basic enablement. The configuration that we completed has set up the service so everything just works with the minimum of oversight. When you need to add users, just purchase licenses and assign the licenses to the appropriate user from your Office 365 account. Mobile device management is organized around line of Business application deployment. At this point, we wanted the Mobile device management enabled so you can proceed to work with your developer on the company application deployment for your smartphone. In the reference link section, we included number of links on how to add additional capabilities to Windows Intune for smartphone management.

Downloading Software from the Administration Center

There are two ways to download software to a desktop for management. The administrator can download the software to each desktop or the user can access the Windows Intune center and download the software. The Windows Intune admin center looks very similar to the Office 365 admin center. To log in to the center, enter the URL "http://account.manage.microsoft.com", and use your Office 365 email address. All Office 365 administrators can access the portal (see Figure 7-43).

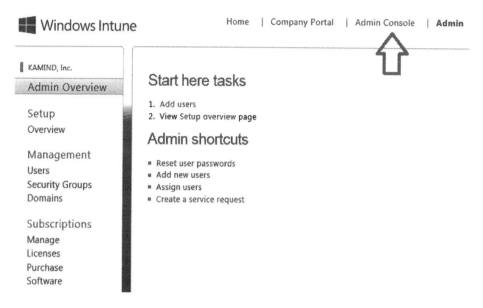

Figure 7-43. *Selecting Admin Console*

Select the Admin Console (Figure 7-43) to access the Windows Intune center and then select Administration (Figure 7-44) to access the client download software screen (Figure 7-45).

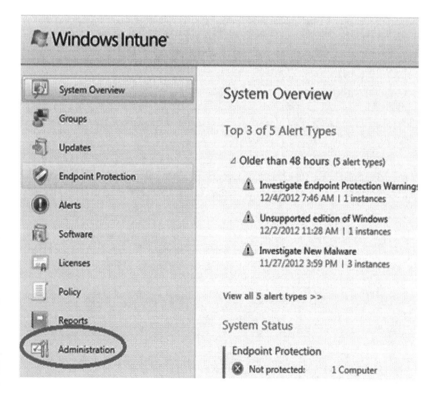

Figure 7-44. *Select Administration to access the client download screen*

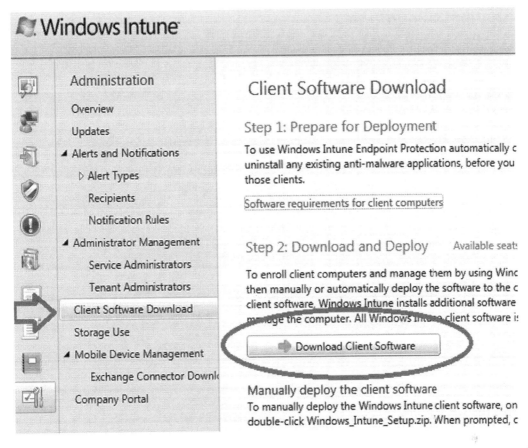

Figure 7-45. *Select "Client Software download" to access software*

Once you have selected the Administration screen, just select Client Software Download to download the client software.

Earlier, we set up the Windows Intune center to generate notification of systems errors and problems. There is no additional configuration we need to do, except download the Window's Intune management software and install it on the desktop devices.

When you download the Window's Intune software from the administration center, make sure you do the following:

1. Save the client software to a folder on your system and unzip it.

2. Uninstall your existing antivirus software; Windows Intune replaces this function.

3. Install the extracted software from the folder that you saved it in Step 1 above.

4. Address any notices that you are informed form the Windows Intune center.

Accessing Windows Intune as a User

Windows Intune provides desktop management, software updates, and antivirus support for up to five devices under a single Office 365 user account. Windows Intune manages Windows desktop PCs and laptops, and smartphones (including Windows Phone 8, Apple iPhone, and iPad devices). To access the Windows Intune site go to `http://account.manage.microsoft.com` and use your Office 365 login. There are two ways to download the Intune client software to a device: using the Company Portal or the administrator console. If you are an administrator and are downloading the software for multiple devices, you must login to the Windows Administration center and link users to devices. If you are having the user self-deploy Windows Intune, follow these instructions below on the download process using the Company Portal.

After you log in, select the Company Portal (Figure 7-46) and register your system. In the Company Portal, select All My Devices and add your system (see Figure 7-47). When you select All My Devices, the devices that you have enrolled in the service will be listed (see Figure 7-48). Select "Add a computer" to download the Windows Intune Management software to add your device.

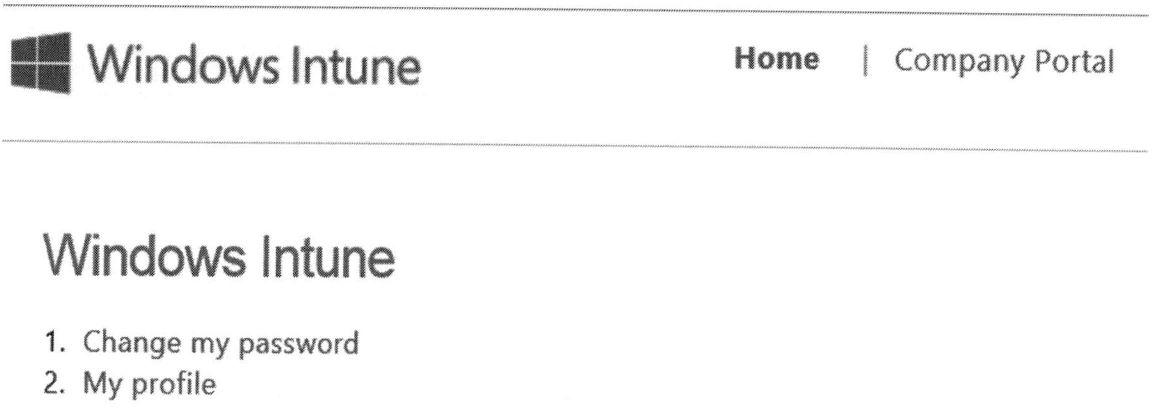

Windows Intune   **Home** | Company Portal

Windows Intune

1. Change my password
2. My profile

Figure 7-46. *Windows Intune Account Portal*

Figure 7-47. *Windows Intune Company Portal*

Figure 7-48. *Windows Intune – Add a computer*

When you add your computer to Windows Intune, follow these simple rules:

1. Uninstall the current antivirus software on your device. Windows Intune provides all antivirus services.

2. Download the software to a directory (not your desktop).

3. Extract all files from the download.

After you download the software, install the software. That is all you need to do. Windows Intune will update your systems with the current updates and repair any system files that were corrupted. Your systems administrator has set up the management of the Windows Intune portal to provide all system updates, deployment of new applications, and antivirus protection.

Most systems do not have all of the updates deployed. Windows Intune will install updates aggressively when it discovers that any systems files on your device are corrupted. This will cause your systems to reboot as updates are applied. It is not uncommon that systems will be behind by 60–90 updates when Windows Intune is first applied or that multiple updates/restarts may be requested in a few hours (when updates are not in sync). Your Intune administrator will set a deadline for updates to be installed. Once the deadline is reached and you have not installed updates, Windows Intune will install the updates for you. If you have a laptop and it is plugged in, it is recommended that you turn off hibernation to allow the updates to be deployed.

Making a Bootable USB

Windows 8.1 Enterprise edition is supplied as part of the Windows Intune subscription. Windows 8 software may be downloaded from http://account.manage.microsoft.com. Log on to the Windows Intune center and download the DVD (ISO) image and serial number associated with your account (see Figure 7-49). You can burn the ISO image to a DVD or a USB memory stick. This document describes the process of making your own bootable memory stick with your Windows 8 image.

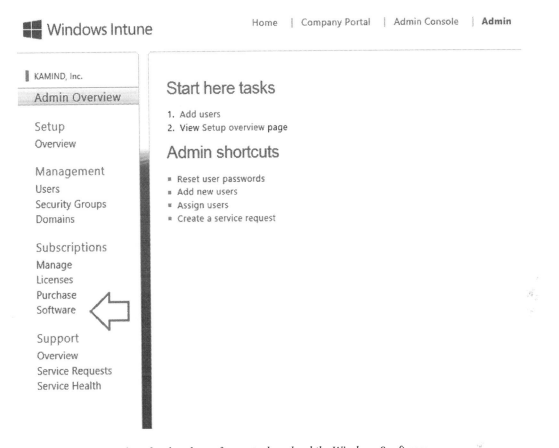

Figure 7-49. *Intune download - select software to download the Windows 8 software*

To create a bootable USB memory stick you will need to expand the ISO image from the Windows 8 download. The tools that you need to create a bootable device are as follows:

1. The Windows Intune subscription software (downloaded as shown in Figure 7-45)

2. A Windows 7 PC (or later) with a USB port

3. A USB memory stick with a size greater than the ISO image (4 GB or 8 GB)

4. An ISO unpack utility (downloadable from the web or can be found as part of any commercial DVD publishing package)

Any memory stick can be used, just make sure the size is larger than the ISO media. The memory sticks that we use are typically 8 GB. This allows us to build a USB stick with the Windows 8 software and have enough room to add the Office 365 and the Windows Intune client.

Preparing the USB Memory Stick

Preparing the memory stick is very straightforward. Follow these steps: Open up a CMD window in Windows 7 (64 bit) or Windows 8, and enter the following commands:

```
DISKPART (enter)
LIST DISK (enter) (this will list the disk devices, such as the USB stick)
SELECT DISK 5 (in our case, the USB was listed as device 5)
CLEAN
CREATE PARTITION PRIMARY
SELECT PARTITION 1
ACTIVE
FORMAT FS=NTFS QUICK
ASSIGN
EXIT
```

At this point the USB memory stick has been prepared to install the Windows 8 software.

Unpacking the ISO Software

Once you have built the memory stick, you need to copy the files over to the USB device. Copy all files including hidden and system files. We use MagicISO to copy the files (see Figure 7-50) from the ISO image to the USB device.

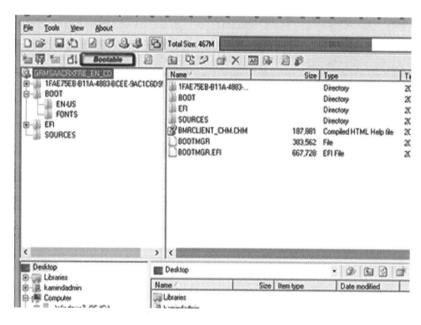

Figure 7-50. *MagicISO - Expansion of the Boot directory of an Bootable ISO image*

Setting the UBS Memory Stick to be Bootable

Earlier, we copied the files to the USB device. At this point, we need to set the USB device to be bootable. You can do this from the USB device or the PC. The setting of the boot sector must be made from the boot directory (see Figure 7-46). To set the boot drive, do the following:

1. Open up a CMD window.

2. Change to the drive letter of the USB memory stick.

3. Change directory to the "boot" directory on the memory stick.

4. Run the command: **BOOTSECT.EXE /NT60 ?:** (where ? is the USB drive Letter).

Now boot the USB and test out the boot image and reboot your PC with the memory stick installed.

Software Key Registration

Windows Intune sometimes requires a manual key registration when you add Windows 8 bootable media. The error displayed on the desktop is a licenses activation error. There are two steps you need to follow to install the key: assignment of the license to the Windows Intune user and the manual activation of the key (if the key is not activated in 24 hours after Intune policies are applied).

Step 1: Retrieve the Key

Your Windows Intune subscription has an option to upgrade the local desktop (or laptop) to Microsoft Windows 8 Enterprise software. If you are using this software download, you will need to retrieve the key from the Windows Intune center. You retrieve the key from the software download section on account.manage.microsoft.com. You can only access the key if you have a local admin account in Windows Intune. Log in to the Intune center, select the Software tab (Figure 7-51), and then expand the product listing and select View as shown in Figure 7-52 to retrieve the Window's 8 activation key.

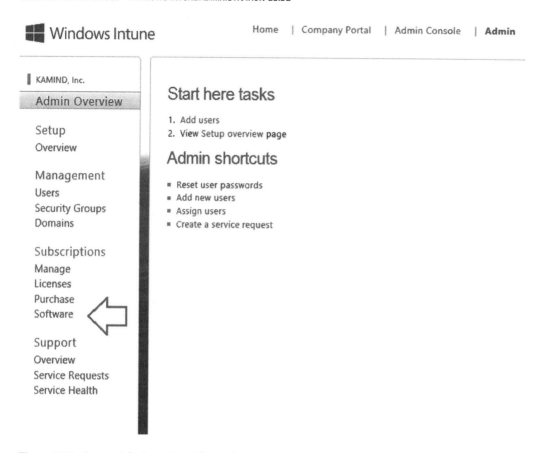

Figure 7-51. *Intune Admin center - Select software*

Download Products

Product Name	Details	Product Key	Download
![Windows Intune] Windows Intune			
- Windows Intune w/ Windows Desktop Operating System (Per Device) (Licenses - 22)			
System Center 2012 Endpoint Protection	View	View	Download
System Center 2012 Config Mgr Client Mgmt License	View	View	Download
System Center 2012 Endpoint Protection with Service Pack 1	View	View	Download
System Center 2012 Config Mgr Client Mgmt License with Service Pack 1	View	View	Download
Windows 8 Enterprise	View	View	Download
Windows 8 Pro	View	View	Download

Figure 7-52. *Retrieving the serial number with the "View" Option under Product Key*

Step 2: Assign an Intune License to the User

Assign the full Windows Intune license to the user account that requires them. Select the user account and assign the key (Figure 7-53 and Figure 7-54).

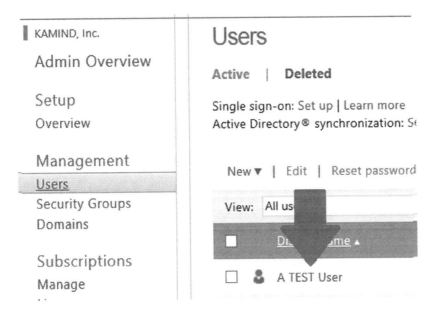

Figure 7-53. *Selecting user to Assign License*

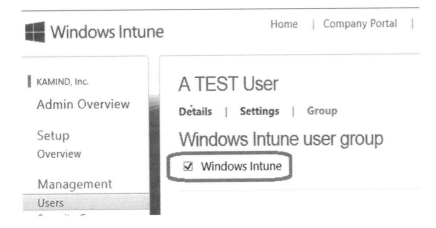

Figure 7-54. *Assigning Intune License*

Step 3: Install the Key on the Local System

To install the key, you need to launch a command prompt as an administrator. In Windows 8, select the command prompt "CMD" icon (from the main Windows 8 screen), then right click, and select the "Run as an administrator" option from the menu bar. This will launch the CMD prompt on the Windows 8 desktop.

Enter the two commands to install the system key retrieved form the Windows Intune Console. In the new command window run the two commands listed below.

```
slmgr.vbs -ipk <your product key here>
```

Hit Enter on your keyboard then type:

```
slmgr.vbs -ato
```

An activation message will be displayed if the serial number is registered and activated correctly.

Reference Links

There is a lot of information about Office3 65 on the web — the issue is finding the right site. The information contained in this chapter is a combination of our experiences in doing deployments and support information that has been published by third parties.

Windows Intune TechNet home page

http://technet.microsoft.com/en-us/windows/intune.aspx

Windows Intune Getting Started Guide

http://www.microsoft.com/en-us/download/details.aspx?id=26706

Windows Intune website:

http://www.windowsintune.com

Windows Intune Online Help:

http://onlinehelp.microsoft.com/en-us/windowsintune.latest

Windows Intune Company Portal for Windows 8:

http://www.microsoft.com/en-us/download/details.aspx?id=40794

Windows Intune Support Tool for System Center 2012 and Phone 8:

http://www.microsoft.com/en-us/download/details.aspx?id=39079

Windows Intune Phone 8 Direct Management

http://www.microsoft.com/en-us/download/details.aspx?id=36174

Next steps

This chapter was focused on the configuration and set up of Windows Intune. Office 365 is interesting to explore and discover new capabilities and there is much more to do depending on your Office 365 configuration. The key chapters you need to review for your Office 365 deployment are:

- *Chapter 5* – SharePoint Administration

  - SharePoint administration and design can be simple or complex depending on your business needs. This chapter provides you with a basic overview of the configuration necessary to be up and running using Office 365 Team Site. This chapter describes Site Design and Construction issues as well as the full SharePoint Administration functions for Office 365.

- *Chapter 6* – Building Your Website

  - Office 365 includes a public facing website, and the necessary developer's tools to build out the website. This chapter's take you from the basic Office 365 site, to a fully functioning website. The Office 365 public facing websites fulfils the basic web needs for 90% of the businesses on Office 365. This chapter describes how to configure and build the public facing website for your business using the integrated Office 365 website tools and SharePoint Designer – a design tool that is included with your Office 365 subscription.

- *Chapter 8* – Office 365 Administration

  - This chapter describes the different administration centers in Office 365 and the most common tools that you would use to administer your Office 365 company. Depending on your Office 365 services, there are five possible administration tools. This chapter focuses on the Office 365, Exchange, and Lync administration centers. The SharePoint and Windows Intune administration centers are described in their own chapters. We close the chapter with using PowerShell to manage your Office 365 environment.

- *Chapter 9* – Compliance and Data Loss Prevention

  - Businesses must adapt their mail document storage systems to correctly process the electronic communication based on regulatory oversight. The Compliance and Data Loss Prevention (DLP) provides this capability to allow businesses to managed there communications, and protect the business from simple mistakes in its electronic communications. Office 365 includes integrated discovery, supports legal discovery, and assists with audit requirements.

## CHAPTER 8

Office 365 Administration Guide Enterprise

In previous chapters we discussed how to move your business to Office 365. We spent a lot of time talking about the three different categories of Office 365 (e.g. Enterprise, Midsize and Professional) and pointed out that you should be looking at the Enterprise Suites as a solution. The main reason why we select the enterprise version is a simple one: you have the flexibility of deployment and your overall costs are reduced, compared with the other plan options.

This chapter is focused on the administration of the Enterprise subscriptions for Office 365. Time is money, and as an administrator, you are looking at the simplest way to accomplish a task. This chapter outlines the common tasks that administrators are asked to perform. These tasks range from renaming users to adding email aliases to creating shared mailboxes to changing the subscription type (see Table 8-1).

Table 8-1. *Office 365 Enterprise Plan Options*

Enterprise Suites	Mix and Match Components	Application and System Options
Office 365 Enterprise E1 Exchange Plan 1 Lync Plan 1 SharePoint Plan 1	**Exchange** Exchange Online Kiosk Exchange Online (Plan 1) Exchange Online (Plan 2)	Office 365 ProPlus Project Online Project Pro for Office 365 Project Online with Project Pro for Office 365 Microsoft Dynamics CRM Online Basic
Office 365 Enterprise E3 Exchange Plan 2 Lync Plan 1 SharePoint Plan 2	**Lync** Lync Online (Plan 1) Lync Online (Plan 2)	Microsoft Dynamics CRM Online Essential Microsoft Dynamics CRM Online Professional Visio Pro for Office 365
Office 365 Enterprise E4 Exchange Plan 2 Lync Plan 2 SharePoint Plan 2	**SharePoint** SharePoint Online (Plan 1) SharePoint Online (Plan 2) SharePoint Online (Plan 1) with YammerSharePoint Online (Plan 2) with YammerOffice Web Apps with SharePoint Plan 1 Office Web Apps with SharePoint Plan 2	Yammer Enterprise **Support Options** Professional Direct Support for CRM Online Enhanced Support for Microsoft Dynamics CRM **System Options** Exchange Online Protection
	Exchange + SharePoint Enterprise K1 (same as K2)	Exchange Online Archiving (EOA) for Exchange Server Azure Active Directory Rights Management

As an administrator, you'll find that your company will need different components and applications to be added to your subscription. The process of adding components (or applications) is simple: you purchase the subscriptions that meet your needs and add the purchased licenses to the user. In the case of having too many licenses, you work with your Microsoft partner to have the extra licenses removed. What if you are on the other suites (Small Business or Mid-size Business)? You do not have the capabilities available to you in Table 1. If you need the capabilities, you must migrate your business to the Enterprise suite – just like you migrated your company to Office 365. The Enterprise family is a different service offering. Our focus in this chapter is on the administration of the Enterprise offering for Office 365.

The first account that is created when you sign up is the global Administrator. The Global administrator account has full access to all Office 365 resources. You can use the PowerShell environment to configure capabilities, or you can use the Graphical interfaces in the various admin centers (Exchange, Lync or the SharePoint) to manage Office 365 capabilities. The only rule to remember is this: to change features using PowerShell or in the administration graphical interfaces, you must have a license (such as Exchange, Lync, SharePoint or other centers) provision to the account to that is being used to change that feature. If a global administrator's account is trying to change features on a subscription area that the account is not licensed to use, that action will not be permitted. PowerShell commands will not work and the Global administrator will be denied access to the GUI command options. Partners, with Delegated Administrator rights by design, do not have a license and cannot access data or have permissions to use PowerShell.

■ **Note** Only selected Microsoft partners have the ability to offer delegated administrator services to their customers. The Global Administrator must approve the rights to a Microsoft partner to act as a delegated administrator. Microsoft Partners that have Delegated Administration capabilities have earned rights to use this service offering.

A good example is using PowerShell to set up a shared mailbox for smart phones. If you **do not** have an Exchange license assigned to the global admin account, the Exchange PowerShell scripts will fail when they make a set-mailbox call. There are many different commands you can use to manage Office 365 with PowerShell.

For example, you can use PowerShell to administer Office 365 (Figure 8-1 – creating a distribution list) or you can use the GUI interface (Figure 8-2). Both interfaces provide the same results; one is much more scalable than the other. As an administrator, you will use both interfaces. The only rule to remember, is that you must have a license assigned to the account that you are usingto grant permissions to the user accounts.

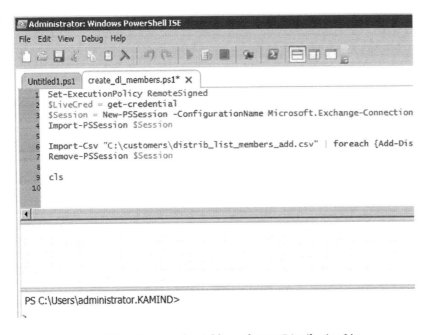

Figure 8-1. *PowerShell Command to Add members to Distribution List*

Figure 8-2. *Office 365 DL list - Add members*

The objective of this chapter is to provide you with the tools and capabilities necessary so you can administer your own Office 365 site, and provide the best level of service to your organization.

▪ **Note** If you have directory synchronization enabled, you cannot edit some properties of the user's mailbox, because it's out of the current user's write scope. This means that the user mailbox must be managed by the on premises active directory.

Preparing to Administrate Office 365

Once you have purchased Office 365, you can begin to administer the company. In Chapter 4, we showed you how to move your company to the cloud and configure your mail services. At the end of the migration steps, we included a check list to verify your Office 365 configuration. This administration section is based on the assumption that you have completed this step.

Final Check List

This information is reprinted from Chapter 4. If you have not verified your configuration, please do this now. These configuration options are discussed in each of the setup and migration steps.

1. If you have a desktop Office 2007/2010, and are using Outlook 2007/2010 (and you are not using Office 2013), run the desktop upgrade for Outlook 2007/2010 from the office 365 software download. If you do not do this, Outlook 2007/2010 will stop working.

2. Run the domain trouble shooting function in Office 365 (select more than 732 hours) and make sure you have all green check marks. (See Figure 4-15). Correct the areas where you do not have green checkmarks.

3. Verify that your Office 365 domain is set to Authoritative and not shared (see Figure 4-31).

4. Verify that you have placed a local DNS record in your on-premise DNS server. You will need to add an "AutoDiscover" CNAME to your **internal DNS** that points to **autodiscover.outlook.com**.

5. Extend the 14-day delete holding time to 30-day delete holding time. Run the PowerShell command. See Chapter 8: Office 365 Administration Guide Enterprise (this one) for information on how to run this command.

   a. Extend 30-day delete for a mailbox

      1. **Set-mailbox user@contoso.com -retaindeleteditemsfor 30**

   b. Extend 30-day delete for the Organization

      2. **Get-mailbox | Set-mailbox -retaindeleteditemsfor 30**

6. The default retention policies **are not enabled** until the archive is enabled. If you **enable the archive** on a user mailbox, the retention polices will begin to execute. Review the chapter on retention polices before you enable the archive.

7. Verify that you configured Yammer to replace Office 365 newsfeeds for your company internal social site.

Common Office 365 Administration Tasks

Office 365 has four administration centers: Office 365, Exchange, Lync and SharePoint (see Figure 8-3) when you have an E3 subscription assigned. There are additional administration centers that are added based on the optional subscriptions. This chapter focuses on areas of administration in Office 365 using Exchange and Lync. The other administration centers (SharePoint, Compliance and Data Loss Prevention and Exchange Online Protection) are discussed as focus topics in their separate chapters. What we have included here are the most common questions that we have been asked about Office 365.

Figure 8-3. *Office 365 Administration center (with CRM option)*

The Office 365 administration areas that we will address are: the Office 365 dashboard and licenses (Table 8-1), Exchange administration (Table 8-2) and Lync/Skype administration (Table 8-3). We wrap up this chapter with information on the configuration of PowerShell. PowerShell is used to configure some functions that are not in the Office 365 GUI.

Table 8-2. *Office 365 Administration functions*

Task	Description
Administration roles	Office 365 supports five different administrator roles. These are Global administrator, Billing administrator, User administrator, Service administrator, Password administrator.
Domain verification (and DNS review)	Domain verification, DNS and service record management.
Adding , deleting, and restoring users	Account creation and user management.
Renaming users (no Exchange mailbox)	Simple steps to rename a user account and change the email address with little impact on the user.
Adding/changing licenses	Subscription/license management.
Security Groups	Domain Security groups management for federated services.
Partner Delegated Administration	Partner Administration management.

Table 8-3. *Exchange Administration Functions*

Task	Description
Exchange administration roles	Review of the different Exchange roles for managing Office 365.
Default user role	Explains the default user roles and permissions.
Conference Room/Resource Room	Explains how to set up and manage a conference room.
Changing a user name and email address	Changing an email is a two-step process. This is how you change the email address of the user accounts.
Adding a user alias	Adding an alias email or changing the default email address.
Shared mailbox	Explains how to create a shared mailbox for the smart phone or Outlook.
Creating a distribution group	Explains the different Office 365 distribution groups a distribution group.
Sending email from an alias email address	Allows the user to send an email form a different email address than the user's own email address.
Smartphone management	User configuration options for Exchange.
Troublingshooting: AutoDiscover	Desktop configuration to ignore Exchange Server.

There are two ways accounts can be created in Office 365: through a manual process (Single user load/Bulk load) or via Active Directory Synchronization Accounts, created through Active Directory process that can only be managed by on-premises Active Directory tools.

There are different types of administrative accounts on Office 365. The root account (first account that was created when you purchased office 365) is a global administrator account. You can create additional global administrator accounts to manage Office 365. Global administrator accounts do not need a license to perform global administration functions. However, the global administration account does require a license to perform administration functions at the functional level (such as Exchange and SharePoint). As an example, if you wish to configure Exchange services or Lync services, you need a Lync and Exchange license assigned to the account. The same is the case with SharePoint. If you do not have a license, or if you are running Active Directory Synchronization, you cannot configure the functions of the service, only the global access controls for the service. Table 8-3 shows a listing of the common exchange functions that you use to manage Office 365.

■ **Note**   If you are using Directory Synchronization, those Exchange functions are controlled by the On Premises Active Directory.

Lync allows you to communicate internally without any configuration. The problem is external communication: The normal configuration is the enabling of communications with external users (Skype and smartphones). The administration topics included below are the configuration changes that are required to address these communications across different external domains. Table 8-4 lists the common Lync configurations that can be changed by a global administrator.

Table 8-4. *Lync Administration Functions*

Task	Description
Setting up Lync federation	Enabling Lync to communicate with non-company users
Configuration for conferencing add on	Adding third party service using outside phone services such as InterCall
Communicating with Skype users	Step by step instructions to enable Lync to Skype integration
Restricting Lync users capability	Restricting Lync capabilities in the admin center

In addition to the administration section, we have also included an overview and usage section on PowerShell. PowerShell is extremely useful if you have to implement unique functions, or have to repeat a set of tasks multiple times. This is not a complete list: There are many more Office 365 commands you can use. Our objective in this chapter is to show you the various options you can use in managing Office 365.

Office 365 Administration Center

The Office 365 Administration consoles are integrated into the top menu bar (Figure 8-4). This menu bar contains the menus of the license functions for the user and the different administration panels that the user account has licenses for. As an example, if the Lync licenses are not assigned, there will be no access to the Lync Administration center. The Office 365 admin center is the main dashboard for the management of Office 365. The Office 365 admin center is used to administrate global functions. These oversee permissions, security groups, domain management, and support and system health. However, Office 365 administration center is also limited if Directory Synchronization is enabled. When Directory Synchronization is enabled, Office 365 acts as a backup to the On-Premises Active directory. In this case, only those functions that are not on the on-premises servers can be modified by Office 365.

Figure 8-4. *Admin Center Selection*

Accessing the Office 365 admin center is simple: just login to Office 365. If you have the permissions, you will land at the administrative dashboard (Figure 8-4). If your permissions are limited, your menu option will be limited to reflect your privileges. The admin center access is based on the permission settings for that user.

Administrator Roles

There are different permission structures in Office 365 depending on which console that you are given permissions to use. The basic permissions of Office 365 are shown in Figure 8-5. There are five different global permissions that may be assigned to user accounts on Office 365. The only account that is assigned a global permissions by default is the first account. This account was created when you purchased the service. All other accounts that are created are assigned user-level permissions. Depending on the size of the organization, it may make sense to assigned different roles for different job functions.

Permission	Billing administrator	Global administrator	Password administrator	Service administrator	User management administrator
View company and user information	Yes	Yes	Yes	Yes	Yes
Manage support tickets	Yes	Yes	Yes	Yes	Yes
Reset user passwords	No	Yes	Yes	No	Yes; with limitations. He or she cannot reset passwords for billing, global, and service administrators.
Perform billing and purchasing operations	Yes	Yes	No	No	No
Create and manage user views	No	Yes	No	No	Yes
Create, edit, and delete users and groups, and manage user licenses	No	Yes	No	No	Yes; with limitations. He or she cannot delete a global administrator or create other administrators.
Manage domains	No	Yes	No	No	No
Manage company information	No	Yes	No	No	No
Delegate administrative roles to others	No	Yes	No	No	No
Use directory synchronization	No	Yes	No	No	No

Figure 8-5. *Office 365 Administrative Roles (courtesy of Microsoft)*

These roles are used to manage large organizations. Small organizations typically assign three roles: Global administrator, Billing administrator and Password administrator. Step back and look at your company, and look at the different roles you can assign to personnel in your company. Microsoft's security model is to assign the minimum role as possible, and grant basic permissions that are required to complete the job. When you assign roles, look at Figures 8-6 and 8-7 and verify that you are providing access at the appropriate level needed to execute the administrative task.

Table 8-5. *Offfice 365 Role Descriptions*

Role	Description
Global Administrator	This is the Company administrator. Users in this role have access to everything or the permission to add them to a dedicated role where they do not have permission (such as discovery management).
Billing Administrator	Access to all financial transactions. Delegated partners do not have access to this information.
Password Administrator	They can reset only passwords of users and other administrators at the same level of permissions.

(continued)

Table 8-5. (*contiuned*)

Role	Description
Service Support Administrator	This is a limited administration role. Users in this rule can only view the portal and assign support tickets. Typically users that are assigned this role have a different role assigned to the different subsystems, such as Exchange (see Figure 8-7).
User Management Administrator	These users can assign licenses and passwords but cannot make changes to other admin accounts that have more privileges than they do.

Office 365 admin role	Translates to this in Exchange Online...	Translates to this in SharePoint Online...	Translates to this in Lync Online...
global administrator*	• Exchange Online administrator • Company Administrator	SharePoint Online administrator	Lync Online administrator
billing administrator	N/A	N/A	N/A
password administrator*	Help Desk Administrator	N/A	Lync Online administrator
service administrator	N/A	N/A	N/A
user management administrator	N/A	N/A	Lync Online administrator

Figure 8-6. *Permission mapping between Office 365 and different services (Courtesy of Microsoft)*

Figure 8-7. *Domain Troubleshooting*

The typical Office 365 configuration leaves one account (usually the root account – the initial Office 365 account) as a Global Admin user without any user licenses. Some organizations will leave this a global admin account and in others this account will be a user account. Regardless of what you do, the first account is the root account. The root account should never be used as a user account. The root account in Office 365 is the base account that is used to create all of the different services that are linked to the Office 365 tenant. As Microsoft has deployed new versions of Office 365, the dependence of the root account has been minimized. We recommend that you do not delete or use this account as a user account.

Microsoft worked around the dependency of the first account by creating a new internal Office 365 group known as the "Company Administrators." All global admins are members of the Company Administrator group. This group is where the base permissions are assigned in Office 365. This internal account reduces the criticality of using the root account as a user account.

Domains

There are no practical limits on the number of domains that can be verified to Office 365 Enterprise. The rules are simple: you need to verify a domain, and you need to assign the domain based on the needs (or Domain Intent). Domain Intent is what the domain services will be configured as; there are three different types of services for Domain Intent. These are listed in Table 8-6 below.

Table 8-6. *Domain Intent*

Domain Intent	Can Mix with	Purpose
Exchange	Lync	Used for Mail services integration.
Lync	Exchange	Used for video and enterprise voice.
SharePoint	-	Used for dedicated SharePoint public site.

Domains: Troubleshooting

When you add a domain, the first step is to verify the domain (see Chapter 4, Setup and Migration). After you verify the domain, add the necessary DNS changes. The DNS changes are standard, so you can add the domain information at the verification step, or after. The key to adding domains is to use the DNS troubleshooter (see Figure 8-7) and to select more than 72 hours (see Figure 8-8).

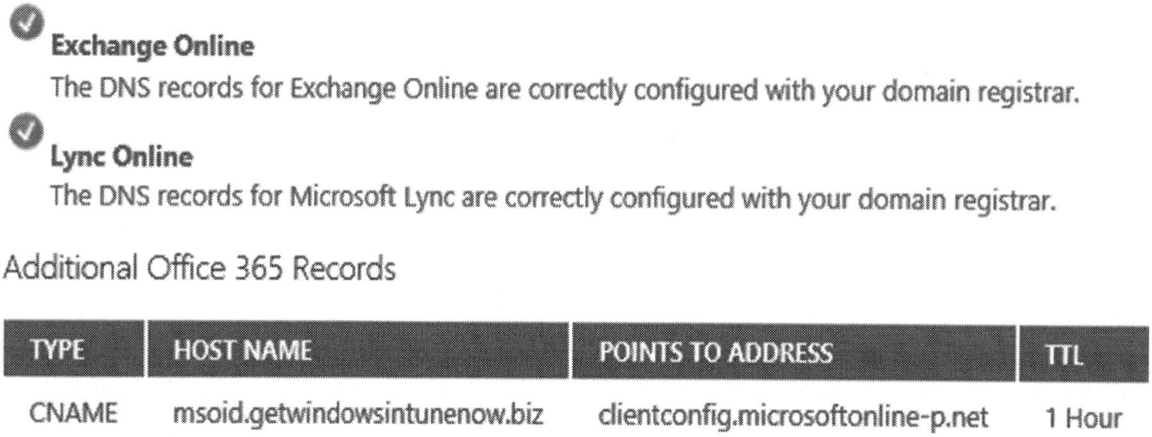

✅ Exchange Online

The DNS records for Exchange Online are correctly configured with your domain registrar.

✅ Lync Online

The DNS records for Microsoft Lync are correctly configured with your domain registrar.

Additional Office 365 Records

TYPE	HOST NAME	POINTS TO ADDRESS	TTL
CNAME	msoid.getwindowsintunenow.biz	clientconfig.microsoftonline-p.net	1 Hour

Figure 8-8. *Troubleshooting Domains*

Once you select the domain and the troubleshooter and the more-than-72-hours options, verify the domain. If the domain is not configured correctly, the domain will show red "X"s and the DNS parameters that need to be changed. Make the changes indicated and re-run the domain troubleshooting tool. Verify the correction has been made and processed by Office 365.

Domains: Standard DNS records

The DNS records (Figure 8-9) are standard for all domains. In this case, we are using the getwindowsintunenow .biz domain. The domain intent is set for Exchange and Lync.

Exchange Online

TYPE	PRIORITY	HOST NAME	POINTS TO ADDRESS	TTL
MX	0	@	getwindowsintunenow-biz.mail.protection.outlook.com	1 Hour
CNAME	-	autodiscover	autodiscover.outlook.com	1 Hour

TYPE	TXT NAME	TXT VALUE	TTL
TXT	@	v=spf1 include:spf.protection.outlook.com -all	1 Hour

Lync Online

TYPE	SERVICE	PROTOCOL	PORT	WEIGHT	PRIORITY	TTL	NAME	TARGET
SRV	_sip	_tls	443	1	100	1 Hour	getwindowsintunenow.biz	sipdir.online.lync.com
SRV	_sipfederationtls	_tcp	5061	1	100	1 Hour	getwindowsintunenow.biz	sipfed.online.lync.com

TYPE	HOST NAME	POINTS TO ADDRESS	TTL
CNAME	sip.getwindowsintunenow.biz	sipdir.online.lync.com	1 Hour
CNAME	lyncdiscover.getwindowsintunenow.biz	webdir.online.lync.com	1 Hour

Additional Office 365 Records

TYPE	HOST NAME	POINTS TO ADDRESS	TTL
CNAME	msoid.getwindowsintunenow.biz	clientconfig.microsoftonline-p.net	1 Hour

Figure 8-9. *Domain DNS Configuration*

Adding, Deleting and Restoring Users

Office 365 supports many features that you can configure through the Office 365 user interface. Some actions (such as setting Shared Mailboxes) are only available using PowerShell. If you are running a Federation service (large organizations) you can use your On Premise tools for Exchange 2010/2013 and Active Directory to configure online services. Changes on user configuration for federated accounts will need to be completed on the on-site servers. Our focus in this chapter is on the user configuration of Office 365 using the Office 365 interface.

There are four primary user operations that you will use for administration:

- Adding single users via the user interface

- Bulk adding using a CSV file and the GUI interface

- Deleting users

- Restoring users

If you need to assign user passwords, you will need to use the PowerShell commands. Typically we load the users using the bulk load options, then we assign the passwords using PowerShell. If you have a federated server (using DirSync or ADFS) you will need to assign those passwords using the on-premises active directory server.

Users: Adding Users via the User Interface

Log in as an Administrator (at www.office365.com or http://portal.microsoftonline.com) as shown in Figure 8-10. Click "Admin" (at the top-right). Next, click "users and groups," then select the "+" sign to add a new user.

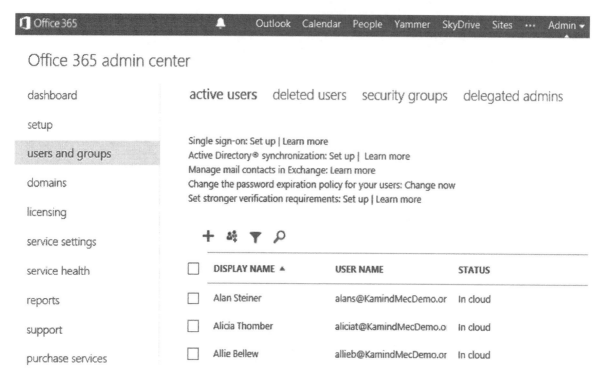

Figure 8-10. *Adding Users to Office 365*

After you select the "+", follow the steps below to add a user.

Step 1 – Add the user information

You must have a first, last, and display name to create a user.

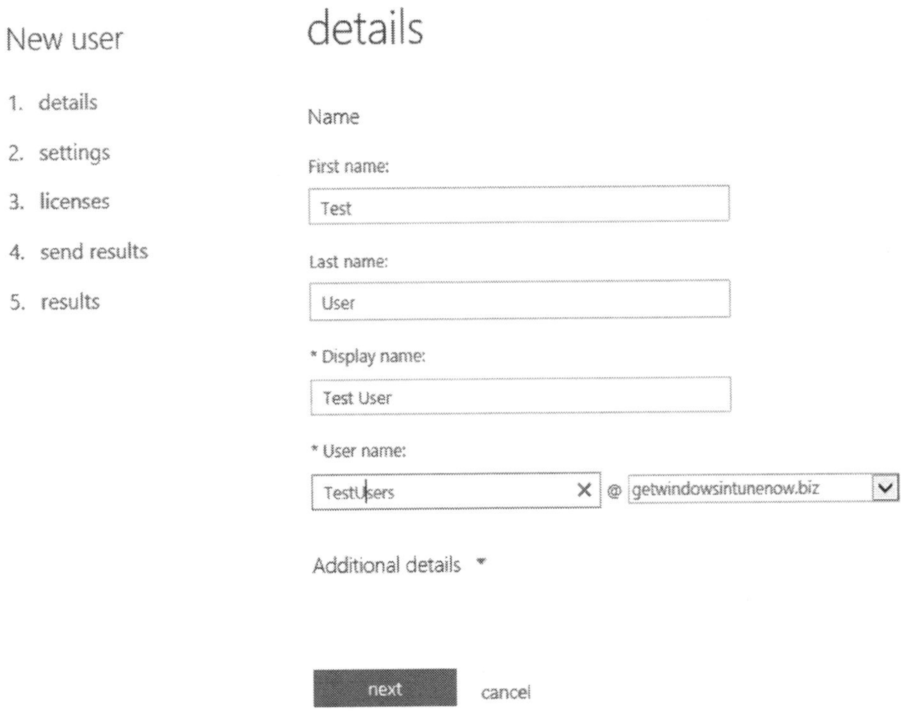

New user

details

1. details
2. settings
3. licenses
4. send results
5. results

Name

First name:

Test

Last name:

User

* Display name:

Test User

* User name:

TestUsers ✕ @ getwindowsintunenow.biz ▼

Additional details ▼

next   cancel

Figure 8-11. *Add the User Information*

Step 2 – Assign the user rights and location

When you add the user, you can assign the role for the user. Only global administrators can assign administrator roles. If you assign a user admin rights, you will need to supply an email address that is not part of Office 365. All administrator users will need to have a cell phone that receives text messages.

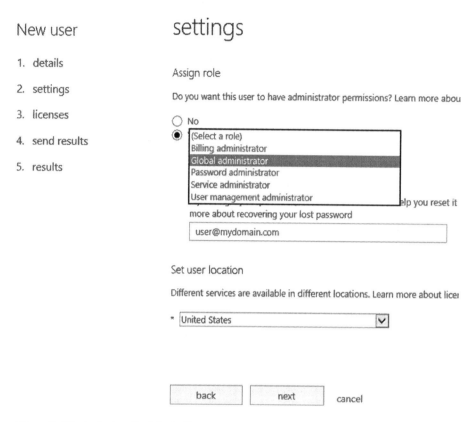

New user

1. details

2. settings

3. licenses

4. send results

5. results

settings

Assign role

Do you want this user to have administrator permissions? Learn more abou

○ No
◉ (Select a role)
   Billing administrator
   Global administrator
   Password administrator
   Service administrator
   User management administrator   elp you reset it
   more about recovering your lost password

   user@mydomain.com

Set user location

Different services are available in different locations. Learn more about licen

* United States   ☑

back   next   cancel

Figure 8-12. *Assigning the Admin User*

Step 3 – Assign the Licenses to the user

You can assign any valid license to the user. You can also selectivity assign access to the various Office 365 services (see Figure 8-13). Select next after your assignment.

Figure 8-13. *Assigning the License to the user*

Step 4 – Setting the password

Once you have created the user, enter the email address (Figure 8-14) for where to send the password for the new user.

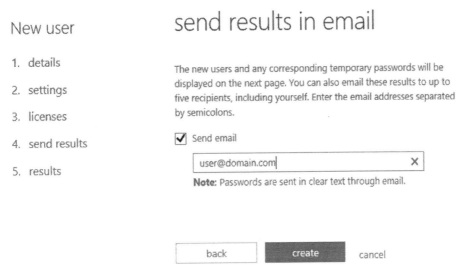

Figure 8-14. *Setting the Password*

After you have set the password, select save to create the user account.

Users: Using the Bulk Loading Interface

You can also add users using the bulk loading option. Bulk loading users requires that you build a CSV file that contains all of the information for all users. The bulk loading tool reads the CSV file and loads all user accounts. To add a group of users to Office 365, select the people icon (see Figure 8-15).

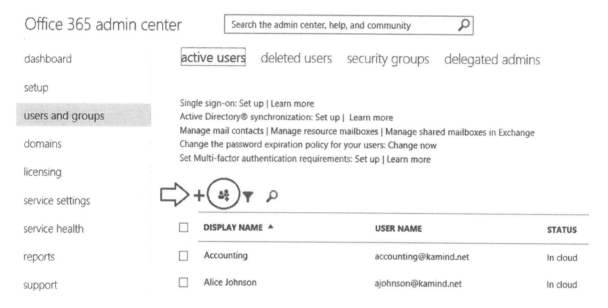

Figure 8-15. *Adding users in bulk to Office 365*

When you start the wizard (Figure 8-16), select the download "sample CSV file" to retrieve the bulk loading template. Fill in the information for a csv file and load the template to load the users. Bulk loading users is a simple process, but you will require licenses to add users to Office 365. If you do not have enough licenses to add users, those new accounts will not be created during the bulk loading process.

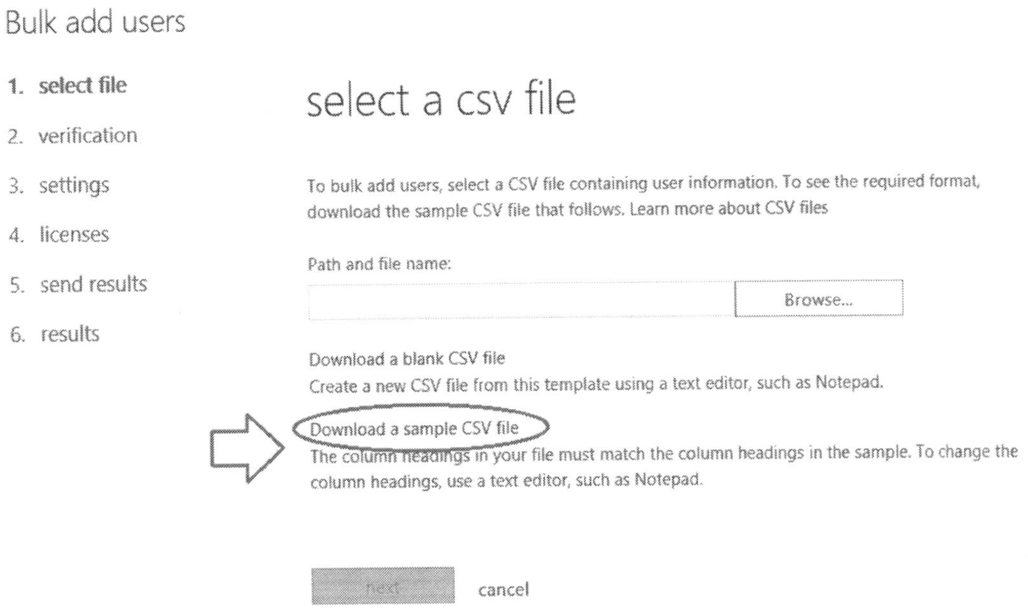

Bulk add users

1. **select file**

2. verification

3. settings

4. licenses

5. send results

6. results

select a csv file

To bulk add users, select a CSV file containing user information. To see the required format, download the sample CSV file that follows. Learn more about CSV files

Path and file name:

	Browse...

Download a blank CSV file
Create a new CSV file from this template using a text editor, such as Notepad.

Download a sample CSV file
The column headings in your file must match the column headings in the sample. To change the column headings, use a text editor, such as Notepad.

next   cancel

Figure 8-16. *Downloading the user csv template for adding users*

Users: Deleting

Deleting users is as simple as selecting the user, then selecting Delete (see Figure 8-17). If the "delete user" trashcan is not present, then the user has been blocked from deletion in Office 365 and you will need to use the PowerShell command to remove the user account. A blocked user account usually happens when a user is placed on legal hold, or when an account was not deleted properly. To remove users that are on litigation hold, you need to remove the in-place hold or the legacy litigation, using PowerShell or the Exchange Admin center. Once the in-place or Litigation hold is cleaned up, you can delete the user. When you delete an account, we recommend that you follow these steps:

1. Remove any legal hold on the account

2. Disable the archive on the account (if you have this feature)

3. Set the user account to the onmicrosoft.com name as the primary address

4. Remove any email alias assigned to the account

5. Remove all licenses from the account

6. Delete the account

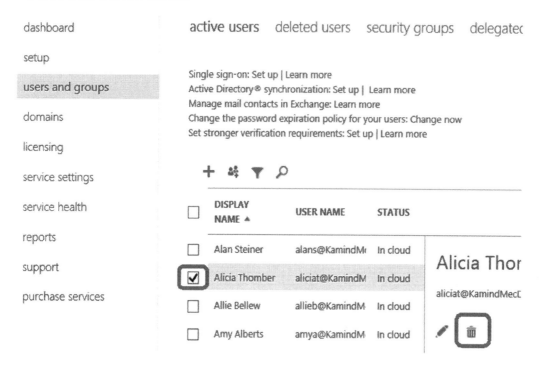

Figure 8-17. *Deleting a user account*

Deleted users can be recovered up to 30 days and are located in the "deleted users" folder. If you wish to remove the user from the Office 365 "deleted users" folder, run the following PowerShell command to purge the user account. If you have not setup PowerShell, see the PowerShell section at the end of this chapter. These PowerShell examples are code snippets and require the necessary credentials to execute (see PowerShell section for detailed setup).

PowerShell commands to return the list of deleted Office 365 users. This PowerShell command returns all the deleted user accounts in the recycle bin with the GUID for the user.

```
Get-MsolUser -ReturnDeletedUsers
```

PowerShell commands to remove the user account from the deleted user folder, using the user GUID:

```
Remove-MsolUser -ObjectId 1b8927dd-1998-4fd9-aefb-7c949351ec9f -RemoveFromRecycleBin
```

Users: Restoring

To restore deleted users, select "users and groups", then select "deleted users". You can then select the user account that you wish to restore. Deleted users will remain in your Office 365 deleted user recycle bin for 14–30 days, depending on the configuration of Office 365. The default retention period is 14 days. Figure 8-18 shows the deleted users restoration option. Just select the user, then restore.

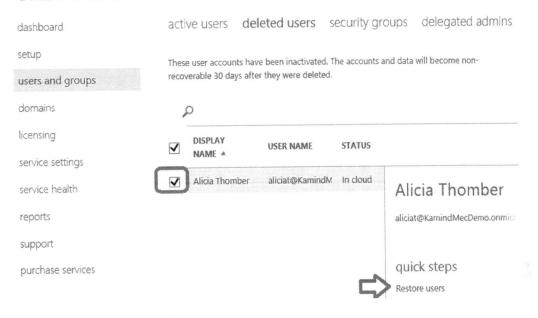

Figure 8-18. *Restoring a deleted user*

Users: Renaming (no exchange mailbox)

Renaming a user display name is a simple process: You select the user account from the Office 365 administration center and you rename the user account (Figure 8-19).

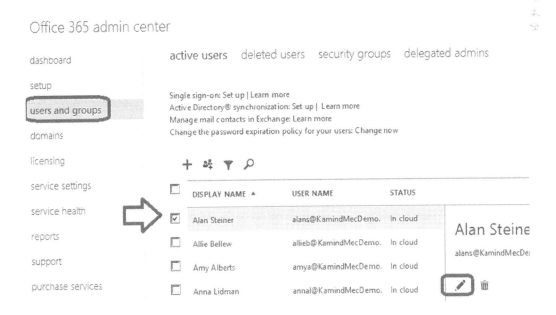

Figure 8-19. *Selecting a user to edit*

Once you select the edit function, then select the area that you wish to change. As an example, you can select the details and change the user name or domain as the primary login address (Figure 8-20) of the user.

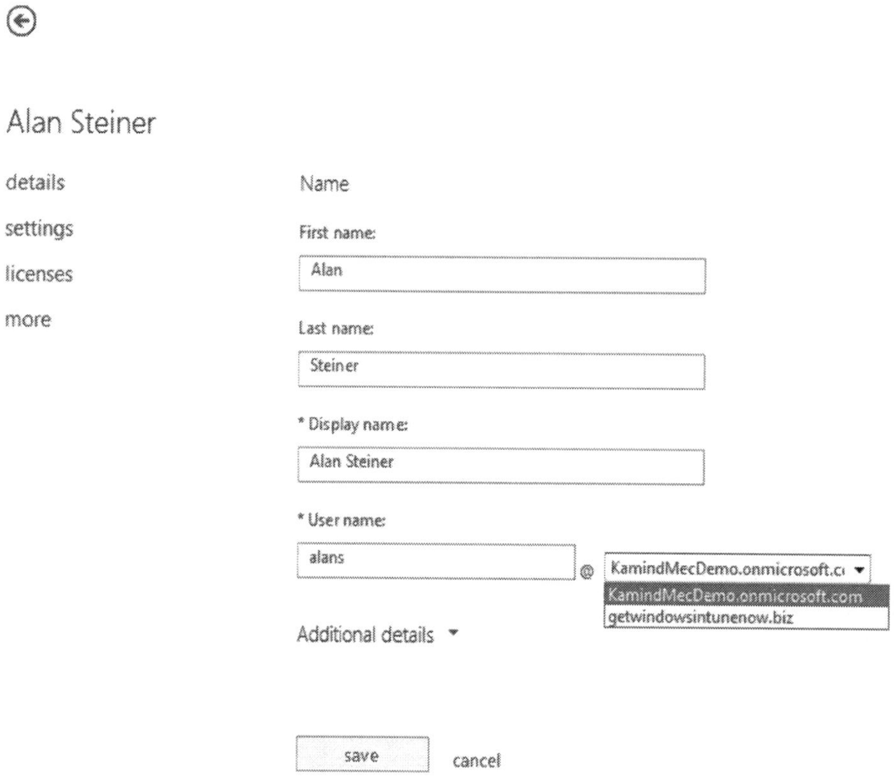

Alan Steiner

details	Name
settings	First name:
licenses	Alan
more	

Last name:

Steiner

* Display name:

Alan Steiner

* User name:

alans @ KamindMecDemo.onmicrosoft.c ▼

KamindMecDemo.onmicrosoft.com
getwindowsintunenow.biz

Additional details ▼

save   cancel

Figure 8-20. *Editing the user login domain*

■ **Note**   If you wish to change the user email address to a different alias, you can do that in the Office 365 admin center – if the alias email address exists in the user account. If the email alias does not exist, any change you make will fail.

If you wish to change the user names and email address, it is a two-step process and requires that the new email address has already been added as an alias before you can change it.

1. Change the user name in the Office 365 admin panel (Figure 8-20)

2. Add the user alias to the user mailbox (see Exchange admin center, Figure 8-40, later in this chapter, for a visual reference)

3. Set the user email address as the primary SMTP address in the Exchange admin center (see Figure 8-41, later in this chapter, for a visual reference)

■ **Note**   To change a user email address, you do not do this from the Exchange admin panel; you perform this function from the Exchange Admin Center. (See Figure 8-32)

Adding/Changing Licenses

Changing licenses is simple in the Office 365 enterprise version. Edit the user in the Office 365 Admin Center, and select the license option (see Figure 8-21). When you select a new license, always select the new licenses first, then unselect the old license and save.

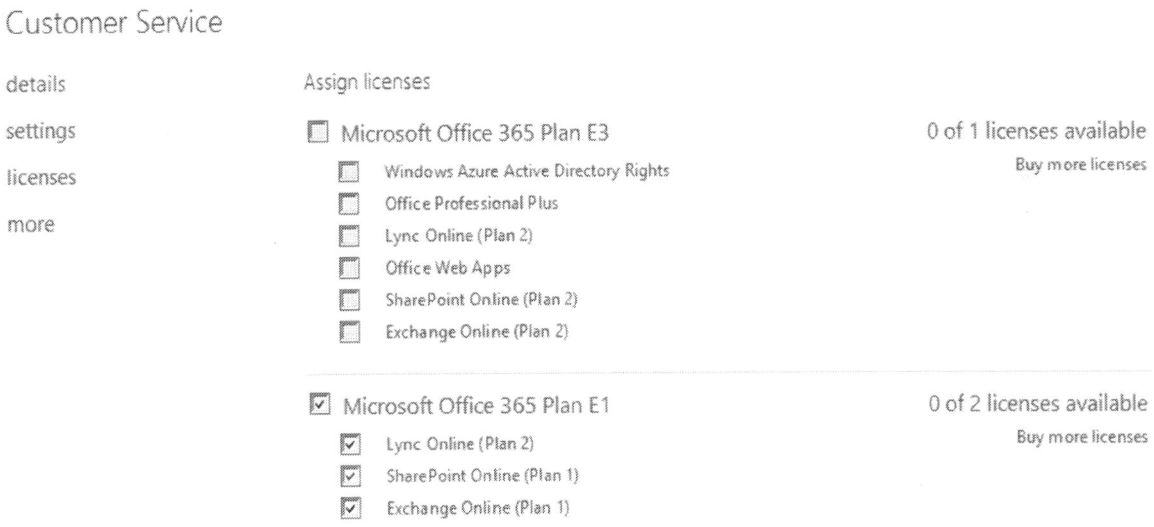

Customer Service

details	Assign licenses	
settings	☐ Microsoft Office 365 Plan E3	0 of 1 licenses available
licenses	☐ Windows Azure Active Directory Rights	Buy more licenses
more	☐ Office Professional Plus	
	☐ Lync Online (Plan 2)	
	☐ Office Web Apps	
	☐ SharePoint Online (Plan 2)	
	☐ Exchange Online (Plan 2)	
	☑ Microsoft Office 365 Plan E1	0 of 2 licenses available
	☑ Lync Online (Plan 2)	Buy more licenses
	☑ SharePoint Online (Plan 1)	
	☑ Exchange Online (Plan 1)	

Figure 8-21. *Setting a new license on an account*

Before you change the license, make sure you have enough licenses. You can check the license status in the subscription settings (see Figure 8-22).

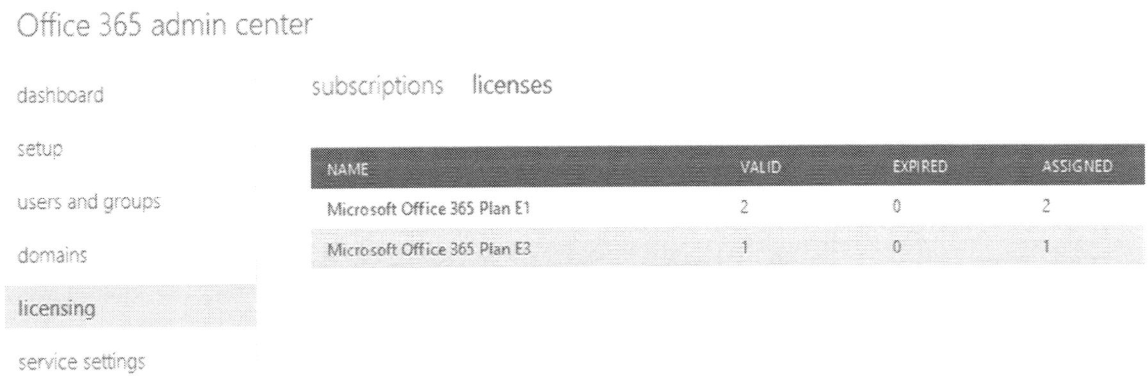

Office 365 admin center

subscriptions   licenses

NAME	VALID	EXPIRED	ASSIGNED
Microsoft Office 365 Plan E1	2	0	2
Microsoft Office 365 Plan E3	1	0	1

dashboard
setup
users and groups
domains
licensing
service settings

Figure 8-22. *License usage status*

Security Groups

Security groups are used to manage permissions globally in Office 365. There are different ways to use security groups: You can use security groups to filter users and administrator permissions (useful in large organizations), and you can also use security groups to manage permissions for different services. SharePoint (as an example), can either use security groups to grant permissions to various site libraries for users, or you can use SharePoint security permissions to restrict access to different libraries in SharePoint. As an example, in large organizations, you can create a security group to isolate users from each other, as well as using security groups to manage access to different federated services (such as Windows Intune and Azure services). There are different ways to use security groups depending on your business needs: Some organizations use security groups to manage SharePoint services. As an example, a SharePoint site is designed, and security groups are created to assign permissions to different areas. The global administrator adds accounts to the different security groups depending on the business requirements. The users added to the security groups inherit the permissions necessary to access the functional areas in SharePoint.

Creating security groups is easy: Sign in as an Administrator; click Admin/Office 365; click "sers and groups/security groups" (see Figure 8-23). Click the "+" to add a new group, or select a group, and edit the group to add an account to an existing group (Figure 8-24). Be sure to click "Save and Close."

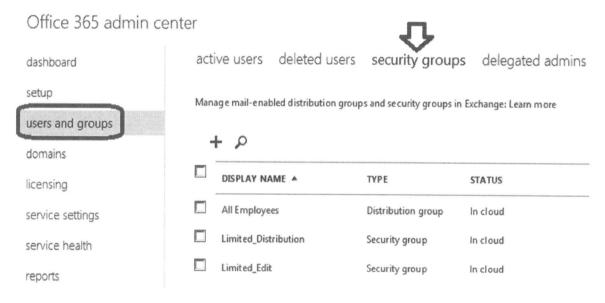

Figure 8-23. *Selecting or creating a new security group*

Limited_Edit

details

members

Available members

Add

Selected members

Remove

	DISPLAY NAME ▲
☐	Alan Steiner
☐	Allie Bellew
☐	Amy Alberts

	DISPLAY NAME ▲
☐	Karen Berg

Remove

Figure 8-24. *Adding to a security group*

The security group wizard shows the account members that are in the security group, and those members that can be added to the security group. Click Members to see the list. Check accounts to add. Click Add to add the account to the list. Be sure to "Save and Close" (at the bottom of the screen) after you have added account(s) to the group.

If you see the error message (Figure 8-25) when you are adding to an existing group, then this group is a mail-enabled distribution group; you can only make changes to mail-enabled groups in the Exchange Admin center.

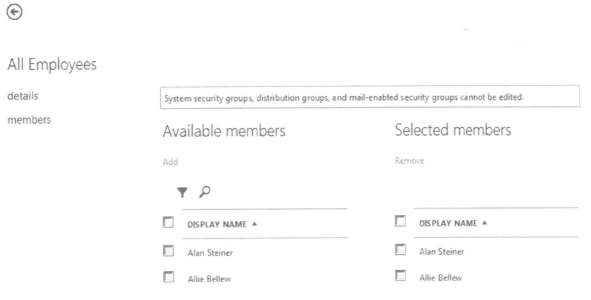

All Employees

details

members

System security groups, distribution groups, and mail-enabled security groups cannot be edited.

Available members

Add

Selected members

Remove

	DISPLAY NAME ▲
☐	Alan Steiner
☐	Allie Bellew

	DISPLAY NAME ▲
☐	Alan Steiner
☐	Allie Bellew

Figure 8-25. *Adding user to an existing group*

Bulk License Assignments

One of the other functions that administrators are required to perform is to make bulk license assignments. You can make bulk user license assignments through the graphical interface by selecting all of the users you wish to change the licenses for, then select "edit" (see Figure 8-26).

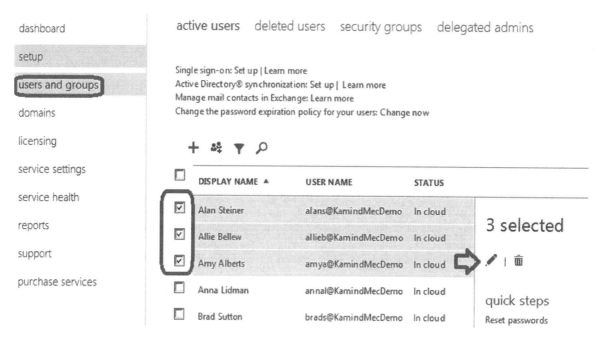

Figure 8-26. *Selecting users for bulk editing*

Once you select the user to change, step through the wizard until you come to the screen that needs to change, then select the new license you wish to add (see Figure 8-27). Select "Submit" when completed.

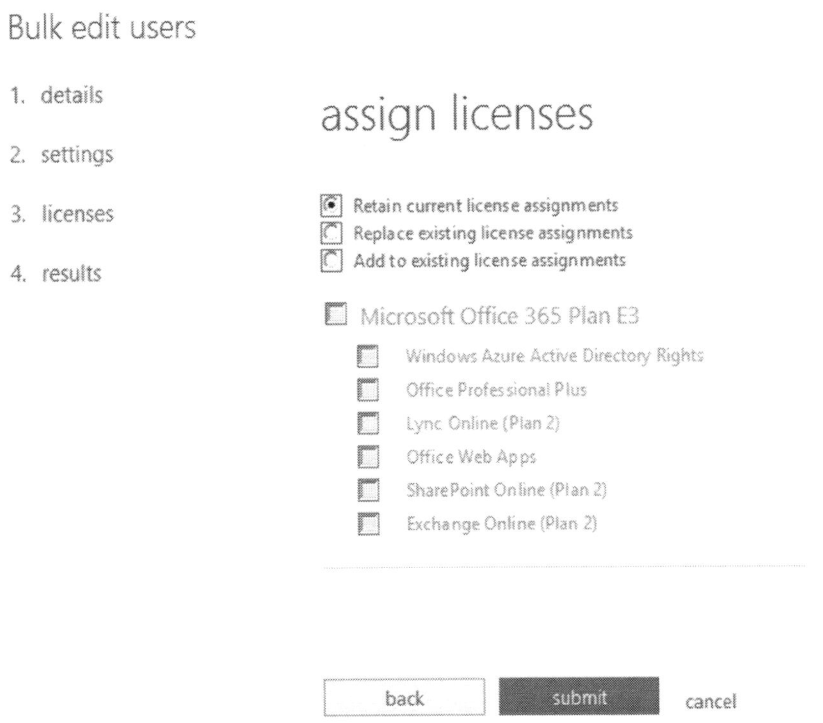

Bulk edit users

1. details

2. settings

3. licenses

4. results

assign licenses

☉ Retain current license assignments
☐ Replace existing license assignments
☐ Add to existing license assignments

☐ Microsoft Office 365 Plan E3

    ☐ Windows Azure Active Directory Rights

    ☐ Office Professional Plus

    ☐ Lync Online (Plan 2)

    ☐ Office Web Apps

    ☐ SharePoint Online (Plan 2)

    ☐ Exchange Online (Plan 2)

| back | submit | cancel |

Figure 8-27. *Bulk license change*

Delegated Administrators

Delegated administrators are trusted advisors. There are two types of delegated administrators: *Microsoft* and *Microsoft partners*. When an Office 365 site is created, no administration rights are granted to any external parties. Microsoft does not have the ability to access user data, unless that right is granted by the account owner.

The account owner (global admin) can add or delete delegated administrator partner (DAP) access in Office 365 as needed (see Figure 8-28). Deleting access is simple: select the account and select delete. The only way you can add a delegated administrator is if the partner sends you a delegated administrator link. Not all Microsoft partners can be delegated administrators: A delegated administrator is a class of partner that has achieved a level of service (as determined by Microsoft) in using Office 365.

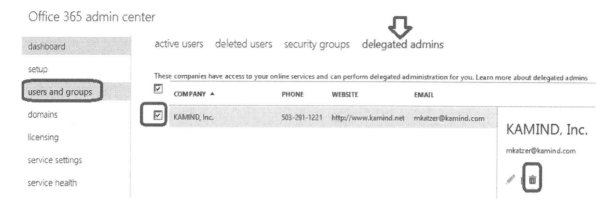

Figure 8-28. *Delegated Administrator Partner - Control Panel*

Yammer

Yammer is a service that is included with Office 365 Enterprise subscriptions. Yammer acts as an internal social media site or discussion board; Yammer content is owned by the company deploying Office 365. This allows an organization to own the social content (and not use a public site - like Facebook) for internal company issues. Yammer is a replacement for SharePoint newsfeed. Access to Yammer is simple: if the user access has been "licensed", the user selects the Yammer link from the Office 365 web interface; Yammer user accounts are then sync'd from Office 365 to Yammer. Once you select the link, you can either invite users to join the Yammer network, or let each user join on their own initiative. Once your users have joined Yammer, the operation is similar to Facebook, except the data is internal to your company and is owned by the company and not in the public domain (see Figure 8-29).

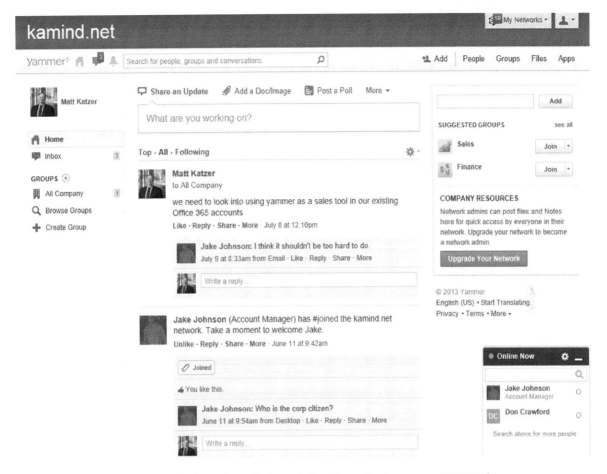

Figure 8-29. *Yammer social media home (sample shown is from the author's company, KAMIND)*

We have only touched on a few areas that are most common on the configuration of an Office 365 company. There are many more issues that you may run into. We only touch the surface of the configuration options of Office 365. The options we explored are the most common options that you use in managing Office 365.

Exchange Administration Center

Office 365 administration sites are added based on licensed features. Exchange (email services in Office 365) is a licensed subscription option. At the beginning of this chapter, we discussed the different Office 365 services (subscription options). Exchange mail services is a subscription option. The global administrator has access by default, but global administrator access is enabled (or disabled) by the roles in the organization. Role-based permissions are controlled in the Office 365 Exchange Administration Center. The Exchange Administration Center (EAC) is located under Admin-> Exchange (see Figure 8-30) below. All of the commands in the following section assume that you are operating in the Exchange administration section.

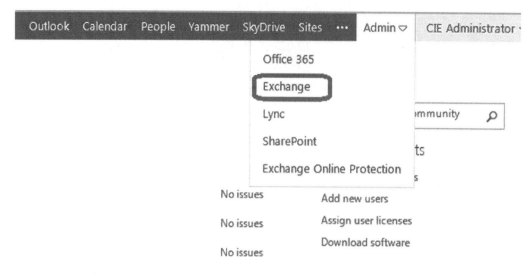

Figure 8-30. *Office 365 Administration Center*

Exchange Administration Roles

The Exchange Administration Center includes a number of administration roles. These roles are used to assign various subtasks to users. The Office 365 global administrator is an organization administrator. The Global administrator may not have permission in some Exchange roles, however the Global administrator can add be added to that role, but that action is audited. In large organizations, the Global administrator accounts are controlled, and user accounts are modified with administrator permissions based on the job roles. As an example, a large company may create a security group of users from one location, and the Exchange administrator is a user in that security group. The Exchange administrator functions are limited to that location as defined in the security group. This is in contrast to a global administrator who has access to all accounts.

In larger organizations, there will be different roles assigned for Exchange, but in small organizations there will only be two roles that are commonly used: the company Administrator role (global admin via the AdminAgent role) and Discovery Management role. Discovery management is discussed in Chapter 9. The Global admin does not have access to discovery management unless that role is granted, and permission has been granted in the discovery SharePoint center.

You can assign any of the administrator roles in table 8-7 to the user mailbox. Our recommendation for assignment of user permissions follows this model:

1. Build a security group for the accounts that will be managed. The user who will manage these accounts should be in the security group.

2. Assign the user Exchange administration permission to the selected account in the newly created security group (Figure 8-31).

Table 8-7. *Exchange Administrator role description*

Exchange Server Role	Description
AdminAgents	Administration agents contain all of the administrators in Office 365 and any other users that are added by the admin. This is where the base Exchange administration permissions are granted.
Compliance Management	Users in this role can configure Exchange compliance policies, such as Data Loss Prevention, as well other Exchange policies or compliance issues (see compliance function in Exchange Admin center).
Discovery Management	This role manages the discovery process. In order to access discovery information, you must be a member of this role.
Help desk	This manages view-only operations and password resets.
HelpdeskAdmins	Manages the help desk.
Helpdesk Agents	Agent that operates the help desk.
Hygiene Management	Manages the Exchange transport services.
ISVMailboxUsers	Third-party application developer mailbox role.
Organization Management	Allows full access to all user mailboxes for any administrative role except for discovery management.
Recipient Management	Role required to move mailboxes in hybrid deployment.
Records Management	Users in this role can configure compliance features such as retention tags and policies.
Rim-MailBxAdmins	Blackberry Mailbox access for BlackBerry messaging servers (only valid if BlackBerry service is enabled on Office 365).
TenantAdmins	Legacy admin role for management of Exchange tenants.
UM Management	Universal messaging management role to integrate necessary functions for Enterprise Voice with Lync.
View-Only Organization Management	View-only privileges for Exchange organzation. Users in this role cannot modify any Exchange properties.

Exchange admin center

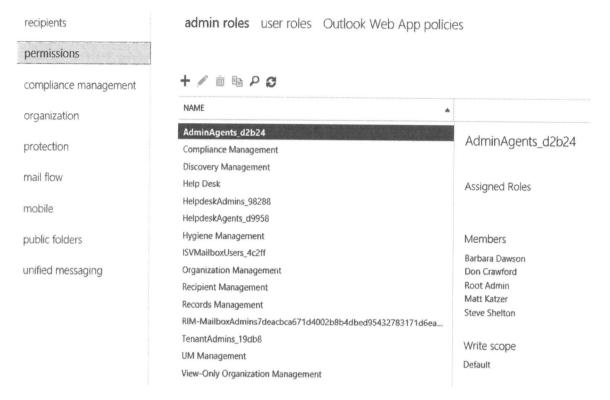

Figure 8-31. *Assigning administrative permissions*

Once you have assigned the permission to the user to manage the Exchange users, you can create necessary user roles (if needed) to manage the group.

Default User Role Defined

All users have a default role assigned to them when they are added to Office 365. The default user role defines the characteristics that the user has in accessing the Exchange mail system. As an example, Outlook web access is defined as a user role. If you don't want to have users access the web mail, you can remove these privileges. The user roles that you can change are listed in Table 8-8 below.

Table 8-8. Default user role assignments

Role Assignment	Description
Contact Information	Allows the user to change their personal contact information.
Profile Information	Allows users to modify their name.
Distribution Groups	Allows user to create Distribution Groups.
Distribution Group Membership	Allows users to modify their distribution group memberships.
Base Options	Allows users to modify basic operations associated with their mailboxes.
Subscriptions	Allows users to change their email subscription options (such as notification of changes to SharePoint etc.)
Retention Policies	Allows users to change the retention policies associated with their email account.
Text Message	Allows users to change their text message (IM) settings.
Marketplace Access	Allows users to change the marketplace access to modify or add remote applications.
Team Mailboxes	Allow users to create their own team mailboxes with other users.

Either create a new role, or modify the existing role, and change the permissions associated with the role (see Figure 8-32). If you modify the default role, you change the role for all users. It is recommended that you create a new role, then apply that roll to the user account (or accounts); to create a new role, select permission, then user roles. Either create a new role (plus sign), or modify the existing role (pencil) (see Figure 8-33).

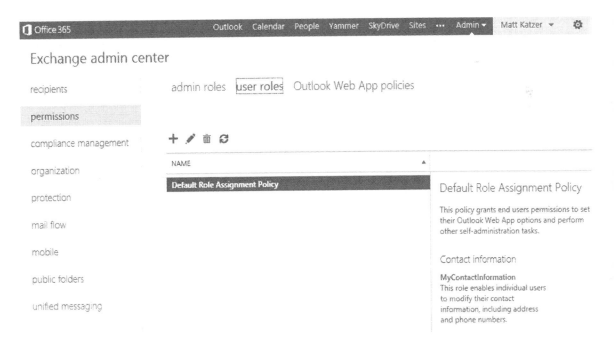

Figure 8-32. Editing the user roles in Office 365

Exchange admin center

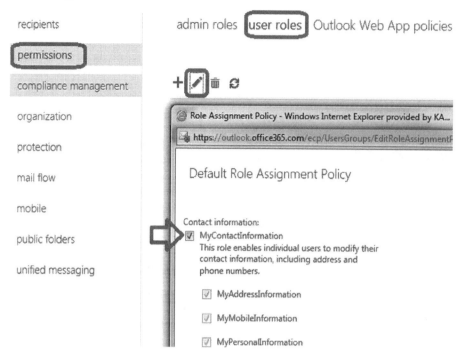

Figure 8-33. *Changing the default user role*

If you create a new role for a user account that is different the other default role, you will need to apply the new role to the user account. Select the "recipients" – "Mailboxes", then the user account. Edit the account and assign the role (see Figure 8-34 below).

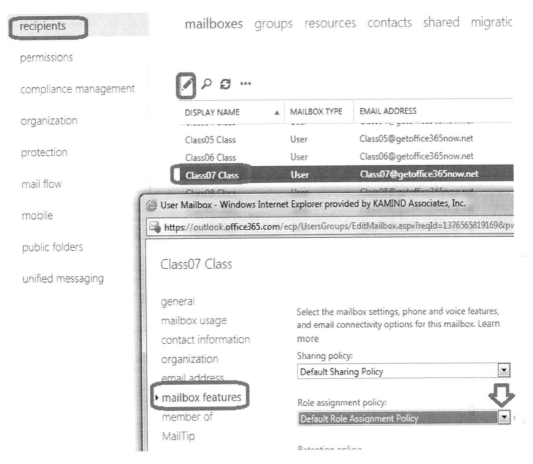

Figure 8-34. *Assign a new role to the user account*

Conference Room: Configuration

Office 365 provides a resource called "meeting room". =Meeting rooms are used to control resources that are limited and need to be managed through scheduling. To set up a meeting resource, log in to Office 365 as an administrator, and select the Exchange (see Figure 8-30, in preceding pages) to access the Exchange Admin Center (EAC).

Creating a conference room is simple: After you have selected the EAC, select Recipient – Mailboxes (in the drop down dialog box in Figure 8-35), and select Meeting Room. This will set up the meeting room with a default configuration (if the meeting room is being used, it will show a busy status). There are additional configuration changes that can be made on conference rooms, but there is no GUI interface. These changes would need to be made using PowerShell.

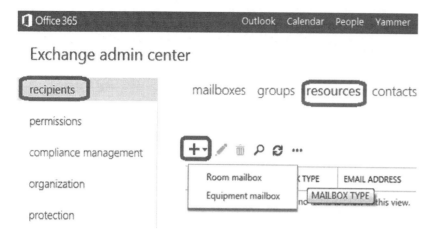

Figure 8-35. *Creating a new conference room*

When you create the meeting room, the first order of business is to assign users that have permission to book the meeting room. These users are called delegate users. You have two options on meeting rooms: allow all users to book meeting rooms (default), or allow restricted users to book meeting rooms. Provide the name of the meeting room and select the appropriate option, then click OK (see Figure 8-36).

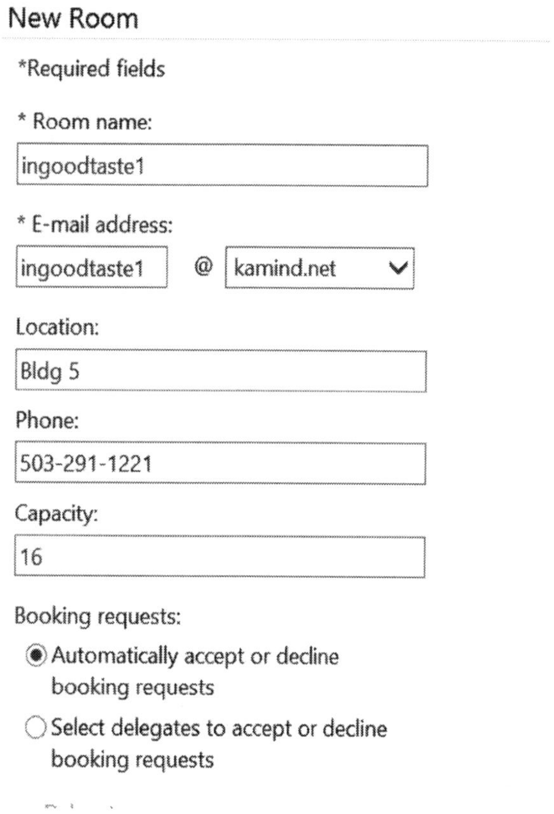

New Room

*Required fields

* Room name:

ingoodtaste1

* E-mail address:

ingoodtaste1   @   kamind.net   ∨

Location:

Bldg 5

Phone:

503-291-1221

Capacity:

16

Booking requests:

◉ Automatically accept or decline
booking requests

◯ Select delegates to accept or decline
booking requests

Figure 8-36. *Configuring a conference room*

The room has been configured with the default setting showing only a busy status. Meeting rooms are very versatile: You can use this function to reserve any type of resource, such as equipment. Remember, meeting rooms are a single device, and having a meeting room resource manages multiple objects. To use meeting rooms to manage multiple objects, you need to create a meeting room for each device. After you have created the room, you can modify the capabilities of the room based on your needs (see Figure 8-37 below).

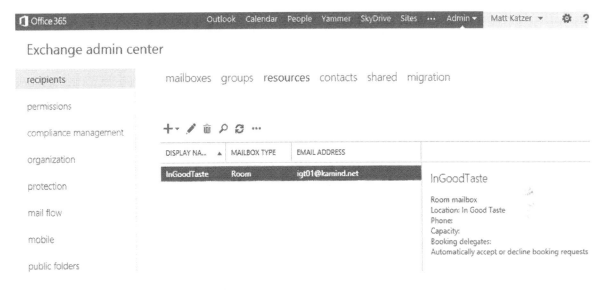

Figure 8-37. *Reviewing conference room characteristics*

Conference Room: PowerShell Modification

Conference and resource rooms provide the basic configuration for use, but there are additional configuration options that can only be done using PowerShell. As an example, the default configuration hides the meeting status and ownership. If you want to make those available, you will need to run the following PowerShell commands (see PowerShell setup at end of this chapter).

Set full details of a conference room using PowerShell:

```
Set-CalendarProcessing -Identity ingoodtaste1 -AddOrganizerToSubject $true -DeleteComments $false
-DeleteSubject $false
```

Set limited details of a conference room using PowerShell:

```
Set-MailboxFolderPermission -AccessRights LimitDetails -Identity ingoodtaste1:\calendar -User default
```

Changing a User's Name / Changing an Email Address

Earlier, we showed how to change the user account properties in Office 365, but you were limited on what you could change based on if there was an alias email address in place. You change the user name in Office 365 administration center (see Figure 8-19 in preceding pages), then you change the user email address in the Exchange center. To change the user email address, click open, select the Office 365 dashboard, then the Exchange admin center (see Figure 8-30 in preceding pages) and follow the steps below.

1. Verify that you have changed the name of the user. If the name is different, change the name in the Office 365 admin center. Do not change the name of the user in Exchange Admin Center.

2. Select Recipients, then Mailboxes and the mailbox of the user you wish to change (see Figure 8-38), then select edit (pencil icon).

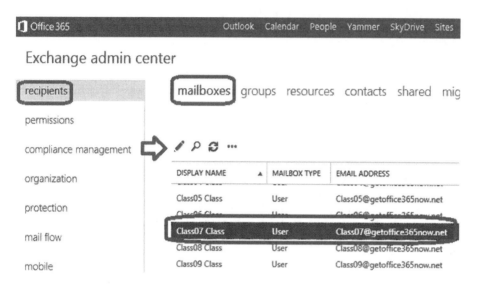

Figure 8-38. *Changing the user's email address*

3. Select "email address" and then the "plus" sign to add the new email address (Figure 39).

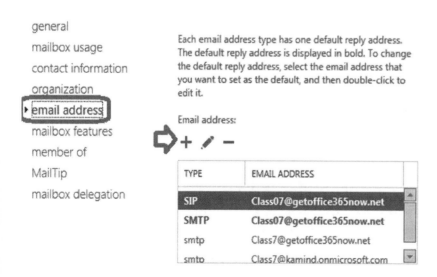

Figure 8-39. *Entering the new email address*

4. To make the address the primary address (the login and reply address), select "Make this the reply" address (see Figure 8-40). The domain on the email must be verified to add the user account.

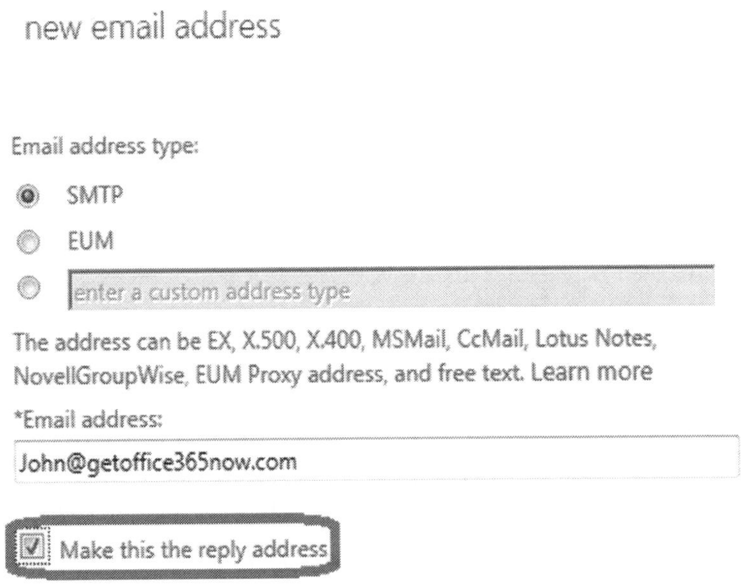

new email address

Email address type:

◉ SMTP

◯ EUM

◯ [enter a custom address type]

The address can be EX, X.500, X.400, MSMail, CcMail, Lotus Notes, NovellGroupWise, EUM Proxy address, and free text. Learn more

*Email address:

John@getoffice365now.com

☑ Make this the reply address

Figure 8-40. *Setting the user email address as the primary login*

■ **Note** When the reply email address is changed, the Outlook user will be requested to log in with new credentials. Outlook recognizes that the user profile is the same, and will link the existing Outlook mailbox to the corrected email address.

Adding an Alias Email Address to a User

It is simple to add an alias email address: Just select the Exchange Admin center, highlight the user account, click edit, then select email address (Figure 8-41). Enter the new email "alias" address for the user. The domain must be verified in Office 365, otherwise the alias will not be added.

Exchange admin center

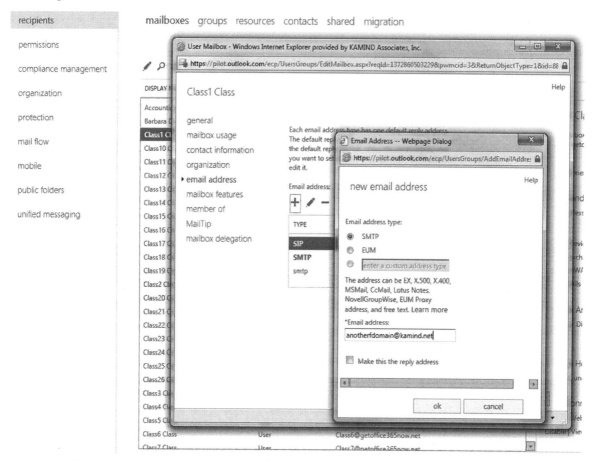

Figure 8-41. *Adding a new email address to an existing email account*

Changing a User Email Account Primary Domain

Office 365 supports multiple different domains and multiple user email aliases per an account. In some cases, an Office 365 organization may need to change to a new domain (e.g. after a company merger or branding change). To make the change for all users is not difficult: all that is required is to verify the domain (set the MX records and Lync records), add the domain to the existing users, and set the reply address to the new email alias. What you cannot do is change the xxx.onmicrosoft.com domain. If you need to change the xxx.onmicrosoft.com domain, you will need to migrate to a new Office 365 organization. To make this change, follow the steps outlined below.

Step 1 – Validate the new domain

Complete a domain validation for the new domain with the domain intent set to Exchange and Lync. Follow the instructions discussed in Chapter 4 and discussed early in this chapter's "Domain" section.

Step 2 – Add the user alias and set the reply address

Add the new email alias to all of the users that will have a domain change. If the user's primary email address is changing, then select the "make this the reply address" option (see Figure 8-42). This will change the user's primary login address to the new domain. This step is no different than changing the user email address to a new address (as discussed earlier).

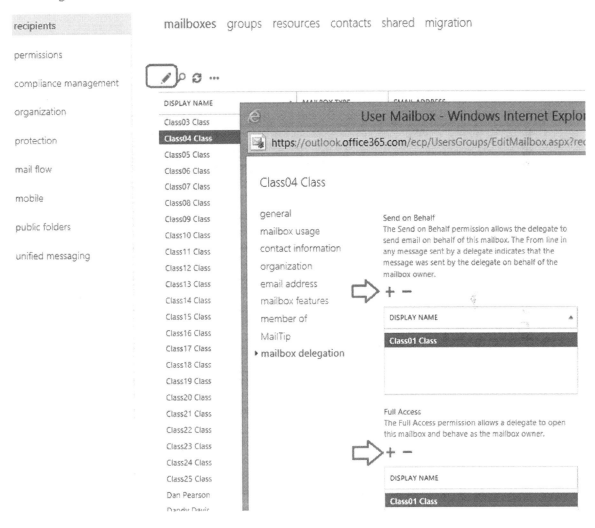

Figure 8-42. *Adding delegated rights to a mailbox*

■ **Note** When the reply email address is changed, the Outlook user will be requested to log in with new credentials. Outlook recognizes that the user profile is the same, and will link the existing Outlook mailbox to corrected email address.

Adding Shared Mailbox

There are two methods for adding a shared Exchange mailbox. The approach you use depends on the capabilities that you want the mailbox to have: In you need to receive information on a mobile device, or of you require the mailbox as an archive for long term storage, then you will need to use a licensed mailbox. If you do not need these features and only want to have access via Outlook, then the mailbox does not need to have a license. We have outlined the choices in Table 8-9 (below).

Table 8-9. *Shared mailbox options*

Approach	Cost (monthly)	Data Size	Capabilities
Shared licensed mailbox	$4 - $8	25GB with 25GB or 100GB archive	Can be received on smartphones (active sync support).
Exchange shared mailbox	$0	5 GB limit	No active sync.

The key decision factor for most users is to receive the information on smartphones. This requirement dictates that you need to use an Office license, rather than a free shared mailbox.

Shared Mailbox: Using with a Smartphone and Outlook

Smartphone devices require active sync connection. You add a shared mailbox the same way you add a mailbox to Office 365. The only issue is that you must assign delegated rights to the users who wish to use the mailbox. This is the same for all user mailboxes. Once a mailbox has been created, you need to assign share rights to the mailbox.

To add a shared mailbox, follow these steps:

1. Purchase an Exchange Plan 1 (or Plan 2) mailbox.

2. Assign a user account to the Exchange email account.

3. Assign user-delegated rights to the mailbox.

Just select the Exchange Admin center, highlight the user account, click "edit", then "select email address" (see Figure 8-43) to be changed (use the pencil). Select "mailbox delegation", then add the user for both "Full Access" and "Send on behalf". Click "ok", when completed, and the mailbox is modified.

Figure 8-43. *Adding a free shared mailbox*

Shared Mailbox: Using Only with Outlook

If you need to add a shared mailbox for use only with Outlook (and you do not want to use a license), you can create a shared mailbox in the Exchange administration center, then add the user as delegated user to the mailbox (like we just did in Figure 8-43).

Select the Exchange Admin center, select "Shared", then create a shared mailbox. In this case, we created a mailbox called CalCompany (see Figure 8-44). Select the mailbox, then "mailbox delegation" and add the users who will access the shared mailbox (as we did earlier – see Figure 8-43). Click "OK" when completed. The shared mailbox will appear in each user's Outlook that was added as a delegated user.

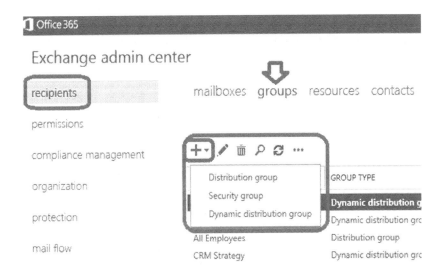

Figure 8-44. *Adding a Distribution group*

Shared Mailbox: Using PowerShell

In some cases, you will need to use PowerShell to set up and configure a shared mailbox. You need to run two PowerShell commands: one to set the permission and the other to set the behavior of the shared mailbox. Once you have modified the shared mailbox, the configuration will be updated in the Outlook client at the next login. In this example, "Identity" is the shared mailbox, and "User" and "Trustee" are the person who has access to the shared mailbox.

Step 1: Add the recipient permissions

```
Add-RecipientPermission -Identity user@kamind.com -Trustee trusted@kamind.com -AccessRights SendAs
```

Step 2: Add mailbox access permissions

```
Add-MailboxPermission -Identity user@kamind.com -User trusted@kamind.com -AccessRights FullAccess
-InheritanceType All
```

Adding a Distribution Group

There are three different types of distribution groups: "Distribution groups", mail enabled "Security groups", and "Dynamic distribution groups". When you add a group (see Figure 8-44), you select a group based on the business role that you wish the group to perform.

There are different views types of group to add, and which group you use comes down to management view. In general, Security groups are not mail-enabled and are managed externally to the Exchange Admin center. Security groups are created in the Office 365 administration center and are managed from Office 365 and not the Exchange Admin center. Typically you will create either a "distribution group" or, if you are a large organization, you create a Dynamic distribution group.

Table 8-10. *Distribution Group Types*

Group Type	Description
Distribution Group	Distribution groups are mail-enabled groups. An email that is sent to the distribution group is sent to all members.
Security Group	Security groups are groups that are used to grant permissions. In some cases, these may be mail enabled. It is recommended that you do not use mail-enabled security groups.
Dynamic Distribution Group	A distribution group that has a variable number of members based on filters and conditions in active directory.

Step 1: Create the Distribution group

In the Exchange Admin center, select "recipients", then select "groups" (see Figure 8-45), add the group ("+" sign), then select the distribution group to be added.

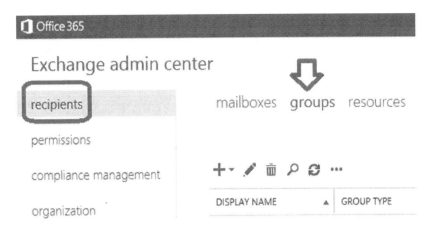

Figure 8-45. *Adding a new Distribution group*

Step 2: Define the Distribution group

Fill in the information about the Distribution group. When you first create the group, leave the defaults in place. You must specify an owner of the group and any initial members that you wish to add (see Figure 8-46).

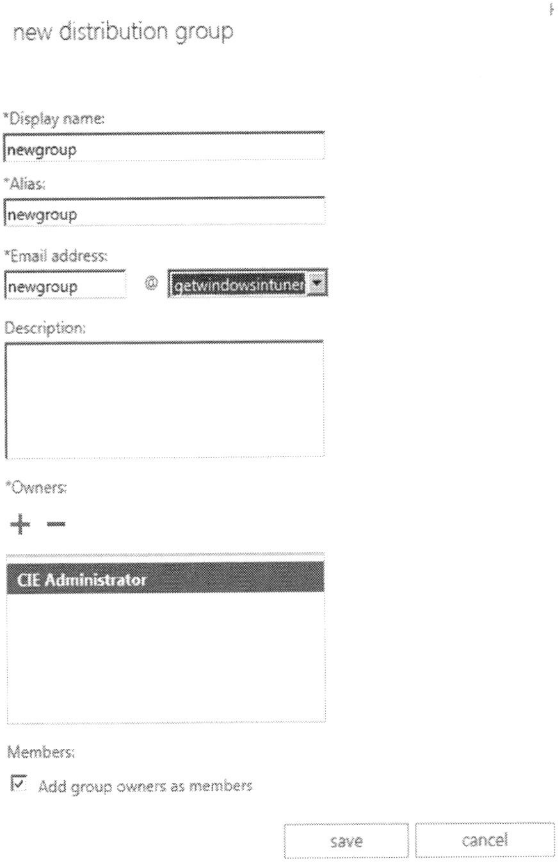

new distribution group

*Display name:

newgroup

*Alias:

newgroup

*Email address:

newgroup   @ getwindowsintuner ▼

Description:

*Owners:

+ −

CIE Administrator

Members:

☑ Add group owners as members

save   cancel

Figure 8-46. *Defining the Distribution group*

Step 3: Enabling the Group for External Access

After you have created the group and saved it, the group is set up for internal access. If you wish to enable the group for external access, you must edit the group and enable the external access options (see Figure 8-47). Select the group, select "edit", and select the "delivery management" option. This is a two-step process: You must create an internal distribution group (and save it) before you can enable it for external access.

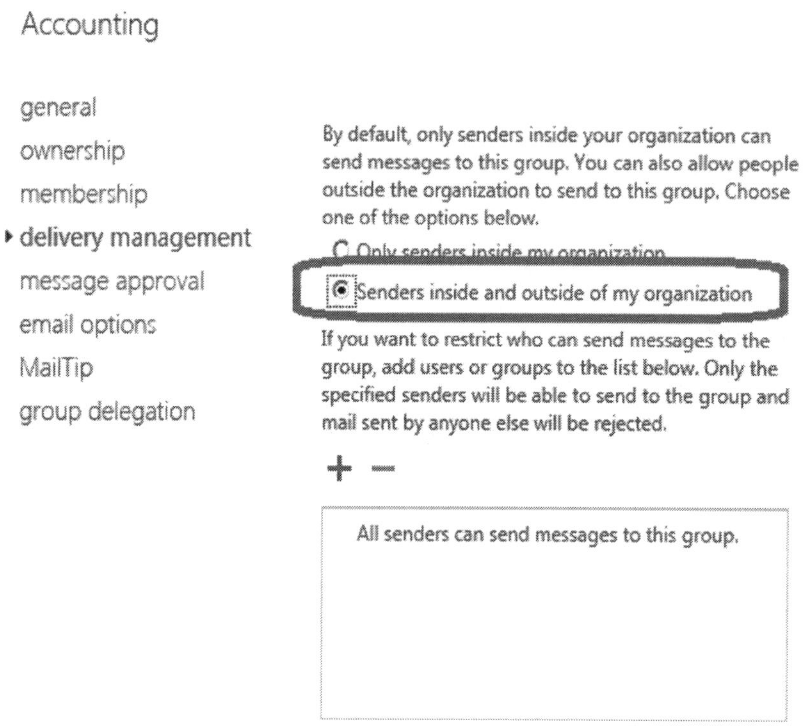

Figure 8-47. *Setting for external delivery*

Using Alias to Send/Receive from Email

You may want to use a different email address to send and receive email. Office 365 is designed to allow only one email address to be used: your primary email address. The way to work around this is to use a distribution list and to grant a user account full permission to use that distribution list using PowerShell. Log in to the Office 365 administration center and under the admin tab, select "Exchange" and follow the steps outlined below.

Step 1: Create the Distribution group

In the Exchange Admin center, select "recipients", then select "groups", and click on the "+" sign to add the Distribution group. Use the email alias as the Distribution group name.

Step 2: Configure the Group to be Added

In the Exchange Admin center, select "recipients", then select "groups", and click on the "+" sign to add the distribution. Since this is a personal alias, add a description and complete the additional steps for the configuration of the group (see Figure 8-48).

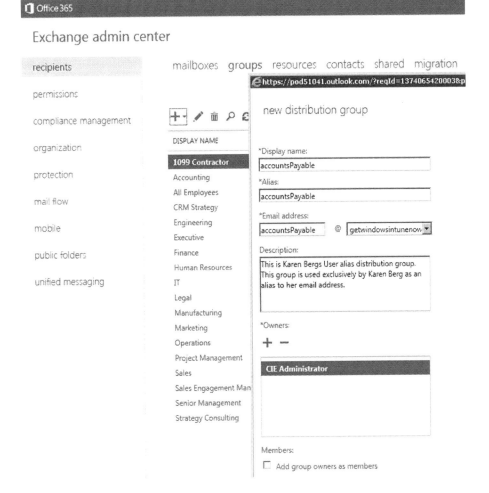

Figure 8-48. *Adding Distribution group*

Add the user, and select the membership options. Since this is an email alias (i.e. an internal group) it is recommended that you restrict it to the individual that is using the group (see Figure 8-49).

new distribution group

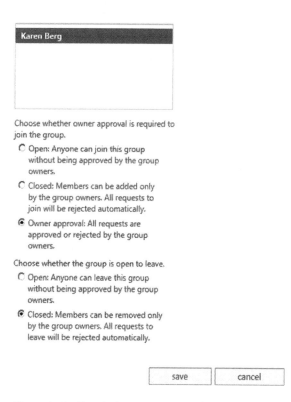

Choose whether owner approval is required to join the group.

○ Open: Anyone can join this group without being approved by the group owners.

○ Closed: Members can be added only by the group owners. All requests to join will be rejected automatically.

◉ Owner approval: All requests are approved or rejected by the group owners.

Choose whether the group is open to leave.

○ Open: Anyone can leave this group without being approved by the group owners.

◉ Closed: Members can be removed only by the group owners. All requests to leave will be rejected automatically.

[save] [cancel]

Figure 8-49. *Restricting access to Distribution group*

Step 3: Enable the Group for External Access

In the Exchange Admin Center, select "group", then "edit" (pencil icon). Select "delivery management", and then enable the mail option (internal only is default) and enable the user for outside of the organization. This is identical for external distribution groups that we discussed earlier.

He

foodovation

general

ownership

membership

membership approval

▸ delivery management

message approval

email options

MailTip

group delegation

By default, only senders inside your organization can send messages to this group. You can also allow people outside the organization to send to this group. Choose one of the options below.

○ Only senders inside my organization

◉ Senders inside and outside of my organization

If you want to restrict who can send messages to the group, add users or groups to the list below. Only the specified senders will be able to send to the group and mail sent by anyone else will be rejected.

+ −

All senders can send messages to this group.

save   cancel

Figure 8-50. *Enabling the group for external access*

Step 4: Grant the Permission to the User

The final step is to grant the permission to the user. There are two ways to do this: either through PowerShell, or by using the Exchange admin center. Select the "In the Exchange Admin center" option, select "group", than "edit" (pencil icon), and select "group delegation". You will need to enter the user account for both *Send As* and S*end on Behalf* (see Figure 8-51). Select "OK", and the user will now be able to use the "From" address in Outlook or in the Outlook Web App to send emails using the alias email address.

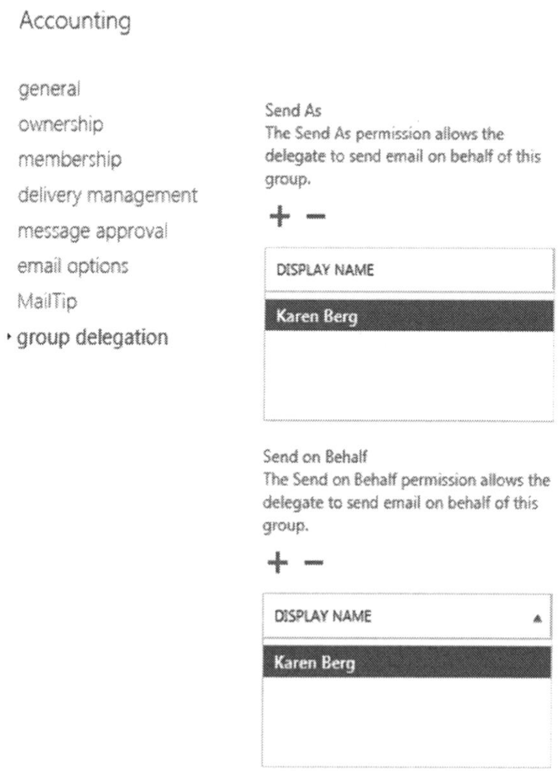

Accounting

general

ownership

membership

delivery management

message approval

email options

MailTip

▸ group delegation

Send As
The Send As permission allows the delegate to send email on behalf of this group.

+ –

DISPLAY NAME
Karen Berg

Send on Behalf
The Send on Behalf permission allows the delegate to send email on behalf of this group.

+ –

DISPLAY NAME ▲
Karen Berg

Figure 8-51. *Setting Send on Behalf options*

You can also grant theses permissions using the PowerShell commands for a shared mailbox. In this case you are using a distribution list and granting full access for its use. Execute the PowerShell command, and give access rights to the user mailbox. The shared mailbox PowerShell command is as follows:

```
Add-RecipientPermission -Identity myfakeemail@domain.com -Trustee myrealeamil@domain.com
-AccessRights SendAs
```

Step 5: Verifying Outlook Configuration

The final step is to send an email from Outlook to verify that you can send a message from an alias. In order for this to work, you must select the email distribution group you created earlier. In our example, we used "Get365". Select "get365" from the group email address book. (If you manually type the email address in, this will fail.) To send an email alias from Outlook, follow the steps outlined below:

1. Open up Outlook, select the "From" drop down, and select the "Other email address" (see Figure 8-52).

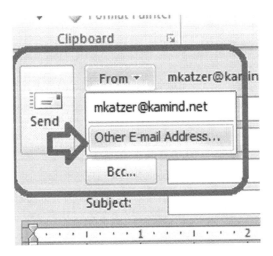

***Figure 8-52.** Selecting From / Other email address*

2.   In the "From" box, select "From" and find the distribution alias (see Figure 8-53).

***Figure 8-53.** Selecting the alias address "Get365"*

3.   Click "OK", and send the email.

In Figure 8-52, we select "Other email addresses", then select the distribution group (see Figure 8-53); you cannot enter the distribution group name in the address bar. The email will not be sent.

Smartphone Management from Exchange

Smartphone devices are controlled with Exchange active sync. The default configuration is to allow users to control their smartphone using Outlook Web App – Options. If you desire to control these options at an administration level, you access this information via the Exchange admin center (EAC), under the mobile option (see Figure 8-54).

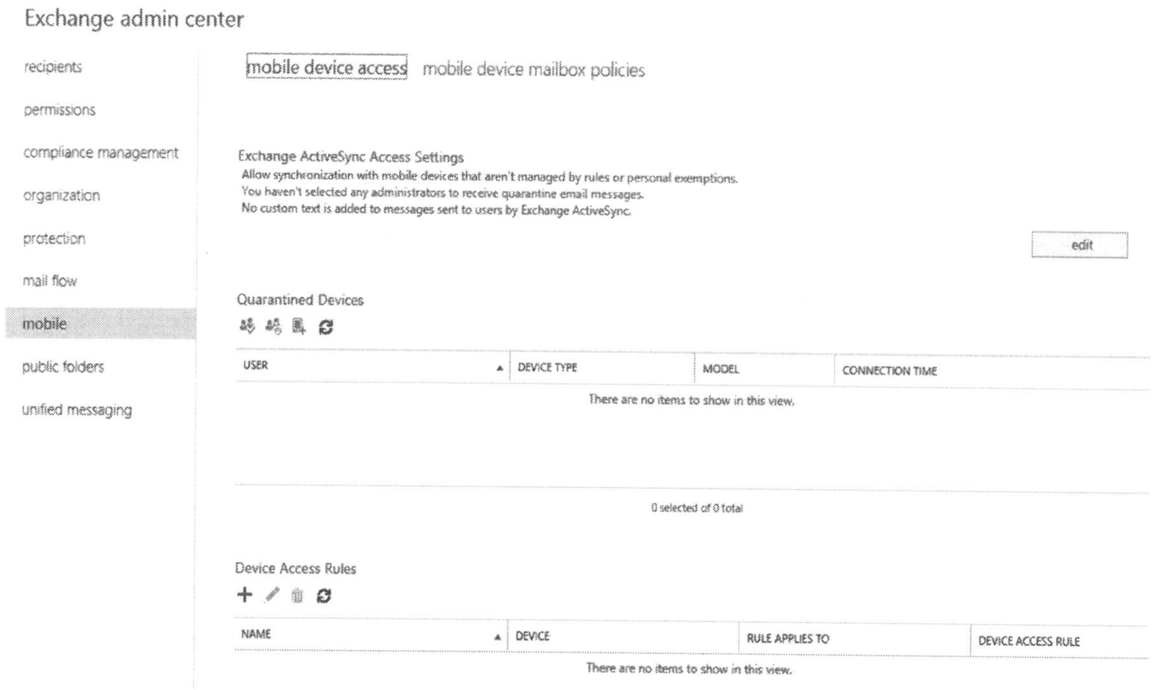

Exchange admin center

recipients

permissions

compliance management

organization

protection

mail flow

mobile

public folders

unified messaging

mobile device access · mobile device mailbox policies

Exchange ActiveSync Access Settings

Allow synchronization with mobile devices that aren't managed by rules or personal exemptions.
You haven't selected any administrators to receive quarantine email messages.
No custom text is added to messages sent to users by Exchange ActiveSync.

edit

Quarantined Devices

USER	DEVICE TYPE	MODEL	CONNECTION TIME
	There are no items to show in this view.		

0 selected of 0 total

Device Access Rules

NAME	DEVICE	RULE APPLIES TO	DEVICE ACCESS RULE
	There are no items to show in this view.		

Figure 8-54. *Mobile device access control*

You can also enable detailed control options on the mobile devices, such as password requirements, password complexity and encryption options. These options are in addition to the Windows Intune Mobile device management policies.

Many organizations wish to limit what users can do with smart devices. In some cases, you may restrict all users from using mobile devices; this is a business planning process issue. It is best to define the business polices and implement them during deployment; The important point here is that you can control the mobile device access to information, if needed.

Troubleshooting: Autodiscover

Autodiscover is the ability of an Outlook client (including your laptop and your smart phone) to discover the location of the Office 365 Exchange Email Server, and to automatically connect to that server (see Figure 8-55). You need to insert the Autodiscover record in the external DNS and the internal DNS. Both records should point to outlook.com (see Figure 8-56).

Exchange admin center

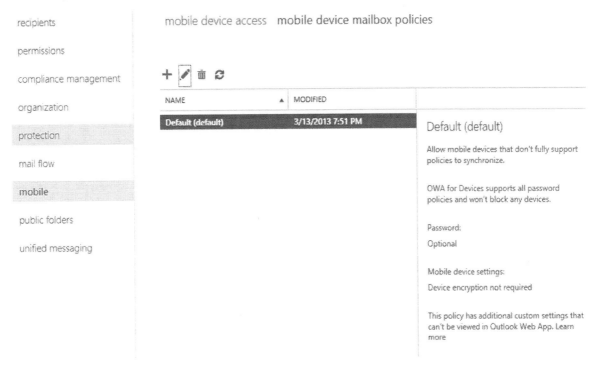

Figure 8-55. *Mobile device policies*

Type	Priority	Host name	Points to address	TTL
CNAME	-	autodiscover	autodiscover.outlook.com	1 Hour

Figure 8-56. *Autodiscover record value*

The Autodiscover process is outlined in Figure 8-57. When an internal client looks up an Autodiscover record, it first determines the Autodiscover record through active directory. If the client is external, it looks up the Autodiscover record from the DNS.

Figure 1   The Autodiscover service process for internal access

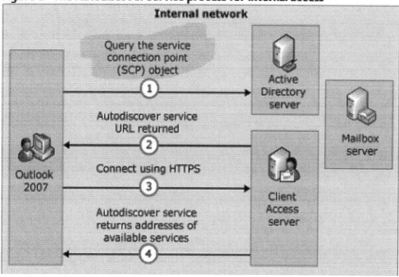

Figure 8-57. *Exchange Autodiscover process (Courtesy of Microsoft)*

If you are on site and you are trying to connect to the Office 365 Exchange Server, the Outlook client will use the Exchange Service Control Point connection object to attach to the local Exchange Server and bypass the external auto discover look up. If you have chosen not to use Microsoft migration tools, you will need to block the local clients from finding the on-site Exchange Server in the auto discovery process, or convert the mailboxes to a Mail enabled user (MEU). The registry entries that must be modified for the clients are listed below (see Microsoft KB article – 2612922).

Equation 8-1. Registry entries to block Service Control Point (SCP) look up.

1. Navigate to the following registry key:
HKEY_CURRENT_USER\Software\Microsoft\Office\12.0\Outlook\AutoDiscover

2. Set the following values for the Value Names listed below:
"PreferLocalXML"=dword:1
"ExcludeHttpRedirect"=dword:0
"ExcludeHttpsAutodiscoverDomain"=dword:1
"ExcludeHttpsRootDomain"=dword:1
"ExcludeScpLookup"=dword:1
"ExcludeSrvLookup"=dword:1
"ExcludeSrvRecord"=dword:1

Lync Administration

Lync is a full featureed communications tool that supports file sharing, web conferencing, voice communications, and many other features (very similar to Skype, but with many more features). Lync integrates into Microsoft Exchange and acts as a phone switch for incoming voice calls. Large organizations use Lync as desktop phone replacements, and allow their users to deploy Lync clients on any mobile or desktop device. Smaller organizations use third-party services such as Connect Solution (www.coso.com) to handle incoming phone calls; Lync supports Enterprise voice (both people can talk at the same time). There are many different characteristics of Lync; it is a powerful and popular business communication tool, and the data it accesses is encrypted between parties.

Setting up Lync Federation

In Chapter 4, we configured Lync to be federated to communicate to external users. The process is simple (see Figure 8-58). Select the "Lync Admin" center from the Office 365 dashboard (under the Admin tab), select "organization" and "external communications", and eLync federation takes one to four weeks to be provisioned for the service. Once the service is provisioned, you are enabled for external communications.

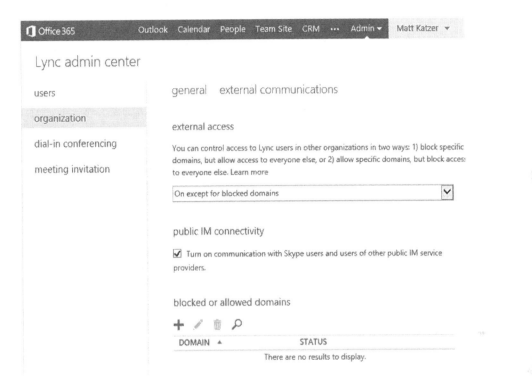

Figure 8-58. Enabling external communications

■ **Note**   It is recommended that you have verified the domain prior to enabling federation. If you enable the onmicrosoft.com domain, there may be some service downtime when you switch over to the verified domain.

Configuration for Conferencing Add-on

There are several different conferencing suppliers for Lync. To find all of the providers, select "Lync administration center", then select the "provider" tab (see Figure 8-60). This will display the list of providers that are certified by Microsoft to work on Office 365. You can contact them directly, or ask your Microsoft partner to do so.

Once you have selected a teleconferencing provider partner, just enter the dial-in information for the user account under "dial-in users" (see menu item in Figure 8-59). Your teleconferencing bridge number will be enabled and will automatically be generated with an Outlook calendar invite, as long as Lync is installed and running on your desktop.

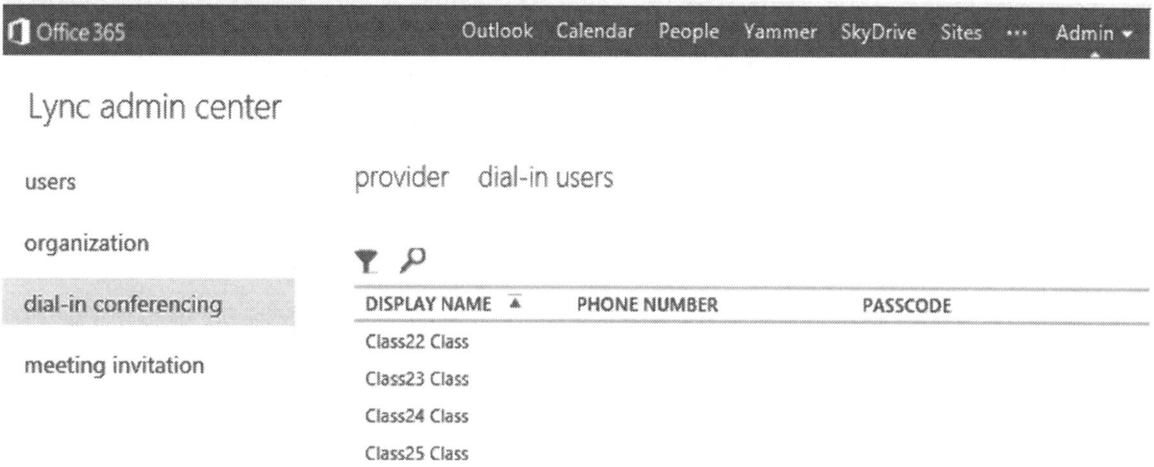

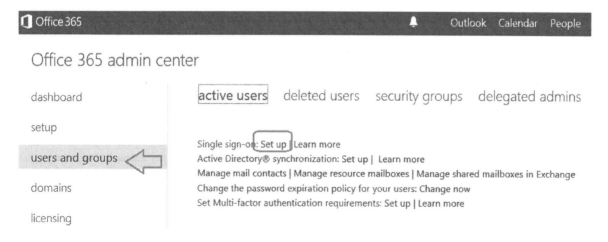

Figure 8-59. *Lync administration center, provoder listings*

Microsoft is adding additional features to Lync; as they add more capabilities, the Lync admin center will be extended with new features.

Using PowerShell

Earlier we briefly discussed PowerShell and the capabilities that it provides you. PowerShell is required for any bulk changes you need to perform, or for special commands that are not part of the Office 365 admin console. Typically we recommend that if your organization has more than 10 accounts then you may find it more convenient to use PowerShell. The account that you will use for PowerShell management is the Global Administrative user account, and the account must have a license in the area that the PowerShell command is executing. As an example, if you are using Exchange PowerShell commands, the global admin account must have an exchange license assigned. If the license is not assigned, then the PowerShell command will fail. The simplest way to install the latest version of PowerShell is to select the "Single sign-on" option (see Figure 8-60). This is the same process that we used in Chapter 4.

Figure 8-60. *Selecting Single sign-on to install PowerShell*

Select step 3, "Install PowerShell" (See Figure 8-61). The PowerShell installation will verify the updates required to support the Windows Azure PowerShell. The only option we are interested in is the installation of PowerShell on your desktop systems. Select the correct version (32-bit or 64-bit) for your system.

Set up and manage single sign-on

When you set up single sign-on (also known as identity federation), your users can sign in with their corporate credentials to access the services in Microsoft Office 365 for enterprises. As part of setting up single sign-on, you must also set up directory synchronization. Together, these features integrate your on-premises and cloud directories.

1 Prepare for single sign-on
Learn about the benefits of single sign-on and make sure you meet the requirements before you set it up.
Learn how to prepare for single sign-on

2 Plan for and deploy Active Directory Federation Services 2.0
Work through the in-depth documentation to deploy and configure AD FS 2.0.
Follow instructions for planning and deploying AD FS 2.0 for single sign-on

3 Install the Windows Azure Active Directory Module for Windows PowerShell
Download the Windows Azure Active Directory Module for Windows PowerShell, which includes cmdlets to establish the trust relationship between your AD FS 2.0 server and Office 365 for each of your domains that use single sign-on.
Learn about installing and configuring the Windows Azure Active Directory Module for Windows PowerShell

- ⦿ Windows 32-bit version
- ○ Windows 64-bit version

[Download]

Figure 8-61. *Installing Office 365 PowerShell*

Once you have installed Office 365 PowerShell, launch the PowerShell module and enter the following commands.

```
Set-ExecutionPolicy RemoteSigned
$LiveCred = Get-Credential
Import-module msonline
Connect-MSOLService -Credential $LiveCred -Verbose
Get-MsolGroup
```

The results of running theses commands should be similar to Figure 8-62.

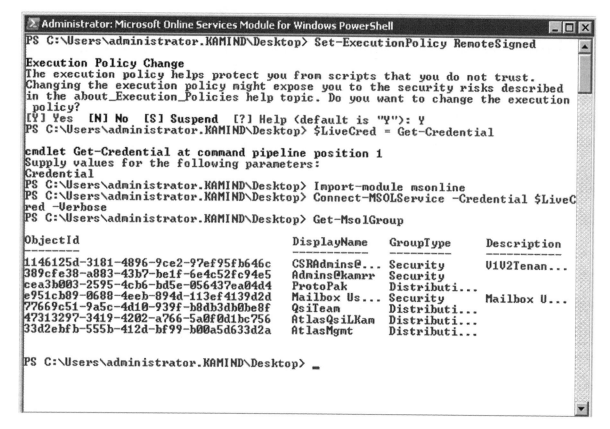

Figure 8-62. *Validating PowerShell commands*

You have completed the base PowerShell set up; now use the above command to validate the installation. If the command above does not work, you have either installed the PowerShell GUI incorrectly, there is a lack of permissions, or you have not installed the desktop connector for Office 365. Using PowerShell requires administrative privileges and a license to be assigned to the account that is using PowerShell commands.

PowerShell: Using the Standard Header

Most Office 365 features can be changed within Office 365 using the service Admin centers (Exchange, CRM, SharePoint, and Lync). Sometimes you cannot make the necessary changes, however, and will need to make changes using Windows PowerShell.

PowerShell can be complex for any user. When using PowerShell with Office 365, you need to use a standard PowerShell header. This standard header will allow you to connect directly to the Office 365 administration interface and make the necessary changes. However, if you do not set up the commands correctly with the remote interface execution parameters, the PowerShell command will fail. The only issue is that the user account that you log in to (for Office 365) must have a license assigned to it. The licensed user can only execute the PowerShell commands for the Office 365 that the user admin account is licensed to use, otherwise it will fail.

We use a standard PowerShell interface that allows the command to run in a PowerShell command prompt, or the integrated systems editor (ISE). The standard command interface (or PowerShell header) can be invoked with this script:

```
Set-ExecutionPolicy RemoteSigned
$LiveCred = Get-Credential
Import-module msonline
Connect-MSOLService -Credential $LiveCred -Verbose

$Session = New-PSSession -ConfigurationName Microsoft.Exchange-ConnectionUri
https://ps.outlook.com/powershell/ -Credential $LiveCred -Authentication Basic -AllowRedirection

Import-PSSession $Session -Allow Clobber

# Insert Other Power shell commands before remove PSSession
#*********
# PowerShell Commands go here
#*********

#Clean up and close the session
Remove-PSSession $Session
```

Once you have verified the functionality of the header script, you are now ready to make the necessary changes in Office 365. This section of the administration maintenance manual lists the type of problems encountered and the PowerShell solution. All that is needed for the user to execute these commands is to use an acocunt--with global administrator rights--that has been licensed with an appropriate subscription (such as Exchange, SharePoint, etc.).

PowerShell: Not Remotely Sign Error

The first time you run PowerShell, you may get an error not remotely signed. To correct this error, you need to enable PowerShell on your system:

1. Start Windows PowerShell as an administrator by right-clicking the Windows PowerShell shortcut and selecting Run as Administrator.

2. The WinRM service is configured for manual startup by default. You must change the startup type to Automatic and start the service on each computer you want to work with. At the PowerShell prompt, you can verify that the WinRM service is running using the following command:

   ```
   get-service winrm
   ```

   the value of the Status property in the output should be "Running".

   a. If the value is not running; you can start the service from the command prompt

      ```
      sc config winrm start= auto
      start winrm
      ```

   b. To configure Windows PowerShell for remoting, type the following command:

      ```
      Enable-PSRemoting -force
      ```

Mail flow should resume in the next two to four hours.

PowerShell: Winmail.dat Problem

Let's say the email is being sent externally to users in an RTF mime format, and the users cannot read the email and see a "winmail.dat" file. The winmail.dat file appears on a client email because Outlook (on the sender) is not installed correctly or there is another Outlook Add-In (on the sender) that is preventing the email form being converted to text. To resolve this issue, either disable the Outlook Add-ins (on the sending device) or uninstall and re-install Office 2007/2010.

If this fails, then as a last resort you can force the Office 365 Exchange server to send only pure text email. This command will force the emails to be sent out as pure text format.

```
Set-MailContact <ExternalEmailAddress or GUID> -UseMapiRichTextFormat Never
```

Verify that the mail format was applied:

```
Get-MailContact | Select <ExternalEmailAddress or GUID> | Select UseMapiRichTextFormat
```

The above command will only display the user email address if it supports RTf format, otherwise, it will display other options.

PowerShell: Enable Audit

The Audit command turns on full tracking for any access to a mailbox. To change the audit state on a mailbox, run this command:

```
Set-Mailbox <Identity> -AuditEnabled $true
```

Set multiple mailboxes for audit:

```
$UserMailboxes = Get-mailbox -Filter {(RecipientTypeDetails -eq 'UserMailbox')}
$UserMailboxes | ForEach {Set-Mailbox $_.Identity -AuditEnabled $true}
```

PowerShell: Verification of Audit Logs

Run the following command to verify the audit log configuration and the time limit configuration. Administrator audit log is on by default, mailbox logs are off by default. Audit logs are enabled for 15 days.

```
Get-AdminAuditLogConfig
```

PowerShell: Mailbox Audit Log search

To perform an audit log search in PowerShell, use the following command. This requires that auditing has been enabled on the mailbox in question:

```
New-mailboxAuditLogSearch  -Mailboxes user@domain.com -Startdate 1/1/2010 -EndDate 12/31/2013
-StatusMailRecipients  manager@domain.com
```

PowerShell: Passwords Forever

Passwords can be set from the user interface. However, when you reset a password, all passwords revert back to the 90-daypassword reset.

```
Get-MSOLUser | Set-MsolUser -PasswordNeverExpires $true
```

▓ **Note**   If the user's password is reset, the policy changes back to 90 days. If you want the forever policy applied, you need to set it again with PowerShell, and every time you reset a password. The Office 365 interface allows passwords to be fixed for up to 720 days.

PowerShell: Get Mailbox Statistics

```
This command retrieves all of the usage data about the userGet-Mailbox | Get-MailboxStatistics |
Select-Object DisplayName,StorageLimitStatus,TotalItemSize
```

PowerShell: Enable Litigation Hold – No Notice

```
There are different legal holds - with notice and without notice. This command places a mailbox on
legal hold with no notice given to the end user.
Get-Mailbox -ResultSize unlimited | Set-mailbox -LitigationHoldEnabled $true
```

PowerShell: Review Permission Assigned to a Mailbox

This command retrieves all of the permission information about the user:

```
Get-MailboxPermission  -Identity user@domain.com
```

PowerShell: Review the Management Role Assignment to a User Account

This command retrieves all of the permissions assigned to different roles in Office 365.

```
Get-ManagementRoleAssignment- -Enabled $True -Delegating $True
```

PowerShell: Display All Mailbox Forwarders

This commands retrieves information about the Mailbox forwards and allows you to turn them on or off.
    Display al Mailbox forwarders:

```
Get-Mailbox | Where {$_.ForwardingSMTPAddress -ne $null} | Select Name, ForwardingSMTPAddress,
DeliverToMailboxAndForward
```

```
Turn off all milbox forwarders:
Get-Mailbox | Where {$_.ForwardingAddress -ne $null} | Set-Mailbox -ForwardingAddress $null
```

```
Turn off a single mailbox forwarder:
Set-Mailbox <emailaddress>  -ForwardingSmtpAddress $null
```

PowerShell: Change Mailbox Permissions

The mailbox permission command is very useful; you can use this on any email-enabled item (such as distribution groups):

```
Add-MailboxPermission -Identity public@kamind.com -User john@kamind.com -AccessRights FullAccess
-InheritanceType All
```

```
Add-RecipientPermission -Identity public@kamind.com -Trustee rajk@kamind.com -AccessRights SendAs
```

PowerShell: Assign License to a User Account

After you directory-sync an account, there may be a need to bulk-assign licenses via PowerShell. To complete this, you need to execute the two PowerShell commands listed below. There are additional PowerShell commands you will also need to run in order to to retrieve the subscription SKUS to use this command. The licenses types must be active.

```
Set-MSOLUser -UserPrincipalName user@domain.com -UsageLocation US
Set-MSOLUserLicense -UserPrincipalName user@domain.com -AddLicenses {tenantid}:ENTERPRISEPACK
```

PowerShell: Bypass SPAM Filtering for Email

Allow all mail to be sent to a mailbox without filtering email using Exchange Spam Confidence Level (SCL) for email processing. This command accepts all email that is incoming that is processed by Office 365 Exchange server Transport Role:

```
Set-ContentFilteringConfig -Bypassedrecipients public@kamind.com
```

PowerShell: Extend the Purges Folder to Greater Than 14 Days

Email in Office 365 will be deleted form the purges folder after 14 days, once the user has selected the item in the delete folder. The item is moved from the delete folder to the purges folder. The default configuration is 14 days. You can extend this to 30 days with the following commands

1.   Extend 30 days delete for a mailbox

```
Set-mailbox user@contoso.com -retaindeleteditemsfor 30
```

2.   Extend 30 days delete for the Organization

```
Get-mailbox | Set-mailbox -retaindeleteditemsfor 30
```

PowerShell: Meeting Room Configuration

To make meeting rooms more useful, you need to add additional user information about the meeting room. The only way to add additional capabilities is to use PowerShell to extend the meeting room options. This example uses the meeting room "ingoodtaste1".

Set Conference room to show "limited details – free & busy"

```
Set-MailboxFolderPermission -AccessRights LimitDetails -Identity ingoodtaste1:\calendar -User default
```

Reference Links

There is a lot of information about Office 365 on the web; the issue is finding the right site. The information contained in this chapter is a combination of our experiences in doing deployments, and support information that has been published by third parties.

Updating Federation certificates on Office 365

http://support.microsoft.com/kb/2523494

How to set up a certificate on IIS 7.0

http://www.iis.net/learn/manage/configuring-security/how-to-set-up-ssl-on-iis

Office 365 Service level permissions

http://community.office365.com/en-us/wikis/manage/535.aspx

Exchange 2013 Role Overview

http://help.outlook.com/en-us/exchangelabshelp/ee441216

Exchange 2013 Built in Roles

http://technet.microsoft.com/en-us/library/dd351266(v=exchg.150).aspx

Next Steps

Your basic Office 365 system has--hopefully by now--been set up and configured. At this point you are 100% functional and ready to move to the next steps. However, your work is not yet complete. There is much more to do depending on your Office 365 configuration. The key chapters that you need to review for your Office 365 deployment are:

- Chapter 5 – SharePoint Administration

  - SharePoint administration and design can be simple or complex, depending on your business needs. This chapter provides you with a basic overview of the configuration necessary to be up and running using Office 365 Team Site. This chapter describes site design and construction issues as well as the full SharePoint Administration functions for Office 365.

- Chapter 7 – Windows Intune Administration

  - The secret to an optimal Office 365 site is the management of the desktop to ensure that updates are current and the user antivirus is functioning. Windows Intune is a desktop management tool that addresses these issues and reduces the administrator's effort in desktop management while improving the user's experience.

- Chapter 9 – Compliance and Data Loss Prevention

  - Business must adapt their mail document storage systems to correctly process their electronic communications based on regulatory oversight. The Compliance and Data Loss Prevention (DLP) features of Office 365 provide the capability for businesses to manage their communications. Office 365 includes integrated discovery and supports legal discovery and audit requirements.

- Chapter 10 – Exchange Online Protection Administration

  - Office 365 is composed of a set of services. The Exchange Online Protection (EOP) service is the front end of Office 365 and handles all of the external email front end processing and filtering. If you have smart devices that email to Office 365, you will use EOP to manage the interaction.

- Chapter 11 – DirSync, ADFS, Single Sign-On and Exchange Federation

  - Active Directory Federation Services and Single Sign-On is the integration of the Office 365 Active Directory with on-premises Active Directory. This allows one sign on (controlled by on-premises servers) to give access to both cloud resources and on-premises resources. Password Sync can be a simpler implementation that meets many requirements. Federation allows on-premises and cloud Exchange servers to work together.

■ ■ ■

## CHAPTER 9

Office 365 Compliance and Data Loss Prevention

Office 365 is a suite of software products that Microsoft Offers as a service subscription. The basis for the service is to reduce the IT costs for business implementation. The major benefit of using Microsoft Office 365 services is that businesses are more focused on the building the business, rather than building IT cost centers.

There are three plans of Office 365: Professional, Mid-Size Businesses, and Enterprise. Compliance, data loss prevention, encryption, and rights management are available only in the Enterprise plan. If you are not on the Office 365 Enterprise plan, the contents of this chapter will not apply to your Office 365 subscription.

This chapter is a compilation of the best-known methods in use to implement a compliant cloud storage system that meets the needs of various regulation entities. It comprises two parts: the compliance capabilities of Office 365 and later implementation. We encourage you to reach out to a Microsoft Tier 1 Champion Partner and engage it as a licenses advisor to help with these features in Office 365.

Overview of Office 365 Compliance and Discovery

Office 365 is built on the principle that the information contained in the cloud service is owned by the business. The data your company places in Office 365 is your data. Microsoft has as strict policy not to mine or process your data for any business purpose. If you choose to leave Office 365 for some other service, the data you leave behind will be destroyed within 90–120 days of your subscription termination.

There are two parts to compliance: Microsoft's management of the Office 365 service, and your business processes in the management of your Office 365 data. Microsoft's management of Office 365 service and their service standards are published on the Microsoft "trust" website (see Figure 9-1, `http://www.microsoft.com/en-us/office365/trust-center.aspx`). If you are looking for a HIPAA (Health Insurance Portability and Accountability Act of 1996) Business Associate Agreement certification or request a copy of the service audit logs, you can request those directly from Microsoft. Microsoft is transparent in its process on Office 365 and built the service around the protection of your company information. This is in contrast to other cloud services that require an intellectual property rights assignment, which allows them to use your information to sell advertising, among other things.

Office 365
Trust Center
Security. Compliance. Privacy.

Learn how we, as an industry leader in cloud productivity
services, are continually taking steps to maintain your trust in
Office 365.

Our commitment to the area of trust is explained through the
five pillars of the Trust Center.

Watch the video to learn more...

Please read the Official Microsoft Blog about Protecting customer data from government snooping.

Your privacy matters

- Your data is not used for our advertising.
- We enable you to collaborate but also give you the ability to control information sharing.
- You own and retain all rights to your data in Office 365.

Learn more

Leadership in transparency

- You know where your data resides.
- We are transparent about who can access your data and under what circumstances.
- If you choose, we keep you updated about changes to data center locations and other audit information.

Learn more

Independently verified

- We stay up to date with today's ever-evolving industry standards and regulations.
- Our service is verified to meet requirements specified in ISO 27001, EU model clauses, HIPAA BAA, and FISMA.
- Our data processing agreement details privacy, security, and handling of customer data, which helps you comply with local regulations.

Learn more

Relentless on security

- Our built-in security features are a result of over a decade of providing and protecting online services.
- We provide flexible security settings that enable you to have control over your information.
- Our security processes monitor, anticipate, and mitigate threats to protect your data.

Learn more

Figure 9-1. Office 365 Trust Center (http://www.microsoft.com/en-us/office365/trust-center.aspx)

Compliance Settings

When we refer to Office 365 compliance, we are referring to the capabilities of Office 365 data governance to preserve and manage information. Compliance and regulatory settings are the services you enable on the Office 365 site and that meet your business need or regulatory requirements. As an example, you can group information into three different categories: compliance, information review, or business data retention:

- Compliance (HIPAA as an example)

  - Rights management and the protection of personal information

  - Encryption of personal information external to your organization

- Information review (regulatory like FINRA (Financial Industry Regulatory Authority
  –www.finra.org) or judicial order)
    - Litigation hold and eDiscovery
    - Email review to meet FINRA requirements
- Business data retention
    - Business processes on age of data
    - Data management: how to archive, how to delete

All information that you keep falls into these categories. For example, HIPAA requires you to manage certain types of data in a way to protect information. To meet HIPAA requirements, you must protect personal information by encrypting the information before it is sent externally to the organization. One of the HIPAA requirements is that the service you are using provides a Business Associates Agreement (BAA) for their services.

Information review typically means that the information is subject to an audit and is immutable—meaning it cannot be changed or deleted by the users or the organization—prior to review. Any type of regulator review requires that the data is immutable. The most common is litigation. When an organization enters into litigation, all information is frozen at that period in time. We refer to that as *litigation hold*. Regulator reviews such as FINRA are nothing more than an extension of a litigation hold.

Business data retention is nothing more than the business processes used to maintain information, subject to the regulatory requirements. As an example, if the business policy (or user policy) deletes information subject to the retention policy, the information is deleted from the user perspective, but may be kept for a very long time subject to the compliance needs of the organization. The user may delete information, but the compliance setting keeps the information in an area where it is immutable and fully searchable and hidden from the user.

The Office 365 administrator has complete control over the configuration of the compliance and retention polices. The administrator can enable these settings and all actions are auditable. The settings can be changed by using the Exchange Admin Center or using PowerShell commands. As Microsoft enhances the Office 365 service, these settings are simplified in an easy-to-use graphical interface.

The rest of this chapter discusses these concepts and provides a step-by-step implementation with examples of data loss protection (compliance), regulatory review (discovery), and business data retention policies. These three areas make up Office 365 data governance.

■ **Note** If you find that you need to perform discovery or mailbox searches, all users subject to search must be on Enterprise Subscription "Exchange Plan 2," and there needs to be at least one E3 subscription to use the Electronic Discovery Center.

Data Governance Concepts

Microsoft provides the management service on Office 365 that meets or exceeds the regulatory compliance. The management of the data in Office 365 (and the subscription types) are managed and owned by the individual users. The Office 365 business owners need to look at the business and decide what makes business sense based on the needs of the business. To put this in perspective, when an external entity looks at email storage, it is considered modifiable by the user and is noncompliant to certain regulations. A compliant systems requires that the mail and document storage systems must be incapable of being modified, or *immutable*. The owner of a mailbox must not be able to go in and delete the information or document. These capabilities are options in the Office 365 enterprise plan and are include at no charge in some of the subscriptions suites (such as the Enterprise E3 subscription).

You are probably familiar with the various CSI and NCIS shows. A key message that these shows highlight lies in the evidentiary collection of information, and that there must be a "chain of custody" regarding information collected. Think of data governance in the same context as you would a murder with the collection of information for the legal prosecution of the suspect. It is all about chain of custody. Data governance on Office 365 is the same. Access to information that is under discovery or access cannot be tampered with. Further, access is recorded and auditable for all those who access the information. This is the data governance model of Office 365.

Archive and retention policies are implementations of our ability to manage the data to meet our data governance needs. Traditional approaches, such as journaling, record information external to the organization structure, and mostly just contain copies of the email communications. This archaic journaling approach does not address the changing landscape of data governance and data management. Journaling does not link data from storage sites and draft documents in an integrated form. Even an archive is nothing more than another mailbox that is used to store information.

Immutability, audit policy, archive/retention, and data loss prevention are all part of the Office 365 data governance structure. It is designed around chain of custody and the preservation of information—information that cannot be tampered with. If it is tampered with, then a full audit trail of access, as well as the original information that was modified, is created.

Before we discuss the practical aspects of the configuration of retention policy and eDiscovery, we need to frame the discussion with a definition of each of the four key areas of data governance to put them in perspective.

Immutability

There has been much written about information immutability, and there are many misconceptions as to what this is and how it is managed in Office 365. The definition is simple: the preservation of data in its *original form cannot be changed and is kept in a form that is discoverable.*

Recall the discussion of chain of custody. The information that you are accessing and providing for data governance needs not only cannot be changed, but you must not have the ability to change it. In addition, any access to the information must be fully traceable. If you access information, the information that you extract will not change the underlining information.

The best example is to look at an email that flows in or is created by a user in the cloud (see Figure 9-2). In this case, information that arrives or is in a user mailbox can be changed and modified by the user. This is the normal process that we use in writing an email. An email that is immutable, on the other hand, keeps all parts of the message in a form that can be fully discoverable through searches. When an email message is drafted, all changes and drafts are kept and not deleted. Nothing is purged—all information is fully discoverable.

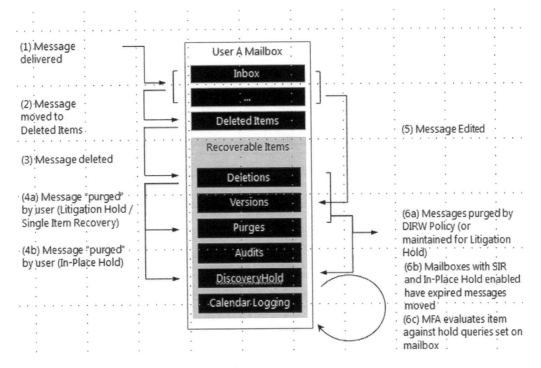

Figure 9-2. Life of an email message

When we refer to compliance, we are referring to our ability to access communications and documents that are immutable. Retention rules are based on business policies in the management of email communications, specifically what email is visible to the user in the mailbox, and what is kept in the archive. For example, you may have a business policy that dictates the movement of email from a user mailbox to an archive if the email is too old, or if the user deletes an email. One company has a retention policy of 90 days; after 90 days, user incoming email is moved into the compliance archive. These retention rules move the mail from the user mailbox (or delete folder) into the archive. These rules can be systems level (user has no control), or they can be local level (user has complete control), or any combination.

Litigation hold is an action that is placed on a mailbox to meet compliance requirements for future discovery and searching. What litigation hold does is to ensure that the data in a user mailbox is immutable. As an example, if the user tries to delete an email, the email is deleted (or purged) from the user's view, but the litigation hold function blocks the email from being deleted in the system and is fully discoverable by the administrator (or compliance officer).

Referring back to Figure 9-2, we see the life of an email in a user mailbox. In Figure 9-2, the user only sees the message in steps 1–3. The compliance officer has access to all transactions in steps 1–6. When a discovery action—a search—is executed, all information is displayed in the search request, including the information in the deleted items, purges, and draft folders.

Audit Policy

Companies in the cloud need to know who has access to their company data. The ability to monitor and produce the necessary reports are part of the Office 365 audit capability. Companies need to do the following:

- To verify that their mailbox data isn't being accessed by Microsoft.

- To enforce compliance and privacy regulations and access by nonowners.

- To have the ability to determine who has access to data at a given time in a specific mailbox.

- To have the ability to identify unauthorized access to mailbox data by users inside and outside your organization.

The ability to monitor the mailbox data is a fundamental part of the Office 365 organization (see Figure 9-3). Once the audit capabilities are enabled (via PowerShell), the audit reports can be generated by the administrator or an individual who has been given this capability.

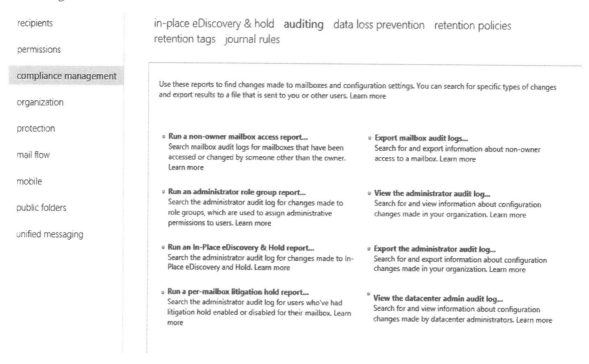

Figure 9-3. *Audit and retention capabilities*

The audit reports are displayed in the search results in the Exchange Administrator Panel. However, if the audit reports are not enabled, the information is not logged. Each audit report contains the following information:

- Who accessed the mailbox and when

- The actions performed by the nonowner

- The affected message and its folder location

- Whether the action was successful

The first step in setting up a compliant organization is to enable the audit capabilities to ensure that you have a complete record of all accesses to user mailbox data by nonowner users. This information is used to supplement future reports. Figure 9-4 provides a descriptive explanation of the terms in the audit reports.

Action	Description	Administrators	Delegated Users
Update	A message was changed.	Yes	Yes
Copy	A message was copied to another folder.	No	No
Soft-delete	A message was deleted from the Deleted Items folder.	Yes	Yes
Hard-delete	A message is purged from the Recoverable Items folder. For more information, see Recover Deleted Items.	Yes	Yes
FolderBind	A mailbox folder was accessed.	Yes	No
Send as	A message was sent using SendAs permission. This means another user sent the message as though it came from the mailbox owner.	Yes	Yes
Send on behalf of	A message is sent using SendOnBehalf permission. This means another user sent the message on behalf of the mailbox owner. The message will indicate to the recipient who the message was sent on behalf of and who actually sent the message.	Yes	No
MessageBind	A message is viewed in the preview pane or opened.	No	No

Figure 9-4. Office 365 audit information (courtesy of Microsoft)

The audit reports that are generated contain detailed information about who has accessed the information and how they have changed it. As you'll see in Figure 9-4, users have different levels of access, and that access can be tracked in audit logs. If a legal hold was placed on the user mailbox, then the search of the user mailbox will show the history non-mailbox owners access. The areas marked "Yes" are those that can be tracked in the audit logs. This is different than the tracking of the information in the discovery center. The discovery center can track all information that is placed on legal hold. The audit logs track the non mailbox owners who access information.

Information Immutability

Information immutability takes this one step further and integrates Lync Communications, and SharePoint documents (as well as SkyDrivePro document synchronization), into the equation. The Office 365 approach is designed to shrink and reduce the amount of information by removing duplicate information. This reduces the complexity of the searches and allows the compliance officer to clearly see the thread of the information and the root cause (if any) of the discovery request. The searched data can be exported in the industry standard Electronic Discover Reference Model (EDRM) standard in an XML format to provide content to a third party. The Office 365 approach is designed to remove duplicate data from searches and does not remove any data from the user SharePoint or email mailbox. The data stays where it is and is immutable.

In Office 365, data governance and compliance is simplified. The scope of the discovery is reduced to the specific set of key words and can be easily restricted to a few users in questions. It is not uncommon that an eDiscovery request on Office 365 would cost 90 percent less than an eDiscovery request using an older journaling system for email communication management.

As you read the rest of this chapter, the discussion on archive and retention polices are built around data immutability to manage an organization's compliance needs. In Office 365, this is referred to as *compliance management*. Administrators are enabled to set up controls based on the business polices of the organization.

Office 365 Archiving and Retention

The term *archive* is overused. It often implies more than what it really is. Archive is nothing more than a second mailbox designed for long-term storage. The relevancy of an archive is based on the business process rules that are used to manage it. This is where immutability and retention policies come into play. Immutability refers to how information is retained (in a form that can't be changed) in the mailbox and the archive. Retention polices (see Figure 9-5) describe the length of time you need to keep the data that is not subject to any legal action (legal hold to guarantee immutability).

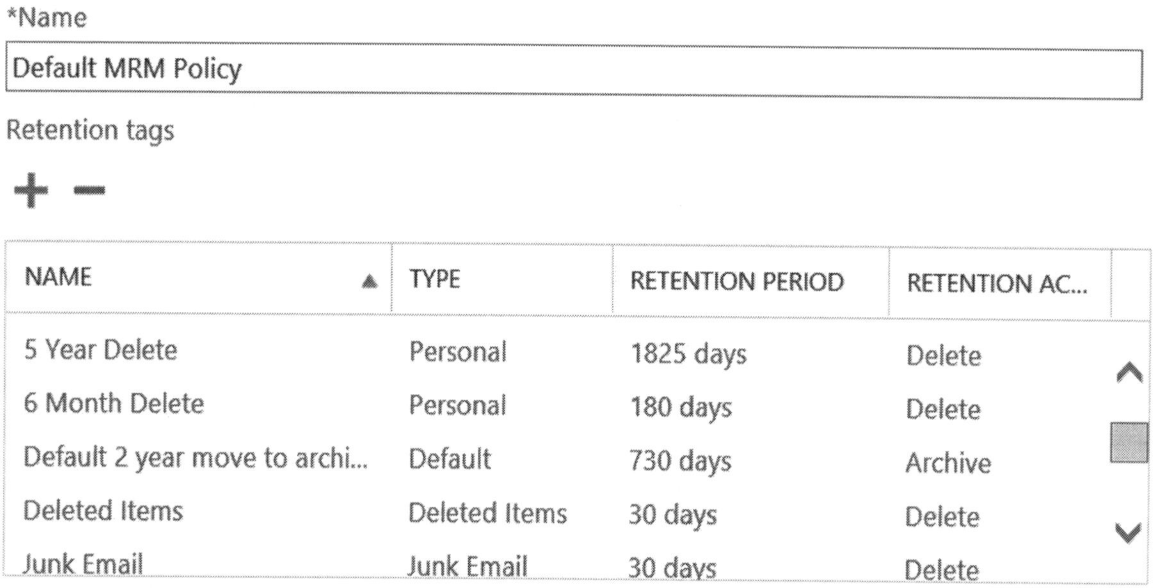

*Name

Default MRM Policy

Retention tags

NAME ▲	TYPE	RETENTION PERIOD	RETENTION AC...	
5 Year Delete	Personal	1825 days	Delete	⌃
6 Month Delete	Personal	180 days	Delete	
Default 2 year move to archi...	Default	730 days	Archive	
Deleted Items	Deleted Items	30 days	Delete	⌄
Junk Email	Junk Email	30 days	Delete	

Figure 9-5. *Sample retention policies*

There are two types of archive in Office 365: personal archives and server archives (see Table 9-1). Server archives can be immutable (meaning they can be configured to ignore any change using litigation hold or in-place hold). Personal archives are stored locally on the user desktop and are not immutable (users can change the contents). The retention policies only refer to the moving of data from the user mailbox to the archive.

Table 9-1. *Archive Size*

Archive Type	Size	Immutable	Retention Policies
Personal	User dependent	No	Personal rules
Server based	50 GB (E1)or unlimited (E3)	E3 or Exchange Plan 2	Server retention rules

Retention Policy

Retention policy is nothing more than the business processes that define the movement of data. Retention polices are a set of rules that are executed concerning a message (see Figure 9-6). Retention policy is a combination of different *retention tags*, which are actions placed on a message. You can have only one retention policy applied to a mailbox. In an organization where you have compliance requirements, retention tags are used to manage the user mailbox information and to control mailbox sizes.

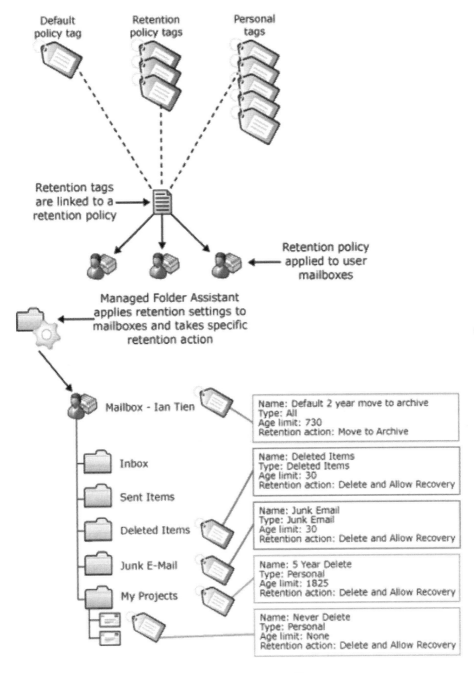

Figure 9-6. Office 365 retention tags (courtesy of Microsoft)

Retention tags define and apply the retention settings to messages and folders in the user mailbox. These tags specify how long a message is kept and what action is taken when a message reaches the retention age. Retention tags are used to control the amount of information that is on the user's desktop. Typically this means that the message is moved to the archive folder or it is deleted. Looking at Figure 9-6, you can see three types of retention tags: Default retention tags, Policy retention tags, and Personal retention tags (described below):

Default:	The default policy applies to all items in a mailbox that do not have a retention tag applied.
Policy	Policy tags are applied to folders (inbox, deleted items, and so on) and override the default policy tags. The only retention action for policy is to delete items.
Personal	Personal tags are only used for Outlook clients to move data to customer folders in the user's mailboxes.

The best way to understand retention policy is to follow the example in our implementation section (later in this chapter). Keep in mind that the implementation of a retention policy directly effects the amount of information kept in a user mailbox. Retention tags (which make up the retention policy) are just another tool used for information management. Depending on your business needs, you may have different retention polices to manage information of different groups in your organization. In one organization we managed, the data retention policy was 90 days, unless the mailbox was placed on in-place hold for litigation or discovery.

Compliance archives may or may not have a retention policy applied to them, but they will have the mailbox placed under litigation hold and the data retention policy of the SharePoint site also placed under litigation hold. User mailboxes that are placed under litigation hold with the external audit enabled meet all compliance requirements, because the data is immutable.

Data Loss Prevention

Data loss prevention (DLP) operates with either a template rule (see Figure 9-7), or with a trigger from the Rights Management Service based on business policy. The purpose of DLP is to execute an action based on rules. DLP does not prevent an individual from doing something bad. All DLP does is to limit the information flow in case someone sends electronic communications to a third party that violates business policy.

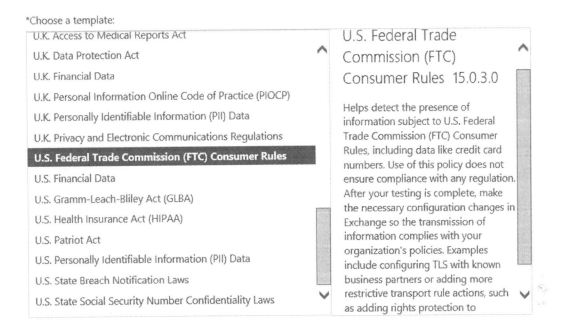

Figure 9-7. Data loss prevention (DLP) templates

What DLP does is minimize mistakes that individuals make in sending information to individuals that do not have a business need to know the information. Add to this capability auditing and discovery, and you will be able to determine which individual had last access to the information.

There are many rules that you can select to implement in addition to the rights management rules on Office 365. Figure 9-7 shows the different templates that can be managed in your organization to control information to meet federal and state regulations. Rights management is the extension of DLP to manage internal documents and information using Active Directory. DLP functions are managed using both the Office 365 interface and PowerShell commands (Figure 9-8)

If you need to...	...use the following cmdlets
Connect to or disconnect from the Rights Management service for your organization.	**Connect-AadrmService** **Disconnect-AadrmService** For more information, see Connecting to the rights management service and Disconnecting from the rights management service
Disable (or re-enable after disabling) the Rights Management service for your organization.	**Enable-Aadrm** **Disable-Aadrm** For more information, see Enabling the rights management service and Disabling the rights management service
Manage the super user feature within the Rights Management for your organization.	**Enable–AadrmSuperUserFeature** **Disable–AadrmSuperUserFeature** **Add–AadrmSuperUser** **Get–AadrmSuperUser** **Remove–AadrmSuperUser** For more information, see Manage super users for rights managed content
Manage users and groups who are authorized to administer the Rights Management service for your organization.	**Add–AadrmRoleBasedAdministrator** **Get–AadrmRoleBasedAdministrator** **Remove–AadrmRoleBasedAdministrator** For more information, see Add, list or remove role-based administrators for rights management
Get a log of administrative tasks that have been performed against the Rights Management service for your organization.	**Get-AadrmAdminLog** For more information, see Download audit logs for Windows Azure AD Rights Management
Migrate your organization to an on-premises AD RMS deployment from the Rights Management service.	**Set–AadrmMigrationUrl** **Get–AadrmMigrationUrl** For more information, see List or set the URL for use in migrating rights managed content to AD RMS
Displays the current Rights Management service configuration for your organization.	**Get-AadrmConfiguration** For more information, see Display the current rights management configuration

***Figure 9-8.** Rights management capabilities (courtesy of Microsoft)*

Setting Up Office 365 Compliance, Discovery, and Retention Policy

Office 365 is very flexible in how the different policies for the management of information can be set up. The problem is where to start. Earlier, we reviewed the different capabilities that you have in Office 365. There are three different areas that need to be configured before you can begin to use the services. The following section outlines the steps required to set up the 365 organization for compliance, discovery, and retention policy. Follow the steps to set up the different features. Note: you will find additional details about compliance steps described in the section "Configuring Compliance."

There are many different views of eDiscovery. What you are trying to avoid is the generation of document pursuit in paper and electronic form to a request. Figure 9-9 is a sample of the old way of producing documents for eDiscovery. This is a sample of what you want to avoid. Litigation is expensive and discovery is very expensive process (from $1–$2) a page. In this example, there were 200,000 pages of documents generated to satisfy a request. Costwise this was $250,000–$400,000 worth of work. Office 365 allows you to create a "discovery center," where you can process the queries, and generate a Sharepoint library that has the information requested in the response. (Recall that we discussed sharing information earlier in Chapter 2 and Chapter 5.) In this case, information was generated for the other side's attorneys that was responsive to the judicial order. Access to the discovery search results can be shared with the other Side's attorneys. This discovery center approach is a lot lower in cost than the traditional document production shown in Figure 9-9.

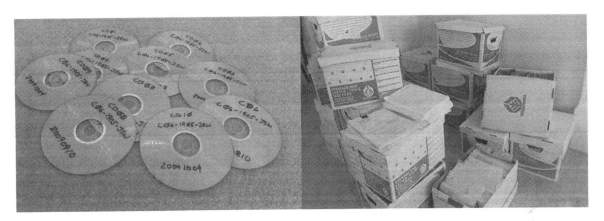

Figure 9-9. *Document production in response to judicial discovery order (approximately 200,000 documents produced)*

Compliance Setup

Compliance management seems very complex, but in reality it is very simple to set up. The starting place is the business process requirements—what information to keep, what types of audits you want, etc. Once these issues are known, then it is a straightforward implementation process.

The process steps are outlined below and described in greater detail later in the "Compliance Example" section:

1. Determine the compliance requirements.

2. Define the users who will manage the compliance activity.

3. Enable encryption (if required by business policy).

4. Enable audit (if required by business policy).

5. Test out the compliance policy with tool tips.

6. Enforce the compliance policy.

Compliance configuration is a simple two-step process: determine the business needs and then implement those business needs. Our compliance example looks at the requirements of HIPAA in the protection of personal information under federal regulation. Compliance can also be used to manage information in an organization, such as with documents that are tagged as confidential.

Discovery Site Setup

Discovery management is more about business process and the collection of information as required by either federal or state regulation, or judicial order. The steps outlined below are described in detail in the section "Discovery Site Example" and require that you have a SharePoint Plan 2 license (for the search query and the reviewer) and the email accounts are Exchange Plan 2. Plan 2 licenses are automatically part of the E3 subscription. The steps to complete the discovery search are outlined below:

1. Define the business policy for the search (regulation review or judicial)

2. Enable auditing

3. Identify who will perform the discovery and review functions

4. Enabling in-place hold (or legal hold) for immutability

5. Compliance and Discovery—using the eDiscovery Search Tool

6. Case-creation process

7. Build the search query

8. Review the information

9. Export the data for review in Outlook

The "Discovery Site Example" section provides a detailed step-by-step example of what is needed to perform a search on the data in an organization to meet regulatory requirements or judicial orders.

Retention Policy Setup

Retention policy refers to how long data is kept in your mailbox before it is moved to the online archive. The way in which retention policy works in conjunction with compliance management seems very complex, but in reality it is very simple to set up. The issue is the business processes in place in the organization to manage information. The steps outlined below are described in detail in the section "Compliance Configuration":

1. Determine the business retention policy

2. Define the retention tags

3. Implement the retention policy rules

Retention policies are business polices. These polices are overridden by any compliance or regulatory requirements for the management of data. The best example of an override policy is how deleted information is handled. The retention policy will delete the information, so the user sees the information deleted in the inbox, but the litigation hold policy will keep the information in place. The deleted information is never deleted; it is just hidden from the user. The hidden information is fully discoverable.

Compliance Example

As discussed earlier, compliance is a combination of regulatory monitoring and business process. In this section, we will walk through the compliance setup for a regulatory problem, protection of personal information. Here are the steps:

1. Select the compliance requirements

2. Define the users who will manage the compliance activity

3. Enable encryption

4. Enable audit

5. Test out the compliance policy with tool tips

6. Enforce the compliance policy

Let's follow the steps for implementation of the compliance policy.

Step 1: Select the Compliance Policy

Depending on the industry that you are in, there are different compliance requirements. To access the Office 365 compliance center, login to Office 365 and follow these steps (see Figure 9-10)

1. Select the Exchange admin center

2. Select data loss prevention

3. Select the "+" sign; select the New form template option

4. Select HIPAA template for data loss prevention

5. Select PI template for personal information

6. Select "test with policy tips" (this will be changed to "enforce" once we are competed our testing)

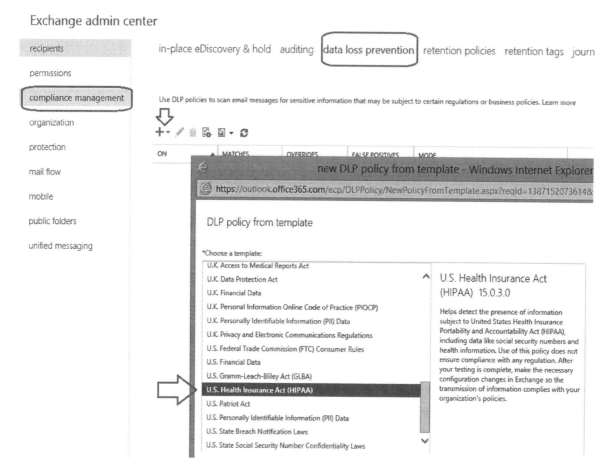

Figure 9-10. *Data loss prevention templates*

Select the polices that you wish to use. You can only add one policy at time. Office 365 will process the polices in the order that they are listed. In our example, we selected the HIPAA and PII (personal information), and then we chose the deploy these policies with "tips" (see Figure 9-11). Tips are notifications to the user that if they continue to send the email, they will be violation of state and federal laws. Office 365 will keep track of the violations in the exchange admin center (under data loss prevention) and on the Office 365 administrator dashboard (under mail control)

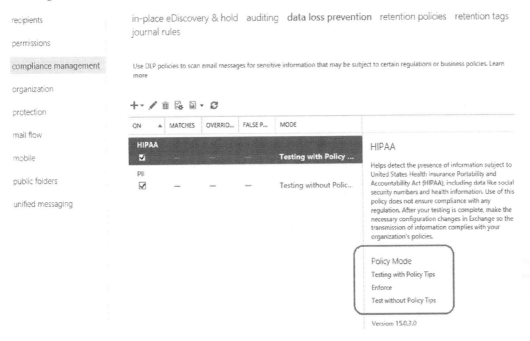

Figure 9-11. *HIPAA and PII with policy tips enforcement*

After you have selected the new DLP policies, then return to exchange admin center, and the "mail flow, rules" screen (Figure 9-12). Verify the order of the rules. Adjust the rules based on your business requirements.

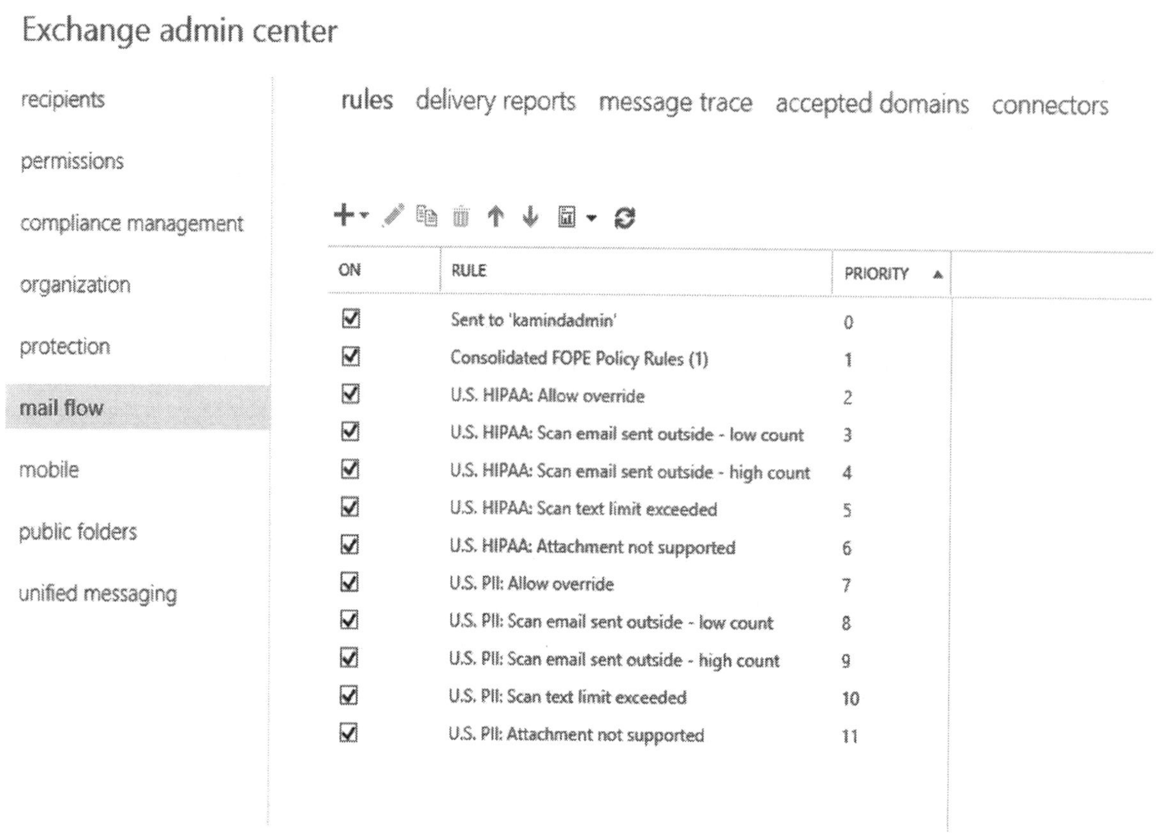

Exchange admin center

recipients

permissions

compliance management

organization

protection

mail flow

mobile

public folders

unified messaging

rules   delivery reports   message trace   accepted domains   connectors

ON	RULE	PRIORITY ▲
☑	Sent to 'kamindadmin'	0
☑	Consolidated FOPE Policy Rules (1)	1
☑	U.S. HIPAA: Allow override	2
☑	U.S. HIPAA: Scan email sent outside - low count	3
☑	U.S. HIPAA: Scan email sent outside - high count	4
☑	U.S. HIPAA: Scan text limit exceeded	5
☑	U.S. HIPAA: Attachment not supported	6
☑	U.S. PII: Allow override	7
☑	U.S. PII: Scan email sent outside - low count	8
☑	U.S. PII: Scan email sent outside - high count	9
☑	U.S. PII: Scan text limit exceeded	10
☑	U.S. PII: Attachment not supported	11

Figure 9-12. Office 365 DLP policy rules

Step 2: Define the Users Who Will Manage the Compliance Roles

Compliance management is role based. To enable and review the information, you must be in the compliance role. To add a user in the compliance role, go the exchange admin center, select permissions, and then admin roles. Select compliance management, and add the user to the compliance management group (see Figure 9-13). Select the pencil icon to edit the compliance roles, then add the compliance officers into the exchange compliance and management roles fields.

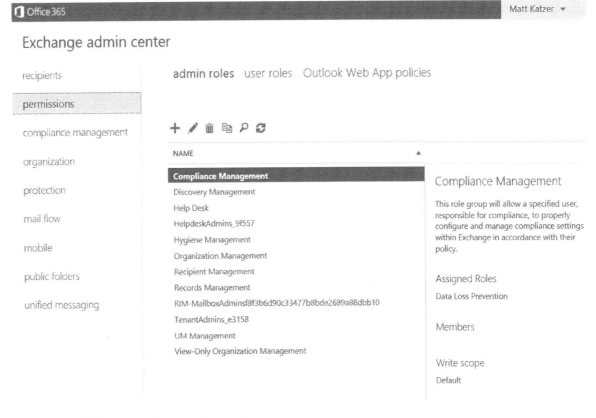

Figure 9-13. *Adding a user to a compliance role*

Step 3: Enable Encryption

Depending on the industry you are in, you will need to enable the encryption of email when information is being sent externally from Office 365. The encryption option is standard in the Enterprise subscriptions, such as E3 and E4, but is optional for other plans.

Any time there is personal information distributed to a party outside of your company, the information should be encrypted. To set up Office 365 encryption, go to the exchange admin center, and select "rules." Create a new rule, then select "apply rights protection to messages" (see Figure 9-14).

Exchange admin center

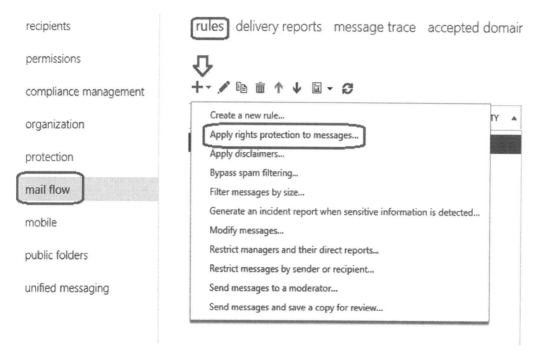

Figure 9-14. *Accessing data rights management rules*

After you have selected the rights protection, enable Office 365 encryption (see Figure 9-15) and apply it to the different transport rules you have in place. Review the policy rules (Figure 9-12 above) and edit the transport rules that you wish to modify. Add an "action" of encryption to those rules. (Transport rules are discussed in detailed in Chapter 10.)

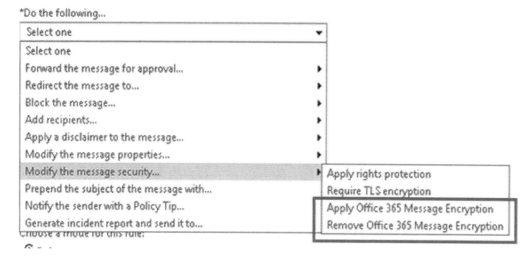

Figure 9-15. *Enabling Office 365 encryption (courtesy of Microsoft)*

Step 4: Enable Audit (Optional)

To start using the tracking methods in Office 365, the first step is to enable external auditing. After this is enabled, you can access audit reports from the Office 365 Exchange control panel. Chapter 6 provides information about setting up PowerShell on your system. The current version of Office 365 does not have an integrated user interface to enable the audit capabilities, so these capabilities must be enabled through PowerShell. You only need to do this to turn the capabilities on, or to disable them. You do not need to perform this function each time you use the search capabilities of Office 365.

To enable mailbox audit logging for a single mailbox, run the following Windows PowerShell command:

```
Set-Mailbox <Identity> -AuditEnabled $true
```

For example, to enable mailbox auditing for a user named Sam Sneed, run the following command:

```
Set-Mailbox "Sam Sneed" -AuditEnabled $true
```

To enable mailbox auditing for all user mailboxes in your organization, run the following commands:

```
$UserMailboxes = Get-mailbox -Filter {(RecipientTypeDetails -eq 'UserMailbox')}
$UserMailboxes | ForEach {Set-Mailbox $_.Identity -AuditEnabled $true}
```

▓ **Note**   Please refer to Chapter 8 for details on installing PowerShell.

Step 5: Test the Compliance Policy with Tool Tips

The first step in compliance policy rule testing is to test out the policy with tool tips. Tool tips inform the user of the DLP rule and request an override before sending the email, as shown in the example in Figure 9-16. The DLP rule that was invoked was about the protection of personal information. The user was sending out the email, and a notice was generated to the user to stop the behavior.

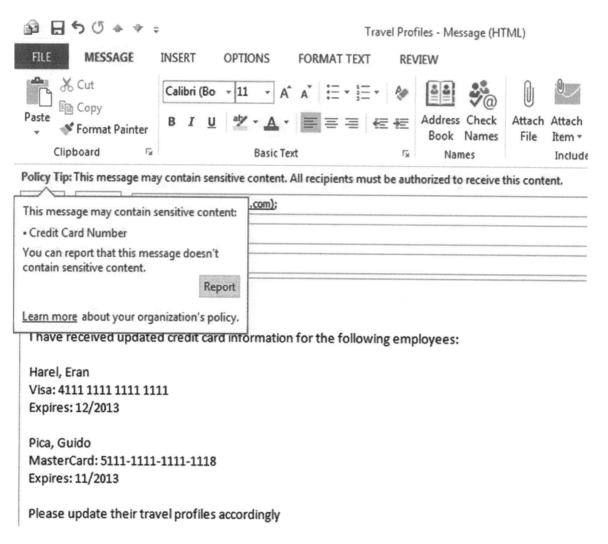

Figure 9-16. *DLP toot tip notice (courtesy of Microsoft)*

Step 6: Enforce the Compliance Policy

Compliance enforcement is simply about preventing the information from being sent by the user. When the enforcement policy is sent, the user is allowed to send the information, but the email is not actually sent. It is instead rejected with an unauthorized notice and returned to the user. To enforce the compliance policy, modify the DLP rules (Figure 9-11 above), and select the "enforce" option.

Discovery Site Example

The discovery process is an eight-step process. There are two ways to complete discovery. You can use either the SharePoint Discovery site or use a PowerShell script. The PowerShell script is used for Office 365 organizations that do not have a SharePoint configuration. This method is discussed in the email scanning example. The steps to use the SharePoint Discovery site are described below:

1. Define the business policy for the search (regulation review or judicial)

2. Enable auditing

3. Identify who will perform the discovery and review functions

4. Enabling in-place hold (or legal hold) for immutability

5. Compliance and discovery—using the eDiscovery Search Tool

6. Case-creation process

7. Build the search query

8. Review the information

9. Export the data for review in Outlook

Step 1: Define the Business Policy for Search

Office 365 integrates a standard electronic discovery function that allows you to scan for any type of information across Office 365. There are two ways you can search for data in Office 365, using the integrated compliance search services via SharePoint services, or through PowerShell. There are two prerequisites necessary before you perform compliance searches; you must:

- Enable the user mailboxes in-place hold (legal hold)

- Enable the audit capabilities of Office 365 (keeps logs of access for 30 days)

Once these features are enabled in Office 365, your Office 365 organization is compliant for all access, both internal and external.

Step 2: Enable Auditing

To start using the tracking methods in Office 365, the first step is to enable the external auditing. After this is enabled, you can access the audit reports from the Office 365 Exchange control panel. Chapter 8 provides information about setting up PowerShell on your system. The current version of Office 365 does not have an integrated user interface to enable the audit capabilities, so these capabilities must be enabled through PowerShell. You only need to do this to either turn the capabilities on or to disable them. You do not need to perform this function each time you use these audit capabilities on Office 365.

To enable mailbox audit logging for a single mailbox, run the following Windows PowerShell command:

```
Set-Mailbox <Identity> -AuditEnabled $true
```

For example, to enable mailbox auditing for a user named Sam Sneed, run the following command:

```
Set-Mailbox "Sam Sneed" -AuditEnabled $true
```

To enable mailbox auditing for all user mailboxes in your organization, run the following commands:

```
$UserMailboxes = Get-mailbox -Filter {(RecipientTypeDetails -eq 'UserMailbox')}
$UserMailboxes | ForEach {Set-Mailbox $_.Identity -AuditEnabled $true}
```

■ **Note** Please refer to chapter 8 for details on installing PowerShell.

Step 3: Identify Who Will Perform the Discovery and Review Functions

There are two roles: compliance management and discovery/records management (see Figure 9-17). Users who perform the discovery function must be in this role.

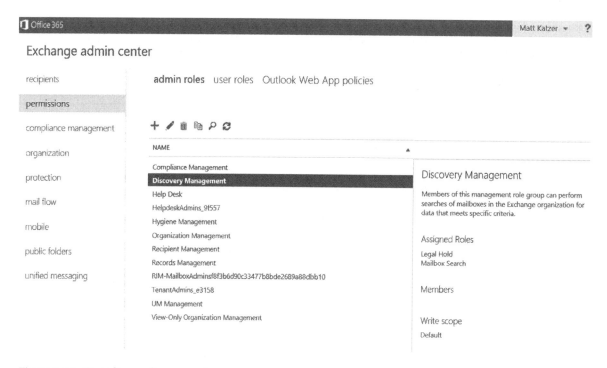

Figure 9-17. *Compliance: discovery roles*

As an example, if you want to have a person to perform discovery and review, you add the person to the Discovery Management role. To add the person (see Figure 9-17), select the exchange admin center, then permissions and admin roles. Select the role (discovery management in this example), then select edit (the pencil icon) and add the person to that role. A global admin can only perform this function if they are added to the role. If you are not added to the role, you will get a PowerShell error, or you will not be able to access the discovery search records.

If you only want the person to perform search review, then you must manually give the person full access rights to the mailbox using the PowerShell script. Their access will only be through the Outlook client and not the discovery search center. Since the "Discovery Mailbox Search" is a mailbox, you use the PowerShell command to access the mailbox.

```
Add-MailboxPermission "Discovery Search Mailbox" -User user@contoso.com
 -AccessRights FullAccess
```

■ **Note**   Discovery management gives the user full access to all mailboxes to perform searches. If you want to restrict access to a small group of individuals, then create a uniquely named mailbox for that discovery and user access. If no mailbox is specified in your search, the default mailbox that Office 365 uses is "Discovery Mailbox Search."

Step 4: Enabling In-Place Hold (or Legal Hold) for Immutability

There are two ways to enable immutability in Office 365: through the Exchange management interface via the discovery search center (in-place hold), or through the use of PowerShell. The common practice is to perform this function by using "compliance management" in the exchange admin center (Figure 9-18). The process to enable compliance center searching is in the following sections.

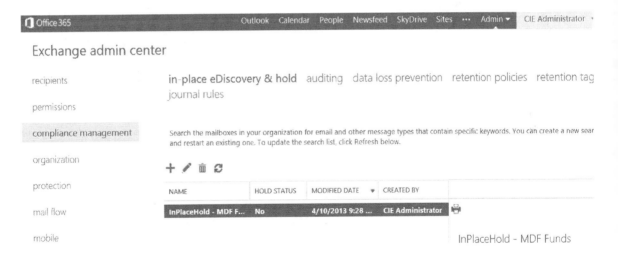

Figure 9-18. *Compliance: in-place hold on user accounts*

Extending Deleted Item Recovery

In some cases, there may be not be a need to enable in-place discovery or legal hold. The business need may be only to prevent the deletion of information for a period of time, until the information is audited. In this case, we are looking for limited information immutability. To accomplish this, we would run a PowerShell script and change the way the user deletes information in a mailbox or a group of mailboxes. This retention script operates on a mailbox (or an archive). Retention tags are used to manage information.

```
Set-Mailbox <identity> -LitigationHoldEnabled $true -LitigationHoldDuration <duration, in days>
```

Also, extend the "delete" purges folder from 14 days to 30 days.

```
Set-mailbox user@contoso.com –retaindeleteditemsfor 30
```

The typical example would be an audit department wanting to have a temporary legal hold on a mailbox for a limited duration (90 days). In the PowerShell example, we place the mailbox on a legal hold status, with a limited duration of time. This is different than a retention policy. Retention policy in Office 365 is used to manage mailbox information (to be deleted) and the movement of data from the mailbox to the archive or the bit bucket.

Step 5: Compliance and Discovery: Using the eDiscovery Search Tool

The Office 365 Global administrator can create an integrated eDiscovery SharePoint Site (see Figure 9-18). This site is only visible to the global administrator and delegated administrator partners (DAP) (if added as a Site collection Administrator). If you are not authorized, the eDiscovery interface is not visible, and access as a DAP is denied. The compliance and eDiscovery center must be created in the Sharepoint admin center; discovery data access is turned off by default. You must be explicitly assigned to the Exchange discovery management group to take advantage of the discovery management functions.

Once you create the discovery center (see Figure 9-19), the users assigned to discovery management need also to be assigned to the discovery management role in the exchange admin center (Step 3 above). Also, the compliance officer must be assigned the role of site collection administrator. All other members of the discover team should be explicitly assigned permission to the discovery center (usually as a contributor). Sharepoint permissions are discussed in detail in Chapter 5."

 Contoso Intranet

eDiscovery Center

Search this site

Cases
   MDF Allocation Case
Subsites
   Misisng $$
   March
Site Contents

 Welcome to the eDiscovery Center

Use this site to create, manage and work on eDiscovery Cases. With eDiscovery Cases you can manage the identification and in-place hold of Exchange mailboxes, SharePoint sites, and other sources of content. You can also create and manage search queries to identify relevant content and then export the search results.

 Create new case

Get Started

1. Grant your legal users permissions to access content across your SharePoint deployment. We recommend creating a security group that contains your legal team members.
2. To discover Exchange mailboxes, ensure your administrator has installed the Exchange Web Services Managed Client on all SharePoint servers and have your administrator configure authentication between Exchange and SharePoint.
3. Give your legal team security group user policy permissions to all appropriate SharePoint Web Applications that contain content you need to perform eDiscovery on.
4. Grant your legal users eDiscovery permissions for the Exchange mailboxes you must perform eDiscovery actions on.

In-Place Hold, Search, & Export

- With in-place holds you can specify SharePoint sites and mailboxes to place on hold. When content is modified or deleted it will be stored in-place until you need to export it.
- In-place eDiscovery search allows you to search across SharePoint sites, file shares, and Exchange mailboxes. Use proximity, wildcards, Boolean logic, and refiners to scope the results to the content you need. Because the search is in-place, your results are live and up to date just like if you were doing a normal Outlook Web Access or SharePoint site search.
- Once you have identified the content you need, you can download it to your local hard drive or file share in a portable native format. Easily download SharePoint pages, documents, lists, and Exchange mailbox data.

Figure 9-19. *Compliance: searching SharePoint site*

If you have not built the compliance search center, refer to the section "Creating Integrated Electronic Discovery in Sharepoint Services." The rest of these steps refer to processes in the Sharepoint discovery search center. At this point, we will assume the following:

- eDiscovery search center is created
- Compliance manager has been assigned as a site collection administrator
- All other team members are assigned the appropriate Sharepoint roles
- All other individuals (IT support services etc.) are removed from accessing the discovery center

Step 6: Case-Creation Process

eDiscovery is organized by cases. Figure 9-19 is the discovery project site. When you create an eDiscovery action, you are creating a case for data organization. A new case is created as a subsite under the compliance discovery site. As an example, if you are searching or reviewing all emails and content for March 2013, then you would select "new case" (Figure 9-20), then fill out the information about the case and assign owners (Figure 9-20).

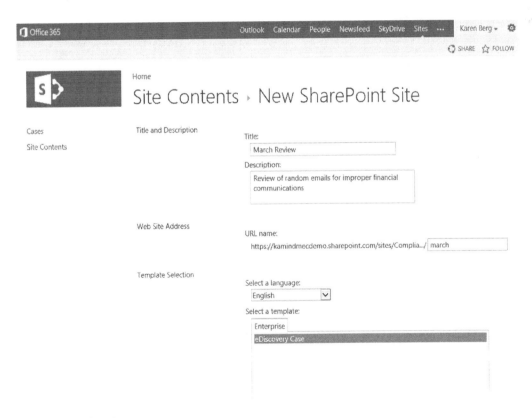

Figure 9-20. *Creating a new case*

There is no difference between an eDiscovery and a compliance archive search. They are the same. Typically, compliance reviews require a sampling of information, and an eDiscovery site is based on a terms request usually from a judicial order (or a FINRA request). The basis of both orders is that the information is immutable and auditable. The site that you select is the eDiscovery site to perform these functions.

NOTE ABOUT PERMISSIONS

- The discovery management role is required to perform discovery queries.

- Delegated access to the mailboxes must be given to the reviewers.

- Reviewers must be given access to the "Case" site that you create.

Before you complete the case, make sure you select "use unique permissions," then select the navigation options to allow the case to be accessed from the main discovery windows (see Figure 9-21). Select "finish" when you have completed the details.

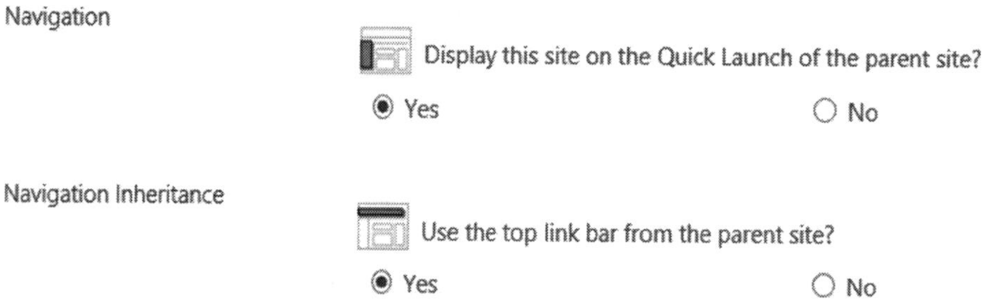

Navigation

Display this site on the Quick Launch of the parent site?

⦿ Yes   ◯ No

Navigation Inheritance

Use the top link bar from the parent site?

⦿ Yes   ◯ No

Figure 9-21. *Menu configuration options*

Your new site has been created, and you can now begin your search queries.

Step 7: Building the Search Query

The first step is to build the eDiscovery set. Select "new item" from eDiscovery set (under identify and hold; see Figure 9-22). If you do not have the ability to select the new item, you are not in the eDiscovery role (Step 3).

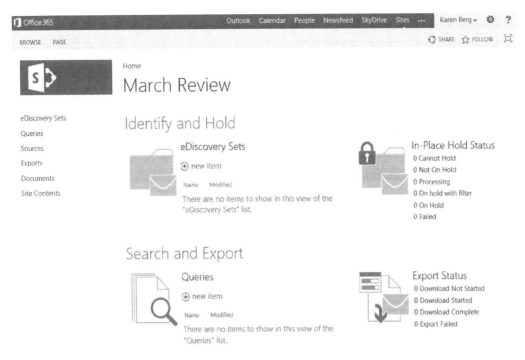

Figure 9-22. New eDiscovery search site for March

After you select new Item, fill out the discovery search request (See Figure 9-23).

Figure 9-23. Defining the eDiscovery set

When you create a discovery set, you are setting up the items so you can search it and bind the discovery set to your query. This allows you to limit your information request to address only the specific issue you are interested in. A typical discovery set invoices these steps

1. Define the name for the discovery set.

2. Add the sources to the discovery set (email addresses and/or locations in SharePoint).

3. In the box under "filter" use any key words you want to use to narrow the search.

4. Set the date range and author (if appropriate).

5. Apply the filter.

6. Select in place hold (the base accounts are already enabled from an earlier step).

The first step is to select the discovery sources (see Figure 9-24).

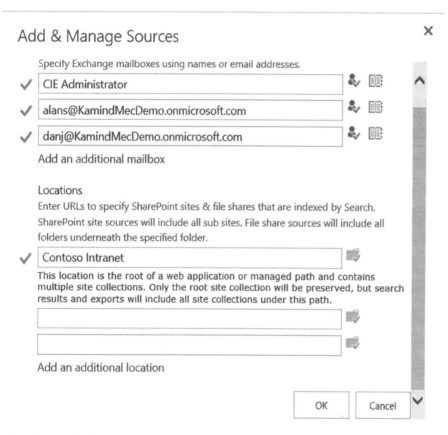

Figure 9-24. Adding sources

Once you have added the sources, just complete the rest of the steps that we outlined earlier, and your discovery set is built. There are no limits to the number of discovery sets you can have. Before you exit the discovery set, make sure you have enabled "in-place hold" for the discovery set you are reviewing. (See Figure 9-25.) Press save and exit. The new discovery set should be displayed after you have saved the query (see Figure 9-26).

○ Enable In-Place Hold
○ Disable In-Place Hold

| Preview Results | Save | Cancel |

Figure 9-25. *Enabling in-place hold on the eDiscovery set*

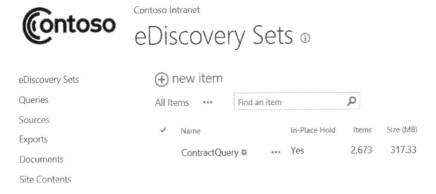

Figure 9-26. *eDiscovery set summary*

Earlier, we discussed the AQS syntax. The AQS syntax is used to build the search request to collect data for review by the compliance officer or discovery technician. This information can be updated in the discovery set. When you access the discovery set the next time, the discovery set will update based on the filter criteria that you have provided. To verify the discovery set, select the item from the list. There is a detailed description of the AQS syntax later in this chapter.

Step 8: Review the Information

To review the raw information based on your filters is simple. Just select the discovery set to verify the information (See Figure 9-27), then select "preview."

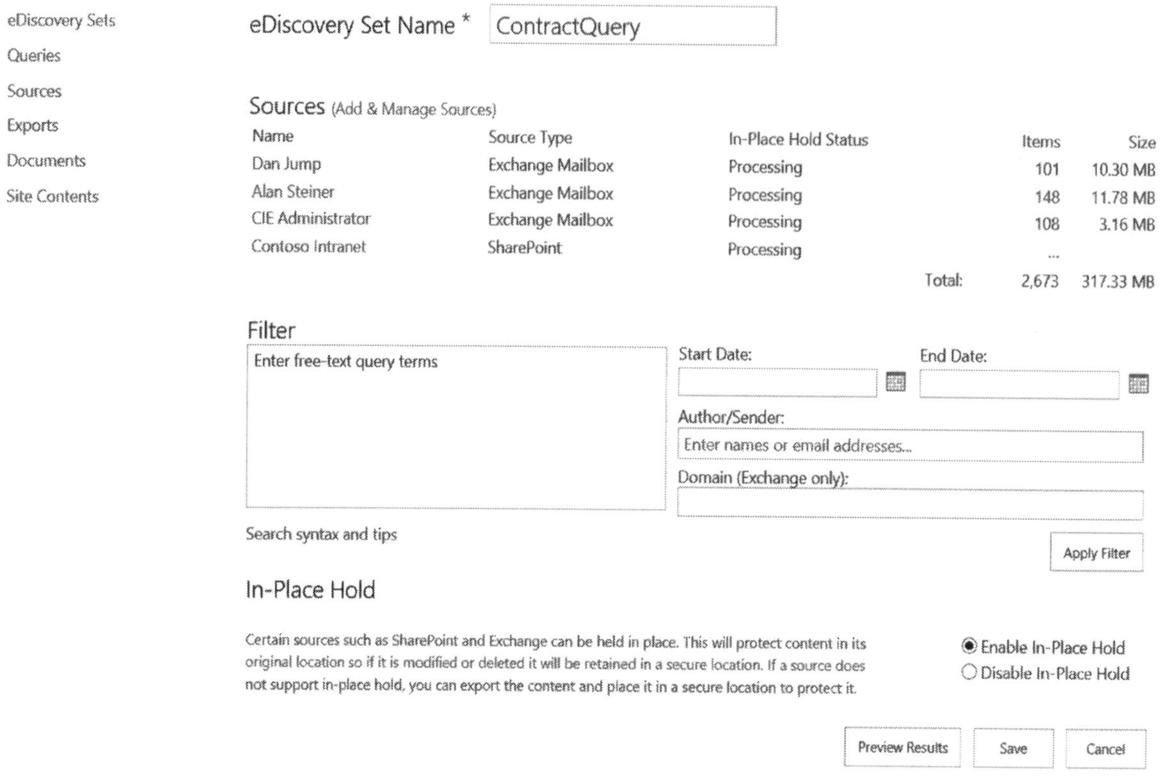

eDiscovery Sets

Queries

Sources

Exports

Documents

Site Contents

eDiscovery Set Name *   ContractQuery

Sources (Add & Manage Sources)

Name	Source Type	In-Place Hold Status	Items	Size
Dan Jump	Exchange Mailbox	Processing	101	10.30 MB
Alan Steiner	Exchange Mailbox	Processing	148	11.78 MB
CIE Administrator	Exchange Mailbox	Processing	108	3.16 MB
Contoso Intranet	SharePoint	Processing	...	
		Total:	2,673	317.33 MB

Filter

Enter free-text query terms

Start Date:

End Date:

Author/Sender:

Enter names or email addresses...

Domain (Exchange only):

Search syntax and tips

Apply Filter

In-Place Hold

Certain sources such as SharePoint and Exchange can be held in place. This will protect content in its original location so if it is modified or deleted it will be retained in a secure location. If a source does not support in-place hold, you can export the content and place it in a secure location to protect it.

◉ Enable In-Place Hold
◯ Disable In-Place Hold

Preview Results   Save   Cancel

Figure 9-27.   *eDiscovery set preview*

After you have selected the preview, select the item in the windows to display in the Outlook web app. This portion of the discovery set is used for verification. There are additional tools in case management that are used to provide more information detail (See Figure 9-28).

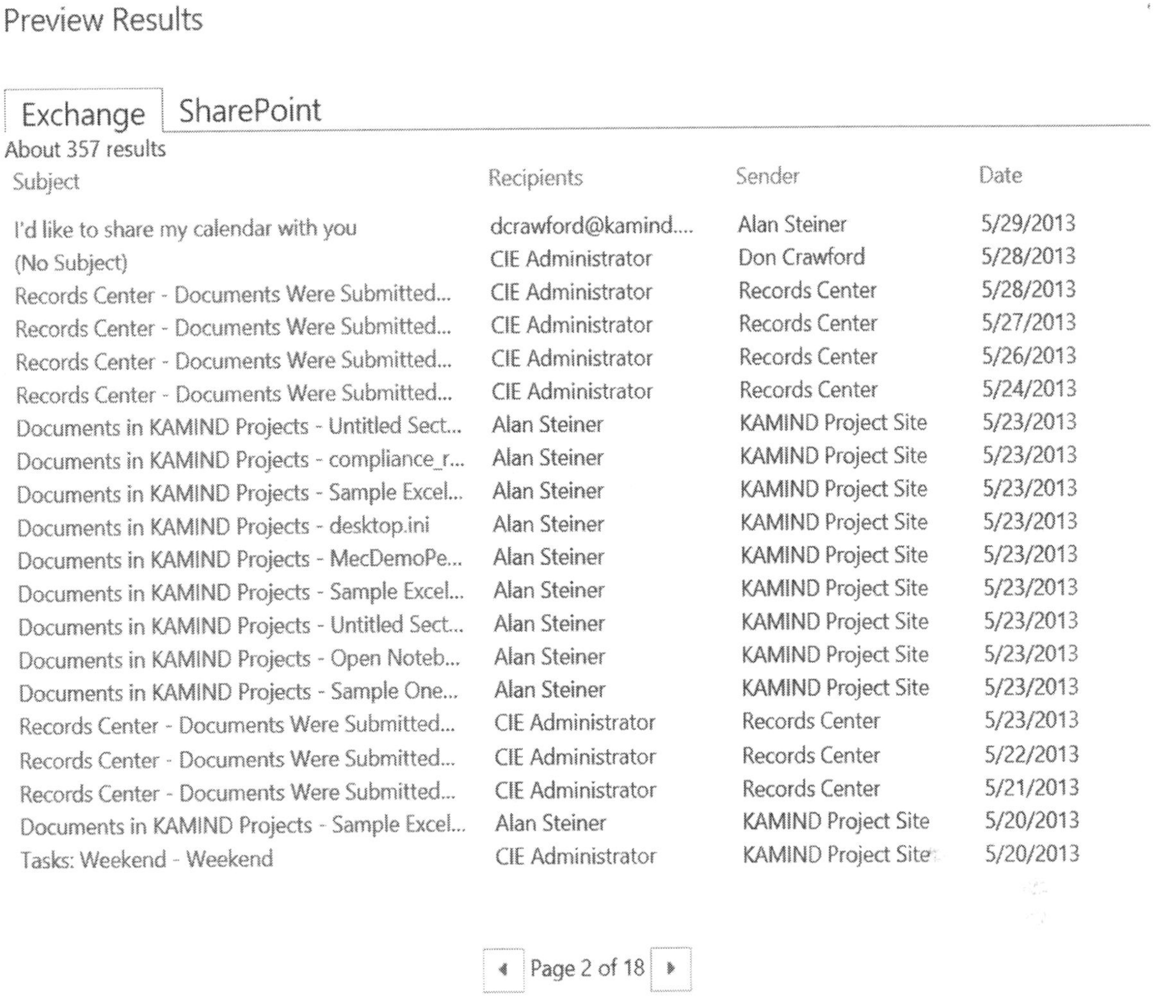

Preview Results

Exchange	SharePoint

About 357 results

Subject	Recipients	Sender	Date
I'd like to share my calendar with you	dcrawford@kamind....	Alan Steiner	5/29/2013
(No Subject)	CIE Administrator	Don Crawford	5/28/2013
Records Center - Documents Were Submitted...	CIE Administrator	Records Center	5/28/2013
Records Center - Documents Were Submitted...	CIE Administrator	Records Center	5/27/2013
Records Center - Documents Were Submitted...	CIE Administrator	Records Center	5/26/2013
Records Center - Documents Were Submitted...	CIE Administrator	Records Center	5/24/2013
Documents in KAMIND Projects - Untitled Sect...	Alan Steiner	KAMIND Project Site	5/23/2013
Documents in KAMIND Projects - compliance_r...	Alan Steiner	KAMIND Project Site	5/23/2013
Documents in KAMIND Projects - Sample Excel...	Alan Steiner	KAMIND Project Site	5/23/2013
Documents in KAMIND Projects - desktop.ini	Alan Steiner	KAMIND Project Site	5/23/2013
Documents in KAMIND Projects - MecDemoPe...	Alan Steiner	KAMIND Project Site	5/23/2013
Documents in KAMIND Projects - Sample Excel...	Alan Steiner	KAMIND Project Site	5/23/2013
Documents in KAMIND Projects - Untitled Sect...	Alan Steiner	KAMIND Project Site	5/23/2013
Documents in KAMIND Projects - Open Noteb...	Alan Steiner	KAMIND Project Site	5/23/2013
Documents in KAMIND Projects - Sample One...	Alan Steiner	KAMIND Project Site	5/23/2013
Records Center - Documents Were Submitted...	CIE Administrator	Records Center	5/23/2013
Records Center - Documents Were Submitted...	CIE Administrator	Records Center	5/22/2013
Records Center - Documents Were Submitted...	CIE Administrator	Records Center	5/21/2013
Documents in KAMIND Projects - Sample Excel...	Alan Steiner	KAMIND Project Site	5/20/2013
Tasks: Weekend - Weekend	CIE Administrator	KAMIND Project Site	5/20/2013

◀ Page 2 of 18 ▶

Figure 9-28. *eDiscovery set review*

The main page of the discovery management site will list the cases that are created (see Figure 9-19). The case we were discussing is the "March" case. The discovery cetners builds a Sharepoint site for case specific discovery actions. Figure 9-29 shows the March case sharepoint site.

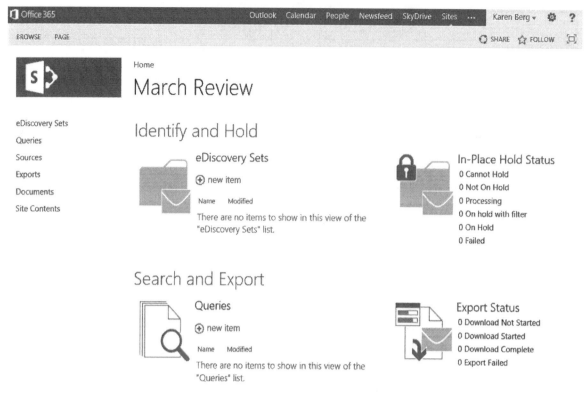

Figure 9-29. *New eDiscovery search site for March*

Step 9: Export the Data for Review in Outlook

You can export the discovery information collected in the session, just select the export function and download the data (See Figure 9-30). Office 365 will download the data as a PST file along with search parameters and statistics. Once the data is downloaded, all that is needed is to open up Outlook and load the file in as a local archive.

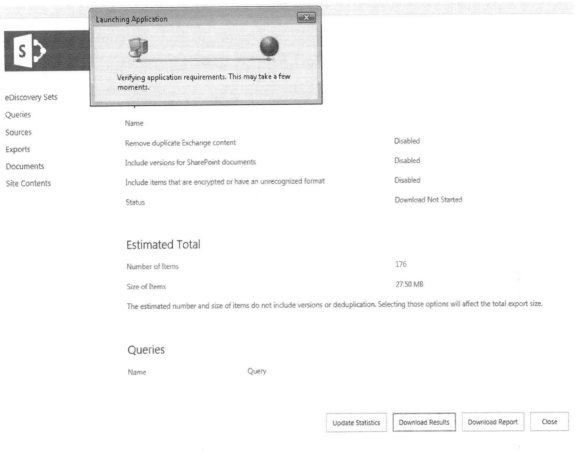

Figure 9-30. *Exporting eDiscovery search*

■ **Note**　The desktop discovery download tool requires that you are `runngin.net` framework 4.5.

The eDiscovery search tool will download the information to your local system (See Figure 9-31). Once the data is downloaded, open Outlook and review the information in detail using the local Outlook tools. You have completed a discovery search request. Open up Outlook (2010 or 2013), and add the downloaded PST archive.

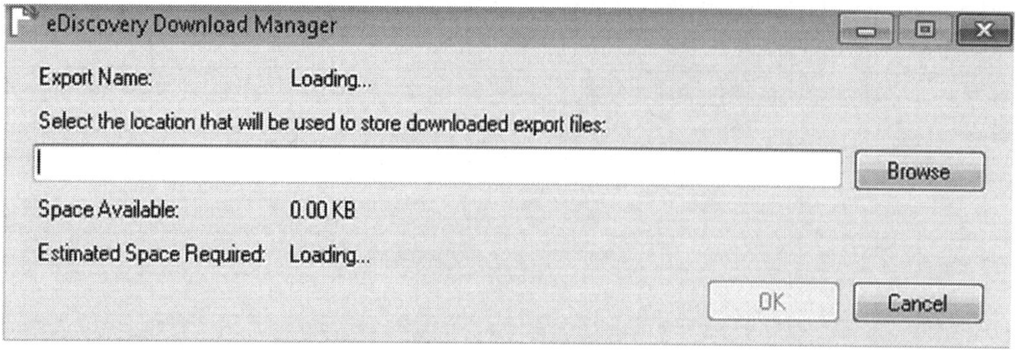

Figure 9-31. *eDiscovery download manager*

Retention Example

Retention policy is about the moving of data from the online mailbox into the archive mailbox. In some cases you may wish to delete emails, in others to preserve them long term. When you are experimenting with retention policies, use a mailbox with a trial set of sample data. If you are afraid of deleting information, then enable litigation hold (or in-place hold) on the account that you are setting up the retention tags. If the retention tags are not set up correctly, information will be deleted.

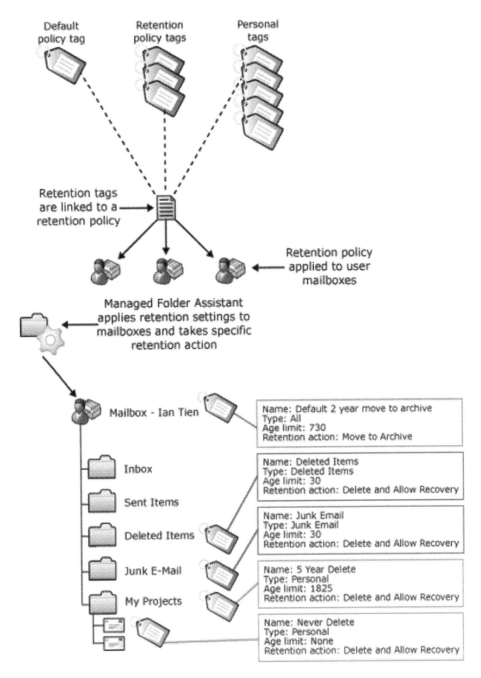

Figure 9-32. Retention tag structure (courtesy of Microsoft)

We are presenting this figure again to highlight that Retention policy is composed form retention tags. Retention tags describe the movement of information in a users mailbox. Legal hold (or in-place hold) is about the immutability of information. If you have legal hold implemented on a mailbox, the retention policy will move information, and information that moved will be removed from the user's view and appear to be deleted to the user, but the data is maintained in a hidden directory for legal search if the legal hold is implemented.

Earlier we designated the retention policy as having three steps:

1. Determine the business retention policy.

2. Define the retention tags.

3. Implement the retention policy rules.

Step 1: Determining the Retention Policy—Four Questions

When you put a retention policy in place, you are putting in place a business process definition for your organization. The retention policy needs to be implemented uniformly across your organization and well documented. You can have different retention polices for different groups, but you should not single out a retention policy for an individual. If you are in a discovery situation, you may place your organization at risk when you do not have a uniform policy.

When we define a retention policy for an organization, we ask the following questions and set up the retention policy rules. Remember that a regulated organization will have a litigation hold component that will overlay the retention policy to ensure data immutability. The four questions that define the retention policy are:

1. How long is information kept in the user primary mailbox?

2. How long is the information kept in the archive mailbox?

3. How long is deleted information kept?

4. What happens to deleted information?

Retention polices are configured in the exchange admin center (EAC). To access the EAC on the Office 365 admin page, select "service settings," choose the Mail tab, then "manage additional settings in exchange admin center." Select "compliance management," then "retention polices" (see Figure 9-33).

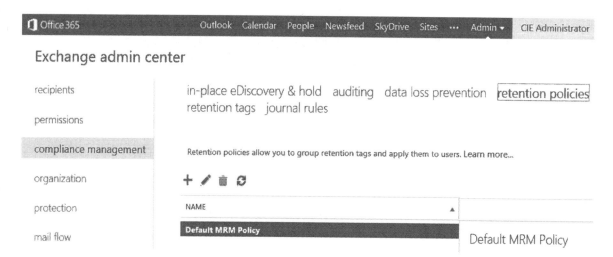

Figure 9-33. *Finding the retention policies*

All Office 365 organizations are set up with the default retention policy composed of a set of retention tags to govern the way data is retained and moved to the archive. Once you have configured your retention polices, you need to enable them for the mailbox. There are two ways you apply a policy: using the graphical user interface and applying to the user mailbox or using a PowerShell commands. (See TechNet link http://help.outlook.com/en-us/beta/gg271153.aspx). The default retention tags are listed in Figure 9-34.

Exchange admin center

recipients

permissions

compliance management

organization

protection

mail flow

mobile

public folders

unified messaging

in-place eDiscovery & hold   auditing   data loss prevention   retention policies   **retention tags**   journal rules

Retention tags are visible to end users and can be used to specify when items in users' mailboxes will be moved to the archive or removed from the mailbox. Learn more...

		RETENTION PERIOD	RETENTION ACTION	
applied automatically to entire mailbox (default)				**1 Month Delete**
applied automatically to a default folder	nal	**30 days**	**Delete**	
applied by users to items and folders (personal)	nal	7 days	Delete	Retention tag type
1 Year Delete	Personal	365 days	Delete	Personal
5 Year Delete	Personal	1825 days	Delete	
6 Month Delete	Personal	180 days	Delete	Retention period.
Default 2 year move to archive	Default	730 days	Archive	Hold for 30 days
Deleted Items	Deleted Items	30 days	Delete	
Junk Email	Junk Email	30 days	Delete	After retention period
Never Delete	Personal	Unlimited	Delete	Delete (Temporarily recoverable)
Personal 1 year move to archive	Personal	365 days	Archive	
Personal 5 year move to archive	Personal	1825 days	Archive	Comment
Personal never move to archive	Personal	Unlimited	Archive	

Figure 9-34. *Default retention tags that make up the default retention policy*

When you first look at the retention tags, they seem to be in conflict with each other. Retention tags are implemented for a folder in a mailbox. This can be at the root (entire mailbox) or a specific folder in a mailbox. Figure 9-34 retention tags apply to different folders. The combination of the retention tags make up the retention policy.

Step 2: Create a New Test Policy

Before you modify the retention tags, you want to build a new policy and pick a set of tags to experiment against a user mailbox. The way retention tags are designed, you do not have the ability to add new ones, only to modify the existing tags.

To build a retention policy, and add a small subset of the retention tags into the new policy, apply the policy to a user mailbox. This will allow you to test out the renetion policy. To create a new policy do the following:

1. In the Exchange Admin center, select "retention policies," then select the "+" sign to create a new policy and assign it a name.

2. Add a retention tags from the list above to build out new test Policy (see Figure 9-35).

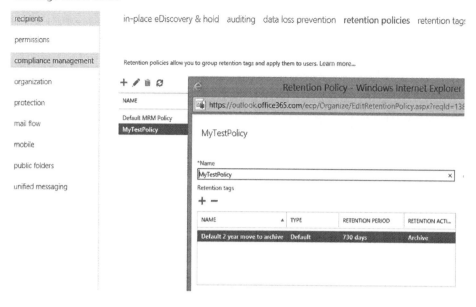

Figure 9-35. *Adding a new retention policy*

3. Save this policy and apply it to a test account to verify the operation. (to apply a policy, select the user mailbox (see Figure 9-36).

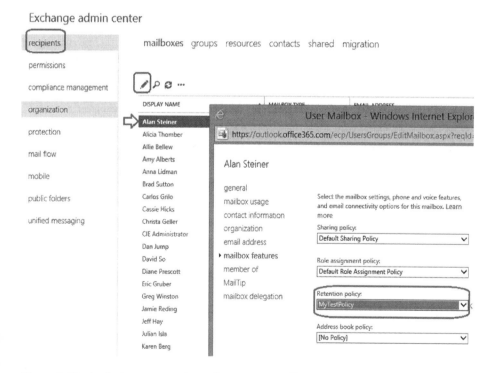

Figure 9-36. *Apply the new retention policy to a test mailbox*

Step 3: Modify the Test Policy

The next step is to modify the test policy and add your new rules to it. Before you change the retention tags, collect all of the current tags you plan to use into the test policy to see how the policy operates. Once you understand how the policy operates, then change the retention tags to meet your business rules. (Remember the four questions. Keep in mind that the tags are global, so changing a tag will affect all retention policies that use this tag.

To change a retention tag, edit the retention tag, and change the properties (se Figure 9-37).

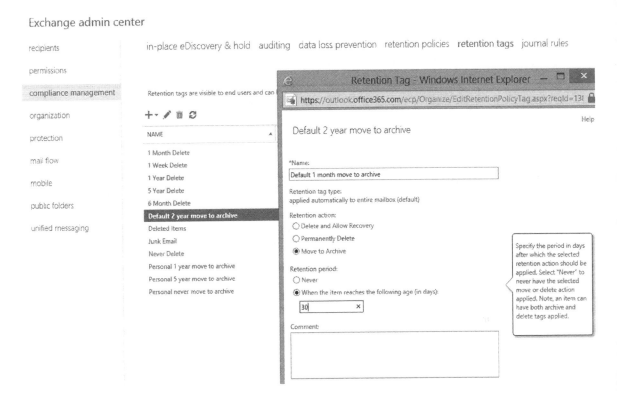

Figure 9-37. *Modification of a retention tag*

In our example, we changed the retention tag to move data from the mailbox to the archive in 30 days. Then apply the retention tag. The changes will replicate in all of the retention policies that are using this retention tag.

Creating Integrated Electronic Discovery in SharePoint Services

The first step in using the integrated eDiscovery SharePoint site in Office 365 is to create the eDiscovery site and assign the permissions. The eDiscovery site is created in the SharePoint admin center. Once the site is created, you can access it directly from the SharePoint admin center, or through a link on your team site. Once you build the eDiscovery site, you need to enable the user to have access to it from the discovery management or the record management group. The default configuration of Office 365 does not assign any user to these roles. To add a user, you need to add the user in Exchange administration and one of the three user roles:

- *Mailbox search role*—Allows users to perform in-place searches

- *Legal hold role*—Allows a user to place a mailbox on hold

- *Discovery mailbox permission*—Allows a user to review the contents of a discovery mailbox

Why do you have multiple eDiscovery roles? Simple. You may have a situation where there is an external person who is required to review the material, but you may not want to give the external person permission to generate the material for review. In this case, you would assign an internal person the permissions to perform a mailbox search and the external resource with full permissions to discovery mailbox results. The external resource most likely will be the other side's attorney or an external compliance officer. This is a very common situation in a compliance audit or sharing of eDiscovery searches.

Step 1: Creating the Compliance Search Site

The compliance search site is created in the SharePoint admin center.

1. To create the compliance site, in the office admin panel, select "service settings," then "sites," and then select "create site collection" (Figure 9-38).

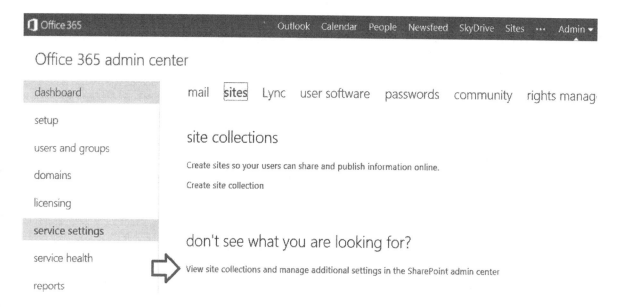

Figure 9-38. *SharePoint site creation*

2. In the site collection, select new site (see Figure 9-39).

Figure 9-39. *creating a compliance site, part one*

3. Once you start the new private site, you select the correct site for your business. In this case, it's an eDiscovery center (Figure 9-40).

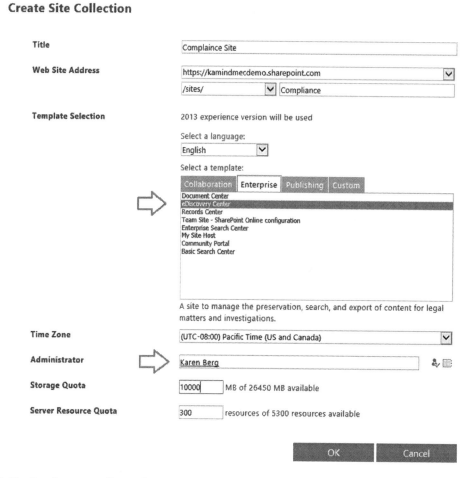

Figure 9-40. *Creating a compliance site, part two*

4. Once the compliance site is created, you can access the site from the SharePoint admin center (See Figure 9-41) or use the https URL for the discovery site.

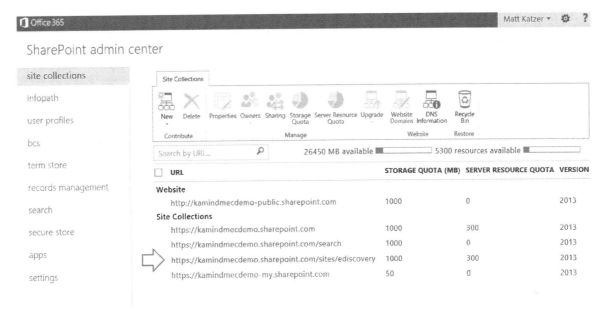

Figure 9-41. eDiscovery SharePoint site: access URL

   a. When you create the discovery site, assign the compliance officer permission as a site
       collection administrator. The other members of the compliance team need to be assigned
       roles as contributing members.

   b. If you invite external individuals to the discovery center, it is better to use a Sharepoint
       licenses and apply explicit rights then to use an external email address invite. This will give
       you a better set of controls for operation.

Step 2: Building a Compliance Search Case

The compliance search site is created in the SharePoint admin center (Figure 41). Once the site is created, the site administrator can access it directly using the site URL https://...../sites/ediscovery/default.aspx or by adding a shortcut on the user's personal site - home page. To use the compliance site, create cases and use them to frame your search request (see Figure 9-42).

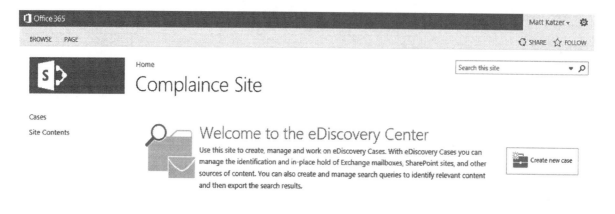

Figure 9-42. *Compliance site: case creation*

Step 3: Linking Exchange Server to the eDiscovery Center

After you create the eDiscovery center, you need to enable the Exchange server for access to the eDiscovery center. This is not enabled by default. If you do not enable the server you will see the following error message when you try to enter a user mailbox: "The connection to the search service application failed."

To enable Exchange search for the case site, do the following:

1. Select the eDiscovery home site that you just created.

2. Select "site settings" under the gear icon (Figure 9-43).

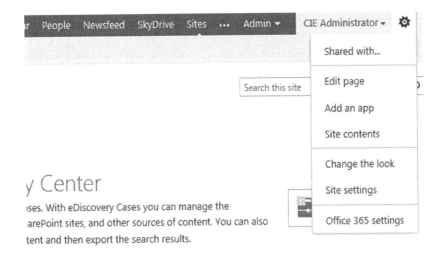

y Center

ises. With eDiscovery Cases you can manage the
arePoint sites, and other sources of content. You can also
tent and then export the search results.

In-Place Hold, Search, & Export

Figure 9-43. Selecting site settings

3. Under "site collection administration," select "search result sources."

4. Select "new result source" (see Figure 9-44), and enter the following:

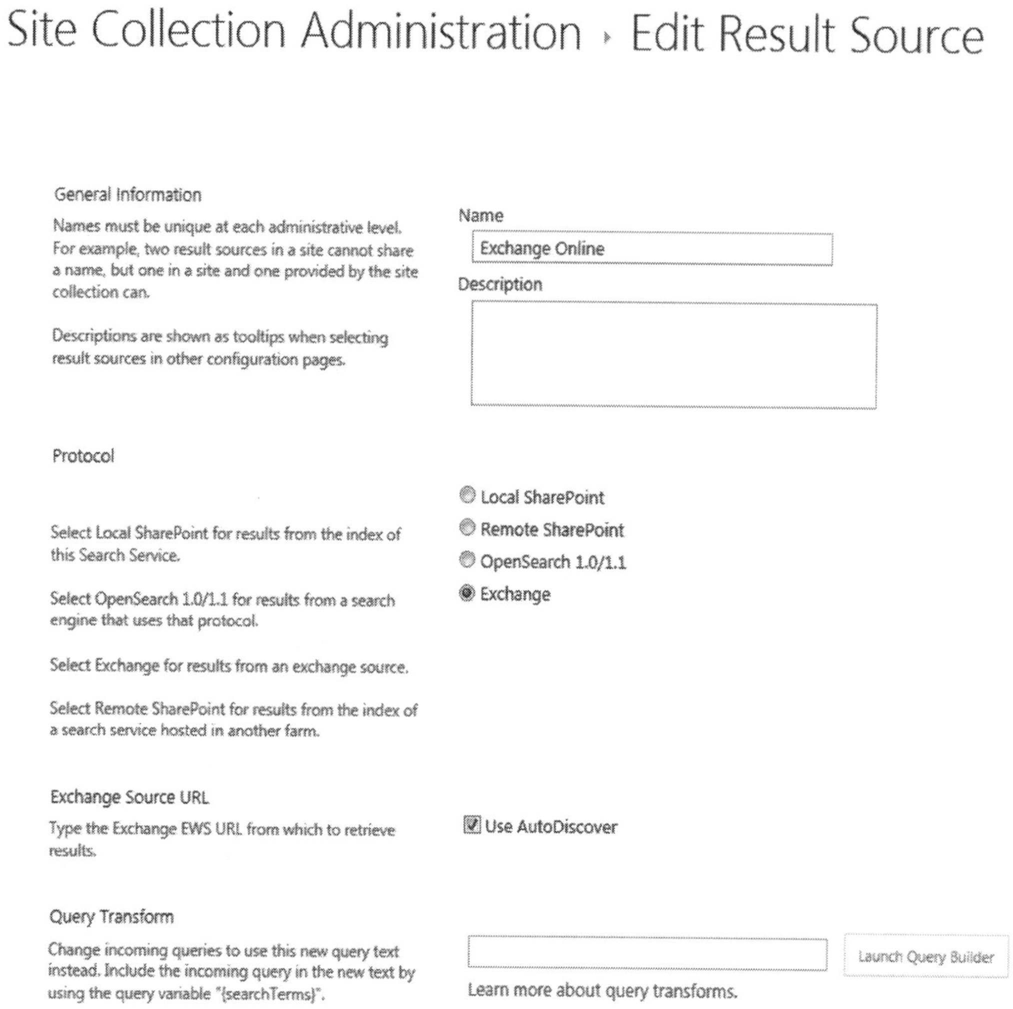

Site Collection Administration › Edit Result Source

General Information

Names must be unique at each administrative level. For example, two result sources in a site cannot share a name, but one in a site and one provided by the site collection can.

Descriptions are shown as tooltips when selecting result sources in other configuration pages.

Name

Exchange Online

Description

Protocol

Select Local SharePoint for results from the index of this Search Service.

Select OpenSearch 1.0/1.1 for results from a search engine that uses that protocol.

Select Exchange for results from an exchange source.

Select Remote SharePoint for results from the index of a search service hosted in another farm.

○ Local SharePoint
○ Remote SharePoint
○ OpenSearch 1.0/1.1
◉ Exchange

Exchange Source URL

Type the Exchange EWS URL from which to retrieve results.

☑ Use AutoDiscover

Query Transform

Change incoming queries to use this new query text instead. Include the incoming query in the new text by using the query variable "{searchTerms}".

Learn more about query transforms.

[Launch Query Builder]

Figure 9-44. *Connecting Exchange server to eDiscovery center*

    a.   Supply a name for the exchange connection.

    b.   Choose "Exchange" for the protocol.

    c.   Select "Autodiscover".

    d.   Clear the Query Transform text box.

    e.   Click "Save".

Discovery Search Using Advance Query Strings (AQS)

Before we address any of the examples, we need to step back for a brief review of advance query strings or AQS. The syntax can become very complex. AQS is provided by the Windows operating system using Windows Desktop Search (WDS). All AQS searches must be fully qualified. A fully qualified search requires that you add a parenthesis every time you add a Boolean operator (AND OR or NOT) to a search query. The Queries are processed based on the location of the parenthesis).

A definitive explanation on this topic exists here:

http://blogs.technet.com/b/exchangesearch/archive/2012/03/10/how-to-use-aqs-to-construct-complex-discovery-queries.aspx

----

Sample AQS Query for Financial Review

You can use the AQS query to address compliance related issues (such as FINRA audit review by the Compliance Officer). The AQS can be any combination of words. The more complex, the longer it takes to generate the query request.

```
(Guarantee OR Money OR Complaint OR Attorney OR Transfer OR Security OR Loss OR Loan OR
Misrepresented OR Unauthorized OR Yield OR Stock OR Bond OR Security OR Percent OR Pay* OR Promise
OR Funds OR Risk OR Secure OR Take* OR Pissed OR Churn)
```

Creating and Exporting Discovery Mailboxes

Your Office 365 site is created with a unique mailbox called Discovery Search Mailbox. This is the default mailbox that is used to handle all discovery requests. To create a specific mailbox for discovery or assign permissions to the discovery mailbox you need to use PowerShell commands in Office 365.

■ **Note**   Discovery mailboxes only have 50 GB of space allocated, and permissions to use them (or see them) are by the discovery management role.

Creating and Accessing Discovery Mailboxes

Since a Discovery Search Mailbox is a mailbox, you can use all of the standard PowerShell commands in accessing the mailbox. The only restriction on discovery mailboxes is that they cannot send or receive email. Discovery mailboxes are designed for one purpose; to act as a store for discovery search request.

To create a new discovery search mailbox, use the following PowerShell command:

```
New-Mailbox -Name <String> -Discovery
```

To list all of the discovery mailboxes (these are not listed in the Exchange management console) run the following PowerShell command:

```
Get-Mailbox -Resultsize unlimited -Filter {RecipientTypeDetails -eq "DiscoveryMailbox"}
```

Likewise, to assign permissions to a specific person as a reviewer, use the Add-MailboxPermission command:

```
Add-MailboxPermission <Display name of discovery mailbox> -User <Display Name> -AccessRights
FullAccess
```

Likewise to find all permissions on a mailbox (remember a discovery Mailbox is just another mailbox), run the Get-MailboxPermission command:

```
Get-MailboxPermission <Display name of discovery mailbox> | Format-Table User,AccessRights,Deny
```

Exporting Information from Discovery Mailboxes

Office 365 does not support Export-Mailbox or Import-Mailbox commands using PowerShell. The only way to export information is to use Outlook. When the user is granted a role in the Discovery Management Group, that user has full access to the mailbox and can add an additional mailbox to Outlook (see Figure 9-45). Once the mailbox is in Outlook, you can export the Discovery Search Mailbox as a PST file using the standard Outlook data export commands to create a PST file:

1. Start Outlook 2013.

2. Select file, then account settings.

3. Select your email account, then change settings.

4. On the change account page, select more settings.

5. Select the Advanced tab and then enter "Discovery Search Mailbox".

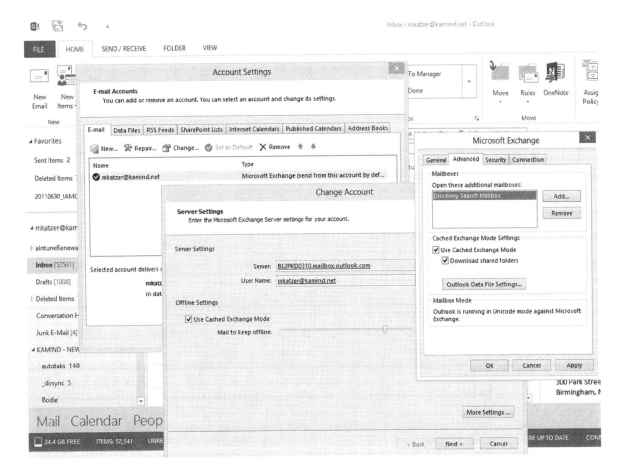

Figure 9-45. *Adding the Discovery Search Mailbox to Outlook*

Once the mailbox is added, it will look similar to Figure 9-46. If the mailbox search information is not present, then depress Shift-F9 to update the mailbox folder from the Office 365 Exchange server.

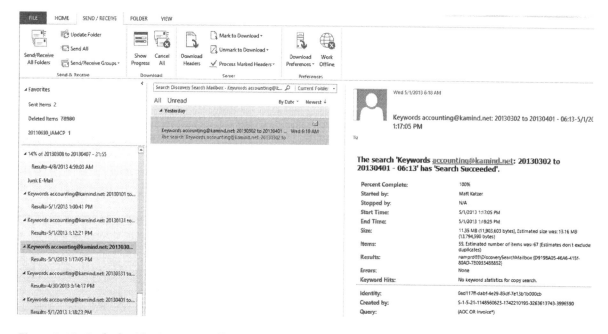

Figure 9-46. *Outlook with Discovery Mailbox Search results*

Reference Links

There is a lot of information about Office 365 on the web—the issue is finding the right site. The information contained in this chapter is a combination of our experiences in doing deployments and support information that has been published by third parties.

Microsoft Office 365 Blog: Latest News about Office 365

http://blogs.office.com/b/microsoft_office_365_blog/

Searching Mailboxes on Legal Hold

http://help.outlook.com/en-us/140/hh125820.aspx

Understanding Legal Hold in Office 365

http://www.networkworld.com/community/blog/doing-e-discovery-message-retention-legal-rec

Understanding Retention Policy PowerShell Commands

http://help.outlook.com/en-us/beta/gg271153.aspx

Understanding Permissions on Discovery Mailboxes

http://help.outlook.com/en-us/140/ee424425.aspx

Search for Deleted Messages

http://help.outlook.com/en-us/beta/gg315525.aspx

Benoit's Corner – Useful Tips and Tricks on Exchange and SharePoint

http://blog.hametbenoit.info/default.aspx

AQS Query Syntax : Discovery

http://blogs.technet.com/b/exchangesearch/archive/2012/03/10/how-to-use-aqs-to-construct-complex-discovery-queries.aspx

Next Steps

Your basic Office 365 systems has been set up and configured. At this point you are 100 percent functional and ready to move to the next steps. However your work is not complete at this time; there is much more to do, depending on your Office 365 configuration. Here are the key chapters you need to review for your Office 365 deployment:

- Chapter 5, SharePoint Administration

  - SharePoint administration and design can be simple or complex depending on your business needs. This chapter provides you with a basic overview of the configuration necessary to be up and running using Office 365 Team Site. This chapter describes Site Design and Construction issues as well as the full SharePoint Administration functions for Office 365.

- Chapter 7, Windows Intune Administration

  - The secret to an optimal Office 365 site is the management of the desktop to ensure that updates are current, and the user antivirus is functioning. Windows Intune is a desktop management tool that addresses these issues and reduces the administrator's effort in desktop management, as well as improving the user's experience.

- Chapter 8, Office 365 Administration

  - This chapter describes the different administration centers in Office 365 and the most common tools that you would use to administer your Office 365 company. Depending on your Office 365 services, there are five possible administration tools. This chapter focuses on the Office 365, Exchange, and Lync administration centers. The SharePoint and Windows Intune administration centers are described in their own chapters. We close the chapter with using PowerShell to manage your Office 365 environment.

- Chapter 10, Exchange Online Protection Administration

  - Office 365 is composed of a set of services. The Exchange Online Protection (EOP) service is the front end of the Office 365 that handle all of the external email front end processing and filtering. If you have smart devices that email to Office 365, you will use EOP to manage the interaction.

- Chapter 11, DirSync, ADFS, Single Sign On and Exchange Federation

  - Active Directory Federation Services and Single Sign On is the integration of the Office 365 Active Directory with on premises Active Directory. This allows one sign on (controlled by on premises servers) to give access to both Cloud and on premises resources. Password Sync can be a simpler implementation that meets many requirements. Federation allows on premises and Cloud Exchange Servers to work together.

CHAPTER 10

■ ■ ■

Office 365 Exchange Online Protection Administration Guide

Office 365 version 2013 is a suite of software products: Software as a Service (SaaS). Customers can purchase Office 365 in many ways, depending on the needs of the organization. Exchange Online Protection (EOP) is one of the service offerings that is included with all of the e-mail services and suites, but it may be purchased separately. EOP is the hosted spam/virus service that processes e-mail communication before it is received by Office 365 mailboxes or on-premise servers, and it is the focus of this chapter.

As shown in previous chapters, the Enterprise version of Office 365 is composed of various services and applications (see Figure 10-1).

Enterprise Suites	Mix and Match Components	Application and System Options

Office 365 Enterprise E1
  • Exchange Plan 1
  • Lync Plan 1
  • SharePoint Plan 1
 	
Office 365 Enterprise E3
  • Exchange Plan 2
  • Lync Plan 1
  • SharePoint Plan 2
 	
Office 365 Enterprise E4
  • Exchange Plan 2
  • Lync Plan 2
  • SharePoint Plan 2
	Exchange
	Exchange Online Kiosk
	Exchange Online (Plan 1)
	Exchange Online (Plan 2)
	
	Lync
	Lync Online (Plan 1)
	Lync Online (Plan 2)
	
	SharePoint
	SharePoint Online (Plan 1)
	SharePoint Online (Plan 2)
	SharePoint Online (Plan 1) with Yammer
	SharePoint Online (Plan 2) with Yammer
	Office Web Apps with SharePoint Plan 1
	Office Web Apps with SharePoint Plan 2
	
	Exchange + SharePoint
	Enterprise K1 (same as K2)
		Office 365 ProPlus
		
		Project Online
		Project Pro for Office 365
		Project Online with Project Pro for Office 365
		
		Microsoft Dynamics CRM Online Basic
		Microsoft Dynamics CRM Online Essential
		Microsoft Dynamics CRM Online Professional
		
		Visio Pro for Office 365
		
		Yammer Enterprise
		
		Support Options
		Professional Direct Support for CRM Online
		Enhanced Support for Microsoft Dynamics CRM
		
		System Options
		Exchange Online Protection
		Exchange Online Archiving (EOA) for Exchange Server
		Azure Active Directory Rights Management

Figure 10-1. Exchange Online Protection - Enterprise Option

The best way to show the flexibility of EOP is to look at a live example on how EOP was used to link two different mail systems together during a migration to Office 365. This situation involved linking Office 365 and Google Docs for a test group evaluation and a migration.

In this example, a client purchases EOP as a filter for two reasons 1) to replace the current solution and 2) as a possible transition to Office 365. However, the client was not sure, and wanted to evaluate the solution. This client had Google Docs users (~150 users). They need to move their mail services before Sept 23, 2013 (The 563-page Omnibus HIPAA rule that was released on March 16, 2013 by the Department of Health and Human Services did not extend the grandfather clause on meeting HIPAA compliance for data services.) All data suppliers must be HIPAA-complaint and supply a Business Associates Agreement (BAA). Google Docs were not compliant, so a BAA was not issued for companies that use Google Docs services.

The solution proposed to the client was to use Office 365 as a replacement for the Google spam/virus scanning solution. The proposed cloud solution was architected as a stepping stone to Office 365. This allowed the company to 1) solve the current need (replace postini) and 2) leverage the EOP integration to evaluate Office 365. This customer purchased test licenses on Office 365, along with the 150 production licenses for EOP. The filtering model (see Figure 10-2) allowed e-mail to run through Office 365, and relayed the e-mail addresses that were not on Office 365 to Google for processing. The customer created an Office 365 test group (following the steps outlined in Chapter 4) and continued to evaluate the business reason for moving to Microsoft Office 365. The business issues were evaluated and the test group voted to move to Office 365, with no downtime before the Sept 23, 2013 deadline.

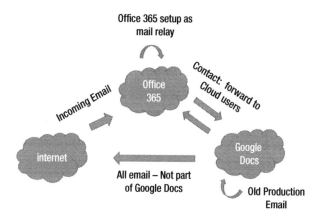

Figure 10-2. *EOP Acting as a Front-End Filter to Google Docs*

How EOP Works

The client was able to use EOP in this manner because EOP is designed with flexibility (see Figure 10-3). EOP works with Office 365 and third-party mail solutions. The focus of this chapter is to expand on the configuration of EOP, which gives you the flexibility to build filtering solutions that will work with your business and Office 365.

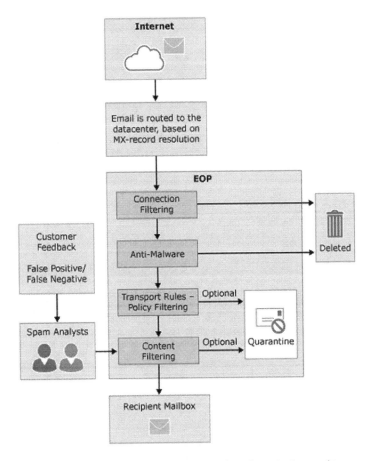

Figure 10-3. *Exchange Online Protection (EOP) Mail Filtering (Courtsey of Microsoft)*

EOP filters spam and checks for viruses before the transport rules and content filtering are checked. This flexibility allows you to add the necessary connectors to third-party services. Earlier you looked at the Google filter case, since this is how we linked the services together. Chapter 9 discussed compliance and Data Loss Prevention (DLP), which will be important here.

The EOP filtering architecture is configurable. The global administrator can configure the following options by using the *mail flow* connectors and the *protection* policies (see Figure 10-4). Some of the policies that can be configured are listed here:

- Send an e-mail notification to a manager upon receipt of an e-mail from a specific sender

- Journal all e-mails to an external archive server

- Copy all e-mails sent to specific users

- Send e-mails to the user junk mailbox or hosted quarantine filters

- Send e-mail through dynamic endpoint encryption (meeting HIPAA requirements)

- Route incoming and outgoing e-mails to a specific destination (via transport rules)

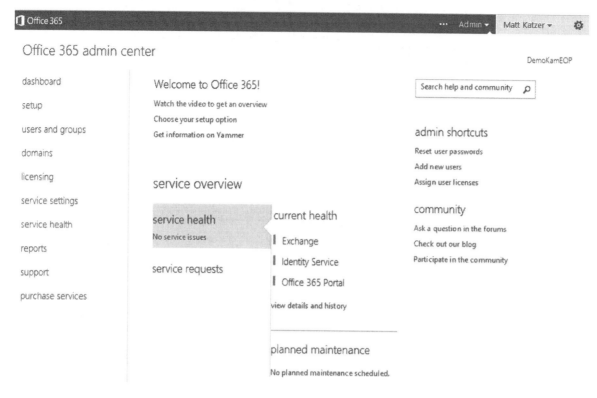

Figure 10-4. *EOP Administration Center*

The complete list of features is Table 10-1. There are some differences between the EOP for on-premises systems versus EOP for Office 365. The configuration in this chapter is a hybrid one, where there is at least one or more mailboxes on the premises or in Office 365.

Table 10-1. *Exchange Online Protection Features*

EOP Features		
Mailbox Location	Role-Based Permissions	Role Groups
Domain Management	Transport Rules	Auditing Reports
Built-In Anti-Spam Protection	Customize Anti-Spam Policies	Quarantine: Admin Management
Quarantine: End User Access	Outlook Junk E-Mail Reporting Tool	Outbound Mail Routing
Secure Messaging with Partner	Safe Listing a Partner's IP Address	Conditional Mail Routing
Hybrid Deployments	Office 365 Admin Center Reports	Excel Application Reports
Message Trace	Delivery Reports	Office 365 Admin Center Access
Exchange Admin Center Access	Data Loss Prevention (DLP)	DLP Policy Tips
Remote PowerShell		

There is very little that the administrator needs to do to configure EOP. The default configuration just works. The Office 365 administrator can configure the EOP to meet the business polices of the organization. This chapter is designed in three parts: setting up EOP for a hybrid organization; configuring EOP spam filters (user and administrator) and customizing the EOP. The majority of Office 365 clients will leave the EOP configuration in its default setup, simply because EOP just works as designed.

Getting Started with EOP: Hybrid or Standalone

If you have already implemented Office 365, you can skip this section. This section is about setting up Exchange Online Protection for the first time and using this as a front-end filter for the on-premises mailboxes (or a replacement for postini on Google Docs). If you have an Office 365 environment setup, the Exchange Online Protection is already configured for you. EOP licenses are contained as part of Office 365 suites and any Office 365-hosted exchange.

Best Practices for EOP Management

Let's get started:

1. Users must be in Office 365. If there is a user mailbox on Office 365, the domain must be set up as a relay.

2. Domains must be listed in accepted domains

3. After you configure EOP, wait 72 hours before you restrict port 25 access

4. Restrict firewall to addresses of the Microsoft Data Center

Steps to Set Up EOP for the First Time

The process of setting up EOP is very similar to that of Office 365. You purchase the necessary subscription. Our recommendation is that any EOP installation should have at least one E3 subscription so the necessary infrastructure is set up for easy migration to Office 365. There are nine steps to set up Office 365, EOP. These are as follows:

1. Sign up for the EOP service.

2. Validate the domain.

3. Load the users.

4. Build the Outbound Connector.

5. Build the Inbound Connector.

6. Change the MX records.

7. Point the on-premise mail connector to the Office 365 smart host.

8. Restrict the IP addresses to Office 365 only.

9. Change the Spam Confidence Level (SCL).

EOP is included with Office 365, but can easily be added to any subscription. The assumption that this configuration is making is that you have a hybrid configuration. Some mailboxes are on Office 365 and the majority of the other mailboxes on different mail services.

Step 1: Sign Up for Exchange Online Protection

Exchange Online Protection is standard on all Office 365 subscriptions. If you have an Office 365 subscription, you do not need to sign up for the service (see Figure 10-5).

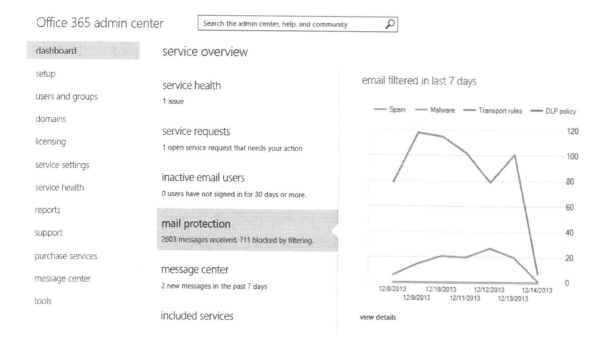

Figure 10-5. *Exchange Online Protection Administration*

If you are new to Office 365 or have an existing trial account and wish to add Exchange Online Protection, you need to link the subscription to your account (see Figure 10-6). To link the EOP to an existing subscription, select the blue "sign in" (by the red arrow in Figure 10-4) to link the Office 365 or Windows Intune account. If you do not have an account, complete the sign-up process to create your first account, and select create and account.

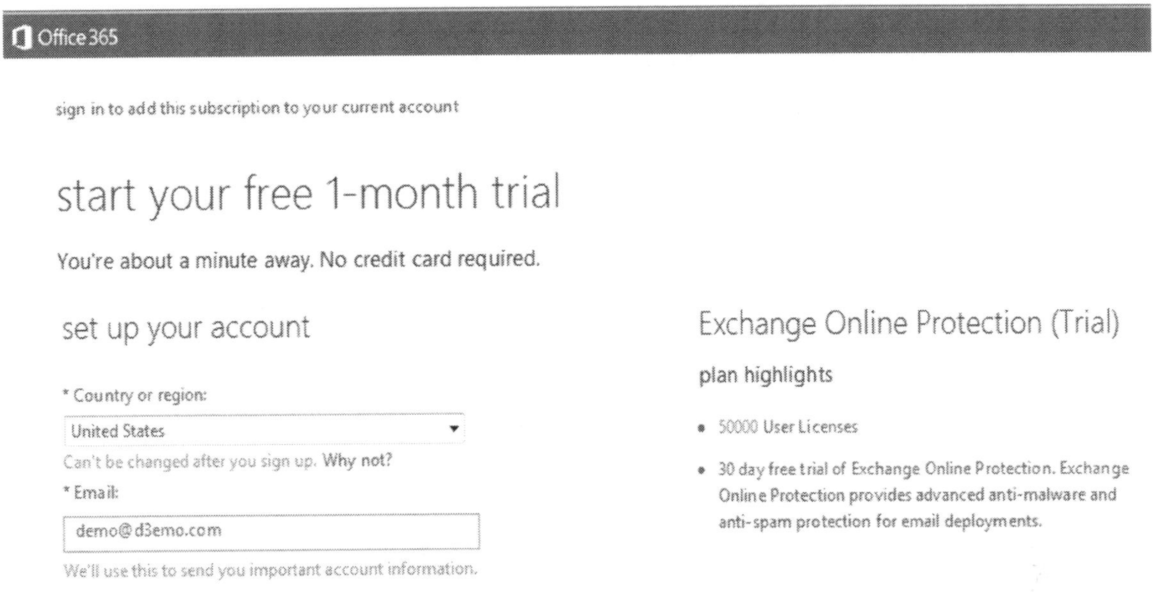

sign in to add this subscription to your current account

start your free 1-month trial

You're about a minute away. No credit card required.

set up your account

* Country or region:

United States ▼

Can't be changed after you sign up. **Why not?**

* Email:

demo@d3emo.com

We'll use this to send you important account information.

Exchange Online Protection (Trial)

plan highlights

* 50000 User Licenses

* 30 day free trial of Exchange Online Protection. Exchange Online Protection provides advanced anti-malware and anti-spam protection for email deployments.

Figure 10-6. *Signing Up for a Free Trial or Paid Subscription*

Step 2: Validate the Domain and Retrieve the MX Records

The first step is to validate the domain name and show proof of ownership. After you show proof of ownership, select Cancel to return to the domain screen (see Figure 10-7) and retrieve the complete DNS records.

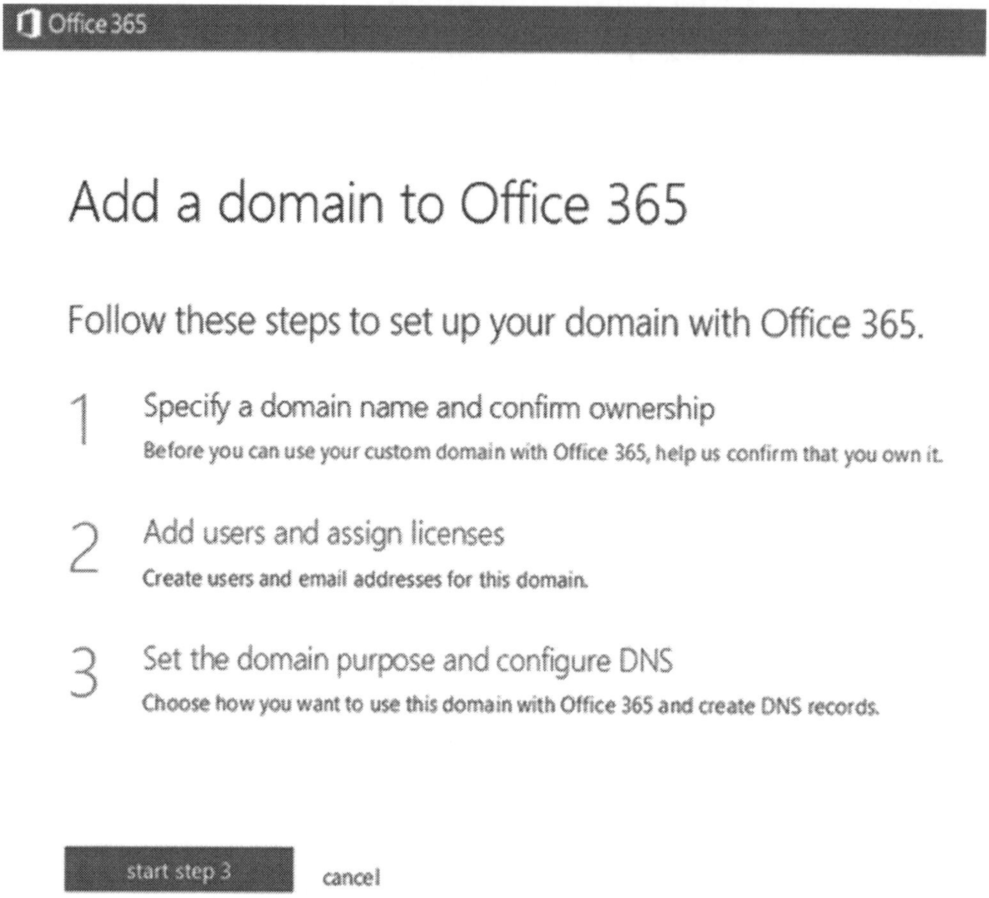

Office 365

Add a domain to Office 365

Follow these steps to set up your domain with Office 365.

1 **Specify a domain name and confirm ownership**
Before you can use your custom domain with Office 365, help us confirm that you own it.

2 **Add users and assign licenses**
Create users and email addresses for this domain.

3 **Set the domain purpose and configure DNS**
Choose how you want to use this domain with Office 365 and create DNS records.

start step 3   cancel

Figure 10-7. *Validated Domain After Users Are Loaded*

■ **Note** If you have an on-premise exchange server, and are planning an Exchange hybrid implementation, follow the instructions in Chapter 11 for adfs and federation. ADFS is a complex migration. Do not proceed with the rest of this chapter.

If you have validated the DNS records, then select Cancel (see Figure 10-8), and retrieve the remaining DNS records to validate them. This will allow you to configure a Hybrid Office 365 configuration.

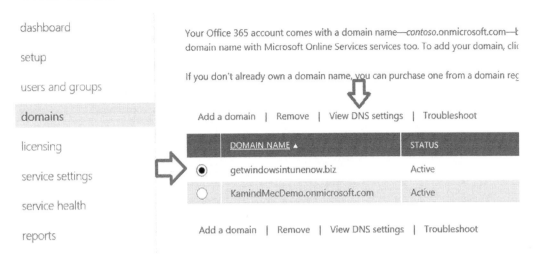

Office 365 admin center

dashboard

setup

users and groups

domains

licensing

service settings

service health

reports

Your Office 365 account comes with a domain name—*contoso*.onmicrosoft.com—b
domain name with Microsoft Online Services services too. To add your domain, clic

If you don't already own a domain name, you can purchase one from a domain reg

Add a domain | Remove | View DNS settings | Troubleshoot

DOMAIN NAME ▲	STATUS
getwindowsintunenow.biz	Active
KamindMecDemo.onmicrosoft.com	Active

Add a domain | Remove | View DNS settings | Troubleshoot

Figure 10-8. *Retrieving the Complete DNS Records*

Step 3: Load the Users

After you have validated the records, you can load the users into Office 365. The users will automatically be assigned as EOP users. When you have a hybrid version, with some users in the cloud and some users on-premise, those cloud users need to have the license manually assigned. The EOP trial subscription is set for 5,000 users.

Step 4: Build the Outbound Connector

There are two connectors to build—the outbound connector and the inbound connector. The outbound connector will route e-mail from Office 365 to the on-site mail server. The inbound connector will route e-mail to the Internet using the Office 365 smart host. The process of making the connectors is to ensure mail flow to the on-site server. This allows an orderly transition of e-mail without any lost traffic. Figure 10-9 shows the mail flow without the on-site server using the inbound connector.

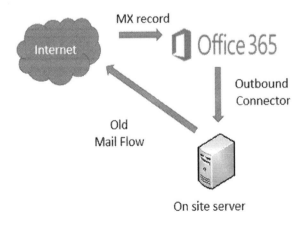

Figure 10-9. *Mail Flow Example*

To set up the outbound connector, select the Exchange Administration Center (EAC). You access the EAC by selecting the Office 365 admin panel, then service settings. At the bottom of the page, select the Exchange Admin Center link located under the heading "Don't See What You're Looking For?" Once you have selected the EAC, select the mail flow and connector (see the red arrows in Figure 10-10).

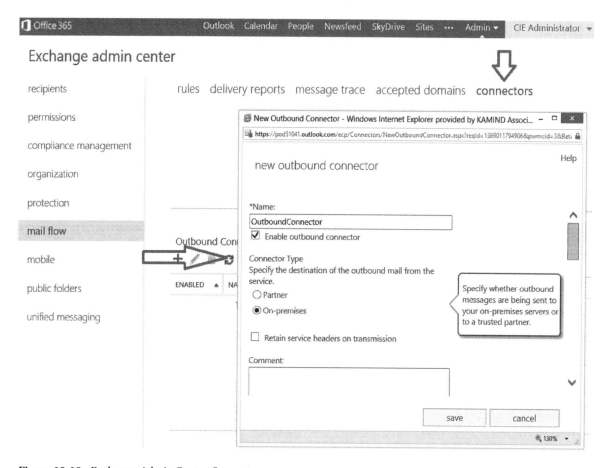

Figure 10-10. *Exchange Admin Center, Connector*

To add an outbound connector, select the + and add the connector. Set the outbound connector values with the following information:

1. Connector name: <Choose a descriptive connector name>.

2. Connector type: <Choose On-Premises>.

3. Connection security: <Choose Opportunistic TLS>.

4. Outbound delivery: <enter the IP address of the on-site server>.

5. Domains : <Add the domains you have validated>.

After you have selected the outbound connector you are ready to receive e-mail and process the e-mail for spam and virus protection. The Office 365 Spam processing needs to run for a seven-day period to learn the mail flow. It is recommended that you do not modify the spam filters for a period of seven days after you have enabled the inbound connector.

Step 5: Build the Inbound Connector

The inbound connector sends mail to the Office 365 smart host. Office 365 processes the mail for spam and virus and then delivers to the destination. There are two steps for configuring the inbound smart host:

1. Configuration and validation of the connector (on-site servers send to Office 365).

2. Locking down the on-site server to only accept e-mail from Office 365 (Step 9).

To add an inbound connector, select the + and add the connector. Set the inbound connector values with the following information:

1. Name: <Choose a unique name for the inbound connector>.

2. Connector type: <Choose on-premises>.

3. Connection security: <Choose Force TLS, and specify the certificate subject name of the certificate from your on-premises environment>.

4. Scope - Domains: <Under Domains, click Add. In the resulting Add Domain window, enter the domain name or leave it blank>.

5. Scope - IP address: <Enter the IP address of the sending on-site server>.

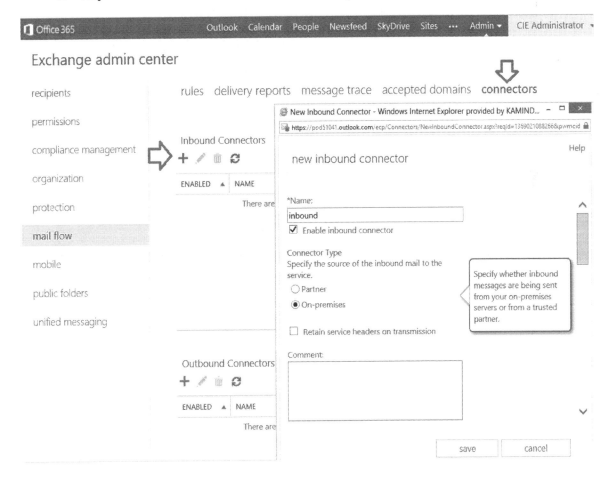

Figure 10-11. Inbound Connector

The inbound is set up to route e-mail from the on-premise server to Office 365. Routing e-mail through Office 365 will help manage the spam configuration.

Step 6: Change the MX Records and Switch to Shared (Optional)

At this point, the mail flow is being configured similar to Figure 10-10. Mail is flowing from Office 365 and to Office 365. At this point, you need to configure the MX records so they point to Office 365. If you have cloud-based mailboxes (in a cut-over test), you will also need to change the domain to Shared mode or non-authoritative (not the primary address for e-mail). You must change the MX records so that they point to Office 365 instead of to the on-premise server.

Once you have changed the MX records to point to Office 365, run the domain setup wizard and select Step 3 (see Figure 10-7). After the domain validation, set the domain intent (see Figure 10-12). Notice that with EOP, there is an option for hybrid mail flow.

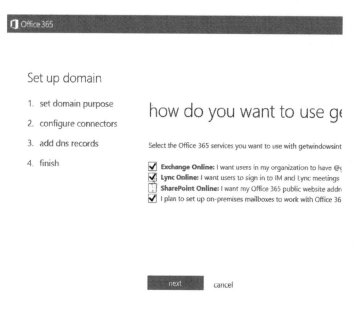

Figure 10-12. Setting the Domain Intent

When you set the domain intent, if you have a domain that is both in the cloud and on-site, you need to also set the mail domain configuration. If this is not set, mail will not flow into the Office 365 account. This is an optional step. Set the domain only if you have cloud mailboxes; otherwise, e-mail may not route to the on-site servers.

If you have mailboxes on Office 365, set the Office 365 mail control to be an internal relay (see Figure 10-13). What this does is sends e-mail to Office 365, then relays what e-mail is not resolved to the on-premise server. Keep in mind the configuration that is normally used is some type of federated account. A federated account will allow calendars to be shared. If the account is not federated, calendars cannot be shared.

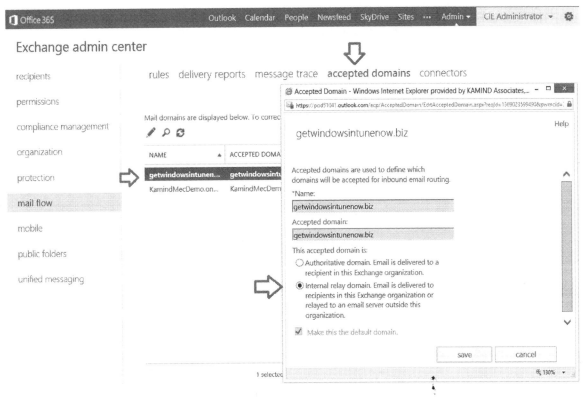

Figure 10-13. *Setting the Domain as an Internal Relay*

Step 7: Route On-Premise E-Mail Through EOP

After you set up the inbound and outbound connectors, you need to change the mail flow to use Office 365. This is a configuration of the on-premise servers so they point to Office 365. See Figure 10-14.

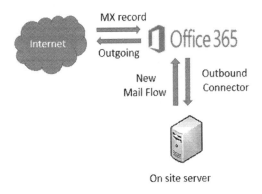

Figure 10-14. *EOP Mail Flow*

Step 8: Restrict Incoming On-Premise Mail to Office 365

After you have configured the on-site server to send and receive e-mail from Office 365, the next step is to restrict the incoming IP address to accept e-mail only from Office 365 (see Table 10-2). Typically, you'd wait 24 hours after the change to the MX records to point to Office 365. This allows the Internet names servers to make the necessary corrections in the redirection of e-mail to the new server location.

Table 10-2. IP Address Restrictions for Office 365 (as of 12/2013)

CIR Routing	IP Address Range
65.55.88.0/24	65.55.88.0/24 = 65.55.88.1 - 65.55.88.254
207.46.51.64/26	207.46.51.64/26 = 207.46.51.65 - 207.46.51.126
207.46.163.0/24	207.46.163.0/24 = 207.46.163.1 - 207.46.163.254
213.199.154.0/24	213.199.154.0/24 = 213.199.154.1 - 213.199.154.254
213.199.180.128/26	213.199.180.128/26 = 213.199.180.129 - 213.199.180.190
216.32.180.0/24	216.32.180.0/24 = 216.32.180.1 - 216.32.180.254
216.32.181.0/24	216.32.181.0/24 = 216.32.181.1 - 216.32.181.254

Select the IP addresses and restrict the incoming server to receive e-mail only from Office 365 and to send to Office 365.

Step 9: Adjust the Spam Confidence Level (After Seven or More Days)

The default spam confidence level is set to level 6. To change the level (increase or decrease in EOP), you will need to run a PowerShell command and set the Spam Confidence Level (SCL) to a different value. The SCL affects the default anti-spam action, which is to move spam messages to the recipient's junk e-mail folder. In the following example, we have waited seven days and decided to adjust the spam confidence level to level 5 (see Figure 10-15). See the section later in this chapter on adding the spam confidence rule and enabling end user spam quarantine.

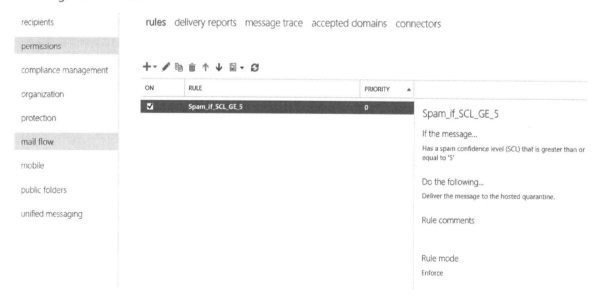

Figure 10-15. Setting the Spam Confidence Level

At this point you have configured Office 365 EOP filters for spam processing. The filters that you set up and configure will handle incoming and outgoing filtering using Office 365 Exchange Online Transport. You can add to the basic setup and adjust the filters as needed.

Modification of Spam Processing

The EOP spam engine can be fully modified by the global administrator. But before you modify the EOP properties, let the default rules handle the spam for at least a seven-day period. This will give the EOP filtering engine time to learn your organization's spam characteristics. To understand how the Office 365 organization is processing spam, just select the Mail Protection link after you log in to the admin center (see Figure 10-16).

Figure 10-16. *Admin Dashboard with Mail Protection Status*

The default settings will address the majority of the spam issues, and the administrator should let EOP process the spam using the default filters for a few days before you begin to tune the filters. The mail protection dashboard (see Figure 10-16) shows the status of the different filters and what is trapping the spam. As an example, we have transport rules enabled, so this is filtering the messages for the quarantine or the junk mail folder. The areas that you can adjust are listed in Table 10-3.

Table 10-3. *Spam Processing Options*

Spam Options	Descriptions
Malware filter	Disposition of detected malware. Keep messages, delete messages, and send notifications.
Connection filter	These are the IP connection filters. The valid and blocked IP addresses are listed. If you are using a trusted third-party safe list, the sender policy is enabled in the settings to bypass spam filter processing.
Content filter	Spam disposition and content process is controlled here. To move spam to user Junk mail (or web-based quarantine), you enable content filtering. International data filters and spam processing options are configured in the content filtering.
Outbound spam	Outbound spam processing options.
Quarantine	E-mails that are in quarantine due to a false positive.

The spam settings are accessed from the Exchange Administration Panel. To access the panel, return the Office 365 administration dashboard, and select the Admin menu link to access the Exchange admin center (see Figure 10-17), then select protection to tune the spam filters.

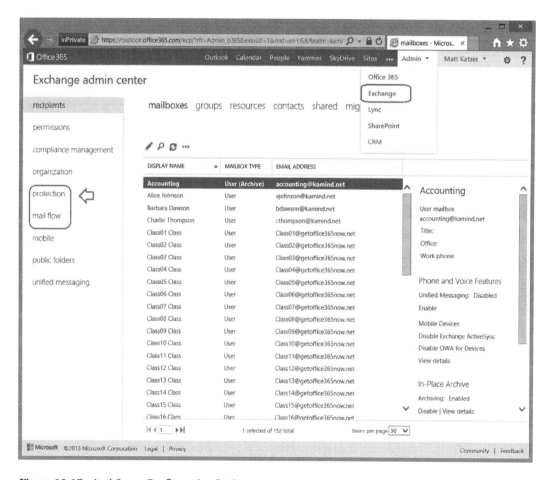

Figure 10-17. *Anti-Spam Configuration Settings*

The administrator can tune any of these filters to reflect the needs of the organization. The filters are set up to cascade on the previous filter (see Figure 10-18). The typical changes after installation involve moving the spam from the junk folder to the web-based quarantine. To change the behavior, you modify the appropriate spam area. In this case of the junk filer, you modify the Content Filter behavior.

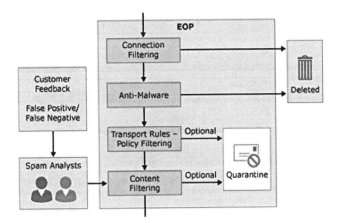

Figure 10-18. *Spam Filter Processing (Courtesy of Microsoft)*

Spam is a growing issue for all users, and to best police spam for your organization, you need to report it to Office 365 technicians. The spam reporting tool is used to report behavior and you can download the tool from `Microsoft.com` (`http://www.microsoft.com/en-us/download/details.aspx?id=18275`). The reporting tool supports Outlook 2003, 2007, 2010, and 2013. Download the corresponding tool for your Outlook client. Once the tool is installed, you can report junk mail on messages simply by right-clicking the message (see Figure 10-19).

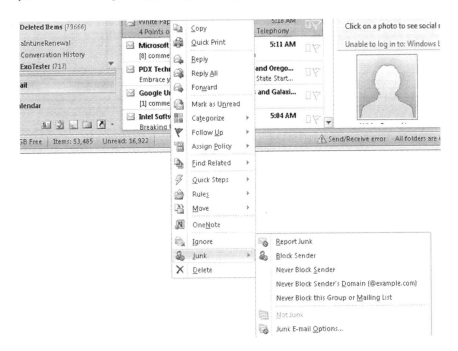

Figure 10-19. *Reporting Junk Mail for Spam Analysis*

When you report junk mail, three things happen 1) the e-mail content is sent to Microsoft for analysis and 2) your organization's spam content ratings are adjusted based on message content type and 3) the message is tagged and is reported as a community reported spam. The community reported spam is the most interesting. E-mail may not be from a true spammer, but if enough people tag and e-mail it as spam in a peer review, that sender's "trust" is lowered. To have a better feel of the spam processing, let's walk through the different configuration options available to the Administrator when managing the Office 365 organization.

Malware Filter Changes

Once you have selected the Anti-Spam Connection Filter policies, there are five areas that you can modify to change the spam headings. These are malware filter, connection filter, content filter, outbound spam, and quarantine (see Figure 10-20).

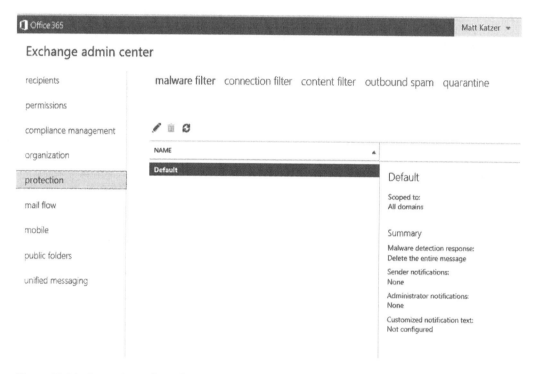

Figure 10-20. *Spam Control Panel*

The Filter property that will have the most impact to you is the content filter. It's the customize filter that is used to define what is spam to your organization.

Typical Changes on a New Configuration

The default spam filter configuration meets the needs of most organizations. The configuration is used for all Office 365 customers, and is open for customization by the administrator. The typical customizations are in the connection filter. This is where you can add trusted senders. As an example, if your voice mail messages are coming from an external server, add the IP address as a trusted sender.

Connection Filter

The connection filters (see Figure 10-21) handle the IP address filters. Typically, three are configured: 1 IP allow list, 2 IP block list, and 3 Safe list. These connection properties are domain in scope. In the voice mail example, this is where you add the connection filter.

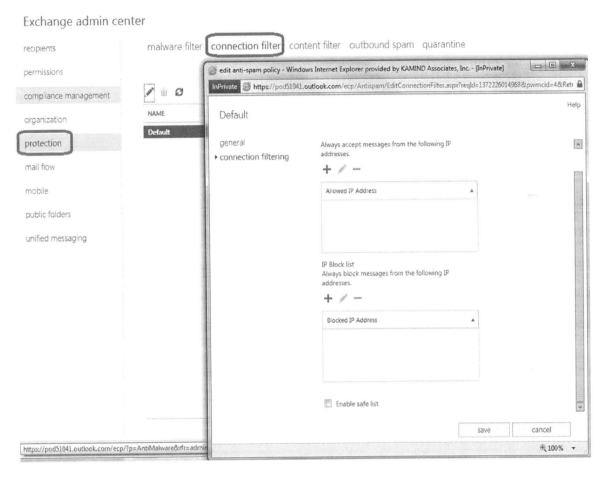

Figure 10-21. *Connection Filter Access*

- *IP Allow list:* This is the IP address list that will be allowed to connect to Office 365. These are trusted senders.

- *IP Block list:* These are the IP address that are being blocked from Office 365 (not trusted).

- *Enable Safe list:* Microsoft subscribes to various third-party sources of trusted senders. Addresses and domains that are on this list bypass spam processing. The normal configuration is off and needs to be enabled by the administrator.

■ **Note** IP addresses must be specified in IP4 format. You can also specify the subnet range using a subnet mask nnn.nnn.nnn.nnn/rr. IPV6 addresses cannot be filtered at this time.

Adding Transport Rules for E-Mail Processing

Office 365 EAC has direct access to the transport rules. You can create additional processing rules that run after the spam. A typical rule would be if you don't want your IP Allow List entry to apply to all your domains, you can create a transport rule that applies to specific domains. To change the transport rules, select Mail Flow and Rules. Select New Rules, and then More Options (after you select a new rule to display the advance configuration). Build the rule based on your needs (see Figure 10-22).

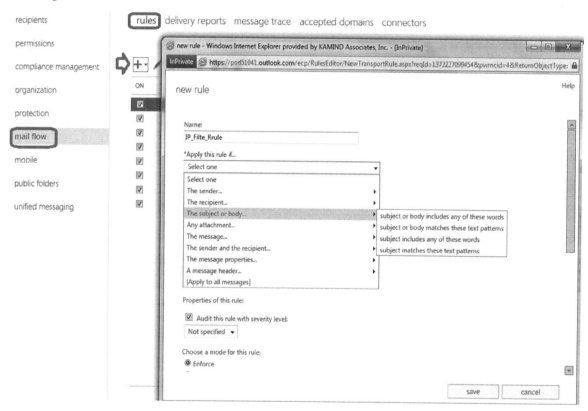

Figure 10-22. *Creating New Transport Rules*

Content Filter Options

The Content filter options govern how e-mail is processed and messages are retained. There are six actions for spam. These actions are:

- Move messages to junk e-mail folder (the default)

- Add X-header

- Prepend subject line with text

- Redirect message to e-mail address

- Delete message

- Quarantine message (not available for individuals at this time)

The default configuration will send all spam to the junk e-mail folder with a default 15 days for deletion (see Figure 10-23).

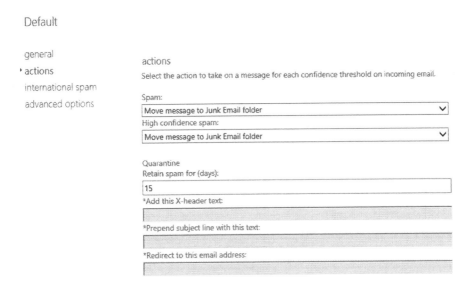

Figure 10-23. Setting Spam Quarantine Options

There are two additional options that the administrator can enable on content filtering. These are the international spam option (foreign language detection) and the advance option. The advance options enable the administrator to block certain message types. As an example, one of the message types is an empty message. A partial list is shown in Figure 10-24.

Figure 10-24. *Sample of Advance Spam Configuration Options*

Fighting Excessive Spam

There are two areas that you can adjust to have an immediate effect on spam processing. This is in changing the Advance Filtering options (see Figure 10-24 earlier) and adding a filter rule to send the spam to quarantine (instead of the user's junk folder). The typical changes that you would make in the spam configuration are highlighted in Figure 10-25.

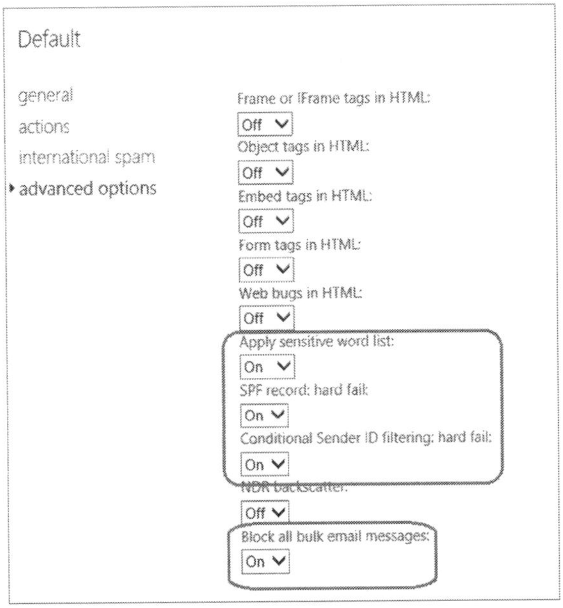

Figure 10-25. *Setting Spam Filter Options*

Moving Mail to Quarantine (Instead of to the Junk Mail Folder)

The default configuration for the spam quarantine is to have the e-mail message delivered to the junk mail folder. The question that is raised is how do you direct the junk mail to the quarantine and bypass the desktop? This is done by setting a new spam confidence rule to be processed at the transport layer. To enable this configuration, you must set up the spam confidence level and the user default profile.

In this example, we set the spam confidence level to 5, so that any e-mail that has a SCL greater than 5 will go to quarantine. Every business is different, and the default configuration of Office 365 EOP is an SCL of 6. To set a new SCL level, go to the Exchange admin center and select mail control. You are going to create a new rule (see Figure 10-26).

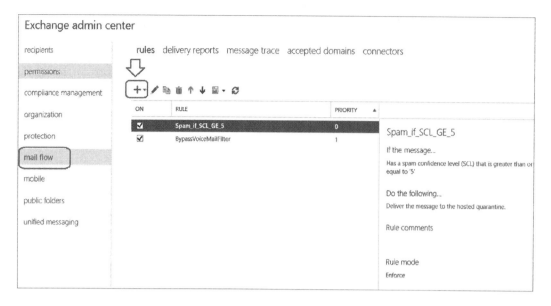

Figure 10-26. Redirecting Spam to Quarantine

In Figure 10-26, select the + to create a new rule and select the Message Rule (see Figure 10-27). Then select message properties (see Figure 10-28) and set the spam confidence level.

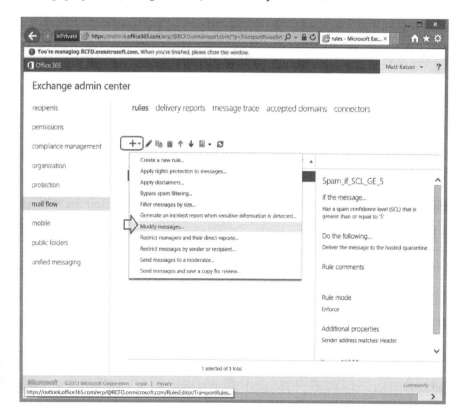

Figure 10-27. Setting Up the Message Filter

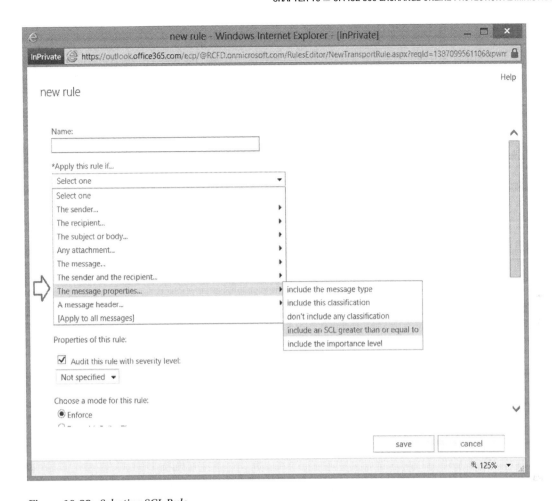

Figure 10-28. *Selecting SCL Rule*

After you set up the message filter (modify properties), select the message properties and set the SCL level. (see Figure 10-28).

The last step is to set up the final rules to send the spam to quarantine (see Figure 10-29). In this case, you want to have all spam over SCL level 5 delivered to quarantine. This is the last configuration change you'll make. At this point, all spam mail is going to quarantine.

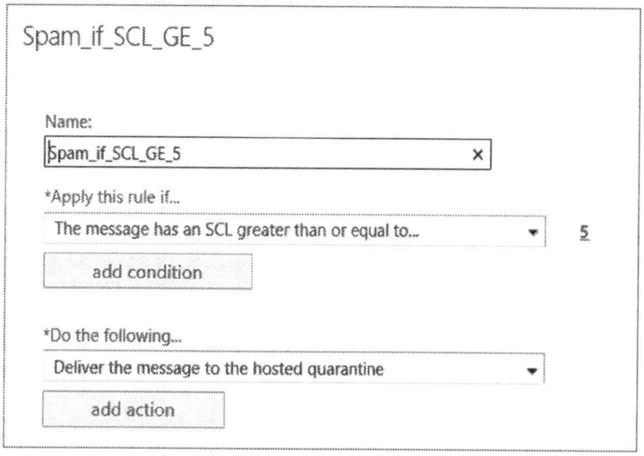

Spam_if_SCL_GE_5

Name:

Spam_if_SCL_GE_5   ×

*Apply this rule if...

The message has an SCL greater than or equal to...   ▼   5

    add condition

*Do the following...

Deliver the message to the hosted quarantine   ▼

    add action

Figure 10-29. *Setting SCL Level for 5 to Deliver All Spam to Quarantine*

User Access to Spam Quarantine

The default configuration for the spam quarantine is to have the e-mail message delivered to the user's junk mail folder after spam processing. As a global administrator, you can have the spam delivered to quarantine or to the global administrator. See Figure 10-30.

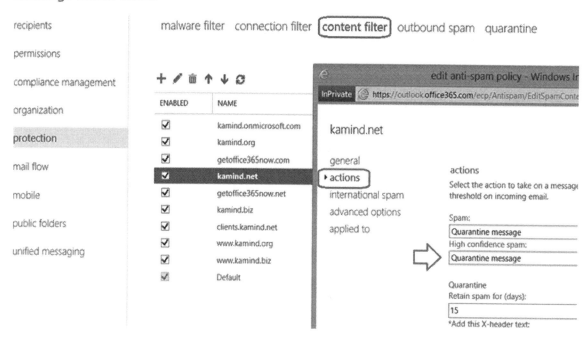

Figure 10-30. *Setting Up Spam to Be Delivered to Quarantine*

Once you set up the spam quarantine option, you can also set up the individual users to receive notification when to check the spam filter (Figure 10-31). To do this, select the domain, then on the right side, scroll down until you see the hyperlink to set the notification days.

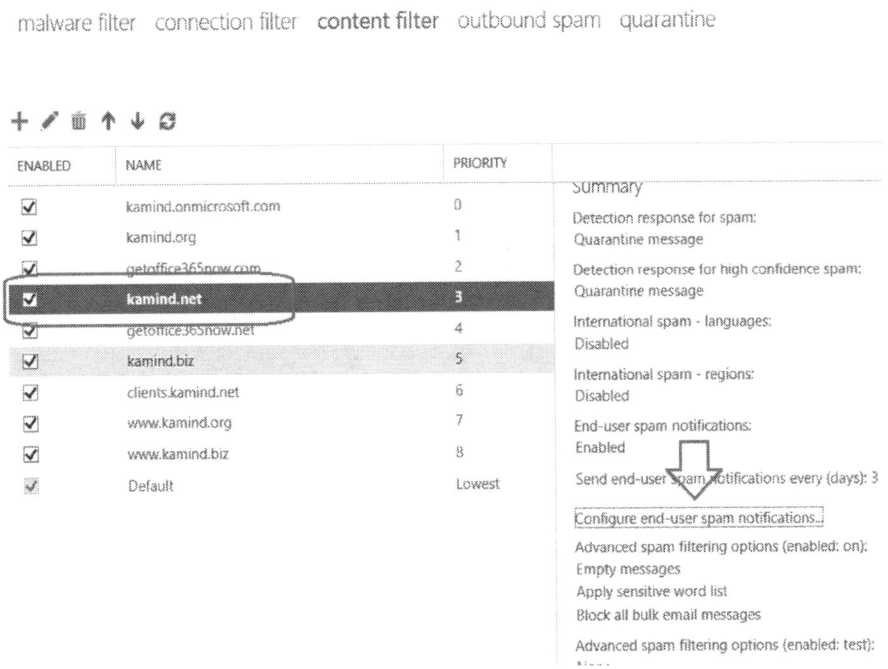

malware filter   connection filter   **content filter**   outbound spam   quarantine

Figure 10-31. *Setting Up End User Notifcation of Spam Messages*

As an administrator, you have full access to the spam quarantine so you can verify the contents of the filter. To look at the quarantine, select the Quarantine tab from the Mail Flow filter (see Figure 10-32).

Exchange admin center

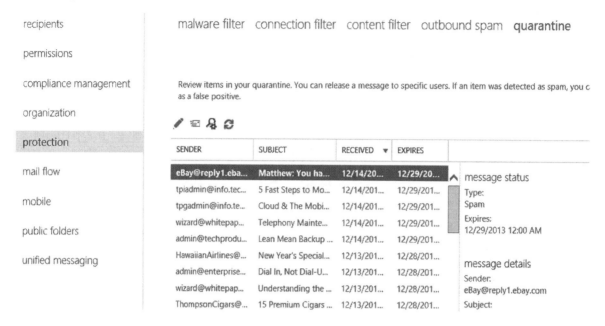

Figure 10-32. *Spam Quarantine*

EOP is being continually extended, and new features are always being added to the service to enhance the operation of Office 365.

Outbound Spam Policy

Outbound spam policy is how you manage notifications that are sent out to third-parties about the spam that you receive (see Figure 10-33). There are two policies—send a copy of suspicious e-mails to an address and send a notice when a sender is blocked from sending out e-mails.

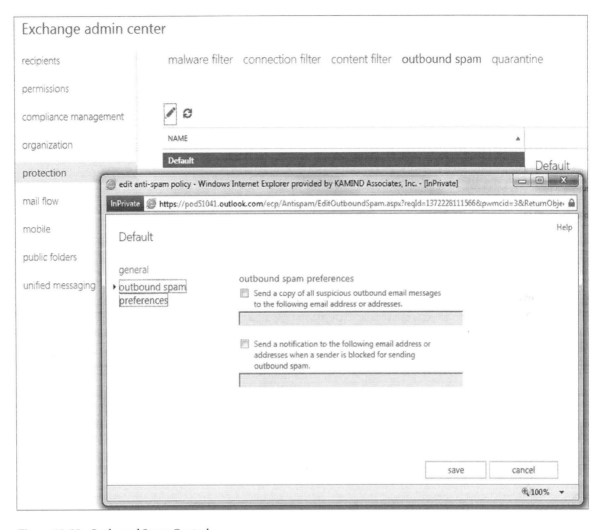

Figure 10-33. *Outbound Spam Control*

- **Send a copy of all suspicious outbound e-mail messages to the following e-mail address or addresses**. These are messages that are marked as spam by the filter (regardless of the SCL rating), and are routed through a risk pool.

- **Send a notification to the following e-mail address when a sender is blocked sending outbound spam**. When a significant amount of spam is originating from a particular mailbox, the mailbox is disabled from sending e-mail messages. The administrator is notified and takes action to resolve the issue.

Sending E-mail from a Device to Office 365

There are different ways to send e-mail from a device to Office 365. The complexity of sending depends upon the devices you are sending the e-mail to. Some devices do not have an embedded SMTP server. They can only perform relay functions. Other devices support a SMTP sender and can directly send to Office 365 (or any other e-mail address on the Internet). All of theses approaches have interesting problems and side effects. The question is which one to use. These four options are listed in Table 10-4.

Table 10-4. *Device Sending Options for Office 365*

Option	Description	Requirements
1	Direct sending form a device using DNS	Sending device supports an SMTP server
2	Sending through IIS to Office 365 internal users	Dedicated Public IP address as a trusted sender
3	Sending through office 365 to External Users	Send as permissions need to be granted to sender
4	Sending through office 365 to External Users using a certificate	Dedicated Public IP address as a trusted sender

Which approach do you use? It depends on what you are trying to accomplish. Most people use the direct send method if they have an on-site Windows server or some other SMTP server. The configuration that always works is when there is an Office 365 integration module present or Directory Synchronization running. These environments with an Office 365 administrator connection always work, provided that you follow these rules:

1. If the e-mail destination is *external*, the sender address must be a valid Office 365 account.

2. If the e-mail destination is *internal*, the sender can be any e-mail address, but the sender must be from the same domain (such as copier@office365account.com).

Office 365 has undergone some significant changes in how on-site devices relay e-mails. This change revolves around the trusted sender. Referring back to Table 10-4, there are four different scenarios for on-site devices to send e-mail to Office 365. We will look at each of these methods.

Preparing Office 365 to Act as an SMTP Relay

There are two mail destinations you can use to send e-mail. The secured destination (requires a login and using port 587) and data is sent via port 587. If you use the unsecured destination, information is sent in clear text, and you use the MX record. When you use either of these records, you add the IP address of the sender so the connection that you are sending from is a trusted sender.

Step 1: Retrieve the Secured SMTP Settings from Your Office 365 Site

Log in to Office 365 and select the settings (gear symbol). Then select options (see Figures 10-34 and 10-35). Write down the SMTP settings for future reference.

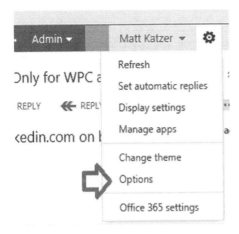

Figure 10-34. *Select Outlook All Options*

Figure 10-35. *Determining the SMTP Settings*

Step 2: Retrieve the MX Record Destination from Your Domain Settings

Log in to Office 365, and select domains. Then choose the domain that you are using for e-mail. Finally, view the DNS settings (see Figure 10-36).

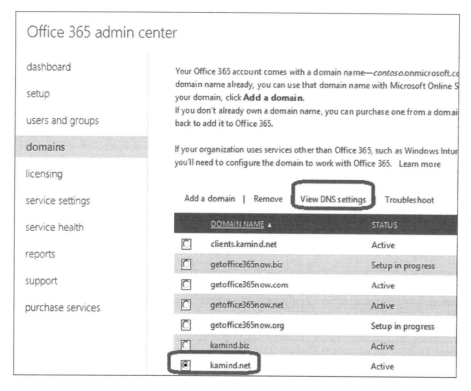

Figure 10-36. *Viewing the DNS Settings in Office365*

After you select View, DNS Settings, copy the MX record for future use (see Figure 10-37). In some cases, it is simpler to send to the mail server directly versus using the smart host. However, this works only if the source domain is from the same domain on Office 365 and the destination address is internal.

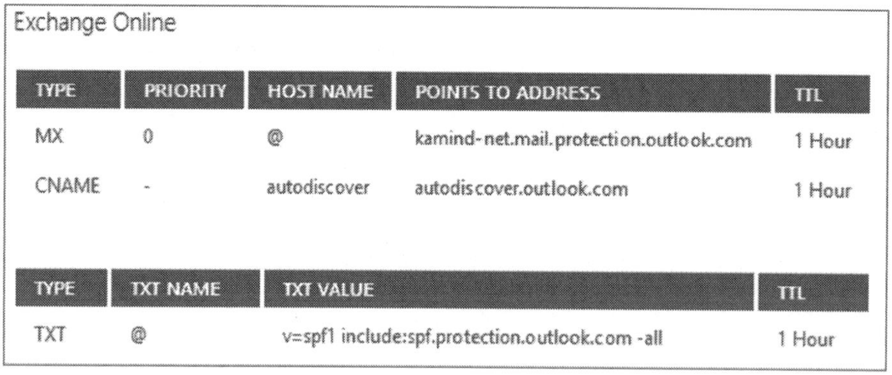

Exchange Online

TYPE	PRIORITY	HOST NAME	POINTS TO ADDRESS	TTL
MX	0	@	kamind-net.mail.protection.outlook.com	1 Hour
CNAME	-	autodiscover	autodiscover.outlook.com	1 Hour

TYPE	TXT NAME	TXT VALUE	TTL
TXT	@	v=spf1 include:spf.protection.outlook.com -all	1 Hour

Figure 10-37. *Displaying the MX Record for the Domain*

Step 3: Determine Your Public IP Address for the Send Connector

If you have a static IP address that the on-site devices uses for Internet access, you need to record that information to be used later as the trusted sender. The trusted sender address needs to be entered into the Exchange Online Protection interface. If you do not have a static IP address, you will need to use an account sent to Office 365. The static IP address will be used as a trusted connector to Office 365.

Step 4: Construct Your New SPF Record

After you have determined the static IP address, you need to build the new SPF record. The static IP address will look like the following (replace the 10.10.10.10 with your static IP address). You will use this information later when you add the trusted connector to Office 365:

```
v=spf1 include:spf.protection.outlook.com ipv4: 10.10.10.10-all
```

Configuring the Device to Send to Office 365

Once you have collected the basic information about Office 365, you are now ready to configure the e-mail for the on-site devices. Table 10-4 contained four different methods to send to Office 365. These methods are:

- Sending from a device using DNS.

- Sending through IIS to Office 365 internal users.

- Sending through IIS and Office 365 to external users.

- Sending through IIS and Office 365 to external users using a certificate.

Which approach works the best? It depends. The best approach is to try the simplest first (the first option), and go to the more complex approach that makes business sense.

Option 1: Sending from a Device Using DNS

This is the simplest approach. Usually the device has a SMTP server built into the device. All you need to do is supply a destination e-mail address, and add the IP address of the sending device as a trusted sender. Follow the steps outlined in the following sections.

Step 1: Configure the Sending Device

Add the destination addresses in the sending device. No special login is required as long as the sending device is only sending to Office 365 and is not using Office 365 as a relay.

Step 2: Configure the Office 365 Inbound Connector

You are using an anonymous connection as a trusted relay, so you need to add the IP address (see Figure 10-38) to Office 365 EOP Inbound connector and the new SPF record to DNS (see the earlier information you collected from Office 365).

Figure 10-38. *Setting Custom Connector*

To add the Office 365 inbound connector, log into Office 365, and select Service Settings. Then select Custom Mail Rules (see Figure 10-38). In Figure 10-39, select Connectors, and then add a new inbound connector. Enter the static IP address.

Figure 10-39. *Adding the Inbound Connector*

Step 3: Configure a Bypass Spam Filter

After you have built the inbound connector, you need to add a "bypass spam" rule so the e-mail traffic will skip the spam filter and connection filtering. To add the Office 365 custom rule, log in to Office 365 and select Service Settings. Then select Custom Mail Rules (see Figure 10-40). Select Rules and then select Bypass spam Filter.

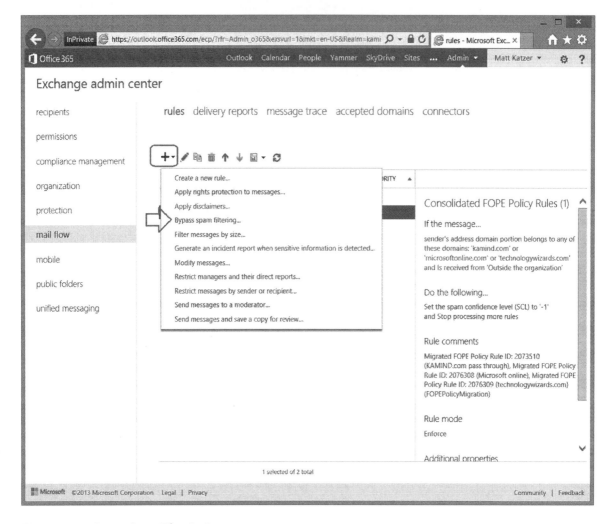

Figure 10-40. Bypass Spam Filter Option

Once you have selected the bypass spam filter options, select "IP Addresses in Any of These Ranges" (see Figure 10-41).

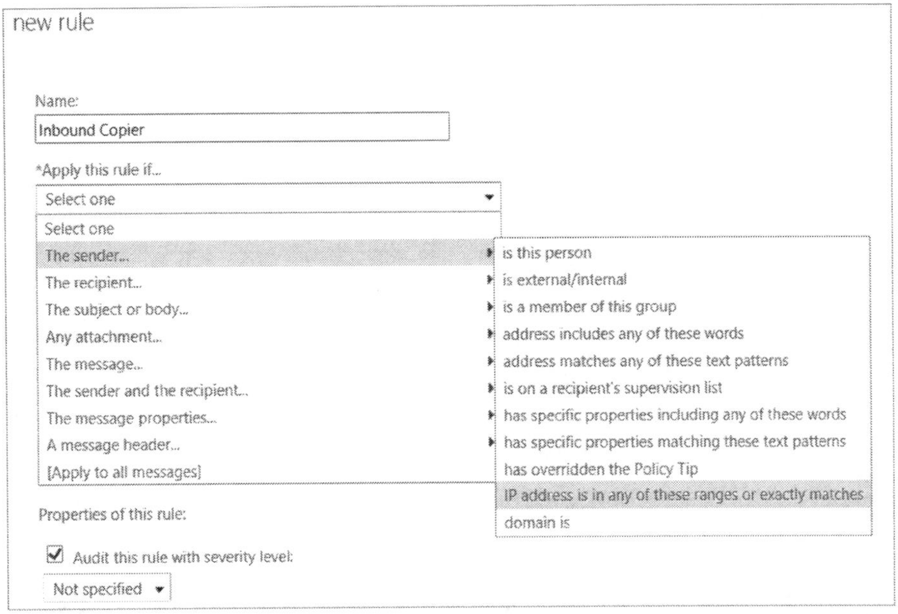

Figure 10-41. *Adding the Bypass Spam Filter Rule*

Enter the selected IP addresses (see Figure 10-42) and save the rule. At this point, any e-mail message that is sent from the device should arrive at the destination e-mail in Office 365.

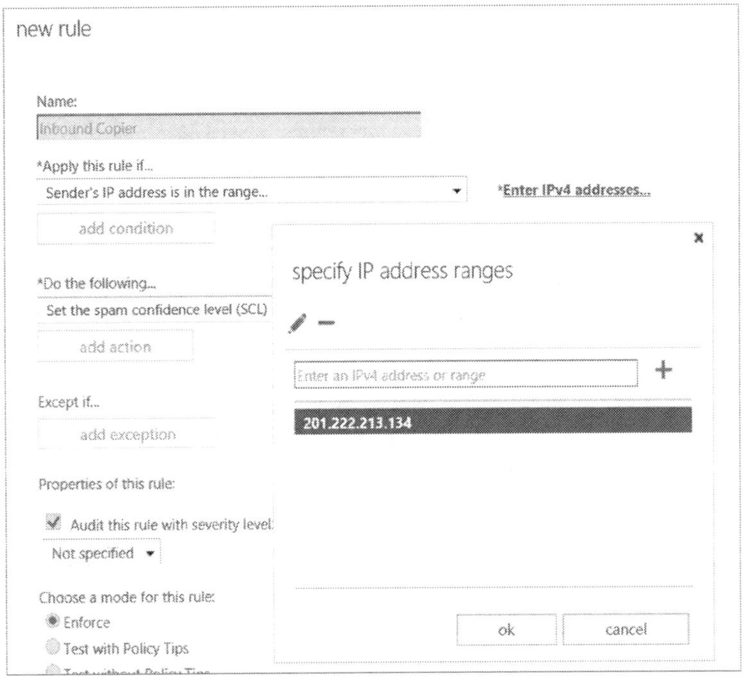

Figure 10-42. *Adding IP Address Bypass for Spam Filter*

If you do not have a device that can relay e-mail to Office 365, then you'll have to add the SMTP server feature to a Windows server in your network (this is option 2). This approach does not require an Office 365 account.

Option 2: Relaying Through a Windows SMTP Server

Relay through an on-site mail sender (such as the SMTP server in IIS) to send mail to an Office 365 account or to the Internet. An example is an on-site copier that has an interface to send directly to an e-mail address. In some cases, you may have a Microsoft Window server on-site, and you can easily add the SMTP mail servicer to this server. The SMTP server is standard with all Microsoft servers and is detailed in this knowledge-based article (see http://support .microsoft.com/kb/2600912) and at the end of this chapter.

If you do not have a device that can relay e-mail to Office 365, add the SMTP server feature to a Windows server in your network. This approach does not require an Office 365 account.

Step 1: Add IIS SMTP Server to Your Windows Server

If you are using a Windows server as a relay, you will need to install the SMTP service; otherwise, you will use the device SMTP service (see Figure 10-43).

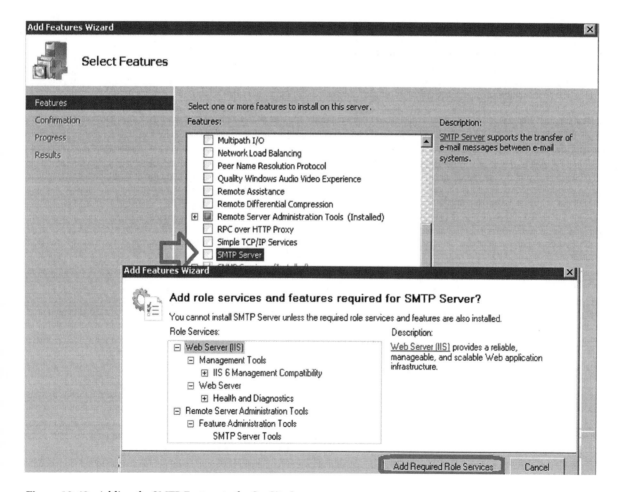

Figure 10-43. *Adding the SMTP Feature to the On-Site Server*

Step 2: Configure IIS Manager

Once you have added the SMTP server, you need to configure it to send e-mails to Office 365. If you have a new domain, you will want to configure this as a new "remote" SMTP domain (see Figure 10-44). Once you have configured the remote domain, select the domain and right-click on properties (see Figure 10-45). Configure the basic services.

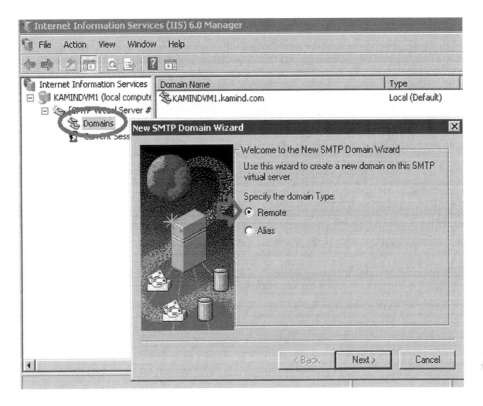

Figure 10-44. *Remote Domain Setup IIS*

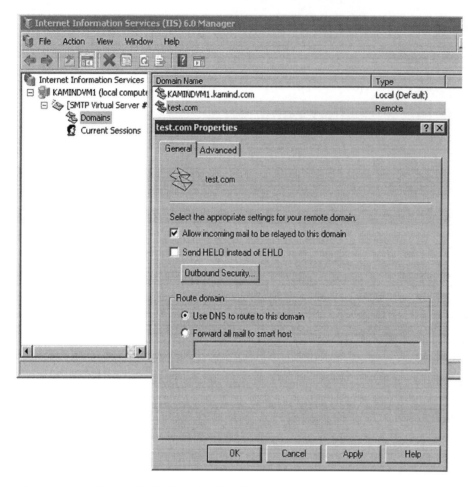

Figure 10-45. *Allowing Mail to be Relayed to the Server*

Step 3: Add Access Information

After you have set up the domain, right-click and select the properties of the virtual server (SMTP Virtual Server #1). Then select the Access tab and then click Relay. Select the computers that can access this relay server. As an example, enter the IP address of all of the devices (copiers and so on) that are using this service to relay to Office 365. Only enter the IP addresses of the devices that you trust—see Figures 10-46 and 10-47.

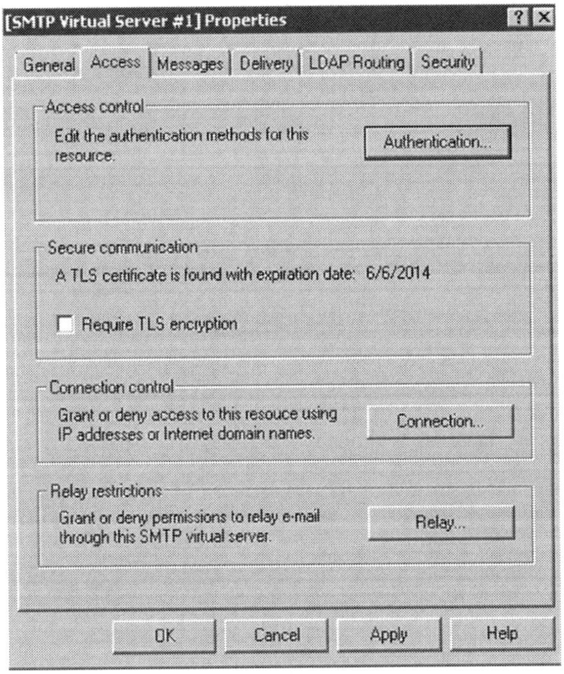

Figure 10-46. *Configuring SMTP Server*

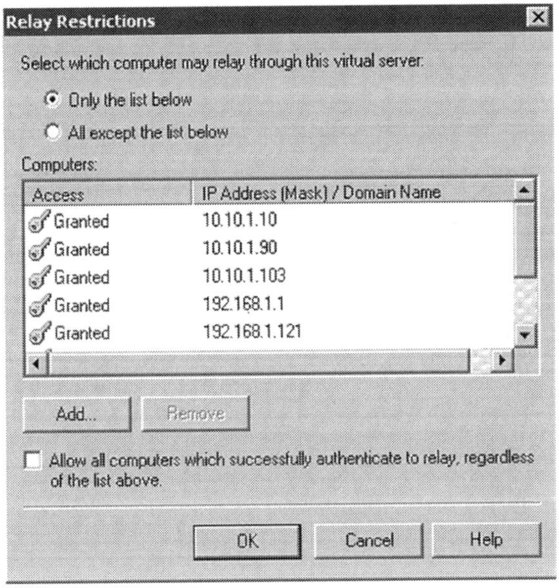

Figure 10-47. *Restricting Access*

Step 4: Set Up Authentication

On the Access tab, select authentication, then verify that anonymous is selected, then select OK (see Figure 10-48). You are using anonymous because you are going to restrict the relay in Office 365 to only allow e-mail relay from a specific IP address.

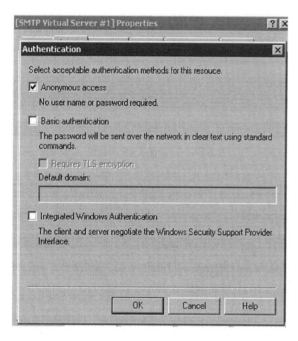

Figure 10-48. *Setting the Access Mode to Anonymous*

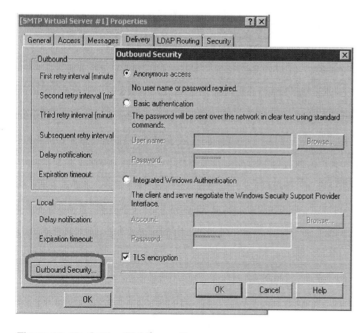

Figure 10-49. *Setting TLS Encryption*

Step 5: Set Outbound Security

Select the Outbound connection and specify the port, as shown in Figure 10-50.

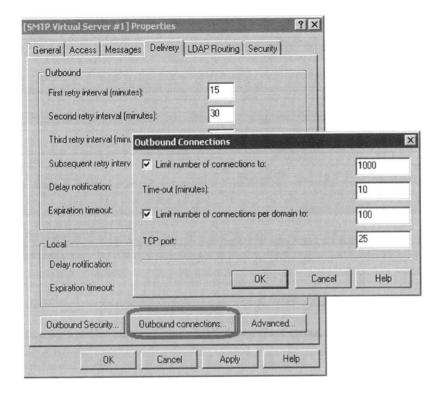

Figure 10-50. *Setting Port Delivery*

Step 6: Configure the Office 365 Inbound Connector

Since you are using anonymous connection as a trusted relay, you need to add the IP address to the Office 365 EOP inbound connector and set the new SPF record to DNS (refer back to the earlier information you collected from Office 365).

To add the Office 365 inbound connector, log into Office 365, select Service Settings, and then choose Custom Mail Rules (see Figure 10-51). In Figure 10-52, select Connectors, then add a "new inbound" connector. Enter the static IP address.

Figure 10-51. Setting Custom Connector

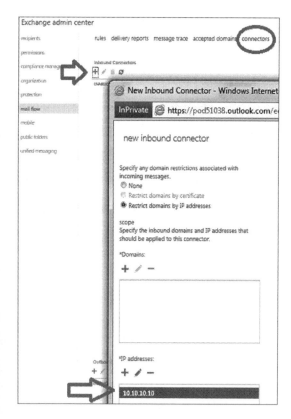

Figure 10-52. Adding the Inbound Connector

Step 7: Configure a Bypass to the Spam Filter

After you have built the inbound connector, you need to add a "bypass spam" rule so the e-mail traffic will skip the spam filter and connection filtering. To add the Office 365 custom rule, log in to Office 365 and select Service Settings. Then choose Custom Mail Rules (see Figure 10-53). Select Rules, and then select Bypass Spam Filter.

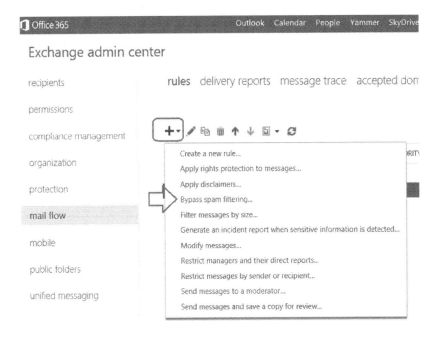

Figure 10-53. *Bypass Spam Filter Option*

Once you have selected the bypass spam filter options, select "IP Addresses in Any of These Ranges" (see Figure 10-54).

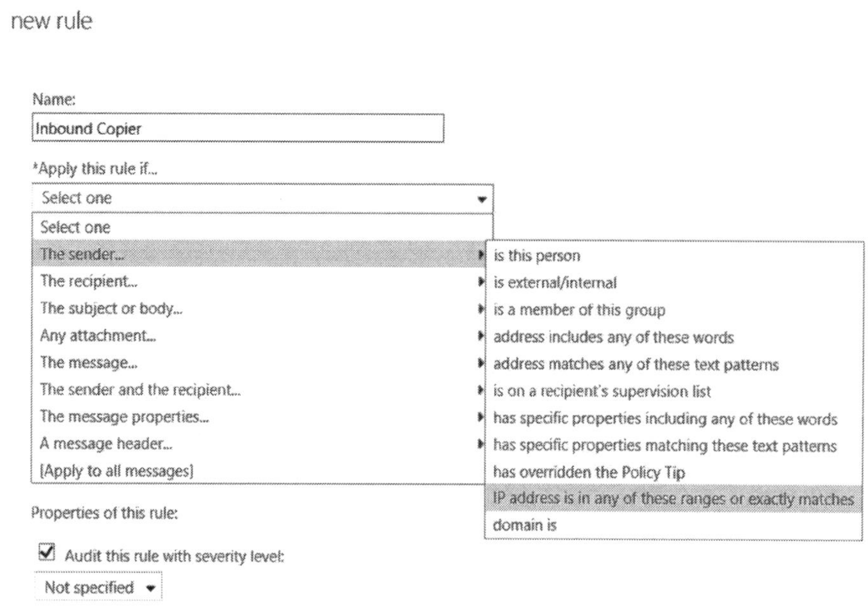

new rule

Name:

Inbound Copier

*Apply this rule if...

Select one	▾

Select one	
The sender...	▸ is this person
The recipient...	▸ is external/internal
The subject or body...	▸ is a member of this group
Any attachment...	▸ address includes any of these words
The message...	▸ address matches any of these text patterns
The sender and the recipient...	▸ is on a recipient's supervision list
The message properties...	▸ has specific properties including any of these words
A message header...	▸ has specific properties matching these text patterns
[Apply to all messages]	has overridden the Policy Tip
	IP address is in any of these ranges or exactly matches
	domain is

Properties of this rule:

☑ Audit this rule with severity level:

Not specified ▾

Figure 10-54. *Adding the Bypass Spam Filter Rule*

Enter the selected IP addresses (see Figure 10-55) and save the rule. At this point, any e-mail message that is sent from the device should arrive at the destination e-mail account in Office 365.

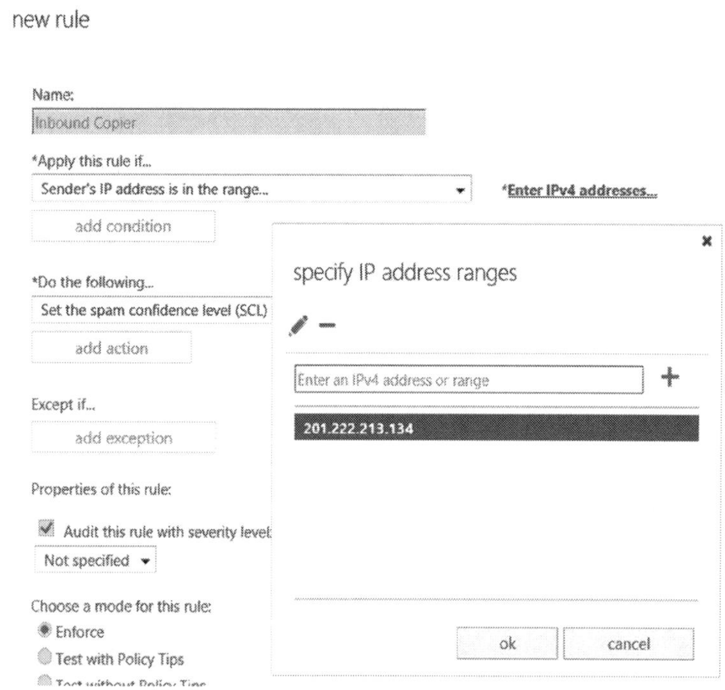

new rule

Name:

Inbound Copier

*Apply this rule if...

Sender's IP address is in the range...	▾	*Enter IPv4 addresses...

add condition

*Do the following...

Set the spam confidence level (SCL)

add action

Except if...

add exception

Properties of this rule:

☑ Audit this rule with severity level:

Not specified ▾

Choose a mode for this rule:

● Enforce
○ Test with Policy Tips
○ Test without Policy Tips

specify IP address ranges   ✕

✎ —

Enter an IPv4 address or range	+

201.222.213.134

ok	cancel

Figure 10-55. *Adding an IP Address Bypass for Spam Filter*

You have completed the configuration of a custom sender, set up the SPF record, and added the IP address to bypass the spam processing. There are some additional rules you need to remember about the sending device:

- The sending device must be from the same domain as the Office 365 destination.

- When you send to an external user, you will bypass Office 365 (see Figure 10-56).

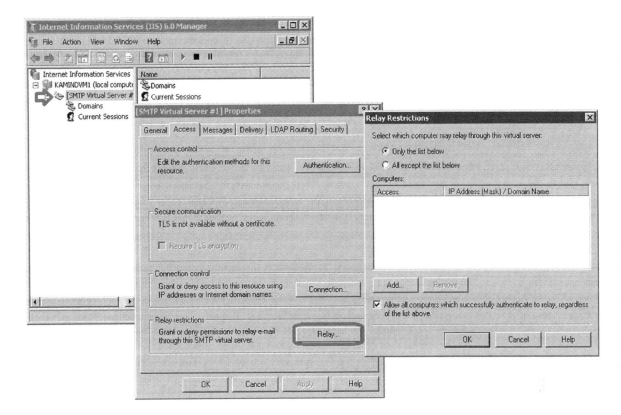

Figure 10-56. *Adding a Default Mail Relay*

Option 3: Sending to Office 365 Using an Authenticated Office 365 User

This configuration is very similar to the Option 1, except that you are going to use an account to send mail to other internal and external users. Why would you use this approach instead of Option 1? There are two possible answers:

- You want to have a log of the content that is being sent to the Office 365.

- You have a dynamic IP address assigned.

There may be other reasons, but 90 percent of the users fall into these two categories.

Step 1: Create an Office Account

Create an Office 365 account in Office 365, or create an account local active directory. Depending on the requirements, if you need to record information for compliance needs, then choose exchange plan 2.

Step 2: Configure the Default SMTP Server

In Option 1, you used the remote domain to relay e-mail to Office 365. In this case, you are going to configure the default server. Select the IIS manager, and right-click on the default domain (see Figure 10-56). Select Access, and then select Relay. Add the local IP address of the machines that are authorized to use this sender.

Step 3: Configure the Default SMTP Server

Configure the Access control to allow all authorized senders to anonymous connect to this SMTP virtual server and relay e-mail through the server. Select the Access tab, and then select the Authentication button. Make sure the anonymous checkbox is selected.

Step 4: Configure the SMTP Smart Host

At the beginning of this section you looked up the user account that you were going to use to act a secured relay, and determine the address. The smart host is at `smtp.office365.com`. Enter the smart host (see Figure 10-57.)

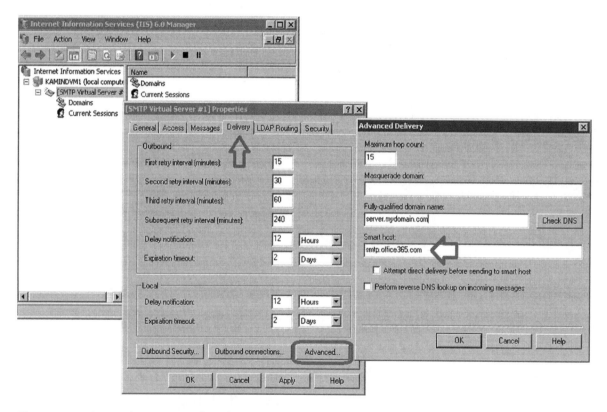

Figure 10-57. *Setting the Smart Host for Relay*

Step 5: Configure the Outbound Connection

The `smtp.office365.com` is not at the standard port. It is located at port 587. In this case, configure the outbound security to use port 587 (see Figure 10-58).

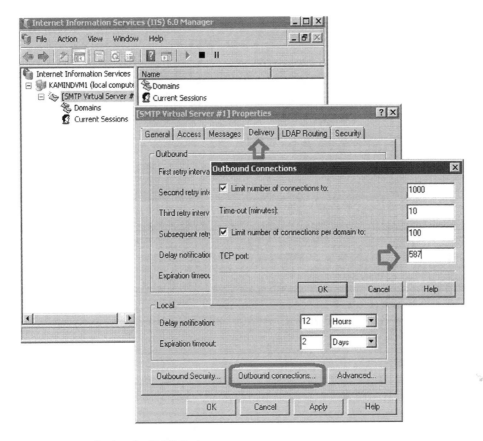

Figure 10-58. *Setting the SMTP Port*

Step 6: Add the Trusted User Account to Send

The next step is to add the trusted user account that will be used to log in to Office 365 and to send messages to internal and external users (see Figure 10-59). This is a trusted user account, so allow only trusted senders to use this relay. Make sure the TLS encryption is checked.

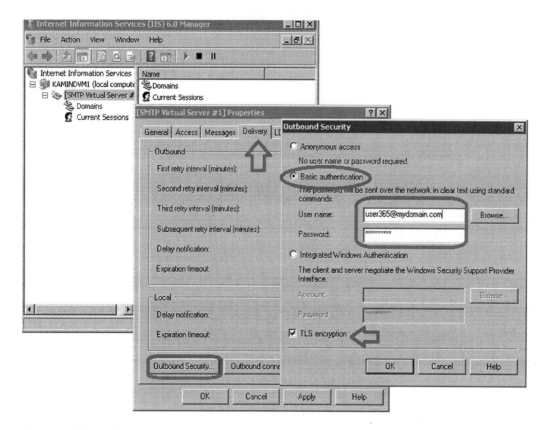

Figure 10-59. *Adding Trusted Users*

Step 7: Optional SPF Record and Inbound Connector

If the IP address of the Internet gateway is not a dynamic IP address, you can add an inbound connector to Office 365. You will use the same process discussed in Option 1, Step 7. Do not forget to add the SPF record for the connection into your DNS zone file.

Step 8: Grant Send as Permissions to the IIS Account

If you are sending to Office 365 and external users (or sending on behalf of another users), you need to grant permission to the sending account (in the SMTP IIS relay server) send as permission. To accomplish this, you need to run the PowerShell command listed here:

```
$LiveCred = Get-Credential
Import-module msonline
Connect-MSOLService -Credential $LiveCred -Verbose

$Session = New-PSSession -ConfigurationName Microsoft.Exchange-ConnectionUri
https://ps.outlook.com/powershell/ -Credential $LiveCred -Authentication Basic -AllowRedirection

Import-PSSession $Session -Allow Clobber
```

```
# Add the permissions to sender to send to the recipient
Get-Mailbox | add-recipientpermission -trustee "IIS user account" - Accessrights sendas
-confirm:$false

#Clean up and close the session
Remove-PSSession $Session
```

Option 4: Sending Through Office 365 to External Users Using a Certificate

Exchange Online Protection uses either IIS or a device sender. If you require encryption you will need to import the public certificate to the device that is sending the e-mail. As an example, if you are using IIS SMTP server discussed in Options 2 and 3, you need to manually import the domain certificate, public certificate. It is recommended that it be a wildcard certificate. You can use a device-specific one, but this adds to the complexity of the task. If you do not use a public certificate for encryption, the e-mail will be sent to Office 365 in clear text, unencrypted.

Step 1: Import the Pubic Certificate

If you choose to use IIS and the SMTP server, you will need to import the certificate into the private store of the computer account. If you are using a custom device, you can import the certificate into the custom sender. Figure 10-40 shows you how to import the certificate into a Windows server using the certificate management (MMC option). When you import the certificate, you import the certificate into the personal certificate store, as shown in Figure 10-60.

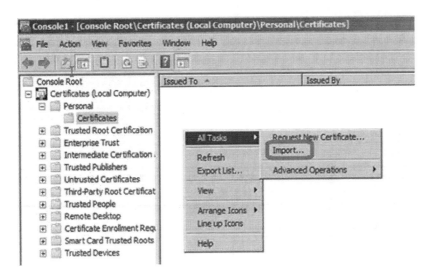

Figure 10-60. *Importing a Certificate into the Private Certificate Store*

Step 2: Configure the Default SMTP Server

In Option 1, you used the remote domain to relay e-mail to Office 365. In this case, you are going to configure the default server. Select the IIS manager and right-click on the default domain (see Figure 10-61). Select Access and then Relay. Add the local IP address of the machines that are authorized to use this sender.

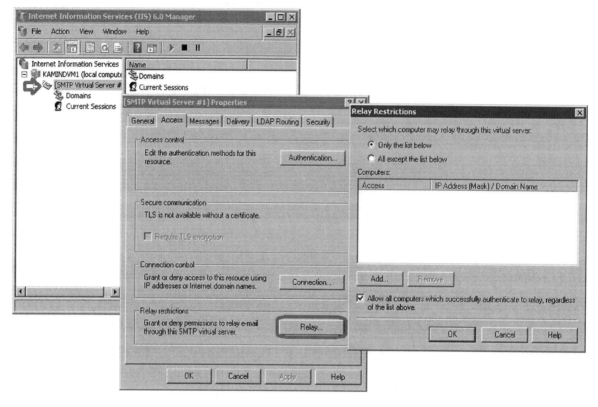

Figure 10-61. *Adding a Default Mail Relay*

Step 3: Configure the Default SMTP Server

Configure the Access control to allow all authorized senders to anonymously connect to this SMTP virtual server and relay e-mail through the server. Select the Access tab, and then select the Authentication button (see the button in Figure 10-61). Make sure the anonymous checkbox is selected.

Step 4: Configure the SMTP Smart Host

At the beginning of this section you looked up the user account that you were going to use to act a secured relay, and determine the address. There are two possible endpoints that you can use. In Option 2, you used the exchange server endpoint. In Option 3, you used the EOP endpoint. The difference in using this approach is that you no longer require an Office 365 account. You can send directly to Office 365.

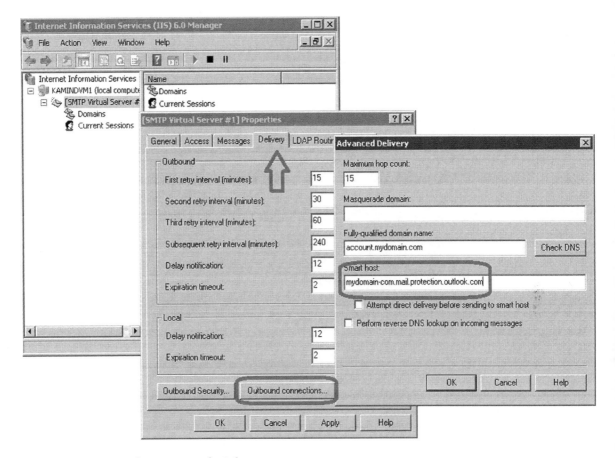

Figure 10-62. *Setting the Smart Host for Relay*

Step 5: Configure the Outbound Connection and TLS Encryption

The SMTP port is the default port 25. With the certificate installed in Step 1, you enable TLS encryption (see Figure 10-63).

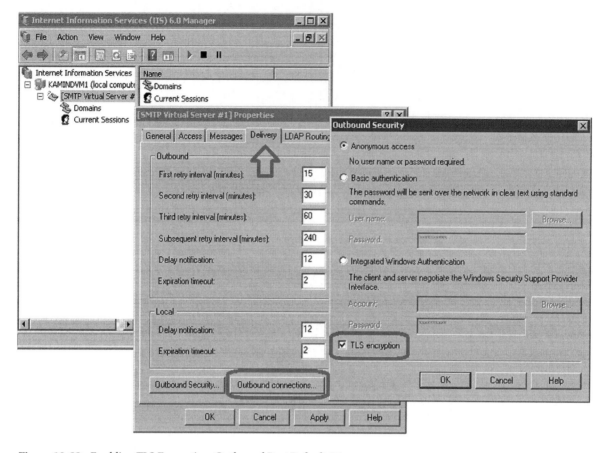

Figure 10-63. *Enabling TLS Encryption: Outbound Port Default 25*

Step 6: Configure the Office 365 Inbound Connector

The EOP connector is configured with a trusted inbound connector that uses the public certificate. To access the admin center, log in to Office 365 and select Custom Mail Rules. See Figure 10-64. Then select the connectors and add an inbound connector (see Figure 10-65).

Figure 10-64. *Selecting Custom Mail Rules*

Figure 10-65. *Adding the Inbound Connector*

To add the Office 365 inbound connector, log in to Office 365 and select Service Settings. Then choose Custom Mail Rules (see Figure 10-66). In Figure 10-67, select Connectors, and then add a "new inbound" connector. Set the following parameters:

- Select a name for the connector

- Select on-premise

- Select force TLS

- Enter the public certificate name

- Enter the static IP address of the external connector

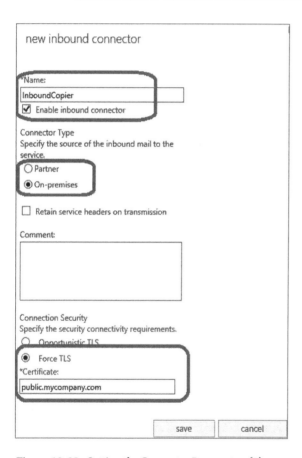

Figure 10-66. *Setting the Connector Parameters (1)*

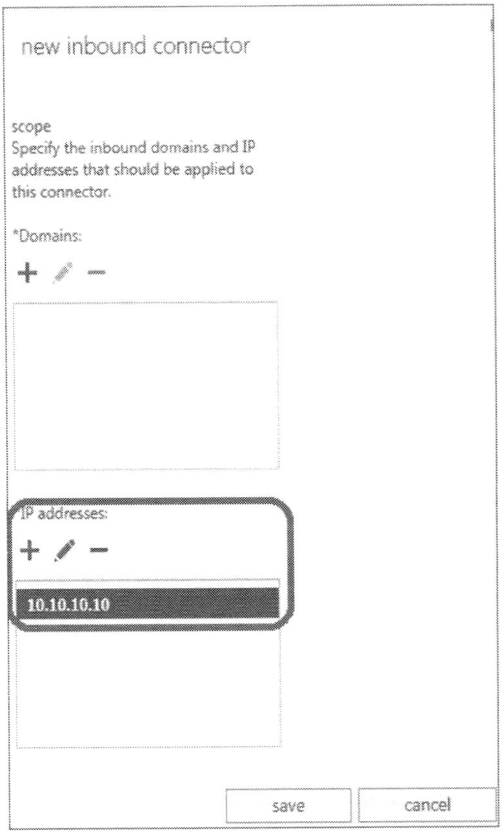

Figure 10-67. *Setting the Connector Parameters (2)*

Step 7: Configure a Bypass to the Spam Filter

After you have built the inbound connector, you need to add a "bypass spam" rule so the e-mail traffic will skip the spam filter and connection filtering. To add the Office 365 custom rule, log in to Office 365, and select Service Settings. Then choose Custom Mail Rules. As shown in Figure 10-68, select Rules. Finally, select Bypass Spam Filter.

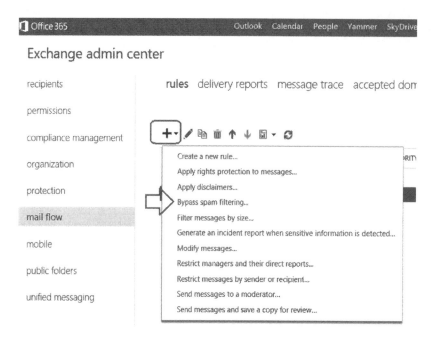

Figure 10-68. *Bypass Spam Filter Option*

Once you have selected the bypass Spam Filter options, select "IP Addresses in Any of These Ranges" (see Figure 10-69).

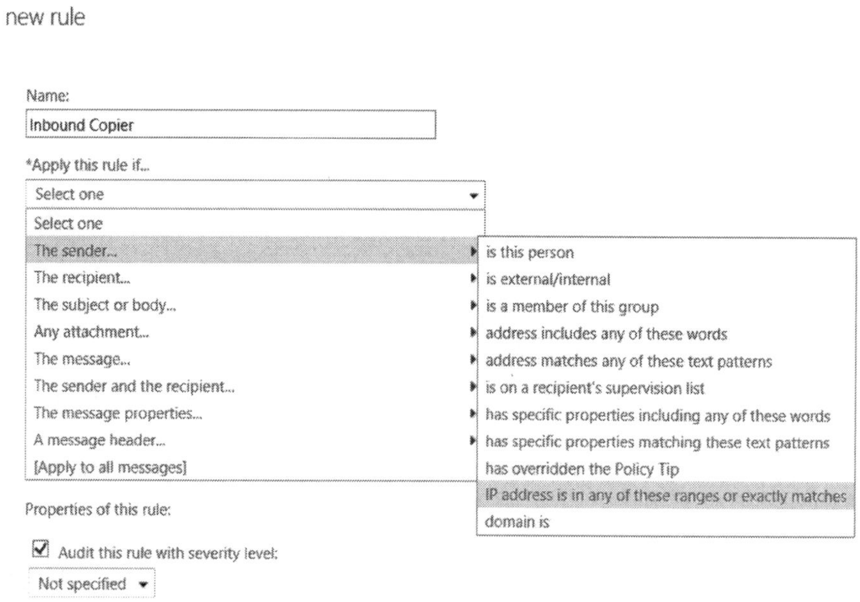

Figure 10-69. *Adding the Bypass Spam Filter Rule*

Enter the selected IP addresses (see Figure 10-70) and save the rule. At this point, the any e-mail message that is sent from the device should arrive at the destination e-mail in Office 365.

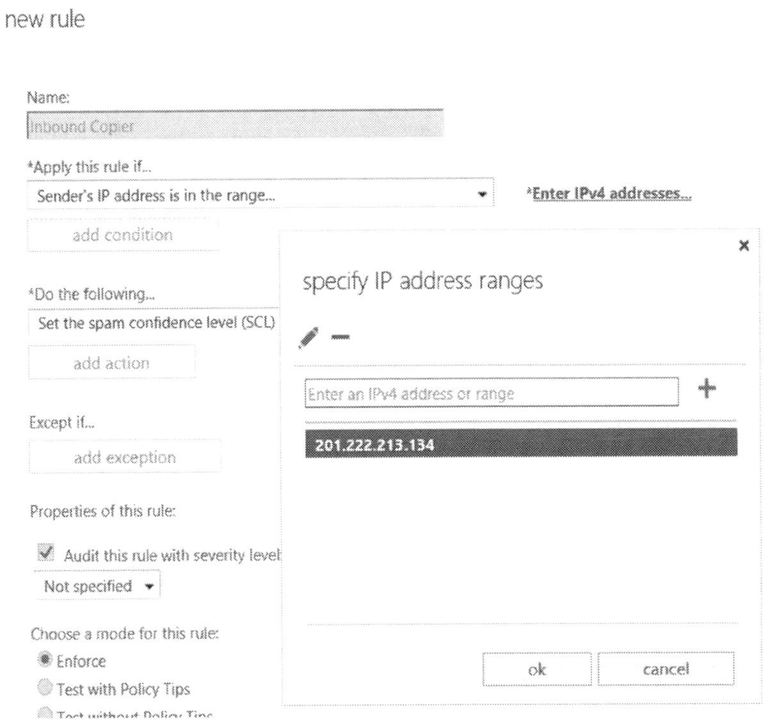

Figure 10-70. *Adding IP Address Bypass for Spam Filter*

Step 8: Optional SPF Record and Inbound Connector

Add the SPF record to your DNS zone file. This will ensure that the messages received in the EOP connector are processed as coming from a trusted sender.

Step 9: Grant Send as Permissions to the IIS Account

If you are sending to Office 365 external users (or sending on behalf of another users), you need to grant permission to the sending account (in the SMTP IIS relay server), send as permission. To accomplish this, you need to run the PowerShell command listed here:

```
$LiveCred = Get-Credential
Import-module msonline
Connect-MSOLService -Credential $LiveCred -Verbose

$Session = New-PSSession -ConfigurationName Microsoft.Exchange-ConnectionUri https://ps.outlook.com/
powershell/ -Credential $LiveCred -Authentication Basic -AllowRedirection
```

Reference Links

There is a lot of information about Office 365 on the Web; the issue is finding the right site. The information contained in this chapter is a combination of our experiences in doing deployments and support information that has been published by third parties.

Exchange Online Protection – Overview

http://technet.microsoft.com/en-us/library/jj723119(v=exchg.150).aspx

Exchange Online Protection – Capabilities

http://technet.microsoft.com/en-us/library/jj723115(v=exchg.150).aspx

Exchange Online Protection – Setting up mail flow

http://technet.microsoft.com/en-us/library/jj723133(v=exchg.150).aspx

Setting content-filtering policies

http://technet.microsoft.com/en-us/library/jj200684.aspx

Spam filter junk mail reporting tool

http://www.microsoft.com/en-us/download/details.aspx?id=18275

Adding the SMTP sender to a Windows Server (2008R2, 2012)

http://support.microsoft.com/kb/2600912
http://support.microsoft.com/kb/2799338

Setting up an SMTP mail relay in Office 365

http://community.office365.com/en-us/wikis/exchange/how-to-setup-an-smtp-relay-in-office-365.aspx

How to set up a certificate on IIS 7.0

http://www.iis.net/learn/manage/configuring-security/how-to-set-up-ssl-on-iis

Next Steps

This chapter focused on the configuration and set up of Exchange Online Protection spam filers. Office 365 is interesting to explore. There is much more to do depending on your Office 365 configuration. The key chapters you need to review for your Office 365 deployment are as follows:

- **Chapter 5** —SharePoint Administration
  - SharePoint administration and design can be simple or complex, depending on your business needs. This chapter provides you with a basic overview of the configuration necessary to be up and running using the Office 365 team site. This chapter describes site design and construction issues as well as the full SharePoint Administration functions for Office 365.

- **Chapter 7**—Windows Intune Administration

  - The secret to an optimal Office 365 site is the management of the desktop to ensure that updates are current, and the user antivirus is functioning. Windows Intune is a desktop management tool that addresses these issues and reduces the administrator's effort in desktop management, and improves the user's experience.

- **Chapter 8**—Office 365 Administration

  - This chapter describes the different administration centers in Office 365 and the most common tools that you would use to administrate your Office 365 company. Depending on your Office 365 services, there are five possible administration tools. This chapter focuses on the Office 365, Exchange, and Lync administration centers. The SharePoint and Windows Intune administration centers are described in their own chapters. We close the chapter with using PowerShell to manage your Office 365 environment.

- **Chapter 9**—Compliance and Data Loss Prevention

  - Business must adapt their mail document storage systems to correctly process the electronic communication based on regulatory oversight. The Compliance and Data Loss Prevention (DLP) provides this capability to allow business to manage their communications, and protect the business against simple mistakes in its electronic communications. Office 365 includes integrated discovery, and supports legal discovery and audit requirements.

■ ■ ■

## CHAPTER 11

Office 365 DirSync, ADFS, Single Sign On and Exchange Federation

An Office 365 site is an organizational unit complete with its own security components and e-mail domain: @<company name>onmicrosoft.com or @<company name>.microsoftonline.com. The Office 365 combination of services and administration is an Active Directory organization. Your onsite equipment may be organized as a Windows Active Directory structure. If you have a large organization, you will have a local security login (Active Directory if you are using Windows Server) to access all of your services and other network equipment. This chapter focuses on the integration of the local Active Directory to the Office 365 Active Directory. There are many different ways to integrate the two different Active Directory structures, depending upon the business requirements. The driving force for integration is Single Sign on (SSO), but SSO has a price with the complexity of the IT infrastructure. Most organizations only need Directory Synchronization with password integration. Table 11-1 lists the different options of Active Directory integration.

Table 11-1. *Active Directory Integration*

Active Directory Integration	Capabilities	Requirements
No Integration	Two separate logins Office 365 and local system	n/a
Sync local AD to Office 365	Integrates Active Directory using sync tool	Requires Directory Synchronization server
Sync local AD and Synchronize passwords to Office 365	Integrates Active Directory using sync tool and enable password write back	Requires Directory Synchronization server with write back configuration
Federate AD to Office 365	Onsite server controls security	Requires a ADFS and Proxy server
Federate Exchange to Office 365	Allows mailbox moves from local to cloud and back	Requires the purchase of Exchange server

The method you choose depends upon the end user experience. Most companies with less than 500 employees choose Directory Synchronization with password integration. The deciding point on Directory Synchronization versus Active Directory is based upon security concerns.

No Integration

No integration of Active Directory is the simplest form of all integration. The Office 365 security structure is independent of the local On-site servers. There is no limit to the size of the organization that uses this model. We have deployed large and small customers with no integration to local services.

Directory Sync with local AD to Office 365

The sync tool for the local Active directly to Office 365 is known as Directory Synchronization or DirSync. This tool is used to replicate the Active Directory to the Office 365 site (see Figure 11-1). The users Active Directory objects are replicated to Office 365. When you assign a license to the user account, the local mailbox is created unless the user account has a local Exchange mailbox. The local user mailbox must be removed from the on premises exchange server before the Office365 user account mailbox is created in Office 365.

	DISPLAY NAME ▲	USER NAME	STATUS
☐	A Test	AtestUser@kamind.com	Synced with Active Directo
☐	adminservice	adminservice@kamind.microsoftonline.com	In cloud
☐	aspnet_wp account	ASPNET@kamind.com	Synced with Active Directo
☐	aspnetuser	aspnetuser@kamind.com	Synced with Active Directo
☐	backupuser	backupuser@kamind.com	Synced with Active Directo

Figure 11-1. *Directory Sync users from Onsite Server*

Active Directory information is synced from the server to the Office 365 tenant. Users that are not synced are represented by a different icon, as shown in Figure 11-1 (see admin user), versus the other users with a sync symbol.

When you set up Directory Synchronization, you are syncing the Active Directory security structure, rules and objects, but you are not syncing the passwords of the local users to the Office 365. Password synchronization requires a separate tool or the implementation of Federation services, known as Active Directory Federation Services or ADFS.

Directory Sync Caution

Microsoft Directory Sync is designed to work with the on-site Active Directory. Your on-site Active Directory user's accounts are synced to the cloud. If the account is synced as a "Mail Enabled Users" or "MEUs," you can create a cloud mailbox. If the user account is not a MEU, you cannot create a cloud mailbox when a license is assigned. By default, if there is an On Premises Exchange server, with a mailbox for the user account, that account is synced as a non- MEU's user account (cannot create a mailbox). If the mailbox does not exist in the cloud, then the e-mail cannot be migrated to the Office 365.

When you use DirSync, you are required to use Microsoft tools to move user information from the local Exchange server to Office 365. At the final step in a Microsoft mailbox move, the AD values of the account are changed to reflect a MEU. These values are:

- *mail*: The primary SMTP of the cloud mailbox.

- *proxyAddresses*: Values from both the On Premises mailbox and the cloud mailbox.

- *targetAddress*: Read from the On Premises mailbox; the value is the primary SMTP of the cloud mailbox. This is converted to a contact when the mailbox is moved.

Once the MS tools (Exchange Server remote move or a cutover move) are used to move a mailbox, the Microsoft tools **delete the On Premises mailbox, and convert the user exchange account to contact**. If you choose to use external tools (such as Migration Wiz), you will need to manually convert the mailbox. Usually the conversion is the deletion of the mailbox and removing of the exchange server. When the proper MEU AD parameters are set and synced to Office 365, the Office 365 mailbox is created (once a license is assigned of the object).

Directory Synchronization (DirSync)

DirSync can be enabled or disabled. However, once you enable DirSync (see Figure 11-2) you are committed to the Microsoft migration process; if you have an On Premises Exchange Server. Even if you choose to disable DirSync, the Cloud AD has already been changed, and it does not revert back. If DirSync is enabled, you are committed to follow through with the Microsoft Migration process. When you disable DirSync, the sync objects revert back to local control, however the AD does not revert to "clean" pre-DirSync state.

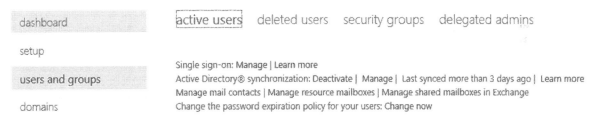

Figure 11-2. *DirSync configuration*

To disable DirSync, just select the deactivate option (next to the "Active Directory Synchronization") on the Directory Synchronization interface. Once DirSync is deactivated, a message will be displayed that takes up to 72 hours for the object to be connected.

Using PowerShell to Stop/Start DirSync

You can also accomplish the same activity by using PowerShell. In this case, you would use the following commands:

1. Turn off the DirSync by running the cmdlet: **Set-MsolDirSyncEnabled -EnableDirSync $false**

2. Assign licenses, create Office 365 mailboxes, and migrate e-mail

3. Turn on the DirSync by running the cmdlet: **Set-MsolDirSyncEnabled -EnableDirSync $true**

Remember, the Office 365 site will stabilize in four hours, and you cannot enable DirSync until the site has stabilized.

Server Types required for DirSync and Active Directory Federation Services

The installation server needs to be 64 bits, and either a 2008R2 or a Server 2012 member server. Directory Sync can be installed on a domain controller (but this is not recommended). ADFS federation servers can be installed on either a Doman Controller C or a member server. The proxy servers can be installed on any server (except domain controllers).

Using DirSync with Password Synchronization

If you desire to synchronize the local Active Directory with Office 365, you can enable password synchronization. The local password is "synced" with Office 365, and the process is encrypted. There are some cautions if this is enabled.

- This password synchronization model is not as strong as a federated security discussed later in this chapter.

- The password can be changed on site and in the cloud (optional).

- If the password is changed in the cloud and the write back is enabled (off by default), this is written back to the on-site Active Directory (AD). Any global administrator can changed the cloud password.

If Directory Synchronization is enabled, the administrator needs to be aware of the limitation on password reset and the impact to it on site security policies. If a strong method of security is required, Active Directory Federation services should be deployed.

Federate AD to Office 365

Federation to Office 365 uses ADFS and DirSync to provide a Single Sign-On password integration. The problem with this approach is that it requires a minimum of four servers to have the necessary robustness to handle Office 365 integration. The security servers are robust and are integrated tightly with Office 365. If the local service that is running the ADFS servers go offline, users will not be able to log in to Office 365 services. The reason for this is simple. The primary domain security control is on site. The Office 365 Active Directory services must validate access with the local domain controller. If the local AD is not online (through ADFS), access cannot be authenticated.

Federate Exchange to Office 365

Federate Exchange to Office 365 allows the local Exchange administrator to use "mailbox move" to move the mailbox from the local server to the Office 365 server. This approach is called a remote mailbox move. Federated Exchange builds upon Directory Synchronization and ADFS.

Next Steps

As you can see there are many different steps you can take, depending upon your need and your overall objective. Regardless of the approach that you take, there are some critical steps for integrating to Office 365:

- Speed of Conversion

- Directory Synchronization – cutover or Federation

- Single Sign On?

- Exchange Migration strategy – Federation?

These different issues and approaches will determine the migration approach you decide to take. In the previous sections, we discussed different cutover migrations. In the following section we will review the steps necessary for Exchange Federation. The first step in this process is to implement Single Sign On.

This Chapter assumes that you want to implement full Active Directory (AD) Federation Services, with Exchange Federation. If you are only going to implement a portion of the integration to Office 365, follow these steps outlined in Table 11-2. The steps are additive. If you choose to implement Exchange Federation, you need to implement all of the previous steps.

Table 11-2. *Implementing the Integration to Office 365*

Deployment Goal	Steps to deploy	End Results
AD Synchronization	Step 1, 2, 3	Onsite AD is synced to Office 365
AD Synchronization with Password	Step 4	On site AD passwords are sync to Office 365
Enable AD Single Sign On	Step 5, 6, 7	AD integrated to Office 365, single login and password
Exchange Federation 2010	Step 8	Exchange integration to Office 365

Steps to Implement AD Sync, Single Sign On and Exchange Federation

Moving toward Exchange Server is a two-step process. The first step is to implement Active Directory Federation services (ADFS) with Directory Synchronization. The second step is to implement Exchange Server (if you desire to have an integrated Exchange service on site). If you choose to only implement ADFS, then skip the Exchange Server section.

Step 1: Verify Active Directory – Exchange Server Status

When you implement DirSync, the mailboxes in the Office 365 mailbox will not be created if there is an Exchange Server installed and active on your network. If you do not have an Exchange Server, and you are planning to configure DirSync, then verify that the Exchange Server is not present in Active Directory. To verify the Exchange Server status, select "Sites and Services" from the Administrator menu. In the Site and services control panel (Figure 11-3), select "Show Services Node." Expand the Active Directory and look for the Exchange Services.

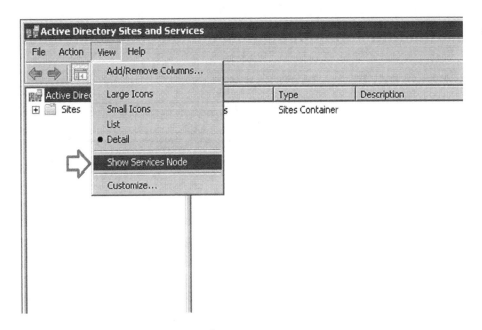

Figure 11-3. *Show Services in Sites and Services*

If the Exchange Server is not present, then the Active Directory will look like Figure 11-4.

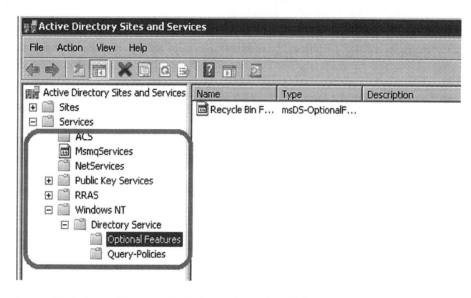

Figure 11-4. *Active Directory - No Exchange Server Installed*

If the Exchange Server was present on your network, then the Active Directory will look like Figure 11-5. If you do not have an Exchange Server and the information is present in Active Directory, the server was not uninstalled. You will need to engage your Microsoft partner or submit a service request to Microsoft to assist you in the cleanup of the improperly uninstalled Exchange Server.

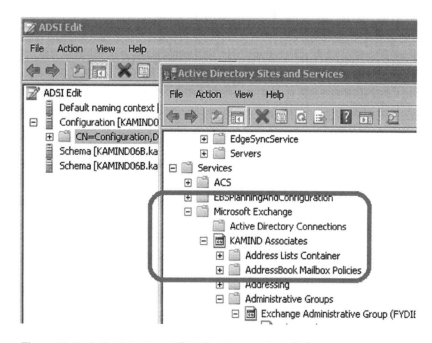

Figure 11-5. *Active Directory with Exchange server installed*

Step 2: Installation of the 3.5 .NET Framework and 4.0 .NET Framework

The Directory Sync and ADFS Integration tool requires that you install the .NET framework 3.5 and 4.0. The .NET Framework is required for access into the compliance monitoring center for Office 365. The .Net 3.5 framework is a server feature (See Figure 11-6) and the .NET 4.0 and 4.5 frameworks are downloaded directly from the Microsoft download centers.

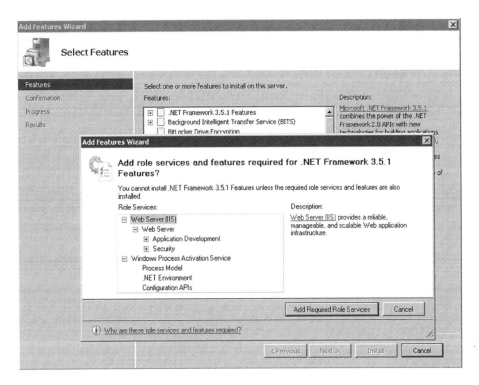

Figure 11-6. *Installation of .NET Framework 3.5 server feature*

Install .NET Framework 3.5

To install the .NET 3.5 Framework, go to your Server Manager, and select "features." Find the .NET 3.51 features and install all of the default features requested (Figure 11-6).

■ **Note**   If you have versions of the .NET framework newer then 3.5, you will need to uninstall the new versions to install the older versions.

Install .NET Framework 4.0

To install the .NET 4.0 Framework, go to Microsoft Downloads (see Figure 11-7) and search for ".Net 4 full web install" and download and save the version of the framework that you wish to use (either standalone or web installer).

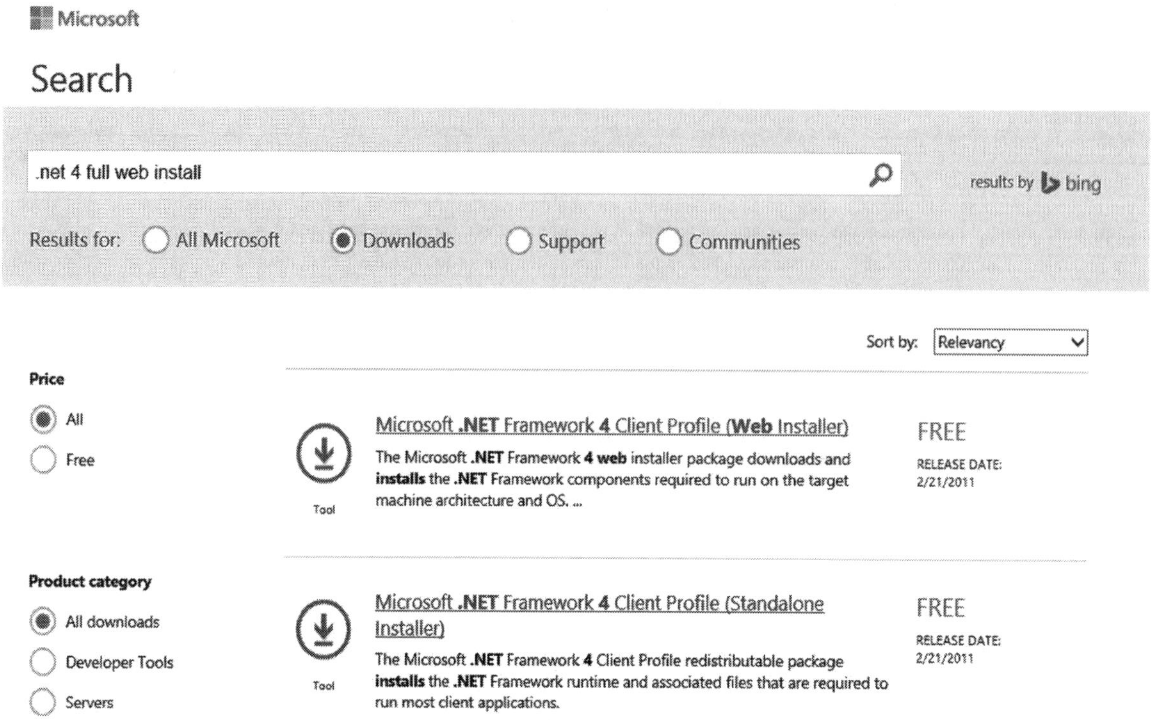

Figure 11-7. *Download .NET 4 Framework from Microsoft Downloads*

Step 3: Create the Admin Accounts

DirSync (and ADFS) will require an Office 365 Global Admin account and an On-Site Domain admin, as well as a member of the Enterprise Admins group. Create these two accounts.

■ **Note**   When you install DirSync or ADFS services, follow these two steps: (1) login as this on-site domain admin account to install the software and (2) download the software, right click and run as an administrator. This account needs to be explicitly added as an *Administrator* on the local machine administrator group (where DirSync is installed), and as a member of the Domain Enterprise Admin group.

Step 4: Clean Up Active Directory

Before you can install either Directory Synchronization Services or Active Directory Federation Services, you need to clean up your Active Directory. The most important step is the validation of the Active Directory and the correction of any Active Directory object. The detailed steps to run this tool are described later in this Chapter under *"Active Directory Cleanup – Check."* It is worthwhile to run the check because the online tool requires all of the necessary system updates required to make DirSync run. One note of caution: before you run Directory Sync, inform your users that the password cannot have any part of the login name, otherwise DirSync will fail. To run the test tool, use the link: `https://onramp.office365.com/` and verify Active Directory configuration. The results of the check will look like Figure 11-8.

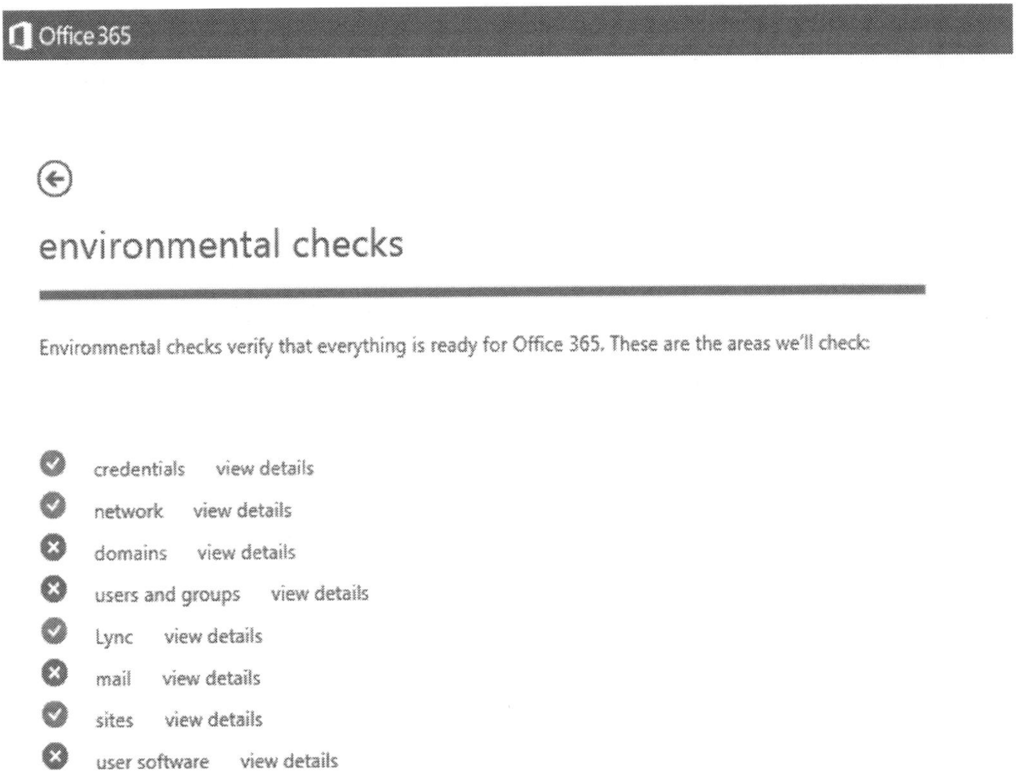

 Office 365

(←)

environmental checks

Environmental checks verify that everything is ready for Office 365. These are the areas we'll check:

- ✓ credentials   view details
- ✓ network   view details
- ✗ domains   view details
- ✗ users and groups   view details
- ✓ Lync   view details
- ✗ mail   view details
- ✓ sites   view details
- ✗ user software   view details

Figure 11-8. Results of AD check using the Onramp tool

■ **Note**   User passwords that have the same name as the users will not sync to the cloud and will fail with the Directory Sync tool.

The Onramp tool will analyze the Active Directory and make recommend changes. You do not need to implement all of the changes before you run DirSync. However, review them and understand why you want to change (or delay) them. The user objects that have errors will not replicate to Office 365. These should be addressed before you implement DirSync and Active Directory Federation Services.

The most common error that you could run into is the "you must have Microsoft online services sign-in assistant version 7.0 or greater" error. If you run into this error, please review the "DirSync: Installation error – Missing Online service Sign in" section later in this chapter.

Step 5: Optional - Extended Active Directory

In some cases, you may wish to have access to the extended Active Directory Object information for Exchange. If you wish to add this to your current environment, then install the exchange server Scheme and Forest extensions. These extensions are installed from the Exchange server installation DVD. You only install the extensions, and not the Exchange Server software.

If you are running Exchange server 2003, then upgrade the scheme to Exchange 2007. If you are running Exchange 2007 or later, there is no need to extend the Scheme, unless you are planning to install a new exchange server. The Exchange 2007 DVD is located on the MSDN Site for download. If you do not have access to the Exchange

Server 2007 DVD, use the Exchange 2010 DVD. To find necessary information on Scheme extensions search for "Exchange 2007 forestprep" and follow the instructions from TechNet. The Scheme extensions can be installed from a production or trial DVD.

Step 6: Install Directory Synchronization

There are four steps required to set up Active Directory Synchronization, the most important step is the validation of the Active Directory and the correction of any Active Directory object. This should have already been completed when you validated the Active Directory.

Figure 11-9. Setup for Directory Synchronization

■ **Note** Make sure you login as an user for the admin service account that will be used to configure the on premises DirSync service. The DirSync service may not install correctly if the service account is configured incorrectly.

To start up synchronization, select users and select setup Active Directory Synchronization (see Figure 11-9). Once you have the setup screen (Figure 11-10), follow the steps indicated. On step 3, select "Activate." This will allow the Directory Synchronization to start on Office 365.

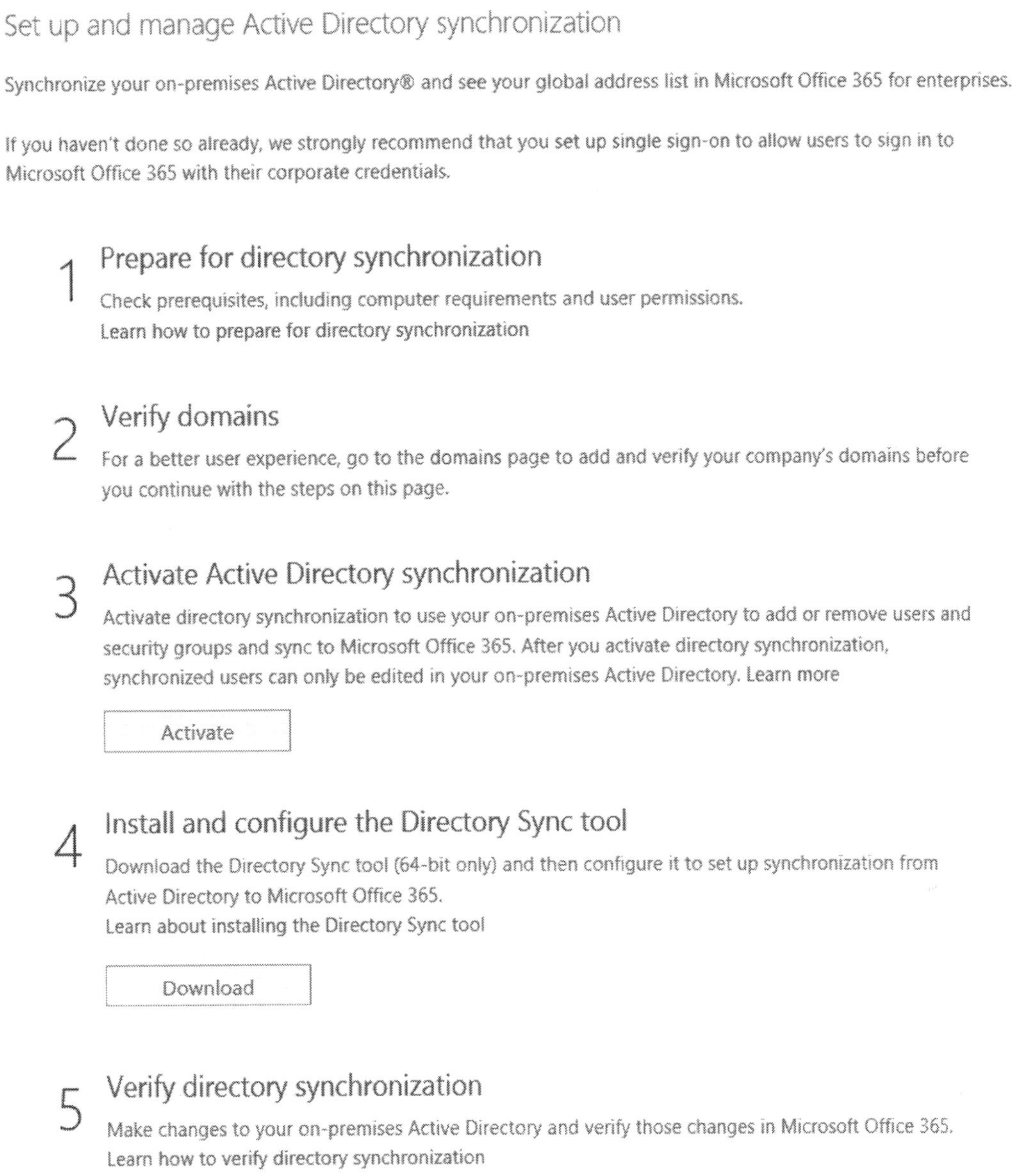

Set up and manage Active Directory synchronization

Synchronize your on-premises Active Directory® and see your global address list in Microsoft Office 365 for enterprises.

If you haven't done so already, we strongly recommend that you set up single sign-on to allow users to sign in to Microsoft Office 365 with their corporate credentials.

1 Prepare for directory synchronization

Check prerequisites, including computer requirements and user permissions.
Learn how to prepare for directory synchronization

2 Verify domains

For a better user experience, go to the domains page to add and verify your company's domains before you continue with the steps on this page.

3 Activate Active Directory synchronization

Activate directory synchronization to use your on-premises Active Directory to add or remove users and security groups and sync to Microsoft Office 365. After you activate directory synchronization, synchronized users can only be edited in your on-premises Active Directory. Learn more

> Activate

4 Install and configure the Directory Sync tool

Download the Directory Sync tool (64-bit only) and then configure it to set up synchronization from Active Directory to Microsoft Office 365.
Learn about installing the Directory Sync tool

> Download

5 Verify directory synchronization

Make changes to your on-premises Active Directory and verify those changes in Microsoft Office 365.
Learn how to verify directory synchronization

Figure 11-10. Setting up Active Directory Synchronization

Review steps 1 – 2, and verify your configuration before you activate and install the Directory Synchronization. The Onramp tool that we ran earlier will also check this configuration. If you are satisfied that you have made the changes in Office 365 and your onsite Active Directory, then activate the Directory Synchronization, and download the Directory Sync tool.

We recommend that for the account you use a unique Office 365 synchronization account (no licenses needs to be assigned). Typically we use the onmicrosoft.com account. It takes four hours before the Office 365 is synchronized with Active Directory the first time (depends upon the number of objects).

■ **Note** The Directory Sync tool must be installed by a domain administrator (see Figure 11-11). Directory Sync reads active directory. The tool permission must be installed by the domain administrator. Make sure you "right click" and run as an administrator to install the Directory Sync tool. Do not download and run!

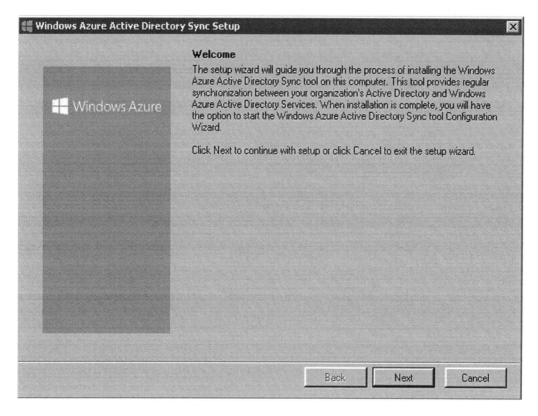

Figure 11-11. Installation of the Directory Synchronization Tools

You cannot reverse DirSync. So if you decide to move ahead with DirSync, your options will be limited. As an example, if you have an on-site Exchange server, the mailbox will not be created in Office 365 and your only choice for migration tools are the ones supplied by Microsoft.

■ **Note** If Directory Synchronization does not install and returns the error "… *you must have Microsoft online services sign-in assistant version 7.0 or greater.*" See the trouble shooting section later in this chapter on how to resolve the issue.

The first step in the installation is the installation of the software and setup of the permission. If the Directory Sync tools do not install correctly, you will need to uninstall and correct the problem. Always download the Directory Sync software and run the installer as an administrator; right click on the download and select run as administrator. If the software correctly installs, the installation will prompt you to start the configuration wizard (see Figure 11-12).

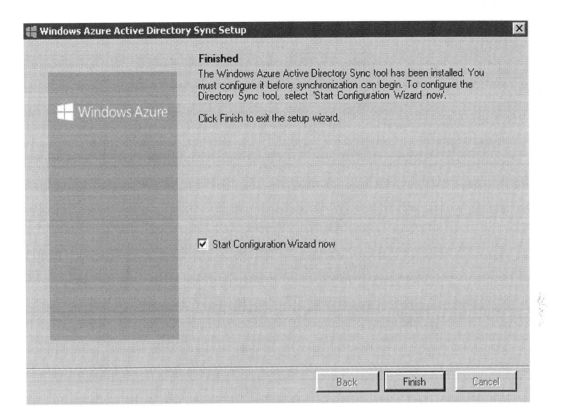

Figure 11-12. *DirSync tool installation of support files*

■ **Note**   If you are installing Directory Synchronization on a domain controller, do not start the wizard during the installation. Un-check "Start Configuration Wizard" and click "finish." Reboot the server, and restart the wizard to complete the Directory Synchronization setup.

After the DirSync software is installed, start the configuration wizard. You will need two accounts (we created theses earlier). The Office 365 is a global admin account and the on-site account is a domain admin that is a member of the enterprise Admin group (see Figure 11-13).

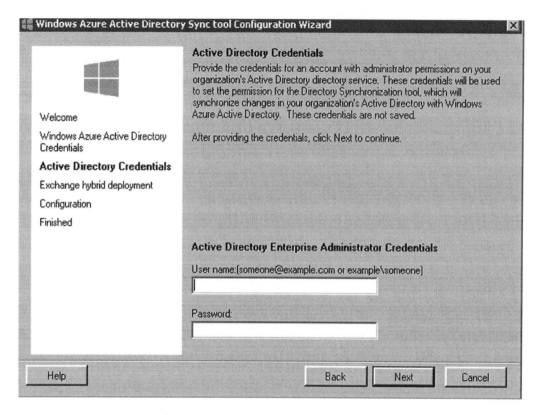

Figure 11-13. *Starting the on line services Directory Synchronization Tool*

The account to use for DirSync is the original admin account that was created when you started your Office 365 site. This account is a super admin account. The login should be the login address (@<domain>.onmicrosoft.com), not the vanity domain (short e-mail address).

The DirSync wizard allows you to enable write back if you have (or are going to have) an exchange hybrid server in place. If you do not have a server that has the capabilities of exchange federation, then this will be grayed out typical Directory Synchronization enablement takes four hours for the initial sync and for larger organizations 24 hours to sync. If there is no exchange server, Figure 11-14 is grayed out.

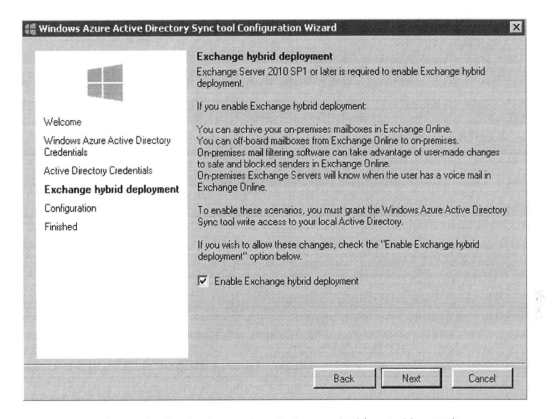

Figure 11-14. *Directory Synchronization - Enabling Exchange hybrid (required for ADFS)*

The Office 365 password synchronization is part of Office 365. To enable the password option, run the wizard and select the password synchronization option (see Figure 11-15). At this point the password changes in the on-site AD will be replicated to Office 365. The password policies will be those from the on-site Active Directory and not Office 365.

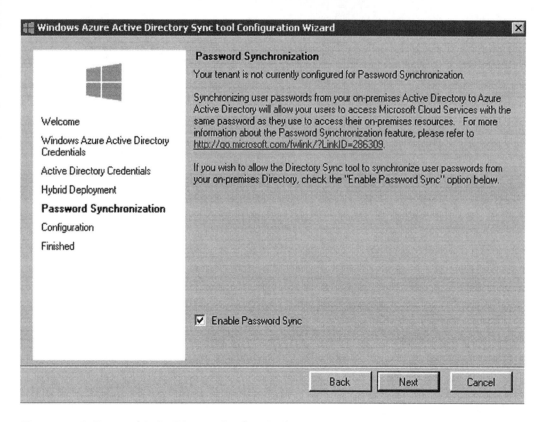

Figure 11-15. *Password Active Directory Synchronization*

Select the password option for synchronization (Figure 11-15), then select "Next." This will begin the final configuration (Figure 11-16) of the Directory Synchronization tool.

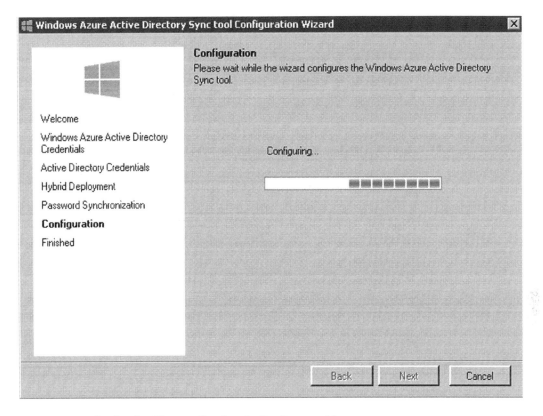

Figure 11-16. *Configuring Directory Synchronization Password Sync*

If the configuration is successful, you should see Figure 11-17.

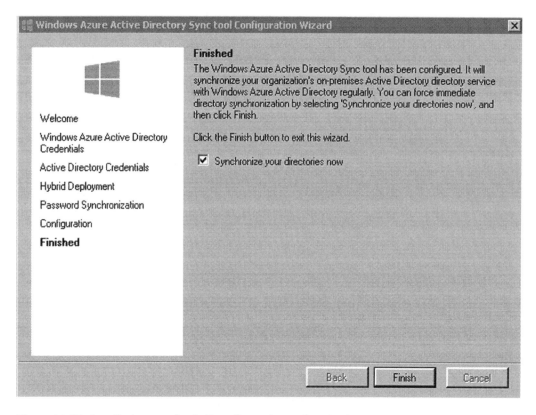

Figure 11-17. Installation completed - Start directories synchronization

If you are running Directory Synchronization, you will notice that some Office 365 fields are grayed out. The user information that is matched to the On-Premises Active Directory, is controlled by the On-Premises servers. As an example, the primary e-mail address and the alias (Proxy addresses) must be set in the On-Premisess Active Directory. The tool to change these items is either the Active Directory add users and computers, or the Exchange management console. In our troubleshooting section we described how to change the values of theses parameters using the Active Directory tool "Add Users and Computers." These tools are located on the Domain Controller.

Step 7: Installation of the Directory Sync Tool

Once you have installed the Directory Synchronization tool, the next step is to install the synchronization client. The synchronization client is useful to see the status of the Active Directory replication to the cloud and to force a replication.

Figure 11-18, shows the path and location of the Miisclient.exe. This is the behind-the-scene tool that manages the Active Directory Synchronization to Office 365.

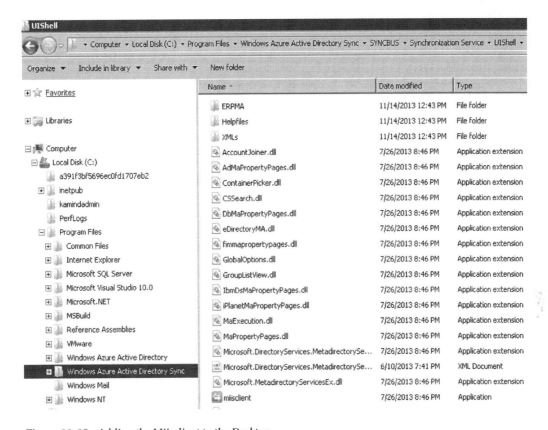

Figure 11-18. *Adding the Miisclient to the Desktop*

Search for the client, and install a shortcut to the desktop. Click on the desktop Miisclient tool, and examine the hyperlinks with the status (see Figure 11-19). The Tools menu has the option to start a full or partial synchronization to/from Office 365. The Miisclient allows you to perform, import, and export object sync.

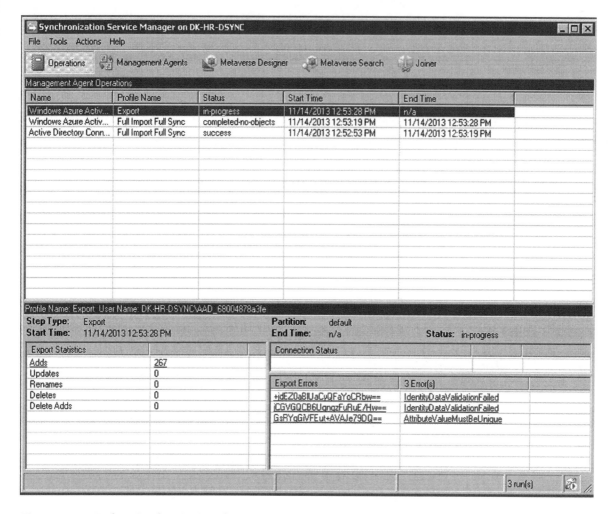

Figure 11-19. *Desktop Synchronization Client*

Force DirSync with PowerShell

You can also use PowerShell to force Directory Synchronization. To use PowerShell, login to the server where the DirSync software was installed, and navigate to the directory C:\Program Files\Windows Azure Active Directory Sync. Right-click on "DirSyncInstallShell" and select send to desktop. This will create a shortcut on your desktop so you can run the PowerShell command "Start-OnlineCoexistenceSync."

Step 8: Verify Active Directory

Active Directory is syncing to Office 365. At this point, you need to verify that the accounts that are syncing are the correct account address. As an example, if the account are online the onmicrosoft.com name, this is one of two issues; 1) the account does not have an internet-routable domain name or 2) there is another account with the same name, and Office 365 could not create the account.

The solution to (1) is to change the account e-mail address in the On Premises sever and in (2) verify that the account is not in the delete users account list. If these users are in the delete user account list, you need to remove it using a PowerShell command discussed in Chapter 8. There may be additional DirSync errors.

DirSync Errors

Directory Synchronization errors do happen (Figure 11-20). These errors appear because incorrect Active Directory data. Before you install DirSync, you need to complete an AD review to check for improper names, and data organization. The DirSync errors will be sent to the admin user account. Once the error is corrected, the error messages will go away.

See <u>Directory Synchronization errors</u> for more information about the errors listed in this email message.
The Directory Synchronization batch run was completed on **Wednesday, 08 August 2012 23:44:38 GMT** for tenant **KAMIND IT, Inc.**.

The following errors occurred during synchronization:

Identity	Error Description	On-premises object ID
testgroup2	Unable to update this object in Microsoft Online Services because the following attributes associated with this object have values that may already be associated with another object in your local directory: ProxyAddresses smtp:mkatzer@kamind.com;. Correct or remove the duplicate values in your local directory. Please refer to http://support.microsoft.com/kb/2647098 for more information on identifying objects with duplicate attribute values.	mWNV5LSY80SSaKuR0cojUg==

Tracking ID: 4f16cd39-e5b8-4f1d-a80d-0b1fac9a3255

Figure 11-20. *Directory Synchronization Error*

Installing Active Directory Federation Services

Directory Synchronization provides the first level integration required for federation services integrating. There are two types of federation: Active Directory federation and Exchange federation. Most business will install DirSync services to address the password to local Active Directory Synchronization. However, some businesses will install full federation services. Before you begin to install federation services, make sure you have the correct server infrastructure in place for single sign-on. The bare minimum configuration is two proxy servers and two federation services. This will provide you the necessary backup when federation services are installed.

■ **Note**   ADFS integration tightly integrates Office 365 with the on-site equipment. If there is a failure of the "on site" equipment, access to Office 365 will be denied for all users. This is why there are a minimum of four servers.

Step 1: Install Active Directory Federation Services

ADFS allows the integration of the On Premises Active Directory to Office 365 (Figure 11-21). In an ADFS environment, the integration is accomplished via relaying party trust. When the domains are federated, the user has a single login environment across both environments (Office 365 and the local Active Directory environment).

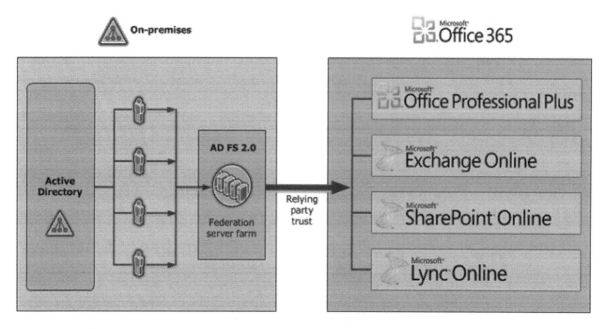

Figure 11-21. *MS Active Directory Federation Services - Courtesy of Microsoft*

The user experience is one of "sameness." The user logs into the local Active Directory or Office 365, and the user passwords are processed by the local on-site security servers. If the user tries to login to Office 365, and the account has not been created in the local Active Directory, then the user will see a screen similar to Figure 11-22.

Figure 11-22. *Single Sign On Example for Office 365 (account login failure)*

Installation Overview

ADFS requires that the **UPN suffix changes to an internet routable address** (your e-mail address). The first step in creating the UPN is to change the way the user accounts are logged into in the local Active Directory. Typically, local AD setup for the local domain is company.local or company.lan. The user login accounts are set up as user@company. local. This will need to change to user@company.com . This is the new UPN suffix that will need to add into the AD.

The following steps listed will set up ADFS integration between the Office 365 and your onsite AD. This is a pretty straightforward process. At the end of this section we address different troubleshooting tools for the testing of ADFS with Office 365.

Adding UPN Suffix to AD

1. Add UPN Suffix to AD and configure for each user

   a. domain.com was used for the UPN in this example

   b. UPNs used for identity Federation can only contain letters, numbers, periods, dashes and underscores.

2. Open AD Domains and Trusts tool.

3. Right-click AD Domains and Trusts and click Properties

4. On the UPN suffixes tab, type the alternative UPN (Figure 11-23) suffix for the forest and then click Add.

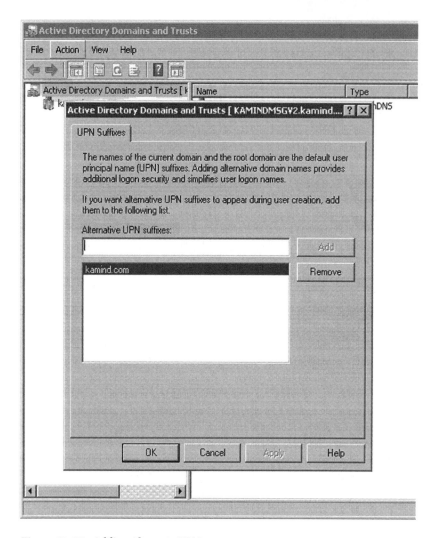

Figure 11-23. Adding Alternate UPN

Setting the User UPN

1. Select Active- Directory user and computers

2. Open user properties, navigate to Account Tab

3. Select the external namespace UPN for the "User logon name" (Figure 11-24).

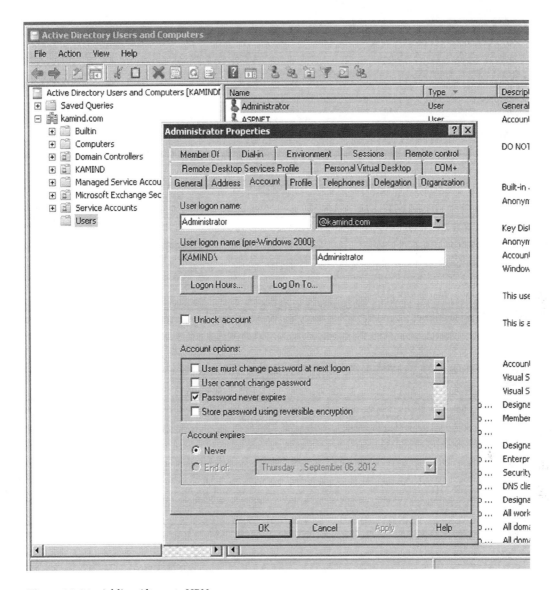

Figure 11-24. *Adding Alternate UPN*

Creating a service account for ADFS

Create a service account for ADFS. This can be a regular domain user, no special permissions needed.

Installing ADFS on a server

1. Add internal ADFS server to AD forest

2. Install ADFS on a domain controller

3. Download ADFS 2.0. During the install process, the following Windows components will be automatically installed:

    a. Windows PowerShell

    b. .NET Framework 3.5 SP1

    c. Internet Information Services (IIS)

    d. Windows Identity Foundation

- Installation

    - On the Server Role Option screen, select Federation Server (Figure 11-25)

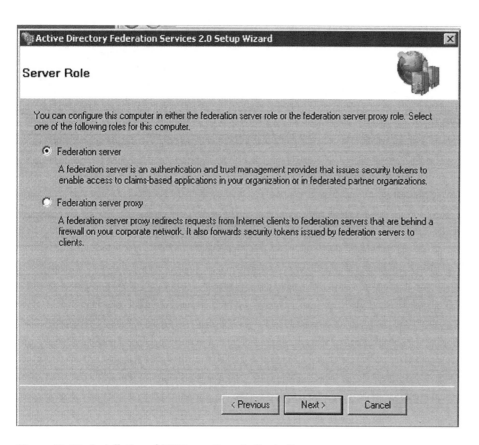

Figure 11-25. Installation of ADFS on a Domain Controller

- Finish the rest of the wizard, this will install any necessary prerequisites

- At the end of the wizard, uncheck box to Start the ADFS 2.0 Management Snap-in

- Adding IIS certificate (Figure 11-26)

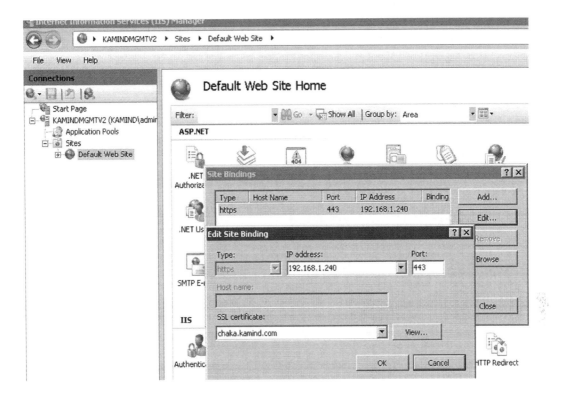

Figure 11-26. *Setting up binding for IIS server*

- Request and provision public certificate through Entrust
- Bind certificate to IIS on port 443 (remove binding for port 80)

Validate the IIS server and bind the certificate to port 443, removing the port 80 binding (see Figure 11-27).

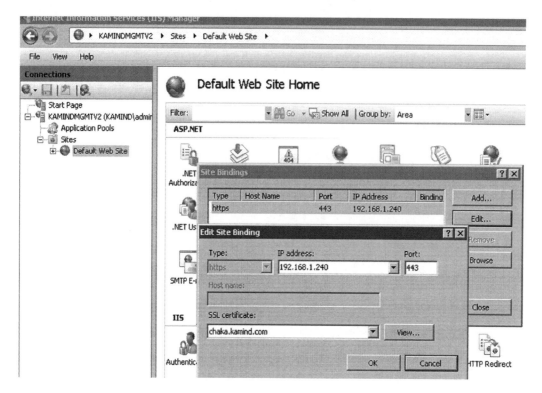

Figure 11-27. *Setting up binding for IIS server*

Configure the ADFS management

Run the ADFS wizard and create a new federation service (see Figure 11-28).

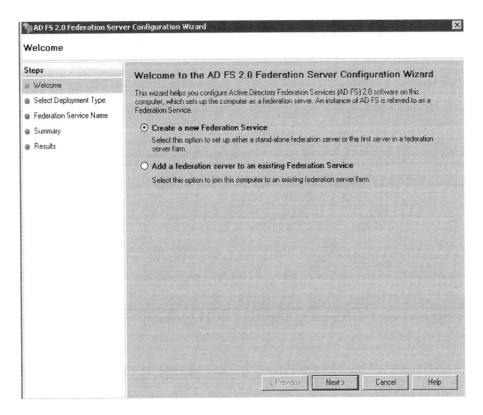

Figure 11-28. Creating a new Federation services

When you install ADFS, the first server installed is a new federation server (see Figure 11-29).

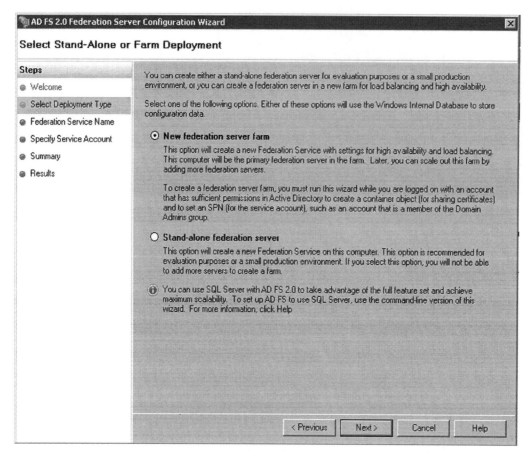

Figure 11-29. *Setting up binding for IIS server – as a farm*

Follow the wizard and install the public name of the federation server or proxy server (see Figure 11-30). Add the local administrator account (see Figure 11-31) when prompted by the wizard.

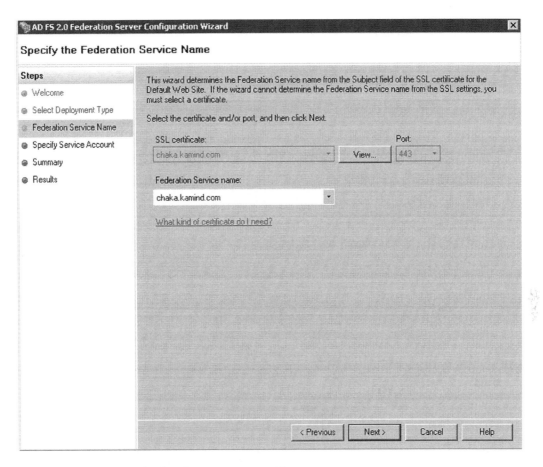

Figure 11-30. *Setting up binding for IIS server to certificate*

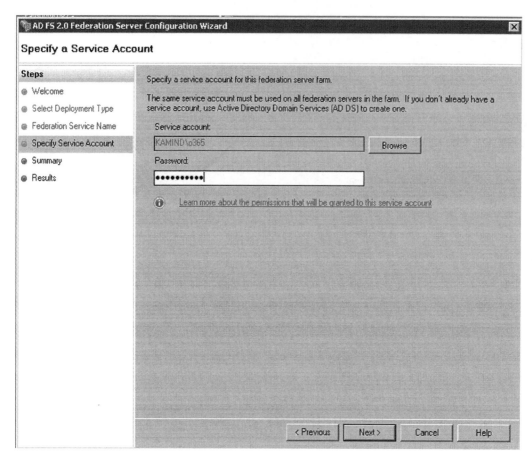

Figure 11-31. *Setting up the service account*

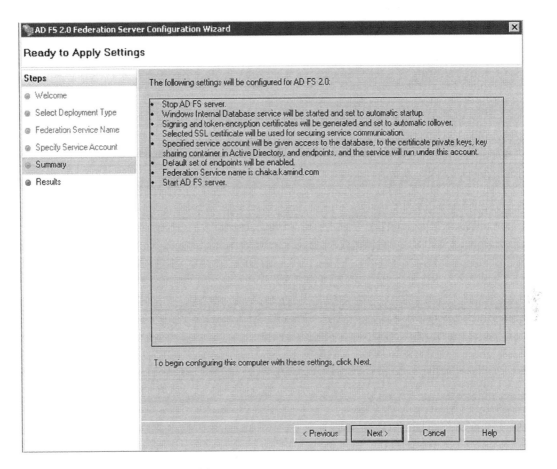

Figure 11-32. Auto Configuration of the ADFS server

ADFS server installation will add SQL Express to your server. Make sure you verify the server components added in case of conflicts (see Figure 11-33). If you have a large number of objects, you will need to use SQL Server to manage the objects.

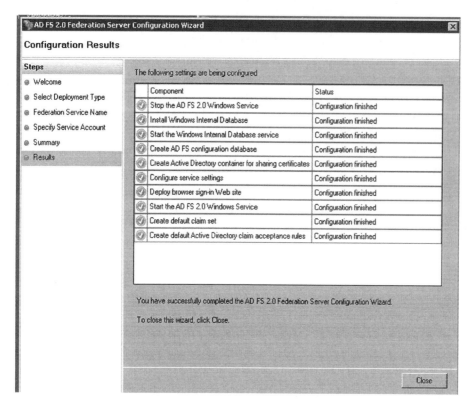

Figure 11-33. Summary of the configuration

If you see any item that comes up with a red X, you will need to troubleshoot the issue before you can enable the Federation operation.

Verify Federation configuration

To verify the domain configuration, just launch the ADFS server in a browser with the URL (`https://<ADFS domain name>/FederationMetadata/2007-06/FederationMetadata.xml`). If the system is configured correctly, then the XML script will be displayed as shown below (see Figure 11-34). Our domain is `chaka.kamind.com`.

Figure 11-34. Partial screenshot showing valid Federation trust

You can also verify the two endpoints to ensure that the ADFS server is configured:

- `https://{your_federation_service_name}/adfs/fs/federationserverservice.asmx`

- `https://{your_federation_service_name}/adfs/services/trust/mex`

The second test to make is ensuring that the event log has the correct event record in place. Check the applications and services logs for the event 100. This will show if the Federation services started correctly. After you have validated the ADFS server, then the next step is to install the Federation proxy server. Make sure you verify the event log (Figure 11-35) and address any errors.

Then, open up the Windows Event Viewer and navigate to Applications and Services Logs > AD FS 2.0 > Admi

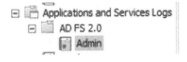

Then check for event ID 100 which should show the Federation Service started successfully:

Figure 11-35. Checking the event Log Status

Step 2: Adding Federation Proxy servers

If you are running a test environment, you do not need to implement a Federation proxy. However, if you are running a production environment, you need to deploy the Federation proxy's. Start by verifying the Federation proxy servers (if you are using them), and make sure you can execute the command, shown in Figure 11-36, from each of the Federation proxy servers. Federation proxy servers can be added at any time; you can add them as part of the deployment steps, or add them after you have implemented single sign-on. From a firewall perspective, all that you are doing is exposing the proxy address to the Internet; versus the federated server proxy address. Figure 11-36 provides an overview of the Federation proxy server deployment.

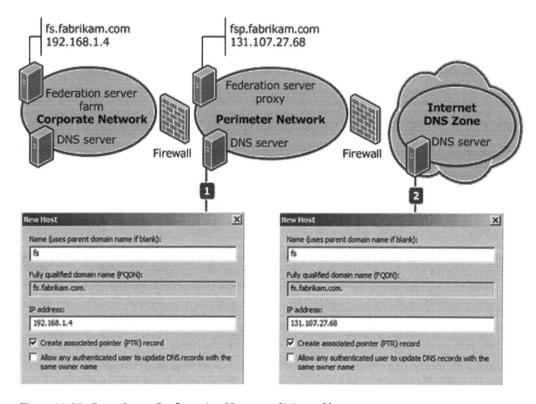

Figure 11-36. *Proxy Server Configuration (Courtesy of Microsoft)*

Install ADFS 2.0 Proxy server

To install ADFS proxy server, you will need to add the public certificate to the proxy server - IIS interface, and have the internal Proxy Servers point to the internal Federation Servers. In Figure 11-36, there is an example with a pair of proxy servers that are load balanced on the network. These proxy servers provide external interface to respond to service request for the internal Federation server. The stumbling block for most ADFS implementation is when you attempt to lock down the Federation interface before testing is completed the proxy servers are blocked and cannot communicate to the Federation Servers. The solution is to add a local host name to the proxy servers to resolve the internal address of the Federation Servers. In Figure 11-36, we have the external servers, and the internal Federation farm. The steps below are necessary to add a pair of Federation proxy servers.

1.   Export a public certificate from the ADFS internal server and copy it to the proxy server

2.   Add a HOST file entry for `ADFS.domain.com` to point to the internal ADFS server

3.   Validating the DNS resolution of `ADFS.domain.com` resolves to the external A record from an internet connected PC

4.   Double-click ADFSSetup.exe (this is the ADFS 2.0 download)

   a.   Click Next on the Welcome Screen and Accept the License Agreement

   b.   On the Server Role Option screen, select "Federation Server Proxy"

   c.   Finish the rest of the wizard; this will install any necessary prerequisites

   d.   At the end of the wizard, uncheck the box to Start the ADFS 2.0 Management Snap-in

5.   Import the certificate in IIS and bind the certificate to the Default Web Site (`ADFS.domain.com`)

6.   Configure the ADFS proxy by selecting the ADFS 2.0 Federation Server Proxy Configuration Wizard

   a.   Enter the Federation namespace (ex. `ADFS.domain.com`)

   b.   Click the Test connection button

   c.   Enter the service account credentials

      i.   Select a long name (`adminservice@<domain>.onmicrosoft.com`) as a service account

      ii.   Make sure the service account has the SPN set correctly

   d.   Finish the Wizard

7.   Log into the portal with UPN credentials. Note that once the UPN login is entered, the password field is grayed out and a link activates to log into the ADFS server

Testing Single Sign On

It is not possible to test out Single Sign On. Once it is on, it is on. The best way to test Single Sign On is to test the various connectivity points around Office 365 with an account. You are basically checking connectivity internally and externally and verify access to OWA and Outlook connectivity.

■ **Note**   If you turn on Federation, this is the point of no return. You are committed at this point.

Turning on Single Sign On

Once you are ready to turn on Single Sign On, all that is needed is to run the scripts listed below. This will enable Single Sign On for the domain:

```
Note: domain: kamind.com, internal server kamindmgmtv2.kamind.com
Account:  need to use the onmicrosoft.com account as the admin account for livecred

Set-ExecutionPolicy RemoteSigned
$LiveCred = Get-Credential
Connect-MsolService -Credential $LiveCred.
Set-MsolADFScontext -Computer kamindmgmtv2.kamind.com
```

```
# - use if new domain
#New-MsolFederatedDomain -DomainName kamind.com
# - use if existign domain
#Add-MSOLDFederatedDomain -domainame kamind.com
Convert-MsolDomainToFederated -domainame kamind.com

#Get Status of federated domain
Get-MsolFederationProperty -DomainName kamind.com

#if the domain does not match Federation
Update-MsolFederatedDomain -DomainName kamind.com
```

The sample output of this command on the domain kamind.com is shown in Figure 11-37.

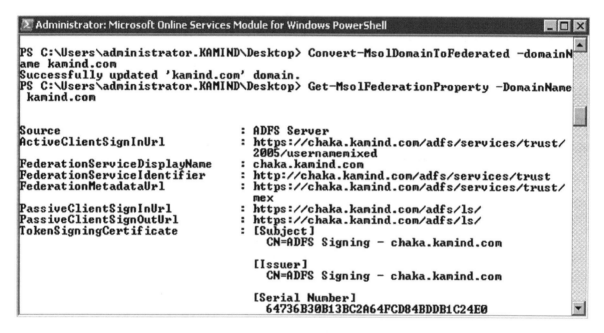

Figure 11-37. *Screen output from successful PowerShell scripts*

After you run these commands, it should look like Figure 11-38.

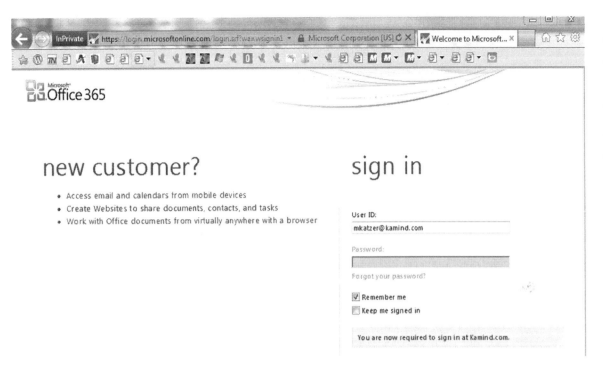

Figure 11-38. *Enabled Federation login*

Add the auto update token certificate

Office 365 tokens update every 20 days. To make sure that the ADFS servers are in sync with Office 365, you need to download the Office 365 meta-data and sync the server prior to the first event (seeFigure 11-39).

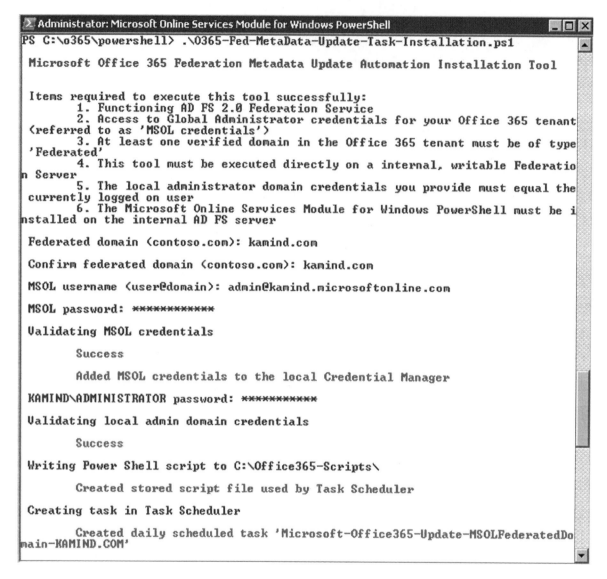

```
Administrator: Microsoft Online Services Module for Windows PowerShell                    _ □ ×
PS C:\o365\powershell> .\0365-Fed-MetaData-Update-Task-Installation.ps1

Microsoft Office 365 Federation Metadata Update Automation Installation Tool


Items required to execute this tool successfully:
        1. Functioning AD FS 2.0 Federation Service
        2. Access to Global Administrator credentials for your Office 365 tenant
(referred to as 'MSOL credentials')
        3. At least one verified domain in the Office 365 tenant must be of type
'Federated'
        4. This tool must be executed directly on a internal, writable Federatio
n Server
        5. The local administrator domain credentials you provide must equal the
currently logged on user
        6. The Microsoft Online Services Module for Windows PowerShell must be i
nstalled on the internal AD FS server

Federated domain (contoso.com): kamind.com

Confirm federated domain (contoso.com): kamind.com

MSOL username (user@domain): admin@kamind.microsoftonline.com

MSOL password: ************

Validating MSOL credentials

        Success

        Added MSOL credentials to the local Credential Manager

KAMIND\ADMINISTRATOR password: ***********

Validating local admin domain credentials

        Success

Writing Power Shell script to C:\Office365-Scripts\

        Created stored script file used by Task Scheduler

Creating task in Task Scheduler

        Created daily scheduled task 'Microsoft-Office365-Update-MSOLFederatedDo
main-KAMIND.COM'
```

Figure 11-39. Adding certificate to On-Site Office 365 ADFS server

1. Download and save the meta data update
    http://gallery.technet.microsoft.com/scriptcenter/Office-365-Federation-27410bdc

2. On the ADFS server, open an Office 365 power shell prompt and enter the command 0365-Fed-MetaData-Update-Task-Installation.ps1

After you have completed the server update, then start the ADFS tool. This will show you that the trust has been installed on the server, as shown in Figure 11-40.

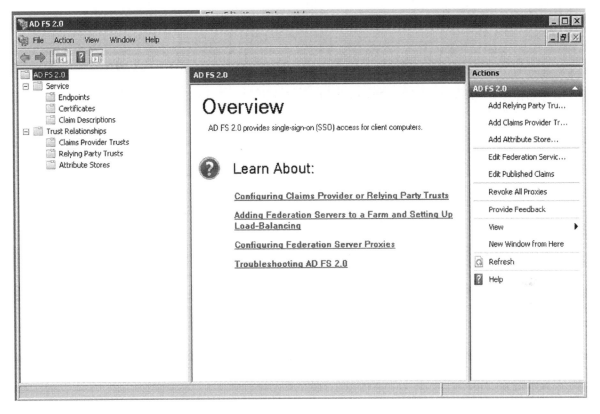

Figure 11-40. *Starting the ADFS tool to verify the configuration – no DB sync error*

Step 3: Federation - Exchange 2010 Integration

After you have configured and tested Active Directory Federation Services, the next step is to federate the Exchange server. Exchange Server allows the movement mailboxes from On Premises to Off Premises using the Exchange Server's remote mailbox move. In Figure 11-41, you can see the Federated Exchange Server (Exchange 2010), with the hub transport setting already created to handle the mail routing in the cloud. The Exchange Management console should look similar to Figure 11-41, if the hub transports are configured correctly.

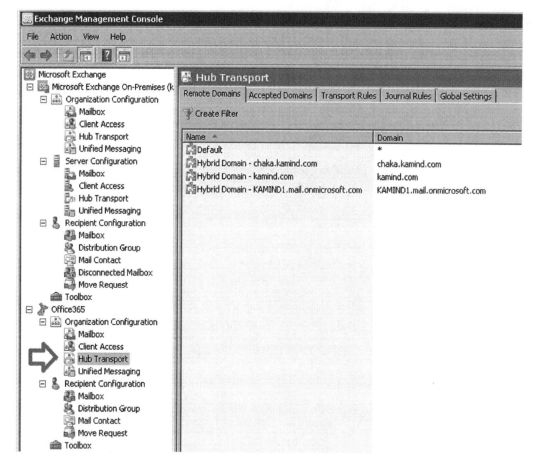

Figure 11-41. Exchange Server setup

Pre-Federation Checklist

Before you begin to federate the domains, it is crucial that your Single Sign On is working, and that your Federated Proxy Servers are in place. Once those are in place and stabilized, you can federate the Exchange Servers. To get ready for Exchange Federation, review these four checklist items, and you are ready to begin Exchange Server deployment:

1. Do you have Exchange 2010 installed?

2. Exchange 2010 Validation – verify your Exchange configuration.

3. Mail flow – How will you route mail (Cloud or onsite)?

4. Compliance and retention – What are your business requirements?

Exchange Server is more about planning than it is implementation. The major change for the users will be the changes for Single Sign On (discussed in the preceding section). Once your users have implemented the changes necessary in Single Sign On, Federation is transparent.

Exchange Server 2010 Installed?

If you currently do not have Exchange 2010 installed, then stop at this point. This document assumes that you have a working Exchange 2010 installation supporting OWA and Outlook anywhere (SSL with RPOC tunnel access).

If you have Exchange 2003, or 2007, you will need to refer back to Chapter 2 if you want to install Exchange 2010, and the steps necessary to accomplish this. This document does not address any Exchange to Exchange upgrades, and assumes that you have a working Exchange 2010 server in production.

To proceed to Step 3, if you have not already upgraded your Exchange 2010 servers to Exchange Server version 2010 service pack 3, please do so. This is required to run Exchange Federation.

Exchange Validation – Steps to check prior to deployment

Before you can begin to implement Exchange Federation, please verify the following:

1. Validate the exchange Connectivity

    a. Run the Exchange connectivity test tool on the Exchange Server web services and RPC. Fix any errors reported (see https://www.testExchangeconnectivity.com/).

    b. Run the Remote Connectivity test tool on the Office 365 Single Sign On Tab. Fix any errors reported.

    c. Verify the external connectivity of Exchange external Url for Web Services, OAB and Active Sync using Exchange PowerShell.

It is import that each of these steps are completed in the planning and testing process before you go on to implement Federation. In some cases, you may decide for business reasons not to correct a problem that was raised by the connectivity/testing tool. In these cases, make sure you understand what the problem is and why you are not going to correct it.

Validate the exchange Connectivity

The best way to ensure your organization is ready for Federation is to run the remote connectivity Federation testing tool. There are three "Exchange Server" tests that we need to execute on this tool. This is on the "Exchange Server tab". (Use a Windows 7 based system for testing.)

1. Microsoft Exchange ActiveSync Connectivity Test

2. Microsoft Exchange Web services Connectivity Test

3. Microsoft Office Outlook Connectivity Test

Each of these tests will validate your Exchange server organization to make sure that your certificates are in place, and any previous deployment issues have been resolved. Typically when we run the tool in a deployment scenario, we do not specific the remote access server. Once you have made changes to your DNS for Federation, you will need to manually specify the server address. In our case, our CAS server is chaka.kamind.com.

The first test is the Exchange ActiveSync Connectivity test. This test verifies your active sync configuration and your certificate configuration (Figure 11-42). Both are needed to allow the Exchange Server remote to move.

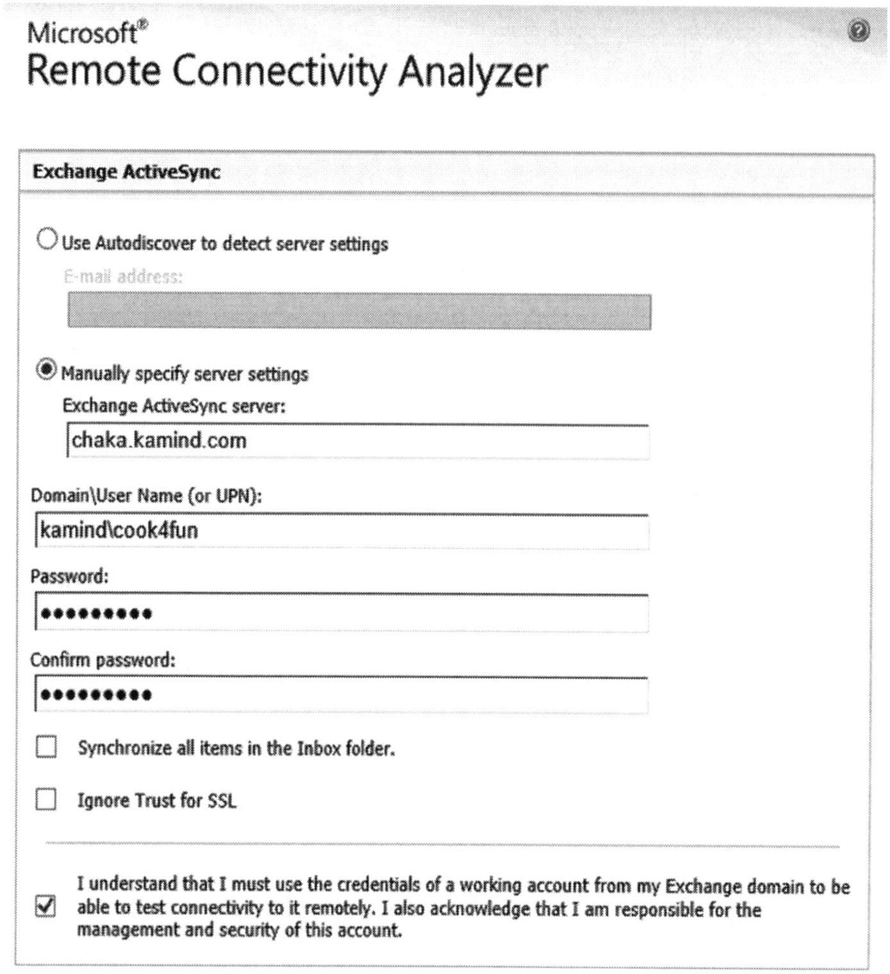

Microsoft®
Remote Connectivity Analyzer

Exchange ActiveSync

○ Use Autodiscover to detect server settings

    E-mail address:

◉ Manually specify server settings

    Exchange ActiveSync server:

| chaka.kamind.com |

Domain\User Name (or UPN):

| kamind\cook4fun |

Password:

| ••••••••• |

Confirm password:

| ••••••••• |

☐   Synchronize all items in the Inbox folder.

☐   Ignore Trust for SSL

☑   I understand that I must use the credentials of a working account from my Exchange domain to be able to test connectivity to it remotely. I also acknowledge that I am responsible for the management and security of this account.

Figure 11-42. *Selecting a user account for testing*

In running our connectivity test, our connection failed with the following error message (see Figure 11-43).

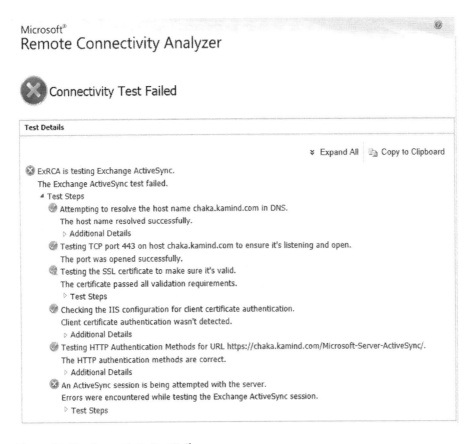

Figure 11-43. *Connectivity Test Failure*

Looking in detail on this error message (in Figure 11-43), we discovered that the accounts we had in our Exchange Server were not set up for RPC and OWA access. So in this case, we need to enable the accounts that were going to the cloud. If the OWA or RPC is not enabled, the account cannot be migrated. Run the second test and verify the Exchange ActiveSync AutoDiscover. (This test will fail once we change the external and internal DNS records).

The other two tests will verify the *web services connectivity* and the *RPC connectivity*. The accounts that you are planning to move to Office 365, must be enabled for ActiveSync and RPC access. Later on you can restrict services using the Office 365 Exchange Management panel.

Step 4: Mail Flow – Decide on how mail will route

Migration can be complex or simple. One of the changes introduced with Exchange Service Pack 3, was the introduction of the integrated Forefront Configuration as part of the Hybrid Federation wizard.

At this point, you will need to decide on your mail flow configuration, based upon your business needs In Figure 11-44, if we select displayed option, Office 365 Exchange Online Protection (EOP), assumes that you will redirect the MX records to Office 365, and EOP will deliver mail to your On Premises server for compliance based upon the transport rules (see Figure 11-45). The transport rules are used to deliver mail to the appropriate destination if there is a On Premises need for compliance logging. EOP configuration is discussed in detail in Chapter 10.

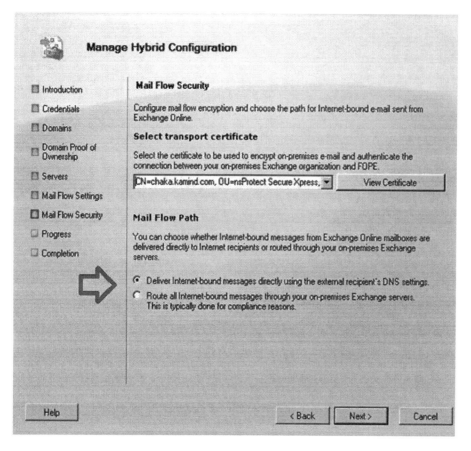

Figure 11-44. *Forefront Mail Flow Selection*

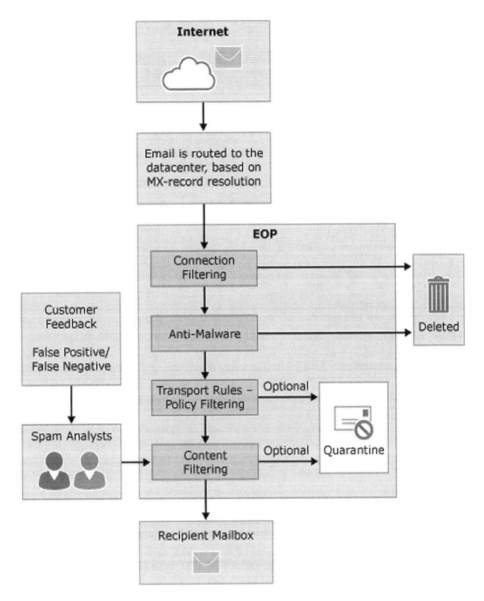

Figure 11-45. *Exchange Online Protection (EOP) Transport Filter*

Step 5: Compliance – What is your email and document retention policy

Compliance is covered in detail in Chapter 9, but to understand how to configure retention policy you need to understand how the Office 365 archive and compliance structure works as compared to traditional journaling. When you think of journaling, such as GFI (or some other service), it is writing out all electronic communication to a third party information store. This happens to all communications that flow into the company from the cloud. The purpose of this model is to ensure that the data that is written to the third party archive is immutable (not subject to change or deleted by the user).

The Office 365 model is different (Figure 11-46). Instead of journaling all communications, you are performing the journal function on a per mailbox basis, and to do this you use a concept of retention rules to control the user mailbox information.   Retention rules specify what happens to the mail in a user mailbox if the email is too old, or the user deletes an email. Typically these retention rules move the mail from the user mailbox into the archive. These rules can be systems level (user has no control), or can be local level, user has complete control.

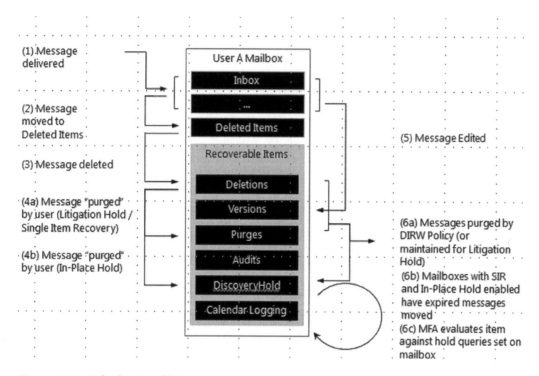

Figure 11-46. *Life of an Email Message*

Litigation hold is an action that is placed on a mailbox to meet compliance requirements for future discovery and searching. What litigation hold does is to ensure that the data in a user mailbox is immutable; and cannot be change. As an example, if the user tries to delete an email, the email is deleted (or purged) for the users view, but the litigation hold function block the email from being deleted in the system and is fully discoverable by the administrator (or compliance officer).

In Figure 11-46, we see the life of an email in a user mailbox. When there is compliance in place, the user only sees the message in steps 1 – 3. The compliance officer has access to all transactions in steps 1 – 6. When a discovery action – a search – is executed, all information is displayed in the search request.

In our hybrid example, we are not changing mail flow to the compliance engine. We are maintaining the mail flow as it is currently define. Later after we migrate to Office 365, we will move the compliance archive to Office 365. To ensure that the mail flow is not change, we adjust the mail flow using the EOP transport rules.

Step 6: Federation – Implementing Exchange Server (2010)

Exchange Server Is not like Single Sign On and Directory Synchronization. You can add Exchange Server after you migrate to Office 365. Likewise, you can remove it if you are 100% cloud based. To use these installation steps, you must install **Exchange 2010 Service pack 3** or later. To Set up Exchange Federation, use the following the steps:

1. Open up the Exchange 2010 management console (See Figure 11-47).

Figure 11-47. *Adding Exchange Management Forest*

2. At the top most node, right-click and select add Exchange Forest.

a. Enter the following information for the new Exchange forest (see Figure 11-48).

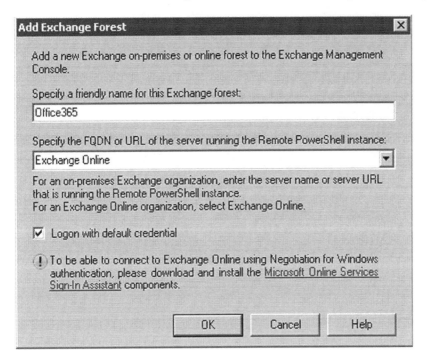

Figure 11-48. *Adding Exchange Forest*

b. Enter the name for the Forest (in this case, we selected Office 365).

c. Select Exchange Online; this will configure the correct PowerShell extension for Office 365.

d. Select "Logon with default credential." When you are prompted, enter the Office 365 credentials for login. The credentials supplied must have a license assigned to the account. If a license is not assigned, some PowerShell commands will fail.

e. Once you have configured the Exchange Forest you will need to verify the commands. To verify the commands, open the Windows PowerShell command prompt (not an online services one).

3. Run the PowerShell commands to verify the Exchange configuration:

```
#Create an Office 365 remote PowerShell Session
$O365 = Get-Credential
$session = New-PSSession -ConfigurationName Microsoft.Exchange -ConnectionUri
https://ps.outlook.com/PowerShell/ -Credential $O365Cred -Authentication Basic
-AllowRedirection
Import-PSSession $Session

#Clean up and close the session
Remove-PSSession $Session
```

a. After you enter the above commands, the output should look similar to Figure 11-49, displaying the status of the remote interface. The purpose of the preceding command is to make sure that the command sequence is valid and that the Exchange 2010 console has the necessary components installed.

```
PS C:\Users\administrator.KAMIND> $O365 = Get-Credential

cmdlet Get-Credential at command pipeline position 1
Supply values for the following parameters:
Credential
PS C:\Users\administrator.KAMIND> $session = New-PSSession -ConfigurationName Microsoft.Exchange -ConnectionUri https://
ps.outlook.com/powershell/ -Credential $O365Cred -Authentication Basic -AllowRedirection
WARNING: Your connection has been redirected to the following URI:
"https://pod51018psh.outlook.com/powershell-liveid?PSVersion=2.0 "
WARNING: Your connection has been redirected to the following URI:
"https://sn2prd0710psh.outlook.com/powershell-liveid?PSVersion=2.0 "
PS C:\Users\administrator.KAMIND> Import-PSSession $Session

ModuleType Name                      ExportedCommands
---------- ----                      ----------------
Script     tmp_d74dfffb-59ac-4e06... {Set-RoleGroup, Set-RMSTrustedPublishingDomain, Disable-UMAutoAttendant,...

PS C:\Users\administrator.KAMIND> _
```

Figure 11-49. *Sample output demonstrating valid PowerShell execution*

4. The next step is the configuration of the Exchange server certificate. You will need to have either a wild card or a server specific certificate. If you do not have a server specific, please refer to the section on creating a new Exchange certificate. At this point you have run the Exchange connectivity test and have installed a server certificate, as well as install the necessary certificates on the CAS server. Once the certificates are installed, they should appear similar to Figure 11-50.

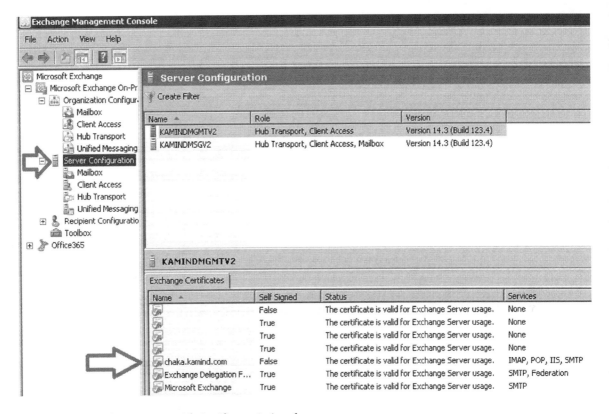

Figure 11-50. Exchange Server with Certificates Assigned

5. Open up the Exchange management console and verify that the Exchange certificates are assigned to the SMTP, and IIS service (see Figure 11-51).

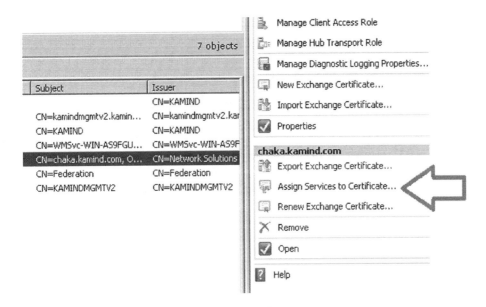

Figure 11-51. Assigning Services to Certificate

a. Select the certificate that is used on the external interface (these services should already be assigned as part of the troubleshooting process with the connectivity wizard).

b. When you run the wizard, select the servers that the certificate is installed and apply all services that you will use. You must select at least IIS and SMTP. If you are prompted to overwrite the default certificate, select NO (see Figure 11-52).

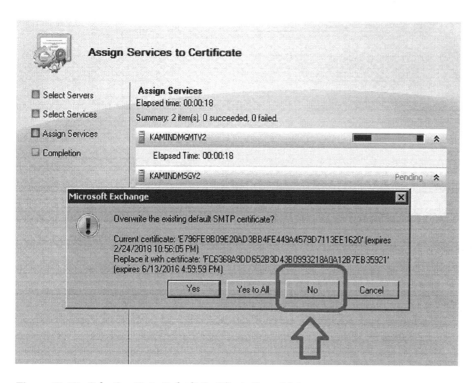

Figure 11-52. *Selecting No to Default Certificate Over right*

6. After you have updated the certificate with the services, the next step is to verify the service. To do this, you will run Exchange PowerShell and enter the command "Get-ExchangeCertificate | fl". Verify that the service attributes include "IIS and SMTP", Status is "Valid" and the RootCA Type is "thirdparty" as shown in Figure 11-53.

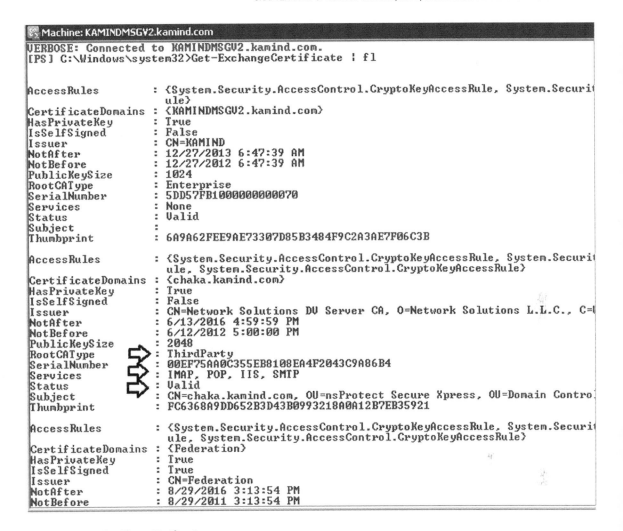

Figure 11-53. *Certificate Verification*

7. After the certificate has been verified, the next step is to verify the external URL end points are installed correctly on the Client Access Server. To accomplish this, run three different PowerShell scripts. The endpoints should already have been resolved in the TestConnectivity verification that we completed earlier. Run the following scripts (see Figure 11-54).

a. `Get-WebServicesVirtualDirectory "EWS (Default Web Site)" | Fromat-Table Name, ExternalUrl`

b. `Get-OabVirtualDirectory "OAB (Default Web Site)" | Fromat-Table Name, ExternalUrl`

c. `Get-ActiveSyncVirtualDirectory "EWS (Default Web Site)" | Fromat-Table Name, ExternalUrl`

```
[PS] C:\Windows\system32>Get-ActiveSyncVirtualDirectory "Microsoft-Server-ActiveSync (default Web Site)" | Format-table
Name, ExternalURL

Name                                                     ExternalUrl
----                                                     -----------
Microsoft-Server-ActiveSync (Default Web Site)           https://chaka.kamind.com/Microsoft-Server-ActiveSync


[PS] C:\Windows\system32>Get-OabVirtualDirectory "OAB (Default web Site)" | Format-Table Name, ExternalUrl

Name                                                     ExternalUrl
----                                                     -----------
OAB (Default Web Site)                                   https://chaka.kamind.com/OAB


[PS] C:\Windows\system32>Get-WebServicesVirtualDirectory "EWS (Default Web Site)" | Format-Table Name, Externalurl

Name                                                     ExternalUrl
----                                                     -----------
EWS (Default Web Site)


[PS] C:\Windows\system32>_
```

Figure 11-54. Sample Output with error

In the example shown in Figure 11-55, the web services virtual directory returns a blank (no value). To correct this, you need to either add the external URL using either the management console or PowerShell. In this case, the External URL was not set correctly on the internal CAS server kamindmsgv2 (see Figure 11-55).

```
Machine: KAMINDMSGV2.kamind.com
[PS] C:\Windows\system32>Set-WebServicesVirtualDirectory -identity "kamindmsgv2\EWS (Default Web Site)" -externalurl htt
ps://chaka.kamind.com/EWS/Exchange.asmx -BasicAuthentication:$True
[PS] C:\Windows\system32>
[PS] C:\Windows\system32>
[PS] C:\Windows\system32>Get-WebServicesVirtualDirectory "EWS (Default Web Site)" | Format-Table Name, ExternalUrl

Name                                                     ExternalUrl
----                                                     -----------
EWS (Default Web Site)                                   https://chaka.kamind.com/EWS/Exchange.asmx
```

Figure 11-55. Set Web Services External URL on CAS server

8. Configure the DNS for Auto discover and SPF txt records

   a. On the Office 365 Admin console select "Domains," then select the domain for the mail records, view DNS settings then View DNS records for the UPN domain (see Figure 11-56).

      i. *Set the External AutoDiscover record*

      ii. *Set the TXT spf records*

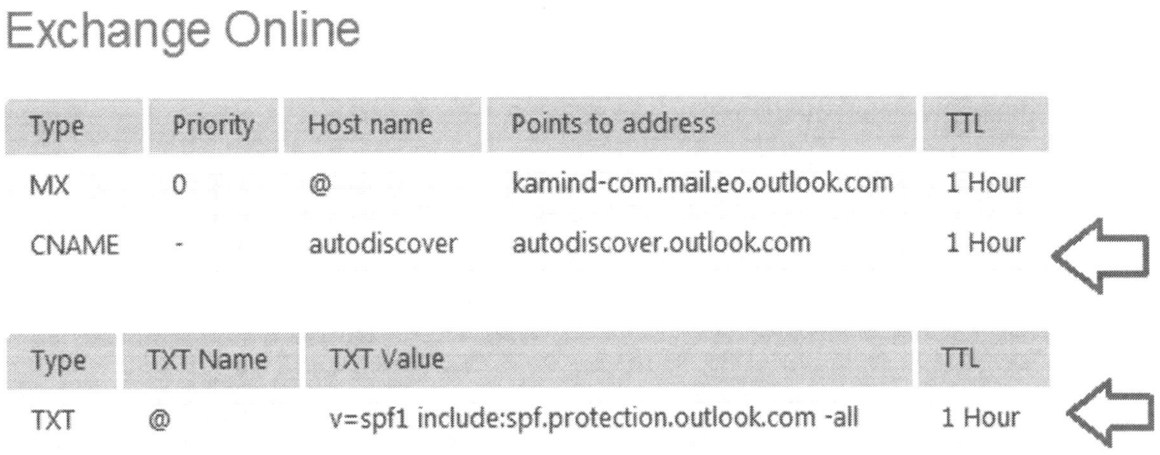

Exchange Online

Type	Priority	Host name	Points to address	TTL
MX	0	@	kamind-com.mail.eo.outlook.com	1 Hour
CNAME	-	autodiscover	autodiscover.outlook.com	1 Hour

Type	TXT Name	TXT Value	TTL
TXT	@	v=spf1 include:spf.protection.outlook.com -all	1 Hour

Figure 11-56. *Setting the External DNS records*

9. Run the Hybrid Configuration Wizard. The wizard will verify the Federation configuration, validate the domain for Federation services, and install the EOP connector.

   a. On the Exchange Management Console, select the Organizational Configuration node, then select the Hybrid configuration tab, then the New Hybrid Configuration (see Figure 11-57).

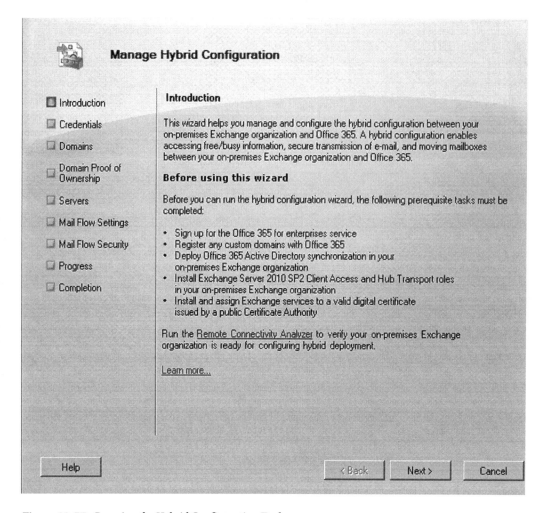

Figure 11-57. *Running the Hybrid Configuration Tool*

    b.   The hybrid configuration will require two accounts to integrate into Office 365; both of these accounts needs to be a member of the "Organization management Role" group for the On Premises server and the Office 365 server.

        i.   *The Office 365 account should be unique. We typically recommend that the account be part of the onMicrosoft.com domain (see Figure 11-58).*

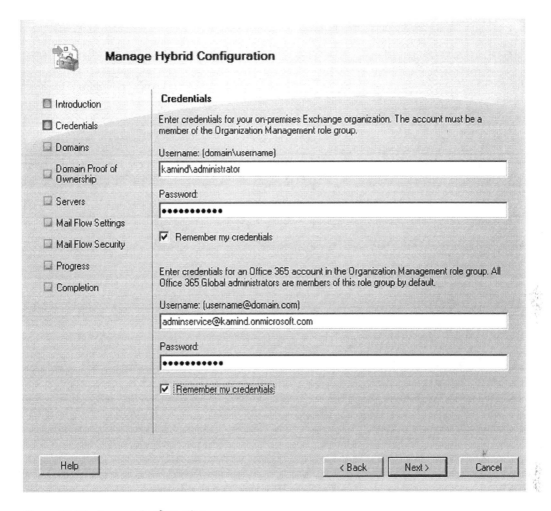

Figure 11-58. *Account Configuration*

  c. Add the domain to be federated (see Figure 11-59).

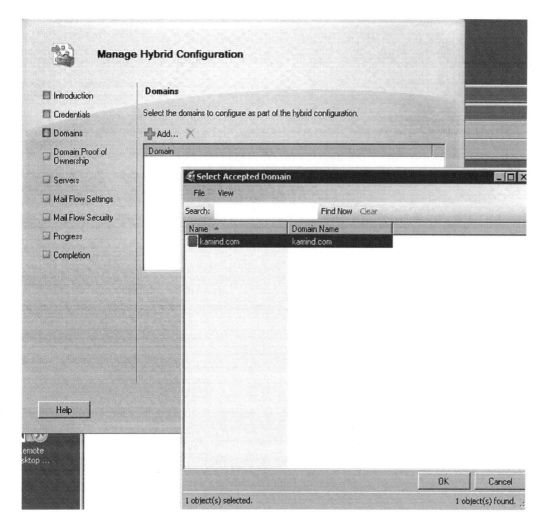

Figure 11-59. *Adding Hybrid domain for Federation*

    d.   Create the validation text record for DNS verification. The text record needs to be copied and installed in the DNS server, so select the check box once the record is entered (see Figure 11-60).

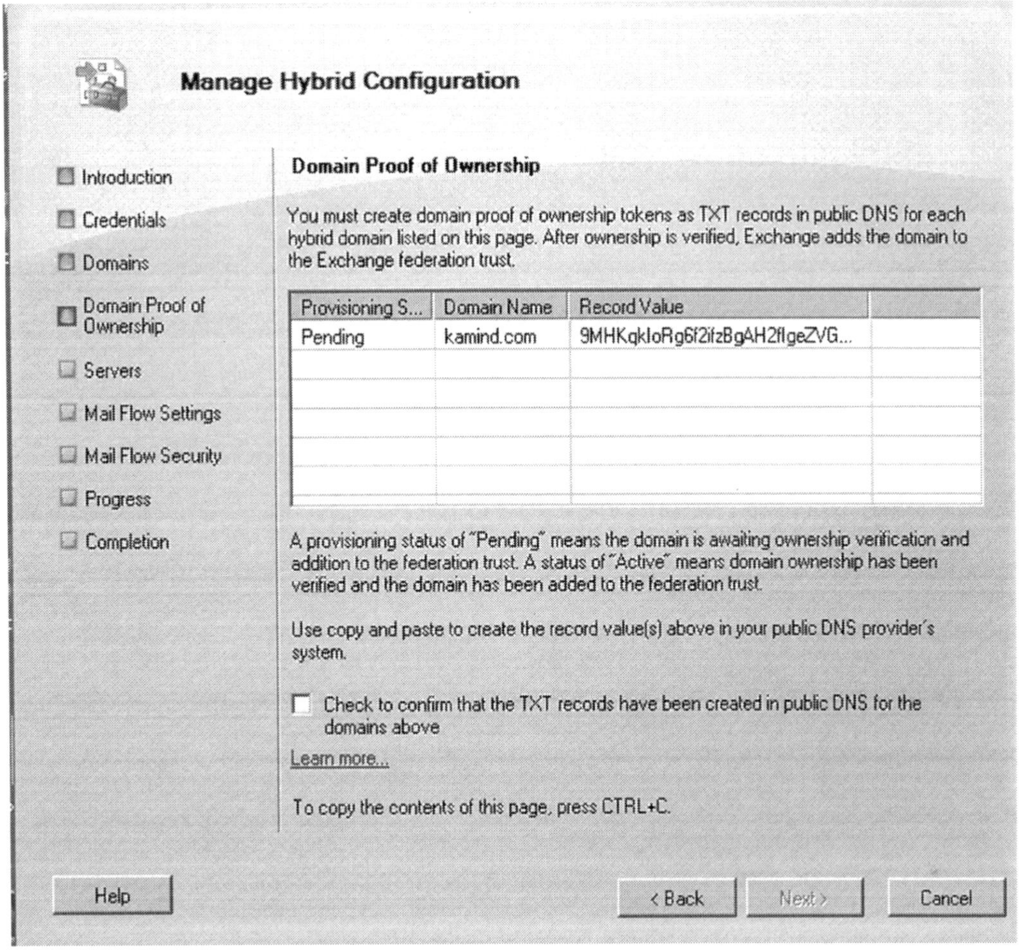

Manage Hybrid Configuration

- Introduction
- Credentials
- Domains
- **Domain Proof of Ownership**
- Servers
- Mail Flow Settings
- Mail Flow Security
- Progress
- Completion

Domain Proof of Ownership

You must create domain proof of ownership tokens as TXT records in public DNS for each hybrid domain listed on this page. After ownership is verified, Exchange adds the domain to the Exchange federation trust.

Provisioning S...	Domain Name	Record Value	
Pending	kamind.com	9MHKqkIoRg6f2ifzBgAH2flgeZVG...	

A provisioning status of "Pending" means the domain is awaiting ownership verification and addition to the federation trust. A status of "Active" means domain ownership has been verified and the domain has been added to the federation trust.

Use copy and paste to create the record value(s) above in your public DNS provider's system.

☐ Check to confirm that the TXT records have been created in public DNS for the domains above

Learn more...

To copy the contents of this page, press CTRL+C.

Help		< Back	Next >	Cancel

Figure 11-60. *Creating the verification text records*

    e.   Add the primary mailbox/CAS server and the hub transport server (Figure 11-61).

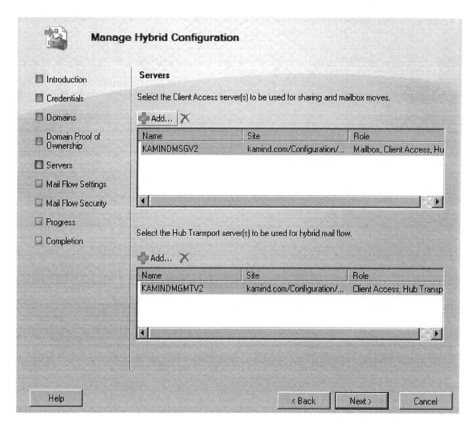

Figure 11-61. *Enter the Mailbox Server and Client Access Server*

     f.   Add the IP address of the external gateway for the EOP send connector to access for
          the on-site hub transport server (SMTP gateway – Figure 11-62).

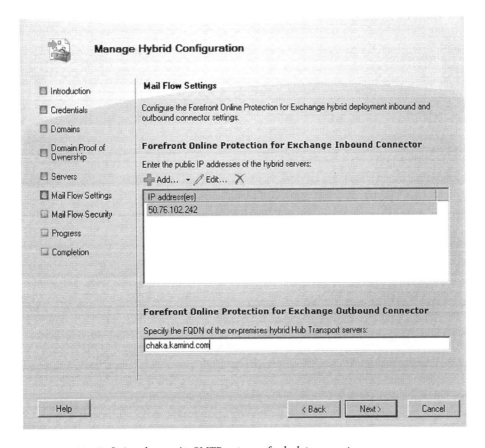

Figure 11-62. Defining the on-site SMTP gateway for hub transport

    g.   Select the EOP mail flow; either Cloud or On Premises.

10.   The Current MX (Mail exchange) records still point to the original location of the On Premises server (Figure 11-63). There are two ways to route mail in a hybrid organization: through EOP or through the existing On Premises server. After you complete the wizard, you will need to add the IP addresses of the EOP send connector to your hub transport server (or firewall).

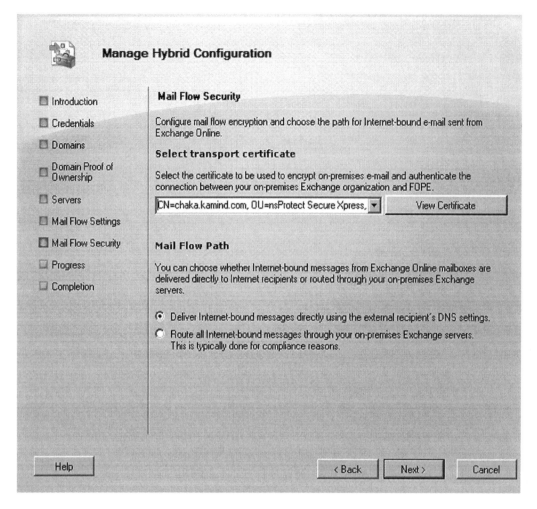

Figure 11-63. *Selecting the EOP Mail flow*

a.   Complete the wizard by selecting "Manage" (see Figure 11-64).

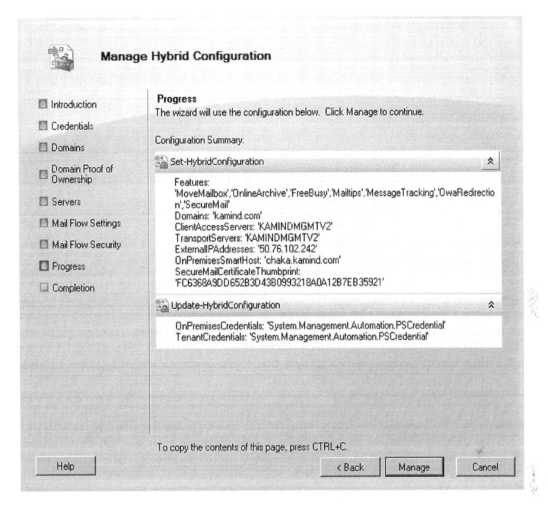

Figure 11-64. *Creating the Federation Interface*

b. The Hybrid wizard is extremely verbose. All information is logged in the directory C:\Program Files\Microsoft\Exchange Server\V14\Logging\ Update-HybridConfiguration.

c. Once you have resolved any errors, the Hybrid Federation connector is created (see Figure 11-65), so click Finish. Once the connector is in place, you can modify the connector as needed.

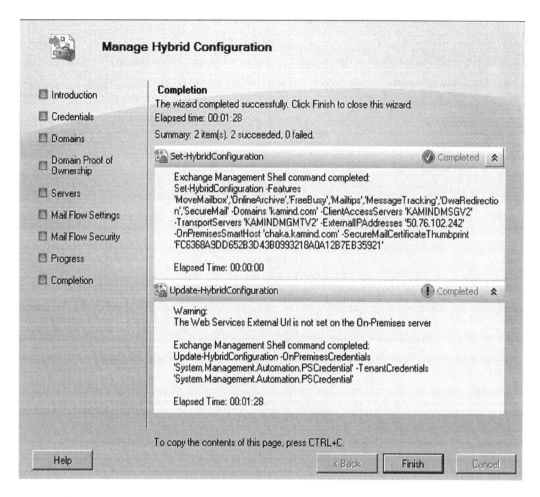

Figure 11-65. Hybrid Configuration - Completion

11.   To verify your configuration, execute the command Get-HybridConfiguration
        (see Figure 11-66).

Figure 11-66. *Validating the Hybrid Configuration*

12. After you have completed the hybrid wizard, you need to add the IP addresses of the EOP gateway to your On Premises firewall to allow the email connectivity. Go to http://technet.microsoft.com/en-us/library/dn163583(v=exchg.150).aspx.

The Hybrid Federation configuration is completed. At this point there are only two steps left for full Federation: testing out mailbox moves and moving the MX records to point to Office 365.

Step 7: Post Federation Testing

Post Federation testing is the verification that the Hybrid deployment is working, and if so the following is true:

1. You can create a remote Mailbox in Office 365 from the On Premises server

2. You can move a mailbox to Office 365

3. You can verify free Busy calendar sharing with the cloud

4. You can verify mail flow by sending a message from Office 365 to premise server

5. You can change the MX records and point the DNS records to Office 365

Change the MX records

After you have completed all of the testing to ensure mail flow is correct, you need to move the MX records from pointing to the On Premises server to Office 365. Once you have competed this step, you will be ready for production deployment using the remote mailbox move. The MX record will look similar to Figure 11-67. Once you have completed the record move, verify the records in Office 365 and then you have completed the Federation configuration.

Exchange Online

Type	Priority	Host name	Points to address	TTL
MX	0	@	kamind-com.mail.eo.outlook.com	1 Hour

Figure 11-67. *Change the MX records*

At this point your Office 365 federation is completed. You can move mailboxes to the offsite server and back to the On Site server. Mail migration at this point is completed by using the remote mailbox move from the On Site server to Office 365.

Troubleshooting

ADFS and Directory Synchronization work well, but you need to address problems when they happen. ADFS problems will lead to the users not being able to login into Office 365 or access any emails. Directory sync issues end up having password mismatches. Most of the issues you run into are at the initial deployment stages. The most common issues that you run into on Office 365 follow:

> Active Directory Readiness Check
>
> DirSync: Installation error – Need Online Service Sign in
>
> DirSync: Active Directory Required user fields
>
> DirSync: Adding Alias Proxy (exchange server not present)
>
> ADFS: Remote Connectivity Analyzer
>
> ADFS: Database errors
>
> ADFS: Hybrid Federation Certificate Problems

There are other issues that you may run into. These are the most common issues that we have seen on Office 365 when you deploy Directory Synchronization or Active Directory Federation Services. Detailed information about the various troubleshooting steps are listed below.

Active Directory Readiness Check

If your Active Directory has gone through a number of upgrades, you should review the Active Directory for readiness – Verification of the structure to make sure it will work with directory sync. The objective here is to validate and repair any Active Directory issues, and to check for other issues that can be addressed later.

1. Select a domain joined workstation or server (preferably the server that you will run DirSync on) and login to start the tool.

2. Follow the steps outlined below (this tool will not work if you have run DirSync).

3. Repair issues as found (through the first four checks: credentials, network, domains and users and groups); any other issues (Lync, mail, sites, user software) can be addressed later.

Step 1 – Sign In with your Office 365 Admin account

Select a domain joined server (used to install this set of check tools). Start a web browser and navigate to: `https://onramp.office365.com/`. Click the arrow by 'Liberate' and Sign in (Figure 11-68) with your Office 365 Administrator account.

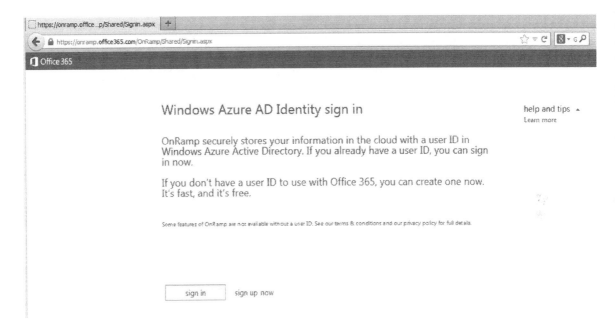

Figure 11-68. Azure AD Identity sign in

Click through the screens and make selections as required. Select "We'll synchronize our On Premises' Active Directory with Office 365" (unless you have a different plan). See Figure 11-69.

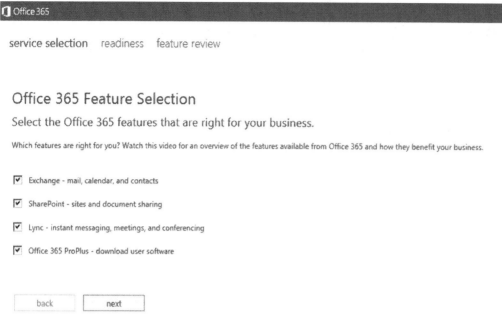

Figure 11-69. *Office 365 feature selection for validation*

Select the exchange migration type (see Figure 11-70). Make sure you check "We'll synchronize our on premises Active Directory with Office 365". This will force the onramp tool to validate your local Active Directory for errors. If you are prompted with a screen on the Migration help, select "I am an IT professional." This will begin the test (see Figure 11-71).

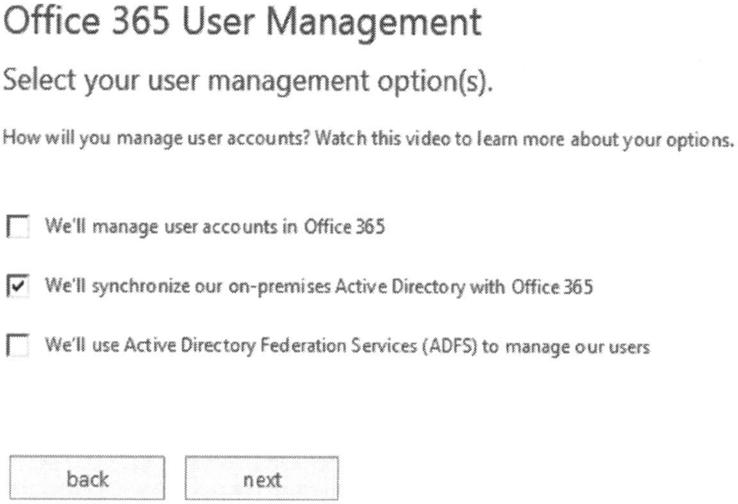

Office 365 User Management

Select your user management option(s).

How will you manage user accounts? Watch this video to learn more about your options.

☐ We'll manage user accounts in Office 365

☑ We'll synchronize our on-premises Active Directory with Office 365

☐ We'll use Active Directory Federation Services (ADFS) to manage our users

[back] [next]

Figure 11-70. *Select Synchronize Active Directory*

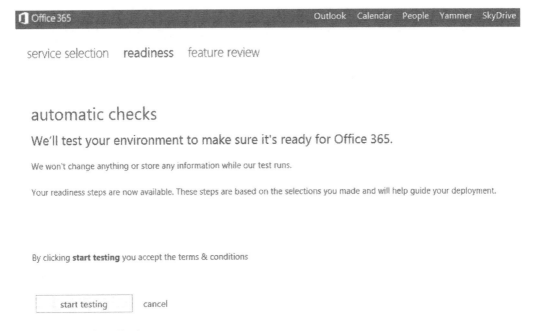

Figure 11-71. *Start Testing*

Step 2 – Install required Software updates

During the readiness test, you will see an analysis of the current environment. To address the issues, click on the necessary software downloads and install the updates. In some cases, you may see an error: "Microsoft online services sign-in assistant version 7.0 or greater" must be installed. If this is the case, refer to the "Troubleshooting" section. You will need to install the Directory Sync tool and re-run the readiness checks (see Figure 11-72).

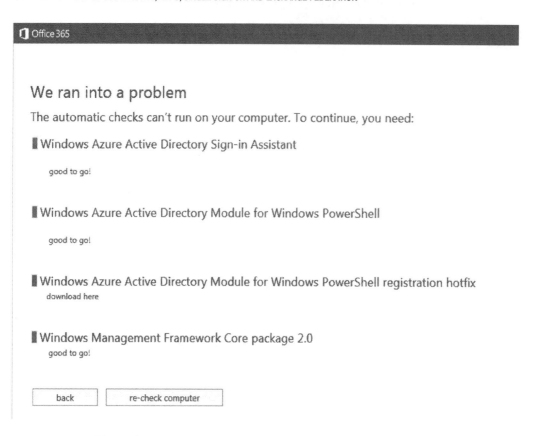

Figure 11-72. *Additional Items to Install*

Step 3 – Run the tests

Run the tests: re-check computer/Check again. For Active Directory we are only concerned about the first four sections (credentials, network, domains and users and groups). You can click on view details to review issues (see Figure 11-73). There are several screen shots of the sections below. DO NOT INSTALL DIRSYNC YET!

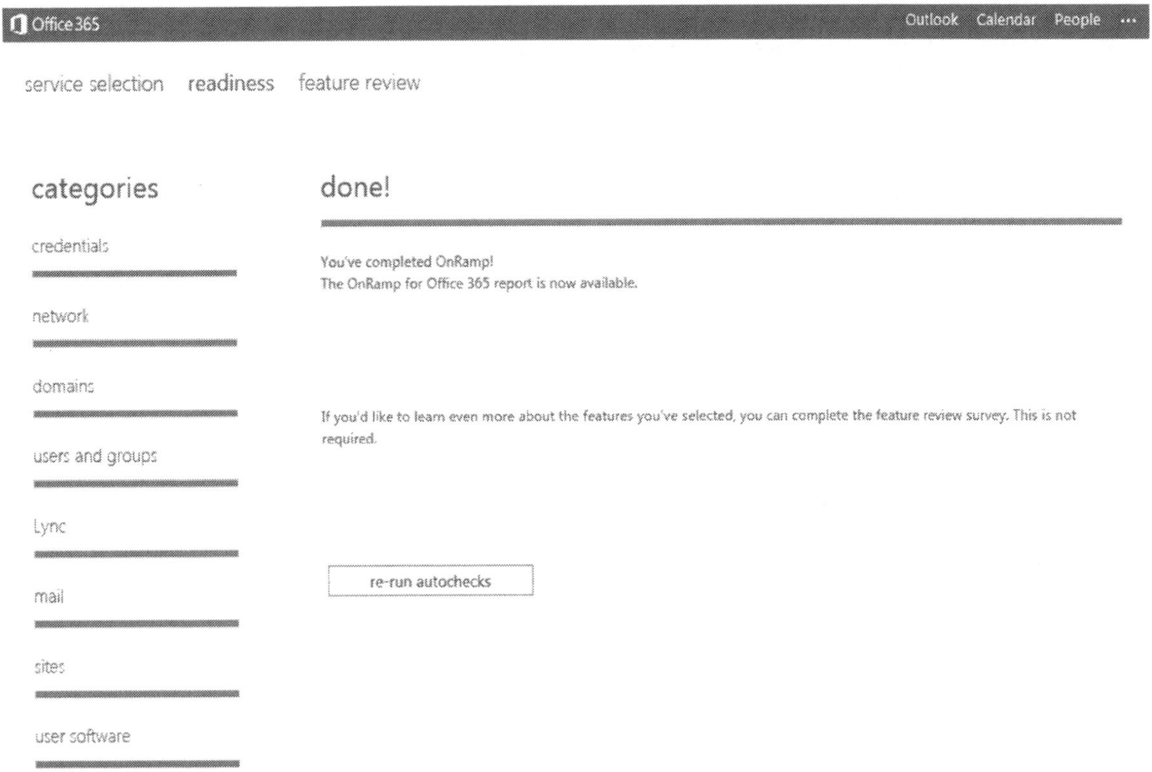

Figure 11-73. Readiness

After you run the test, you should see a summary on the readiness checks (see Figure 11-74). If you view the details, this action will show you how to correct the problems you may discover.

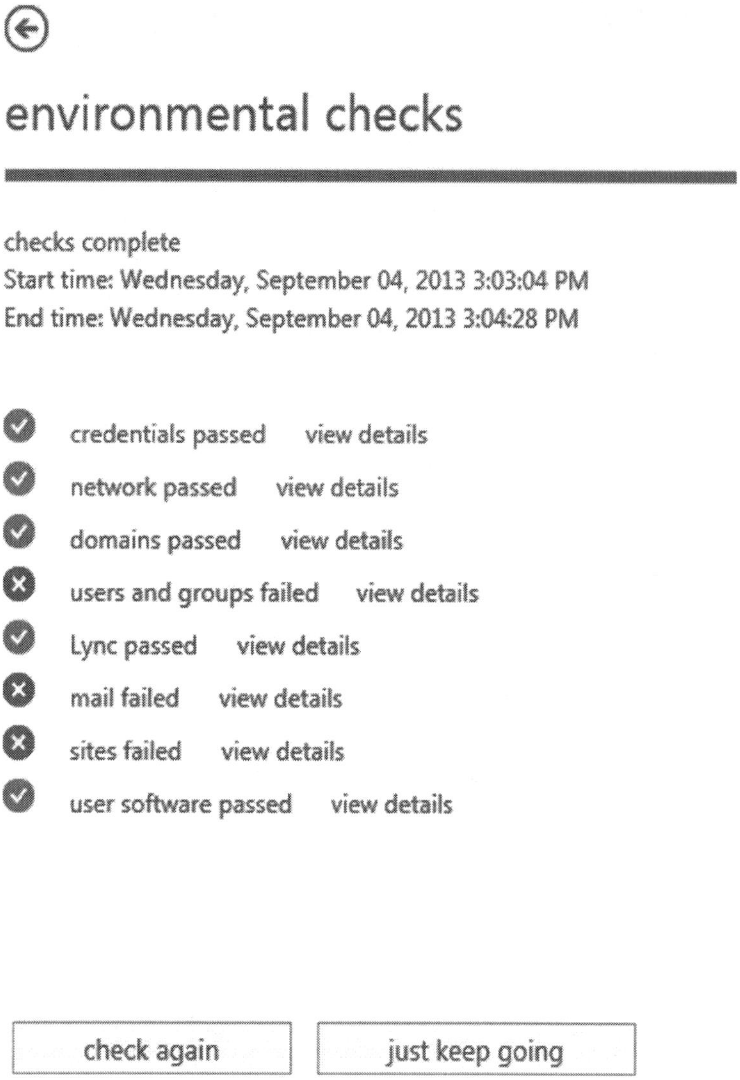

environmental checks

checks complete
Start time: Wednesday, September 04, 2013 3:03:04 PM
End time: Wednesday, September 04, 2013 3:04:28 PM

✓ credentials passed   view details

✓ network passed   view details

✓ domains passed   view details

✕ users and groups failed   view details

✓ Lync passed   view details

✕ mail failed   view details

✕ sites failed   view details

✓ user software passed   view details

check again		just keep going

Figure 11-74. Environmental checks

Step 4 – Research and Repair issues

You can check each failed requirement. The two areas to focus on are the network configuration and the User and groups Active Directory objects.

Lync issues are network related (see Figure 11-75 and Figure 11-76)

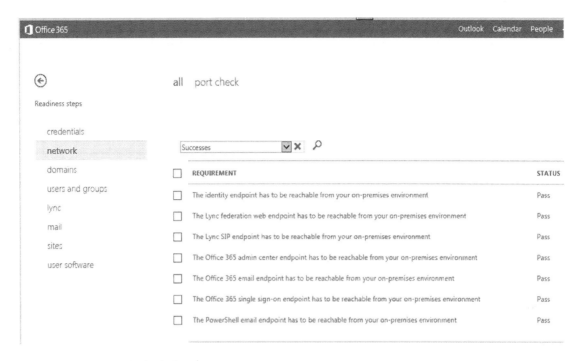

Figure 11-75. *Network Checks for Active Directory*

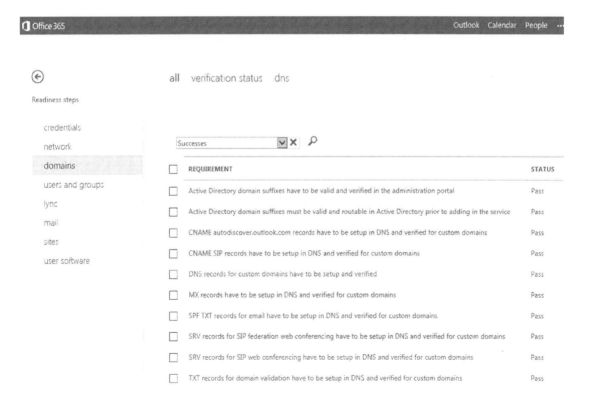

Figure 11-76. *Domain Verification*

Active Directory user issues (see Figure 11-77)

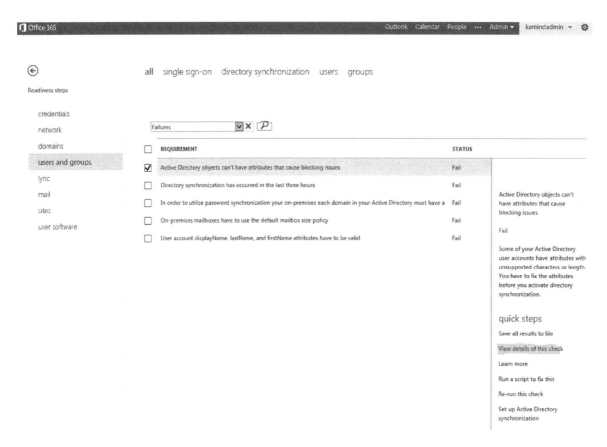

Figure 11-77. *User Verification check*

Review the details of this check on Active Directory and repair the objects that need to be repaired. In Figure 11-77 (see yellow), view the details of the check and take corrective action. The errors you fix at this stage will save you hours later on once you have implemented Directory Synchronization.

DirSync: Installation error – Missing Online service Sign in

One of the common errors that you may run into is the "you must have Microsoft online services sign-in assistant version 7.0 or greater" error (see Figure 11-78). The only way to address this is to manually install the Active Directory Sign On component.

Figure 11-78. *Active Directory Installation Error*

To install this component:

1. Go to the microsoft download center and search for "Microsoft Online Services Sign-In Assistant for IT Professionals" (`http://www.microsoft.com/en-us/download/details.aspx?id=28177`)

2. Download and install the desktop sign tool

3. Restart the Directory Synchronization installation.

The DirSync tool should install correctly.

DirSync: Required Active Directory User fields

Once you have identified all of the errors in Active Directory and cleaned the object up, you will also need to verify the user data. Directory Sync requires certain attributes to be configured correctly for the object to be replicated to Office 365. Active Directory Directory Sync requires that the user account must have the following attributes filled out (First Name, Last name, Display name and Email Address).

To set these parameters, go to Active Directory Users and Computers, select the user object, and then change the properties of the user above with the required information. All Active Directory objects that are being replicated must have this change, otherwise the mailbox will be replicated as `<company>onmicrosoft.com` (see Figure 11-79).

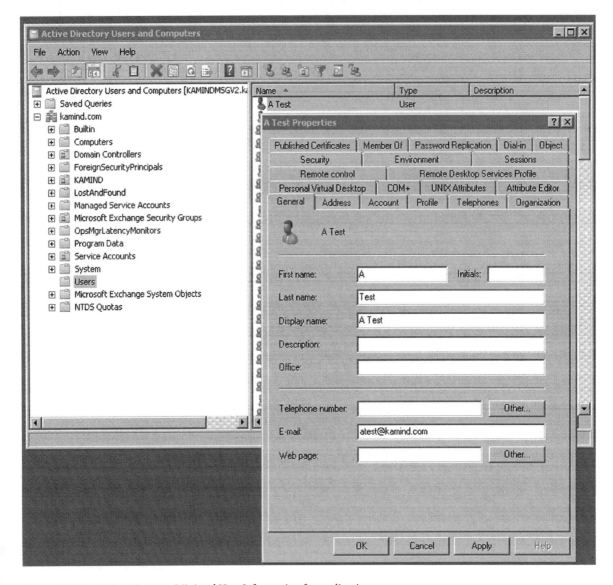

Figure 11-79. *Active Directory Minimal User Information for replication*

DirSync: Adding email Proxy Addresses

Active Directory organizes email address and proxy addresses in the format "`smtp:tom@domain.com`". Remember that case is important in the smtp header. A "SMTP:" in uppercase is the primary email address and the "smtp" in lower case is the alias address. In Figure 11-82, an e-mail address was added. This is the primary e-mail address so it will be replicated at "`SMTP:atest@kamind.com`".

If you do not have an Exchange Server, how do you add or modify the smtp proxy addresses (or alias)? There are two ways to do this; use the Exchange Server MMC client to modify the Active Directory, or use ADSIEDIT (located in the domain controller administrator tools group)to make the changes. You can also use the Active Directory User and Computers, and make the changes in the attribute editor. ADSIEDIT works the same way, just select the user object and make the changes.

To use Active Directory User and Computers, you must enable the Advance Features (under view, select "Advance Features"). The property dialog should look similar to Figure 11-80. Select the "Attribute Editor" tab, then select "Filter" and "Show only attributes that have value" (see Figure 11-81).

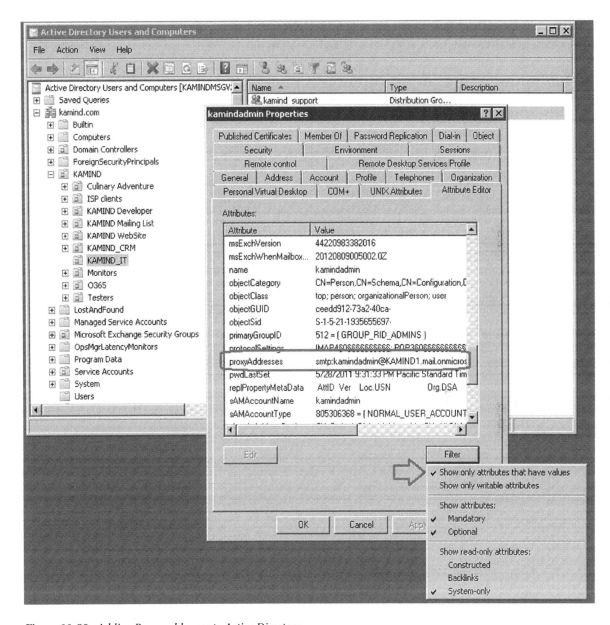

Figure 11-80. *Adding Proxy addresses to Active Directory*

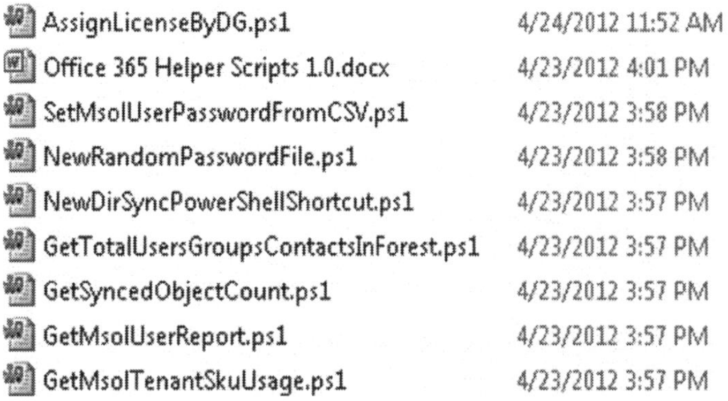

AssignLicenseByDG.ps1	4/24/2012 11:52 AM
Office 365 Helper Scripts 1.0.docx	4/23/2012 4:01 PM
SetMsolUserPasswordFromCSV.ps1	4/23/2012 3:58 PM
NewRandomPasswordFile.ps1	4/23/2012 3:58 PM
NewDirSyncPowerShellShortcut.ps1	4/23/2012 3:57 PM
GetTotalUsersGroupsContactsInForest.ps1	4/23/2012 3:57 PM
GetSyncedObjectCount.ps1	4/23/2012 3:57 PM
GetMsolUserReport.ps1	4/23/2012 3:57 PM
GetMsolTenantSkuUsage.ps1	4/23/2012 3:57 PM

Figure 11-81. *DirSync Related PowerShell Scripts - May 2012 - Helper scripts*

Select the "proxy addresses" and select Edit (see Figure 11-81). Remember, you can only enter the alias. Do not change the primary address in the attribute filed. The primary address can only be changed in the user properties. When you change the user properties, additional fields in Active Directory are updated. Once you make the changes, save them and DirSync will replicate them, or you can manually replicate the changes.

DirSync: Using PowerShell Licensing Scripts

Microsoft Online Services has released a number of PowerShell scripts that assist users in the migration to Office 365 while using DirSync. These scripts provide detailed information on the usage of Office 365, and allow you to assign licenses and other parameters to users in bulk (see Figure 11-81).

To add licenses, you need to collect information about your Office 365 organization. The script, *GetMsolTenantSku* generates a report (see Figure 11-82) on the usage of the licenses, and the Office 365 organization name that use the license. To add a license to a DirSync object is a two step process: 1) determine the license that is being used, and 2) assign the license to the DirSync object.

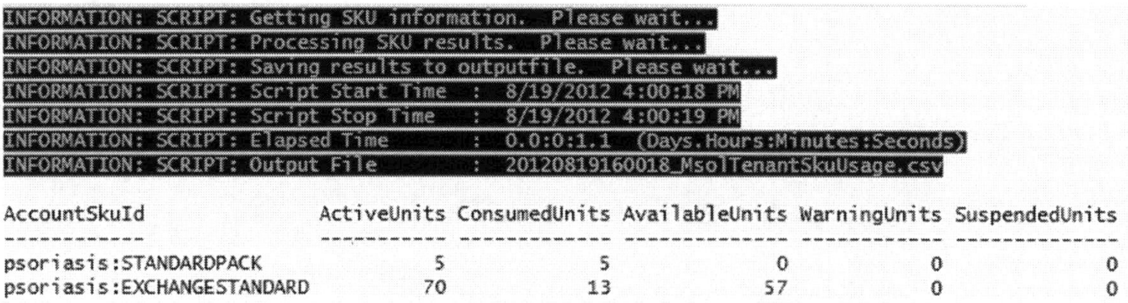

```
INFORMATION: SCRIPT: Getting SKU information.  Please wait...
INFORMATION: SCRIPT: Processing SKU results.  Please wait...
INFORMATION: SCRIPT: Saving results to outputfile.  Please wait...
INFORMATION: SCRIPT: Script Start Time   :  8/19/2012 4:00:18 PM
INFORMATION: SCRIPT: Script Stop Time    :  8/19/2012 4:00:19 PM
INFORMATION: SCRIPT: Elapsed Time        :  0.0:0:1.1  (Days.Hours:Minutes:Seconds)
INFORMATION: SCRIPT: Output File         :  20120819160018_MsolTenantSkuUsage.csv
```

AccountSkuId	ActiveUnits	ConsumedUnits	AvailableUnits	WarningUnits	SuspendedUnits
psoriasis:STANDARDPACK	5	5	0	0	0
psoriasis:EXCHANGESTANDARD	70	13	57	0	0

Figure 11-82. *Determining the licenses that are in use*

ADFS – Remote Connectivity Analyzer

ADFS issues are usually based on permissions, passwords or wrong UPN parameters. When you are using ADFS, you are changing from using a "non-routable domain" to a routable domain. If you have this problem, what you will see is a login prompt on the Federation server. Your account credentials will be rejected. If you have this message, how do you fix the Single Sign On? The first step is to run the Remote Connectivity Analyzer to verify connectivity (see Figure 11-83). This section reviews some of the common ADFS errors and troubleshooting steps to correct the ADFS error.

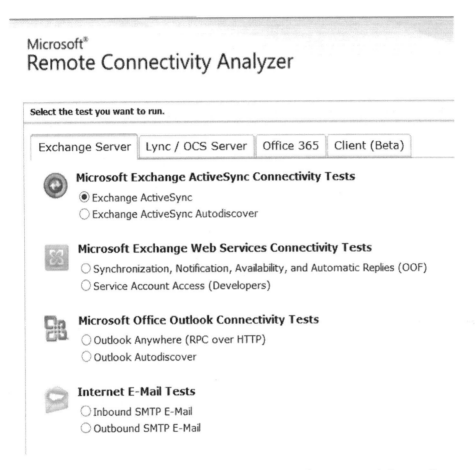

Figure 11-83. Connectivity Test Tool (https://www.testExchangeconnectivity.com/)

ADFS: Database Error

If the ADFS services has a synchronization error, or the SSO stops working, you may need to recreate the ADFS integration database. To create a new database, you will need to run the wizard. The wizard is located on the server where ADFS is installed:

```
<drive:\>Program Files\Active Directory Federation Services 2.0\ FsConfigWizard.
```

When you run the wizard, you are following the same steps, with the exception of the need to delete the existing ADFS database. Here are the steps to follow:

1. Select "New Federation Server farm"

2. Select next – the SSL certificate should still be valid

3. If prompted, delete the data base

4. Enter the service account

5. Select next and correct and errors `d

You will receive an error message because the existing ADFS website is in place (see Figure 11-84).

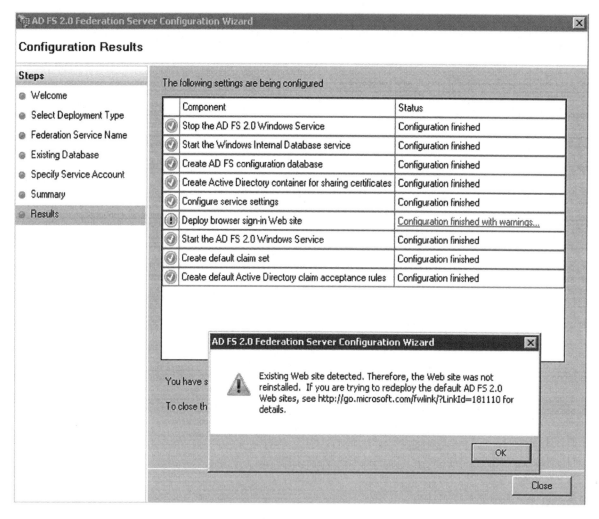

Figure 11-84. *ADFS reinstallation Warning message*

For the final step, you will need to reconnect Office 365 to the local server by running the following PowerShell scripts:

```
Note: domain: kamind.com, internal server kamindmgmtv2.kamind.com
Account:  need to use the onmicrosoft.com account as the admin account for livecred

Set-ExecutionPolicy RemoteSigned
$LiveCred = Get-Credential
Connect-MsolService -Credential $LiveCred.

#Get Status of federated domain
Get-MsolFederationProperty -DomainName kamind.com

#if the domain does not match Federation
Update-MsolFederatedDomain -DomainName kamind.com
```

After you have run the scripts, start up the ADFS configuration tool and it should connect up to the Office 365 services (see Figure 11-85). If you have an error, check the proxies and rerun the PowerShell scripts.

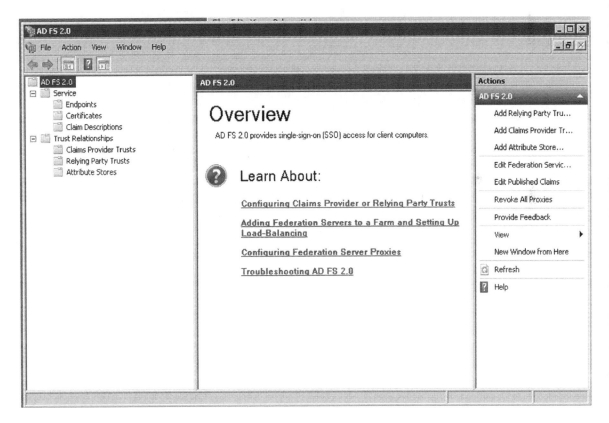

Figure 11-85. *Starting the ADFS tool to verify the configuration – no DB sync error*

ADFS: Hybrid Federation Certificate Problems

A common error when the Hybrid wizard does not complete is a failure of the certificate (see Figure 11-86). The wizard looks for all names to be on the certificate, so you can have a failure if you are using a third party certificate that is not complete.

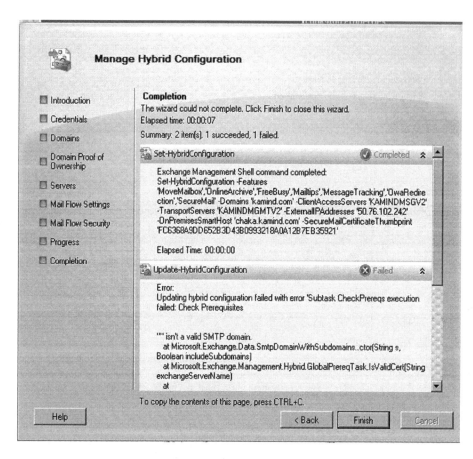

Figure 11-86. *Hybrid Certificate Error*

To verify that this is a certificate error, use "Get-FederationInformation –Domanname <enter domain>" (see Figure 11-87).

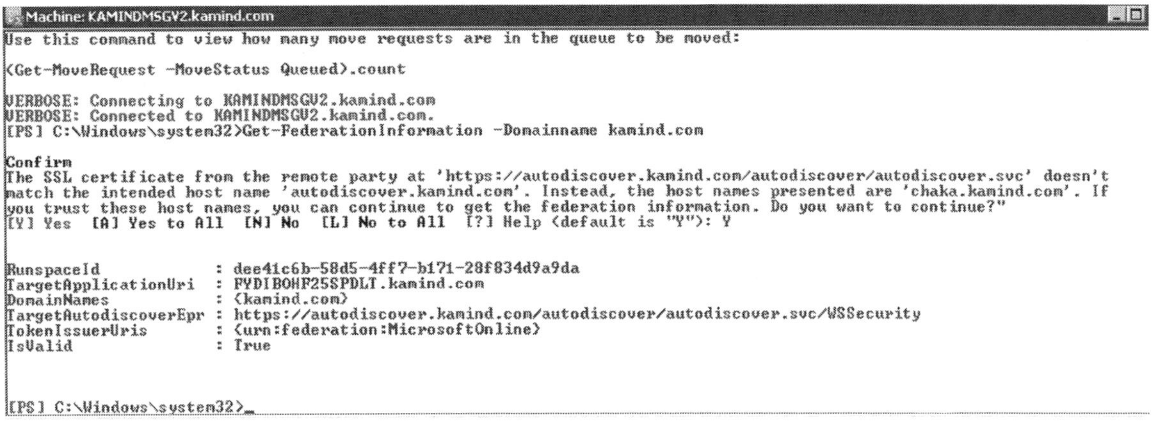
Machine: KAMINDMSGV2.kamind.com
Use this command to view how many move requests are in the queue to be moved:
(Get-MoveRequest -MoveStatus Queued).count
VERBOSE: Connecting to KAMINDMSGV2.kamind.com
VERBOSE: Connected to KAMINDMSGV2.kamind.com.
[PS] C:\Windows\system32>Get-FederationInformation -Domainname kamind.com
Confirm
The SSL certificate from the remote party at 'https://autodiscover.kamind.com/autodiscover/autodiscover.svc' doesn't match the intended host name 'autodiscover.kamind.com'. Instead, the host names presented are 'chaka.kamind.com'. If you trust these host names, you can continue to get the federation information. Do you want to continue?"
[Y] Yes [A] Yes to All [N] No [L] No to All [?] Help (default is "Y"): Y
RunspaceId : dee41c6b-58d5-4ff7-b171-28f834d9a9da
TargetApplicationUri : FYDIBOHF25SPDLT.kamind.com
DomainNames : {kamind.com}
TargetAutodiscoverEpr : https://autodiscover.kamind.com/autodiscover/autodiscover.svc/WSSecurity
TokenIssuerUris : {urn:federation:MicrosoftOnline}
IsValid : True
[PS] C:\Windows\system32>_

Figure 11-87. *Checking the Federation Certificate credentials*

The PowerShell command returns the Federation error for the SSL certificate. There is only one way to address this and that is to purchase a new SSL certificate with the appropriate name on the certificate. In general, wildcard certificates are used hybrid domains.

ADFS: Single Sign On (SSO) User experience

The SSO experience for the user is a seamless integration that assumes that the user has a system that is integrated into a Windows Active Directory. When the user logs on to the local system and authenticates with Active Directory, the user login credentials are passed through to the Office 365 side (see Figure 11-88).

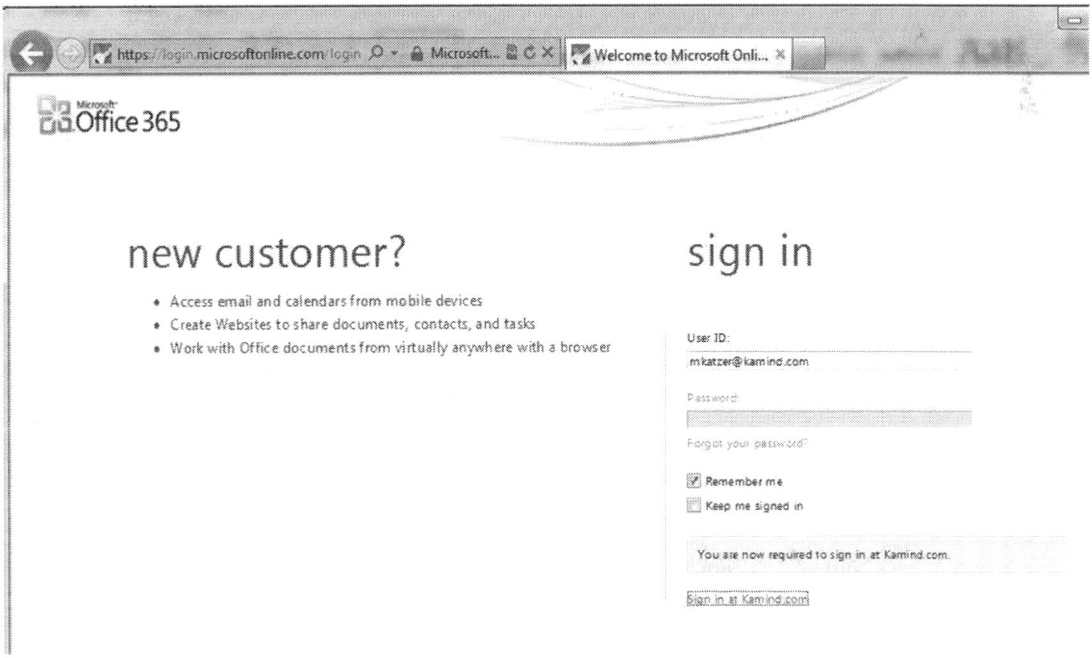
https://login.microsoftonline.com/login
Welcome to Microsoft Onli...
Office 365
new customer?
Access email and calendars from mobile devices
Create Websites to share documents, contacts, and tasks
Work with Office documents from virtually anywhere with a browser
sign in
User ID:
mkatzer@kamind.com
Password:
Forgot your password?
Remember me
Keep me signed in
You are now required to sign in at Kamind.com.
Sign in at Kamind.com

Figure 11-88. *Office 365 redirection to local server*

Non Domain login

All logins to the cloud are authenticated by the local domain controller. When a user logins to www.Office365.com, the login credentials are sent to the On Premises Federated Domain Controller (via ADFS) to login. The user will see the preceding response. If the user systems is configured correctly, the user login will be automatic (see Figure 11-88); if not the user will be required to authenticate (see Figure 11-89).

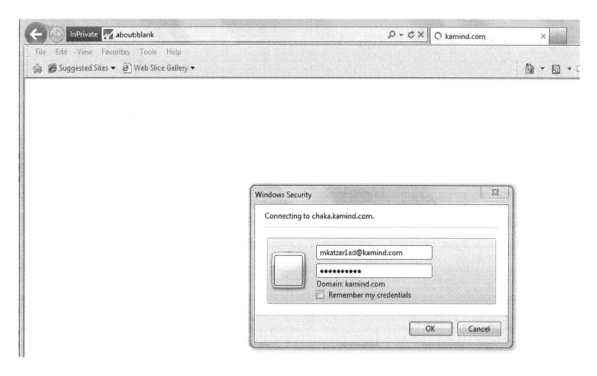

Figure 11-89. *User login redirected to local domain controller*

Domain login overrides Web login

The local systems login overrides the Office 365 account login. In the preceding case, if we login as one user on our local computer, and we try to login as a different user in Office 365, the Office 365 login will override with the current Active Directory account. As a practice example, in Figure 11-47, we used the web login mkatzer1ad@kamind.com, but the client login to the Active Directory was kamdinadmin@kamind.com.

When the security credentials are checked with the local server and system, the user account that is connected to the cloud is the account that the user is logged into locally. The caution here is that you will need to use devices that are not attached to a domain in order to migrate between different Office 365 accounts (in the same domain).

Reference Links

There is a lot of information about Office 365 on the web, the issue is finding the right site. The information contained in this chapter is a combination of our experiences in doing deployments along with support information that we have assembled along the way.

Microsoft Office 365 blog – Latest news about Office 365

```
http://blogs.office.com/b/microsoft_office_365_blog/
```

Exchange Deployment Assistant (2010) – Q/A on deployment of Office 365

```
http://technet.microsoft.com/en-us/exdeploy2010/default(EXCHG.150).aspx#Index
```

Benoit's Corner – Useful tips and tricks on Exchange and SharePoint

```
http://blog.hametbenoit.info/default.aspx
```

Directory Synchronization Tool Update

```
http://technet.microsoft.com/en-us/library/jj151800.aspx
```

Troubleshooting Free and Busy

```
http://support.microsoft.com/kb/2555008
```

Windows Azure Active Directory – validation (http://support.microsoft.com/kb/)

```
2461873 - (http://support.microsoft.com/kb/2461873/)
```

You can't open the Windows Azure Active Directory Module for Windows PowerShell

```
2494043  - (http://support.microsoft.com/kb/2494043/)
```

You can't connect by using the Windows Azure Active Directory Module for Windows PowerShell

```
2587730 - (http://support.microsoft.com/kb/2587730/)
```

Authentication error when you use the Set-MsolADFSContext cmdlet in the Windows Azure Active Directory Module for Windows PowerShell

2279117 - An administrator cannot add a domain to an Office 365 account

```
2515404 - (http://support.microsoft.com/kb/2515404/)
```

Troubleshoot domain verification issues in Office 365.

```
2618887(http://support.microsoft.com/kb/2618887/) - Error when you try to configure a second
federated domain in Office 365: "Federation service identifier specified in the AD FS 2.0 server is
already in use."
2578667 - (http://support.microsoft.com/kb/2578667/) "Your organization could not sign you in to
this service" error and "80045C06" error code when a federated user tries to sign in to Office 365
```

Exchange server 2013 – extending Active Directory Attributes with forestprep and domainprep

```
http://technet.microsoft.com/en-us/library/bb125224(v=exchg.150).aspx
```

Next steps

Your basic Office 365 systems has been set up and configured. At this point you are 100% functional and ready to move to the next steps. However, your work is not complete at this time; there is much more to do. Depending on your Office 365 configuration, the key chapters you need to review for your Office 365 deployment are as follows:

- **Chapter 7** – Administration of Windows Intune

  - The secret to an optimal Office 365 site is the management of the desktop to ensure that updates are current, and the user antivirus is functioning. Windows Intune is a desktop management tool that addresses these issues and reduces the administrators' effort in desktop management, and improves the user's experience.

- **Chapter 8** –Administration

  - The administrator's job is never completed. This chapter contains the useful information for common task such as configuration of SharePoint permission, using different types of PowerShell scripts for configuration of the Office 365 sites and other tips and track that we used to make Office 365 work without any support calls

- **Chapter 9** – Compliance, Discovery and Rights Management

  - Securing our data is critical to all businesses. How do you keep data, where is it kept and how to you deal with discovery issues assorted with compliance. The new Data Loss Prevention (DLP) features (and encryption options) provides the necessary tools to meet the regulatory needs of today's business. This chapter reviews the different approach to control data loss, data retention and compliance.

- **Chapter 10** – Administration of Exchange Online Protection

  - Mail routing and configuration of the Office 365 SPAM filters is not easily understood. This chapter contains useful information on setting up EOP, adding policies to the message filters, using Encryption and controlling mail flow. If you are doing any migrations where you need to cut over 100% to Office 365 and redirect mail to the old email servers, this chapter addresses those and other Forefront Online protection issues.

Glossary

The following list of glossary terms are covered in this book.

AAAA record—Part of the Domain Name System (DNS). Normally returns a 128-bit IPv6 address.

Active Directory (AD)—Active Directory is a database designed to store information about your Microsoft network environment, including users, groups, passwords, user contact information, and network configuration. It is normally replicated across your network.

AD FS—Active Directory Federation Services extends Active Directory to off-premises applications and systems (outside the firewall). AD FS allows single sign-on.

alias—An e-mail address that points to another e-mail address. People outside the system can e-mail to an alias address. You can have as many alias addresses as you wish in Office 365.

app—A component of a SharePoint page, such as a document library or list. A type of Web Part.

A record—Part of the Domain Name System (DNS). Normally returns a 32-bit IPv4 address.

Autodiscover—Part of the Domain Name System (DNS). Autodiscover describes the name (IP address) of where a program such as Outlook can find the Exchange server for a given e-mail account. Implemented as a CNAME record, it may have to be implemented on a DNS local server as well as at the domain registrar. For Office 365, the initial Exchange server address is `autodiscover.outlook.com`.

BPOS—Business Productivity Online Standard Suite (the previous name and version of Office 365).

browser—Web browser, such as Internet Explorer, Firefox, Chrome, or Safari.

cloud—Any off-premises service that is maintained by a third party. Examples include Hotmail and the Microsoft Online Services: Office 365.

CNAME record—Part of the Domain Name System (DNS). Alias of one name to another.

coexistence—In a coexistence migration, the mail flow (via the MX record) remains through the original e-mail server as test groups are migrated to Office 365. Mail flow is redirected to Office 365 at the end of the migration.

content type—A content type defines the attributes of a SharePoint list item, a document, or a folder. There is a content type per site collection. It could be considered as a "collection of columns for reuse" in other lists or document libraries. Content types are inherited. See Reference Links page.

core business software—The software that is the heart of the business. This could be the point-of-sale software for a retail store or the order tracking system for a warehouse. It is the software that runs the business.

cutover—In a cutover migration the mail flow (via the MX record) is redirected to Office 365 for the entire organization at one time.

DirSync—Directory Sync allows an Active Directory to be synchronized to another Active Directory. In the Office 365 world, an on-premises Active Directory is synchronized (now including passwords) to the Office 365 Active Directory for your tenant.

distribution groups—Distribution groups (formerly known as distribution lists) are lists of e-mail addresses. E-mailing to a distribution group sends the e-mail to each user in the group. A distribution group can be for internal e-mail only or available to the outside world.

DNS—Domain Name System; also the protocol used by the Domain Name System. Used to look up additional information (or translate) a name to an IP address. See also A record, AAAA record, CNAME record, MX record, SPF record, SRV record, TXT record, and www record.

document—A Word, Excel, PowerPoint, or other type of file within a SharePoint document library. A document may have independent permissions.

document library—A set of documents within a SharePoint site. In many ways, a document library is a specialized list that contains the document and associated meta-data. A document library is separate from a page but usually is displayed on a page. When you select and display a specific document library, the page ribbon shows actions that can be performed in the document library or folders and documents within it, such as setting permissions or deleting an item. A document library may contain folders and documents.

Document Set—Document Sets are a feature in SharePoint Server 2013 that enable an organization to manage a single deliverable, or work product, that can include multiple documents or files. A Document Set is a special kind of folder that combines unique Document Set attributes, the attributes and behavior of folders and documents, and provides a user interface (UI), meta-data, and object model elements to help manage all aspects of the work product. See Reference Links page.

domain name—Often referred to as "custom" or "vanity" domains, this is the name of an organization on the Internet, used for its e-mail and web site. A domain name is maintained (and reported to the rest of the world) by a domain registrar. Examples of domain names are kamind.net, microsoft.com, or getoffice365now.com.

domain registrar—An organization that maintains your domain information, for example: eNom, Network Solutions, or GoDaddy. See also DNS.

EBS—Essential Business Server.

e-mail migration—The process of moving existing (historical) e-mail to a new e-mail service.

Essential Business Server—A configured three-server solution (Exchange, SharePoint, Systems Center) for companies with 75 to 400 employees. Microsoft canceled this offering on March 4, 2010. One of the factors was the cost per employee, as compared with the Microsoft Cloud offering.

Exchange Federation—A mechanism for trust between Exchange servers.

Exchange Federation remote mailbox move—A form of e-mail migration between federated Exchange servers. In Office 365, this is normally between an on-premises Exchange server and the Office 365 Exchange server(s) of your tenant.

Exchange Online Protection (EOP)—A Microsoft service that filters incoming e-mail for spam and viruses. Formerly known as Forefront Online Protection for Exchange (FOPE), this service is included in the hosted Exchange area of Office 365. There are several controls that can be used to customize the service.

Exchange public folders—A method of sharing information within an organization, using the Exchange server as the database. Contrast with SharePoint.

Exchange server—A Microsoft Services software product that receives, stores, and forwards e-mail (and other information, such as calendars, contacts, and folders) for an organization. A user typically sees the e-mail, calendar, and contacts through a client, such as Outlook, or through a web browser. Hosted Exchange is Exchange servers maintained by an external service, such as Office 365.

exe file—Executable file. These cannot be stored (directly) in SharePoint; use a .zip file.

external contacts—External contacts are contact information about people outside an organization.

folder—Similar to a folder on your PC. Part of a SharePoint document library. Folders may have independent permissions. A folder contains documents.

FTP—File Transfer Protocol. When implemented by an FTP server, it is a method used to share files. There are security and usability issues. See SharePoint as an alternative.

Hybrid Coexistence—Hybrid Coexistence could be considered as a type of migration. In the Office 365 context, an organization's e-mail can be stored either in the organization's on-premises Exchange server or the Office 365–hosted Exchange server for the tenant. After establishing Exchange Federation, an administrator can move users' e-mail boxes to and from the cloud.

immutability—The preservation of data in its original form is "immutable" (cannot be changed) and is kept in a form that is discoverable.

IP address—Internet Protocol Address—the numeric address of a device or service.

KAMIND—IT cloud consultants.

legal hold—Legal hold is an action that is placed on a mailbox to meet compliance requirements for future discovery and searching.

list—A set of items within a SharePoint site. You can think of a list as a bunch of rows and columns with potentially a data value at the intersection, like a spreadsheet. There are specialized lists that have special properties. A list is distinct from a page but usually is displayed on a page. When you select and display a specific list, the page ribbon shows actions that can be performed on the list or items in it, such as setting permissions or deleting an item. Special list types include Task List or Calendar List.

Lync—A communications client tool included in Office 365 that supports text, voice, and video communication with a whiteboard, shared programs, PowerPoint, shared monitors, and polls to one or more people. Can be used for planned or ad hoc meetings, person-to-person communication, and even remote support.

mail flow—Mail flow describes how a particular piece of e-mail flows from the sender to the receiver. See also MX record.

meta-data—Additional data stored about/with a SharePoint item, for example, the date and author of a document. This data is searchable.

Microsoft Domain Name—The prefix for `.onmicrosoft.com`. This is also the basis of your SharePoint site; for `xxx.onmicrosoft.com` the SharePoint site is `xxx.sharepoint.com`. This cannot be changed, nor can it be moved between different Office 365 plans.

Microsoft Online Services—Services provided by Microsoft, including Office 365 and Windows Intune.

migration—Copying data (typically e-mail, calendar entries, and contacts) from your existing environment to Office 365.

MX record—Part of the Domain Name System (DNS). An MX record tells the outside world the location of your mail service (name or IP address).

Office 365—The brand for the collection of Microsoft Cloud Services. Office 365 includes hosted Exchange e-mail, Lync Enterprise voice, SharePoint, and several software options. It is generally considered "Software as a Service."

Office 365 ProPlus—The current version of Office Professional, presently Office 2013. This is the full Office product and can be installed on up to five devices (under the same login), such as your work desktop, laptop, a Mac, and a home computer.

Office 365 Wave 14—A version first released in July 2012.

Office 365 Wave 15—A version first released in March 2013.

off-premises—Often used as a synonym for *cloud*, this actually denotes hardware devices and software that are located outside of your company location (off-site).

on-premises—This generally refers to equipment, computing resources, or people that are located at a company location (as opposed to at home or on the road).

on-site—People or equipment that is located at a company location (as opposed to at home or on the road). Usually a synonym for on-premises.

Outlook profile—The Outlook client reads Outlook profiles that contain the e-mail accounts that are to be included in this execution of Outlook.

page—A SharePoint page is what you see with your web browser. You can have multiple pages within a site. Generally, a site presents a default page that users will think of as "the site."

permissions—The "who can do it" aspect of SharePoint. Permissions are set on a site, list, document library, etc. Permission levels include None, Read, View, Contribute (Read and Write), and more. A particular user must have "permission" to do that activity on that item, for example, to be able to update the item.

pilot/test group—A group of users who are to be migrated. The first pilot/test group should include raving fans and naysayers and should be designed to test as many combinations of users' needs, to ferret out issues early in a migration.

POP mail—POP stands for *Post Office Protocol*. It is a protocol (method) of transferring e-mail from an e-mail server to an e-mail client. In a practical sense, each e-mail client receives its own copy of the e-mail. The effect is that you must frequently delete an e-mail from each client after it has been received. Contrast this with Exchange server, where e-mail is stored on the server, and the protocol allows an action (such as deletion or movement to a folder) on an e-mail to be reflected immediately on the Exchange server.

PST Export / Import—A PST file (the file extension for an Outlook personal information store file) stores e-mail on your computer. It can contain archived e-mails or current POP mail. Export is a process in Outlook that copies e-mail from a mailbox to a PST format file. In the context of Office 365, PST Import is the Outlook process that copies a PST file to the Office 365–hosted Exchange server. It is a method of e-mail migration.

push install—An automated installation that is set up by IT to push updates to the desktop, with no user interaction. Software updates are pushed and automatically installed.

security group—A security group is a type of Active Directory object that can be used to grant permissions in SharePoint.

SharePoint—SharePoint is Microsoft's document-storage and content-management tool. SharePoint was first released in 2001. Originally, SharePoint was used as an enterprise's on-premises intranet. SharePoint was included in Small Business Server and in the original Microsoft cloud offering: BPOS. The version with Office 365 is SharePoint Online.

SharePoint is fundamentally a web server that presents web pages to your browser (Internet Explorer, FireFox, Chrome, Safari, etc.). The SharePoint data (structure, permissions, sites, your documents, etc.) is hosted on SQL servers that are maintained by Microsoft within their secure environment."

single sign-on—Single sign-on (SSO) provides a single sign-on to an organization's computing resources, using Active Directory Federation Services (AD FS).

site—A SharePoint site is a collection of SharePoint "apps" and Web Parts (components), such as document libraries, lists, tasks, blogs, pictures, templates, and text that are presented to a user at a particular URL as a page. A site is within a particular site collection. An example is a project site.

site collection—This is a collection of SharePoint sites. With the Enterprise plan you may have multiple site collections within your tenant. Site collections have sets of properties that are the same for all sites within a site collection and which may be different between site collections.

site contents—Contents of a SharePoint site. The site contents page shows lists, libraries, and other apps and subsites that are associated with this site. This page is a helpful reference to your site structure. Access to this screen appears as a link on a site page or as a drop-down choice under the "gear" icon at the top right of the screen. Only items that you have permission to see will show.

SPF record—Part of the Domain Name System (DNS). "Sender Policy Framework" is an e-mail system to help prevent e-mail spam. The SPF record (normally implemented as a TXT record) describes which hosts are allowed to send from the domain. In Office 365, the sender is `spf.protection.outlook.com` for your domain.

SRV record—Part of the Domain Name System (DNS). An SRV record describes the location (protocol and port) for a given service at a host. Office 365 Lync requires two SRV records for correct implementation.

SSO—Single sign-on provides a single sign-on to an organization's computing resources, using Active Directory Federation Services (AD FS).

subsite—A SharePoint subsite is simply a site under (within) a site. You can nest sites until you confuse yourself.

tenant—This is your Office 365 account, including hosted Exchange, Lync, SharePoint, and your Office 365 Active Directory. The first account that you create when you first purchase Office 365 is the "owner" of your tenant. This account should be an admin account, not a person. This account does not normally require an Office 365 license. Relating to SharePoint, all of your site collections are within your tenant. You can have any number of domains within your tenant (with e-mail accounts), but you will have only one root SharePoint URL: `https://xxxx.sharepoint.com`.

TXT record—Part of the Domain Name System (DNS). A TXT record can contain any type of text. See SPF record. For Office 365, a TXT record is also used to prove domain ownership. (A specific TXT record is added by the domain registrar for your domain.)

URL—Universal resource locator. The specific universal address for a web page, it is essentially a specific location within a domain within the World Wide Web. (This doesn't necessarily mean that you can see it from anywhere; there can be security restrictions.) Examples are `https://kamind.sharepoint.com` or `http://getoffice365now.com`.

virtualization—A server or desktop operating system running on a virtual host. The server or desktop operating systems are running in a hardware-agnostic mode, because the hardware services are supplied by the virtual host.

Web Part—SharePoint components that can be inserted into a page (part of a site). Web Parts are very powerful and can interact with other sites and data outside of SharePoint.

web site—A SharePoint web site is a specialized site collection that can be seen by the outside world (public facing) through a standard URL (such as `http://getoffice365now.com`). You may only have one web site within a tenant.

www record—Part of the Domain Name System (DNS), it provides the name or IP address of a web server for a given domain name.

Index

▓ E

▒ T, U, V

▒ W, X, Y, Z

Get the eBook for only $10!

Now you can take the weightless companion with you anywhere, anytime. Your purchase of this book entitles you to 3 electronic versions for only $10.

This Apress title will prove so indispensible that you'll want to carry it with you everywhere, which is why we are offering the eBook in 3 formats for only $10 if you have already purchased the print book.

Convenient and fully searchable, the PDF version enables you to easily find and copy code—or perform examples by quickly toggling between instructions and applications. The MOBI format is ideal for your Kindle, while the ePUB can be utilized on a variety of mobile devices.

Go to www.apress.com/promo/tendollars to purchase your companion eBook.

Made in the USA
Lexington, KY
17 August 2015